Sir Donald Bradman
A biography

Previous books by the author include

Cricket Books: Great Collectors of the Past
The Cricketer's Book of Crossword Puzzles
England v Australia *(with Ralph Barker)*
The World of Cricket *(with E. W. Swanton and Michael Melford)*
A Portfolio of Cricket Prints

A jubilant Sir Donald Bradman at the Hilton Hotel in London in 1974, when he visited England to attend a charity evening as guest of the Lord's Taverners.

Sir Donald Bradman
A biography

Irving Rosenwater

B T Batsford Ltd   London

He did not mean to be just one of the stars, but the sun itself.
R. C. Robertson-Glasgow
on Sir Donald Bradman

ISBN 0 7134 0664 x

Printed in Great Britain by The Anchor Press Ltd
and bound by Wm Brendon & Son Ltd
both of Tiptree, Essex
for the publishers B T Batsford Limited
4 Fitzhardinge Street, London W1H 0AH

Contents

List of Plates

Preface

Let us remember that a biographer, like a novelist, proves nothing at all if he tries to prove anything. There are biographies with a theory just as there are novels with a theory. They are merely unconvincing bores.

André Maurois in 1956

This is a book about Sir Donald Bradman. Beyond one brief chapter towards the end, and what the reader may care to deduce from a remarkable cricketing life, it makes no attempt to discover the secret of his genius, for not even Sir Donald himself would be able to discover that. He was asked often enough in his playing days to supply the answer, and he could no more do so than could Scott or Macaulay or Conrad or Milton, if asked. Genius is compounded of many things, from endowment to waywardness, and from perspiration to flair. Not being susceptible to definition, it will not readily yield its mystery. On the whole we must accept the reminder of Carlyle that 'genius is ever a secret to itself'.

Nor does this book attempt to show that Sir Donald Bradman was the greatest batsman who ever lived. That verdict, in any event, is by no means universally held. The true answer, like the true definition of genius, is not possible to reach. In his own era, the name of Bradman stood like a colossus in the domain of batsmanship. But so, before him, did the name of Hobbs, and the name of Trumper, and of course the name of Grace. When Sir Donald Bradman's first-class career was already five years behind him, Sir Henry Leveson Gower declared that if any batsman was greater than Hobbs he would like to have the pleasure of watching him. Admittedly 'Shrimp' was a Surrey man and one of those responsible for picking Jack Hobbs for his first Test in England: but his remark was made at the end of a long life of fairly close proximity to many of the world's leading cricketers.

It could only be an act of adulation that could claim for any batsman the title of the 'greatest' who ever lived. There can be no doubt that Hobbs never sought it, and most certainly Trumper never did so. W.G., in his genial and earthy way, probably considered the soubriquet of 'The Champion' to be properly bestowed on him: but did he not so plunder fast bowling and slow bowling and professional bowling and amateur bowling as to make any rivals for that claim seem puny? And did not Billy Murdoch once say of him: 'I have never seen his like and never shall'?

It is distinction enough, surely, to be spoken of in the same breath as the greatest batsmen of all time. On figures alone the Bradman record is prodigious. Figures are not, by a long chalk, everything in cricket: but they are *something*, and mean more than their detractors would have us believe.

Figures can no more be kept out of the Bradman story than House of Commons orations out of the Churchill story. Churchill made a few dull and uninspiring speeches; Dickens was capable of banal plots and wooden characters; and Bradman played some bad and uncharacteristic innings – but not too many of them! The extremes of brilliance and badness should always be balanced in an account of a man's art. But let it be remembered that D. G. Bradman ended his first-class career, which spanned 20 years, with an average of 95·14, and finished even better in his 52 Tests with 99·94. No wonder the term 'Bradmanesque' became a new adjective in the language.

Neville Cardus once tried to rationalise the skill of Bradman, and found it – so he said – easy to do. He called it 'the sum total, or synthesis, of all that has for years been developing in batsmanship, just as the *Queen Mary* is the sum total, or synthesis, of all that for years has been developing in the science of shipbuilding'. That was a noble tribute – but it still did not explain his secret! Why did Bradman reach this special position and not any other batsman?

Most great batsmen have a high plateau of performance which takes in a limited portion of their career and which distinguishes it, in historical perspective, from their other years. In Bradman's case he had no such high plateau – or, at least, if he did, it was the entire decade of the '30s which, apart from his comparatively short post-war farewell, effectively comprised his first-class career. Thus there was no appreciable striving for the peak and certainly no lingering on the stage too long. No one else, of course – not even Grace or Hobbs or Hammond – was at the top for such a large proportion of his career. Bradman was virtually never anywhere else but at the top.

Without an initial sympathy for the subject of this biography, it would have been infinitely more taxing to write. It is by no means intended, however, as a work of hagiography. Archangels undamaged make tiresome reading. There is no such thing as the perfect man, any more than there is the perfect cricketer. It would be wrong to expect a reader to believe in one.

Just as authors so often have their own way of writing their life story, in their books, so cricketers in a sense write their own biography in their play. Sir Donald Bradman went further and produced three volumes of autobiography, as well as much other writing, not least his newspaper contributions. Of Sir Donald's own books, the most invaluable source material has naturally been provided by *Don Bradman's Book* (Hutchinson, 1930 and 1938), *My Cricketing Life* (Stanley Paul, 1938) and *Farewell to Cricket* (Hodder and Stoughton, 1950), though none of these works has been slavishly followed, and without being able to add at least as much again by way of fresh facts and data, this present book would not have justified being undertaken. It is now 30 years since the biography by A. G. Moyes appeared (Harrap, 1948): and it was time for a fresh book. The Moyes work – as no doubt will be the judgment on these following pages also – had some faults. The 1930 tour of England, when Bradman held sway as perhaps the most amazing sportsman in the world, was covered in three pages: and that really could not be right. Because the 1930 tour was the cornerstone on which all Bradman's subsequent fame was founded, it is covered more generously here.

The other major work that must here be acknowledged is B. J. Wakley's *Bradman The Great* (Nicholas Kaye, 1959), which, though not a biographical work *per se*, is nevertheless a book which, within its scope, can never be surpassed. It is a monument in figures to Bradman's great career, scrupulously and devotedly compiled.

It has been the serious endeavour in this book never to tamper with the truth for the sake of some trivial effect, a treason unfortunately not unknown in some writing on the game. It is a biography of Sir Donald Bradman, not a history of the Bradman era. Nor is it a history of any special features of the Bradman era, like the bodyline furore, except of course in so far as that and like features affected the attitudes and conduct of Bradman. It was a fact, of course, that bodyline did affect Bradman very much indeed: as much as the Home Rule campaign affected Gladstone or friction over Holstein affected Bismarck. To that extent bodyline has had to be given proper attention. If it is true that biography should deal with events that throw light on character, then those events have been related. Not all the events in Bradman's life do that. Above all, what I consider the besetting defect of so many cricket biographies has, I trust, been rigidly avoided – the dispiriting and laborious recital of the day by day (indeed, it sometimes seems, over by over) progress of each and every Test match in which the hero has taken part, culled from a former account, regardless of the hero's role, and in reality a monumental exercise in the boring and worthless. Often such tiresome accounts can only be included to bolster a slender subject matter.

I have not hesitated to make use of contemporary quotation, especially when this illuminates the methods and habits of Bradman the batsman. He rose to batting eminence so early, and stayed there for so long, that every critic, whatever his credentials, passed some sort of judgment on Bradman's style (or lack of it!), on his strengths and on his weaknesses, or why he was likely to succeed – or to fail! – in a forthcoming venture. Some of these views were almost certainly tailored to journalistic expediency: some editors, and many readers, were more likely to be entertained by the prospect of the emperor being toppled than reigning on in assured serenity. Men who are very good at what they do are so often natural breeders both of detractors and of partisans. In the 1930s Winston Churchill and Donald Bradman were as good examples as any. The school of Bradman-baiting grew almost into an industry as Bradman's career advanced, in Australia at any rate. The early triumphs, so vociferously hailed, served only to put him on a pedestal from which it was a temptation to seek, even if in vain, to depose him. Much of the criticism of Bradman in his career was irresponsible, even if honestly expressed. But on the other hand there were many, especially Test cricketers, who had the highest credentials to talk – and many of these were as often proved wrong as right. It all made a fascinating exercise in the exacting process of cricket prophecy, with the piquant presence always of the real probability that D. G. Bradman would render his more arrogant and adventurous critics quite foolish.

No biography of a major figure can be written without a good deal of help from others. I have spoken to or corresponded with a large number of people with first-hand knowledge of Sir Donald, and those persons' help has normally been acknowledged in the text. At the same time, I have long agreed with the Proustian view that the people one meets are not their true selves; and in any event even allegedly good memories are notoriously unreliable. On balance I have more frequently (but not inflexibly) preferred to stay with the written evidence.

In response to the published notices of my intention to write this book, I received a large number of letters from well-disposed correspondents, whose generous observations are also gratefully acknowledged. So many indeed responded that although I have not been able to use directly all the material placed at my disposal, every incident and every moment has shed some light on the man who is Sir Donald Bradman and is therefore part of this book.

I have derived great benefit from reading and have made use of many books, newspapers and periodicals, mainly English and Australian. All quotation has been acknowledged in the text, for which I wish to thank all concerned.

So far as books are concerned, there are literally hundreds that make some mention of Bradman, many at considerable length. While most of them have been consulted, either briefly or otherwise, those contemporary writers to whom I am most particularly indebted are Sir Neville Cardus, Sir Pelham Warner, J. B. (Sir John) Hobbs, J. H. Fingleton, P. G. H. Fender, R. C. Robertson-Glasgow, Ray Robinson, D. R. Jardine, Bruce Harris, W. J. O'Reilly, R. S. Whitington and Harold Larwood. I am especially indebted to Ian Peebles and his publishers, Collins, for permission to quote the passage from *Spinner's Yarn* that probes the Peebles–Bradman confrontation of 1930. Others, naturally, have also been quoted and duly acknowledged.

Individuals whom I would like to thank in particular are the Hon. John Rossiter, Alex Bannister, Ralph Barker, Rev. Timothy Biles, T. C. J. Caldwell, J. D. Coldham, Stephen Green, J. T. Ikin, J. C. Laker, L. Livingston, S. J. E. Loxton, F. G. Mann, D. P. B. Morkel, Alan Percival, Miss Netta Rheinberg, Mrs Dorothy Robinson (of Kotara Heights) and Ray Robinson. I would also like to thank my valued friend, Geoffrey Copinger, for allowing me to ransack his library without demur; another valued friend, Gordon Phillips, for undertaking the not inconsiderable task of preparing the index; and yet another valued friend, Geoffrey Saulez, for unravelling discrepancies concerning Bradman's catches in his career – a fruitful source of mystification in many cricketers' records! My gratitude goes also to Mrs Gillian Rowland-

Clark for her courage in agreeing to decipher a none too easy manuscript and in producing an immaculate copy for the printer.

Finally, my most genuine gratitude goes to Sir Donald George Bradman, for having lived his life the way he has and for having made such an inspiring biographee. He has had no romantic private life, to whet the appetite of biographers or playwrights; and indeed his private life is as little documented as his public life is profusely so. He emerges as an extraordinary example of a self-made man who has very properly long held the stage as a legend in his own lifetime.

I.R.
London
March, 1978

1 The Child and the Youth

Youth is a wonderful thing; what a crime to waste it on children.
                                    George Bernard Shaw

At the close of the year 1904 Australia was a young and expanding Commonwealth. Mr George Bradman and his wife Emily could feel satisfied with
their young family of three girls and a baby son. Had they chosen to call a
halt to their family-building at that stage, the world would never have heard
of Don Bradman, and the course of cricket history in the twentieth century
would have been vastly different. Instead, they added one final member to
the family, another baby son, the fifth child, christened Donald George. He
was born four years after the fourth child, and he was to soar above all his
contemporaries in skill and fame.

The future captain of Australia and shatterer of world records was born
at Cootamundra, in the sheep and wheat country of south-east New South
Wales, on 27 August 1908. On exactly the same day, in a three-room house
in the hills of south-west Texas, was born Lyndon Baines Johnson, who also
was destined to rise to the top of the tree and become President of the
United States. It is an interesting reflection that the fame and fortune and
active career of one – the sportsman – had run its full course and had its
fullest meed of public acclaim whilst the repute of the other – the politician –
was still virtually unknown.

The municipality of Cootamundra, in Harden county, is getting on for
200 miles south-west of Sydney. It is a delightful part of the Australian outback. To have produced Sir Donald Bradman is far and away its greatest
claim to fame. In the early years of the century, cricket was certainly played
there, as it was in almost every country district, but the population was
small and the opportunities limited. Bradman himself played only one
innings at Cootamundra in his life – and scored only one run. This was at
the very end of the 1927–28 season, when he was already an inter-state
cricketer and had already notched his first two centuries in the first-class
game. Arthur Mailey, between drawing cartoons for a Sydney paper, took
his side, the Bohemians, on a country tour and included the 19-year-old
Bradman who, at Cootamundra, got off the mark, as was his wont, with a
single, and was then sadly run out. So, out of more than 50,000 runs that
flowed from the Don's bat in first-class and minor cricket in his prolific
career, the place of his birth saw but a humble single.

The origins of the Bradman family are very ancient. They can be traced
back many hundreds of years to a tiny triangle at the southern tip of the
Cambridgeshire–Suffolk border, formed by the villages of Withersfield and

Haverhill in Suffolk and Horseheath in Cambridgeshire. Around there to this day a good many of the family still reside. They are – and always have been – aware enough of their most famous representative in Australia, and Donald George alone, out of all of them, has risen above the ordinary. The original version of the name was spelt equally as Bradman and Bradnam (the final three letters in reverse order), and under the name of Bradnam the family still thrives in that small corner. In that part of the world, folk readily admit that they are not too careful in spelling their names, but there is not the smallest doubt at all that Sir Donald Bradman's ancestors derive from that portion of England. When he played at Cambridge as a 21-year-old on his first tour of England in 1930, he took the opportunity to trace his forbears in that region and met several persons by the name of Bradnam, including the foreman on a farm at Horseheath, the farm belonging to the grandmother of Dr C. T. E. Parsons, now of Bury St Edmunds, who has kindly supplied some of these details.

Sir Donald Bradman's great-grandparents, on the male side, John and Lucy Bradman, lie in the parish churchyard at Withersfield. John Bradman was an agricultural labourer who was born in 1806 or 1807, and his wife was a year younger. They were both born in Withersfield. After their marriage they lived at 26 High Noon Lane, Withersfield, where they raised a large family – they had at least four sons and four daughters, and perhaps more, as not all survived childhood. That house in Withersfield – the home of Sir Donald Bradman's grandfather – in due course became the village post office; and, when Donald Bradman made his first visit to England in 1930, that very house, appropriately enough, was still occupied by a member of his family – Mrs Tilbrook, a niece of Don Bradman's paternal grandfather (she was born a 'Bradnam'), who lived there with her husband. When an aunt of Mrs Tilbrook got in touch with Don Bradman, he replied that he had often heard his father speak of Withersfield and added in his letter that his father had told him the family in earlier days had spelt the name as 'Bradnam'. By the middle of June in 1930, the village of Withersfield was bubbling over with excitement at Don Bradman's march of triumph and the young record-breaker's photograph decorated the walls of every little inn.

It was Sir Donald Bradman's grandfather, Charles Bradman – he is actually recorded as being christened under the name of Bradman, and not the alternative version – who emigrated to Australia from Suffolk as a youth of 18 – just approaching his 19th birthday – early in 1852. He, the eldest son of John and Lucy Bradman, was born at Withersfield early in 1833 and was baptised at the parish church there on 26 May that year. Like his father, and like indeed his younger brothers, Charles Bradman was an agricultural labourer.[1] The time that he emigrated was one of great agricultural depression in East Anglia, and perhaps there was some attraction in the news of

---

[1] Whether Charles Bradman's labours ever allowed him to play cricket would be a pleasing piece of intelligence to know. Young boys in Withersfield at the time were certainly fully

the gold discoveries in Australia. Although Victoria is usually associated with the 'gold rush' (and Victoria certainly had by far the richer and more accessible fields), the first discoveries, in early 1851, were actually made in New South Wales, near Bathurst, at Ophir and later Turon. Small groups of agricultural workers from East Anglia (as well as from many other parts) banded together to go to Australia, anxious to divorce themselves from the agricultural serfdom that would otherwise be their inevitable lot – and the sole member of the Bradman (or Bradnam) family to go was Charles.[1] Unlike many who made the journey from England to Australia in the 1850s, Charles Bradman's venture was a wholly voluntary one – and a wholly honourable one! The number of immigrants claimed by Australia in 1852 was 95,000, seven times that of 1851. Nearly all of them were from the British Isles – most of them making for the goldfields of Victoria. Something under 9,000 of them, however, went to New South Wales, and Charles Bradman was among them.

The Bradman family at the southern tip of Suffolk was a big one – several others of that name were living in Withersfield in the middle of the nineteenth century apart from the household of John and Lucy. They spilled over, too, across the nearby border into Cambridgeshire, at Horseheath in particular: though there are some who claim that the 'spilling over' was the other way, and that Cambridgeshire is the county of origin of the Bradmans. If this be so, this gives to Cambridgeshire yet another high distinction in its nineteenth-century cricketing fame – when Thomas Hayward and Robert Carpenter and Diver, Tarrant and Buttress all helped Cambridgeshire for some years to be one of the strongest counties in England. Tom Hayward junior was born there – the first man after W.G. to score a hundred centuries – as was of course the greatest century-scorer of them all, John Berry Hobbs. And so, by geographical accident, are linked the names of Hobbs and Bradman, two master batsmen of the twentieth century, two knights of the cricket field.

Sir Donald's grandfather, Charles Bradman, spent the rest of his days as a New South Welshman, and a highly respected New South Welshman at that. In 1860 he married Elizabeth Biffen, who was ten years younger than him, at Berrima Church, near Mittagong. Elizabeth Biffen, Sir Donald's grandmother, though she was only a teen-aged girl when she married, developed into a woman of very strong character. Extremely capable in days when life was not easy, she ran her household with an admirable control, and in particular was an expert needlewoman. (In due course all

---

employed as agricultural labourers from about the age of 10. Cricket is recorded in Suffolk (in the centre of the county, certainly) at least as early as 1743; and at Haverhill, only two miles from Withersfield, farm servants were playing the game in 1786.
[1] One of Charles's brothers – this time under the name of 'Bradnam'! – went north and settled in South Shields, where the family prospered and grew. Several persons reside in that district today named 'Bradnum', who may be related. In 1930 Don Bradman also had a great-aunt living in the Manchester district.

three sisters of Don Bradman loved needlework.) A New South Wales girl, Elizabeth Biffen was born at Mittagong, though her family originally came from Camden, south of Sydney, in Macarthur sheep country, where there still reside many members of the Biffen family, a good number of whom were and are dairy farmers. She and her husband, Charles Bradman, after residing in Mittagong, eventually settled in 1873 at Jindalee, in New South Wales, and not long afterwards, the third of their three sons was born – George Bradman, father of Sir Donald. Jindalee was a village that has long since disappeared, some seven or so miles to the north of Cootamundra, though the name survives today as a shire of New South Wales. Charles Bradman spent the last 34 years of his life living there, gaining much esteem as a small farmer in the Cootamundra district (the officially approved name then was actually Cootamundry). Sir Donald himself never knew his paternal grandfather, for he died, at the age of 74, in October 1907 (at Jindalee) – ten months before Sir Donald was born. At the time of his death Charles Bradman left six children: the eldest a son, followed by four daughters, and the youngest, his second surviving son, George. (There had also been a further son, who had died young, before George's birth.)

George Bradman, Sir Donald's father, was born – like Sir Donald himself – at Cootamundra, on 29 November 1875. His first abode was the old Bradman home at Jindalee, which was taken over in due course by George Bradman himself when his father, Charles, got on in years. George's elder brother was 14 years his senior and, unlike him – who left home after a quarrel over land with his father – George got on exceedingly well with his father and proved a most responsible young man. Sir Donald Bradman's father actually married when he was 17 years of age, with his father's consent, his bride in 1893 being Emily Whatman, herself an Australian by birth, as were her mother and father. Emily Whatman, Don Bradman's mother, was the sixth of nine children – four boys and five girls – born to William George Whatman and Sophia Jane Whatman (both of whom were born in New South Wales). Emily herself was born on 6 September 1871 on a farm at Mittagong Range, called Comerton Park. The Whatmans were a large farming family, going back many years, in the Bowral–Mittagong area of New South Wales. Emily Whatman was living there when she met George Bradman while she was on a visit to Cootamundra. The marriage was a highly successful and happy one and lasted for 51 years, until the death of Mrs Bradman a few days before Christmas, 1944.

George Bradman was still living at Jindalee when he married, and where he practised farming; but in due course he and his wife moved a little distance away, to Yeo Yeo (still near Cootamundra), between Wallendbeen and Stockinbingal, on what is today known as the Friendly Way – a modern appellation all but rejected by the local community. The Bradmans lived in a cottage at Yeo Yeo, on land owned by George Bradman. It was the first home of Sir Donald Bradman.

Yeo Yeo – the 'Yeo' is pronounced as in 'yeoman', the whole name therefore like the child's toy – is what in England would be termed a tiny railway halt, and it might interestingly be emphasised that contrary to popular belief, Sir Donald Bradman never lived in Cootamundra at any time in his life, though he was born there, as were his elder brother and his three sisters. He was actually born in a nursing home at 89 Adams Street, Cootamundra, which still stands, now for some years as a residential dwelling. Perhaps 'nursing home' is a little too grandiose a title for what 89 Adams Street was in 1908, for it was actually the home of the local midwife, Mrs Eliza Ellen Scholtz, known to all as 'Granny' Scholtz, and it was she who delivered Donald George Bradman on Thursday, 27 August 1908, and indeed nursed him as a baby. Her role in the history of twentieth-century Australian cricket has gone unsung, but she deserves some permanent mention here, if only for a job well done! 'Granny' Scholtz, who delivered four of the five Bradman children (all except the youngest of Don Bradman's three sisters, Elizabeth May) was a remarkable woman in her own right, and was within a few weeks of her 93rd birthday when she died in Sydney in August 1939, thus knowing of many of the great triumphs of the boy she nursed. Bradman always sent her a telegram on her birthday.

There is no plaque on the house in Adams Street to record the event. Australians do not go in for plaques of this kind, either in the big cities or in the little towns, though at one time a journalist did have the notion of placing a plaque there. The house is now an attractive and well-maintained one, freshly painted in a decor of black and white.[1]

After Donald Bradman was born, his mother returned, with her new baby, to the cottage at Yeo Yeo: that cottage, too, still stands – the first home of Sir Donald Bradman – though for a long time now in a state approaching ruin. By Australian standards of those days the home was reasonably substantial – in fact, in two sections, amounting to virtually two cottages, connected by a covered way. At one time in 1976 it appeared that the site might be saved from complete decay by the Cootamundra Lions Club, who considered the removal and restoration of the cottage, but before the end of that year the project had been abandoned as too costly.

The day of Don Bradman's birth was not the most propitious in the annals of batsmanship. In England Hobbs made 5, Ranji 0, Fry 7, Hayward 9, Mead 1 and Woolley 5. Clearly there was a balance to be redressed! The year 1908 was also the final year of the great W. G. Grace's career in first-class cricket – Bradman was born four months after his last appearance and two months after W.G.'s last century in any cricket. Thus Don Bradman's birth so soon after W.G.'s departure from the scene may be regarded as an instance of nature's law of compensation. At Yeo Yeo in the meantime George Bradman continued as a farmer – a wheat and sheep farmer and a

---

[1] As the career of Don Bradman unfolded, various unfounded claims were made as to his alleged place of birth. In 1937 it was claimed that he was born in Walthamstow, on the eastern edge of London – and Carpenter Road there was even named! But he was positively born in Cootamundra.

successful one. He was also something of a mechanical 'expert', extremely gifted with his hands – a characteristic he passed on to his elder son, Victor – and he did much to assist the local farmers around Yeo Yeo to improve their farm mechanisms.

In late 1910 or early 1911 – the evidence is not certain, but it points more to early 1911 and at all events it was when Don Bradman was at the age of two – the Bradman family moved from Yeo Yeo to Bowral, 82 miles by rail south-west of Sydney. The move was dictated solely by the health of Mrs Bradman. Don Bradman's mother was never robust, and the particularly healthy climate of Bowral – which has led to its development as a popular tourist centre – was to be to her benefit. Bowral is in fact considered one of the finest health resorts in the Southern Highlands, its climate at all seasons of the year being unusually invigorating. (The name comes from the aboriginal word meaning 'high', no doubt because of its altitude of 2,210 ft.) Bowral, where an English team had first played in 1886–87, was in due course to become proudly and permanently identified with Don Bradman – 'the Bowral Boy'. It was still on the small side when the Bradmans moved there: the 1911 census revealed its population as 1,751 and its dwellings 364 – respective figures not wildly removed from what were to become an average seasonal aggregate and top score for Don Bradman!

Don Bradman was not only the baby of the family but, as time was to show, its smallest member in stature. Photographs of his father as a cricketer show him to be tall, strong and broad-shouldered, and, in middle age, as a bespectacled, somewhat stern man with a furrow between his brows, something like 6 ft. in height and of sober dress. The facial characteristics of Sir Donald Bradman in his middle age are certainly those of his father. Donald's brother Victor Charles, who lived on Mount Gibraltar, Mittagong, and who died at the age of 55, was over 6 ft.; his three sisters, in order of age, Islet, Lillian and May, were all reasonably tall – and D.G.B. himself, 'the little man', when fully adult, only 5 ft. 6¾ ins.[1] He was almost exactly the same height as his mother.[2] Many fine batsmen in Australia's history have been short in stature – Alec Bannerman, Murdoch, S. E. Gregory, Duff, Macartney, Collins, Hassett, Harvey, Craig, Walters and others. If placed on a scale when he entered big cricket, Bradman's 10 st. 4 lbs. would have been swamped more than double by Warwick Armstrong's 21 st.

---

[1] The three Bradman sisters in due course became respectively Mrs Islet Whatman, of Mittagong; Mrs Lillian Sproule, of Campbelltown, near Sydney; and Mrs May Glover, of Fivedock, Sydney, and later Mittagong. The eldest sister, Islet Nathalie (and eldest of the five children) died in Wollongong Hospital on 3 August 1977 at the age of 83.
[2] The height of Sir Donald Bradman has sometimes been given in print (though a precise figure is most often avoided) as 5 ft. 8 ins. That is the figure Sir Donald quotes himself. Ray Robinson, however, has been consistent in giving it as 5 ft. 6¾ ins. – a height not the result of any measurement but which he admits is 'a visual impression'. Stan McCabe was 5 ft. 8 ins. and Bradman was not as tall. Rodney Marsh is 5 ft. 8½ ins. and Sir Donald is certainly not as tall as Marsh. Lengthy efforts some years back by Ray Robinson to determine the true height of Bradman from the records of the Australian Air Force and Army proved, alas, abortive.

Just as W. G. Grace's father and maternal uncle ('Uncle' Pocock) were lovers of the game and proficient in some degree as players, so the young Don Bradman was likewise fortunate in his family surroundings. His father began his new life in Bowral as a carpenter, doing much of the carpentry work for one of the town's leading builders, Alf Stephens, at one time Mayor of Bowral and captain and President of Bowral Town Cricket Club. Alf Stephens was a man in due course to play a role in the life of D. G. Bradman and it was the practice wicket that Alf Stephens built at his home in Aitken Road, Bowral, that Don Bradman – among many local players – regularly used for a practice session. George Bradman never ceased to acknowledge the debt that was owed to Alf Stephens in the development of his son Don's cricket. Don Bradman and Alf Stephens remained close friends until the end of Alf Stephens' life. He died in Bowral in 1973 at the age of 86. Alf Stephens was a cricketer, albeit a minor one. And George Bradman, Donald's father, was a cricketer too. 'Just a useful all-rounder', he protested once, when asked about his cricket. An enthusiastic cricketer, he had played at Cootamundra, before moving to Bowral, but irregularly. With limited opportunities, he scored his fifties – but never a hundred – without ever threatening to set the Murrumbidgee on fire. He once won a medal for bowling. He played for Bowral Town in numerous matches, but had turned 40 before he did so and was never a regular member of the side. For many years he acted as umpire for Bowral Town Cricket Club, and in due course was to find himself umpiring while young Donald acted as scorer for the side. George Bradman, like his father at Jindalee before him, was a highly respected local resident of Bowral, playing a very full part in community affairs. He became known locally as 'Pop' Bradman in the process of years. His sporting interests, apart from cricket, extended to rifle shooting, where the good Bradman eye was in evidence: in his middle years George Bradman shot regularly in competition for the Bowral Rifle Club. There was, however, no specially unusual cricketing talent to pass down to his son. Donald's elder brother by four years, Victor, was, if anything, below average as a player. But the paternal enthusiasm and willingness was present – and, of equal significance, Mrs Bradman had two brothers, George and Richard Whatman, who, though certainly some way below first-class ability, were respectable players by local standards.

Opinions vary as to which of the two Whatman brothers was the better cricketer. The matter is not important, for both were immensely keen and played important roles in the development of their nephew Don's cricket. Richard Whatman was born on 15 September 1867 and George William Whatman on 28 March 1875, both on the same farm at Mittagong Range (Comerton Park). Richard was a dairy farmer just out of Bowral, with a milk run, delivering milk direct from his farm to town homes in Bowral. George, too, was a dairy farmer and vegetable grower near Bowral. Both of them captained Bowral Town Cricket Club, George for some time, and as an opening batsman, useful medium-pace bowler (as well as a very good wicketkeeper!) he was the driving force behind the Bowral Town side for many years: perhaps he was not too far short of the standard of first-grade cricket in Sydney. It was George Whatman who once said: 'If you want to become a good cricketer, you've got to practise at least an hour every day.' Richard, also an all-rounder, captained Glenquarry C.C., about six miles from Bowral, and played much of his cricket for them, as well as a good deal for Bowral and many other clubs in the district. (He was also a great tennis enthusiast.) Richard had half a cricket pitch constructed at his home at Hordern's Lane, off Kangaloon Road, Bowral, where those who wished to do so batted and bowled – while the dog fielded. Young Donald Bradman, in his teens, went there regularly for practice. 'Dad taught him a lot', recalls Richard Whatman's widow, now in her 100th year. Richard Whatman was Don Bradman's first coach, and even after Bradman left school and got his first job in Bowral, after he had finished the day in the real-estate office he would go off to Hordern's Lane for practice. Richard was enormously proud of his nephew, Don. When Bradman went abroad with Australian sides, Richard Whatman would sit up all night to listen to the Tests broadcast from England. Indeed, in 1930 he purchased his first wireless set for that purpose. (There were four Whatman brothers in all. One, Sydney Eldridge, died when very young. Another, James, did not play cricket. Only Richard and George were involved in Don Bradman's development. Richard Whatman died at Tamworth, New South Wales, on 23 August 1941, aged 73, and George died some dozen or so years ago in Sydney. Likewise, Sir Donald Bradman's parents are also dead. His mother died, after a three months' illness, in Campbelltown Hospital, near Sydney, on 16 December 1944, aged 73 (she had been living in Campbelltown with her daughter Lillian). Her husband, Sir Donald's father, survived her for 16 years, before he died, aged 85, after a short illness, on 18 April 1961, in Berrima District Hospital, Bowral (now known as Bowral and District Hospital) – immediately opposite Bradman Oval.)

Thus it can be seen that if Sir Donald Bradman can be said to have inherited his cricket skill at all, certainly some of the credit must go to the brothers Whatman. Sir Donald's mother, too, was a player of sorts – a left-hander both with bat and ball – who often played cricket with her two brothers in the yard at one of Richard Whatman's country properties. She was not lacking in encouragement when it came to her son Donald's cricket, and, as it happens, Don Bradman was in due course to score his first hundred on a turf pitch with a bat bought for him, as a present, by his mother. At all events, counsel and encouragement were never far away from the youthful Bradman. Recalling Mrs Bradman, one of Sir Donald's sisters has recently said: 'We sometimes wondered where she got her wisdom from. We could all go to her with any problem; none of us was afraid of her, and she always gave us the soundest advice. All the children inherited her common sense.'

Don Bradman's first home in Bowral was in Shepherd Street, at an existing property bought by his father, and to which George Bradman –

moving there with his wife and three girls and two boys – made additions and improvements. The house was (and still is) situated on the corner of Shepherd Street and Holly Street, a typical timber-framed weatherboard Victorian bungalow, with the distinctive bull-nosed curved iron verandah which extends round three sides. (Today it is no. 52 Shepherd Street, though the house was not numbered when the Bradmans lived there.) The Bradman family lived at Shepherd Street until 1924. It was where the young Don Bradman grew up. It was where, at the age of 9 or 10, Don Bradman had an old kerosene tin for a wicket in the back yard. When he arrived home from school, he would get his mother to bowl for him. He would first throw his small leather bag, with his school books, that was strapped to his back, up the small passage in front of the kitchen door – with a resounding bang, calling at the same time to his mother, as he gathered his bat, 'Come on, mum.' Mrs Bradman would co-operate; and her left-handed deliveries would be duly played by young Donald. 'At the age of eight or nine he was a very fair bat', recalled Don Bradman's father in January 1930. And no doubt he was.

The family moved to 20 Glebe Street, Bowral, a short distance from Shepherd Street, in 1924. This was a home that George Bradman helped build himself, having first bought the plot. It was an attractive cottage, containing five rooms and a kitchen (as it still does), with a garage at the rear which George Bradman used as a workshop. George Bradman and his wife lived there until 1943, and the house has not been structurally altered since, other than the modernisation of the interior. It immediately looks out on to Glebe Park, and it is literally possible, with no great effort, to throw a cricket ball on to what is now Bradman Oval – just slightly to the right of Don Bradman's old home.

At both Shepherd Street and Glebe Street, regular musical evenings were held every Saturday – 'wonderful sing-songs', as Don Bradman's sister recalls them – to which many of the neighbours were invited. Young Don Bradman learnt to play the piano – taught by his sister Lillian, herself in due course to become a professional teacher of the piano: and of this instruction, Lillian's younger sister, with sororal pride, has said: 'Lily didn't give him much teaching, either. He was as good at that as he was at cricket.' There was a strong musical tradition on both sides of the family, whether Bradman or Whatman. Don Bradman's father especially was a keen musician, who played the violin, either by ear or from music, most capably. Young Don himself preferred the violin as a boy, before turning to the piano. Don Bradman and his late cousin, Hector Whatman, frequently played the violin together. Don Bradman's mother, who never received any musical instruction, played by ear both the piano and accordion; both the Bradman boys played the piano, and *all* the Bradman children were able to play *some* instrument. (In addition, Richard Whatman played the violin at country dances and house parties, and George Whatman was a violinist too.) The piano at Glebe Street gave Don Bradman much pleasure and his skill aspired to a more than ordinary standard.[1] Even with jazz music he showed remarkable delicacy of touch. On the ship to England in 1930 he was often in the music lounge entertaining passengers at the piano. In 1930, too, his piano-playing featured on a gramophone record that he made in London. In 1934, on arrival at Southampton of the ship bringing the Australians to England, and while the gangway was being lowered, Bradman entertained the team in the music-room on the piano, playing popular tunes, to which his fellow-cricketers sang. Right through the tour he played on a variety of tinkling instruments in many a country hotel to help in sing-songs for the team. In England in that same year he actually played – as an amateur – with the professional dance band of Ben Oakley, who recalls that his band of six were then playing regularly at the Thatched Barn on the Barnet by-pass. During matches in London, some of the Australians went there in the evenings for a swim in the pool, but Don Bradman was attracted to the band and asked if he could play the piano with them. 'I asked him if he could read music', recalls Ben Oakley, 'and he said "Of course." From then on he came at every opportunity he could from cricket, and he was a very good, in fact excellent, professional standard.'

In his younger days Bradman was even a minor composer of sorts. He wrote a song entitled 'Every Day is a Rainbow Day for Me' that was introduced during the performance of the pantomime *Beauty and the Beast* at the Grand Opera House in Melbourne in February 1931. The song, described as 'pleasantly melodious and sentimental', was accorded an enthusiastic reception and Bradman was called to the stage to bow his thanks.

Don Bradman's childhood days in Bowral were neither more nor less remarkable than those of scores of other Australian country boys. Sir Donald has called them 'normal boyhood days'. They were normal enough, it is true, in that he went to school, played his games and honoured his parents. What made them something less than normal was his questing spirit, his inability to be idle – and his determination to fill his spare hours with *something* that was either challenging or productive. The Bradman homestead, at both Shepherd Street and Glebe Street, was not in a row of terraced houses, where boys would be neighbours and become natural friends. The young Don Bradman was a choirboy at St Jude's Church (an Anglican church) in Bowral and attended Sunday School there. Away from school, the young Bradman had his elder brother and sisters for company, but was more often left to his own devices. He preferred that. He loved to be out of doors, and with a schoolboy's sense of improvisation he devised that novel if primitive form of cricket practice that has become celebrated in the lore of

[1] In the lounge at 20 Glebe Street, where the Bradman musical evenings were held, there is still a piano – and an organ as well. The organ occupies the spot where the Bradman piano once stood. The house has had only two effective owners – George Bradman and the purchaser from him after Mrs Bradman's death, Andrew Wright, a local Bowral baker and café owner, who died in 1957 and whose widow, Mrs Mima Wright, is now the owner, residing there with her son-in-law, William Lyle.

Bradman's childhood. At the back of his home at Shepherd Street he would throw a golf ball against the brick base of an old water tank a few yards away and try to hit the rebound with a small cricket stump. The ball came back at different speeds and at different angles, and there was no flat-faced bat to meet it. Sometimes a tennis ball was used, but the golf ball was speedier and smaller and more of a challenge. The exercise, to be successful, demanded footwork, judgment and a nimble brain. It required patience above all. Until the boy Bradman could strike the rebound three times out of four he was not satisfied. By way of variation, throwing practice was gained by aiming a golf ball at a certain spot on a rounded rail of a fence. Between the Shepherd Street property and the adjoining Holly Street property, there was a paling fence, against which Bradman regularly threw his golf ball, aiming in the first place for the rail. When the ball missed, it would hit the paling fence – as a result of which the neighbours in Holly Street time and again complained about the palings being broken. But Donald Bradman continued to throw – though his aim improved so that he hit the rail rather than the palings. The complaints stopped! The increasing accuracy of the throws were to be reflected in time on the cricket fields of Australia and England. This thick wooden rail produced catching and fielding practice, and with the old water tank helped to develop a ball sense and co-ordination that at first merely pleased its owner but was soon to acquire a much larger significance. Long hours were spent with the golf or tennis ball – hours always spent alone – and almost by the accidental force of circumstances did the young Bradman pursue his methods that were to fit him for bigger and nobler things.

It would be wrong to suppose that any boy could merely follow this formula and become a champion cricketer of the world. That can no more happen than can childhood doodlings make a Picasso. But youthful practice has more than once paid handsome dividends. Colin Bland, one of the world's great fielders, used to practise for hours, picking up and throwing at a stump with a hockey net behind it on his farm in Rhodesia. Among the country boys of New South Wales there had been C. G. Macartney, who used a small bat of cedar wood to face up to the apples bowled to him by his cricketing grandfather in West Maitland – a distinct advantage over solitary practice. England's own Champion, W. G. Grace, had had a whole family – as well as three dogs – to help out in the virtual all-the-year-round practice at Downend; and he (and all the Grace boys) had advantages above the ordinary in being introduced to good cricket so young. W.G. played for West Gloucestershire v Bedminster at the age of nine. (It was in fact just one day after his ninth birthday.) Don Bradman at that age, though he had natural talents, had not advanced very much beyond using the limb of a gum tree as a bat in the playground of his junior school.[1]

---

[1] At the M.C.C. dinner to the Australians in May 1938, Don Bradman revealed that at one time his ambition was to be a house decorator. What he decorated in the process of years, of course, was the game of cricket at its highest level – as no man did before him.

The fact remains, however, that however unpropitious the conditions, Don Bradman was unusually keen on cricket: and with his peculiar temperament it was unlikely that any ordinary happenings would stifle that keenness. Bowral was not to know that it had in its midst a cricketer of future greatness, and this was perhaps just as well, for he might have been treated as a kind of circus exhibit, pampered, spoilt – and, far worse, coached to his possible detriment. As to Bradman's coaching, much has always been made of the absence of it, but this is true only in respect of formal coaching in Bowral. Just as Denis Compton was coached, and coached assiduously, when he went to Lord's, so Don Bradman was coached when he went to Sydney. But by then, of course, he was already a batsman in his own right, albeit somewhat unpolished and crude. The initial steps had been his own, the further steps acquired by watching, and the final steps achieved by coaching.

Don Bradman attended two schools in Bowral – the Primary School in Bendooley Street between the ages of five and ten, and then Bowral Intermediate High School which then (but not now) immediately adjoined the junior school. According to the New South Wales Education Department, the High School was then known as the best country Intermediate High School in the State. With home-made bats (a euphemistic term) and chalk-marked wickets in the school yard, the young padless cricketers felt their way on nothing remotely resembling a genuine 'pitch' and with a composition ball. Sometimes the junior Bradman would be allowed to join the seniors in their play, a privilege he gratefully embraced. It was all, however, demonstrably primitive: but they were the best facilities the school could provide. More importantly, these occasions at least provided an early insight into cricket and into the meaning of games in general. He started playing – very primitive cricket – at the age of seven or eight. He believed there were always plenty of boys better than him and he could never understand why they did not make more runs. It may have been more a matter of temperament than technique.

Bradman's ball-throwing exercise was also practised by him on his way home from school in Bowral. He normally went home alone (by choice) and used to throw a golf ball against the rounded telegraph poles in the town. The ball would come back at varying angles – and if he missed, it would mean a tedious recovery. The young Bradman's accuracy produced fewer and fewer misses the more frequently he practised this.

There was no organised cricket against other schools when Don Bradman was at Bowral, but sports afternoons did see scratch sides from within the High School itself oppose each other. On only three occasions in all – and they were very much exceptions to the norm – did Bradman play against another school. The first of these matches, and the first real match of his life, was when he was 11 and was played on the football field, rather than on the cricket ground, at Glebe Park, Bowral – an arena that was destined to be renamed one day the 'Bradman Oval'. The diminutive Bradman, at number four in the order, had to go in to stop a hat-trick. If genius is an infinite capacity for taking life by the scruff of the neck, young Bradman displayed it that day, for he fearlessly made 55 not out. It is interesting that thus early in his career his wicket could not be captured. He never really looked back from then. It was season 1919–20.

The following summer (1920–21) was to see two major highlights in the young Bradman's life. He was to score his first-ever century and was to have his initial sight of a first-class match. His school twice played Mittagong School – close rivals – that season, and in the first of the matches, on Mittagong's ground, Bradman scored 115 not out in a total of 156. He was 12 years old, and it was the first of the 211 centuries he was to score in all types of cricket in his fabulous career. Bradman's school won, and he was pardonably proud. In the return match, when Mittagong were again defeated, Bradman made 72 not out. He was proving a match-winner already – and a mighty hard cricketer to dismiss. The future was hidden from him, as it is mercifully hidden from us all, but that century at Mittagong, when he made all but three-quarters of his side's runs, was the first milestone on the highway to fame. (A daughter of Alf Stephens and a Bowral contemporary of Don Bradman recalls that a little later other schools refused to play the Bowral School 'if Bradman was in the team'. It is a fact that Mittagong made a formal request to Bowral High School to leave Bradman out of its team, or they would forfeit the match.)

It should be remembered that when Don Bradman was at school, there were no opportunities for boys from schools of his status to be taken in hand for organised coaching. This may have been a blessing in disguise. No one ever told Don Bradman how to hold a bat – and consequently no one ever told him how he must alter his grip or his stance. (When he was later so instructed, he would have nothing of it.) It was not until September 1930, when Don Bradman was already, even at 22, a legend in the game, that a systematic and comprehensive coaching scheme was put into execution by the New South Wales Cricket Association, drawn up by the Association's master coach, George L. Garnsey. This was a new scheme and included for the first time – from November 1930 – boys from High and Intermediate High Schools and country cricketers. If Bradman had been born ten years later, he might well have been part of this scheme.

In February 1921 Don Bradman, wearing knickerbockers and under the careful guardianship of his father, went from humble Bowral to mighty Sydney to see the Sydney Cricket Ground for the first time in his life. It was the fifth Test between Australia and England; and the young schoolboy, whose name was still unknown, in the midst of the enormous crowd, was overwhelmed by it all. His imagination was fired – by watching Woolley bat and by watching Macartney bat, and by being taken in one of the intervals by his father to look – from the outside – at the Sydney pavilion. Young Donald and his father saw the first two days' play, before George Bradman had to attend his business at Bowral. But those two days included a memorable 170 by C. G. Macartney, the last 139 of them before a Saturday crowd of some 30,000. Never had Don Bradman seen such batting or such a mass of people. Sir Winston Churchill, ever the great phrase-maker, once referred to the 'sharp agate points on which the ponderous balance of destiny turns'; and that afternoon at the Sydney Cricket Ground, as a 12-year-old boy holding his father's hand peered into the august pavilion, was surely one of the great turning-points in the life of D. G. Bradman. The boy was not only impressed – he was quite overcome. 'I shall never be satisfied until I play on this ground', he told his father.

Boyhood ambitions more frequently fail than fructify. And these words on this page appear here only because Don Bradman meant what he said. There have not been many idle pronouncements made by Don Bradman in his life (at least if there have been, very few have come down to us) and thus early in his life one can see the seed of ambition which was to germinate and thrust relentlessly, so that finally nothing in the world could stand against it. Did not the young Disraeli, in his father's library, imagine himself a modern Richelieu or a second Napoleon? And did not Napoleon himself, at only nine and a half, declare his intention to want to grow up like the Corsican patriot and general, Paoli?

Those two days at the Sydney Test were the only two days of first-class cricket that Bradman saw before becoming a participant himself. His father may well have smiled, as Don Bradman himself has put it, 'with affectionate tolerance', at his son's bold assertion of ambition in 1921. But just as George Bradman was a man who did not choose that failure or lack of ambition should play any part in his own sphere of life, so – as he was to learn before very long – Donald was of like mould.

Meanwhile Don Bradman continued to go to school at Bowral, his only real cricket coming during a weekly sports afternoon when he would play in scratch matches between the boys, the two and a half hours of cricket being designed, if possible, to give each side roughly an equal period in the field and at the wicket.

Don Bradman's sporting education, pleasurable as it was to him, was not of course the main reason for his presence at school. Though not an outstanding scholar, he was by no means a poor one either. If anything, he was above average. His restless mind was always absorbing something or enquiring along fresh paths. He was an alert little boy, never then – as he has never been since – given to idle dreaming. He read a lot and acquired a basic mastery of words and sentence structure that was to stand him in good stead for the rest of his life. He was a capable talker, and a most capable writer, at a very early age. He obtained his Intermediate Certificate at a younger age than most other boys and won a gold medal at school for exceptional ability in mathematics. That was his best and favourite subject. He was to prove, on the last day at Headingley in 1948, that he was a mathematician as well as a cricketer. He had a head for figures, 'and whenever the master was doing a sum on the blackboard, I used to try and race him in my mind to see if I could work out the answer before he did'. Thus early was there the desire to excel. Bradman was a quick learner, whether in the classroom or on the cricket field – early in his career Jack Ryder said he was the quickest learner in the game – and his learning always had an object, to make him better than he had been. He had the seeds of genius as a youth; not academic genius to set aflame the seats of learning, but the sort of genius that excites and probes and anticipates and reaches upwards.

At the age of 12 and 13, Don Bradman used to act as scorer for the local Bowral Town team – an adult team, of course, that played in the Berrima District Competition and in other competitive matches in its own area of New South Wales. His own father was often standing as umpire. It was a privilege for the young Bradman to act as scorer, no doubt granted him partly through his father's position and partly through his uncle, George Whatman, being the Bowral captain. The inevitable occasion arose, as it has arisen so many times in the lives of young scorers, that the team found itself one short: and Don Bradman's uncle was duly obliged to draft his nephew into the team, young as he was. He was actually 13 years old. They were some six miles out of Bowral, at Moss Vale, so it was either ten men for Bowral or a full side including Bradman. The scorer, in his short white knickerbockers, became cricketer for the day. On a matting-over-concrete pitch, he batted at number ten, with a full-sized bat, and proved once again – on this, his first appearance in adult cricket – how difficult was his wicket to capture. According to one of those playing in the match, Bradman 'dabbed them here and there'; he didn't hit with much power – but never looked like getting out. On this Saturday in 1921–22 he was left with 37 not out when the innings ended. As was normal, matches were played over successive Saturdays, and the following week, in the second innings, he scored 29, again not out, having been allowed to open. This had all been satisfactorily auspicious, for Moss Vale were as good a local team as Bowral might face. In the very few relatively important matches in which he had so far taken part – as a schoolboy and as a cricketer among men – Don Bradman had played five innings and had been not out all five times. In fact he became known as 'not out' Bradman in Bowral. In the course of time, when Bradman left Bowral to reside in Sydney, a Sydney cricket writer reminded one of the local players that the little township had lost Bradman for good. The reply was swift: 'And good riddance, too; we never could get him out.'

Whether by way of reward for his display at Moss Vale, but certainly as an act of encouragement, one of the Bowral team, Sid Cupitt, made a present to Don Bradman of one of his old bats. It was cracked and it was too big: but it was the first real bat Don Bradman ever owned. His father's carpentry sawed three inches off the bottom of it. It had a splice and it could score runs. 'That bat meant almost everything in the world to me', recalled Don Bradman later. But he was too young yet to become a regular playing member of the Bowral club.

In 1922–23 he was still too young for serious cricket and there were no teams in Bowral catering for his age-group. In 1922, when he was 14, he left school and took his first job as a clerk in a real-estate office in Bowral's main street, Bong Bong Street. (The firm is no longer in existence, but was situated on a site immediately to the right of the present Post Office there.) He worked for Mr Percy Westbrook – a great encourager of Don Bradman's cricket – who traded under the style of Davis and Westbrook (in Sydney, Deer and Westbrook). Percy Westbrook was a great lover of sport himself, an enthusiastic tennis player but in particular a bowls player of considerable repute, who had been singles champion of New South Wales and had been in his prime before World War I. For over 20 years he was a leading bowls personality in the State. As an employer Mr Westbrook was kindness itself, at least in allowing young Bradman every scope for his sporting interests. These, at the age of 15 and 16, were centred far more on tennis than on cricket. In the season of 1923–24, Don Bradman played no cricket at all, devoting himself exclusively to tennis, at which he was by no means a poor performer. Tennis and cricket became rivals for his attention and for his time. He was chosen for local representative tennis tournaments and won at least one local championship. His uncle, Richard Whatman, gave him unlimited access to his own tennis court. He became a very successful player. No doubt Percy Westbrook was quietly pleased. Whether Don Bradman, had he forsaken cricket, would have become a Davis Cup player is not too fanciful a thought, with his special temperament and sporting aptitude. (When Jack Crawford, the Australian Davis Cup player, saw Bradman competing in the tennis tournament on the ship coming over to England in 1934, he expressed the view that, with a little practice, Bradman would be a match for anyone in England or Australia outside the first ten.)

His sport in fact was far from confined to cricket. At school he had been the mainstay of the tennis team and was a fleet forward for the school rugger XV. (Over 40 years later he confessed he would have liked to have gone on to play Rugby Union, but he was far too small.) As an athlete he won the 100 yards, 220 yards, 440 yards and 880 yards events at one and the same school athletics meeting. He also won the goal-kicking contest in his division. Like his father, he was a good rifle shot. In fact he loved all sport, and at an early age was attracted even to golf, and would go caddying frequently as a boy in Bowral. After leaving school he was an all-round sportsman in Bowral. Group Captain E. J. Palmer, who now lives in Lincoln, knew Bradman well in those days in Bowral and recalls not only his skill at cricket and tennis: 'At one stage he took up golf and I seem to remember in a match he produced a drive of 412 yards. I several times played table tennis with him and was reduced to laughter, because he cut the ball to such an extent that I had no idea where it would go. I also seem to remember that, young as he was, he drove a car superbly and could, perhaps, have been a world champion racing driver.' If the recollection of the length of that Bowral golf drive is accurate – or even nearly accurate – it represents a most remarkable performance. But it is certainly true that before he came to England in 1930 people frequently marvelled at his prodigious drives at golf.

Remarkable performances were never unusual in Bradman's life, and he indeed was a highly proficient golfer, in due course to win the championship of the Mount Osmond Country Club (South Australia) in both 1935 and 1949. By the time the Second World War came, his golf handicap was down to three, and after he retired from cricket it went down to scratch. In 1952, at his club in Adelaide, he achieved a hole in one at the 150-yard seventh. Ray Robinson, incidentally, has related – to illustrate rather Don Bradman's nerve than his all-roundedness – an incident that confirms his skill in a motor car: 'I once saw him careering at 70 m.p.h. or more along the country highway from Bowral, his home town, in a sports car belonging to "Wizard" Smith the racing driver. He coolly took bends at speeds which professional drivers in following cars could not match, despite much swaying, skidding and screeching of tyres.'

The season of 1924–25 was once again largely, but not exclusively, devoted to tennis. Bradman was now aged 16, approaching something of a crisis in his sporting life, imbued with a love for cricket and finding pleasure, and success, in tennis. Towards the end of that summer he joined the Bowral Town Cricket Club, still a boy among men. And, as if the jealous mistress that is cricket was anxious to punish those whose allegiance may have strayed, he was granted a duck in his very first innings for Bowral on his return. He was at least a true cricketer now, with such a score to his name. An innings of 66 (top score) for Bowral v Wingello before the end of the season put him in a happy frame of mind to look forward to the next cricket season: and although tennis was not completely left behind, cricket was now restored in his favour and to its rightful place in his priorities.

2 A Future Dawns

The present interests me more than the past, and the future more than the present.

Theodora Campian in *Lothair*

Don Bradman had his eye on the future when he decided to throw in his lot with cricket. At the age of 17, in the 1925–26 season, he first showed that amazing prolificness in run-getting that was to characterise his whole career. He was still living at Bowral and it was his first full season with the Bowral Town team. He was its youngest regular member. His brother Victor played in the side – it was his first season; his two uncles, George and Richard Whatman, played in the side; Mr Cupitt, who had given him his first cricket bat, played in the side; and he knew all the players well, even though most of them were many years removed from him in age. It was nothing fresh for him to be the youngest member of the side – even at school this had been the case, and he prospered well enough in that role.

Young as he was, it was clear enough that he exhibited certain qualities even away from the field of play. Just one month after his 17th birthday, at the end of September 1925, at the annual general meeting of the Bowral Town C.C., Don Bradman was elected the club's hon. secretary – his first administrative post in cricket. That he assumed the position with a characteristic sense of responsibility is exemplified by the particular meticulousness he showed while secretary in getting Bowral's scores sent to the local newspaper (the *Southern Mail*): this was in sharp contrast to the other Berrima District sides, whose scores were only rarely, and spasmodically, recorded in the press.

Bradman had still had no formal coaching – there just was no formal coaching available – when he took his place in the Bowral team. What runs he had hitherto scored had been through his own methods, as yet uncultivated but in the main effective. His most productive stroke was a lofted on-drive, a typically attacking shot that he was not to discard even when his batting acquired much more polish in the first-class arena. He had few pretensions to style, but he was pragmatist enough to accept the importance of the arithmetic in the scorebook. Those who hold that style is all have a good deal to explain in Donald George Bradman.

What success he had enjoyed as a boy in and around Bowral had necessarily to be tempered by the modesty of the bowling he encountered. Country bowlers of high talent occasionally did emerge, but they were positively *rarae aves*; and, in addition, young Bradman's skill had never yet been tested on a turf pitch. Bradman learned his cricket on concrete wickets, with coir or canvas mat covering. One such country bowler was, however, waiting in the wings to greet Don Bradman in 1925–26. He was W. J. O'Reilly, then a 19-year-old student at Sydney Teachers' College and a member of the Wingello side, where his family lived. Strangely, it was in Bowral that in the course of time O'Reilly was to hold a teaching appointment.

Bowral were due to play Wingello over two successive Saturdays, the first day's play to be at Glebe Park, Bowral, on the ground later to be known as the 'Bradman Oval'. When the sides had met the previous season – and when Bradman had made 66 – O'Reilly was not in the team. He very nearly did not play in the 1925–26 game either, for he was on his way home by train, from Sydney to Wingello, when his plans were altered for him. O'Reilly has described it thus:

> As the train stopped at Bowral I heard a voice calling out: 'Bill O'Reilly, get out, please.' I looked out to find the railway stationmaster from my home town diligently searching the train for me. When I called to him he excitedly informed me that the Wingello cricket team was playing Bowral on that afternoon and that I was selected to play. I told him that I had no cricket gear with me, but he smilingly observed that he had thought of all that before he had left home and that he had paid a hurried visit to my mother who, God bless her, had supplied all the necessary.
>
> On leaving the train I was given a detailed account of a Bowral boy who had been showing excellent form with the bat and who was likely to supply such formidable opposition that the lads from my town thought that my services should be enlisted for the fray.

O'Reilly's services, alas for Wingello, did not meet with the success that was expected of them. O'Reilly asserts that he twice had Bradman dropped in the slips (by the Wingello captain) before he was 30, but admits that not another chance came from the Bradman bat. By the close of that first day, Saturday, 9 January 1926, Bradman had scored 234 not out in $2\frac{3}{4}$ hours, hitting 4 sixes and 6 fours in his final 50 runs. O'Reilly had a full seven days to contemplate on this indignity. 'I just could not assimilate the knowledge that a pocket-sized schoolboy could have given me such a complete lacing. I spent the rest of the week which followed in trying to work out what it was that had gone wrong with my bowling to allow such an indignity to happen.' Though Bradman had passed the schoolboy stage, he was still certainly 'pocket-sized' – and O'Reilly was the first of a great string of fine bowlers to marvel and ponder over the skill of this diminutive batsman. When the game was continued the following Saturday, this time on the Wingello Recreation Ground, Bradman was bowled without addition by a leg-break from O'Reilly, first ball. This match marked the first meeting of Bradman and O'Reilly and also, of course, the first mammoth score that Don Bradman had achieved. That it was not to be the last he very quickly indeed proceeded to demonstrate.

As a record individual innings for the Glebe Park ground at Bowral, Bradman's score was beaten on 12 March 1932 by a young batsman named

Walter Horne (who was then still attending the High School) with 235 not out in 185 minutes for Exeter v Bowral 'A' grade team in the knockout competition for the Woodhill Shield. Walter Horne was actually to play against Don Bradman when Bradman toured the Bowral area with his Sydney club, St George, over Easter, 1933, and scored a modest few runs: but his name, alas, made no further deep impression on cricket history.

At the age of 70 W. J. O'Reilly returned to that ground at Bowral on 4 September 1976, where he had been so severely tested more than half a century before. He bowled one ball that day – to his old adversary, Sir Donald Bradman, aged 68. It was a symbolic event to mark the opening of the new Bradman stand at the rebuilt ground, now with a turf pitch instead of the concrete one on which the young Bradman had made his 234 runs in 1926. At a nostalgic dinner the night before, Sir Donald said: 'I have some wonderful memories of Bowral. The life that fate marked out for me took me away but I have always retained my love for the place.' Sir Donald took the opportunity of having a look at his old home in Glebe Street, where he had lived with his parents and his brother and sisters. The Bradman home was a small and smart brick house, attractively set against trees, and almost adjoining the cricket ground at Glebe Park. The house, inevitably older now, still stands – a reminder, together with the cricket ground that now bears the famous batsman's name, of Bowral's early association with the Bradman legend. Glebe Park had been opened in February 1909, shortly before the Bradmans arrived in Bowral, and in 1934 the land was purchased by the council. In 1938 it was proposed to rename the area 'Bradman Oval', at the suggestion of the Bowral Cricket Club. This was formally done in 1947, after the hiatus of war, when the new turf wicket was first used, it having been laid the previous year.

Apart from his innings of 234 in 1925–26, Don Bradman had also made scores of 105 and 120 that season before Bowral played Moss Vale – the ancient rivals – on the Moss Vale ground in the final of the Tom Mack Cup in May 1926. In the semi-final, against Bundanoon, Bradman had scored his 120: he had made it on the first day of the match (10 April), but due to successive Saturdays being washed out, this game did not end until 8 May – hence the late start for the final between Bowral and Moss Vale. In this final Bradman played a spectacular innings of exactly 300, spread over three successive Saturday afternoons – 15 May, 22 May and 29 May – and achieved as an opening batsman. Play was restricted to 2 p.m. until 6 p.m. each Saturday, and on the second Saturday Bradman took his score from 80 to 279. When he was finally caught on the boundary, on the third day of the match, for 300, he had shared a second-wicket stand of 374 with his uncle, the captain George Whatman, who went on to make 227.[1] Don

---

[1] The precise number added by Bradman and his uncle for the second wicket is complicated by discrepancies in different versions of the score. One report states 374, but also says the first wicket fell at 145 and the second at 529 (i.e. 384 added). From further versions the stand could have been 373 or 377. No scorebook survives to settle the point.

Bradman's innings was a new record score for that district of New South Wales, and the first triple-century recorded there.

Playing in that match at Moss Vale – down as last man in the order for Bowral but going in at number ten because one man could not bat through injury – was a player never destined to make a mark in the game, but who was remembered in later years with much fondness by Don Bradman. His name was Alf Stephens (he scored 7 not out in the huge total against Moss Vale) and he and young Bradman were of course good friends. He was also, of course, the Bowral builder for whom Don Bradman's father had done a good deal of carpentry work. Before Don Bradman ever left Bowral for Sydney, and with Test cricket not yet on the horizon – though perhaps not impossibly far away – Alf Stephens told the precocious Bradman that if he were ever chosen to go to England, he, Stephens, would be there to see him. His word was duly kept, for he was in England in 1930 to see many of Bradman's great triumphs, and it was with Alf Stephens and his wife that Bradman relaxed, away from cricket and away from the team, just before the first Test of 1930.

Bradman's triple-century earned him a rare visit to Sydney. His mother had promised him a new bat if he scored a century in the final against Moss Vale, while his father and uncles had promised him a new cricket shirt, boots and a blazer. To acquire the new bat, which had been conclusively earned, Bradman went off with his father to one of Sydney's biggest sports stores – where, most curiously, Bradman himself was in due course to be employed – and was so long and choosy in his deliberations that many dozens of bats were put before him for his youthful inspection before he was satisfied. Neither the salesman nor the country lad nor his indulgent father could have foreseen the importance of the occasion. But Don Bradman was not to be hurried; and he eventually picked a 'Roy Kilner' bat, made by the Yorkshire firm of William Sykes, on whose very bats – again most curiously – the name of Don Bradman himself was in due course to appear.

After his innings of 234, and most especially after his 300, Bradman's name began to reach the world beyond the small township of Bowral. The triple-hundred was given some mentions in the Sydney newspapers, not least because of the unending saga that the match was presenting – it lasted in all for five weeks, not ending – Bowral won by an innings and 338 – until 12 June, an abnormally late date in an Australian season. There was no real reason, however, why anyone – in Sydney or anywhere else outside Bowral – should be unduly impressed by such brief paragraphs. It had always been a feature of country cricket in Australia, and still is, that extraordinary feats should be performed, and there are literally thousands of such unusual incidents, with either bat or ball, on record that have been passed on for their curiosity value to a city newspaper. They made interesting news items and nothing more. The statisticians may have noted them, but they were too frequent even for them. The extreme variety of the circumstances in which such feats were achieved made any valid judgment from a distance quite meaningless. But Don Bradman's overall record for the season of 1925–26 most certainly did have some meaning. His serious cricket career was well and truly under way. In Berrima District matches alone he averaged 109·44 from 985 runs, scored in only 12 innings. In all matches that season he had 21 innings (eight not out) and made 1,381 runs, including four centuries, at an average of 101·38. He was, of course, at the top of the Bowral batting (as well as second in the bowling) and he also won badges for fielding and taking most catches in the season for Bowral. In all matches he actually took 51 wickets at 7·8 apiece with his leg-breaks and held 26 catches.

Before his debut in the Sheffield Shield in December 1927, Don Bradman was to score more centuries and break more records in what was already becoming for him the almost absurdly non-demanding realm of minor cricket; and from the point of view of his development as a cricketer no season was more important to him than that of 1926–27. He began it as a virtually unknown country batsman: he ended it as one who was being spoken of in the best circles in Sydney in terms of admiration and excited expectancy. It was the transition season of his career, when he first played in Sydney, when he first played on a turf wicket, when he first played in the same matches as Test cricketers. The significance of that Australian summer, and its effect both on the 18-year-old Bradman himself and on the future of Australian cricket, makes the recording of some of Bradman's more important exploits in it of more than ordinary interest. He was growing up as a cricketer, and growing up fast – in the sound and critical school of New South Wales cricket of the '20s, where those at the very top kept a mature eye on those at the very bottom.

Because Bradman's subsequent career as a first-class batsman was so phenomenally successful, the biographical and autobiographical writings about him have tended to concentrate much more on his big cricket: but the more one looks at the year after he passed his 18th birthday, the more clearly it can be seen how meaningful it was in shaping his life. He played no first-class cricket in that year, of course – though the determined, ambitious Bradman later confessed to a tinge of disappointment at being overlooked. But by the end of 1926–27 he was positively knocking at the door.

He began that season as he ended it, playing for the Bowral Town club. In between his ambition had been fired – or perhaps re-fired, as he remembered again that visit as a 12-year-old with his father to the Sydney Test match. By the close of the Australian summer of 1926–27 Bowral – if not in fact then in spirit – was left behind him. It all began, rather ironically, in the New South Wales Cricket Association's search for bowlers, a department of the game in which New South Wales – and Australia – at that time was rather deficient. The State selectors arranged a series of practices at the Sydney Cricket Ground and invitations were sent out by the N.S.W.C.A. to a large number of specially selected junior players. When the names of these players were published, it was seen that they were all grade cricketers playing for first-grade Sydney clubs (the normal quarry for talent) – with a single exception. Little could anyone have guessed the miraculous potential of that exception when they read the simple words: 'An invitation has also been forwarded to Don Bradman, the Bowral colt, to attend the Cricket Ground next Monday. His achievements have been extraordinary, and he is deserving of a really good try-out.'

The invitation naturally caused something of a stir in the Bradman household. Coming from the secretary of the New South Wales Cricket Association, it was in the nature of a royal command. Don Bradman, on the appointed day, made the journey to Sydney accompanied by his father. Not many words, it appears, passed between them. 'I know', Don Bradman later wrote, 'I was chiefly full of joy that such a chance was coming my way, and full of eagerness to make the most of it.'

A splendid muster of young players turned up at the Sydney nets on that Monday, 11 October 1926. Bradman, of course, was there, with his father watching – as were the New South Wales selection committee, consisting of Messrs A. G. Moyes (who was later to write Bradman's biography), R. L. Jones and H. Cranney, all three then still practising cricketers and all of long experience. Among former Test players present, assisting and encouraging, were C. T. B. Turner, Harry Donnan and Dr H. V. Hordern. The young bowlers were certainly examined closely, but when the untutored Bradman's turn came, oblivious of who was watching him, and for the first time away from his hard wickets, he forced others to notice him. 'The youngster *looked* a batsman', recalled Johnnie Moyes later, and a press report, mainly surveying the young bowlers who were put through their paces that day, managed to get the newcomer's initial wrong but passed this prophetic verdict: 'J. Bradman, a young batsman from Bowral, was also present, and his display was so impressive that H. Cranney, of the Cumberland Club, invited him to play with the club. Bradman possesses an excellent defence, and should make many runs when he masters the turf wickets. He watches the ball closely and is not afraid to hit the over-pitched ball. His doings will be closely watched.'

Harold ('Mudgee') Cranney, who had been elected a New South Wales selector at the beginning of that season, obviously knew a cricketer when he saw one. He himself was a hard-hitting batsman for Central Cumberland – the club's full name – in first-grade cricket in Sydney and a useful slow bowler who had been connected with the Cumberland club nearly 20 years, was still playing for the first team, and had done much to foster the game in that district. He now saw a supreme chance to foster it further. Hence his approach to lure Bradman to Cumberland – the first positive recognition that a star was on the horizon. Cranney had been an occasional former opening batsman for New South Wales, good enough to score 70 and 144 against South Australia in 1921–22, but before the end of 1926 he had said he would shortly resign as a State selector as he was to move to Tamworth. Had he been successful in capturing Bradman, it would have been his last – and greatest – act for Cumberland. Bradman in fact accepted the invitation to play first-grade cricket with Cumberland that season, but very quickly – and before he actually played a game – the negotiations fell through as he was unable to afford the loss of time and expense of weekly visits to Sydney, and the Cumberland club had no fund from which to pay his expenses. What a player they allowed to slip through their fingers! And how they had only themselves to blame for the almost unrelieved run of failure that was to come Central Cumberland's way – 15th in the first-grade table in 1927–28, out of 16 clubs; 14th in 1928–29; 15th in 1929–30; 15th in 1930–31; and 14th in 1931–32. And what a bolstering to their finances they tossed away! Harold Cranney, incidentally, lived to admire the entire span of Bradman's genius, and died in January 1971 at the age of 84.

Back in Bowral, Bradman was still scoring runs. On 30 October he made a splendid 170 (retired) against Exeter, 'in which he did not give the semblance of a chance and never looked like losing his wicket'. The selectors in Sydney, looking for bowlers, could not omit Bradman from their discussions. In point of fact New South Wales were badly in need of batsmen too, and thus it came about that Bradman was invited to play in a one-day trial match, under the auspices of the N.S.W.C.A., to give promising juniors a chance before the State side was selected to play Queensland at Brisbane. Bradman played for the Possibles v Probables, 27 players in all taking part, and as the occasion marked the first innings he ever played on the Sydney Cricket Ground No. 1, or indeed on any first-class ground, the brief result of the match may be of interest:

On 10 November 1926, at Sydney
Possibles   237 for 10 dec. (D. Mullarkey 64 ret., D. G. Bradman 37*, H. C. Steele 36, J. N. Campbell 5 for 79):
Probables   302 for 9 (A. F. Kippax 58, A. A. Jackson 53 ret., D. Seddon 47, N. E. Phillips 42, G. S. Amos 3 for 33).
Probables won by 65 runs.

In this match Bradman played for the first time against the 17-year-old Archie Jackson, who that season scored heavily for both Balmain and New South Wales. A year younger than Bradman, he went into the Sheffield Shield side later that month because he was already playing first-grade cricket in Sydney – not an indispensable qualification for inclusion, but one to which the selectors have always attached major importance. For all Bradman's optimism and comparative success, it was really too much to expect to be chosen for the State after a net and one solitary outing on turf. But he had certainly once again made a good impression, even though his captain, H. C. Steele, had put him in at number seven and the pre-arranged time for a declaration had left Bradman, as it were, in mid-air. This was the verdict of the *Sydney Morning Herald*:

One of the successes of the day was D. Bradman, the young Bowral player, who batted for 97 minutes and remained not out for 37. Bradman's success was all the more gratifying when it is considered that he was making his match debut against first-class bowling. Although a trifle on the slow side, Bradman showed supreme confidence, and the further he went the better he shaped. He was one of the few batsmen to leave his crease to the slow deliveries of Campbell, whom he played well when that bowler was meeting with considerable success.

Campbell was a googly bowler with the Gordon club who, together with R. L. A. McNamee (Randwick), was promptly chosen for the Shield side. Bradman faced both these bowlers, as well as another New South Wales bowler in Hal Hooker (Mosman), and his good innings could have done him no harm in the eyes of the new State captain, Alan Kippax, who also led the Probables.

The following day the three N.S.W. selectors, who had of course watched the one-day trial, announced the side to play Queensland – and Bradman was not among them. They were probably right not to rush him too soon, but they had far from forgotten him. R. L. Jones, for one, mindful that the Cumberland offer had fallen through, quickly approached his own club, St George, with a view to acquiring Bradman. 'Dick' Jones – a highly honoured name in the history of the St George District Cricket Club – was himself a member of the side, by no means a weak side: but it would have called for a side of exceptional talent not to want to welcome Don Bradman.

Meanwhile the young batsman made a further stride forward when he was selected to play for the Goulburn district team against South Coast at Goulbourn on 13 November, in a trial match in connection with the selection of the Southern Districts team for the forthcoming Country Week matches in Sydney. Bradman made top score for Goulburn (62 retired) and took four for 35. He was duly selected to visit Sydney with the Southern Districts team – the only Bowral player included. He had fully deserved selection, for he had so far never failed in any of the tests before him.

Sir Donald himself has told of his dilemma, having been selected also for the Country Tennis Week in Sydney. The battle between cricket and tennis had not yet been finally resolved. The tennis authorities were as anxious as the cricket ones to harness his skill. Both Country Weeks in Sydney came but once a year. Ideally at that time the young, fit and keen Don Bradman would have gone to both. His employer, Percy Westbrook, however, allowed him only one week away – and Bradman chose the cricket one. Whether it was because the cricket week was first on the calendar cannot be certain, and it is idle to speculate on the course Don Bradman's life would have taken had he thrown aside the chance of his first week of cricket, under influential eyes, in Sydney. A few of cricket's cognoscenti may have recalled his name as the teen-ager who made some extraordinary scores in country cricket in New South Wales in the '20s, just as many other teen-agers have done both before and since. On the other hand, his flirtation with tennis may have no more than delayed his ultimate emergence as a cricketer of genius – depending, one may suppose, on the consequences of the tennis week in Sydney. At all events, tennis was now set aside conclusively in favour of cricket, and Don Bradman's choice cannot have given him too many sleepless nights since.

The annual Country Week cricket carnival in Sydney, wholly conducted on turf wickets, was a great occasion for the players chosen. Eight teams competed in November 1926, with the N.S.W. selectors again watching. It was the only Country Week that Bradman played in, for thereafter he was no longer a country player. A combined City side played a combined Country side as the final match of the carnival.

It would be nice to record that Don Bradman had an unending run of successes in this important week, but apart from the final match against the City his scores were strictly moderate. On the first day he made his best score (43) and added 95 for the second wicket with his captain, L. W. Sieler, a Marulan player, who had been to Sydney several times. Bradman was caught and bowled by Eric Weissel, a batsman from Cootamundra, where Bradman himself had been born. It was Weissel who later that week scored a magnificent 218 not out for Riverina v Far North, having been missed behind the wicket before he had scored! He later became a great Rugby League footballer, and his son, Bruce Weissel, who became school principal at South Berkeley, a Wollongong suburb, was for many years one of Tamworth's finest all-round sportsmen, playing against the West Indians in 1960–61 and against the M.C.C. in 1962–63.

Bradman's performances for Southern Districts in Country Week of 1926 were as follows. He batted at number three each time:

		Bowling
22 Nov. at S.C.G. No. 1	43 v Riverina	0–13
23 Nov. at S.C.G. No. 2	24 v Far North	1–52 and 1–21
24 Nov. at Parramatta Oval	41 v Western Suburbs–Cumberland	0–12
25 Nov. at S.C.G. No. 1	27 v Newcastle	4–44
26 Nov. at Manly Oval	25 v Western Districts	1–40

Thus he averaged 32 with the bat, away from the concrete wickets he was used to and against the pick of the country bowlers of New South Wales other than his own region. It may not have been a triumph in the acknowledged Bradmanesque fashion, but he never actually failed in any innings. His first captain in Sydney, other than in the one-day trial match, was L. W. Sieler (brother of Aub Sieler, the tennis player), who captained Bradman in each of the above five matches. L. W. Sieler represented New South Wales 2nd XI v Victoria and Queensland and his grandson, Alan Sieler, has played much Sheffield Shield cricket for Victoria. He remembers the considerable promise that the 18-year-old Don Bradman showed in that Cricket Week in Sydney: 'I found Don a silent worker, obviously at his age a deep thinker, a fine boy, a good sport, with quick reflexes. The game was treated by him as a business, with great ambition to succeed.'

By this time 'Dick' Jones had had his answer from the St George committee. They would play Bradman in their first-grade side, and as he was already in Sydney he made his debut for the club on the Saturday of cricket week, 27 November, against Petersham – one of the strongest bowling sides in the competition – at Petersham Oval. Batting at number five, Bradman marked his first appearance in grade cricket with a century, scoring 110 (9 fours) in 110 minutes before being run out attempting an impossible run. It was his first century on a turf wicket and he shared a stand of 197 for the fifth wicket with Clarrie Targett (150*), bringing St George to 389 for six at the close. (On the same day C. G. Macartney and A. G. Moyes, both early supporters of Bradman, were scoring 78 and 59 respectively for Gordon v Marrickville at Chatsworth Oval.) Bradman had used the bat he had so fussily chosen in Sydney a few months before, and though he sadly broke it when his score was 98, it says something for his temperament that he went quickly on to his hundred.

R. L. Jones, who had been in the St George team when his talented acquisition made his auspicious debut above, deserves a special word of praise in the Bradman story. What Bradman did for St George – he averaged 91·57 for them over seven seasons – was largely due to Jones initially pressing his claims, doing so as well in his role as New South Wales selector. Most Sydney clubs would have snapped Bradman up, but after having very nearly lost him to Cumberland, Jones acted promptly. He had been the first captain of St George on their elevation to first-grade status in 1921 and was a good batsman and wicketkeeper, but his influence as an administrator was his greatest strength. He helped pick the Australian side for England in 1930, and the success of Bradman must have given him special pleasure. He died in Sydney in 1966, but his name is remembered in St George as one of its greatest sporting personalities. Sir Donald himself has never forgotten 'Dick' Jones.

To return to the young Bradman, there was one day left in Sydney to round off Cricket Week before returning home. This was on 29 November, when Bradman was a member of the combined Country side – still under the captaincy of L. W. Sieler – against the City team, captained by the great C. G. Macartney. The day was a great success for the number three batsmen of each side – Macartney and Bradman. The game was on the Sydney Cricket Ground No. 1, and of City's 301 for eight declared, the 40-year-old Macartney made 126, showing all his old artistry – and what an object lesson that must have been. The Country side replied with 171 for seven, of which Bradman made a 'free and dashing' 98, with nine fours, before being caught off the last ball of the match. He put on 82 for the fourth wicket with a player named Frank Cummins (a Hunter River batsman and later to play with Bradman in North Sydney and New South Wales sides), who made only 19 – the next best score of the innings. The prolific Eric Weissel this time got only a single. The busy Sydney carnival was over.

In the last week of December 1926, Bradman took eight for 36 and scored 103 (retired) against a visiting Sydney team at Bowral, having already been selected to play for New South Wales 2nd XI against Victoria 2nd XI at

Sydney starting on New Year's Day, 1927. He was top scorer in the first innings with 43 before the future Test bowler, Hans Ebeling, dismissed him. Before that season was out, Bradman broke his own local record score with a shattering innings of 320* (including 6 sixes, 1 five and 43 fours), scored on successive Saturday afternoons – 21 and 28 May 1927 – for Bowral against Moss Vale in the final of the Picard Cup, played at Lackey Oval, Moss Vale. This match was not in the Berrima District Competition proper, but the same local teams took part. The new mammoth score by Bradman was described as an 'amazing innings' compared with his previous season's 300, such had been his advance in the course of twelve months. He was a State 2nd XI player and a Sydney first-grade player by now, and Moss Vale simply reeled under his onslaught – so much so that steps were taken to bar any first-grade player from future participation in such competitive matches.[1] Bradman's average in the Berrima District Competition and Picard Cup in 1926–27 was 186·66, and naturally he topped the Bowral batting in this his last season with the club. Meanwhile, to the end of the Sydney season, he had continued to play on Saturdays for St George, for whom he averaged 48·16 in his debut season, finishing second in the batting. In all forms of cricket in 1926–27, he scored 1,576 runs, including five centuries, at an average of 71·63.

Thus ended for Don Bradman a busy and significant summer – his last in wholly minor cricket before his great days ahead. Though he had yet to make his first-class debut, he was a 'name' – at least in Sydney – but he was still essentially a player of one-day games, with no chance of mid-week practice on turf.

---

[1] Great as was Bradman's score for the district, it was beaten twice in the 1939–40 season, firstly at Bradman Oval, Bowral (the old ground at Glebe Park, where Bradman first encountered O'Reilly), by Clive Goodfellow, who opened the innings for Bowral v Robertson – both 'A' grade teams – and carried his bat through the innings for 333*, all in a single afternoon on 12 December 1939; and then on 20 April 1940 when Harold Burgoyne, a second-grade batsman, scored 393* for Moss Vale v Sutton Forest at Old Park, Moss Vale, in the second-grade knock-out competition final.

3 Steps to Fame

On looking back at the season in which Don Bradman made his debut in first-class cricket – 1927–28 – there is one striking feature that does much credit to the triumvirate of New South Wales selectors that summer, Messrs R. L. Jones, A. R. Ratcliffe and E. L. Waddy. They did not choose Bradman straight away; nor did they choose him, when they eventually did so, with an imposing array of big innings behind him that would have made his selection obligatory or inevitable. Indeed, had he *not* been selected to make his Sheffield Shield debut when he did, there would have been no public clamour and very little private comment. Bradman, as the new season of 1927–28 unfolded, played himself in somewhat modestly, still travelling from Bowral to Sydney for his games with St George, with whom he was now playing his first full season. For two and a half months his name – despite what private ambitions he may have harboured – was nothing more than one of the many players among the 16 grade clubs of Sydney. Something like 200 players had ambitions, greater or smaller, to aspire to the New South Wales side. He was *known*, of course, but still had to prove himself in the probationary school of first-grade cricket. Bradman's name was very far from being on everyone's lips.

His cause was helped by C. G. Macartney's announcement on 18 October 1927 of his decision to retire from first-class cricket, a decision that was not unexpected but which for all that left a conspicuous gap in the State side. Alan Kippax, as was his wont, began the season by taking a side to the country: Bradman was not in it. Arthur Mailey then took a Sydney team to Singleton: Bradman was not in that either. Twelve months later it was to be unthinkable that these country tour captains should not put Bradman down as a very early member of their embryonic lists – but in September, October and November of 1927, Don Bradman was not only not in demand but still very much feeling his way in senior cricket, albeit with a firm enough eye on bigger things.

He may have ended the previous season with Bowral with an average soaring a long way past the 100-mark, but that did not prevent him beginning the new season for St George with innings of 4 and 7 (clean bowled each time) against Petersham. When the names were given out of the New South Wales squad to practise for the State's forthcoming first-class matches (against the New Zealanders and the other States), Bradman was not among them, although as many as 29 cricketers were chosen. On this evidence, it might be taken that in the middle of October 1927 he was still not regarded as being one of the best 29 cricketers in the Sydney grade competition, and it is unlikely that the selectors would have rejected him merely on account of his having to travel from Bowral. Nor would they have rejected him on the grounds of precocity of age, for he was already past his 19th birthday. It may well have been that they did not choose to rush him into first-class cricket, but that does not explain his absence from the squad of 29. That Bradman, however, was by no means out of their thoughts was to be demonstrated soon enough.

At the very next opportunity after this summary passing over, and with what now seems a typical Bradman riposte, he scored 130* for St George v Paddington (including the bowling of J. M. Gregory) at Hampden Oval, full of fine drives against the slow bowlers in particular and containing no chance until he was past his century. It may well have pleased Dick Jones of St George, but if he then tried to press Bradman's claims for the State side, he did not succeed.

Bradman was accordingly not selected for New South Wales's first match of the season, against the New Zealanders returning from England. In the event he was hardly missed, for New South Wales, in less than a day, hit up 571 in the astonishing time of 278 minutes (123 runs an hour) and the man whose place he might have taken, Archie Jackson, made 104 in 72 minutes. This match, incidentally, marked W. J. O'Reilly's debut in first-class cricket – exactly seven weeks before Bradman's. The travel-weary New Zealand bowling was hardly in the top flight, but the mammoth score – and, more importantly, the way it was obtained, at 7·3 runs per eight-ball over – gave some indication of the sort of batting side at whose door Bradman was knocking. Good as it was, it was not consistently in such form, however, and with some men nearing the end of their careers, there was still room for fresh blood. Bradman also was omitted – and the omission again gave no reason for surprise – from New South Wales's next match, the opening Shield match of the season, against Queensland at Brisbane, where the New South Wales batting could muster no more than 167 – off only seven fewer overs than were required for the 571! This was an astonishing reversal of form, especially as the batting personnel were very nearly the same in each match. There were also, it should be added, no New South Wales 2nd XI matches for which Bradman might be picked, the solitary inter-State fixture for the 2nd XI that season being against Victoria at the end of January.

Meanwhile, back in October and November, Bradman had made scores of 7 v Randwick and 2 (this as an opener) v Sydney University, and as a first-grade cricketer he was becoming a disappointment. At least he seemed nothing above the ordinary. Between these two failures, however, he played in a minor match that must have jogged afresh the memories of the selectors. Country Week in Sydney had come round again, and following the annual habit, one day was set aside for the country teams to play the Sydney grade teams, which always combined in pairs for this purpose. Bradman played for the combined St. George–University side against Riverina at Hurstville Oval – and scored 125* as an opening bat. (Riverina, incidentally, proved eventual winners of that Country Week carnival, with an unbeaten record.) This was on 16 November, and Bradman was not to know that exactly a month later, on 16 December, he was to be a first-class cricketer.

His selection for the State side was not straightforward, even when it came about. The team to leave Sydney for the southern tour (to Adelaide and Melbourne) consisted of 12 names – but not Bradman's. J. M. Gregory and H. S. B. Love then informed New South Wales they would be unable to make the tour, and thus it came about that their two places were filled by Don Bradman and Albert Scanes, both St George players, the one of course with no first-class experience at all, and Scanes, a cakemaker in Sydney, with a solitary Shield match behind him the previous season when he helped fill the side before the New South Wales members of the 1926 team to England had got back home.

It was a fresh adventure for Don Bradman when he left Central Station, Sydney, on Monday morning, 12 December 1927, as a member of a Sheffield Shield side for the first time. Whether he would play in either Adelaide or Melbourne was still not certain. Either he or Scanes was considered the likely 12th man, and Bradman himself later said, so far as the Adelaide game was concerned, 'in the normal way I was to have been twelfth man'. Bradman was, incidentally, the only one of the 12 New South Wales players entirely new to first-class cricket.

Advantage was taken of the newly opened railway line to Broken Hill to send – for the first time – the Shield team there on its way to Adelaide. Broken Hill was then a silver-mining town with a somewhat primitive cricket arena at Jubilee Oval, but a large crowd turned up to see the State side in the one-day match against a Barrier District team on 14 December. It was the first match Bradman ever played with a Sheffield Shield side, and he probably played only because Archie Jackson was ruled out through a boil above the knee. Batting at number four on a concrete pitch, Bradman scored 46 before being stumped, and shared a stand of 97 for the fourth wicket with his captain, Kippax. It was probably the only time in his adult life that Bradman batted in a serious match wearing ordinary civilian shoes, for the sprigs in his cricket boots proved absolutely unsuitable for the surface on which he played.

This southern tour with New South Wales provided a number of new experiences for Bradman. He spent a night in a train for the first time and, on leaving Broken Hill, went outside his native State of New South Wales for the first time in his life. This minor landmark was achieved on the night of 14–15 December, and Don Bradman saw Adelaide – his future home – for the first time at about 10.30 a.m. on 15 December 1927. The following day, with Archie Jackson's boil no better, Don Bradman made his debut in first-class cricket against South Australia at the Adelaide Oval.

Bradman was fortunate in having a hard and true wicket on which to play his debut innings in the first-class game – though the prospect of facing Grimmett was a formidable one. Moreover, the weather, at least on the first two days, was excessively hot – the game began in a temperature above 90 – and Bradman himself was suffering from an injured finger. His captain, Kippax, twice had to retire on the opening day through sun sickness. Bradman went in to bat for the first time in the first-class game two overs before tea on the first day against South Australia – at number seven in the order, to join his St George team-mate, Albert Scanes, at 250 for four, Kippax having retired. He went in to face Grimmett and Whitfield, and received his first ball from Grimmett. He opened his score with a pull to the boundary off Grimmett in his first over – the first of about 3,000 boundary strokes that Bradman was to make in his first-class career. He actually hit two fours off Grimmett in that first over, and reached his fifty after tea in 67 minutes. His first partnership in first-class cricket realised 48 with Scanes. By close of play Bradman was 65*, out of 150 since he had come in, in an hour and three-quarters, and New South Wales were 400 for seven. By a strange coincidence, on the very same day at Melbourne Victoria also scored exactly 400 – for only two wickets, and Ponsford was not out with 234. The next day Ponsford was to make the new world record score of 437, little knowing that a debutant named Bradman had just arrived on the scene who was to take that, and many other records, under his wing before too many seasons were to pass.

Back at the Adelaide Oval, while Ponsford was making history at Melbourne, Bradman was also making his first niche in the record books of the first-class game with a century innings on debut. He did it before a Saturday crowd, in sweltering heat, and reached three figures by stepping well back and pulling 'Perker' Lee to the boundary at deep fine-leg – Bradman had the satisfaction of watching the ball hit the fence without troubling to run. His hundred had taken him 161 minutes, somewhat below his career average, but understandably so. With the last man as his partner, Bradman was caught off a cut at third slip for 118 in just over three hours. He had been very anxious to do well in this innings, and he had triumphed at the first time of asking. His innings had been chanceless. On reflection it seems that he must have had in mind the familiar nursery maxim, 'begin as you mean to go on'.

Patsy Hendren was watching the innings – he was in Adelaide as coach to the South Australian Cricket Association – and no doubt remembered it on his second view of Bradman a season later, when the youthful prodigy made 87 and 132* for New South Wales against the M.C.C. George Hele was umpiring in Bradman's first match, and recalls the occasion as follows: 'He was only a teenager then, just a bright, happy, smiling boy with a world to conquer. I could tell, that day in Adelaide, that New South Wales had discovered yet another champion to follow the long line of Charles Bannerman, William Murdoch, Victor Trumper, Charles Macartney, Reggie Duff, and

Alan Kippax. Don was a cordial kid who seemed to love batting more than anything in life – even more than fielding along the boundary, in which he took great joy. The quality which impressed me most was his confidence in himself, even in the company of Alan Kippax, the New South Wales captain, Tommy Andrews, Arthur Mailey, Bert Oldfield, and other established players. His fielding impressed me even more than his batting in that game at Adelaide Oval. His throw was so fast and so accurate, its speed quite astounding from one so small.'

Alan Kippax, in that first innings at Adelaide, had become Don Bradman's first partner in a century stand in first-class cricket – they added 111 for the eighth wicket on the Saturday morning at well over a run a minute. Bradman was outscored by Kippax on that occasion, but that was not often to be the case thereafter. It was the first of 164 partnerships of 100 or more that Bradman was to share in first-class cricket – and his most prolific partner in these stands was indeed Alan Kippax, who took part in 15 of them. Grace and efficiency were combined when these two were together, and Kippax was to remain Bradman's captain in the New South Wales side throughout the whole of Bradman's playing association with that State.

The 118 at Adelaide, good as it was, was wisely received with some caution by those who remembered how frequently a century on debut had proved the kiss of death to a first-class cricketer. It is amazing how rarely, in the long list of names of such players, has the successful debutant gone on to achieve any lasting fame in the game. There have, of course, been a few notable exceptions: and the name of D. G. Bradman was the most triumphant exception of them all.[1]

Bradman's footwork, not least against Grimmett, was the outstanding feature of his batting thus early in his career. The Special Representative in Adelaide of the *Sydney Morning Herald* thought that his cut stroke (which eventually dismissed him) was his weakest stroke in general, though he prophetically went on: 'But the rapidity of his advance from the matting wicket standard he was accustomed to only a season ago leaves no room for doubt that he will acquire an all-round mastery at no distant date.'

Bradman, still with a bruised finger, scored 33 in just over an hour in the second innings at Adelaide before Grimmett bowled him. But his place in the side for Melbourne was now secure. On arrival there, the New South Wales team attended the funeral of J. V. Saunders, the great Australian bowler, on the afternoon before their match against Victoria. It was of course Bradman's first visit to Melbourne. He was to produce some of the finest performances of his career on the Melbourne Cricket Ground, but on this occasion scored only 31 and 5. Here he took his first catch in first-class

---

[1] Bradman was the 16th Australian batsman to score a century on his debut in first-class cricket. The other 15, not many of whom advanced to further repute, were, in chronological order, as follows: C. S. Gordon-Stewart, C. W. Rock, J. O'Halloran, L. W. Pye, H. G. S. Morton, W. McPetrie, A. G. Moyes, N. L. Gooden, F. Hyett, N. F. Callaway, J. Bogle, E. B. Forssberg, D. Mullarkey, S. C. Wootton, H. O. Rock.

cricket, which ended an almost flawless innings of 202 by Ponsford: it was a comparatively easy catch over Bradman at mid-on, which he had ample time to run for. In the same match Woodfull made scores of 99 and 191*. Bradman was seeing both him and Ponsford for the first time.

Don Bradman learnt to admire – and to respect – the bowling of Grimmett from his very first encounter with him at Adelaide. In the process of years, Grimmett was to capture Bradman's wicket as many times as any other bowler in first-class cricket: he actually shared this distinction with Hedley Verity – ten dismissals each of Bradman. All ten Grimmett dismissals were of course on Australian wickets. Grimmett certainly conceded his runs, and indeed his centuries, to Bradman, but it is undeniably true that Bradman's average in opposition to Grimmett was a very great deal lower than against any of the other great bowlers of his era. When he was interviewed by Ashley Mallett in 1976,[1] Grimmett claimed that Bradman was 'no good against good length leg-spin'. To maintain that Bradman was 'no good' against *any* type of bowling is, perhaps, overstating the case. He was, to go no further, good enough to score a century on debut against it. Grimmett said: 'He wouldn't use his feet to me to get to the pitch of the ball. Rather like Garry Sobers of this era, he was anchored to the crease.' In fact Bradman's footwork is not often called into question – and neither Bradman nor Sobers have need to be ashamed of their footwork or of the runs they amassed. But Grimmett was always a passionate upholder of the skills of bowlers, and would share none of the adherence to the magic appeal of batsmanship, an appeal nurtured by Bradman in particular in his prime. Grimmett – has any bowler, incidentally, ever had a name more full of Dickensian suggestiveness? – has always preferred the bowler to emerge victorious in any stories between batsmen and bowlers, and he has himself told how, at Sydney once, when he was being severely punished by Bradman, he hit on the idea of bowling only googlies at him – 'and it had him in trouble from the start'. He continued: 'He tried to go on punching instead of getting used to the new form of attack, and so he lost his wicket. It seemed that the Sydney Hill crowd had realised what was going on, because when I switched to googlies one of them called out, "Why don't you bowl him some more leg-breaks, Clarrie – he likes them!" '

There was more than just cricket in the fortnight that Don Bradman was on tour with the State team at the end of 1927. He was the 'new boy', and he found himself not just playing but travelling and living with men who were ripe in the ways of the world as well as in the ways of cricket. To them Bradman was the raw country youth, fit material for initiation ceremonies and practical jokes. He was not yet an awesome record-breaker and there was no reason to suspect he would be. Big scores in Bowral and Moss Vale cut very little ice with the veterans of the first-class arena. The most they could envisage was that he would make some big scores for the State and

---

[1] *World of Cricket* (Sydney), January 1977.

become one of them. Meanwhile they discovered he could play the piano. Was this, they asked him, why his back muscles were in such good shape for cricket? As the train from Sydney proceeded on its long journey, the young Bradman was asked to play on an imaginary keyboard and remove his shirt so that his back muscles could be studied. In the hotel at Adelaide they asked him to do it again, on a real piano – a topless artist of the '20s – while non-cricketing guests were enlisted for the process of 'judging'. He was sent on a fruitless errand one night from the team's hotel in the centre of Adelaide to the seaside suburb of Glenelg, some eight or so miles away – all then strange territory to him. Sometimes Bradman laughed, sometimes he did not.

It is often the case that the biter is bit: and those who sought in that December of 1927 to discomfort the young and untried Bradman, before very long found themselves discomfited to the painful extent that they were quite removed from their long-accustomed positions as popular public heroes and supplanted by this country boy who methodically and ruthlessly put them in the shadows by his uncompromising mastery. The springs that motivate men's actions can never be determined for certain, and Don Bradman would have emerged as a great batsman in first-class cricket without the events of that December. Whether he would have proceeded along his path so relentlessly and so determinedly is open to question – a question that cannot be answered, but, even if it contains only a grain of relevance, puts into some perspective the astonishing career of Bradman. He did not forget these incidents at his expense as he looked back on his first season, and determined to answer them the way he knew best – with his bat.

The remainder of Bradman's first season in first-class cricket, now as a regular member of the State side, saw a mixture of poor and fine batting. He made a duck, first ball, when he made his Sydney debut in Shield cricket, playing across a ball from F. J. Gough, a Brisbane insurance officer and a second-string slow bowler for Queensland, who was then averaging about 80 runs per wicket in Shield cricket. Bradman had made up his mind to play the ball to mid-on (as Kippax had just done) before even it was bowled: and he paid the penalty and learned a lesson at the same time. Thus the first ball he ever received in first-class cricket on the Sydney Cricket Ground – where he was to become an unparalleled idol – bowled him!

He scored his first century on the Sydney ground in his final Shield innings of the season – 134*in 3¾ hours in a crisis against the Shield winners, Victoria, including Blackie and Ironmonger. He was one of eight players to score a century in that match, and on the first day he had played before the biggest crowd of his life so far – a then record Shield attendance of 30,386. As to that hundred, it was said at the time: 'Probably there are many more accomplished batsmen, so far as stroke equipment is concerned, in Sydney grade cricket, but none who has the temperament to go in as he did when wickets were falling before lunch and stay there in defiance of a Victorian attack.'

Bradman, by the way, made his debut in Shield cricket in the very season

in which matches were limited in duration for the first time – to four days of
5½ hours and a fifth day of 2½ hours. The leading batsmen on the Australian
stage at that time had all been brought up in Sheffield Shield matches where
time had never been of the essence. In his debut season Bradman finished
second to Kippax in the New South Wales Shield averages. The difference
was a very large one – Kippax averaging 80·70 and Bradman 46·22. It was
a good, but not sensational start. Within a year Bradman was taking second
place to no one, and many of the State records, not least those held by
Kippax, began to fall with inexorable regularity into the lap of Bradman.

It may also be instructive to record that in Don Bradman's debut season
in the first-class game, the New South Wales Cricket Association paid their
Sheffield Shield players an allowance of £1 per day when they were playing
in Sydney (Sundays excluded), and 25 shillings per day when they were
away. Some players genuinely could not afford to play for the State. In
Bradman's particular case he had the added burden of rail fares between
Bowral and Sydney – a consideration that was no concern of the State
executive. There was, however, always the prospect – for those good enough –
of a lucrative tour to England, or at least some local repute in Sydney to
assist business advancement.

Five-day Sheffield Shield matches imposed a fresh strain on Bradman that
he had never before known. His 'marathon' matches as a youth had been
spread over successive Saturdays and his grade cricket in Sydney was likewise a Saturday matter. The tiresome process of travelling back to Bowral at
the end of each day's play at the Sydney Cricket Ground could not have
failed to prompt thoughts of moving to Sydney. In grade cricket in 1927–28,
after turning down an overture to join the somewhat weak Northern District
club, he topped the St George batting for the first time, but his average of
58·71, like his average for New South Wales, gave no indication of the
avalanche to come. He played in more matches for St George this season
(nine in all) than in any other season with them, for thereafter his first-class
absences ate substantially into the Sydney grade programme. After his first-
class debut, he ended up the season with scores of 22 v North Sydney, 65* v
Balmain, 47 v Manly, and 87 v Randwick (and against Manly had his best
bowling figures in all his eight seasons in Sydney grade cricket – four for 55).
Thus he scored only a single century in ten innings for St George, and
though he aggregated over 1,100 runs in all types of cricket that season, his
century ratio – four hundreds in 32 innings – was positively the lowest of his
entire career. In minor matches alone, where he had hitherto been so
frequently dominant, he scored two centuries in 22 innings.

His impact had not been quite sufficient to gain him a place in the
Australian side that toured New Zealand under V. Y. Richardson in
February–April 1928, though he, P. M. Hornibrook and J. Scaife were
named as reserves. Bradman had played in only two first-class matches when
the tour selectors, Hugh Trumble (Victoria), Tom Howard (New South
Wales) and Richardson himself (South Australia), announced the names on

29 December 1927, and thus to be even a reserve after eight days of first-class experience was a distinction most rapidly gained. (Vic Richardson, of course, was the fielding captain throughout Bradman's 118 at Adelaide.) In the event no vacancy in the side occurred, and Bradman did not go to New Zealand. Instead, he made the first of many country tours of New South Wales in the company of capable cricketers. A short visit was made to the familiar pastures of Bowral – the team being mainly St George players – to open the new turf wicket at Loseby Park, where a great deal of money had been spent by the council to improve amenities. In the first week of April, Bradman embarked on a 12-day tour, embracing Easter, with Arthur Mailey's team of New South Welshmen, called the Bohemians, who included State cricketers in T. J. E. Andrews, E. L. Waddy and C. O. Nicholls, as well as Mailey and Bradman. Mailey had been taking teams to the country for some years, and this tour of the South-Western Districts of New South Wales was a highly unpropitious one for Bradman, who played in all seven matches (there were just 11 players in the party) and mustered just 77 runs, average 11! Highly un-Bradmanesque! These matches were played at Parkes, Canowindra, Cowra, Grenfell, Cootamundra, Canberra and Dudauman; and at Bradman's birthplace, Cootamundra, he was run out for 1. It was on this tour, when the results did not matter too much, that Tommy Andrews instructed Bradman in the arts of running and calling, weaknesses that had been quickly spotted by the pundits in Sydney. The tour ended just in time to enable Bradman to attend a smoke social in Sydney in honour of the marriage of his State captain, Alan Kippax.

Thus ended D. G. Bradman's last summer as a resident of Bowral. He was now a first-class cricketer, aged 19, with two Sheffield Shield centuries behind him. 'It began to appear', he later recorded, 'that whatever the future might have in store for me lay chiefly in my bat.'

The season of 1928–29 was to prove something of a watershed in both the story of Australian cricket and the story of Don Bradman. It was the season in which the Australian eleven had to be practically rebuilt: at its start the old school of Australian cricketers were in the ascendant; by its close – and after a 4–1 defeat by Chapman's touring side – youth had been given its chance and there was healthy optimism as eyes looked towards 1930, an optimism that events were to justify. Don Bradman played his part in this rejuvenescence of Australian cricket, and to some extent he was fortunate that his first full season in first-class cricket coincided with the presence in Australia of a strong Test team from England and the complementary necessity for Australia's selectors to find new and worthy members, especially batsmen, for the national side. At all events, he began the season as a youth of 20 with five Shield matches behind him at the modest average of 46, but ended it securely on the cricket map, already a celebrity with a new record aggregate of runs for an Australian season and a certainty for the next tour of England in 1930.

S.D.B.–D

If the good fortune of circumstances had a hand in sending Bradman so swiftly to the top of the tree, his own skill – and his own ambition – were equal to meet the challenges. He advanced meteorically in 1928–29, partly because he was given the opportunities and partly (perhaps substantially) because of his firm determination to get into the Test side, knowing well enough that Test opponents from England came out only every four years. If any one season was to be more important to him than any other in the early years of his first-class career, he knew it must be 1928–29. His primary task was to make his place permanent in the New South Wales eleven – a task eased by the State's encouragement of enterprising young batsmen. His second task – and this was less than a year since he had first stepped on a first-class field – was to do well enough to be picked for the Tests. Was this wishful thinking? Or arrogance? Or the special brand of Bradman ambition? Bradman himself explained it thus:

> You may say this sounds like presumption on the part of a youth whose experience of first-class cricket was so very small, but it had been done before – the great left-hander, Clem Hill, was a Test player in his teens – and I see no need for apology in anyone having a reasonable belief in himself, coupled with ambition.

That really was the key to Bradman's emergence as a Test cricketer and as a world champion – the belief in himself, an unshakeable belief, coupled with permanent ambition. That unshakeable belief, many years later, caused him to give a classic and unique reply to Neville Cardus's enquiry as to what he attributed his success as a batsman. The Don, quite simply, and truthfully, said that he could not conceive the possibility of a bowler getting him out.

In September 1928, a few days after his 20th birthday, Don Bradman took an important decision. He left Bowral and the care and company of his parents, and took lodgings in Sydney. The constant journeying from Bowral to Sydney to play cricket for St George or for New South Wales, despite a good railway service, was becoming oppressive and wasteful – a 5 a.m. start to arrive back in Bowral about midnight. Like nearly every Sydney grade or State cricketer, he realised the enormous advantage of living in Sydney. The move, just before the start of the crucial 1928–29 season, had two important effects. The first, and comparatively minor one, was that practice on turf wickets would be available to him during the week for the first time, a luxury denied him in Bowral. The second, and decisive, effect was that he now knew irrevocably that he had thrown in his lot with the game of cricket. His future depended on cricket, and depended on his making a success of the life he had chosen. To go to Sydney was a serious step – it might, with a lesser being than Bradman, have proved disastrous. 'Yet', he wrote, 'I was happy – deep down in me was a certainty that I had done the right thing. I felt that it was the only course whereby I could the more surely expand, and so was content, rich in my belief of the future.'

Here, at 20, in a strange city, was Bradman showing all his good sense and nurturing his ambition with the same calculation that was to characterise his later career. Just as was to be the case when he was first to arrive in England – cricket before all else – so it was when he arrived in Sydney. His character, under the wise influence of his mother and father, had already been formed. He set out, quite unashamedly and unambiguously, to get into the first Test side at Brisbane.

On going to Sydney, Bradman spent his first six months with Mr and Mrs G. H. Pearce at their home at Concord West. G. H. Pearce was an insurance inspector with the well-known Australian firm, A.M.F. Insurance Society, and in the course of his duties frequently visited Davis and Westbrook in Bowral, who were local agents for A.M.F. Don Bradman saw him regularly on these visits and formed a close friendship with him, and his offer to house the young Bradman in 1928 was gladly accepted both by Bradman and his parents.

The commercial value of Bradman's name was as yet virtually nil. He himself might have been confident enough that he would ascend to the heights, but even the best judges could not foresee what an astonishing future he was to enjoy. No one, when he arrived in Sydney, clamoured for his services. (This was soon to change.) He still had to provide himself with an income, and in this respect he was fortunate to continue his association with his Bowral employer, Mr Percy Westbrook, who fortuitously chose at that moment to open a new office in Sydney of his real-estate business. When Don Bradman informed him that he had definitely chosen to move from Bowral to Sydney, Mr Westbrook offered him the post of Secretary of the company (Deer and Westbrook) in Sydney. From that position came Bradman's salary, though as a 20-year-old immersed in cricket aspirations, he did not of course truly perform the functions of a bona fide Secretary.

Living in Sydney at that time was J. C. Davis, the distinguished editor of the Sydney *Referee* and authority on Australian cricket, who had then seen every Test in Australia for more than 30 years. He had seen the young Bradman score his 134 not out in a crisis against Victoria at the Sydney Cricket Ground at the end of January 1928, and was impressed with him. He probably also saw him in one or more innings for St George, and at the beginning of October 1928, Bradman having been selected for the Rest in the forthcoming Test Trial at Melbourne, Davis sent over the following assessment of Bradman for a London evening paper. It should be remembered that at that date Bradman had played in no more than five first-class matches and had finished a very modest 14th in the Sheffield Shield batting averages of 1927–28:

It is years since I met a young player possessing such a fine temperament for big cricket. He hails from Bowral, a southern town, where he learnt the game and built up a reputation for making centuries, not by barn-dooring but by batting as it was known when Harry Graham and R. A. Duff flourished.

Like that nimble pair, he is exceptionally quick on his feet, and gets into the slow bowling with skill and relish.

Bradman has a good defence and fine strokes on both sides of the wicket. He represents the old type of batsman as distinct from that, so common in these times, with the two-eyed stance and the monotonous push to leg.

As Bradman is a keen and splendid field, generally in the outfield, and a good batsman, at the pinch he is potentially a Test match cricketer.

At the pinch! Well, Mr Davis was to know a little more within the next few weeks, as indeed was the rest of the world. It was for Archie Jackson that J. C. Davis fell over backwards – Jackson, who had 'much of the Trumper grace and timing' and who was 'nearer to the Trumper ideal than anyone else'. It is true that Jackson exceeded even Kippax in artistry, but it is also true that the selectors chose to ignore him until the fourth Test of 1928–29 (by which time the series had already been decided and Australia had been badly hit by injuries) while opting for Bradman at the first opportunity.

The comparison with Harry Graham – so naturally audacious a batsman to be styled 'The Little Dasher' – had been made a month earlier by 'Third Man', *The Cricketer*'s special correspondent in Australia, who saw Bradman as one of those 'in the running', but no more, for a place in the Tests:

Bradman, of New South Wales, shapes as if he has the brains to know what to do with the bowling, physical ability to do it, and the courage to carry it out. He is a product of a rural district, but, though aggressive, is not agrestic. Fearless footwork is the foundation of his batting, which is eminently sound. Australia needs another Harry Graham, and Bradman may be the man.

Australian critics have always had less evidence than Englishmen on which to base their judgments. Bradman had played in only five first-class matches, and in them had scored two centuries and been out five times for under 20. He had scored only 416 runs, but had made them at more than 35 an hour off his own bat, and had only just missed selection – in his debut season in first-class cricket – for the strong Australian side that left for New Zealand in February 1928. Added to his impressive record in lesser cricket and the basic soundness of his style, his early ventures in the first-class arena entitled him at least to be 'in the running' for some honours in 1928–29.

It seems that the departure from Bowral had no unsettling effect on Bradman, who found his feet in Sydney smoothly enough if his opening score for St George is any evidence. On the first Saturday of the new season he reached his century in 130 minutes against Gordon at Chatswood Oval, ending the day with 106 not out. When the game was continued the following week he was bowled for 107, but the start was good enough. (After 6 October, owing to his commitments in first-class cricket, Bradman was free to play for St George again only once before the first week of April.)

Then, in the most important game of his career so far, the Test Trial at Melbourne in mid-October, when he played for the Rest of Australia v Australia, he failed dismally. It must have been as big a disappointment for the selectors as for Bradman. In both innings he was unimpressive: and he made only 14 and 5. After the first innings débâcle, when Bradman's side were all out for 111, Ponsford said that the Rest batsmen exaggerated the importance of the occasion – little consolation, to be sure, to either Bradman or his colleagues. To make matters worse, the M.C.C. side had now disembarked from the *Otranto* and had begun in good form at Perth. The whole continent was talking cricket, and interest in the forthcoming Tests was tremendous. When the M.C.C. got to Adelaide for their second match, the President of the South Australian Cricket Association, Mr H. Fisher, said that Chapman's side was regarded as 'the strongest since the war' – and Don Bradman, if he read that verdict, could only have pondered on the sudden decline, just when it particularly mattered, of both his form and his prospects. There are not many big matches in the Australian programme to play oneself back into form. 30 November at Brisbane was only a little more than a month away.

Any momentary doubts had to be swept away now or never, and Bradman proceeded to do that triumphantly and decisively in his first Shield match of the season, on his debut in Brisbane – at the Exhibition Ground, where the first Test was due to be played – against the luckless Queensland, who were to suffer such crippling punishment from the Bradman bat in the years to come. For the first time in his career in first-class cricket he batted in his favourite position of number three – and he responded brilliantly with a century in each innings. (He had batted at number six in both innings of the Test Trial, and never higher than number six in any of his big matches of 1927–28. For St George he was batting at number four.) His scores of 131 and 133 not out against Queensland – he surpassed his first innings score with the winning hit on the final morning – put a fresh aspect on Bradman the cricketer. His will had triumphed, and he returned to Sydney with all the confidence he wanted.

Now he was to face his biggest test of all. On 2 November, the day after his Brisbane lustre, his name was announced in the New South Wales team to play the M.C.C. at Sydney. There was a week to go, but he could not turn out for his club on the intervening Saturday as he had been absent in Brisbane when the first round of those matches had been played the week before.

A feature of Bradman's limited career up to now had been the manner, fortuitously or otherwise, in which he had been enabled to see at close quarters big innings compiled by his contemporaries in the first-class game. In only seven matches he had seen as many as 20 hundreds scored (not including four scored by himself) and he saw, and no doubt learnt from, a variety of techniques in the process. For his own New South Wales side he had seen innings by his captain, Kippax, of 315 not out, 143 and 134; two hundreds in the same match (and brilliant ones) by Archie Jackson; and even a hundred by Oldfield. He had fielded out to nine first-class hundreds by opponents, including – in only the second match of his career – scores of

202 by Ponsford and 99 and 191 not out by Woodfull. Among others, he had also fielded through centuries by Hendry, Ryder, Rigg and the fine Queensland right-hander, Cecil Thompson (158 not out). All this may indicate an over-perfection of wickets in Australian cricket of the time or perhaps a paucity of good bowlers, but there is little doubt that Bradman was the sort of young cricketer who would readily absorb all the best in what he saw and remember it to his advantage. He never forgot, for example, the strokes of Macartney and Woolley that he saw as a 12-year-old boy: and he must certainly have benefited by watching, so early in his own career, such practitioners as Kippax, Ponsford, Woodfull and Jackson. It cannot be certain quite how *much* benefit he obtained, however. For in Bradman's case he had certainly formed his own ideas of batting before he had seen any of the great celebrities of his time, apart from the view of the Test match in 1921. He never copied any other cricketer's methods. As Robertson-Glasgow once wrote of him: 'Bradman is an incurable original, a *gamin* who gleefully longed to join the pirates, and became captain of them all.'

As his first confrontation with English cricketers approached, he made no secret of wishing to see Hobbs in action. A few days before, against South Australia in Adelaide, Hobbs had reached 50,000 runs in his career and held the world record of 158 first-class centuries. But after seven strenuous days' cricket against South Australia and Victoria, he stood down from the match against New South Wales. This match is always a big event in a touring side's programme, and Chapman's team arrived in Sydney via some winning and losing moments at the Melbourne Cup (when Hendren backed the winner and Sutcliffe's bet finished last) to be greeted by some famous New South Wales names, including Noble, Turner, Kelly, Kippax, Oldfield, Syd Gregory and Sydney Smith. Warren Bardsley made the ominous pronouncement that the State had unearthed a cricketer named Don Bradman, whom the M.C.C. would have to watch.

If Bradman did not see Hobbs in action, he saw plenty of M.C.C.'s other batsmen. Hammond scored 225, Hendren 167 and Jardine 140 – and M.C.C.'s total of 734 for seven declared was the highest total Bradman ever fielded through in his life, subject only to the Oval Test of '38. Bradman's own contributions were formidable – 87 and, in the follow-on, 132 not out in only 2½ hours. With an undefeated century from Kippax – the pair put on an unbroken 249 for the fourth wicket – he saved the game. Thus he scored a century on his first appearance against an M.C.C. team, scored in intense heat and against Larwood, Tate, Hammond and Freeman. He had also played before the biggest crowd of his life so far – a record day's attendance for the S.C.G. (apart from Tests) of 43,117 were present on the Saturday and 84,703 in all. It was a landmark in his career: runs impressively and quickly scored against the most important team he had so far encountered and against an attack keyed up to concert pitch. Despite his uncertain start to the first-class season, he had now amassed 502 runs in his three matches at an average of 125·50 – enough to anticipate the coining of the word 'Bradmanesque', which had not yet been used, and certainly enough to put him firmly in the selectors' list for the first Test against England. A new champion was positively emerging, and the objective which he had set himself when he left Bowral only two months before – to play himself into his very best form and to get into the first Test side – was now well towards being achieved. The remarkable string of centuries which Bradman had made in junior cricket he was now carrying into the first-class game. And he was still only 20.

It should be added that until the final stages of the New South Wales game, Chapman did all in his power to get Bradman out. It was no help to the M.C.C. to see this young hopeful take a hundred off their attack and give himself confidence for the Tests. But according to Hammond, who was in the field, 'young Bradman looked as if he could stay for ever . . . None of our bowlers could do any more than feed him runs that day.' That was to become the common complaint of bowlers for 20 years to come. That Sydney match, too, marked the first meeting on the cricket field of the two most puissant run-makers of the 1930s – Hammond and Bradman. Hammond put on record that Bradman's name was unfamiliar to him before that match, and when he first saw him in the field – 'a slim, shortish boy with a grim, nervous face' – he looked 'not very formidable'. It was a lightning return from mid-off by Bradman that ended Hammond's innings in that match – run out. By the end of the game, with 219 runs under the belt of the 'not very formidable' boy, Hammond conceded that 'most of us realized that here was a batsman'.

Australia also realized that here was a batsman, and moreover one with the exact temperament for big cricket. He had shown he was an aggressive driver, had strokes on both sides of the wicket and could jump in to slow bowling very quickly. His strokes revealed confidence and certainty. When he drove, he drove hard; and when he cut, he cut hard. He could leg glance or drive past the bowler with equal versatility. His defence, which had always been good, was now likened to Woodfull's. And he was a magnificent outfield – a department in which Australia was then notably deficient. He was nicknamed the 'Century-maker' around this time, a ready sign that he had arrived on the scene, and that nickname was soon to give way to the more familiar and intimate 'Bowral Boy'. The whole cricketing world was soon to speak of the 'Bowral Boy', and when a young man has achieved a national nickname he has achieved, in a sense, more than a knighthood. A man may have a knighthood and be unknown to the world. To win a nickname is to be famous. It is the tribute of the public.

Bradman's stature in Australian cricket in the middle of November 1928 – and he was not yet then a Test cricketer – can be readily gauged from a small incident at the Sydney Cricket Ground that month. During the Australian XI v M.C.C. match (which followed immediately on the New South Wales game), Bradman had some articles of clothing stolen from the dressing-room – his N.S.W. No. 1 blazer, his N.S.W. No. 1 cap, and a pair of cream trousers. No other player in the match had anything stolen: the thief's eyes were on Bradman's items alone. No doubt there still exist somewhere, secreted guiltily from sight, the blazer, cap and trousers of the young 'discovery' of 1928–29. The articles were never returned, and a month later the N.S.W.C.A. delegates decided to replace the goods.

Bradman, by the way, in that Australian XI match, duly got his first sight of Hobbs, and saw him pass fifty in each innings. Bradman himself was easily top scorer in the first innings with 58 not out, when he emerged with great credit from his ordeal against J. C. White, who bowled beautifully and with astonishing accuracy under conditions all in his favour. White bowling into the breeze and making the ball dip from the off into the wicket set a new problem for Bradman. He mastered it carefully – very carefully, for his fifty was the slowest of his entire career (2¾ hours) and he took 77 minutes to score 20. But he saved his side from disaster with a brilliant defence which completely dispelled any remaining doubt there may have been about him as a batsman. He had now scored 277 against the M.C.C. – for only one dismissal. Charlie Macartney said he was now quite satisfied that Bradman had clinched his Test place. Sydney Southerton's immediate verdict that evening on Bradman's innings was clear and prophetic:

> It left the firm conviction that here shines Australia's brightest new star – a man who undoubtedly will make his mark on English wickets in future tours.

Bradman had one of his earliest experiences of public speaking on the first day of the Australian XI v M.C.C. match, when he made a gracious reply during the luncheon interval to the presentation to him by the N.S.W.C.A. of a cricket bag in recognition of his two brilliant hundreds against Queensland. He was soon to become a confident speaker, displaying all the qualities of a clear and concise mind.

The Australian selectors for the Tests of 1928–29 were Warren Bardsley (New South Wales), Dr C. E. Dolling (South Australia), J. S. Hutcheon (Queensland) and E. E. Bean (Victoria), all former first-class players. To this quartet belongs the distinction of introducing Don Bradman to Test match cricket, though in all conscience Bradman virtually selected himself. The team for the first Test at Brisbane was due to be announced on the Monday of the Australian XI match v M.C.C. (19 November), Bradman's average for the season when the selectors foregathered being 140. Even so, the ways of selectors, then as now, could never be forecast with certainty: and Bradman's youth and comparative lack of experience (only nine first-class matches) might have gone against him. Prior to the 1928–29 series getting under way, youth had not been madly popular with Australian selectors, and the meteoric rise of young batsmen had been more a phenomenon of the nineteenth century. (Charles Kelleway, who was to be one of Bradman's colleagues in the first Test, was playing first-class cricket *before Bradman was born*. Test cricket in Australia in 1928–29 was commonly accepted to be 'an old man's game' – which made the success of Bradman, just around the corner, all the more thrilling and inspiring when it did come, not least to Australia's youth.)

Bradman himself has related how, on that fateful Monday, after the day's play at the Sydney Cricket Ground, he waited in his lodgings for the announcement on the wireless of the selected names. He did not know that the selectors deliberated for three hours, well into the night, and all he and the Australian public were told was that the announcement was delayed and would be broadcast later. The young Bradman – who had an innings to face on the morrow against Larwood, Tate, White and co. – took himself off to bed and told his landlady he would see the news in the morning papers. It so happened that the bedroom adjoining his had a wireless set tuned loud, and within ten minutes of being in bed Bradman heard the names broadcast on station 2FC – in alphabetical order, his own name being first.[1] He was the first St George cricketer in history to be selected for a Test side.

Bradman was not yet in the side – critical opinion thought that either he or Hendry would be 12th man, though it turned out to be Oxenham – but at the very worst he was on the brink of a Test career. 'I cannot say that I was unduly elated', Bradman recalled. 'I was not conscious of excitement, but of course was pleased that I had accomplished a task which I had definitely set out to do.' So ambition was realized and a cool head maintained. Ten years later, when Bradman looked back on the occasion in his autobiography, it all seemed very mattei-of-fact and inevitable: 'My chief feeling was, if I remember aright, that I had accomplished something I had set myself to accomplish, and that was that.' He might almost have added Q.E.D. – had there not been much more to demonstrate and achieve beyond the initial selection.

Bradman's first Test match coincided with the first Test match ever played at Brisbane – where no English touring team had ever been beaten in any sort of match in history, the first English side having played there in 1882–83. Cricketers pay little heed to this sort of tradition, however; and in the rainy season in Queensland, with local weather prophets indeed predicting a tropical storm during the match, anything could happen. Test pitches in Australia were then left open to the elements once the match had begun, so any prospect of rain could not have been welcomed by the debutant Bradman. Bradman's two fine matches at Sydney must have been in Chapman's mind when he told the *Sporting Globe* of Melbourne before the match: 'We are under no delusions regarding the strength of our opponents. We know we shall have to fight very hard for victory, but we have a very strong team.'

Chapman's 'very strong team' duly inflicted on Australia the heaviest-ever

---

[1] The practice was that the selectors chose 12 names, without nominating a captain. Then a sub-committee of E. E. Bean (Victoria), H. W. Hodgetts (South Australia) and T. H. Howard (New South Wales) picked the captain, in this case Jack Ryder, a surprise choice and not a reigning State captain. There were many critics of this cumbersome procedure, cricketers claiming the job of selecting the captain to be one for the national selectors. The Board of Control relented in mid-season, and for the fourth and fifth Tests authorised the selectors to appoint a captain when choosing the team.

runs defeat in Test history. The margin was 675 runs. It was a disaster, a sinking to the depths by Australia who, in the words of Monty Noble, were 'out-manoeuvred, out-generalled, and out-played'. In the first innings Bradman, held back by his captain while wickets were falling on the Saturday evening, went in on the Monday morning to play his first innings in Test cricket with the score at 71 for five. He played with a confidence the other Australians lacked and hit Hammond for three successive fours. But after 33 minutes, his first Test innings ended. Tate had noticed that Bradman was strong on the leg side and was anxious to score as quickly as possible. With a well-disguised action, he pitched him a tempting-looking ball on the leg stump which appeared to be identical with previous deliveries. It was, however, Tate's slower ball and caused Bradman to hit too soon. He missed it and was clearly lbw. He made 18. His was one of eight lbw dismissals in the match. The predicted rain duly arrived – over half an inch during the fourth night – followed by hot sun, and Bradman had his first-ever experience of a truly sticky wicket when he went in a second time. He had never even seen such a wicket before, let alone played on one.[1] It was in fact so hopelessly sticky that his fate, and Australia's, was certain. The novelty of a drying pitch was too much for Bradman – he lasted only four minutes on it, and was caught for 1, deceived by a change of pace by White and spooning the ball gently to silly mid-off. Australia were all out in 25.3 overs for 66. 'Not up to Test match standard', was the verdict of Kelleway on Bradman after the match.

Bradman never forgot the painful memory of his baptism in Test cricket. It was not merely the magnitude of the defeat, nor his own small contribution of 19 runs (Ponsford made only 2 and 6). It was the policy of Chapman of batting a second time with a lead of 399 and not enforcing the follow-on. The crowd were disgusted and the critics divided. Moreover Australia were two men short, Gregory's knee having gone and Kelleway ill with ptomaine poisoning (though in a realistic finish both might have batted). Chapman batted on and on for just under six hours beyond his lead of 399 to set Australia 742 to win – against what turned out to be the impossible odds of a death-trap of a wicket.[2] It had been a torrid grounding for a youth of 20. Bradman often thought of this match when in later years his critics charged him with playing 'too hard'. He played to win, to be sure. But so did A. P. F. Chapman at Brisbane in '28.

Bradman's first outing in Test cricket gave no one an inkling that he would annex one Test record after another and become the greatest run-getter of his day. Maurice Tate regarded Bradman as his 'rabbit' and playfully accused Jack White of 'poaching' him in the second innings at Brisbane

---

[1] In January of the same year he had played on a pitch damaged by rain against Queensland at Sydney (and scored 13) but it was in no way comparable in viciousness to the Brisbane pitch.
[2] At that time 742 was the greatest fourth innings total ever set a side to win a Test. It has since been exceeded only once, when West Indies were set 836 on a perfect pitch (and drew) against England at Kingston in 1929–30.

before Tate could attack him himself. Unfortunately for Tate – and for many other English bowlers – Don Bradman overheard the reproof. Tate's sense of humour was lost on the young Bradman. In the first innings Tate had bowled 26 balls to Bradman for one snick to leg for four, then got him lbw. He had also got him lbw (also for 18) in the Australian XI match at Sydney. Tate did not think highly of Don Bradman's batting then – he was 'apt to play across the ball a lot', thought Tate. When the M.C.C. players discussed him before the Test, Tate held he had been lucky to make his hundred for New South Wales for 'he plays cross-bat'. When the tour of '28–29 ended, Tate is alleged to have said to Bradman: 'You'll have to keep that bat a bit straighter when you come to England, or you won't have much luck there.' Don Bradman was the sort of man to remember remarks like that.

When he had gone up to Brisbane a few days before the first Test, Don Bradman had to face the first of many rumours that circulated about him during his career. Statements were published that he was likely to join a sports goods firm in Brisbane and live permanently there and thus become eligible to play for Queensland in first-class cricket. He was naturally pounced upon as soon as he arrived in Brisbane and duly interviewed – and he promptly said that he had no intention 'at present' of leaving New South Wales. Whether Queenslanders held out some prospect for the future from that remark is just possible – fresh in their minds were Bradman's two hundreds on the Exhibition Ground less than a month before – but nothing was to come of it. Instead, Queensland suffered a worse punishment than any other Australian State at the hands of Bradman, who scored 13 centuries (including six of 200 or more) in his 23 innings against them and averaged 141·85 against them throughout his career.

In the Brisbane Test Bradman had been on the losing side for the fifth time in his ten first-class matches. He was learning, at the right age, what a tough mistress cricket could be. Would he get another chance? The selectors, before they left Brisbane, gave out a preliminary selection of 13 names for the second Test at Sydney, and Bradman's was among them. He was the only young cricketer included – the average age of the 13 was 39. A storm of criticism greeted the names, and from Sydney came an extraordinary outburst against the selectors from none other than the Australian Board of Control's own chairman, Aubrey Oxlade: 'Four selectors for Australia's Test team is most unsatisfactory', he said. 'I have always advocated an odd number of selectors because I believe this would obviate deadlock.' The 1928–29 season proved the only one in Australian cricket history when there were four selectors.

Bradman was omitted from the second Test, to his great disappointment, on the morning of the match. He was appointed 12th man. Ryder told him the news in the dressing-room a quarter of an hour before the start. It was the one and only occasion in Bradman's life in *any* cricket, first-class or minor, that he was made 12th man. The decision was not by any means the great howler that later generations might choose to call it. But the effect was that the selectors were attacked again for their rejection of youth. The youngest men in Australia's team were Ponsford and Nothling, both 28: the other nine were over 30. Warren Bardsley, an early and constant admirer of Don Bradman, later disclaimed any share in the dropping of the youngster: but understandably none of the other selectors cared to talk about it. It was jocularly remarked that those same selectors, when Bradman's great exploits of 1930 became known, contemplated changing their names by deed poll!

Bradman was a long way from idle in the second Test, for Ponsford had a bone broken in his left hand by Larwood on the first day, which put him out of the match, out of the series, and left him with a permanently crooked little finger. Thus, after fielding for 14½ hours against England at Brisbane, Bradman had the further pleasure of fielding – as substitute – for over 11 hours at Sydney while England amassed what was then the highest total ever made in Test cricket (636), this fresh record against Australia following immediately on the record defeat at Brisbane. The experience, however, gave him the opportunity of fielding through a second double-century by Hammond within six weeks, and of witnessing his first (and Hammond's first) double-hundred in a Test. In the short second innings Bradman made the only 'sub' catch of his life, holding Tate at mid-off.

E. L. a'Beckett, aged 21 and at Melbourne University and with a fine local record, and Bradman himself were the youngsters brought in for the third Test at Melbourne. Warwick Armstrong, in his role as critic, did not approve the recall of Bradman. In one of the less distinguished pronouncements of cricket history, he went into print the day before the match as follows:

> For his batting I should have preferred Harris to Bradman, who will probably be a good player later but, I think, is not a Test player at present.

(Gordon Harris was the South Australian opening bat who had played in the Test Trial at the beginning of the season, scoring 6 and 51, and was made 12th man for Ryder's XI in the trial match of the following season. He made 1,733 runs in his career in the Sheffield Shield, in 48 innings, at an average of 36·87. He never played in a Test. In due course he and Bradman were to become fellow-selectors for South Australia.)

If Armstrong did not consider Bradman a Test player, he had good cause to revise his opinion a week later. For Bradman scored 79 and 112, both without a chance, on his recall at Melbourne, and was never again omitted from an Australian Test side, other than through illness, until his retirement. Moreover, unlike most other players with lengthy spells in a Test side, there was never even the darkest hint (except, oddly, on a future occasion from Armstrong!) that he might be dropped. Only an occasional malicious barb, backed by no knowledge, called for his dethronement. For 20 years he was to reign as a colossus.

It was said at the time that it was on the recommendation of many prominent critics, and with an eye to future tours, that Bradman was given his second chance in the 1928–29 series. How closely the selectors heeded the critics, even those who spoke confidentially, cannot be certain. But had he not been chosen at Melbourne, he would assuredly have come back before the season was over. As it was, even before the end of the Melbourne Test, it was publicly said of Bradman that 'in him Australia undoubtedly possesses the keystone around whom the team of the coming generation will be built'. It was that Melbourne Test that really marked the start of Bradman's career as a world-beater. His confidence in his own powers was restored as to never thereafter to be forfeited.

His combined time at the crease in Melbourne was seven hours 21 minutes, and he faced more than 500 balls – all faced so impressively that comparisons with the youthful exploits of Clem Hill and Trumper were on everyone's lips. Oh, how much of the genius of Bradman Melbourne was to see! When he reached his maiden Test hundred at half-past five on the fifth afternoon – with an all-run four handsomely driven through mid-on off White – the tumult of cheering and demonstration of enthusiasm lasted fully two to three minutes. 'In fact', recorded Jack Hobbs in his diary, 'there was such a demonstration that we all sat down on the field while Oxenham walked down the pitch and shook Bradman's hand.' At this stage, Bradman (aged 20) was carefully nursing Oxenham (aged 37) and indeed was bearing on his young shoulders the burden of the Australian innings. He was then, at 20 years 129 days, the youngest player ever to score a hundred in Test cricket – it was the 178th Test match in history – being six months younger than Clem Hill had been in 1897–98. He was to hold the record for only a month, from 3 January to 4 February, when Archie Jackson, aged 19 – 'that "Rupert Brooke" of Australian batsmanship' – annexed it in the following Test.

Apart from Sir Robert Menzies, there have not been many Australian Prime Ministers who have gone into print on the game of cricket. One who did so was W. M. Hughes, who was Prime Minister from 1915 to 1923, and a useful enough batsman himself in his time, and who in 1932 published an article on 'The Best Test Match I Ever Saw'. 'I have always been a devotee of the game', he wrote, 'and have never missed seeing a Test match when opportunity offered. I have seen some great games, but taking all in all the 1929 Test match in Melbourne stands out in my memory the most vividly.' Of Bradman's role in that match he wrote as follows:

> As he came out the crowd gave him a tremendous reception. Little more than a boy, his name was in all men's mouths. The crowd had come there to see *him* bat. They were not to be disappointed.
>
> He had made 79 in the first innings, but he was to do still better in his second. He was a delight to watch. His footwork was wonderful, his timing superb, he was master of every stroke. The experts around me that day compared him with Trumper, some holding he was not in the same class, others strongly contending that he was Trumper's equal. But none denied that he was a wonderful batsman. Indeed, that could not be denied in the face of that flick of the wrist with which he

sent the ball travelling like a cannon shot to the boundary, reminding one of Ranjitsinhji.

. . . In Melbourne in the 1929 Test match Bradman . . . played a glorious innings of 112, and the great crowd cheered him again and again.

If the first of Don Bradman's 29 Test centuries brought scenes of great cheering at the Melbourne Cricket Ground, the reception of the news in Sydney was even more remarkable. New South Welshmen had resigned themselves to the departure from the stage of Macartney, and the new 'baby' – the Benjamin – of the Australian team, with all his audacious strokes and spectacular scores, was their new idol. As was common in the big cities of Australia, certain newspaper offices in Sydney – like the Sydney *Sun* in Martin Place – erected a large scoreboard to record the ball-by-ball progress of the Test match in Melbourne, and the street was crowded with a vast concourse of people watching Bradman's score progress towards the hundred. When the deed was done, there was joyful pandemonium:

> Thousands of hats were joyously tossed into the air. Women waved handkerchiefs and umbrellas. Motor-cars opened their throttles with mighty honks. People on passing trams cheered and clapped their hands, and tram bells clanged.

The Bradman legend was born.

For all the enthusiasm, Bradman was again on the losing side in Melbourne. He actually chased the winning hit, a four to long-on by Geary. The ball was later presented to Bradman, with a gold shield on it, by the Victorian Cricket Association to mark his first Test match hundred. That hundred, and the manner of its getting, was the great gain for Australia from their defeat. Since the First World War only Ponsford had scored a century for Australia under the age of 25. That old campaigner, E. W. Ballantine, was one of many who commented on the remarkably confident style of Bradman's 112: 'His strokes radiated beautifully round the wicket like the spokes of a cart wheel.' He went on to record:

> This boy, who has not yet attained his majority, entered the list of century makers in Tests under amazing conditions, batting more like a mature and experienced Test player than a recruit, giving no suggestion of rawness.
>
> He has a fine variety of strokes and is able to change his tactics according to the state of the game.
>
> He came in after Kippax and Ryder had lost their wickets and matters were looking serious for Australia. He had scored 24 when Woodfull, the Australians' 'sheet-anchor', departed, and from that point he carried a great weight of responsibility on his own shoulders.
>
> Woodfull had nursed Bradman, but later the boy nursed Oxenham in turn, engineering the bowling with judgment and success.
>
> Many of the famous cricketers of the past are inclined to see nothing in the form of the present-day players that compares favourably with that of the old 'giants' of the game, but Bradman is certainly one of the brightest and cleverest batsman of the century, being seldom in difficulties – on plumb wickets in any case.

Bradman had now been recognised as a force in international cricket: but even so, his huge future scores and unprecedented career could still not be foreseen. The range of his strokes was a pointer. He played the ball more in front of the wicket than was the custom of the then modern generation. He was always looking for runs, and his placing was masterly. He hit the ball hard, though his defence, when called upon, was rock-like. He could play fast bowling and slow bowling. (In J. C. White's triumphant tour of 1928–29, no one played him better than Bradman.) His footwork was perfect, as was his judgment of length. His hooking was venomous, and his driving and cutting ruthless. Above all, his temperament was unquestionable. He had courage and assurance and played with his brain as well as his bat. His only real weakness at that time was his running between the wickets.

Yet again, in the Melbourne Test, Bradman had watched, as a fielder, a double-century from the bat of Hammond, and whether these three great innings by an opponent in fairly rapid succession – 225, 251, 200 – re-awakened in Bradman his appetite for mammoth scores, the fact remains that before the month was out he quite shattered the calm of the Sheffield Shield season with an enormous and awesome innings of 340 not out. He made it – without a chance off any bowler – for New South Wales v Victoria at Sydney, thus choosing a fixture of high importance in the domestic calendar. The English team were in Adelaide when the news came through, and even Maurice Tate must have given it some respect. If they were quietly confident that no English attack could suffer an innings of such proportions, they did not yet know their Bradman. Within 18 months he was to hit virtually that score against England in a Test match, over 90% of it in a single day. The mammoth innings was the first double-century of Bradman's first-class career and an ominous portent of what the Bradman bat had in store. In brief the innings could claim the following:

i   It was the longest innings, in point of time, in Bradman's life – eight hours eight minutes.
ii   It was the highest score ever made on the Sydney Cricket Ground. (Later broken by Bradman.)
iii It was the record innings for New South Wales v Victoria. (It still is.)
iv   It was the record innings for New South Wales in the Sheffield Shield. (Later broken by Bradman.)
v   It was the record innings in first-class cricket by a player under 21. (This remained a record until 20 February 1974, when Aftab Baloch exceeded it with his 428 for Sind v Baluchistan in a Qaid-i-Azam Trophy match at Karachi. Baloch was 20 years 325 days at the time, though Bradman had been a few months younger at 20 years 151 days.)

Between 14 December 1928 and 16 January 1929 Bradman had either been playing cricket, been at the nets or been travelling on hot and tiring train journeys – with very little rest; and he almost did not play in that

Shield match against Victoria. He felt he needed a break. He was persuaded to play by a personal friend – and everyone, except the Victorian bowlers, was glad he did. In the match before, against South Australia at Adelaide, Kippax had made Bradman an opening batsman in each innings, with an eye on Australia's need for a capable opener in the absence of Ponsford. The experiment was a total failure – he batted less than a quarter of an hour in all for scores of 5 and 2. A week later he was back at number three against Victoria, and so did he relish the familiarity as to hit up his triple-hundred. He score it, by the way, with a brand-new bat that was never used again thereafter – Bradman kept it as a souvenir. Among the first of the many messages of congratulation he received was a letter from the grand-nephew of W. L. Murdoch, whose 321 in February 1882 – also for New South Wales v Victoria and also from the number three position – had been the previous highest score on the Sydney Cricket Ground.

This triple-century was Bradman's first real indication in the higher echelons of the game that the world had a remorseless record-breaker in its midst. It was an exercise in ruthlessness that hitherto had been confined, in Bradman's case, to minor cricket. But only in Bradman's case – for it is important to appreciate that Bradman's entry into first-class cricket coincided with the era of colossal scoring in Australia. Ponsford could boast two quadruple-centuries and over 1,000 runs in only four innings. Hammond, on his first tour of Australia, showed a penchant for 200s. Woodfull liked to bat for as long as he could, and so did Kippax. The 400 total was common-place in Australia, and 500, 600 and occasionally 700 by no means unusual. Those who have criticised the apparent avariciousness of Bradman should remember that it was not he who began it.

Bradman duly played in the fourth Test at Adelaide in February 1929, scoring 40 and 58 (run out) and being at the crease when Archie Jackson reached his brilliant hundred in his first Test innings. The two young men, who were born a year apart, represented the new era of Australian batsman-ship. Both were instantly recognised as having the stuff of greatness in them. They travelled together from Sydney to Adelaide, stayed in the same hotel (but not with the rest of the team) and talked cricket to their mutual advan-tage. 'No two fellows were ever so keen or enthusiastic', was the 'old hand' Bradman's recollection. Today Sir Donald is still moved to poignancy in recalling those times and the memories of his young colleague who was to die at 23.

On the final day at Adelaide, after Australia had lost by 12 runs, Warwick Armstrong generously conceded the merit of the young Bradman: 'He is a fine batsman, and will be a still finer one. To-day he never allowed the crisis to worry him.' His batting proved beyond any doubt that he had the right temperament for the highest class of cricket.

In the fifth Test at Melbourne – an eight-day affair and the longest game of cricket Bradman took part in in his life – he was on the winning side in a Test for the first time. He also cemented his love-affair with Melbourne by scoring another century. He batted altogether in ten Test matches on that ground and scored nine Test hundreds there. This time, when runs were badly needed, it was 123 out of 183 – i.e. he scored twice as fast as his partners and extras while he was at the crease. All his 123 runs were actually scored in partnership with his St George club-mate, Alan Fairfax, who contributed 55 to the 183. In the course of his innings (which, incidentally, was the 50th Australian century recorded against England on Australian soil) Bradman passed the record aggregate of runs for an Australian season in first-class cricket, Aubrey Faulkner's 1,534 for the touring South Africans in 1910–11, which had taken Faulkner 27 innings. Bradman beat it in 23. In the second innings, when he and his captain, Ryder, saw the team home, the aggregate was advanced to 1,690 runs – still, 50 years later, a record.

Bradman's average for the season was 93·88 – remarkable at that time, but to become commonplace in the Bradman saga. In Sheffield Shield matches (he missed only one, through being on Test duty) he averaged 148·83. From one from bottom place the year before, New South Wales now won the Shield by a huge margin, a triumph not only for the players but for the new team of selectors, Messrs R. L. Jones (St George), A. R. Ratcliffe (Glebe) and R. C. M. Boyce (Gordon). Although he could play only four innings for St George, he topped their averages with 65·25, and in recognition of his and Fairfax's entry into Test cricket the club gave a dinner at Hurstville on 13 April 1929, attended by past and present players of St George. A gold fountain pen was presented to Bradman. There was also a joint Bradman–Fairfax testimonial fund opened, well supported in the St George district especially, and buttons displaying Bradman's photograph were sold at a shilling each. A committee representing the citizens of Fivedock (a district of Sydney) was also formed to organise a testimonial to Bradman. He also scored more runs – including two centuries – for a strong N.S.W.C.A. side that toured the country districts at the end of the summer. His actual successive scores were 34 at Newcastle, 128 not out at Tamworth, 117 at Singleton, and – was it an All Fools' Day joke perpetrated on him by the umpire? – a duck, lbw, as opening batsman v Hunter River at West Maitland on 1 April 1929. The successful country bowler was one G. Bell, and though the correctness of the verdict in his favour was held gravely in doubt by many at the ground he had nevertheless achieved what had eluded Messrs Larwood, Tate, Geary and White all season![1] Bradman's minor cricket yielded him very nearly 1,000 further runs on top of his record first-class aggregate, so that he ruled off the season with a final composite total of 2,616 runs at an average of 76·94. It was very satisfactory, to say the least.

Don Bradman's fielding was as much a feature of his advance in the 1928–29 series as was his batting. On his Test debut, at the Exhibition

---

[1] Bradman also took five wickets in an innings twice on this tour, in each case against sides batting 13: in the second innings v Tamworth he took five for 34, and he preceded his 117 v Singleton at Howe Park with five for 57 – all five 'bowled'.

Ground, Brisbane, the only run out in the match was effected by Bradman. Mead cut Grimmett hard just after lunch on the opening day and he and Hobbs ran two. As Bradman, on the boundary edge, had not then fielded the ball, a third was attempted. 'This was a tremendous risk', reported Reuter, 'and, on seeing Bradman pick up brilliantly, the batsmen hesitated in the middle of the pitch. The wicket was as good as thrown away. Bradman, true to his reputation as a fine outfielder, made a beautiful return, and Hobbs was well out when the wicket was broken.' Hobbs, who was batting at his best and had made 49, very rarely in his career misjudged a run sufficiently to run himself out. He said he was unaware who the fielder was on the boundary. 'Had I known of his reputation in the field I would not have responded to Phil's call for a third run. The ball came whizzing in to the wicket-keeper like a gun-shot. I was easily out.' The next man in, Walter Hammond, was probably less surprised. He was already an early-season victim of the Bradman throw. Hobbs was to return the compliment at a most crucial stage in the fourth Test at Adelaide, which Australia lost so narrowly, just when Don Bradman seemed capable of winning the match. Bradman's dismissal was the turning-point of the game. England were *never* to run him out again.

Of that fourth Test match of '28–29, one of the umpires, George Hele, has recorded an amusing reminiscence of Bradman's throwing skill. 'After lunch one day during the Adelaide Test of that summer I was about to straighten the stumps so that play could resume. "Leave them as they are a second, George," Don called. He was standing at square-leg with the ball in his hand. With three successive throws he hit the one stump visible to him three times, then ran off to the boundary chuckling to himself.' Not many cricketers could do that in the 1920s. Not many can do it today, when fielding skills are generally superior. In 1949, a few weeks after Don Bradman – by then a knight – stepped from a first-class field for the last time, Herbert Sutcliffe said of him that he was the finest fielder and best thrower he had ever seen.

When his first full season of first-class cricket was over, Don Bradman, aged 20, could count himself something of a celebrity – a young hero of the nation, who had achieved much and who promised much more. A likeable, intelligent and modest young man, he had now to begin to adapt his life to the 'Bradman legend'. In May 1929 he made a 'celebrity tour', visiting various North Coast parts of New South Wales to give cricket instruction to the boys at Taree High School and other places. At Wingham one Saturday afternoon, he performed the traditional celebrity's role of kicking off in the first local football match of the season.

Watching the Test series in 1928–29, on a journalism-cum-business visit to Australia, was P. G. H. Fender, one of the most perceptive critics of the day. He was in the midst of his long reign as Surrey captain. He was watching from the press-box in Australia, and at the same time preparing his book that was published by Faber and Faber in 1929, *The Turn of the Wheel*. Fender's well-known criticisms of Bradman's batsmanship in 1928–29 became even more well known in the light of Bradman's subsequent triumphs. They became exaggerated to the extent that people averred that Fender said – which he did not – that Bradman 'wouldn't get a run in England in 1930'. But there was certainly an unusual virulence in what Fender did say about Bradman in his initial season of seeing him, and Bradman himself was not unaware of the strength of that censure.

There is no evidence that Fender ever met Don Bradman in Australia in 1928–29 (and indeed Fender has confirmed that they never then met); and all Fender's criticisms were technical criticisms based on what he considered to be undeveloped batsmanship, relying too much on the pull shot and late cut.

In his regular cables to both the London *Star* and the old *Daily News* in 1928–29, Fender was consistently cautious in his praise of Bradman's batting, taking almost an exaggerated care to draw attention to minor weaknesses and to emphasise chances and half-chances. 'He seldom seemed in difficulties . . . yet frequently he made uppish uncontrolled strokes which are chances unless they steer clear of a fielder.' (13/3/29). 'During the Jackson–Bradman partnership, England were extremely unlucky, Bradman alone making six mis-hits, which were catches just out of the fielders' reach.' (4/2/29). 'Bradman made some nice strokes, but Tate had him at his mercy.' (3/12/28). 'Bradman played well, though he was very slow, and when trying forcing shots frequently made them dangerously.' (31/12/28). 'Duckworth should have stumped Bradman when the batsman was 5.' (16/3/29). This sort of minor obsessiveness did not extend to other players, and was in marked contrast to the attitude towards Bradman of other cricketer-commentators on the 1928–29 series, including A. E. R. Gilligan, Lord Tennyson and Frank Woolley (the last two giving, for what they were worth, their lengthy comments from England). On the very last day of the series, Fender still did not think much of Bradman – though there was a glimmer of hope: 'Jackson is Australia's greatest batting find. Bradman, though unsound now, is quite capable of rectifying that.'

When Fender's book on the tour came out, the famous verdict of 'brilliant but unsound' was delivered. It is a verdict that has been quoted many dozens of times since. Even on Bradman's century in the fifth Test at Melbourne, Fender wrote: 'Bradman is such a curious mixture of brilliant and very mediocre batting. He will make a number of glorious shots, and then, in attempting another, he will fluke the ball in some totally different direction to that intended, and practically always just out of a fielder's reach.'

Fender's final judgment – a strong but unfavourable verdict – is quoted *in extenso* from his book, not necessarily to suggest its falsity (that would be an impertinence) but to suggest rather that genius is not subject to the ordinary laws of criticism and can effectively flout them with its own chosen proportions of 'brilliance' and 'unsoundness':

Bradman was one of the most curious mixtures of good and bad batting I have ever seen. In Brisbane he made one grand shot off Tate to the square-leg boundary in the first innings and a collection of others of a most inferior brand. During the rest of the series he improved, making more shots of the truly magnificent type, but never being able to avoid either the really bad ones or the badly made ones. One would see him cram half a dozen or more shots, worthy of the greatest, into a couple or three overs, then two or three times running he would completely mis-time, mis-judge, and mis-hit the ball. One minute one would think him a grand player, and the next he would look like a schoolboy.

If practice, experience, and hard work enable him to eradicate the faults and still retain the rest of his ability, he may well become a very great player; and if he does this, he will always be in the category of the brilliant, if unsound, ones. Promise there is in Bradman in plenty, though watching him does not inspire one with any confidence that he desires to take the only course which will lead him to a fulfilment of that promise. He makes a mistake, then makes it again and again; he does not correct it, or look as if he were trying to do so. He seems to live for the exuberance of the moment. Only time will show whether the mellowing and steadying effect of experience will make or mar.

What time did show, of course, was that Bradman was to average 139·14 in his first Test series in England, 102·84 in his entire Test career in England, and 99·94 in his Test career against all opponents. The constant repetition of error was not noticed – or at least not commented on – by others. Ryder indeed said there was no quicker learner in the game than Bradman.

In the 1928–29 season Bradman encountered for the first time 'ultra-modern leg-theory' – the term employed by the *Sydney Morning Herald* cricket correspondent – in the Sheffield Shield match against South Australia at Sydney, the final Shield match of the season, in March 1929. The perpetrator was the man who had the distinction of being the first to take Don Bradman's wicket in a first-class innings – J. D. Scott, the South Australian opening bowler, whom the *Sydney Morning Herald* correspondent had also seen employing this style at the start of that season in the Test Trial at Melbourne for the Rest of Australia v Australia – in both cases Scott being captained by his Sturt club captain, V. Y. Richardson. In the trial match, Bradman was on the same side as Scott (who was wholly unsuccessful in his efforts to contain Ponsford), but at Sydney Bradman opposed him – and duly scored 35 and 175. The second innings was a brilliant one, and Bradman hooked Scott in particular unmercifully. Scott took no wickets in this Shield match with his leg-theory attack (Jackson, his one victim, was not out to it) and it was a comprehensive failure. To Bradman certainly it was food and drink. The fact probably was that Scott was neither quite fast enough nor quite accurate enough. He was beyond his best days and, past his 40th birthday, in the veteran stage. He had made his first-class debut in December 1908. In that same 1928–29 season, Scott also – significantly – bowled his new style of leg-theory against the M.C.C. side at Adelaide in the second match of the tour, despite its apparent lack of success a few days before at Melbourne. This time, with Jardine a spectator, it was employed specifically against Hammond, Scott having seven men on the leg side and two on the off. Hammond countered it with no difficulty at all, scoring a brilliant 145 and simply murdering Scott's 'special' leg-side bowling. Scott abandoned it against the other batsmen and emerged from the match with one for 145, his solitary victim coming from a good-length ball. Scott's efforts must be viewed as somewhat feeble, and would not be worthy of recall had not events four years later caused people to remember them and ponder. Scott himself, in the aftermath of 1932–33, defended himself vigorously against charges that he had bowled 'bodyline', but admitted he had bowled short against New South Wales in Sydney in March 1929, but not with the intention to bowl against the batsman. Tommy Andrews was the New South Wales captain on that occasion, and as his side averaged 38 per wicket throughout the match, he was not over-concerned.

The 1928–29 Australian season also saw the first criticism of Harold Larwood's leg-stump bowling and the ominous forecast of the 'risk of unpopularity in Australia' such tactics might bring. Warwick Armstrong certainly took Larwood to task for his bowling in Australia's second innings on the last two days of the second Test (when Larwood's bowling was watched by Bradman as 12th man), and this is what Armstrong cabled to London from Sydney concerning Larwood at the conclusion of that match:

> Yesterday and to-day he appeared to be bowling deliberately at the batsmen. He has great pace, and could afford not to bowl at the man.
>
> If he continued these tactics the spectators here might think there were more sporting ways of getting results, and it would be a pity if a player like Larwood ran the risk of unpopularity when he has the talent to send the ball up differently.

Larwood has himself admitted that he used 'leg theory' – deliberately rising balls on the leg stump: the word 'bodyline' at any time was a malicious one in Larwood's vocabulary – in the fourth Test at Adelaide in 1928–29, with five or six men on the leg side, against Bradman and Jackson. It is extremely doubtful whether Larwood himself would have contemplated a renewal of this form of attack (which had proved expensive and not especially fearsome) four years later. But under the direction of a new captain, he was to come to see it as the bowler's only real chance to rebel against pitches that held out only slender hope.

Wisden remained silent on any allegations against Larwood either in the Sydney Test or at any other time on the tour. But M. A. Noble was more forthcoming in 1929 in giving his impressions of Larwood in *The Fight for the Ashes*: 'Despite his direct method of attack on the wicket, however, at times he is not over-particular where the ball goes, delivering it well outside the off stump, outside the leg stump, or direct to the body or head. The working of his trap is easily discernible from the pavilion, for a man is always placed in a likely position to bring about the batsman's downfall in case of a mishit. It may be that this method is adopted to impress the faint-hearted with the possibilities of injury, and so cause them to draw away or nibble at the ball instead of boldly facing it with the bat well in front of the body or allowing the bumpy ones to pass harmlessly over the wicket. However, as he is not overfast, such methods should not achieve much success against class batsmen, and in the long run should prove too expensive to be persevered with.' Noble was to be proved not quite correct.

Before leaving 1928–29, a word should be said about Don Bradman's early coaching. This is a somewhat delicate matter and not simple to resolve. 'I was not coached as a boy', Sir Donald himself has recorded. 'There was nobody to coach me and facilities just weren't available.' And elsewhere: 'No one taught me to play cricket. I was not coached. I found out for myself, and perhaps it was the best way.' It is undoubtedly true that as a schoolboy, and during his entire period at Bowral, he was never formally coached but followed his own natural style and learnt by practice and by watching others. Therefore, by the time he came to Sydney he was already a self-made batsman. But he was not yet the complete batsman, and there seems to be some positive evidence that he was coached in Sydney by the New South Wales coaches. When he scored his innings of 87 and 132 not out against the M.C.C. at Sydney in November 1928 – the first meeting of his life with an English team – Sydney Southerton naturally took it upon himself as the Reuter representative covering the tour, to find out something about Bradman and his background. His sources now cannot be known, but Southerton was a careful journalist who, as a senior agency man, was obliged to maintain a jealous regard for the accuracy of his facts. Reuter's reputation demanded it. At all events, the cable from Southerton in Sydney that went all over the world on 13 November 1928 included the following:

On the return from England of Collins's team in 1926 Bradman was picked for coaching under the N.S.W. scheme then instituted with the present tour in view.

How well C. T. B. Turner, Harry Donnan and J. B. Searle have done their work is shown by Bradman's performance to-day.

For some time he was overshadowed by Jackson, who is not such a solid type of batsman, and he suffered from not having all the strokes at his command.

His defence, however, has always been very good and has been likened to Woodfull's. The N.S.W. coaches taught him how to attack bowling as well as defend himself against it.

They were rewarded by a remarkable string of centuries which he made in junior cricket, and he has carried this tradition with him into top-class cricket.[1]

---

[1] Turner and Donnan were the well-known Test players. James Searle, the eldest man of the three, was wicketkeeper in J. Davis's New South Wales side in New Zealand in 1893–94, and he was the N.S.W.C.A.'s full-time professional coach from 1 October 1927 on a six-days-a-week engagement throughout the summer. He coached assiduously and his methods were highly spoken of in Sydney. His early cricket was with the old Surry United Club on the Albert Ground, the Domain, and Moore Park, and he later played for Redfern, with Spofforth. He fractured a leg in colliding with a fence in a trial match at Sydney for an Australian team due to visit England. For about 30 years he ran a highly successful sports depot in Sydney, frequented by many leading cricketers, and for some years was vice-president of Manly. Also one of the pioneers of baseball in New South Wales, he died on 28 December 1936, aged 75.

Later in the year, further reports definitely speak of Bradman having been 'taken in hand' by the New South Wales coaches under the Association's coaching scheme. 'At that time', it was said, 'Bradman, although obviously a natural cricketer, possessed little more than a strong but untutored defence, and the coaches at once set to work to "pull him out".' No contradiction of these reports ever appeared.

At the end of the 1928–29 season the question of Don Bradman's continuance as a player with St George was raised, for he was not residing within the district of the club as was necessary under the system then in force in Sydney cricket, whereby for cricket purposes the city was divided into defined areas of residence. (Several grade players in Sydney at that time certainly did successfully evade the residential rule and played for clubs outside the district of their residence. For the prominent players, and most especially for the Test players, this was less easy.) The young Bradman had established a happy relationship with the St George club which he was reluctant to sever. Likewise St George were most anxious not to lose him. Accordingly, Australia's new young batting star moved into the appropriate district of Sydney to keep himself qualified for St George – and, at the instance of 'Dick' Jones, he moved into the welcoming home of Mr and Mrs F. M. Cush at 'Ellimatta', 172 Frederick Street, Rockdale, not far from Hurstville Oval. Frank Cush, a member of a large family firm of timber merchants, was then hon. secretary of the St George club, a post he had held since the club's initial entry into first-grade cricket in October 1921 and which he was to hold in all for 25 years, until after the Second World War. He was also at that time a St George delegate to the New South Wales C.A. – in all he was a delegate from the 1921–22 season until his resignation on 11 November 1965. Little could Frank Cush have known, when this 20-year-old boy brought his bags across his doorstep, that he had a future chairman of the Australian Board arriving in his household. For that matter Cush could hardly have anticipated that he himself would one day be Board chairman. Altogether it was a piquant situation that was, in the process of years, to call for mutual congratulation.[1]

Don Bradman enjoyed the privacy of the Cush home until he left Frederick Street on his marriage in April 1932. He has always acknowledged the enormous debt due to the Cushes for the guidance and goodwill they so generously dispensed, quite apart from the material comforts provided.

---

[1] Frank Cush's career as an Australian administrator was a highly distinguished one. Apart from over 50 years as an office-bearer with St George (including the Presidency from 1946 to 1968), he was Hon. Treasurer and also a long-serving member of the Executive Committee of the New South Wales Cricket Association (and a life member from 1943), likewise Hon. Treasurer of the Australian Board of Control (1935–1946) and a N.S.W. delegate to the Board in an unbroken spell from 1930 to 1958, ended only by ill-health. He was Chairman of the Australian Board of Control, 1955–57, and was elected an honorary life member of the Marylebone Cricket Club in 1962 for his distinguished services to cricket administration. In the New Year Honours of 1 January 1963 he was created O.B.E. for his lengthy membership of the Australian Board. He had also been a useful batsman and fine fielder for St George in second-grade matches in the 1920s. His late brother, Herbert H. Cush, was President of the Glebe club in Sydney.

Lady Bradman has more than once remarked how frequently over the years Sir Donald has paid spontaneous tribute to the help he received from Frank Cush and his wife at just that time in his life when it was specially needed.

By the time the Australian winter of 1929 had arrived, Don Bradman was not only a cricketer of international standing but also a young man in demand as a popular hero, and bearing all the burdens – and privileges – that popular heroes bear. Well before the winter arrived, his repute and meteoric success had attracted the business world, a natural enough phenomenon in a sports-conscious country that was prepared to extend to youth the sort of hero-worship that knew no reasonable bounds. (In the fifth Test at Melbourne, when Bradman, aged 20, and Fairfax, 22, walked in to tea on the fourth afternoon, it was written of the pair that 'great Pompey in his passage of Rome had nothing on them'.) Bradman, through his youth and through his prowess, was more than a conventional asset – his name had a money-earning potential that could be exploited with high success among the sporting public. In February 1929 – it was actually during the Adelaide Test – he was approached by and negotiated arrangements with a firm that called itself 'The Premier Sports House of Australia', Mick Simmons Ltd, of George Street in Sydney's Haymarket, not many doors away from the offices of the New South Wales Cricket Association. The firm, which still thrives healthily, had been founded in the 1870s and prided itself on its service to the public. As a sports shop it was in the highest bracket, and with Bradman attached to its staff it could hope to remain there.

Bradman's new post coincided with the closing down by Percy Westbrook of his Sydney real-estate office, and thereafter, at least up to the war, Bradman's life was to be occupied with cricket, stockbroking, and the various off-shoots of cricket, including writing, broadcasting, advertising, and sports goods promotion. In this last-named role, he spent the English summer of 1929, mainly as a traveller in various parts of New South Wales on behalf of his new employers.

The 1929–30 season contained three momentous highlights for Don Bradman. In order of occurrence, they were a superb Test Trial at Sydney, when he made 124 and 225; the breaking, a month later, of the world record individual score in first-class cricket with 452 not out against the luckless Queensland; and – the most momentous of all – selection in the Australian touring side for England. To gain this final objective, all else in Bradman's adult life thus far had been subordinated. The team was due to be announced at the end of January 1930 – by a stroke of good fortune, after the completion of the whole of New South Wales's Sheffield Shield programme (but not the programmes of the other three States). Thus Bradman had the maximum opportunity of showing the selectors his worth. It need hardly be said that he took it brilliantly and decisively.

Before the first-class season began, Bradman was a member of a strong New South Wales Cricket Association team, captained by C. G. Macartney, that toured western country centres and played five matches against Orange, Dubbo, Parkes, Far West, and Bathurst between 21 October and 28 October. Bradman played in all five matches, but only in the first – before a record crowd at Wade Park, Orange – was he at the crease with Macartney, and then only briefly in a stand of 11. Bradman's scores on the tour were respectively 5, 88, 76 (as an opener), 50, and a faultless 84. Handsome crowds and handsome hospitality were at all these country centres – 3,000 turned up at Dubbo and 3,500 to see Far West at Parkes. Macartney was very pleased with it all, and no doubt Bradman was as well: he scored more runs than anyone. On 15–16 November (on the way back from the Sheffield Shield fixture in Brisbane) Bradman played under W. A. Oldfield's captaincy for a New South Wales XI v Newcastle at the local Sports Ground at Newcastle and made top score of the match with a brilliant 111, reaching his hundred in 90 minutes. It was a great Saturday treat for the locals.

The new season, whilst it was to contain the announcement of the all-important names for England, lacked the significance of the previous one, when there had of course been an English Test team in Australia. This time it was to be a domestic season, apart from the brief passage through Australia of Harold Gilligan's M.C.C. side on its way to New Zealand. They played one match in Sydney, against New South Wales, in which 1,607 runs were amassed at an average of 73·04 per wicket – which was then, and still remains, the record wicket-average for any first-class match in Australia and in any match involving an M.C.C. side abroad. In no other match in Bradman's career was the average per wicket so high. The excellence of the Sydney pitch had much to do with it, and before the season was out Bradman was to take the fullest advantage of it by performing the remarkable feat of scoring 1,085 first-class runs *on the Sydney Cricket Ground alone*. His average there that season was 180·83. This is the highest aggregate ever made by a batsman in a single season on a single Australian ground, and Bradman himself never approached it again.[1]

Bradman's contribution to the run-harvest in the M.C.C. match was a highly attractive and chanceless 157. He was out before tea on the first day, having scored 86 in the afternoon session. His captain, Kippax, also scored a hundred, but was truly outpaced, making 51 of the 149 stand for the third wicket. 'Bradman's innings eclipsed anything we had seen before in Australia', recalled Maurice Turnbull. 'The others were always giving us a chance of getting them out . . . but Don Bradman played some glorious back-shots reminiscent of Charlie Macartney, and hardly missed a ball at which he struck.' Turnbull himself was out, for exactly 100, to a brilliant return catch by Bradman, low down – the only 'c and b' effected by Bradman in his first-class career. In this match, too, Bradman had a longer sight of Frank

---

[1] The only comparable instance is the 1,013 runs scored on the Melbourne Cricket Ground by W. H. Ponsford in 1927–28. They comprised four innings – 437, 202 and 38, 336 – his average thus being 253·25.

Woolley than he had had as a 12-year-old at Sydney in 1921. Woolley scored a glorious 219 – his farewell innings on his favourite Sydney ground. On an 80th birthday tribute to Frank Woolley in 1967, Sir Donald said of this 219: 'It remains one of the most majestic and classical innings I have seen, with every stroke in the book played with supreme ease.' More important, Bradman's own technique was making big strides. Of his own innings of 157 it was observed: 'He has more stroke accuracy than at any time last year, which means that he has acquired even surer balance and consequently better timing.'

The trial arranged at Sydney to assist the Australian selectors in picking the side for England was an altogether remarkable affair for Bradman. As a reversal of his sad experience in the trial of the previous season, it could hardly have been more comprehensive. His position for the touring side could not have been in serious doubt, although some detractors – Australians as well as Englishmen – were still prepared to find fault with his methods and predict failure for him on the more variable wickets of England. Old Trafford and Lord's would not be the same as Sydney and Melbourne. This was undoubtedly true: but for the moment Bradman could hardly do otherwise than score prolifically on such pitches as he encountered. In the trial match his prolificness approached a cornucopia. He played for Woodfull's XI v Ryder's XI and scored 124 and 225 (and was still on the losing side!) It took his total to 506 in his last three innings, compiled at 51 an hour and averaging 50 an hour in the trial match alone. However allegedly unsound his methods may have been, they certainly produced runs and produced them quickly. At the close of the second day in the trial he was 54 not out in the first innings, out of 99 since he had come in – that was Saturday evening. On Monday morning he made another 70 before lunch before being last man out, brilliantly caught one-handed in the gully, and, in the follow-on, opened the innings with Woodfull. At close of play he was 205 not out out of 341 for two in a trifle over $3\frac{1}{2}$ hours. Thus he had scored 275 runs in the course of the day's cricket, in 325 minutes. It is not generally appreciated, amid the statistical excellence of the performance, that Bradman's runs that day were scored in a most intense heat, as the whole of New South Wales sweltered in a most trying heat-wave. In Sydney that afternoon a temperature of 98·4 degrees was recorded – a mere trifle to the 107 degrees at Singleton! – and at the Sydney Cricket Ground itself the air was thick with dust after tea, a great trial for the players (as well as for nearly 5,000 spectators). Around this period, with Bradman past 150, induced perhaps by the prevailing conditions, he indulged in outright slogging – a rare thing for him in a match of importance – which did not bring him the haven of the pavilion, however, for he survived his only chance to the deep field when 203!

His aggregate for the day (275) was second only to his personal best of 309 runs in a day at Headingley in 1930. Altogether – and this must be one of the most phenomenal facts concerning Bradman's batting – he scored 200 or more runs in a single day *on no fewer than 27 occasions* in his first-class career:

an unprecedented performance, and one which one can safely say is not likely to be exceeded.

If his century and double-century in the trial match did not give rise to a great deal of fuss outside Australia, Bradman was now set to cause not a ripple but a tidal wave to engulf the cricket scene. His performance at Sydney on Saturday, 4 January, and Monday, 6 January, could not have been foreseen either by Bradman himself, ambitious as he was, or by his most fervid admirers, or by the closest students of the game in Australia. He scored 452 not out, to create a new world record for a first-class match. His employers, Messrs Mick Simmons, would, one supposes, have given thousands for him to do just what he did.

This was the innings that put Bradman on a pedestal in the eyes of the world. For all the triumphs that were to come, nothing quite had the glamour and the impact of the world record score. People who had never before heard his name began talking of Don Bradman. It was not simply a statistical landmark: it was a landmark in the sporting history of Australia. It turned Bradman into the most famous 21-year-old in the world, scaling hitherto unimagined heights – and with his sights firmly fixed on much else.

The world record might have come to Don Bradman the previous season, when he scored his undefeated 340 against Victoria and when his captain in that match, Tommy Andrews, was really obliged to declare late on the second day after the New South Wales innings had lasted nearly ten hours

A specimen of the neat manuscript of Bradman – part of his life story that he wrote for *The Star* in England in 1930.

and reached 713 for six. Bradman's not-out partner at the declaration was Jack Fingleton and they had already added more than a hundred together. No bowler had caused Bradman to give any chance, so the prospects of more – and easy – runs for him were bright. That innings proved to Bradman that huge scoring was possible in five-day cricket and marked him down as a potential record-breaker. All that was needed – given the mighty skill of Bradman – were the correct circumstances whereby the interests of the side were not prejudiced by the accumulation of a tremendous score. Those circumstances were present when New South Wales played Queensland at Sydney in January 1930.

Bradman's attitude to record-breaking remained consistent throughout his career, and he put down his thoughts early on – in his first book (*Don Bradman's Book*), published after the 1930 tour of England:

> I do not set much store on the making of records, and throughout my whole career I have made it a rule, and have never departed from it, always to play for my side, and not for myself. I have never placed my own interest before the interests of my team, and if I made a new record I have been glad, but mainly because I have felt that my side needed the runs.

So far as his 452 not out was concerned, he did go on to say in his book the following:

> On this occasion, however, I definitely and deliberately set out to establish a record. The highest individual score in first-class cricket was the one record I wanted to hold, and the opportunity came my way in this match.

So there it was: a definite and deliberate assault on W. H. Ponsford's 437, made against Queensland in December 1927 – and which had been put together, somewhat coincidentally, on precisely the same two days as Bradman himself played his first innings in first-class cricket and scored 118 on debut. Don Bradman confided to Mrs Cush over the week-end that he was going after the world record.

Bradman had been caught behind the wicket for 3 in the first innings against Queensland, when he was an opening bat. He went in first wicket down at 22 in the second innings, when C. W. Andrews – the Maitland cricketer now with Mosman who was later to join Queensland – was out. Fairfax also soon left, at 33, but with Kippax a huge stand developed which put on 272 for the third wicket in 145 minutes, when McCabe became another sound partner. At the close of the second day, Bradman was 205 not out in 3¼ hours out of a total of 368 for three. This gave New South Wales a lead of 376. The Queensland bowlers had not sent down one maiden, and Bradman had not given one chance.

Bradman spent that Saturday evening quietly, and rested on the Sunday – when the thought of passing Ponsford's 437 occurred to him. As Bradman himself wrote later: 'Everything was just right for me: the state of the wicket, the state of the game, the state of my health. Also I was in the mood for runs.' Everything went like clockwork on Monday, though when 264 he gave his first half-chance (in more than four hours' batting) when Thurlow, at forward mid-on, failed to move at all to attempt a catch off Rowe's bowling. Bradman sped to 310* by lunch, when the total was 551 for five – his side now 559 ahead. Any declaration now by Kippax could not be delayed in all conscience beyond tea. So all depended on the afternoon session, and Bradman needed a further 128 to make the record his own. (Ponsford, by coincidence, was actually taking his own score to 110 on the same morning at Melbourne, without knowing of the drama that was building up 450 miles away.) Bradman had reached his 300 in 288 minutes – the fastest of the three triple-centuries of his career in the Sheffield Shield – and his 310* at lunch had come in 301 minutes. He was in prime form. After lunch he passed the previous best score of his life (and the previous best score on the Sydney Cricket Ground) – his 340* of 12 months before – a landmark warmly applauded by the crowd and recognised even by umpire George Borwick, who shook hands with Bradman. He then passed the previous best score for New South Wales – C. W. Gregory's 383 at Brisbane in 1906–07 – and then reached his 400 in 377 minutes. Although very few quadruple-centuries have been recorded in first-class cricket (only seven in all), Bradman's time to this great figure was, and remains, the fastest on record.

Bradman now had only the world record before him. He was still full of energy, and running superbly fast between the wickets. When he was 391, he had sprinted an all-run four; and was proving particularly skilful in retaining the strike. Then the moment came. At 3.45 p.m., sweaterless and with sleeves rolled up, he went from 434 to 438 with a ferocious hook sent bouncing to the square-leg boundary off a short-pitched ball on the leg stump from Thurlow, and the deed was done. 'I established the only record upon which I had set my heart.' The crowd went wild with delight. Bradman's partner, the wicketkeeper H. L. Davidson, raced up the pitch to congratulate him, and one by one the Queenslanders shook the new record-holder's hand. O'Connor, the Queensland captain, called for three cheers – and it is doubtful whether before or since on a first-class field a cricketer as young as 21 has had this honour accorded him. Even to Bradman, that distinction was not to come again until 1948.

Among those watching was the cigar-smoking Charles Bannerman, aged 78, and in the closing months of his life – the first of New South Wales's great line of batsmen and the first century-maker in Test match cricket. For years he had had his special place in a corner of the members' stand at Sydney and had seen and met every man in an Australian eleven who had played on the S.C.G. How he must have marvelled at the prolificness of this new champion. They were photographed together at the ground that afternoon, the old man's hand on the young man's shoulder. The one had played his cricket with Spofforth and Murdoch and Blackham and Boyle. The other, before his career would be over, would be on the field with Miller and

Harvey and Lindwall and Barnes. It is a photograph that Sir Donald has treasured to this very day.

Bradman was chaired to the gate at the end of his record innings by the chastened Queensland fielders and ran to the dressing-room when Kippax declared a few minutes before tea with a lead of 769. What Leo O'Connor, the visiting captain, thought about it all is not recorded – his poor bowlers had managed only a single maiden over between them in more than seven hours of bowling! Kippax had left himself 9¾ hours to dismiss Queensland, or see them score 770 to win. They were all out for 84 in less than two hours. Bradman himself had scored 452*, out of 739 while at the crease, in 415 minutes, and his new record innings consisted of 49 fours, 13 threes, 46 twos and 125 singles. 'I was not excited', recorded Bradman about the occasion, 'and I cannot say that I suffered any reaction. My feeling was one of complete satisfaction.'

He was lucky, of course, that he had a Sunday intervening between the two parts of his innings, otherwise his stamina might have been at risk. As it was, he showed no visible signs of tiredness at all at the end of his innings, during which he gave only two half-chances. 'My own memories are that the first thing I did when I got to the dressing-room was to have a cup of tea, and that I then felt perfectly fit to take my place in the field.' And elsewhere: 'Physically, I was so comfortable that I felt I could have gone on indefinitely.' He had certainly shown no discernible strain at the crease. 'If there was any strain, it was masked by his boyish smile', said one writer. As to his imperturbability that afternoon, one of the Queensland bowlers remarked: 'He never turned a hair.'

The Queensland bowlers turned a hair or two, that is certain. Towards the end their bowling 'was on the verge of complete impotence' – they conceded 6½ runs an over throughout the innings, and on the Monday alone Bradman himself scored at 4·25 per over. (Hornibrook and Oxenham, it should be remembered, were not available to make the trip to Sydney.) The fielding, however, was 'of a remarkably high order', otherwise Bradman might have topped 500. The official attendance to witness the new record was 7,848, a good crowd for a Monday, and they naturally gave Bradman a great ovation on his return. Indeed, his reception was described as the greatest ovation ever heard on the Sydney ground, which may have been an exaggeration but which reflected the euphoria of the occasion. As his score grew larger and larger, so the crowd on that Monday at Sydney swelled. There were only 3,000 there at the start of play, but 5,000 by lunch-time – and as he was still not out, and with a triple-century behind him, very nearly another 3,000 turned up after lunch. The two parts of the innings may be set out thus:

4 Jan. 1930	205 out of 346 in 195 mins.	22 fours	63·07 runs p.hr.
6 Jan. 1930	247 out of 393 in 220 mins.	27 fours	67·36 runs p.hr.
	452*out of 739 in 415 mins.	49 fours	65·34 runs p.hr.

The speed with which the new world record was compiled may be readily gauged by the following table:

First   100 in 104 minutes
Second 100 in 81 minutes
Third   100 in 103 minutes
Fourth 100 in 89 minutes
Last   52 in 38 minutes

One further point must be mentioned. Despite his handsome rate of scoring, there was never a trace of wildness in Bradman's batting. 'It was an instance', said the *Sydney Morning Herald*, 'of sheer resolution and machine-like steadiness. . . . Bradman throughout held himself well under control.' Arthur Mailey, who was watching the innings for the Sydney *Sun*, said much the same thing. He sent off a short piece to that afternoon newspaper shortly after a quarter past three that day:

> At the time of writing Bradman was past his fourth century. In the Melbourne 'Herald' office I can imagine one William Ponsford, earphones attached, trembling with anxiety, awaiting the news that his record score of 437 has been brushed right off.
>
> Bradman seems to be intent on making records to-day, and providing he can get partners to stay with him for half an hour or so, he should have a number of new ones to his credit.
>
> Although Bradman scored at a fast rate, he did not deliberately attempt any wild strokes. Half-volleys were driven quickly and firmly, and anything short on the off was cleverly guided down the gully for one or two. No bowler troubled him to any extent.
>
> Hurwood, who had bowled finely throughout the day, was certainly respected, but Bradman was always his master.

Thus, once again, Bradman had set himself a task and he had achieved it. In this feature of his character, especially in one so young, lay much of the secret of his success. No mountains were too high to be climbed. Indeed, the more notable the objective the more resiliently Bradman seemed to respond. This trait was to accompany him throughout his career. It helped him to conquer even ill health. Without it he might never have returned to Test cricket in 1946 or led his great side in England in '48.

It should be emphasised that although Bradman's quadruple-century was a deliberate record-breaking attempt, there was never a hint of slowness in the innings. His respective hundreds, set out above, would have been admirable in *any* conditions; and the whole innings was scored at the exemplary rate of 65 an hour off his own bat. When he reached the 400-mark – at which point even one of the umpires applauded! – he proceeded through the crucial stage of approaching and beating Ponsford's score *at almost breakneck speed*: he went from 400 to the record 438 in less than half an hour! He clearly was not exaggerating when he recalled later that year that 'the mood to make runs was on me'! Ponsford had taken ten hours 21 minutes to score his 437. When Bradman took his score to 438, he had been batting six hours 46 minutes.

It was from Ponsford, nevertheless, that one of the first telegrams of congratulation arrived. It came from Melbourne on that Monday afternoon: 'Congratulations on your great feat. A batsman of your ability deserves the honour.' Only a month before, Ponsford had fielded through Bradman's two innings of 124 and 225 in the trial. When in due course – in January 1959 – the world record individual score was exceeded by Hanif Mohammed's 499 in a Qaid-i-Azam Trophy match at Karachi, one of the first telegrams of congratulation likewise came from the previous record-holder, Sir Donald Bradman.[1]

As New South Wales won the match against Queensland with seven hours 48 minutes to spare, Bradman's mammoth score had not jeopardised his side's chances. Indeed, it is the *length* of a batsman's innings rather than the runs it produces that can affect a side's prospects: and the six hours 55 minutes that Bradman was in occupation was by no means a marathon stay by Australian standards. Ponsford himself had twice well exceeded that period, even after the limitation on time had been introduced to Sheffield Shield cricket.[2] Bradman's own captain, Kippax, had batted for six hours 28 minutes in scoring 315* (also against Queensland at Sydney) in 1927–28. And under Bradman's own captaincy, C. L. Badcock was to play an innings of nine hours 47 minutes in a Shield match in 1935–36, which his side still won. In the course of the onslaught against Queensland on 6 January 1930, New South Wales were scoring consistently at more than 100 an hour – they reached 500 in 301 minutes, 600 in 353 minutes, and 700 in 411 minutes. Bradman's own three century partnerships in the innings were all achieved at a very fast rate:

> 272 for 3rd wicket in 145 minutes with Kippax
> 156 for 4th wicket in 81 minutes with McCabe
> 180 for 6th wicket in 93 minutes with Allsopp

It was the habit of the New South Wales Cricket Association to make modest presentations to their players in recognition of a specially good

---

[1] Hanif Mohammed's world record innings was played on a coir matting pitch, and Sir Donald's innings of 452* still remains the highest in first-class cricket *on turf*. Hanif's 499 lasted ten hours 35 minutes. The Bradman record had come perilously close to being toppled in December 1948, when B. B. Nimbalkar reached an undefeated 443 for Maharashtra at Poona, at which point his opponents, Western India States, took the rare course of conceding the match. This was at lunch-time on the third day of a four-day match, and the Maharashtra captain said he certainly intended to bat on after lunch, despite being 588 ahead. It was with this knowledge that the visitors conceded the match – and in so doing left intact for another decade the world record of Bradman.

[2] From the 1927–28 season all Shield matches were limited in duration for the first time – to five days, with 2½ hours' play only on the fifth day. This condition was changed from the start of the 1930–31 season, when Sheffield Shield matches were limited to four days, as they have remained ever since. Thus the entire span of Bradman's career as a Sheffield Shield cricketer was played under time-limit conditions, with the consequent necessity to remain conscious of the clock. The importance of the time factor was appreciated and implemented by Bradman with a savagery of purpose achieved by none of his contemporaries in the Sheffield Shield.

performance. They must have been pleasantly taxed on what to provide on this unique occasion, and they settled on a rose-bowl, suitably inscribed, which still resides with Sir Donald. The innings was also recognized by a gift from Bradman's club, St George, of a silver paperweight in the shape of a boomerang mounted on a gold kangaroo, presented to him at a public farewell function before he left for England. Despite some staggeringly large innings played in minor cricket in Australia over the years, this innings of Bradman's still remains the record in *any* cricket within the borders of New South Wales, first-class or otherwise.

The world was suitably impressed with this quadruple-century – except Colonel Philip Trevor of the *Daily Telegraph* in London. He had never seen Bradman bat, though he had had a very close first-hand contact with Australian conditions as manager of an M.C.C. side, but as far back as 1907–08. He was apt to pontificate somewhat and, with some disdain, he foresaw no limit to individual or team scores in Australia. No doubt, he said, Bradman will live to break his own record or see it broken. He doubted whether his new feat was comparable in actual merit with MacLaren's 424 (which was made, he failed to note, against an attack with only two recognized bowlers); and, with commendable patriotism, informed his readers, irrelevantly, that England still held the best score ever, with 628 not out by the schoolboy Collins in 1899! (If only Trevor had known it, he could have made much of the fact that Bradman's record was made with an English bat, manufactured in Yorkshire! How he would have loved to have told his readers that! But even the *Daily Telegraph* correspondent did not know *everything*!)

Bradman's name was now pencilled in on most people's lists for the team to tour England. At the same time his critics persisted. Charles Kelleway, veteran of 26 Tests, was one of several who had criticised Bradman in 1928–29: 'They'll find him out. He uses a cross bat.' There had also, of course, been Fender and Tate. Now, even with his newest triumphs, it was written of him in Australia: 'This country lad, with his cross bat, will be no good on English wickets.' So many people said that he played with a cross bat that there must have been some truth in it. 'Quite true!' said Learie Constantine later. 'He did – and he does. Many of his scoring shots are so unorthodox that he ought to be unfrocked. The only thing is – where is the bowler who can unfrock him?' That was at the root of it – the phenomenal number of runs and the virtual impotence of bowlers in the face of them. At the end of one of the most memorable innings of his career – his 160 against Middlesex at Lord's in 1934 – the Cricket Correspondent of *The Times* said: 'Cross-batted some of his strokes may be, but oh the time he has to play them!' A. C. MacLaren condemned Bradman's cross-bat driving after his 206 at Worcester in 1934, but Bradman was still the first Australian to reach 2,000 runs that season and finished top of the averages. Bradman's bat was often not straight during the Headingley Test of that year, but he scored 271 runs in a day! In the previous Australian summer, 1933–34, he certainly played an unusually large number of shots with a cross bat in the Sheffield Shield competition – in which he finished with an average of 184! It seems that if unorthodoxy is sufficiently *confident*, it will succeed – as, for example, Charlie Macartney so often proved. Australians used to say of Macartney that 'The Governor-General makes his own laws', and if it brought centuries in its wake, why could not Bradman do the same? A great many fine batsmen have in fact 'made their own laws', but disparagers have too often chosen to ignore that they have also been thoroughly steeped in the basic principles of proper batsmanship. These things are mentioned for, despite all Bradman's fame and world-wide adulation in the early months of 1930, there was not an entirely unanimous chorus of optimism for his prospects in England that summer.

Don Bradman himself, with much modesty, once said that he was quite prepared for the disappointment of his name being omitted from the 1930 selections for England. But the chances of it happening, even in an uncertain world, were nil. The public outcry would have been shattering, and Australia's selectors might well have had their sanity questioned. The selectors, by the way, included one St George man, R. L. ('Dick') Jones, one of those responsible for bringing Bradman to Sydney. He had watched Bradman's ruthless rise to fame, often at close quarters: and if, through their common club and State allegiance, Jones had tried to be especially impartial, the sheer numerical weight of Bradman's performances must have outrivalled Jones in eloquence. Together with Jones (New South Wales), the 1930 tour selectors were Dr C. E. Dolling (South Australia) and Jack Ryder (Victoria). When the due date for the announcement of the names arrived, Bradman's figures in first-class cricket for the season stood as follows:

Innings	N.O.	Runs	H.S.	Av.	100s
13	2	1,400	452*	127·27	4

– naturally, by a big margin, ahead of any other player in both aggregate and average. McCabe's 632 runs came next, and the next best average was Jackson's 75·87.

The names of the 15 players were officially announced by R. A. Oxlade, the Australian Board chairman, from the New South Wales Cricket Association rooms in Sydney at 3.15 p.m. on 30 January 1930 (after there had been a 'leak' in some newspapers which the Australian Board viewed 'with grave concern' and which caused close questioning of the selectors themselves). Don Bradman and his brother Victor were out rabbit-shooting near Bowral at the time. On their way home they learned that Don's name was in the party. 'The Bowral Boy' had made good. He and his family were delighted, his parents taking a proper pride in the honour accorded their youngest child. Bowral itself, of course, took an almost equal pride in their young candidate for the hall of fame; and before he sailed off on his first venture abroad, the Mayor presented him with silver entrée dishes (as well as a little useful spending money!) at a public farewell enthusiastically attended, at the local theatre, by many who had watched him grow up since a child.

There was always a certain amount of parochialism in Australian cricket. Hugh Trumble, then secretary of the Melbourne Cricket Club, was quick to deplore Ryder's omission – but not, for example, to praise Bradman's inclusion. One was a Victorian and one a New South Welshman. 'On an English tour', he said on 4 February 1930 – and he said it in Sydney of all places – 'at least one forcing batsman is needed. Ryder is a strong, forceful batsman of this type. His inclusion would have helped the side in the time-limit matches.' What sort of batsman did he consider Bradman? Even a large group of prisoners in a Melbourne gaol signed a protest at Ryder's exclusion!

In England, strangely, there were still some reservations about the selection of Bradman. Maurice Tate, always good for a quote, was sought out by the press on the strength of having played against 13 of the 15 in the recent past. After praising the choice of Jackson, he went on: 'Bradman is more of a defensive batsman, and his success will depend on how he settles down in the different conditions over here.' Tate was entitled to his opinion on the 'defensive' nature of Bradman's batsmanship, but surely it was the very height of inanity to proclaim that a batsman's success would depend on how he 'settled down'. *Of course* it would so depend – and that was precisely true of *every* touring cricketer who came to England, whether in 1930 or any other year. What Tate was merely saying was that if Bradman was to get a lot of runs he would be doing well; but if he got few runs he would be doing badly! Poor Tate was always willing – often too willing – to give a view. But there was seldom, alas, much profundity in his offerings.

The Times wrote warmly of Kippax and Jackson, 'the stylists of the team', but discreetly played safe so far as Bradman was concerned. 'Bradman is of a different type. He may be the biggest success of the tour; on the other hand he may fail. Like Richardson, he attacks the bowling, and is a very fine stroke player. How he will fare when the ball is turning remains to be proved, but on a hard wicket he should be very dangerous indeed.' These were words that were cautious, bold and prophetic at the same time: a good journalistic mixture that left readers to put down their money and take their choice!

M. A. Noble, puffing at his pipe, gave himself time to think about the matter. He was a marvellous and highly perceptive critic who had learned much about the strategy and tactics of the game from his first inter-state captain, Tom Garrett, and later, briefly but significantly, from Harry Trott in Test matches. He was not always right, of course, but he was fearless and honest and respected. When the Australian side landed in England, Noble gave such a masterly analysis of Bradman's batsmanship that no apology is made for quoting it *in extenso*:

> Bradman is a batsman who, at times, defies orthodoxy and at others subscribes faithfully to it. He is not of the common order. He will play a ball off the wicket to the on-side with a cross bat as easily as the ordinary player would play it back to

the bowler. People wonder how he does it. I think I know two of the 'hows'.

First, he possesses a wonderfully quick eye; secondly, and this is, perhaps, the more important attribute, he never attempts the stroke off an impossible ball. If the ball is only just short of a good length he plays it correctly, but let it be a little bit shorter and off it speeds to the boundary.

The same stroke can be made just as powerfully, more accurately, and with much less risk with a straight bat. One wonders, therefore, what will happen when the sight focus is slightly out of gear and the muscular reaction less responsive.

A short delivery to most batsmen is a signal to the right leg to move across the wicket, thus bringing the body into a correct position, that is, facing the ball ready for any eventuality.

At times Bradman turns on the right foot, swings the left away to the leg side, and cracks the ball hard between the on-side fieldsmen. This is a dangerous position, and personal injury might easily result. Also it is quite possible to be bowled off the body.

An even greater weakness, however, is his careless dropping of the bat to a good-length ball just outside the off-stump. No effort is made to score, nor does he move his feet; he simply allows the ball to hit the bat.

I suppose this is really a defensive action, but it is a dangerous one, for if the ball keeps low or turns ever so little from the off there is great risk of its being snicked into the wicket. Yet these uncertainties of his batting will probably be much modified by association with clever bowlers on undependable wickets.

Bradman is an intelligent cricketer. His batting is free and attractive, and he scores in all directions. Quick on his feet, he is the despair of slow bowlers. Leg-breaks and googlies have no terrors for him, for he goes down the pitch after them and extracts their venom before they have time to bite. At the same time his defence is very sure, a fact he has proved many times when he has solidly played his team out of danger and then opened out in his own aggressive, quick-scoring style.

Provided that these two boys [Bradman and Jackson] strike form - and I can see no reason why they should not - England will have a treat the like of which they have not tasted from Australia since Charlie Macartney's brilliant performances in 1926.

Bradman may indeed have had weaknesses - which cricketer has not had them? - but, as Noble said, he had intelligence too: and rarely, at that time or at any other time, did Bradman's intelligence let him down. Noble's analysis was written specially for the London *Evening News*, and it is interesting that their own 'Cricket Expert', Harry Carson, could not find himself able, a few months before, to accept that Bradman (or Jackson) could rival Macartney: 'The man the Australians will miss most is Macartney, and it is doubtful whether Bradman or Jackson has quite the experience of cricket to take the game over as the "Governor-General" could and did . . . I am sure Macartney will be woefully missed.'

At the time the side was announced, Bradman's entire first-class career read with an impressiveness that the figures in no way falsified:

Innings	N.O.	Runs	H.S.	Av.	100s
47	9	3,506	452*	92·26	13

This gave him the best average of any first-class cricketer in the world. The only players remotely approaching him at that moment were W. H. Ponsford, with an average of 74·11 from 8,004 runs, and George Headley – at the very beginning of his career – who had then played only 13 innings for 932 runs, average 71·69. (It was Headley of course who was soon to acquire the soubriquet of 'the black Bradman': to Learie Constantine, however, it was Bradman who was 'the white Headley'!)

Bradman had scored his 3,506 runs at exactly 39 an hour, but in the 1929–30 season alone (that is, up to the touring team's announcement) he had scored at 47·97 an hour off his own bat. Not many Australians – not even his detractors – chose to apply the adjective 'defensive' to his batting.

To the above figures, Bradman added three further innings before he left Australia for England, all for the selected touring side – 20 and 139 v Tasmania, at Launceston and Hobart respectively, and 27 v Western Australia at Perth. At the T.C.A. ground at Hobart an aperitif for the future was provided when Bradman and Ponsford were at the crease together for the first time in their lives. Both were in the sort of form to make any bowlers shudder – Ponsford scored 166, Bradman 139, and between them they put on 296 for the second wicket (ended only by a run out) in 2½ hours, 62 of them at one stage in only 15 minutes, and 100 in 47. Bradman, despite his wonderful form, was outpaced by Ponsford in this initial association – and there was hardly an occasion in the entire season of 1929–30, in any sort of match, that this happened to Bradman, and it rarely happened in his entire career. Overnight they were neck and neck, 70 apiece since they came together. But next morning Ponsford scored 83 to Bradman's 69 before they both fell at the same total. There may have been something significant in this – the elder man, who had been allowed to enjoy the world record for only a few days over two years and could discern a new, inexorable domination that would put him and all others in the shade, deciding to show this young genius that W. H. Ponsford was also a name to be reckoned with. Both these batsmen had the highest mutual regard for each other, and Bradman considered Ponsford's play to have 'no weakness'. They had in common, of course, an appetite for huge scores that seemed insatiable. They had also in common the doubtful distinction of being the target of the jealousies of others. Both were immensely gifted cricketers, and as a partnership they were merciless in their concentration, alertness, versatility and prolificness. They were to occupy the stage as partners for only a brief period of four years (1930–34) and perhaps only on their second tour of England together did they dominate as a pair: but when they did so, they produced for spectators a joint display of footwork that was as marvellous to behold as the runs that followed. Certainly in 1934 English bowlers found Ponsford every bit as difficult to get out as Bradman. Sheffield Shield bowlers found them both equally impossible to master. Robertson-Glasgow once observed: 'Because Bradman will always be remembered is no reason why Ponsford should be neglected; when the sun rises it is a mistake to forget the moon.' The measure of Don Bradman's greatness was his capacity to overshadow Ponsford, who was not only a superlative batsman but one who himself possessed positive record-breaking propensities.

In the Hobart pavilion at lunch-time on that Saturday, Bradman was present at the unveiling by C. J. Eady, the old Test player, of an enlarged photograph of Joe Darling, who had done so much for Tasmania's cricket and its public life since he had gone to live in Hobart. It could not have occurred to anyone, as Darling was replying with much pride, that one of the most junior members of his audience would one day become the first man – and so far the only man – to captain Australia against England in more Tests than Joe Darling's 18.

The trip across Bass Strait to Tasmania had been the first time Bradman had become a 'sailor' – and he did not enjoy the experience. The trip was made in the splendidly appointed passenger-ship, *Nairana*, which then plied regularly between Melbourne and Launceston. Before leaving Port Melbourne, Bradman's name and fame had preceded him to both Launceston and Hobart. He was given a royal reception on both grounds, where of course opportunities to witness the leading Australian players were naturally very limited.[1] A return by sea-tossed boat to the mainland preceded a laborious five-day train ride from Melbourne to Perth for a final farewell match against Western Australia – Bradman's first visit to that State. The Perth ground was a primitive arena to what it is today, but the hospitality afforded the cricketers – including a civic reception and a visit to Government House – was a fitting *bon voyage* from Australia.

There had been a whole series of farewell occasions, of course, most notably in Sydney. On the night of 26 February Bradman was entertained – and it was *quite* an entertainment – at Sargent's Cafe, Market Street, by the directors and employees of Mick Simmons Ltd. Over 200 were present, including Stanley McCabe (who was later to succeed Bradman at the firm); and the hero of the evening himself was presented with a wardrobe trunk, suitably inscribed, as well as a set of cut glassware subscribed by the employees. Over the tables there floated balloons inscribed 'Bon voyage, good luck, Don'. The following night, at the Hotel Wentworth in Sydney, the N.S.W.C.A. entertained in sumptuous fashion the six New South Wales members of the touring team at a dinner attended by many great cricketers and prominent citizens. Bradman spent his last two nights in New South Wales with his parents at Bowral before, on 6 March, he joined the train at Moss Vale on which the Queensland and other New South Wales members were travelling to Melbourne. Before he was to set foot again in his native State, he was to astonish the world even more than he had done already.

---

[1] The practice of Australian touring sides visiting Tasmania as their first port of call before leaving for England began in 1926. The cricket was normally neither over-serious nor over-demanding (and sometimes not of first-class status) but it served the useful purpose of introducing as team colleagues players from different States who had hitherto known each other only briefly. Bradman himself played in Tasmania again before leaving for the tours of England in 1938 and 1948.

The young Private Donald Bradman was at that time among the names of volunteers for the new militia of the Illawarra Regiment (New South Wales) and he duly applied for, and was granted, extended leave to make the tour of England. When triumph followed triumph later on in 1930, a proposal was made to the commanding officer of the regiment that Bradman be induced to study for a commission. This did not come about as cricket assumed a greater and greater role in Bradman's life.

So, the farewells having been made in Sydney and in Bowral, Don Bradman, the new batting wonder of the age, was on his way to England. The colossal number of 3,619 runs had been amassed by him in all matches, major and minor, in that Australian season of 1929–30, as many as 2,135 of them (average 112·36) in the comparatively taxing conditions of first-class cricket and first-grade cricket in Sydney. For St George he set new standards, averaging 109·80 from his seven innings (two not out) and twice beat the existing club record (175 by R. J. Louden in 1927–28) with innings of 180 not out v Glebe in October and 187 v Randwick in February. This 187 was scored on Bradman's favourite Sydney Cricket Ground No. 1, and was made out of 325 in only 140 minutes in the face of some brilliant fielding. St George actually scored 390 for seven in 190 minutes, and at one time Bradman and Albert Scanes added 50 in 16 minutes. In his limited appearances for St George that season, Bradman scored 549 runs, and he and Alan Fairfax became the first St George cricketers ever to tour England. His first-grade average was the highest among all the Sydney clubs – there were 16 in all competing – and it was the first time a St George player had achieved this distinction. It was also the first time a St George player had recorded an average of 100 in a season since the club entered first-grade competition in 1921–22. In the course of time, Bradman was to set fresh records for St George both for aggregate and average. His record 187 for St George was the culmination of a brilliant spell in which he actually made five centuries in five successive innings in minor cricket, the last three of them in four days, amassing 541 runs for once out in those four days, as follows:

Wednesday, 12 Feb. 228* for Gladesville Mental Hospital v *Sydney Morning Herald* at Gladesville Hospital

Thursday, 13 Feb. 126 rtd for St George–Marrickville v Riverina at Hurstville Oval

Saturday, 15 Feb. 187 for St George v Randwick at S.C.G. No. 1

He did not play on the Friday! Only one chance was given in all the 541 runs. And they were scored at the rate of 98 an hour off his own bat! The 228* was made in only two hours by some colossal hitting on to or over surrounding buildings and over trees into the streets nearby. It was a small ground, to be sure, but he had 12 fielders against him and there were no sixes awarded (five being the maximum): he ended his innings with 4, 1, 5, 4, 5, 1, 4, 5, 4, 5 off the last 12 balls he received. Next day, during the country week carnival in Sydney, the grade clubs combined to play each country team, and Riverina faced an XI from St George and Marrickville. Bradman hit 23 fours in 70 minutes before he retired with 126. (It might here be mentioned that most other Sydney players in minor cricket at that time retired – against lesser opponents in non-competitive matches – when they had made 50 or 60. If Don Bradman seemed specially favoured in being allowed to go on to his century, and beyond, the answer lay in the astonishing speed at which he scored. For him to retire after, say, half an hour, with 50, would teach his opponents little and deprive the spectators of much. He almost regularly would reach his century quicker than one of his colleagues would reach 50. For the best example, perhaps, a match on the Sydney Cricket Ground on 3 December 1930 may be cited. It was the annual match between the combined Great Public Schools and a N.S.W. Cricket Association XI. Bradman did not go in until after tea in this one-day match, but reached 50 in 21 minutes and 100 in 46 minutes, before being caught at cover, hitting at every ball, for 110. Earlier Jack Fingleton had retired with 57 in 53 minutes, and the other opener, the left-handed B. M. Salmon (also a Shield cricketer), made 53 in 66 minutes – innings of a positive snail's rate alongside Bradman.)

Bradman's first-class runs alone in 1929–30 totalled 1,586 – only one other man in Australia reached even 800, S. J. McCabe with 844 – and his first-class average of 113·28 quite swamped the two next best of 77 by Woodfull and 70 by Jackson. There was a curiosity in the Sheffield Shield figures that year. Bradman averaged 111·75, and the next best average in the country (64·57) was also by a New South Welshman, Arthur Allsopp: Allsopp, who played in all but one of the Shield matches, totalled 452 runs – precisely the number scored by Bradman in a single venture to the crease!

From that momentous day when he learned he was one of the Australian side for England – 30 January 1930 – Don Bradman, with the sound common sense that was typical of him, began to keep a personal diary of events and impressions, in particular as they affected the touring side. Don Bradman was cricketer foremost and diarist very much secondarily, but he had a shrewd eye for the future and if – with the connivance of the gods – he would make a success of England, his diary entries would provide invaluable material for a written record of the tour from his pen. So it indeed proved. If the voluble minority would be shown to be right and his trip to England ended in forgettable mediocrity, his diary entries would be a form of diversion and a practice in literary effort at the very least. At all events he wrote up his diary day by day.

For one so comparatively young, Bradman took everything connected with his cricket – and therefore connected with his future – with the utmost seriousness. His mind was methodical and practical. *The Cricketer's* 'Third Man' said of him when the team was chosen: 'Sturdy and full of pluck, Bradman is a pugnacious batsman, with cricket wisdom of one greater than his years. His rapid footwork and powerful strokes fulfil the unspoken

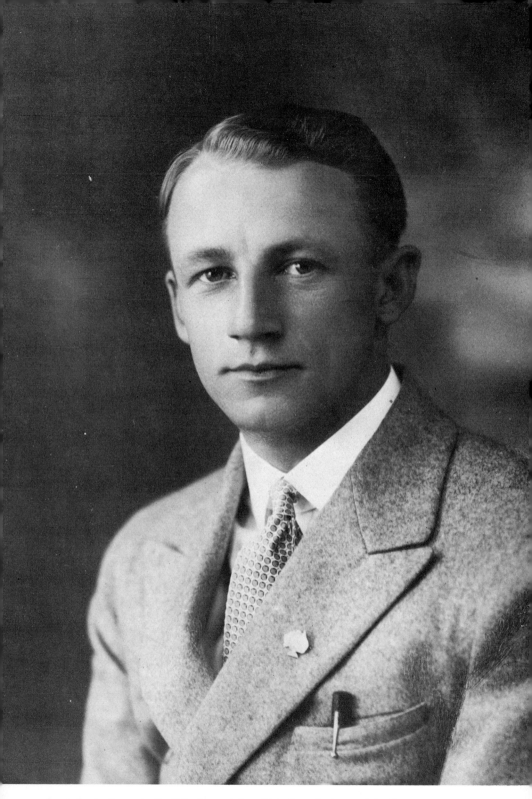

1 An early studio portrait of Bradman, taken (it is thought in 1930) by **Bassano**, the portrait photographers, then of Dover Street, London.

2 Sir Donald Bradman's parents – a photograph taken at Bowral in November 1930.

3 A unique role for D. G. Bradman –
fulfilling the duties of 12th man for the
only time in his life, for Australia v
England in the second Test at Sydney,
December 1928.

4 Bradman's first Test innings at
Melbourne. He is seen here, left, going
out to resume his partnership with
J. Ryder, his first Test match captain,
at the start of the second day's play in
the third Test against England, 31
December 1928. Bradman scored 79.

5 Don Bradman and his first captain in first-class cricket, Alan Kippax. This photograph was taken at Aylestone Road, Leicester, in 1930.

6 The young Don Bradman, on his first
appearance at the Oval in May 1930,
plays a ball along the ground to M. J. C.
Allom in the slips. On this day Bradman
scored an undefeated 252 against Surrey,
captained by P. G. H. Fender, whose
earlier criticisms of Bradman's methods
had become notorious. The wicketkeeper
above is E. W. J. Brooks.

7 The young record-breaker receives the
plaudits of Yorkshiremen. Bradman
returns to the pavilion after his
magnificent 334 in the Headingley
Test of 1930. It was the first innings of
his life on the ground, where he was to
average 192·60 during his career.

8 Above left: two Australian sporting champions – Don Bradman, right, watching Walter Lindrum at play at Thurston's Billiard Hall in London at the end of the 1930 tour of England. Note the unusual positions of the pockets on the table.

9 Not the work of a machine! Bradman in his prime displaying supreme human effort in driving Quintin McMillan during his 219 for New South Wales v the South Africans at Sydney – scored in well under a day on 7 December 1931. Bradman has left the crease with all the confidence of a man unable to contemplate dismissal. H. B. Cameron is the wicketkeeper.

10 Above: a business rendezvous in Sydney, 1931. Don Bradman, right, with Mr Claude Spencer, who handled the negotiations between Bradman and the Lancashire League Club, Accrington. Neither Accrington nor any other league club ever secured Bradman's services.

11 A typical off-side stroke by the youthful Bradman. This photograph has been prepared for the characteristic 'cut out' depiction of sporting personalities prevalent in the 1930s.

promise of his correct stance and high grip of the bat-handle; and he is tireless. Bradman drives a lot and bangs anything short to the leg fence with great force. The only uncertain element in his batting is the way he sometimes makes a tentative tap at a ball just outside his off stump, but a batsman of his great resource should be able to eliminate this "if" stroke on wickets from which the ball comes at varying heights.' 'Third Man' was also ready to put the doubters in their place: 'Those who look for the crudities in Bradman's methods, described by Fender, will need to make a microscopic scrutiny, because improvements in his style have made him an even greater batsman than he was last season . . .'

Those who chose to be impressed by figures rather than technique had literally thousands of runs to go by. The *Daily Pictorial* of Sydney, in its issue of 20 February 1930, revealed the remarkable fact that Bradman had scored in excess of 10,000 runs in all matches since his 17th birthday. It gave his full aggregates season by season, and if the final month of the season be added on, Bradman's record in major and minor cricket up to the time the *Orford* sailed from Fremantle was as follows:

	Innings	N.O.	Runs	H.S.	Av.	100s
1925–26 (aged 17)	21	8	1,318	300	101·38	4
1926–27 (aged 18)	27	5	1,576	320*	71·61	5
1927–28 (aged 19)	32	5	1,155	134*	42·77	4
1928–29 (aged 20)	42	8	2,616	340*	76·94	11
1929–30 (aged 21)	43	10	3,619	452*	109·66	13
	165	36	10,284	452*	79·72	37

What other Australian – or what cricketer from any land – had left for his first tour of England at the tender age of 21 with such a mountain of runs already behind him?

These figures also illustrate the dramatic – and deliberately planned – advance he made (admittedly with more opportunities) in the crucial season of 1928–29, from which time he never looked back. His 37 centuries included seven scores of 200 or more, four of which reached 300. Brilliant as all these figures were for a mere youth, his *first-class figures alone* when he left Australia showed his average, from 50 innings, to be 90·04. As was always the case with Bradman, his first-class figures were always more impressive than his minor ones.

Everything, naturally, was new to Don Bradman on his first venture abroad – the prolonged days at sea, the ship games (just before the *Orford* crossed the equator Bradman's youthful skill at tennis saw him defeat Hurwood 6–1, 7–5, in the final of the deck tennis), the traditional stop in Ceylon for some cricket and a sight of an ancient Buddhist temple; and then on to Suez, Cairo, Port Said, Italy, Switzerland, France and England. The ship's dance floor held little attraction for Bradman – perhaps he considered his footwork satisfactory enough – but he was not shy, among his friends, to entertain on the piano. In Cairo and nearby Gizeh he visited the Sphinx (demonstrably more enigmatic than any bowler he had encountered) and the Pyramids and the famous Mosque of Mohammed Ali, followed by a tour of the Cairo bazaars and his first – and only – camel-ride. Most of the Australian team tackled a camel. None chose to go back for more!

The route from Naples to the Channel was overland – a help to the bad sailors (including Bradman), though fortunately the journey up to then had been mercifully calm. Bradman thus saw and admired the Vatican City; St Peter's, Rome; the grave of Keats in the Old Cemetery in Rome; and the Colosseum. The eeriest of all experiences was when the team – each cricketer carrying aloft a lighted taper – followed a mediaevally-clad monk through the dark labyrinthine passages of the catacombs of St Sebastian, in which lay stone coffins and heaps of bleached bones. Then Bradman saw La Scala, Milan; one of the versions of 'The Last Supper'; rode through the St. Gotthard tunnel; and viewed Paris from the top of the Eiffel Tower. Outside the Australians' hotel in Paris, the fresh-faced Stanley McCabe dug Bradman in the ribs and pointed to the magnificence of the Champs Élysées in front of them. 'Bradman', he said. 'You could make 490 not out right there in the middle of the road, and nobody in Paris would be the least impressed. You'll stand a chance of becoming a fine cricketer some day, but in Paris you will just be Bradman.'

The only cricket played since leaving Australia had been a one-day game at Colombo on 2 April against All-Ceylon on the C.C.C. ground. The sequence of Australian visits to Ceylon had, like the trips to Tasmania, started on a regular basis in 1926, though the earliest Australian side to play in Ceylon had been the 1884 side to England, and the 1921 Australians *would* have played there had not their ship put into port too late. The attractions in 1884 had been Bonnor, Murdoch and Giffen: in 1930 the attraction was D. G. Bradman. The biggest crowd ever seen at a cricket match in Ceylon turned up for him. He made a sound, if sedate, 40 in his first innings outside Australia, while both Ponsford and Woodfull got half-centuries. The 'real' Bradman, the murderer of bowling, was not on view. Bradman, most unusually for him, was out 'hit wicket' – a form of dismissal in first-class cricket that was to befall him only once, and that as far on in his career as 1947–48. The successful Ceylon bowler was the old Royalist boy, Neil S. Joseph, primarily a batsman, on his first appearance for Ceylon. Don Bradman was to play only once more in this delightful island, at the end of his career in 1948.

Travelling across the world in the same ship as Bradman in 1930 was the man the new record-breaker was to succeed in public esteem as the epitome of skilful and audacious stroke-play – C. G. Macartney. He was going to England to write for the *Daily Mirror*. What sort of joy – and what sort of punishment? – would have been seen had Macartney been a player in the same side as Bradman?

Snow, rain and sunshine had been the lot of the Australians in rapid succession as they crossed Europe in mid-April 1930. Amidst strange tongues and strange ways, it had all been something of an interesting and pleasant diversion. Now the serious adventure was directly before them – and before Don Bradman. What would he make of it?

4 Debut in England

Circumstances! I make circumstances!
Napoleon Bonaparte

The year 1930 was as full of interest, of major and minor dramas, as any other year of modern times. While Marlene Dietrich sizzled in *The Blue Angel*, and *Cakes and Ale* came on the market, people were still not ready to accept as real the threats of new wars. The R 101 airship was destroyed in flight; the B.B.C. first attempted television broadcasts; M. Briand proposed a 'United States of Europe'; and the worst floods in history laid waste the Yangtze Valley in China. On the cricket fields of England, Donald George Bradman made his bow.

It was the most astonishing first appearance in England of any cricketer in history. Though eleven cricketers appeared in every side Bradman played for, and though Grimmett took 29 wickets in the Test series (and 144 on the tour) and Woodfull's captaincy was immaculate throughout, all eyes and pens were firmly focussed on the Sydney marvel, with the rest of the players satellites revolving around the sun. As early as the first Test at Trent Bridge, the newspaper headlines were already talking in bold type of 'Bradman v. England'. On the last morning of that match, a man in the crowd uttered a prayer to Tate: 'Please bowl him out, Maurice!' – and, so that there should be no mistake about his intentions, 'Bowl him middle stump.' Bradman made 131, by a long way – by more than 100 runs – the lowest of his four centuries in the series.

Bradman took England by storm that summer and introduced a new dimension into batsmanship. It became the fashion thenceforward to go to a Test match with a record book in one's pocket and watch tradition and the old landmarks go by the board. As R. C. Robertson-Glasgow was later to write: 'Like his fellow-countryman Walter Lindrum in billiards, he sought and achieved a numerical standard not previously contemplated.' There were reservations before Bradman landed in England about his skill. By the end of the tour he was unarguably the most remarkable cricketer to have arisen since the war. All batting was judged in the light of Bradman's mastery: and compared with that, other cricketers were merely human. Bradman was a miracle in flannels. 'Will he one day', asked P. F. Warner in November of 1930, 'play an innings of 600 or 700, and put the aggregates of Grace and Hobbs and their number of centuries, in the shade?' No wonder a good-humoured and enthusiastic Englishman proposed to start a 'Fund for the Assassination of Bradman'!

Of course the impact Bradman made in 1930, on both seasoned England cricketers and on the ordinary man in the street, was tremendous. He was lionised wherever he went, and to the end of his playing days in England his absence from a match brought intense local disappointment. With typical national masochism, English crowds came back again and again to see him tear their bowlers to ribbons. In 1930 he became the nearest thing to a magnet that cricket spectators had known. Even the King, in his message of congratulation to Woodfull on the success of his side, singled out one man among the Australians: 'It was a great pleasure to His Majesty to meet them, to see them play, and to have the opportunity of watching Mr Bradman bat.'

Naturally in 1930 bowlers all over England were striving their hardest for the distinction of dismissing Bradman: if not for a low score, they would settle for a high one. Many strove in vain, of course, and no one all summer got him for a duck. Maurice Tate dismissed him for 1 in the second innings of the Lord's Test, but he had made 254 in the first innings: and on the next occasion Bradman and Tate were in contention Bradman scored 334. When the Australians went up to Bradford after the Test match at Lord's, Bradman was boasting an average of 99. All England had been revelling in his run harvest. But the wily, 46-year-old Emmott Robinson, with the first ball he bowled to him, had him lbw for 1 after only eight minutes, and to this day the weavers and grinders at Park Avenue talk of the mighty roar that greeted the Don's downfall: there was no sense of chagrin at his departure, but a full Yorkshire pride – and the matter could not have been engineered by a firmer favourite than Emmott Robinson. 'Ahr Emmott's shifted 'im', was the popular cry. But the Don being the Don had a score to settle. By chance his very next innings was also on Yorkshire soil, in the Test match at Headingley. Nobody 'shifted 'im' quickly there, Yorkshireman or other-wise. By the end of the first day he was past his triple hundred.

Bradman in 1930 rose to the very summit of batsmanship, and had already attained immortal fame, at an age when most other batsmen were still feeling a tentative way in the lower reaches of domestic cricket. Nature endowed him with wonderful health that year (which was not to be his lot on every tour of England). A full eleven of powerful Australian batting strength could be named of those who, at Bradman's age in 1930, had not yet made their bow in Test cricket – Bardsley, Collins, Iredale, Armstrong, Noble, Ransford, Darling, Ryder, Kippax, Woodfull and Ponsford. 'Bradman is a cricket phenomenon. We have nothing like him', said Lord Harris at the end of the 1930 series. Such was Bradman's great certainty in keeping the ball on the ground that summer that among all his 2,960 first-class runs he hit only two sixes – and one of those was off a no-ball. *The Times*, in praising his brilliance at Headingley, said: 'He does not merely break records; he smashes them . . . The most ardent advocate of brighter cricket could ask no more of him, except, perhaps, that he should occasion-ally – say rather oftener than once in a hundred or so – put a ball in the air.' That was a heartfelt plea, and Bradman only *very* occasionally complied.

Responsible people quickly recognised he had revolutionised the game. There were remarks – made innocently enough, but later to acquire a terrible ominousness – that something would have to be done to curb his powers, in some such way as the anchor cannon was banned in billiards. The revival of underhand lobs was suggested, and the skill of Jephson recalled. Bradman might well have been out to a lob, but in all likelihood after passing 200. More seriously, P. F. Warner wrote, after the shattering 334 at Leeds: 'We must, if possible, evolve a new type of bowler and develop fresh ideas on strategy and tactics to curb his almost uncanny skill.' (In the bodyline bitterness these words were to be menacingly held up before an unsuspecting Warner.) At the same time Trevor Wignall echoed the rampant despair by declaring: 'I honestly believe that if he made up his mind to stay in for the whole of a four-day match he could do it.'

Before the end of September all the traditional caution of *Wisden* had been thrown to the wind and it was publicly made known that Bradman would be one of the Five Cricketers of the Year – a not exactly unpredictable fact, but for all that a unique violation of what has always been a closely guarded cricket secret. Before he left England, more rumours were circulating about Bradman than about any previous cricketer who had been on tour – principally that he had become engaged to an English girl and that he would return to England to play for a county as an amateur. 'They are mere yarns', said Bradman, dismissing them, while further rumours grew. He was going up to Oxford, said some: the fortunate college was not named, though there could hardly be any doubt he would get his blue as a Freshman! (If a typical Bradman innings had been added to Pataudi's 238 not out in 1931, how Cambridge would have suffered!) *Punch* inevitably depicted him in 1930 as Gulliver among the Lilliputians.

The story of the 1930 tour began, as was to be the pattern from that year for Australian sides in England, at Worcester.[1] There were no preliminary practice matches for the Australians that year, and Don Bradman's first opportunity to face a ball on British soil was in the nets at Lord's, which he did within 24 hours of his arrival in England. The team had spent Tuesday, 22 April, sightseeing in Paris, then crossed the Channel next day to arrive in London – in a steady drizzle – on the Wednesday evening. The day of arrival (ominously?) was St George's Day. The Hotel Cecil now being defunct,[2] Don Bradman's first night in London was spent at Sir Gilbert

---

[1] No Australian side had ever opened its programme at Worcester before. The South Africans of 1929 had been the first touring team to start off there, and in due course nearly all visiting sides began their first-class fixtures there. When, in the '30s, the counties were asked whether they would wish regularly to entertain the tourists for the opening match of the season, Worcestershire were the only county to say they would be happy to do so. The Worcester tradition for the Australians persisted until 1972. Thereafter matches arranged in 'geographically convenient groups' were favoured by the Australian Board for tours of England.

[2] This august landmark of the capital, between the Strand and the Embankment, had been the 1921 and 1926 London headquarters of the Australians and had been the venue of the

Scott's luxurious Gothic folly, the old and spacious Midland Hotel, above St Pancras Station, which transformed itself from a hotel into offices in the mid-1930s and is now the headquarters of British Transport Hotels. The usual luncheons and receptions to welcome a touring side followed, and Tom Webster produced a characteristic menu-card for the luncheon in the Australians' honour at the Savoy Hotel by the British Sportsmen's Club – and then on that same day, on the afternoon of 24 April, Bradman practised at Lord's for the first time, on a soft and unfamiliar wicket. As many as eleven of the Australians were on their first tour of England – their aggregate youth caused them to be nicknamed Kelly's crèche – so there were reputations in plenty to be made or marred.

On the Saturday, 26 April, after further practice at Lord's, the Australians lunched at Wembley as guests of the Football Association before joining over 92,000 spectators that afternoon to watch Arsenal beat Huddersfield Town 2–0 in the Cup Final. It was the first of four Cup Finals that Don Bradman witnessed at Wembley – he was to see the matches also in 1934, 1938 and 1948 – and was memorable, apart from the football, for the passage over the ground of the German airship, Graf Zeppelin, on her way to Cardington, looking like a long, silver cigar – the first visit of a Zeppelin to England since the war. At Wembley Stadium, however, she sailed so dangerously low over the huge crowd that official questions were promptly asked as to why this was allowed. Spectators at Wembley could see the passengers leaning out of the windows waving handkerchiefs, and could distinguish men from women. A tragedy of catastrophic dimensions could have occurred had there been a mishap.

The start of the tour proper was now in sight. Two more days of nets at Lord's, then the departure for Worcester on the Tuesday afternoon. On Wednesday morning, 30 April, the game against Worcestershire began – with Don Bradman one of eight newcomers in the Australian side. The Worcestershire committee had arranged for a British Movietone News picture to be made of the match, but they could not have anticipated that one of the newcomers was to announce himself in the most emphatic manner possible. The debut innings of Bradman on British soil became, in retrospect, highly significant both for Bradman himself and for Australian cricket. It set the mental tone for the tour by at once putting Bradman on the best of possible terms with himself and illustrating that Bradman was as anxious to deal in big scores in England as he was in Australia. His 236 was not just another double-century: H. H. Massie had scored 206 in his first innings for the Australians in England in 1882, and a brilliant innings it was too – but it achieved not an atom of significance compared to Bradman's score. If anything, Bradman's innings was a declaration of intent, a warning and a

---

great Centenary Dinner held by the M.C.C. in 1914 to celebrate the centenary of Lord's Cricket Ground. A fast-fading memory today, the Hotel Cecil was sold, to the regret of many, the sale proceeds announced in 1930 amounting to £1,622,705.

lesson at the same time – a warning to bowlers up and down England and a lesson to those who had said his methods were too unsound for England.

Peter Jackson, of Worcestershire, then only 18, and one of the few men who bowled against Bradman on both his first and last tours of England, remembers his initial impression of Bradman in 1930: 'As I first saw him walking briskly to the wicket he was a small, compact and wiry man who soon proved that he was very quick on his feet, that he picked up the length and flight of each delivery in almost the first few feet of the delivery. In his early style he was decidedly unorthodox but very sure. None of the old English "straight bat" type. He rarely hit the ball in the air and his runs came all round the wicket. Although two successive deliveries may have been almost identical, that did not mean they would be hit in the same direction.'

At the end of his first day's cricket in England, Don Bradman was 75 not out, having batted for an hour and a half in the company of his captain, Woodfull, who made 95 not out that day. Woodfull's innings, as was to happen so frequently on that tour, whatever its numerical value, was not the one that was scrutinized if Bradman was his partner. Woodfull, anyway, was a known quantity on English wickets. Even before Bradman had reached his first century in 1930, and on the evidence of his first 75 runs alone, the authoritative H. J. Henley pronounced on him as follows in the *Daily Mail*: 'Bradman, as a newcomer, was specially interesting. He at least has not been overrated. He seems to have every stroke in the cricket book, from the long-handled drive to the short-armed hook, and he revives the almost lost art of the late cut. Also he jumps out to slow bowling. There are very big possibilities about this square-shouldered, thick-set boy of twenty, but from the England point of view there is one consolation – Worcestershire bowling isn't England bowling.'

So immediately, after 90 minutes at the crease, the threat of Bradman was writ large across English cricket. He was then aged 21 of course (not 20), and when he took his score to 200 next day he became – as he still is – the youngest Australian to make a double-century in England, three weeks younger than Trumper. He was out for 236 out of 413 in 276 minutes, an innings of great certainty. Although it was true that Worcestershire's bowling was certainly not the strongest in England, Bradman did eventually play the same sort of innings against bowling that *was* the strongest in England. Worcestershire had played H. A. ('Barmy') Gilbert, the old Oxford blue and ornithologist, against the Australians – in his day a fine bowler and who had finished second to Fred Root in the Worcestershire bowling in the 1929 championship. Don Bradman simply murdered him, and he never played a first-class match again.

Wilfred Rhodes watched that innings of 236 at Worcester, and when shortly afterwards he met up with his old Yorkshire colleague, Waddington, he said: 'Abe, I have just seen the greatest batsman the world has ever seen.' 'Nonsense', replied Waddington (and it was a term of temerity in the presence of Rhodes). 'Never again will there be anybody as good as Jack

Hobbs.' Years later Waddington recounted the conversation. 'It was not long, however, before I was convinced that Rhodes was right', he said. 'Bradman is the greatest batsman I am ever likely to see.'

Bradman's declaration of intent at Worcester was not only reflected in his big score but by his words and actions off the field. He told Fred Root in that first match that before leaving Australia he had made up his mind that cricket was *the only object* of the tour so far as he was concerned – and that, of course, was merely a synonym for getting runs and runs and more runs. Bradman admitted at the earliest opportunity that social functions were neither especially to his liking nor in the framework of his priorities in England: he intended to limit them 'as far as was consistent with decency'. After the first day's play at Worcester, the Australians attended a reception at the Guildhall at the invitation of the Mayor of Worcester and the Worcestershire captain, the Hon. John Coventry (who had to stand down from the match with a severe cold, Major M. F. S. Jewell captaining in his absence). Don Bradman had excused himself and was away strictly by 9 p.m., to get straight to bed. Beau Vincent, of *The Times*, retained a special memory of the young Bradman on the verge of his triumphs in 1930: 'It was on his first visit to this country, and it was the evening before the first match of the tour at Worcester. He was sitting in front of the fireplace in the public writing-room – alone and thinking. And I feel that all through his illustrious cricket career he has always been thinking, concentrating upon what has to be done. Master of himself, just as he had unquestionably been the master of bowlers.'

During the torrid series of 1932–33, Fred Root looked back at the one and only occasion he had played against Don Bradman (at Worcester in 1930) and spoke of his methods as he saw them at first hand, without, however – as was to be so common – distinguishing leg theory from bodyline: 'His footwork would do credit to an expert dancer and enables him to make use of his left shoulder. When he first experienced my leg theory method at Worcester he was palpably puzzled, but he eventually overcame it by his magnificent footwork, and was finally driving inswingers from the leg stump past extra cover. There is no temerity about Bradman's methods. He does not suspect a trap in a half-volley, long hop, or full toss, and his method of defence is to attack. As a bowler I can readily vouch for the efficacy of such a theory. Nothing upsets the average bowler so much as to be hit hard and often. Even the leg theory wilts under punishment, and I have always maintained that if batsmen will "go for it" this attack loses half its terrors.' (*Daily Mail*, 13 January 1933.)

'Does George Geary turn the ball a lot on English wickets?' That was the first question Don Bradman asked – he put it to Fred Root – when he arrived at New Road on May Day in 1930. He was still in the midst of his innings against Worcestershire, but he was already playing in his mind his next innings against Leicestershire. At Aylestone Road, on a 'Geary wicket', he duly scored 185 not out in 5¼ hours and would almost certainly have got another double-century had not rain ended play for the day (and for the match) at 5.30 on the second afternoon. He was merciless on Geary, pulling and driving him to all parts of the ground, and in one period of 20 minutes he scored 33. So far Bradman had scored 421 runs in ten hours in England, spread over only two innings. The object of the tour for him, after only a week of battle, was being fulfilled in abundance. 'It is joyous to see Australia's second Trumper in his varying phases', commented the *Morning Post*.

Of practically every match on that 1930 tour of England there is at least one Bradman story to be told. His third innings was against Yorkshire at Sheffield, on his first wet wicket in England. George Macaulay, when he sent down his first ball to Bradman, turned to Bill Bowes and said: 'I can get this fellow caught and bowled.' He did. But Bradman had made 78 before he achieved it. It was George Macaulay, by the way, who summed up Bradman prophetically enough in 1930: 'He's a good 'un. I bet he gets many a million on good wickets.'

The fact that Bradman passed his 1,000 runs before the end of May in 1930 (the first tourist ever to do so and still the youngest of any of the small band to achieve it) was a triumph of determination and opportunity. It was certainly not inevitable, in spite of Bradman's propensity for run-gathering. In fact it very nearly did not happen. His innings against Leicester-shire and Surrey were cut short by rain, and he did not play in the Australians' first match in London, at Leyton. In his first innings at Lord's (v M.C.C.) he dragged a ball into his stumps when 66, and a week later, on his debut at the Oval, scored a wonderful 252 not out in gloomy conditions against Surrey, at one period actually scoring 51 out of 52 with Fairfax and reaching 200 out of 289 while at the crease. When his stand with Fairfax had reached 100, Fairfax's share was only 22. That innings – scored on the fullest expanse of the Oval and made on the only day that play was possible in the Surrey match – took Bradman to 922 runs on 24 May, and was most carefully com-piled for the benefit, in particular, of P. G. H. Fender, the Surrey captain, whose published criticisms of Bradman's batting methods in the 1928–29 series had certainly not been forgotten by the young Australian. They were not forgotten by the not so young Australian either, for Bradman remembered that innings and the motive behind it to the end of his career and beyond. Outside the Tests, it was probably his best innings of 1930, with a chance only at 207. He scored 116 in boundaries alone that day and made his runs at 52 an hour off his own bat.[1] One must suppose that P. G. H. Fender was suitably impressed or at least had a plateful of food for thought. 'He didn't tell us what he thought of the innings', recalls Bert Lock, 'but though Bradman kept

---

[1] Bradman actually scored 114 between lunch and tea and 110 between tea and close – the first time he had scored 100 runs in a session of play in England (though he had gone very close when he added 98 before lunch on the second day at Worcester). According to an eye-witness at the Oval, Bradman's chance at 207 was the first time he hit the ball in the air: it went to short square-leg, Bert Lock, who was so surprised that he dropped it. It had been arranged that the pitch be covered on Saturday night and the whole of Sunday, so had play been possible on Monday Bradman would have had a dry pitch to play on.

cutting balls to third man and we all kept saying he would soon be caught, the innings can only be described as magnificent.' The paying gate that day was 8,611, and it was the first of many great performances Oval crowds were to see from Bradman. In all the many years that Fender captained Surrey, from 1920 to 1931 and a few times after that, Bradman's 252 not out was easily the highest score ever made against him when he was leading the side at the Oval. Also fielding out to the innings that day was D. R. Jardine. It was the first and last double-century from Bradman's bat through which Jardine fielded.

Fender, in all fairness, had indeed started to repent in advance of Bradman's onslaught at the Oval: but even so, it was only a partial repentance in which he still could not bring himself to admire Bradman. At a wine trade luncheon in the middle of April, he declared that every Australian batsman was a perfect stroke-player and had only to discover the particular strokes he could use to advantage in England in order to shine. (He wisely did not share the view of many that the Tests were almost a certainty for England.) In the *Observer* on 27 April he looked back on the decline of Australian cricket since 1921, viewed the 1928–29 Tests as trials for 1930, and said: 'This season we shall see the new generation, and I feel convinced that some of the players now visiting us for the first time bear names destined to be landmarks not only on this tour but in cricket history.'

One of that new generation lived up to Fender's words on 24 May. Bradman, at the end of his 252*, seemed as fit as ever – he had even been anxious to run a fifth run for a hit by Fairfax towards the end, but the cautious Fairfax declined. It was quite some departure from the Oval that evening for Bradman. These days private cars in the forecourt carry the players through the Hobbs Gates or a team coach awaits them outside. Bradman went back to his hotel that Saturday the modest way, by underground – and he did not lack company in the short walk from the pavilion exit to the Oval station. He took a longer while to reach the station than he normally would to reach double figures, struggling through a crowd of admirers, especially boys, some of whom fought to catch the same train and refusing to leave the carriage until Bradman got out at St Pancras. Then Bradman celebrated his double-century in his own way – with a cup of tea – before going to the theatre, where Percy Fender entertained the Australians and his own Surrey team. Next morning Bradman was up bright and early to keep a golfing appointment at the Shirley Park Golf Club, near East Croydon!

The dramatic circumstances in which Bradman actually reached his 1,000 for the season are well enough known. He still required 46 more runs on the morning of 31 May, when Woodfull lost the toss to Lord Tennyson at Southampton. Bradman then owed nearly all to Grimmett, who took seven for 39 to dismiss Hampshire by mid-afternoon. Then, for the one and only time in his 120 first-class innings in England, he went in as opening batsman – with rain-clouds hovering above. The opportunity seemed lost when play could not be resumed after tea, with Bradman 28. 'The hands of the pavilion clock', recorded Bradman, 'were simply rushing round to six-thirty, and there we were looking at the rain coming down in torrents. The weather had baulked me.' Not quite, for a brief resumption of play was possible and Bradman made runs as quickly as he could. When he was 39 more rain fell, and his aggregate was now 993. 'I could not have complained if umpires and players had rushed pell-mell to the pavilion. That excellent sportsman, Lord Tennyson, who was captain of Hampshire, decided on one more over. I saw him approach the bowler, and although I have no exact knowledge of what he said, I think I could make a good guess. At all events, I had first one full toss to leg and then a "long hop", both of which I sent to the boundary, and then we bolted for shelter.' Within five minutes the ground was under water.

The bowler was Jack Newman, and the over that Saturday evening was left uncompleted in torrential rain. But the deed had been done. Hampshire had been generous, and Lord Tennyson in particular: his role in the proceedings was to have a certain sad repercussion 18 years later.

The due acclaim from the public for Bradman's great feat – there were 9,000 at Southampton after tea that Saturday – was literally washed away, for no sooner had he reached the 1,000 runs than the entire crowd was making desperate efforts to escape the downpour. The hasty exodus from the field was something of an anti-climax, but the runs were in the book, even if the ground was under water. The Hampshire bowlers had gone all out to dismiss Bradman until he wanted those final seven, and Lord Tennyson, asked whether Newman's simple deliveries were intentional, smiled broadly in reply: 'Perhaps the wet ball slipped out of his hand.' Percy Chapman, with a touching degree of optimism, that evening said of Bradman's feat: 'I am delighted, but I hope he gets rid of all his runs before the Test matches start!'

Oddly enough, Bradman had batted – as if by mathematical precision – precisely a day *in toto* to reach his 1,000 runs: 24 hours exactly. His personal rate of scoring to the end of May was thus 41·70 runs per hour. These, of course, were his first 1,000 runs on British soil, and to no other scorer of 1,000 by the end of May can that proud distinction be attributed. Hammond and Hallows, then the two most recent performers of the feat, each sent a message of congratulation. The full sequence of Bradman's scores which gave him his 1,000 by the end of May is as follows. The first 75 of his 236 at Worcester were scored in April, and he therefore scored 926 within the month of May itself – another record, which still stands, for any single month's cricket by a touring batsman in England.

It is interesting that without exception, in every one of the nine matches he played to reach his 1,000, he faced at least one bowler – sometimes more than one – who was good enough in 1930 to take 100 wickets in the season: so Bradman's passage was by no means along a glissade of uninterrupted ease.

v Worcestershire	at Worcester	236 in 4 hours 36 minutes		
v Leicestershire	at Leicester	185* in 5 ,, 17 ,,		
v Yorkshire	at Sheffield	78 in 1 ,, 40 ,,		
v Lancashire	at Liverpool	{ 9 in 19 ,,		
		{ 48* in 1 ,, 29 ,,		
v M.C.C.	at Lord's	{ 66 in 1 ,, 50 ,,		
		{ 4 in 20 ,,		
v Derbyshire	at Chesterfield	44 in 1 ,, 25 ,,		
v Surrey	at Oval	252* in 4 ,, 50 ,,		
v Oxford University	at Oxford	32 in 1 ,, 0 ,,		
v Hampshire	at Southampton	47* in 1 ,, 14 ,,		

1,001 in 24 hours 0 minutes

By the end of May, Bradman's dominance over his fellow-tourists was already ruthlessly established. The eight batsmen of the side at that moment sported averages as follows:

	Innings	N.O.	Runs	H.S.	Av.	100s	50s
D. G. Bradman	11	4	1,001	252*	143·00	3	2
W. H. Ponsford	11	3	604	220*	75·50	2	1
W. M. Woodfull	8	0	442	133	55·25	2	3
A. F. Kippax	11	4	296	57	42·28	0	2
V. Y. Richardson	9	0	289	100	32·11	1	0
A. G. Fairfax	9	3	179	53*	29·83	0	1
A. A. Jackson	12	1	275	64	25·00	0	2
S. J. McCabe	8	0	142	91	17·75	0	1

The senior wranglers, even at this stage of the tour, were in a paradise of their own – and Bradman had not even begun his record-breaking Test series of 1930. It is an interesting curiosity, by the way, that in the first ten matches played by the Australians that year, not a single hundred was scored against the side – a better record in that respect than even the 1921 and 1948 sides, and the best by an Australian side in England this century. Before the end of the tour Bradman's personal haul of ten first-class hundreds was to exceed the total number of centuries – eight – scored by the entire array of batsmen pitted against the side.

Don Bradman had the privilege of meeting the King for the first time on the Sunday before the first Test of 1930. The King had attended the Cup Final at Wembley which Bradman had watched three days after he arrived in England, but His Majesty's presence there was a very late decision – indeed, taken only at about 2 p.m. on that very Saturday – and none of the Australians was presented to him. On Sunday, 8 June, the Australians lunched as guests of Viscount Downe, a former pupil in R. A. H. Mitchell's house at Eton, son and nephew of former M.C.C. Presidents, and who might well himself have become President had he not died so comparatively young the year after. The Australians were entertained to lunch by Lord and Lady Downe at Hillington Hall, King's Lynn, on the borders of the Royal estate in Norfolk, having journeyed there by car in the morning. The agenda for the afternoon was Sandringham, where Bradman and other Australians (except Jackson and a'Beckett), having been taken there by Lord Downe, were received by the King and Queen. The whole occasion was quite informal, and the King, speaking freely of cricket past and present, revealed the keenest interest in the tour. Woodfull had a genuine friendship with King George V and whenever they met they would chat more as two old friends than as monarch and subject. On this occasion the Australians were given the freedom of the grounds, and Bradman was one of those who inspected the gardens and stables, the King's dairy, the new museum and the stud farms, and the church. The King congratulated Bradman on the fine tour he had so far enjoyed. As a memento of their visit to Sandringham, the Australians collected the best of the snapshots taken there, placed them in a handsome, leather-bound album, with gold-tooled decorations and the Australians' colours, and presented it to Their Majesties. (Queen Mary had specially asked for copies of the pictures.) The young Don Bradman's signature is one of those that adorns this singular piece of cricketana, now safely housed in the Photograph Collection among the Royal archives at Windsor Castle.

This royal diversion came in the midst of the match against Cambridge University at Fenner's, played over the Whit week-end – a match that has a small part in the Bradman story, for it was the most successful of his first-class career in which he starred as a bowler. Outside minor cricket he bowled only occasionally (and then expensively), though he did once bowl Hammond, in his prime, in a Test match at Adelaide – albeit with a full toss! Bradman bowled slow leg-breaks and googlies, though he never liked to be spoken of as a bowler at all. His understanding of the art, however, was complete: and never more so than when he became captain of Australia. 'Batsmen', he said in his retirement, 'may often save matches and sometimes win them, but more often it is the bowlers who are responsible for victories.' Before he came to England in 1930, Bradman had taken nine first-class wickets in Australia, including that of Patsy Hendren on the first occasion he played against an English team. Prior to Fenner's, he had already bowled at Aigburth, Chesterfield and on the Christ Church ground at Oxford, collecting three wickets in those three games. At Cambridge he had figures of three for 35 and three for 68, bowling 28 overs in all and dismissing so good a batsman as E. T. Killick in both innings. At Scarborough in September he dismissed Leyland, Wyatt and Tate in the same innings, which served to give Bradman tour figures of 12 wickets at 25·08 – and fourth place in the final averages!

On the team's first full day in London, W. L. Kelly, the manager – a Melbourne auctioneer who had played for Victoria before the First World War – said to a gathering of cricketers in the old, commodious library of Australia House: 'Our job is to win back the Ashes. It is up to Australia to do it, and I feel that if we have no casualties and the team play up to their best form we have as good a chance of regaining the Ashes as you have of retaining them.' (Mr Kelly, incidentally, a superb manager, was to live through and admire the entire career of Bradman, dying in Melbourne in 1968 at the grand age of 92.)

Don Bradman, the glittering star, was one of those to whom Mr Kelly and all Australia looked on the eve of the first Test at Trent Bridge. Maurice Tate's prognostication as to Bradman's batsmanship had been that his success in England 'will depend on how he settles down in the different conditions over here'. By the second week of June, Bradman could feel more than satisfied with the way he had settled down. No tourist to England had ever before entered the first Test of a series with as many as 1,230 runs to his name, and this still remains a record for a tourist.[1] Bradman was the most talked-of man of all the players on either side before the match, and he invested the Australian party with even more glamour than Australian sides normally had. During the early morning of the first day of the Test, the street in Nottingham that contained the Australians' hotel was jammed with people for well over an hour. Outside the hotel where the England side were staying, only a handful of onlookers gathered. (The Australians stayed at the Black Boy, in Long Row, in the centre of Nottingham. The hotel, one of the best-appointed in the city, was opposite the Council House, where then – as now – 'Little John' sonorously struck the hour. It is still recalled as a local curiosity how Woodfull caused the chimes to be silent during the night so as not to disturb his sleeping team. Those were the days before visiting teams began to stay at the huge Bridgford Hotel (opened in June 1966), on the bank of the Trent, overlooking the ground. The site of the Black Boy, which closed its venerable doors on the night of 8 March 1969 is now occupied by Littlewoods Stores.)

Don Bradman went out to play his first Test innings in England before a Saturday afternoon crowd of some 23,000 at Trent Bridge in 1930 – it was a full house, with the gates shut – and on a wicket that perfectly suited Maurice Tate. There had been rain followed by sun. Bradman, having had one life off Tyldesley when 7, played on to Tate after a quarter of an hour for 8. He was uncertain, even nervous. He never looked comfortable. He was, with all the unpredictability of cricket, reduced to the commonplace. 'Tyldesley bothered him', said Cardus, 'Tate tormented him until mercifully bowling him with a breakback to which Bradman held out a bat as limp as it was crooked.' If anyone at this point had chosen to venture that this batsman, before the series was out, would upset all previous standards of run-getting, an amused tolerance might have ensued. Maurice Tate, at least, made no recorded comment – he was obviously proud enough, however, for when he came to write his autobiography four years later he titled his chapter on the 1930 Tests, 'I Bowl Bradman'. But before the match was through, Bradman

---

[1] Charles Hallows, of Lancashire, in 1928 entered the first Test v West Indies with his season's aggregate at 1,273 runs. He had achieved that in 19 innings, compared to 14 by Bradman, and the first Test in 1928 began on 23 June, ten days later than the 1930 date.

had given due warning: his 131 in the second innings was easily – by more than 50 runs – the highest score of the match, and all the time he was in, for four hours 20 minutes in all, England's cause was in danger.

The unbeaten Australians met their first defeat of the tour in the Trent Bridge Test. It was to be the only game they lost all summer. It turned out also to be the only Test on English soil in which Don Bradman scored a century and was on the losing side. In fact it was the only match *of any kind* in England – Test or otherwise – in which a Bradman hundred was linked with defeat. Although it was not always the case on Australian wickets, in England (apart from Trent Bridge 1930) a Bradman hundred was a positive guarantee against defeat. Before very long, indeed, people were to come to the view that Bradman's very inclusion in a side was sufficient to give it the stamp of impregnability. As a match-winner throughout his career, of course, Bradman was to stand alone. As A. G. Gardiner was to write of him in 1938: 'He can make any team of crocks formidable against any challenge. So long as there is someone left to keep the other wicket intact, no game is so hopeless that he cannot snatch victory out of the jaws of defeat. And his value to his side is not limited to the centuries he scores. It was said of General Kléber that merely to look on him made men brave, and in the same way Bradman's presence in a team gives it the spirit of victory.'

Four days were allotted to Test cricket in England for the first time in 1930, and England won at Trent Bridge with less than an hour to spare. Bradman on the final day looked as though he might well win the match for his side, for at lunch Australia needed 231 with 240 minutes left and seven wickets in hand, with Bradman (12 short of his hundred) and McCabe together. Both were batting beautifully, the two youngest players in the match. The pitch, moreover, was lasting well – that particular pitch had not been used for any purpose for four years and had been most carefully groomed for this occasion. But if Australia thought their luck was going to hold and they would get the further 231 to win, the superstitious among them remembered that the Test had begun on Friday the 13th, that it was the 13th match of the tour, that it was Chapman's 13th Test against Australia, and that even the digits of the opening day (13.6.30) added up to 13! Australia duly lost. Copley's famous catch to dismiss McCabe began the decline, but the googly from Robins that deceived Bradman clinched it. The crucial ball was described by Cardus as 'one which the most skilful man might not be able to achieve even on his luckiest day'. But Bradman had played an innings 'that will have to be remembered with the great classics of the past', wrote Trevor Wignall. 'He will not be twenty-two until next August, but here he is with only Jack Hobbs, who is old enough to be his father, competing with him for the distinction of being described as the world's greatest batsman . . . Pouring praise on Bradman is so much the equivalent of gilding the lily that one hesitates to say much more about him, but chiefly because his side was in such a tight corner his latest effort must of necessity be considered the best of his young career.' A day later he wrote prophetically enough: 'He will do many more remarkable things before this summer is over.'

Bradman's 131 at Trent Bridge (the first century ever made against England on that ground) meant of course that he had scored a hundred in his first Test match in England – something that, while not unique, had eluded such great names as Trumper and Hill and Macartney and Bardsley and Woodfull and Ponsford. It was the first of his 11 centuries in 19 Tests in England, 'a splendid fighting innings, which will take its place in cricket history' (P. F. Warner). Bradman himself was disappointed at his mis-judgment of the ball that bowled him, but such was the praise for his score from every quarter that one might have thought Australia had won. The Bradman relentlessness was there to the full, utterly efficient, utterly sound and utterly threatening. As this was his first Test in England, one further initial impression may be permitted.

On that last tense day, with Bradman hoping – and England fearing – that he might win, or at least save, the match for Australia, one of those watching was the late James A. Jones. He is not known to cricketers, but is celebrated – and quite rightly so – in journalistic lore for his quite brilliant column, 'Courts Day by Day', that bejewelled the pages of the *Evening News* for so many years and was recognised in Fleet Street as one of the most remarkable of all daily columns. The supreme ease of his style was as much in evidence at the cricket ground as in his familiar magistrates' courts:

We look at Bradman with something like despair. He is a beautiful craftsman, we know; not a genius like Jack Hobbs, of the debonair bat, but a man who brings utility to its highest pitch: and there is hardly a man in this hushed multitude who is not praying for him to get out . . .

But Bradman stays and stays.

He is like a robot. Runs come to him as if they were being manufactured by a slow but infinitely efficient machine. And though the Englishmen crouch around like panthers, they seem powerless to stop this implacable progress . . .

The robot falters for a moment. The ball fizzing from the impish stretch of turf beats him completely.

He turns round and looks at Duckworth with a startled expression. It is only for a moment; the machine begins to work again, and soon it has scored the highest individual score in this historic match . . .

We are back on the rack once more. The run-machine is in gear and nothing can stop it. Chapman has got his lucky cap on – a thing gaily striped, which has been a charm to him since he became England's captain.

But for once it will not work . . .

Bradman makes his century, as he was bound to do from the very start. We give him a cheer. So do the Englishmen. Then we lean forward once more, and watch with strained eyes.

Bradman was lionised when he left the ground at the end of the match, and again as he walked out of his hotel that evening to go to the railway station in Nottingham. His average for the tour was 105·30. He had scored more runs than any batsman in England, and had almost certainly received more critical praise and public adulation than any visitor to England before him. It was by no means the end. Indeed, the Bradman legend was just gathering pace. There were four Test matches to go, and indeed the 'run-machine' was in gear with nothing to stop it. Even the English weather had no effect on Bradman. Poor a'Beckett had not been well since he landed, Woodfull and Hurwood had suffered from colds, and Richardson and Oldfield were troubled with hay fever. Fairfax soon after landed in hospital and Ponsford was on a milk diet. Grimmett developed gastritis, but rapidly recovered, and poor Archie Jackson was never really well, though the English climate was not to blame in his case. A slight chill, quickly shaken off before Worcester, was all that Bradman had suffered. Then came Wimbledon weather, and Bradman took the opportunity of renewing his keen interest in tennis by visiting the famous tournament just before the second Test at Lord's.

What Bradman did at Lord's can be summed up – but not exactly dismissed – in a single phrase: He played the most perfect innings of his life.

The superlatives had been cascading forth since Worcester. There seemed nothing left. And now Don Bradman, off the mark first ball with his customary single, proceeded to make the highest score ever recorded in a Test match in England and the highest score by an Australian in a Test match in the world – a quite brilliant 254, renowned by no means simply for its numerical size but for the sheer perfection of its stroke-play and footwork. Not a chance was given; hardly a false stroke was made; never once was the ball lifted off the ground. That such perfection should have been maintained over a period of more than $5\frac{1}{2}$ hours – albeit bisected by a Sunday – showed Bradman to possess not only a buoyant faith in himself but the most remarkable qualities of concentration and single-mindedness. Maurice Tate bowled heroically, but to Bradman nothing seemed impossible. He treated the England bowlers as if they were novices at the nets. Rarely can England bowlers have been given such scant courtesy. In more recent years West Indians such as Weekes, Sobers and Richards have on occasions played at the highest level with something approaching contemptuousness in the way they have dismissed the ball with apparent ease to the boundary. This mark of utter and merciless domination was born in Test cricket at Lord's in 1930, and it was Bradman who gave birth to it. His dazzling skill literally left some of the critics at a loss for words – and they admitted it! Jack White, a Test selector giving himself the best of all close-ups and who took his full share of punishment in that innings, remarked later that in his opinion Bradman, had he wished to, could have played every ball he bowled before it bounced – an amazing testimony to footwork that was indeed exceptional. J. C. White was made to seem a real Somerset straggler that day. Bradman's very first ball in that innings was driven firmly to long-off – 'an impertinent crack', recalled Cardus years later, 'and when he finished the stroke he was close enough to J. C. White to see the look of astonishment on the bowler's face.

Nobody had dreamed in England then of using feet with impunity to J. C. White.' On another occasion, looking back at that first ball, Cardus said: 'This was the beginning of the most murderous onslaught I have ever known in a Test match.'

For his *Manchester Guardian* readers that day, Neville Cardus – even when Bradman was half-way through his innings, not out 155 on Saturday night – wrote that 'young Bradman knocked solemnity to smithereens and attacked with a bat which might well have appeared excessively care-free even on the smooth lawn of a country house cricket match . . . The advent of Bradman was like combustible stuff thrown on fires of batsmanship that had been slumbering potentially. The bat sent out cracking noises: they were noises quite contemptuous. Nearly every ball was scored from: maiden overs seemed beyond the reach of possibility. . . . When he batted eleven men were not enough. Lord's was too big to cover; holes were to be seen in the English field everywhere. Chapman tried his best to fill them up, but in vain. . . . Bradman to-day established himself amongst the authentic batsmen of England and Australia of all time. Quality does not need to argue itself; we feel it intuitively the moment we see it. Until to-day I had looked at Bradman's batting as a thing of promise; I have now seen signs of a glorious fulfilment.'[1] Some people said that Bradman was not an artist in his innings at Lord's – as Duleep had been for England on the first day – but a craftsman: but if so, they conceded he was a brilliant and faultless craftsman. Frank Chester, one of the umpires, later recorded: 'I left the Lord's Test in 1930, after watching Bradman, firmly convinced that he was the greatest batsman of all time.'

Bradman began that 254 'as if he had already made a century', said P. F. Warner. Bradman himself recalled: 'This was my first Test at Lord's, and I was naturally very anxious to do well.' He went in, as at Trent Bridge, before a Saturday crowd, and was able to 'do well' enough to reach the fastest fifty of his Test career. (He reached fifty altogether 42 times in Test cricket.) It took him 45 minutes, a time he was to equal the following winter in Australia. For the first time in his career – the first of a record six occasions – he scored a century in a single session of play in a Test, going from 54 at tea to 155 not out by close of play. He and Woodfull had added 231 for the second wicket at exactly 90 an hour, and on Saturday night Australia were 404 for two. Archie MacLaren condemned the England bowling tactics (he condemned most of England's tactics in the match) and charged Tate with

---

[1] Cardus had indeed been not too certain of Bradman before Lord's. At Aigburth against Lancashire he had seen him out to McDonald for 9 'to a stroke of incredible cheekiness. He actually moved across to the off and tried to hit a fast ball from McDonald to square-leg for four. He was bowled middle stump; Macartney would have condemned the stroke as entirely unorthodox, Trumper would have waited until he had reached at least fifty before attempting it'. Even on the final day of the Trent Bridge Test Cardus had written (perhaps with an eye on his Mancunian faith and readership?): 'Neither Bradman nor Ponsford exactly looked to be great batsmen, yet both of them are beaters of MacLaren's highest score. From this morning I concluded their superiority with MacLaren is strictly statistical.'

playing the batsmen *in* rather than getting them *out*. Jimmy Catton, who was working with MacLaren on the *Evening Standard*, opined, no doubt correctly: 'Some grumbled, some criticised, and some were very wise after the event.'

On Monday Bradman had his eye on R. E. Foster's 287, the then record score in England–Australia Tests. When Tate achieved a maiden over to him, there was a tremendous cheer. When 191, made without the ghost of a mistake, Bradman tried to play a ball from Hammond to the on: whether or not he changed his mind is uncertain, but the ball actually went through the slips – an unbelievable circumstance if indeed Bradman had not intended it: it was no chance, it was along the ground, but in the midst of such total perfection there were some persons anxious to cry out he had erred! When he passed 200 an Australian admirer from the crowd picked up the ball and kissed it! Even Percy Fender was bowled over and called the 254 'as perfect an example of real batting, in its best sense, as anyone could wish to see'. Sir Donald himself still singles that innings out as technically the best of his career. 'Practically without exception every ball went where it was intended to go, even the one from which I was dismissed, but the latter went slightly up in the air, and Percy Chapman with a miraculous piece of work held the catch.' It was a superb one-handed catch, at full stretch at extra-cover swooping to his right, off a very hard hit. It ended an innings of genius.

Plum Warner now called Bradman 'the champion batsman of the world' – a slightly longer title, but distinctly reminiscent, of the one given to W.G. 'He stands', said Warner, 'on the threshold of what, given good health, must surely be a career which will equal and probably surpass that of any other batsman.' L. V. Manning, noting that Bradman was only 21, asked: 'What will he achieve before he unbuckles his pads for the last time?' For the record, his innings of 254 was watched, in wonderful weather, by about 31,000 on the Saturday and 32,000 on the Monday, including members – and including Warren Bardsley, who saw surpassed his 1926 record (193*) of the highest score for Australia in a Test at Lord's – and they all gave him a memorable ovation on his return. Tom Webster drew a cartoon of the rear view of a retiring cricketer which he captioned: 'A charming picture of a batsman returning to the pavilion. This is a picture treasured by every member of the English eleven. It is Mr Bradman.'

Most of the records Bradman set up at Lord's were to be broken in an even more remarkable – if slightly less perfect – innings less than a fortnight later at Leeds. But that 254 still remains the highest Test innings played at Lord's, and at 21 years 307 days Bradman still remains the youngest cricketer ever to score a double-century in England–Australia matches. 'There is no longer any necessity to talk of him in connection with Victor Trumper or Charlie Macartney', wrote Trevor Wignall. 'He resembles both at moments, but the most sensible way to refer to him now is by stating that he is Don Bradman, which merely means that he occupies a niche of his own.'

Australia won the second Test at Lord's, of course, and the harbour ferries in Sydney heralded the news at 3 a.m. with 'Cock-a-doodle-doos' on their sirens. Even at that hour of the morning there were thousands in the streets waiting for the scores to be posted. Their own New South Welshmen had contributed five players to the victorious team – but the one who was pre-eminent, the toast of all Sydney, was Donald George Bradman.

The gargantuan appetite of Bradman for runs was now a *fait accompli* at Test level. No one *dared* imagine that this innings was a flash in the Test match pan. He had made huge scores against club bowlers, Sheffield Shield bowlers, and Test trial bowlers in Australia; he had devastated the English counties. Now he had turned his attention to the highest class of cricket of all. He did it with the sort of purpose that spelt despair – there was a certain resignation, even before he went to Leeds for the third Test, that he was bound to beat 'Tip' Foster's 287. The surprise was that he did not beat it at Lord's. This is not – and was not – said with hindsight. It was being forecast before the Lord's match was over. 'What's the use?' asked a man in the crowd as Bradman batted relentlessly on in his 254. One by one the England bowlers came on and retired defeated. To the unconquerable Bradman, some of the bowling seemed as easy as schoolboys' under-arms. One of the spectators that day, the late Mr H. F. Mathews, of New Malden, recalled the impact: 'I well remember, when he reached 250, the people around me expressing their amazement, and dismay, very volubly, when what must have been a cockney retorted: "Blimey, what are you worrying about? It's only a quarter of a thousand." ' Well, a quarter of a thousand wasn't going to be enough for Bradman at Headingley, any more than it was going to suffice on several other Test match occasions in the future.

Bradman had not had a bat in his hands for more than a week (while he had a private look around London and enjoyed the Wimbledon finals) when he motored up to Yorkshire through pre-motorway England and booked in at the Queen's Hotel, Leeds, for the third Test of 1930. The brief respite from cricket was to prove beneficial. Friday, 11 July, at Headingley, was the day the Don overflowed.

Of all the distinguished performances in the long history of Test cricket, Don Bradman's great feat of scoring 309 runs in a day off his own bat, as he did on the first day at Headingley, must rank very high, if not at the very top. This was achieved not merely in a Test match, but in the very highest form of Test cricket – between England and Australia. England's bowling was stronger than at Lord's – Larwood and Geary were now in the side – and Bradman had to go in, as was very far from the case at Lord's, after Australia had lost a wicket to the 11th ball of the innings. Bradman made England's bowlers, according to one observer, 'look cheaper than dirt' and 'served them all as though they were novices in a backyard'. He was 105 at lunch, 220 at tea, and 309 at the close – with power to add. Such indeed was the fearful domination he had imposed, and so fresh did he seem at the end of it all, that it was seriously put into print that night that there seemed no reason at all why he should not score a further 300 on the morrow. Bradman

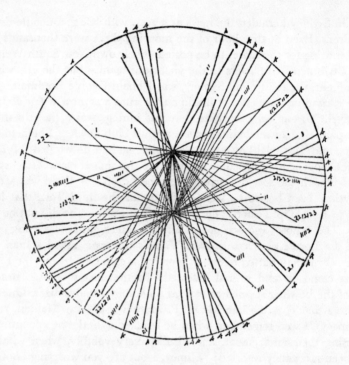

The famous innings of 334, scored by Don Bradman as a 21-year-old against England at Headingley in 1930. This is W. H. Ferguson's chart depicting the scoring-strokes of 46 fours, 6 threes, 26 twos and 80 singles. Ferguson was one of the scorers in every one of the 52 Tests in which Bradman played.

recalls the occasion more modestly: 'I consider I was very lucky to strike my best form on an ideal batsman's wicket, and if I thought about it at all it was that the morrow could look after itself.' In fact on the morrow he was out for 334.

This was the first innings of Bradman's life at Headingley, and his century before lunch on the first morning of a Test linked his name with the only previous performers – Trumper and Macartney. These three brilliant New South Welshmen held this distinction to themselves until October 1976, when Majid Khan joined them. Macartney, incidentally, was watching the innings from the press-box. Bradman reached his hundred before lunch with 13 minutes to spare – *precisely* the same margin that Macartney had given himself on the same ground four years before. This margin remains a world record for the first morning of a Test, for Trumper (v England at Old Trafford in 1902) reached the hundred-mark with only five minutes to spare, and Majid Khan (v New Zealand at Karachi in 1976–77) did so with seven minutes to spare. Oddly enough, out of only four instances of a century before lunch on the first day of a Test, W. M. Woodfull had the distinction of batting at the other end throughout two of them (Macartney's and Bradman's). In batting feats of this nature, the bowling rate must always be relevant: and it is important to note that in the two hours' play before lunch on the first day at Headingley in 1930, 46 overs were delivered. By way of telling comparison, on the first day of the England–Australia Test at Headingley in 1977, in the same two-hour pre-lunch period, 28 overs were delivered.

In well over a hundred double-centuries that have now been scored in Test cricket, Bradman's time to 200 that day – in 214 minutes – remains the fastest. When he beat Foster's England-Australia record of 287, he had been batting $5\frac{1}{4}$ hours compared to Foster's seven hours. The runs poured forth like a cataract in inexorable flood – straight drives, off drives, cover drives, on drives, square-leg hits, hooks, cuts and all else. 'To mention the strokes from which he scored most of his runs is to go through the whole range of strokes known to a modern batsman', said *The Times*. 'Once or twice he demonstrated an idea which is not generally understood, but at no time did he take anything approaching a risk, and he cannot have hit the ball in the air more than three times during the day. It was in fact an innings so glorious that it well might be classed as incomparable, and how the Yorkshiremen loved it.'

Indeed to every ball that day he had *some* stroke – he hit 42 fours on that first day alone – and Pelham Warner said next morning that such was his quickness of foot that he seemed able to force any ball, however good its length. 'To call him a run-getting machine', said Warner, 'as he has been called, is a poor compliment; that rather implies that the runs are ground out with a roar and a clash and a clatter, while as a fact he makes his runs easily and smoothly and naturally, with the mark of genius throughout. He is never flurried or in any apparent hurry, and yet runs come from his bat almost as fast as bullets from a machine-gun; there has never been a batsman who in match after match has claimed such a huge proportion of the runs scored. You may talk of Alexander, Hercules, Trumper and Macartney, but this young Australian is a super-batsman and the equal of any-one.'

By the end of that evening most of the 20,000 present must have thought likewise. Among those who long retained happy memories of that day was A. J. Richardson, of the 1926 Australian side, who had travelled to England on the same ship as Bradman and who had crossed the Pennines to watch, being pro again that year with Bacup. Among the schoolboys watching was Leonard Hutton, aged 14, sitting on the hard Headingley benches. He had batting ambitions himself, and had just made the Pudsey St Lawrence first eleven. One day he was to play an even bigger innings in a Test match. Among the professional critics watching (even though perhaps not the most technically gifted) was the *Daily Express* man, Trevor Wignall, seeing yet more magic from Bradman, and he confessed he found it 'difficult to avoid exaggeration when writing of this amazing youngster, but there must be many like myself who now think that cricket has never known anyone like him'. He went on:

There still appear to be those who question Bradman's right to be described as the most marvellous batsman of his time. He may not have the correctness of Hobbs or the perfect artistry of Woolley and Duleepsinhji, but what does this matter when he can get his runs against the best bowling in England in the manner of shelling peas?

I can easily remember such stars as Spooner, Ranjitsinhji, Trumper, and others of the truly great, but no one of them was better than this astonishing boy from a hamlet in Australia. If he has a fault at all, it is that he makes cricket look too much like child's play, and at the rate he is progressing he will soon have to be handicapped, as are billiards players, before he starts to score.

It is either compelling him to owe 100 or blindfolding him that will stop his gallop. It is impossible now to speak of one of his strokes being better than others, for he cuts with the same brilliance and sweetness as he drives, while he has some shots that have never been seen before.

Well, they used to say that W.G. should be made to play with a smaller bat. Now the new champion of cricket was likewise considered to be too good for his contemporaries.

When he came off the field with his undefeated 309 that day, shepherded back by police and eluding attempts to shoulder him in triumph, he was too shy to appear afterwards before the cheering crowd around the pavilion. In the dressing-room he carefully placed his bat in a bag and asked for a cup of tea. He was smiling and showing no sign of strain. He is alleged to have remarked on entering the dressing-room – at least his vice-captain, Vic Richardson, said so – that it had been 'a good bit of practice for tomorrow': the remark gained prominence, but Sir Donald denies that he said it. One remark *was* made, however, in an unmistakable East Yorkshire accent, when Bradman reached his 300 and acknowledged the long round of applause: 'Why, noo, if it's a fair question, what diz tha think tiv him?' The reply came: 'Why, Ah think, wiv a bit o' practice, t' lad 'll mak a cricketer!'

There are countless stories about that three hundred in a day – unusual in the Bradman saga, for anecdotes did not readily attach to him during his career. Richard Tyldesley, rubicund and rotund, did more than his share of running that day. Bradman seemed to be picking on him, especially, for wherever he fielded, poor Tyldesley was forced to chase the ball to the boundary, ponderously and perspiringly – the ball for ever just beating him to the edge. The slight downhill slope at Headingley did not help. 'He's damned good, isn't he?' said someone to Tyldesley at the end of the day. 'He's no good to me', came the rueful reply. Tyldesley was in his benefit year, but he derived no benefit from Bradman's innings that day.

Seth Kilner, father of Roy and Norman, went across from his home at Stairfoot to see that first day's play. He always remembered Bradman going down the wicket to a ball, slipping, and having fallen flat and had his intended shot frustrated, nevertheless managed to late cut the ball for four. Jack Hobbs recalled how monotonous it became, on each succeeding 50 and 100, for the England players to keep saying: 'Well played, Don.' (Bradman's *slowest* fifty all day, by the way, took him 75 minutes, his third: to atone for his slackness, he hit the next in 40!) Maurice Tate always believed that he all but bowled Bradman with the first ball he bowled to him which, he said, 'missed the off peg by a coat of varnish'. There seems to be no other evidence to support this, and Sir Donald cannot recall it. Harold Larwood has gone even further and claims he actually 'dismissed' Bradman for a duck in that innings, but the claim – in public at least – was not made until 24 years later (when both umpires were dead), when Larwood wrote it in a newspaper article in July 1954. It has never been supported by any of the players or the 20,000 spectators present. He set it down again in his auto-biography in 1965. 'Even before he had scored I had him caught behind the wicket', said Larwood. 'There is no doubt in my mind, he was palpably out. Everyone around the wicket appealed, even Jack Hobbs, the fairest man I ever met on a cricket field.' Larwood is certainly mistaken. For one thing he did not bowl at Bradman that day with his score at 0, and Hobbs was certainly fielding at cover to Larwood, and fielded either there or on the cover boundary all day. A few lines further on in his book, Larwood spoke thus of appeals for a catch behind in English cricket of 1930: 'It was the practice in England for only the bowler and those close around the wicket in a position to see or hear to appeal.' This alleged incident was at a time when Bradman's arrival at the crease brought almost a ball by ball descrip-tion of his movements in the newspapers, and the entire – and not incon-siderable – press contingent at Headingley seems to have failed to notice the appeal or alternatively to have conspired to suppress it. Bradman did make mistakes, however, at 141 and 202, in each case skying the ball to mid-on, but no fielder touched it. His only real chance was when 273, a little before six o'clock, when Duckworth dropped a hard offering off Geary behind the wicket – only the third time he had actually been dropped in more than 15 hours' batting in the series! The Don smiled broadly, and Duckworth looked daggers.

Earlier in the tour, in the beautiful Skinners' Hall in London, Surrey had given a dinner to the Australians, presided over by H. D. G. Leveson Gower, the Surrey President, who – thinking as much of his role as Chairman of Selectors – confessed: 'Sometimes I dream that Bradman will never be dismissed for less than 150 in the Test matches . . . but it is only a dream.' That was before the series began. The dream had now become a nightmare, and the England selectors were as powerless to stop Bradman in 1930 as their successors were to prove in later years. ('Shrimp's' predicament at Bradman's hands was, however, preferable to the black-edged letter he received threatening him with death if he did not include Sandham in the Leeds Test! He thought it prudent perhaps not to tempt the fates too overtly, and included Sandham in his side to play the Australians at

Scarborough at the end of the season. There, Sandham dropped Bradman off a sitter at mid-on!)

Leveson Gower might have derived some consolation from Archie MacLaren – they must have both shaken their heads in unison after that Bradman effort of the first day at Leeds. With touching faith, MacLaren, after the Lord's defeat, opined: 'Doubtless Larwood and Sutcliffe would have made a very big difference. When they return I feel sure there will be different scoring cards at Leeds.' The major difference was that Bradman was not satisfied with a mere double-hundred. Larwood's analysis at the close of the first day was 0 for 103. In the midst of the onslaught George Duckworth looked at Maurice Tate: 'I thought you could get him out in England off that cross-bat shot, Maurice?' It was hardly a time for chiding or joking. Bradman was interviewed at the end of the day and said: 'My feet are awfully tired, but I could have gone on if it hadn't been the close. I am happy to have beaten the record, but happier still to think that Australia is in such a good position.' He went, by the way, to his 2,000 for the season with his last shot that evening – at that time the youngest player in history to reach such an aggregate.

Bradman's personal detractors – and they were beginning to muster their ammunition by then – made much of the fact that Bradman did not throw any wild party on the night of his triple-hundred. He was not even at the hotel bar. Instead, after dining, he was in his own room listening to music (and probably writing). This was precisely the relaxation he required, best suited to his temperament. Beer-drinking, not one of his habits at any time, would have been his *last* desire. 'Was I expected to parade the streets of Leeds?' asked Sir Donald in his autobiography.

Ben Barnett said of Bradman in 1961: 'If he made a century he would get back to the hotel at night, have dinner and then go to his room to write.' Ben Barnett knew the Don on tour in 1934 and 1938, but it was just the same in 1930. On that Friday night at Leeds he was almost certainly bringing a little further up to date his life story, which he had by then contracted to write. One of the Australian team in that match suggested to Bradman that he should 'give a dinner for the boys' when it was known that Bradman had gained a handsome reward – mentioned a few lines hence – at Leeds. Bradman's reply spelled out his shrewdness: 'If I gave you fellows a dinner every night from now until we got home to Australia you would only say what a fool I am!' And no doubt they would have done.

Next day – the third Saturday in succession in the series that his batting had been on display – he was caught behind the wicket off Tate for 334, then the highest innings in any Test and still the highest for Australia. He removed his cap to deafening applause as he walked back. He had scored his runs at 52 an hour and had hit 46 fours (still an England–Australia record). 'We can still hardly believe that it is true – that this master of cricket, so icily aloof from human failings, has erred at last', wrote James A. Jones. The other Mr Jones – R. L. Jones, of St George, and one of Australia's selectors – said in Sydney: 'I never had any doubts, but his record is beyond my wildest dreams.' That Saturday in Sydney a movement was started to subscribe to a public testimonial for Bradman.[1]

On the Headingley field itself, Bradman became £1,000 richer that afternoon. At the fall of Sutcliffe's wicket Alec Hurwood, the 12th man, took a telegram out to Woodfull: 'Kindly convey my congratulations to Bradman. Tell him I wish him to accept £1,000 as a token of my admiration of his wonderful performance. (Signed) Arthur Whitelaw, Australia House.' Woodfull handed the telegram to Bradman, who read it and put it in his pocket. Mr Kelly, the manager, replied: 'Bradman on field. Kindly accept deepest gratitude on his behalf wonderful generosity.' Bradman also wired, as soon as he could, hoping to convey his personal thanks later. Arthur Ernest Whitelaw was an Australian by birth – from Auburn, Victoria – who had played some minor cricket himself when living in Melbourne. A middle-aged man of much charm, he had gone to England some 14 years before and had acquired a fortune as a member of the firm of Fleming and Whitelaw, soap manufacturers. Well known for his generosity, he said: 'I thought Bradman's performance merited such recognition as it would be useful to a young fellow on the threshold of his career. Boxers get much more for far less important achievements. We must encourage our cricketers in every way possible, since cricket is the greatest of all games. This is not so much a gift as a mark of appreciation on behalf of Australians.' Towards the end of the tour, in the ballroom of Australia House, at a ball in honour of regaining the Ashes, Mr Whitelaw presented Don Bradman with his £1,000 and gave each member of the team an ashtray. Bradman's gift, incidentally, was in itself £400 more than any Australian player's fee for the entire tour.

And how did Mrs Emily Bradman herself, Don's mother, take it all in Bowral? There was high excitement there as each successive triumph of the Don came through on the radio, and the Bradman home was in a simmer of activity as neighbours called constantly to enthuse over the newest success. 'If these records continue much longer I don't know how I am going to

---

[1] Bradman's highest innings in Test cricket consisted of 46 fours, 6 threes, 26 twos and 80 singles. The successive scoring-strokes in his 334, as set out in the scorebook in the possession of the Yorkshire C.C.C., read as follows : 2421144214143214411444124141112141241111121 441214414242111141111213242411414112242411224411111411111114143111414211143122112114412111211134141141114443111411244. The transcription here printed is accurately reproduced: but it is a classic example of how even the best regulated scorebooks, and on the most important occasions, can be – and alas too often are – incorrect. Although the strokes certainly add up to 334, Bradman is shown to have gone from 219 to 223 with a four, and likewise from 308 to 312. He most positively *was*, however, 220* at tea and 309* at the close on the first day. The scorer for England was Brownfoot (Billy Ringrose being away with the Yorkshire first XI at Bath and Swansea), and while possibly the Test score may have been copied into the Yorkshire scorebook at a later date, with all the hazards that copying entails, it is more likely to have been *bound* in, together with the Yorkshire second XI matches, found in the same bound volume. An examination of Ferguson's original ball-by-ball scoresheets, housed in Sydney, reveals the error. Brownfoot was correct up to 219*, but omitted Bradman's final single before tea. On the following morning Bradman's remaining 25 runs came as 4311141244, not as Brownfoot recorded it.

stand it', said Mrs Bradman as the Leeds news became known. 'I am so worked up and excited when Don is playing in the great matches that I don't know what I am doing. All the villagers hurry round, and while the news is coming through on the radio we chat and argue for hours. . . . Scores of telegrams have been pouring in congratulating me about Don. . . . Although I am so proud of him – and what mother would not be? – I am not the least afraid of his success turning his head as it might do with most young fellows. I know my Don would think too much about his mother to let success spoil him.' Not for years had Bowral been in such a state. The local hotels reported splendid business and, as one report put it on the day after his 334, 'if the toasts drunk to his health and long life count for anything Bradman bids fair to put Methuselah's record for longevity where he has already put most of the cricket records.'

It might here be emphasised that there was always the strongest bond of affection between Don Bradman and his mother. Bradman's three main interests in life at that time could legitimately be set down as cricket, playing the piano, and his mother. Throughout all his activities in England in 1930, he never failed to write a weekly letter to his mother, telling her of his adventures. And, though it is little known, he took careful steps to make proper financial provision for his parents early on in his cricket career as soon as he began earning money through his skill as a batsman.

Would Bradman have scored 300 runs in a day in a Test match now? When, in a television broadcast in 1971, the view was expressed that he might well have done so, several sound judges were quick to come forward in support. Of course, over rates, field placing and captaincy in the 1970s is quite different from the '30s: but B. A. Richards scored 325 in a day at Perth in 1970–71 in a Sheffield Shield match. Genius has demonstrated time and again that it is subject to no laws. And the power to surprise – nay, to astound – that Bradman showed in his prime should never be forgotten. Sir Donald Bradman himself recalled in 1967, with a certain amount of wonderment, how 'without batting an eyelid, one modern player told me I wouldn't get the runs I did if playing today because the bowling and field placing are more scientific'. Without bringing his own genius into the argument, Sir Donald said: 'I believe any champion of any era would have been a champion in any other era. It is purely a question of adaptability.' Maurice Tate after the war used to be asked what his bowling tactics were when Bradman came out after tea at Headingley, roaring towards his triple-century. Did he make plans to pin his down? 'Pin him down?' Tate would ask with incredulity. 'Of course not! I bowled every ball to bowl the little devil out!' In other words England attacked all day – and Bradman attacked likewise. (Tate, by the way, had been the major sufferer in the innings of 334, and more than half the runs actually came off him and Larwood. Bradman's full Headingley plunder was achieved as follows: 93 runs off Tate, 84 off Larwood, 56 off Geary, 53 off Tyldesley, 27 off Leyland, and 21 off Hammond. If Vic Richardson's observation of Bradman's earlier innings at Lord's –

that he 'had scored enough for three batsmen' – was true, what was the reckoning at Leeds? Bradman's scoring rate in his 254 at Lord's had been 45 an hour. He had raised that quite comfortably to 52 an hour at Leeds. He scored his 334 off only 448 balls – a rate of 74·55 runs per 100 balls off his own bat. Of his 46 boundaries, by the way, as many as 34 were in front of the wicket – a wonderful testimony to his spirit of aggression. When Len Hutton batted for more than 13 hours at the Oval in 1938, only 16 boundaries were in front of the wicket. Bradman's 46 fours were taken from all the bowlers put against him – none escaped – Larwood being hit for 14 of them, Tate 13, Geary 8, Tyldesley 6, Leyland 3, and Hammond 2.)

Neville Cardus had been watching Bradman's progress of triumph in the 1930 Tests with ever-increasing wonderment – writing this time from the spot instead of from Cross Street. Despite his press-box uncertainty at Trent Bridge, he had been quick enough to know that Bradman's 131 there 'will be by no means his highest score against England this summer'. After the miracle of Leeds he sat down to compose what has since become his celebrated 2,000-word study of the 21-year-old Bradman and one of the classical gems of cricket literature. It was timed to appear on the morning of the Old Trafford Test and spread itself across six columns of the *Manchester Guardian* – six out of the seven columns in all. What good judgment that great newspaper had; and what great skill did Cardus bring to his task. He wrote as 'Cricketer', of course, but deliberately with book publication in view in due course; and four years later the essay appeared, with some small amendments, in *Good Days*, where it thrilled a vast new audience and does so still to those who are both fresh to it and familiar with it. 'The really astonishing fact about Bradman', said Cardus, 'is that a boy should play as he does – with the sophistication of an old hand and brain. Who has ever before heard of a young man, gifted with quick feet and eyes, with mercurial spirits and all the rapid and powerful strokes of cricket – who has ever heard of a young man so gifted and yet one who never indulged an extravagant hit high into the air? Until a year or two ago Bradman had seen little or no first-class cricket. Yet here he is to-day, bringing to youth's natural relish for lusty play with a cricket bat a technical polish and discretion worthy of Tom Hayward. A mishit by Bradman – when he is dashing along at 50 runs an hour – surprises us even as a mishit by Hayward did when he was in his most academic vein. How came this Bradman to expel from him all the greenness and impetuosity of youth while retaining the strength and alacrity of youth? How did he come to acquire, without experience, all the ripeness of the orthodox – the range and adaptability of other men's accumulated years of practice in the best schools of batsmanship? . . . If Bradman develops his skill still further – and at his age he ought to have whole worlds to conquer yet – he will in the end find himself regarded not so much a master batsman, but as a phenomenon of cricket.'

There were those in 1930 – as there were to be for ever more – who accepted the runs of Bradman but not his methods. Cardus dealt with that on that July morning in the 'M.G.' by ending his cultured discourse with this peroration:

> He has all the qualities of batsmanship: footwork, wrists, economy of power, the great strokes of the game, each thoroughly under control. What, then, is the matter with him that we hesitate to call him a master of style, an artist who delights us, and not only a craftsman we are bound to admire without reserve? Is it that he is too mechanically faultless for sport's sake? A number of Bradmans would quickly put an end to the glorious uncertainty of cricket. A number of Macartneys would inspire the game to hazardous heights more exhilarating than ever. . . . But this is a strain of criticism that is comically churlish. Here have we been for years praying for a return of batsmanship to its old versatility and aggression; we have been desperate for the quick scorer who could hit fours without causing the game to lapse into the indiscriminate clouting of the village green. In short, we have been crying out for batsmanship that would combine technique and energy in proportion. And now that a Bradman has come to us, capable of 300 runs in a single day of a Test match, some of us are calling him a Lindrum of cricket! It is a hard world to please. Perhaps Bradman, by making a 'duck' in the Manchester Test match, will oblige those of his critics who believe with Lord Bacon that there should always be some strangeness, something unexpected, mingled with art and beauty.

Well, Bradman didn't quite oblige his critics with a duck in the Manchester Test but, as we shall see, he was reduced to the most abject ordinariness there, contrary to every expectation.

Headingley had been a fresh exercise in superlatives for the critics, and they must have been thumbing their Rogets feverishly, with a mixture of trepidation and despair, as Old Trafford approached. With wisdom after the event, people were crying that all this should have been foreseen, for Bradman was playing precisely these strokes at Worcester in April. He was, it was true: but blocking the shots was the puzzle. Ferguson's scoring charts, even if the England players had asked for a sight of them, would have been doubtful aids in solving the problem. A feature of Bradman's genius was always an ability to place a ball between fielders with unerring precision. Bradman had now scored five centuries against England in his last six Tests, and each had been an improvement on the last – 112, 123, 131, 254, 334. To say this sequence could not go further was something no critic dare surmise in mid-July 1930. That was the measure of Bradman's potency. He had played in only three Tests in 1930 and already he had comfortably outstripped the aggregate of any previous Australian in a completed rubber.

It seemed that the Almighty – personified temporarily in the shape of I. A. R. Peebles – decided England should have a breather at Old Trafford. 'England was a little afraid of the young man by that time', recalled Walter Hammond. His average for the tour was 106 and in the Tests alone 145! But Bradman's nerve was quite shaken at Old Trafford by his first ball from Peebles, which all but bowled him and went for four byes – had the larger stumps been in use he would have been bowled, thinks Peebles – and within minutes it was plain he could not detect the googly from the leg-break. Fast or medium-pace bowling had been nourishment to Bradman; and slow bowling had normally held no terrors. This however was certainly a strange hazard. He gave a chance to Hammond off Peebles when 10, was beaten again next ball, and was then caught off Peebles by second slip off a late cut. He had made 14 in half an hour, undoubtedly his most uncertain innings of the summer. The roar from the crowd was deafening. The failure defied – as to many it still does – logical explanation, for leg-breaks and googlies were 'picked' successfully enough by Bradman at all other stages of his career. But none of the Australians could pick Peebles that day. Ian Peebles himself has given his explanation in his recent autobiography, *Spinner's Yarn*:

Much has been written about this duel and many commentators have been very generous to me. Over the years I have given the matter a good deal of thought and imagine that I see it in proper perspective. I believe I bowled my best, especially the leg-break, and I am sure Don could not pick my googly. That being said, there is one more important factor. It is that, for the first time in his life, Don was seeing a slow, soft English wicket. Any good Yorkshireman would have met with little difficulty on it but, to the batsman brought up on fast Australian wickets, it had always been a problem at first sight. Curiously enough it was the one type of pitch upon which Don never looked at ease, presumably because he didn't really apply himself to what, for him, was a rare and not very important matter. Bill Ponsford, with a good strong top hand, was always a great player on soft wickets – as Don must have been had he tackled them seriously.

Bradman had played against Peebles twice previously on the tour, v M.C.C. and v Oxford University, when there had been no such trouble. Peebles did not get his wicket in either of those matches, but at Oxford had him 'caught' off a no-ball – only to be struck next delivery for six off another no-ball, which was the first six Bradman hit in a first-class match. At Manchester it was almost total surrender to Peebles. As soon as Bradman was out the match looked to be a genuine contest again – which Bradman had certainly never allowed it to look at Lord's and at Leeds. 'The whole of these Test matches centre on Bradman', wrote Harry Carson before Old Trafford, 'and the general opinion is that if we cannot get him out in three overs we may have to wait three days.' Carson foresaw a contingency he confessed might be remote: 'It is just possible that Peebles might find something Bradman does not like.' He was right. He did.

There wasn't an excessive period for self-congratulation after Old Trafford, for in the next match Bradman promptly reached a chanceless hundred against Somerset – the 20th century made for the Australians in all matches on the tour, of which Bradman had made nine. He shared his first three-figure stand of the tour with Jackson (231 in 215 minutes for the second wicket) and his average was still over the 100-mark when he set off for Swansea for the Bank Holiday fixture with Glamorgan. The late Dai Davies, in his book published a year before his death, told a splendid story of Bradman's first appearance in Wales. Bradman went in with three-quarters of an hour to go on the Saturday evening:

The first ball I bowled him just shaved his off stick. It was so close that the wicket-keeper, Trevor Every, made no attempt to take the ball, believing it would have bowled Bradman, and it went for four byes. I knew I had him in my sights but after only one more over I was absolutely flabbergasted when Turnbull told me abruptly: 'Put your sweater on!' I just couldn't believe it, and said: 'What's the matter with you? Let me have another go at him. I'll get him out next over.' Turnbull looked at me hard and said: 'That's what we don't want. Can't you see we've got to keep him in for Monday?' We were in such terrible financial straits that winning the game had to come second to pulling the crowd. Needless to say, Bradman was not out at close of play. On Monday there was a gate of 25,000, and the match receipts were £4,500, the highest figure taken at a county game through-out the season. Glamorgan's share of the gate was £2,500, and Turnbull had been dead right. The county showed a small profit at the end of the season for the first time since the previous Australian tour of 1926.

At Northampton in Bradman's next match, A. E. ('Taffy') Thomas, a fine medium-pace right-hander, was promised a 'fiver' – the conventional handsome inducement of the time – if he could get Bradman first ball. On a very sticky wicket, he was within a hairsbreadth of doing so. Having dis-missed Jackson, Thomas's next ball all but bowled Bradman: which, considering that Bradman was top scorer in a disastrously low innings, might have made the Australian total a laughable one. As it was, never in his entire career did Bradman take a 'first ball' in England. At the other end Jupp's off-spinners perplexed Bradman over after over. He struggled to 20 at lunch, then played on to Jupp in the second over afterwards, and the Australians were all out for 93, to the astonished delight of a 10,000 crowd. Only four boundaries were hit by the tourists, two of them by Bradman. Such is the glorious uncertainty of cricket that it was left to Northampton-shire, comfortably bottom of the table that year, to dismiss the Australians for their lowest score of the tour. It was at Northampton that Bradman received a letter, without delay, addressed simply: 'Mr Don Bradman, Champion Cricketer, England'.

Before the Oval Test began, England's bowlers shuddered at the public announcement that it was no secret that Bradman would attempt to break his own record for the highest individual score in Tests – the match, with the series still level, was to be a timeless one. Ben Bennison, who was helping Bradman write his life story, later recorded: 'When he proceeded to the Oval, we were quite prepared to see him get as many as 500 runs; and when, at Kennington, he passed the 200 mark, we doubted whether there was any finality to his run-getting.' The Oval wicket, moreover, had been most carefully looked after that summer. Some people thought that S. F. Barnes – at the age of 57 – should be brought into the England side to combat Bradman. He was still bowling brilliantly that summer for Staffordshire, and had just taken six for 6 and six for 23 in the match against Denbighshire, followed by seven for 20 v Lancashire II. The South Africans of 1929 had declared him the best bowler they had met all tour. In 1930 he was to finish easily at the top of the second-class averages with 51 wickets at 5·74, while for Rochdale in the Central Lancashire League he took 89 wickets at 8·22. There were no Bradmans opposing him, to be sure, but he was still a force and extremely fit. Leslie Duckworth, Barnes's biographer, wrote in 1967: 'I shall always hold it against the M.C.C. that no opportunity was created for Barnes and Bradman to oppose each other on the field, even though, in view of Barnes's age, they would not have been meeting on equal terms. Nevertheless, to have seen Barnes bowling against Bradman would have been worth going a very long way but, alas, it did not happen.'

What *did* happen was that Bradman scored 232 in the Oval Test in 7¼ hours, with only a single chance at 82, and broke more and more records in the process. He took his average for the series to 139·14 and his aggregate to 974 runs – still a record aggregate for a Test rubber. No batsman before had ever had such an average in an England–Australia series, and only Geoffrey Boycott since (in 1977, with more than 500 fewer runs) has bettered it. Bradman had made off his own bat more than a third of the runs scored by Australia's batsmen. His innings at the Oval was spread over three days, and on successive mornings he made 85 and 98 before lunch. In Bradman's home town of Bowral, a girl named Dorothy Pickle gasped and swallowed the fountain-pen with which she had been jotting down the scores when Bradman's century was announced on the wireless. She was rushed to Sydney Hospital, where her first words on regaining consciousness some hours later were: 'He's a great boy, isn't he!'

The 'great boy' had gone a long way towards winning the match, and the Ashes, for Australia. On the day of victory, Woodfull – on his birthday – mentioned only *one* of his players by name in an interview: 'We owe a tremendous lot to Bradman, who is surely one of the world's greatest batsmen.' The innings of 232, for which he batted longer than in any other innings on his four tours of England, not only gave Bradman the record – which still stands – of most double-centuries in a Test series: it also gave him at that time the record number of double-centuries by an individual in *all* Test cricket. In August 1930, only Hammond, among other cricketers, had scored even two double-centuries. Bradman thereafter simply surged forward with Test double-hundreds, and at no time from 1930 to the present day has he not been the world record-holder. His 974 runs in the series had come in only seven innings. So good a batsman as Gordon Greenidge, the West Indian opener, had scored precisely that number of runs in his Test career at the close of his highly successful series in England in 1976 – but Greenidge's 974 runs had taken 23 innings: a comparison a little unfair, perhaps – but Greenidge was, and is, a highly distinguished performer with the bat who began his Test career with 93 and 107 in the same match and made three centuries in successive Test innings against England.

By the close of the third day at the Oval, Bradman was 130* – surging towards the possibility of 1,000 runs in the series, and already a legend in the game, whatever the future had in store. The innings impressed Cardus immensely: 'It was as quiet as his innings at Leeds was energetic. . . . We have now seen Bradman the brilliant and Bradman the shrewd, playing four-day cricket and cricket that takes no heed of the clock. In these different circumstances he has shown command over the appropriate methods; his versatility is astonishing, and he is indeed a great batsman, though I still doubt whether he yet is equal to the challenge of a great spin bowler on a bad wicket.'

On the fourth day of the Oval Test – 20 August – Charles Bannerman, the first Test centurion of them all, died in Sydney, close to the cricket ground. He had been one of those who had watched young Bradman climb to the top. This was the very day Bradman had established the new record aggregate for a series, and scored what was then the highest Test innings at the Oval, exceeding the 211 of one of Bannerman's early colleagues, W. L. Murdoch (also, incidentally, a man with Cootamundra connections, for he used to live there). Cricket, then as now, could never be divorced from its past: but as the old champions were passing on, new ones were rising in the sky. Another old champion – an English champion – was then in his 48th year, and of him that August the *Daily Herald* remarked: 'At the moment that Jack Hobbs is preparing to end his great career Bradman is ready to wear the mantle. This mere boy is leaving behind records on which we thought any cricketers could safely rest.'

The time for superlatives was – mercifully for those whose task it was to concoct them – drawing rapidly to a close with the series over. At least there would be a breather until the next series. It had been easy for the writers to go overboard, but there had been nothing like Don Bradman on the sporting scene in all their experience. On the Sunday at Leeds, Trevor Wignall resignedly considered how Bradman's performances had affected him and his colleagues: 'Bradman, indeed, has become a menace to the gentlemen of the Press. Even with four dictionaries at our elbows he leaves us gasping. I am almost inclined to suggest, much as I like him, that he be deported to his own country, and kept there.' More significantly, Wignall had this to record:

And I am tempted to say also that to-day he is the greatest athlete or sporting figure in the wide world. If this is doubted please tell me who can be compared with him. Are men like Bobby Jones, the golfer, Tilden, the tennis player, Guest, the sculler, Schmeling, the fighter, or Gallacher, the footballer, actually in the same class? I am ready to say definitely that *they are not*! The nearest approach as a doer of great deeds to young Donald is Bobby Jones, but when he swings his driver or mashie he has nothing to beat except, perhaps, a puff of wind.

When Bradman is batting he has the bowling might of the earth opposed to him, and in addition he has a wicketkeeper and nine fielders ever on the alert. Jones never has a sticky or powdery wicket to contend with, but all sorts of funny things can happen to Bradman when he is making cricket look like a pastime for infants. It was pointed out to me this morning that a wicketkeeper is scarcely necessary when he is batting. The majority of stumpers estimate that in a long day's play they will be called on to stop four balls out of every six. That, I understand, is how George Duckworth views the matter. But he will agree that when Bradman was immediately in front of him he did not handle one ball in ten. Even when deliveries are wide of the wicket Bradman jumps out at them, and I honestly believe that if he made up his mind to stay in for the whole of a four-day match he could do it.

He has most of the cricket records in his bag now at the age of twenty-one, and what he will have accomplished by the time he is thirty is perhaps best left to the imagination. I have no hesitation in calling him the world's greatest athlete, and I am nearly tempted to throw everything overboard and write him down as the most remarkable the world has ever known.

If a *Daily Express* judgment may not have been to the liking of all, then few could have taken exception to the *Morning Post*. P. F. Warner, on the evening Don Bradman scored his 232 at the Oval, wrote for his next morning's edition: 'As for Bradman, he is a genius. What Bobby Jones is to golf and Lindrum to billiards, Bradman is to cricket. Grace, Hobbs and Spofforth were others. Bradman is such a wonder that if he was batting on the tramlines of Vauxhall Bridge Road he would make a hundred and probably three hundred. . . . He has already attained immortal fame, and must be a tremendous influence on the future of the game. One trembles to think what lies in store for bowlers in the next 15 or 20 years.'

Bradman's tour figures in first-class matches as he left the Oval at the end of the series – amid much mobbing and hero-worship – were:

Innings	N.O.	Runs	H.S.	Av.	100s
30	5	2,522	334	100·88	9

This is yet another record, for no touring batsman from any country, either before or since, has amassed such a total by this stage of a tour – that is, by the end of the final Test. At that same moment only three other members of the Australian party had reached even 1,000 runs – Woodfull (1,339), Ponsford (1,228) and Kippax (1,129). By the time the team dispersed in September, the averages were to reveal something quite extraordinary: if the second highest run-scorer – Kippax with 1,451 – *had been allowed to double his aggregate*, he still would not have reached Bradman's total! Not even of George Headley, who carried so much batting on his own shoulders, could this ever be said.

It may be instructive at this point to set out exactly off which bowlers Bradman amassed his record aggregate of 974 runs in the 1930 series. The runs were scored at slightly over 40 an hour off his own bat, which was a faster rate than he was scoring against the counties that summer. It was also a full dozen runs an hour better than his initial Test series of 1928–29. Despite his speed of scoring, Bradman did not hit a single six in the Tests of 1930.

His 974 runs came as follows:

Off Tate	–	238 runs from	461 balls
Off Larwood	–	137 runs from	147 balls
Off Hammond	–	115 runs from	268 balls
Off Tyldesley	–	102 runs from	189 balls
Off Peebles	–	72 runs from	120 balls
Off Robins	–	70 runs from	87 balls
Off White	–	66 runs from	86 balls
Off Geary	–	56 runs from	88 balls
Off Leyland	–	45 runs from	60 balls
Off Allen	–	34 runs from	34 balls
Off Woolley	–	22 runs from	23 balls
Off Wyatt	–	17 runs from	17 balls
		974 runs from	1,580 balls

Bradman therefore scored at better than a run every other ball – actually a run every 1·62 balls. This compares, in the 1930 series, with a run every 3·15 balls by Woodfull, every 2·49 balls by Ponsford, and every 2·55 balls by Kippax, these being the leading scorers. Actually McCabe (210 runs in the series) scored at a better rate than Bradman – a run every 1·47 balls: but Bradman's average was virtually four times that of McCabe.

Bradman's contribution towards winning the series was far more than his 974 runs and his average of 139·14, monumental though those figures were. It was Bradman, on the Saturday afternoon at Lord's, who turned the tables on an England side in the ascendant and did it so ruthlessly and conclusively that England never again recovered their old poise all summer. England's confidence – not just for the match, but for the series, and, it may be argued, for the decade – was almost clinically cut away in two and three-quarter hours. Australia lost the first Test and faced a total of 425 in the second. Bradman's batting then quite overwhelmed England, and whether it was quite realised at the time or not, he was setting history on a new path. The Bradman era of great Test match scores was inaugurated at Lord's, and from that same innings Australia rose mightily to the position of great strength that was to go hand in hand with the Bradman mastery. There is no doubt, from all the evidence that can be mustered, that the Australians were collectively in decidedly low spirits after the Trent Bridge defeat, and indeed right up to lunch-time on the Lord's Saturday. One of the touring party called themselves in June 'a three-man team'. Before that crucial Test at Lord's, Australia had won only *one* out of the last 11 encounters with England. 28 June 1930 saw the end of England's dominance: and it was Bradman who ended it. To adorn the occasion – as if to salute its historical import – he played an innings as near to perfection as could be. That Saturday at Lord's was Bradman's – and Australia's – most significant moment of 1930. By the time he passed 300 in a day at Leeds, he had already fashioned the new course of cricket history. But it was at Lord's that the fashioning was done.

By the end of the series P. G. H. Fender had little option but to concede that Bradman was 'an enormously improved player as compared with 1928–29, and has already made his place among the great ones of the game'. He generously recorded: 'Until we saw Bradman this summer, I do not think that any of us realized that it was possible to be so really brilliant without taking risks. I know of no English batsman to-day who is capable, for any long period, of forcing runs against Test bowling at such a pace, without taking risks which one knows will, sooner or later, get him out.' But, for Fender, Bradman *still* was not to be compared with Trumper or Macartney!

The strife of the Test series was now over, and what might have been looked forward to as a pleasant and carefree close to the tour, in the final days of August and early September, lay ahead. In fact, a match of tremendous tension followed at once when the touring side went to Bristol to play Gloucestershire in what turned out to be one of the most exciting games played in England between the wars and the only tie ever to be played by an Australian side on tour. On a bowler's wicket, runs were never easy throughout – Bradman hit only one four in nearly two hours in his first innings of 42. The Australians needed 118 to win in the fourth innings on the last day, and with an altered batting order, Bradman was still in at lunch, his side needing 51 to win with seven wickets in hand. Parker and Goddard had opened the bowling – 'You can do it on your own on this wicket', Beverley Lyon had told them – and were never taken off for the whole three hours of the innings. When Parker bowled Bradman for 14, to make the score 81 for six, the cheering was so loud and so lengthy as might have hailed an actual win. Bradman, with 6,000 others at the ground, then watched the last four wickets fall, in a fever of excitement, at 86, 108, 115 and 117, to produce the first tie in which he participated. (In the final season of his career, 1948–49, his own testimonial match at Melbourne was also a tie, though there was still one wicket to fall in the last innings.)

Before a crowd of over 13,000, Don Bradman spent his 22nd birthday in blazing sunshine at Canterbury – and confronted, for the first time in England, the not easily distinguishable leg-breaks and top-spinners of A. P. Freeman.[1] When that match against Kent began, 'Tich' Freeman had taken 252 wickets in the season, exactly 100 ahead of the next best in England (C. W. L. Parker's 152). He certainly troubled Bradman more than once, and got him lbw just before lunch for 18, the raising of 'Sailor' Young's finger heralding another burst of tremendous enthusiasm from the crowd. The scorebook shows Bradman, in the second innings v Kent, as 205 not out: but it does not show how desperately close he was to being lbw again to Freeman at the very start of that innings. As it was, another world record came to Bradman at

---

[1] Bradman's birthday was the occasion of day-long congratulatory messages arriving at the St Lawrence ground, the game being held up once while a Post Office messenger ran out with a telegram to Bradman.

the St Lawrence ground with his sixth double-century of the season. It is a record that still stands. By then also – actually during the desperate second innings against Gloucestershire – he had become the highest scorer for the Australians on a tour of England, exceeding Victor Trumper's 2,570 runs of 1902. That total had taken Trumper 53 innings: Bradman passed it in 32.

The night before the Australians travelled north for their final fixture of the tour, at Scarborough, the President of M.C.C. and former Lord Mayor of London, Sir Kynaston Studd, gave the side a farewell banquet at the Merchant Taylors' Hall in Threadneedle Street.[1] Many distinguished cricketers were present – Lord Harris and Ranji both spoke – and Bradman met for the first time Sir James Barrie. He was to meet him again in 1934, but on this 1930 evening in London, Bradman provided some good material for Barrie's speech. A few days before, at Folkestone, Bradman had passed 3,000 runs in all matches on the tour. In that bewitching accent of his, and puffing at a cigar throughout, Barrie jested at the young Don's expense: 'The next man in is . . . Sir Kynaston made me out a list of the various combatants, and he told me that when I mentioned this name it would be received with hearty but hollow cheers. The name, so far as I can make it out, is Mr Badman. I feel very sorry for Mr Badman. I do not doubt that he meant to do better. (Laughter.)[2] When the Australian team return home they will be met, as we can well imagine, by countless thousands of Australians all straining at the leash to hear from Mr Woodfull which side won, and when they hear there will be tremendous rejoicings. The team will be taken to hotels and public places and feasted – all with the exception of Mr Badman. He has carried this plan of his of not knowing how to get out to such an extent that he now cannot get out of anything. He won't be even able to get out of the ship when all the others are merry and bright. We now leave him pacing the deck, a dark and gloomy figure.'

At the Scarborough Festival (the first since the death of C. I. Thornton) Bradman's wonderful tour of 1930 came to an end. It might have finished on the inglorious note of a first-ball duck had Wilfred Rhodes's mid-off, R. E. S. Wyatt, been a little quicker. Bradman tried to drive Rhodes and uncharacteristically lifted the ball. He went on to 96, which included two further chances off Rhodes. The oldest bowler Don Bradman faced on his

---

[1] Earlier in the day the Australians had concluded their match against the Club Cricket Conference at Lord's – a most interesting fixture, taking place for the first time. That remains the only occasion that the Australians have played the C.C.C. at Lord's. The fixture was well attended, and Bradman (dropped at square-leg when 4) made top score, playing for the first time under the experimental larger wicket used extensively in club cricket in London that summer (as well as in county matches), which was favoured by the Australian Board of Control, and which became law the following year. Bradman made 70 in 80 minutes, being splendidly caught at first slip by the Conference captain, Frank Whitehead (Hornsey) off S. Nazeer Ali (Indian Gymkhana). Bradman stated at the time that he thought the Conference bowling distinctly better than that of some of the counties.
[2] By an astonishing coincidence, and almost certainly unknown to Sir James Barrie, there was actually a cricketer by the name of Badman playing regularly at that time – E. A. Badman, an opening batsman for the Sports Club in Colombo, Ceylon.

four tours of England was also one of the best. In 1963, on the balcony at Headingley during the Test match, Wilfred Rhodes said the hardest batsman he ever bowled against was Don Bradman in 1930. 'You couldn't keep him quiet.' But what a finish to a career it would have been for Rhodes had luck just tilted his way! For his own part Bradman saw enough of Rhodes in 1930 – Rhodes at the age of 52 – to know what a great bowler he must have been. When the biography of Rhodes was written nearly 30 years later, Sir Donald was invited, in December 1959, to contribute the Introduction. He did so with warmth, humility and pride, observing that 'one of the tragedies of sport is that a young player such as I was in 1930 is unable at an early stage of his career to absorb the knowledge, background and history of contemporaries who have adorned the stage for a very long period but are just about to leave it.' There were young players opposed to Sir Donald himself in his final months on the first-class field. But they, one must trust, had as little cause to ask 'Who is Don Bradman?' as the youthful Australians of 1930 had cause to ask 'Who is Wilfred Rhodes?'

By September 1930 Donald Bradman was a national hero of Australia. The country lacked a popular sporting hero, and he filled the gap to perfection. He was still not the complete cricketer for all his achievements, but he had overcome the testing ordeal of a tour of England with colours flying so high as to be almost unbelievable. Australians – or Englishmen for that matter – have never chosen to categorize their batsmen as truly great until they have proved themselves on the varied wickets that comprise an English season: and Bradman had proved himself at the first time of asking, in a way to lift him above all his contemporaries, Australian and otherwise. Before the summer of 1930, the highest average by a cricketer on his first tour of England had been 57·65 by Woodfull in 1926. Bradman averaged 98·66. Such an average at that time had never been known in England. His aggregate of 2,960 runs in first-class matches (and 3,170 including minor matches) was not only the highest in England that year but was – and is – the highest by any overseas batsman on any tour of England. Almost every county fielded their strongest side against the Australians – a practice in those days all but obligatory – and the combined cricketing knowledge that was pitted against Bradman at the crease was colossal. Bradman himself observed how thoroughly the professional cricketer in England knew the game and how much more than in Australia a bowler bowled to his field and combated a batsman. In mid-tour – after his magnificent Test at Lord's – the *Morning Post* was moved to say that 'Bradman is a sort of reincarnation in miniature of Grace in his youthful prime'. A later writer aptly remarked that in 1930 Bradman made 'Wisden's Almanack look as out of date as a fashion book of the naughty nineties'.

In the year from September 1929 to September 1930, in *all* matches, first-class and minor, he unbelievably made no fewer than 6,789 runs. Lest anyone should chance to suppose this figure a misprint, it is arrived at in this way:

	Innings	N.O.	Runs	H.S.	Av.	100s
1929–30 in Australia	43	10	3,619	452*	109·66	13
1930 in England	38	6	3,170	334	99·06	11
	81	16	6,789	452*	104·44	24

But even this prodigious aggregate for a year's cricket was to be surpassed by Bradman before the 1930s were much further advanced. His appetite, like his skill, was truly unlimited.

The experience of England could not but have an effect on Bradman. At an age when most other young men were just beginning to feel their way in the world, he was already virtual master of all he surveyed. 'It would be hard indeed to find a chink in his armour', said Pelham Warner at the end of the tour. Bradman in 1930 confirmed to himself – and to the world – that he loved making runs and that he loved conquering bowlers. That, in its turn, delighted the crowds who, accordingly, delighted in him. A champion is always popular, and Bradman was lionised in England in 1930. When the Australians visited Manfield Hospital, Northampton, the nurses gave three cheers for Bradman, and insisted on being photographed with him alone, to the exclusion of all others. Amy Johnson, fresh from her triumphal solo flight to Australia – she actually landed at Darwin on the day Bradman scored his 252* against Surrey – visited the Hove ground specially to meet Don Bradman, and this pair, who had so firmly captured the public imagination via the appeal of youth, were duly photographed together in front of the tea tent. Without the iron hand of William Lucius Kelly, the Australian dressing-room would have been invaded more than once by fervent admirers. The lionising potential of Bradman was to manifest itself in due course in all sorts of things – Bradman shirts, bats, pads, boots, gloves, ties, shoes, hats, special drinks, dances, and even lolly sticks for children. In October 1930 it was announced that a super cinema was being built in Sydney to be called 'Don Bradman Theatre'. Clergymen even preached about Bradman, taking him as their text. And parents in Australia named their babies after him.[1]

Bradman's phenomenal success in 1930 was all the more real by the virtual certainty that it was no flash in the pan. This cricketer did not throw his wicket away after reaching his century, and it seemed unlikely that he would be doing so in the future. Those with perception could see that here was not only a cricketing phenomenon but an administrative phenomenon too, for how many people would now be flocking to grounds to watch this batsman at work? And for how many years would this boy, still only 22, hold sway? Bradman not only altered cricket but he altered cricket watching and cricket thinking, and it all came about through the unprecedented triumph of 1930. To quote P. F. Warner again at the close of that tour: 'No

---

[1] Probably only philatelic practice of the time prevented him becoming the first cricketer to feature on a postage stamp: Australia did celebrate contemporary highlights of that period with stamps on Kingsford Smith's world flights (1931) and the opening of Sydney Harbour Bridge (1932).

cricketer has ever done so much at his age, and to what heights he will eventually attain is an interesting speculation; he seems to have brought run-getting to a certainty.'

It was this very 'certainty' that made Bradman different from his fellows. He did not seem subject to the natural laws of batsmanship, or if he was, he flouted them with a disdainful bat. He did not have bad patches and he did not have bad luck. What he did have was immense skill and immense public appeal. Out of all this came the 'differentness' with which the Don was labelled from 1930 onwards. The label was correct, for the Don *was* different. He never tended to make close personal friendships with any of his cricketing colleagues, whether in Shield matches or on tour. Perhaps only C. W. Walker, the South Australian wicketkeeper who was to die in action in the war, and T. W. Wall, were exceptions to this. The 1930 side in general saw Bradman as above the team, not of the team. It is true he was not one to share his success with others – the first night of the Test at Leeds was evidence enough – and he disliked collective celebration anyway. That may not have been the typical Australian's way, but it was Bradman's choice. It strained his relationships with his fellow-tourists, and some jealousy of his endless success may not have helped. Few cricketers would care to admit to jealousy of another player, but by 1930 Don Bradman had proved he was not merely 'another player' but was a cricketing Caruso or Forbes-Robertson, always likely to give a top-class performance. The sheer relentlessness of the Bradman march had never been known in Grace or Fry or Ranji or Hobbs or Trumper or Stoddart or Macartney or Hill. Only perhaps Ponsford had shown similar traces, and he was put firmly in his place with the arrival of the Don. Admiring a man's excellence is not the same thing as approving it. It was impossible not to recognise the prowess in Bradman's batsmanship, but when it positively put into the shade the hitherto normally accepted prowess of others, those others could have been only human if their response included elements of resentfulness and jealousy. The increased practice of record-keeping, fanned into a journalistic and public pastime directly through Don Bradman's record-breaking, served further to push Bradman higher up the scale and to push other batsmen lower down it.

Bradman in England in 1930 had matured very perceptibly. He was perfectly at ease in talking to pressmen (despite the dangers of violating his contract) and confirmed himself, although one of the youngest members of the party, as a most confident public speaker. When the team were playing Lancashire at Aigburth in May, Bradman took himself off in the evenings, with Fairfax, to see some boxing at the Liverpool Stadium. Replying to a welcome, Bradman entered the ring to address the crowd: 'We cricketers sometimes get fed up with our own game. We like to see something more exciting for a change. I cannot complain of any lack of thrills in the past two days.' He was given a great reception – but Fairfax could not be coaxed to speak! Bradman also made cinema and theatre appearances, which were really business ventures, though his keen brain and good sense always prompted him to say the right things. On the night Australia regained the Ashes in August, Bradman appeared on the stage of the now defunct Stoll Picture Theatre in Kingsway and made a speech to such a tumultuous reception that no wonder a fresh rumour began that he was to embark on a stage career! He spoke of the pride of the Australians in recovering the Ashes and paid a fine tribute to Hobbs (who had made it known he had just played in his last Test). 'It will be a long time before the world finds another cricketer such as Hobbs', said Bradman from the stage. 'He was the master cricketer of all time, and from all viewpoints.' These appearances – and Bradman appeared also in 'talkies', delivered broadcast messages and posed for photographs – were exercises in diplomacy as well as turning Bradman into a capable business man. He also negotiated the sale of the book and serial rights of his life story, and while the rest of the side were in seclusion at Downside School before the first Test, he paid a business visit to the Horbury (Yorkshire) headquarters of William Sykes Ltd, manufacturers of the 'Don Bradman' autograph bat. His business opportunism extended to his having on exhibition in a shop window in Leeds the bat with which he made his 452* – this as a prelude to the Headingley Test, while all Leeds (and all England) were wondering what he was going to do. Then he promptly went one better. Having duly made 334 at Leeds, he then placed *that* bat on view in Finnigan's sports window in Deansgate, Manchester, for the enthusiasts gathered in the city for the fourth Test (though he might have been wiser to have taken it to the ground with him instead!).[1] He also made a gramophone record (of two popular tunes on the piano and a brief address on cricket) at the Columbia Gramophone Company studios in London, played a little golf and a little billiards, watched Walter Lindrum at play at Thurston's – and wrote ceaselessly throughout the tour, both private letters and material for publication. He found time even to be coached on the billiards table by Lindrum in London.

Just before the war R. C. Robertson-Glasgow recalled his first meeting with Don Bradman in one of his regular pieces for *Men Only* (when that publication was edited by Reginald Arkell). The recollection is well worth quoting:

> I first met Bradman, during the 1930 Folkestone Cricket Festival, in the writing-room of an hotel. I had rushed into it to dash off some postcard, and, as I addressed it, my eye caught a huge pile of letters; next to them – almost *under* them – sat Bradman. He had made his name in cricket. He was fresh from triumphs against England at Lord's and the Oval. And now, quiet and calculating, he was, he told me, trying to capitalise his success. I wished him luck, and suggested he might need a secretary. He has since told me that his business efforts on that evening in Folkestone were not in vain!

[1] As to Bradman's cricket bats in 1930, incidentally, he arrived back in Australia without a single one. He had arrived in England in April with quite a selection of the finest bats and during the tour many others were given to him. All were eventually 'begged' by various organisations for use as prizes in charity raffles. A few of the bats remained in England, but most were distributed on the long sea journey to Australia.

How Bradman found time for all these extraneous affairs in the midst of a full programme of cricket is testimony to the disciplined way he organised himself. His success on the field naturally bred confidence and, in the eyes of his colleagues, enabled him to act in a manner the other cricketers dare not adopt. Woodfull, Grimmett, Kippax and Oldfield had all rejected tempting offers to write for English newspapers – their contracts forbade it – but Bradman took the risk of writing, even if it was at first restricted to his career in Australia. From his writings and other sources, estimates varying between £2,000 and £5,000 were put out as the likely sum by which Bradman would profit.

Bradman's relations with his manager were said to be less than cordial as the tour drew to its close. At Canterbury Bradman laughed off rumours that he was to be 'carpeted' on his return to Australia – and promptly scored a double-century next day. (There was a certain youthful 'cockiness' about Bradman at this time, which some of the England players had noticed in Australia in '28–29.) But Mr Kelly said he could not very well pass over Bradman's apparent defiance of the Board of Control. The other players felt it inevitable. In view of its impending significance, it might be as well here to set out the relevant clause relating to writing contained in the lengthy and detailed contract signed by each member of the touring party before the 1930 tour of England:

> Neither the manager, treasurer, nor any player shall accept employment as a news-paper correspondent, or do any work for, or in connection with, any newspaper or any broadcasting, and no member of the team, other than the manager, shall directly or indirectly, in any capacity whatsoever, communicate with the Press nor give any information concerning matters connected with the tour to the Press or any member, servant, or agent thereof.

Bradman had certainly passed over material to a literary agency with a view to it being serialized, and this material consisted of a straightforward account of his early life and cricket career in Australia and detailed impressions of his experiences in England and of the matches in which he played. Prima facie this seemed an obvious breach of his contract, but Bradman considered he was in order by stipulating that none of his writings on the tour itself should appear before the team were back in Australia. All this material was also to form the contents of his first book – *Don Bradman's Book* – that Hutchinson were to bring out in November. He had been assiduously compiling the chapters all through the tour.

It should be said that because of the 'hot property' that Bradman became while he was in England, it was he who was approached by the literary agency. They put the offer before him and, rightly or wrongly, he agreed. He was paid a lump sum for all his rights, book rights and serial rights, English rights and Australian rights. The serial rights for England were then sold to the London *Star*. *The Star* scooped not only its evening paper rivals but scooped the world in being the first to serialize the life of Don

Bradman.[1] (Some Australian papers later carried the story.) Bradman did not choose *The Star*, for he had relinquished any say in the matter when he sold his rights, and it was the agency who negotiated with *The Star*, from whom presumably it could obtain the best terms. Bradman obtained no payment at all from *The Star*. He also engaged in no promiscuous writing on the tour, for which no doubt he might have gathered extremely fat fees – but which unarguably would have landed him in hot administrative water.[2]

Has anyone at so young an age, incidentally, written his life story? In the post-war future, Nureyev was to publish his autobiography at the age of 23, and among cricketers another great crowd-puller, Dennis Lillee, brought out his book at 25, as likewise had Doug Walters before him. But in 1930 it was neither the fashion for young sportsmen to bring out their stories nor was it the fashion for *anyone* to sign a publishing contract at 21. So far as life stories go, is this yet another Bradman record?

For a young man of 21, even one with Bradman's resolve and talent, it was not possible simply to sit down during a Test tour of England and write a full-length book, polished and presentable, for public consumption. Bradman was assisted with his 1930 book by a professional journalist, Ben Bennison, a well-known Fleet Street figure on both sides of the First World War. He was a Lancastrian who lived in Dulwich, and in his time was Sports Editor of the *Daily Telegraph*, sporting editor of the *Standard*, and assistant editor of the *Sporting Life*. He had certainly written on cricket – which he once described as 'my passion, if not my religion' – but more prominently on association football and boxing. Bennison's function officially was to 'edit' Don Bradman's book, which effectively meant to write it, or re-write it, to satisfy the reading public. Bennison, like Bradman himself, did not believe in frills or fancies or deep philosophies, and *Don Bradman's Book* was highly successful as a result. In looking back on the venture in his own book of reminiscences, *Giants on Parade*, in 1936, Bennison said:

> In my collaboration with Bradman I necessarily saw much of him. I found him more than a profound student of cricket – he was the conqueror of cricket. He set out and meant to be king. He succeeded.
>
> A more serious young man or one richer in power of concentration I have not met. He did not play cricket for the mere joy of playing cricket. Cricket was his profession, and his unswerving purpose was to reach the top. He loved the roar of the crowd and rejoiced in his triumphs, but quietly, as will a business man chortle over a big deal. A curious mixture, Bradman, for though his personal wants were few,

---

[1] The exclusive daily instalments in *The Star* began on 4 August 1930 and continued to 20 August. The story stopped at the point of Bradman's selection for the 1930 tour. The story of the 1930 tour itself, in accordance with the condition laid down by Bradman, did not appear until the Australians were home. *The Star* carried these instalments (and also Bradman's articles on technique) between 3 November and 17 November 1930.

[2] Newspapers, even in those days, could pay the most handsome fees for something they wanted. The *Daily Mail* in 1931 concluded a £7,800 contract for Winston Churchill to write them a weekly column over a period of a year, and in 1928 Churchill had contracted with *Nash's Pall Mall* to write 12 magazine articles on 'Personages I have Known' at a remuneration that exceeded his annual salary as Chancellor of the Exchequer.

he sought everything worth having with a frankness and honesty that compelled admiration.

He was a boy of Bowral, who, having set out upon a great adventure, was determined to make every capital out of it so that he might return to his modest home with a future assured. To the last ounce he knew his value, not only as a cricketer but as a man . . .

Bradman confessed that he was neither stung nor hurt by his critics, but, as well he might, he took a positive delight in leaving them worse than confounded, and I ever suspected that the while he piled on the agony against our bowlers, he roared inwardly. His phenomenal batting, and the remarkable bowling of Clarence Grimmett, during the 1930 Australian tour, are an imperishable memory.

From the evidence of Ben Bennison's reminiscences, he certainly collaborated with Don Bradman over his 1930 book. Bradman, on the other hand, by no means left the entire exercise to him. Certainly so far as the initial articles in *The Star* were concerned – which formed the basis of the subsequent book – Bradman drafted these in his own hand, and normally that initial effort was so good that it was used as the actual copy forwarded to *The Star* for serialization. Fortunately, Bradman's manuscript was always exceptionally legible. At that stage, indeed, Bradman had deliberately declined any professional help, despite the urgings of friends. Bradman further refused to allow any of his articles as submitted to *The Star* to be altered. A staff man on *The Star* itself recorded in 1930: 'Phrases which had been written in he struck out. He did not deny their truth, but to each one of them he said "This is not me. Anybody who knows me knows I couldn't talk like that, and I certainly couldn't write like that." '

Bradman's own diary, of course, was his most powerful ally in his writings. Very few people were allowed even to glance at its pages, but one close friend who *was* given the privilege said at the end of the 1930 tour:

Every night, no matter how tired he felt, Bradman kept his diary up to date. It is a wonderful book. He has entered in it his impressions of English cricket and players, the towns he visited, and the various personalities he met.

I was amazed at the neatness of the penmanship and the diversity of idea. Very few things seem to escape Bradman's notice. He is a very keen observer, and expresses himself so clearly and quickly that I feel sure, if the diary could be published just as it is, it would be a world's 'best seller'.

He makes entries about his hobbies, too. These include piano-playing – perhaps you did not know that he is a fine pianist – golf and tennis. Bradman told me that at one time he seriously considered taking up tennis and dropping cricket. That, of course, was before he became world-famous.

But you can take it from me – Bradman's diary is a most interesting book, for it is instructive as well as being a reflection of places, games and people as they appear to him.

The excellence of Bradman's memory should also here be noted, for that too aided him considerably in his writings. Certainly by 1930 he had become renowned as the possessor of such an amazingly good memory that he was compared to music-hall artists who challenge their audiences to pose them questions. In fact his own touring colleagues did hurl constant posers at him, and their regular comment of 'Ask Bradman' was their method of gathering authoritative facts. He could remember almost anything of interest that he heard. He could also remember such things as his overnight score in matches, bowling changes, and how his colleagues fared. He carried in his head telephone numbers and addresses of friends and all those small facts that most people put on paper. He was not only a remarkable cricketer!

Before leaving the subject of income from the tour, Bradman was due to receive under the terms of his contract – in common with all the other players – a total fee of £600 for the visit – £50 before leaving Australia, £400 during the tour (but not more than £80 per calendar month), and £150 on return to Australia. This final balance could be forfeited to the Australian Board wholly or in part if the report on each player was not satisfactory.

For all the care and legal expertise that went into the drafting of the 1930 tour contract with the players – and the hand of the Board chairman, solicitor Aubrey Oxlade, was very much apparent – it could not be certain whether Bradman's arrangements amounted to an actual breach or only a moral breach. The writing in any event, it is fair to say, was wholly unexceptionable and could in no sense have brought either the game or the Australian team into disrepute. The philosophy behind the Board's contract – and the justification for the many and stringent conditions it imposed – had been to protect the good name of Australian cricket. It is highly unlikely, as much in 1930 as today, that any agency or publisher would have settled for the cricketer's story *without* his comments on the tour which his compelling presence turned into such a huge success.

The matter was to be resolved before the year was out by the Board of Control in Australia.

5 The Legend Expands

Like a second W. G. Grace he has changed the conception of first-class batting, opening avenues hitherto untrodden, suggesting possibilities till now unsuspected.
R. C. Robertson-Glasgow on D. G. Bradman, 1930

Don Bradman left England and the scenes of his great triumphs on 27 September 1930, telling an interviewer at St Pancras Station before he went: 'It isn't goodbye, it is only au revoir. I hope to be back in 1934, if my cricket is still good enough.' Note how carefully he phrased his sentences – to contain a sensible and cautious rider. All his sentences had been similarly carefully phrased throughout 1930, whether he was talking to a public audience or penning the pages of his book. He joined the *Oronsay* to sail to Australia, and among the passengers were Mr and Mrs C. G. Macartney. Several of the team joined the ship later at Toulon.

The arrival back in Australia heralded such scenes of enthusiasm for Bradman as to be very nearly a repeat performance by Australians of the welcomes they gave to Amy Johnson for her solo flight from England to Australia a few months before. Bowral made it known that they were to hold a welcome home carnival for their famous son, and a good deal of money they expended on the preparations. The *Oronsay* docked at Fremantle on 28 October and the players were driven to Perth for a civic reception by the Lord Mayor at the Prince of Wales Theatre, where Bradman was besieged and kissed by a bevy of women. After lunch by the Western Australian Cricket Association at the Palace Hotel, Bradman spent half an hour signing autographs for a fresh group of women and girls. Wherever he appeared he was mobbed. It was the start of a very hectic week.

Meanwhile Bradman had sought and obtained permission from the Australian Board to make his own way across Australia and home, independently of the rest of the team, and at the Board meeting in Sydney on 18 September his employers, Mick Simmons, had been granted permission for him to travel by air from Adelaide to Sydney. Bradman accordingly parted company with the rest of his colleagues at Perth, while the *Oronsay* sailed on to Adelaide without him. This procedure happened to result in Bradman arriving in Adelaide, Melbourne and Sydney in advance of the other members of the team, which was interpreted – especially with the enormous spotlight thrown on his every movement – as a calculated effort to steal all the thunder. Bradman neither sought nor could he control the public applause that came his way. Indeed, on his way home, at Goulburn, he was too frightened to accept even an invitation for a cup of tea lest there be some sort of reception – and he only went for his cup of tea on the promise there would not be one. A Queensland cricket official said that Bradman's individual journey was 'an insult to the other members of the team', and the manager, Mr Kelly, made a private protest at Bradman being allowed to make his trip while Kelly knew nothing of it. In fact the permission had come from the Board chairman himself, Mr Oxlade. 'The Board of Control has taken Bradman out of my hands', complained Kelly. Whether or not the manager had yet drafted his report on the 1930 tour, it now seemed certain that Bradman would not escape scot free in it for any alleged misdemeanours, however minor.

Some of the other players, perhaps bolstered by the confidence of their home surroundings, were beginning to talk about Bradman. Some were particularly hurt that he accepted an offer to write newspaper articles. 'He is the best batsman in the world', said one of the team in Adelaide, 'but that is where he finishes. He did not spend twopence during the tour.' At the S.A.C.A. luncheon to the team at the Adelaide Oval – in Bradman's absence – Mr Kelly, responding to the toast of the Australian XI, said that the one indispensable man in the side was Grimmett: 'He was the outstanding success of the team.' There is no evidence that Kelly even mentioned Bradman's name. This was in Grimmett's home city, it is true, which may also have accounted for Vic Richardson's remarks on the radio from Adelaide a few days later: 'We could have played any team without Don Bradman, but we could not play the blind school without Clarrie Grimmett.'

All this was very trying, but it was something the young Don Bradman was beginning to learn to live with. Unbridled adulation and virulent criticism were to be his companions for a decade. The Board in Sydney seemed to be on his side – at least until they sat in judgment on him after receiving W. L. Kelly's report. But with or without the report, there is no denying how the public felt about Bradman.

The adulation side of events, considering that Bradman was but one member of a successful touring party, probably went beyond reasonable bounds. His return in triumph to his homeland was likened to a successful Roman general returning from the wars. The *Daily Express* in London, upholding the virtues of team spirit, deplored the passionate welcomes that Bradman was receiving in Australia: 'More is the pity then to see Bradman treated and behaving as though he alone won the Ashes.' But Bradman himself, whenever he addressed a crowd, was most careful to emphasise the parts played by others. A packed audience that gave him a tumultuous reception at the Theatre Royal in Perth heard him say that the success of the team had not been due to individual triumphs but to the team spirit prevailing throughout the tour: 'If credit is due to any player more than another, it should go to our captain, Billy Woodfull.' Later that season, during the fifth Test at Sydney, when the New South Wales Cricket Association presented Bradman with a smoker's stand in recognition of his 334 at Leeds, Bradman emphasised in reply that individual batting records could not be made but for the assistance of the batsmen at the other end.

The interstate platform at Adelaide railway station was thronged with people to see Bradman arrive there from Perth. When he emerged, police had to protect him from the crowd. (He had previously been given a civic reception when the train passed through Port Augusta.) During all this excitement, the *Oronsay*, with Woodfull and company aboard, was still ploughing its way across the Great Australian Bight. When the ship reached Adelaide, Bradman was already fulfilling his own programme. He broadcast a racy account of the England tour on Adelaide radio and appeared before a Saturday night audience on the stage of the Regent Theatre. Next morning he left by plane for Melbourne.

A vast crowd of some 10,000 massed at Essendon Aerodrome to greet him. It was only the circumstance of the plane arriving two hours later than expected that caused some of the crowd to go home. Even so, many hundreds rushed the plane almost before it stopped. Curiosity and hero-worship accounted for most of the crowd. Cricketers were conspicuous by their absence, though Warwick Armstrong was there to welcome Bradman – who had all but been lost in the mêlée when he landed, only a strong posse of police enabling him to reach a lorry draped with the Australian flag that was to serve as a platform. The next day Melbourne admirers presented him with a cheque for £100 at the Tivoli Theatre.

Bradman had flown with the well-known – and ill-fated – Pilot Shortridge on the monoplane Southern Cloud. (Don Bradman was an intrepid young man to opt to fly, even though the choice had been made by his employers in Sydney and even though Pilot T. W. Shortridge was recognised as one of the finest pilots in Australia, with over 4,000 flying hours and more than 460,000 miles to his credit. However, some $4\frac{1}{2}$ months later Shortridge, his assistant pilot and six passengers in the Southern Cloud disappeared on a regular mail flight from Sydney to Melbourne in severe weather conditions, and the most desperate searchings failed to resolve one of the most baffling mysteries in the history of Australian aviation.) Bradman and Shortridge took off again, this time on a bumpy trip, from Melbourne to Goulburn: and at last Don Bradman was back in his native State. It was the cricket season again, just as it had been eight months before, when he had left it. At Goulburn, Bradman was greeted by his father and brother, who had travelled by car from Bowral, and it was to Bowral of course that they all drove off together. Bowral's welcome could not match in size those of Perth, Adelaide and Melbourne – in fact only ten policemen were required to control the crowd – but Bradman was naturally accorded a civic reception when he arrived there on the afternoon of 4 November. The band played 'Our Don Bradman' as the hero of the hour, together with his mother, father, sister and brother, walked to the dais in the Corbett Gardens where the civic dignitaries were already gathered. Speeches of welcome were made by the Mayor (Alderman Sheaffe), by Alderman South (acting president of the Moss Vale and Southern Districts Cricket Association) and by Alderman Westbrook, Bradman's former employer. In Bradman's modest reply, he said he appreciated none of the welcomes more than Bowral's that day because he was aware of its sincerity.

Sydney still awaited him, and he arrived there on Guy Fawkes Day to face a crowd of some 2,000 outside the premises of Mick Simmons in George Street when he drew up. There were a few more police in attendance here than at Bowral. At Sydney Town Hall that night he received a momentous ovation. He was presented with a special model roadster, a two-seater Chevrolet car, of which only six had been made in Australia. This was a gift from General Motors (Australia) Ltd. On the Town Hall stage, alongside Bradman, Mr Mark Gosling, Chief Secretary of the newly elected New South Wales ministry, made a speech. 'Bradman is the Phar Lap of cricket', he said. 'Mr Lang and Mr Lyons are looking for new taxation schemes, and I would suggest that they might impose a tax on centuries, and make Don pay a super-tax on every second century.'[1] Bradman in reply said he had made up his mind to score a century in the Shield match starting that week – a threat he duly carried out! – but if he was bowled first ball for a 'blob', they would have to blame Mr Gosling!

This was a reminder that the serious business of first-class cricket was on the agenda, and also perhaps a reminder that there were other players in the State as well as Bradman. (By comparison with Bradman, Archie Jackson's arrival in Sydney – on the night Bradman was in Bowral – was notably unostentatious. Even his mother was taken by surprise and arrived home to find her son explaining to his father how he got out in one of the big matches in England.)

Bradman played in the Sheffield Shield match in Sydney on 7 November with no practice whatsoever since his departure from England, but was in no difficulty against the South Australian bowling. He scored 61 and 121. For his first innings on Australian soil since his now historic tour, a crowd of over 8,000 gave him a great reception and the South Australian fielders clapped him all the way to the wicket. His 121 took only 142 minutes, watched by more than 12,000. Only splendid catches in each innings got rid of him. This was the first time he had played in a first-class match with the larger stumps and, as he had found against the Club Cricket Conference at Lord's a few weeks before, it made little difference to his batting.

St George, basking in the pride of Don Bradman's achievements, hired the Victory Theatre, Kogarah, for a welcome home concert to him and Alan Fairfax on the night of 10 November. Every seat in the theatre was

---

[1] The comparison with Phar Lap, a racehorse then on everyone's lips, was a high compliment. Phar Lap was one of the most notable thoroughbreds ever to race on Australian turf, and as far on as December 1976 was still described by an Australian journalist as 'the charismatic champion, forever to remain unsurpassed in the realm of turf greatness'. He had, on the day previous to Don Bradman's arrival in Sydney, won the Melbourne Cup, part of a sequence in 1930–31 of 31 wins in 33 races (he came second in the other two). His mounted figure is now a popular tourist attraction at the National Museum, Melbourne. John T. Lang was the newly elected Premier of New South Wales; and J. A. Lyons, then the Acting Federal Treasurer, was a future Prime Minister.

taken and many distinguished cricketing and civic personalities were present. It was an outstanding success, and Bradman and Fairfax were each presented with a club blazer amid great cheering. St George, of course, had never had a personality like Don Bradman, and the club history records: 'Crowds at our games grew in numbers to reach record proportions for attendances at grade matches, so great an attraction was the magic of Don Bradman.'

The Jack Ryder Testimonial match at Melbourne in November 1930 brought a fresh novelty – for the first and only time in his life Bradman had to face the bowling of Arthur Mailey in a first-class match. And the 44-year-old veteran, still rarely bowling a loose ball, still tempting batsmen with his magic flight, duly seized the opportunity to dismiss Don Bradman (exactly half his age) in each innings of the match. He completed the operation with a brilliant 'c & b'.[1] Bradman made no excuses: Mailey's subtleties were still to be reckoned with. This was a moment to savour for the sentimentalists – the wonder boy Bradman falling to the man who had once dismissed Victor Trumper at Redfern Oval. No bowler had the distinction of dismissing both these batsmen in a first-class match, though several bowled against both and among them Wilfred Rhodes came very close to doing it. Mailey shared with Hanson Carter the pleasure of playing on tour abroad with both these master batsmen, the two veterans completing the 'double' together in North America in 1932. (Mailey had also been present at many of Bradman's triumphs in England in 1930, and watched his discomfiture against Peebles' leg-breaks at Manchester. 'I suspected', said Mailey years after, looking back on his Melbourne confrontation with Bradman, 'that he had a flaw somewhere in his armour when facing top-spinning leg-breaks.')

This fixture for Ryder, in which Bradman scored 73 and 29, very nearly provided the one and only occasion that Bradman and Macartney participated in a first-class match together. The selection of the Rest of Australia side had been made by the Victorian selection committee in October and they had chosen Macartney and publicly announced his name. This was while Macartney was still a passenger on the *Oronsay* travelling back from England. However, within a few days of arriving in Australia, Macartney announced his inability to play on business grounds – and Melbourne and many others were saddened. A match starring both Bradman and Macartney would have been a tremendous public draw, for it was the opinion of many Australians, and New South Wales adherents in particular, that Macartney's retirement from first-class cricket had been premature. He was still a force in Sydney cricket. Even in March 1932, at the age of 45, in a first-grade match at Chatswood Oval, he reached 50 in 16 minutes and scored an astonishing (and chanceless) 94 in 32 minutes for Gordon v Paddington. But four-day

---

[1] This was Mailey's final first-class match of his career, and Bradman's wicket was the last he ever captured. Nine days later Mailey gave a lecture in Sydney on 'Spin Bowling', and as the only spin bowler in Australia who had thus far captured Bradman's wicket twice in a match, his already considerable credentials were no doubt, in the eyes of his audience, higher than ever.

cricket would doubtless not have suited his legs. He was, however – in his 50th year – to play his final first-class cricket as vice-captain of the Australian side in India in 1935–36, when he scored nearly 500 runs in all matches (including two four-day ones!), with a masterful century at Jamnagar and several lesser displays that are still remembered by his surviving opponents. He and Bradman in the early 1930s did occasionally play on the same side together in minor cricket – they both scored half-centuries, for example, for Macartney's team v a colts side at the Sydney Cricket Ground in February 1932, and occasionally Macartney captained New South Wales Cricket Association XIs with Bradman in the side. In war-time matches in Sydney, Macartney once again was to show astonishing form. In a one-day match at Trumper Park, Paddington, on 4 January 1940, he made top score of the day with a dazzling 81 for the original A.I.F. side v Second A.I.F. On 14 September 1940 he scored a most brilliant 50 for his own team v Gordon at Chatswood Oval, for patriotic funds, recalling all the splendour of his great days. He was then aged 54.

During Bradman's second innings of 29 in the Ryder Testimonial – an innings played on 18 November – he became the first man in the history of the game to reach an aggregate of 4,000 runs in a calendar year, a year that had started with the memorable match at Sydney in which he had annexed the record individual innings in first-class cricket. Although this particular distinction of reaching 4,000 runs in a calendar year was later also to be achieved by H. Sutcliffe (in 1932), W. R. Hammond (1933), D. C. S. Compton and W. J. Edrich (1947) and L. Hutton (1948), Bradman remains the youngest player to do so, at the age of 22. His final aggregate for the calendar year 1930 (4,368 runs, av. 97·06) remains a record for an Australian.

Before the Test series of 1930–31 got under way – it was the maiden series between Australia and the West Indies – the administrative rumbles still had some more of their course to run. The Australian Press Association and Reuters correspondent with the Australian side in England, Geoffrey Tebbutt, brought out a book on the tour and the first copies were available in early December. In his agency role in England, Tebbutt had been scrupulously objective, as befitted an A.P.A. and Reuter man. Released of his shackles for his first (and only) cricket book, he took some bold journalistic lunges not least against Bradman, whose immense popularity with the English public was not echoed, said Tebbutt, by his team-mates. The £1,000 gift at Headingley did not help. 'Still', wrote Tebbutt, 'they did not begrudge Bradman this handsome recognition. Their grievance was that Bradman had been rather less than human in the way he took success. Having made a score as gigantic as that at Leeds, and in the course of it having shattered so many records, surely the natural thing for the happy warrior to do would have been to bask in the sunshine of his team-mates' admiration, to have shown some human joy in achievement. And when to sporting success is added the manna of a small fortune, the inclination towards even the mildest of "celebrations" ought to be irresistible. But not with Bradman. I believe he spent that night of triumph alone in his room, playing the phonograph! As one of the Australians said to me later: "He is not one of us." That did not worry Bradman. There was no open breach, he was content to lead a life aloof, and Mr Kelly lacked the firmness to take the situation in hand before it got beyond him.'

The timing for the release of these words in Australia could not have been worse – the morning of the first Test. Bradman was then in 'Grimmett country' in Adelaide, on a day moreover that Grimmett took six of the seven wickets to fall in the Test. There were no doubt those ready to swear by Richardson's view – that Grimmett was the real 'king' of the Australian side. To cap it, Bradman was out for 4 next day. Tebbutt's strictures were now common knowledge. Whatever Mr Kelly's attitude towards Bradman may have been, he was touched to the quick by Tebbutt's accusation of weakness against him and, like an angry tiger in his Melbourne lair, drafted a riposte which he swiftly put out and which had the effect, at least publicly, of healing any breach that may have been suspected between Bradman and his touring manager. Kelly and Bradman closed ranks, as it were, in the face of a common enemy. Kelly's statement was as follows:

Mr Tebbutt is quite wrong. There was no breach between Bradman and the other members of the team, and Bradman did not lead a life aloof. He attended all official functions and many others with members of the team. He certainly did not go about as much as the other players, for two reasons – he was writing a book, and owing to his remarkable success, he received a large amount of correspondence which compelled him to remain at his hotel at night to answer it. There was no necessity for a display of firmness on my part as far as Bradman or any other member of the team was concerned throughout the tour, but I certainly did have to be firm to keep out Mr Tebbutt and one or two other Pressmen who were continually trying to push their way into invitations meant solely for the Australian team.

At the same time Geoffrey Tebbutt himself did not remain silent. He, too, in turn, was stung into action by Mr Kelly's remarks. Tebbutt had remained behind in London to see his book through the press, among other things; and *The Star* there – which, through its serialisations, had a special interest in maintaining the public image of Bradman – at once sent a representative to see him. Mr Tebbutt was very willing to talk, and he stuck firmly to his guns. His attitude to Bradman was thus given to *The Star*:

It is most unfair to have taken that paragraph away from the rest of the chapter which I devoted to Don, and then to criticise it.

Don is a friend of mine, and I am quite certain that, if he read the whole chapter, he would not be annoyed. I came over from Australia on the same boat with the team, and went all over England with them during the tour.

Therefore, I got to know a lot about them, and, since I claim that in the book I have written the whole truth, I mentioned the fact that Bradman was aloof. I stick to that. He certainly was.

He mixed quite happily with the rest of the team on the field, of course, and at all the 'official' functions which he had to attend, but he attended very few other social functions with them. There was no quarrel about it, though. He just went his way, and the rest of the team went theirs.

But I did not emphasise that in my book. The paragraph, as a matter of fact, was purely a matter en passant, mentioned quite near the end, after I had said very many nice things about him.

I am going to send Don a copy of the book by the next mail, and I am quite sure that, when he has read the whole chapter, he will not be annoyed, and our friendship will remain as firm as ever it was.

Apart from Geoffrey Tebbutt's book, apart from allegations of stealing the limelight, and apart from a disastrous start to a new Test series, there was still the matter of Bradman's writings to be adjudicated upon by the Board. His last three innings before the adjudication was announced – comprising his three first-class matches of December 1930 – perhaps give some indication of his state of mind: 4, 258, 2. (He had also scored at the beginning of December, before these three innings, a remarkable 110 in a one-day match for N.S.W.C.A. v Great Public Schools at Sydney.) He was still of course a batsman of high genius, but high genius perhaps can be unsettled more readily by petty diversions than can mediocrity.

If Adelaide was disappointed by his failure in the first Test – caught cutting in the slips for 4 – they were to be compensated at once by another vast Bradman avalanche. His 258 against South Australia all came in one day, and Grimmett took some terrible punishment. The great tormentor of English batsmen in 1930 was on this day rendered 'practically innocuous', his analysis at close of play being 26–0–120–1. Was this a Bradman answer to his Adelaide detractors? V. Y. Richardson fielded out to that innings, and eventually ended it – the only man to clean bowl Bradman in a Shield match that summer.[1] Bradman and Jackson added 334 for the second wicket at virtually 90 an hour. It was the highest partnership that Grimmett, as a bowler and fielder, had to endure in his life.

Bradman had taken the care, and extended the courtesy, of writing to the Board about his alleged journalistic misdemeanours in England, putting the facts before it and explaining his view of the matter. By the second week of December it had leaked out that Bradman had *not* received his final tour payment of £150, while his five New South Wales colleagues on the tour certainly had. Kelly's report had by then been forwarded to the new chairman of the Board, Dr Allen Robertson. The new chairman was a Victorian, but in the event State partisanship was to be of no consequence in the issue.

The Board held a two-day meeting at Melbourne on 29–30 December, and the Bradman adjudication and announcement was made on the second day. Bradman was in Melbourne for a Shield match, which ended on 29 December. With the administrative sword of Damocles hanging over him,

---

[1] Bradman falling to Richardson was even more remarkable than it may now seem – for in his entire career of 78 Sheffield Shield matches, Richardson took only two wickets! Bradman was the second, his first victim having also been a good batsman, Dr Roy Park, of Victoria, as far back as 1919–20, though as captain Richardson did not often put himself on to bowl.

he made 2. He stayed behind in Melbourne, and next day was called into the Board's room for a period and was asked various questions during a long discussion on his writing. One can imagine what Bradman was thinking. 'I have done everything that could have been asked of me, perhaps more. I have scored more runs in a Test series than ever before. I have done my full share towards Australia winning the Ashes. I have never been unfit and never been in an "incident" on the field.' He did not *say* these words, of course, but he could have been forgiven for thinking them. The manager's report complained that Bradman had broken the Board's clause quite straightforwardly because while the team were in England articles by Bradman appeared in a London newspaper. There were other allegations against Bradman concerning autographed photos and the making of a film; but these were brushed aside by the Board. The members were unanimous that publication of the articles *was* a breach of the contract, and it was decided on a majority vote to fine Bradman £50 and censure him. Bradman was again summoned into the Board's room and informed of the result before it was made public.

Considering that the Board made a net profit of £21,825 on the tour of England – a figure that was known to them when they met in Melbourne[1] – and considering that Bradman's presence had done much to add to attendances and bolster that profit; and considering further that Bradman was at all times fit throughout the tour and at all times gave of his very best, the practical task before the Board was a delicate one. They were divided over the penalty to exact, and in the end compromised. It was said that Bradman emerged from the judgment hall with a broad smile: perhaps he had already decided, as he shortly told some of his friends, that he would get back that £50.

This was Bradman's first skirmish with the Board and he acted with great decorum throughout, scrupulously avoiding any public pronouncements in advance of the hearing that might prejudice either side. After it was over, he slept on it for a few days and then said: 'Had I thought for one moment that I was violating my contract with the Board I would not have written that book. At the time I did not think I was committing a breach. I am still of the same opinion. . . . However, I must abide by the Board's ruling. Naturally, I am extremely disappointed. Nevertheless, I am prepared to accept their decision in the proper spirit. . . .' (Under the terms of his 1930 tour contract, Bradman had no right of appeal against the Board's decision. They rendered themselves 'the sole authority' in deciding the issue and their decision was, as each player agreed in advance, final.) The *Daily Herald* in London ran an article entitled: 'Hands Off Bradman', and expressed the sentiments at least of the British public:

---

[1] This was a record profit at that time for any touring side in England and exceeded the 1921 tour profit by £4,208 and the 1926 tour profit by £1,114.

Bradman is evidently suffering from a combination of hero worship and official irritation. Apart from one brilliant innings he has dropped entirely from the superb standard he displayed in England. The fact that one half of the Australians expects him to score centuries while the other half regards Bradman as a bad boy must have an adverse mental effect on one who, after all, is a mere schoolboy. Everyone wishes Bradman quick and safe deliverance from officialdom. He is an asset to cricket.

Perhaps fearing that the criticisms of Bradman would turn into a *cause célèbre* and result in prolonged public hostility towards the Board, the Board chose to shroud Kelly's report with a veil of impenetrable secrecy and resolutely refused to allow even the New South Wales Cricket Association to have a copy. The fact that Bradman was to receive £100 instead of £150 was probably anyway in itself enough to condemn the Board before Bradman's adoring public.

'I know that my concentration during that season fell away because of these extraneous matters', said Bradman in due course – and the man whose average in Test cricket was 103 began the series against the West Indies in 1930–31 with 4 and 25 in the first two Tests. Learie Constantine put it down to good fast bowling and good catching. Had the catching continued to be good, Bradman would have been out for only 4 in his third innings of the series in the third Test at Brisbane. He put a superbly fast delivery from Constantine straight into second slip's hands, and second slip – the unfortunate Birkett – dropped it. By close of play he was 223 not out – the highest score for Australia in a Test on Australian soil. He had given not a semblance of another chance. Griffith, who had dismissed him for 4 at Adelaide and was soon to give him his first Test match duck, on this day was punished for 0 for 100. Trumper once scored 208 runs in a day in a Test in Australia, and R. E. Foster 214; but Bradman's 223 in a day still remains a Test record in that country. Constantine had him caught next morning hooking a bumper without addition and his innings has gone down as the highest ever played at the Exhibition Ground, Brisbane, in its brief history as a Test venue. One trifling curiosity of this innings was that when he was in the 140s Bradman used three different bats, changing his first when 144 and his second when 149. Looking back on the disaster of the dropped catch only two years later, Constantine reflected: 'I have often wished that I could field in the slips to my own bowling and never so much as on that day.'

If officialdom was irritated by Bradman, the cricket public of Sydney – not forgetting their excitement during the broadcasting of Bradman's Test triumphs from England – had made their views quite unambiguously known when over 22,000 of them gave him a quite remarkable reception when he walked out to bat in the second Test on New Year's Day. Twice on his way to the crease the cheering was renewed: and it was only a little sad that he was to disappoint them by staying in for only 40 minutes for 25.

Between the third and fourth Tests, Bradman became a cricketer once again instead of an administrative pawn – his 'quick and safe deliverance from officialdom' had been achieved. He celebrated with a devastating 220 against Victoria at Sydney, of which the first 208 came in a single day. He roared past his 1,000 for the season, an aggregate only George Headley was to achieve that Australian summer – 31 days later and in 11 innings more than Bradman. This 220 was Bradman's 12th double-century in the 28 centuries so far in his first-class career – an astonishing percentage. When Hammond scored the 12th double-century of *his* career – at Melbourne in 1932–33 – it was his 71st century in all first-class cricket. When Jack Hobbs had made *his* 12th double-century – at Southampton in 1926 – it was actually his 134th first-class hundred. There was no cricketer in the world, and there never has been, who was so adept as Bradman at going on and on to build huge scores after reaching his hundred.

Learie Constantine on that tour confided to umpire George Hele that the West Indians 'accepted Bradman's customary century. It was the dismissal of the other batsmen on top of this which was the problem'. The fourth Test at Melbourne saw another 'customary century' by Bradman – a fine, fast and glorious 152, his eighth century in his last 12 Tests. Melbourne had not seen a century from Bradman's bat in any match since Chapman's side was in Australia. *Wisden* unaccountably said that he batted for 4¾ hours for his 152, but this does Bradman a great injustice for it was in fact the fastest century innings he played in his Test career, at virtually a run a minute. (The scorebook time was 154 minutes.) He scored 60 out of 89 in 76 minutes on the second morning on a sticky pitch, and on the first evening had reached his fifty in three-quarters of an hour, equalling his Lord's effort of the previous June. Towards the end of his innings, with Bradman going very strongly, there was a strange incident when he and McCabe both found themselves at the same end when the wicket was broken at the other. Bradman deliberately, it is thought, ran off the ground, but was recalled by the umpire, who had given McCabe out. A few minutes later Bradman gave a catch in the deep.

This 152 in the fourth Test of 1930–31 was Bradman's 100th innings in first-class cricket, at which point he had scored 7,948 runs – another record. (His next 100 innings were to prove even more prolific, realising 8,391 runs; and the third hundred innings of his career were, incredible to relate – for they took him well into the post-war period – even more prolific still, with 8,711 runs. Truly a record without parallel!)

Bradman's actual career figures after 100, 200 and 300 innings in first-class cricket – all record aggregates for the respective landmarks – were as follows:

Innings	N.O.	Runs	H.S.	Av.	100s
100	15	7,948	452*	93·50	29
200	23	16,339	452*	92·31	60
300	38	25,050	452*	95·61	103

By way of comparison, the previous highest aggregate after 100 innings was held by Ponsford, before the advent of Bradman the heaviest run-getter in the game. Ponsford's figures after 100 innings were:

Innings	N.O.	Runs	H.S.	Av.	100s
100	7	7,196	437	77·37	28

These were quite magnificent figures by Ponsford (taking him into the 1928–29 season) and illustrate his ill-fortune in having an even mightier run-getter follow so close on his heels and eclipsing what would otherwise have been a far greater fame. Ponsford, eight years Bradman's senior, was the original huge run-amasser of the 1920s and the first man to make colossal scores a habit (both for Victoria and for his club, St Kilda). Not even Don Bradman twice topped 400 or made 1,000 runs in four consecutive innings. Let it also not be forgotten that O'Reilly considered Ponsford the most difficult batsman he bowled against, more difficult than Bradman – a view held likewise by Grimmett. The Ponsford–Bradman mentality of ruthless dedication to run-getting can be exemplified in Ponsford's remark when he played on a ball from outside his wicket to disturb his stumps, having made 352 out of 614 (for three) in six hours against New South Wales in 1926–27: 'Well', he said. 'I *am* unlucky.' If Sir Donald Bradman might object to being thus linked with Ponsford's philosophy, it can only be because Bradman allowed neither unlucky nor lucky elements to enter into his thinking while at the crease. On their form in 1930–31 Bradman was the best batsman in Australia on good wickets, followed by Ponsford. However, when the wicket was helping the bowler, it was the view of Ray Robinson that Ponsford was Australia's best. But over the full careers of these two batsmen, for a player of Ponsford's magnificent ability to be relegated to a secondary role was proof indeed of Bradman's genius.

Learie Constantine had tried very hard all tour to dismiss Bradman for a low score, and at last he did it in the return match with New South Wales, just before the tour ended, when he knocked Bradman's off stump out of the ground for 10. Constantine remembered this dismissal all his life and was never reluctant to regale a willing hearer with the lurid minute-by-minute details of Bradman's short stay and discomfiture at his hands. In his first book, *Cricket and I* (1933), he went through his bowling that day wicket by wicket, giving 250 words to the dismissal of Bradman. After the war, in his next book, were a further 250 zestful words on how he first 'fed' and then tricked the Don to destruction. That was not all. In a later book, through an editorial oversight, he had two further lengthy goes at this selfsame dismissal, all expressed with the sort of relish reserved for the cat commandeering the cream! Constantine always held his bowling that day, when all his six victims were bowled, to have been the best of his career. The philosopher in Constantine might well have reflected on nature's daily distribution of her favours and penalties: while he was enjoying one of his greatest of days, very close to the Sydney Cricket Ground that very afternoon there died another great public entertainer, Dame Nellie Melba (who had sung in London before the 1921 Australian side). Australians adored their favourites, whether singers or cricketers.

The first o against Bradman's name in Test cricket came in the fifth Test at Sydney, a match which Australia lost by 30 runs against two declarations. G. C. Grant's courage in declaring when only 250 ahead, even on a bad pitch, was to be admired, knowing that Bradman was in the side against him, to say nothing of Ponsford, Woodfull and Kippax. Not many captains have taken such a chance with Bradman and got away with it. Herman Griffith – a short man who could bowl formidably fast – clean bowled him round his legs for o after ten minutes – and dragged Bradman's Test average for his career down to 94! It was his first duck in a first-class match for over three years and something he had avoided in his previous 98 innings. Tied down – a condition Bradman hated instinctively – he made 'an almighty cross-bat swipe', said Constantine. Photographs confirm the inelegance. Had Bradman been allowed to get an early single, as was his wont, he might so easily have won the match for Australia.

It is interesting that two administrative changes at the start of the 1930–31 season had little effect on the glut of runs from Bradman's bat. Wicket-covering was re-introduced by New South Wales for that season and the larger stumps were used for the first time in Australia (though not in matches played by the West Indian tourists). Actually in matches played with the smaller stumps he averaged 62·50, from ten innings, and with the larger stumps, in eight innings, 99·62! Under either size of wicket, he was able to exceed 200 in a day! (In addition, Sheffield Shield cricket was now limited to a maximum of 22 hours over four days instead of 24½ hours over five days: but Bradman's speed of scoring remained notably high – his 695 runs in Shield matches came at 46 an hour.)

Bradman's appearances for St George in 1930–31 were almost entirely eliminated by the calls of representative cricket. He played only three innings for them, and as he was twice not out, his average equalled his aggregate – 215! Between his Test match duck and a tour of Northern Queensland, he squeezed in one match for them and scored a brilliant 116 not out in 97 minutes v Marrickville at Hurstville Oval, having wholly rescued the side when he went in at number seven with the score at 50 for five. (St George recovered to declare at 213 for seven.) He very sportingly played in this match, though suffering the after effects of having six teeth extracted the previous evening – hence his low position in the order.

With the West Indians having left for home and the Sheffield Shield season over, Bradman ended his summer as a member of a strong side that Alan Kippax took on a tour of Northern Queensland in March and April. For some seasons past Kippax had taken a side there, and the 1931 side included six Test players. Whatever the fame or otherwise of Bradman and his colleagues they were paid 10 shillings a day to cover incidentals and loss

of salary, while their accommodation and travel were paid for.[1] Touring in
Australia is very different to touring in England – it took the side six days to
travel by boat from Sydney to Brisbane and then from Brisbane to
Townsville before the start of the tour was in sight. Bradman scored four
hundreds – 103 v Cairns, 113 v North Queensland, 107 v Ayr, and 148* v
Mackay – two of them on turf and two on concrete. At Cairns he had an
astonishing match: apart from his 103, he had made 90 in 55 minutes in the
first innings and took 10 wickets in the same match (4–13 and 6–43). In the
one-day game at Ayr, he took 6–23 before scoring his century. The tour was
due to last seven weeks, but half-way through – v Central Queensland at
Rockhampton on 18 April – Bradman turned to intercept a ball at mid-on
and his ankle 'turned'. He was taken by ambulance to Rockhampton
Hospital and was there for six weeks. He had scored 651 runs (av. 81·37)
and – having been given the ball more frequently than in major matches –
had taken 33 wickets at 10·12 each, which left him, unusually, at the top of
the bowling. At one stage of the second innings at Cairns he took four for 1
and came within a whisker of doing the hat-trick – mid-on dropping an
easy catch off the crucial third ball! McCabe hit 50 sixes on the tour, and
Kippax's average was in the 90s.

At the close of the Australian season of 1930–31 Don Bradman, despite
almost 18 consecutive months of cricket, with only the sea journeys to and
from England as real respite, seemed as fresh and as fit as ever, apart from
his ankle injury. When Arthur Richardson, a regular purveyor of cricketing
intelligence between Australia and England, arrived in England in the
middle of April for another season with Bacup, he said that Australian
cricket was 'very stale' and singled out *Bradman alone* of the 1930 Test team
who did not seem to him to be tired.

Richardson was wise enough in such matters and was almost certainly
correct, but other people, prompted among other things by Bradman's duck
in the final Test, were wondering about his future. The *Sunday Chronicle* got
their special correspondent in Sydney to investigate, and, though he was
unaware of Bradman's four hundreds in Queensland, he concluded in mid-
April 1931 that Bradman had been losing his punch. 'Is Don Bradman to
slip off his cricket pedestal?' he asked. 'Are the celebrations and business
worries that followed his triumphant return home from England getting him
down?' He went on:

> Ever since he got back here from England Don has been surrounded by business
> worries. He holds an important job with a firm of sports outfitters, flies round in
> 'The Red Peril' – the car presented to him at Sydney Town Hall by an American

---

[1] These tours, undertaken to encourage cricket in the lesser centres and produce for them
some revenue, entailed an enormous amount of travelling – and there were only 12 players,
including a player-manager! By way of comparison, the allowance to Australian cricketers
in the Test matches that season against the West Indies was £30 per match plus rail fares
and sleepers.

combine – attends luncheons and dinners, writes newspaper articles, and receives presentations.

. . . Previous to the English tour Don was never seen in the field or the street without a smile. To-day he wears a worried look . . .

Friends of his agree that Don has tried to do too much during the past 12 months, and that, unless he winters quietly, he will be burnt out by the time the English team visits these shores.

Don Bradman, however, at the age of 22, was not one to burn himself out quickly, and what others might not attempt to do, he often took in his stride. He was not to be measured, as his deeds confirmed time and again, by ordinary standards. (Before the next English team was to visit Australian shores, incidentally, Bradman was to have two marvellous seasons against the visiting South Africans and on tour in North America.) The diagnosis of 'business worries', at least in 1930–31, was a journalistic exaggeration. His clash with the Board had certainly been a worry, but once that was behind him he enjoyed life. At the same time there were undeniably being sown in Sydney the seeds of future tensions that were one day to force Don Bradman to vacate that city and seek serenity elsewhere.

Bradman's ankle injury actually proved to be a little more obdurate than the doctors expected. For a long period he had to spend two hours a day with the masseurs. The news of his indisposition was seized on by none other than the moguls of Hollywood, quick to sense even the smallest possibility of Bradman's career being in jeopardy. In early August 1931 Bradman admitted he had had offers from Hollywood to go on the stage: but he declined them in the full expectation of being at the nets again for the new Australian season.

While Don Bradman was nursing his ankle back to strength in 1931, a fresh controversy was preparing to burst about his ears. The Lancashire League wanted his genius. Quite who approached whom in the first place is not easy to pin down precisely. The President of the Lancashire League, the late Mr Edward Crabtree, a prominent mill-owner from Todmorden – a great President who did much to bring the Lancashire League into prominence – said in 1934 that 'the first approaches were made by Bradman to the Lancashire League, not by the League to Bradman'. One of those closely concerned with the negotiations at that time, the present distinguished President of the League, Mr Jack Isherwood, says anent Mr Crabtree's remark that he 'cannot say yea or nay' to that. Learie Constantine, who had begun his league career with Nelson in 1929 and who had seen Bradman often enough in 1930–31, was certainly the intermediary in the very early negotiations and reported on Bradman's suitability as a potential league cricketer – presumably quite favourably. Bradman himself had an intermediary in Sydney, a friend, Claude Spencer, whose handling of the matter instead of Bradman personally would, it was hoped, attract less publicity. 'It was all very secret', recalls Mr Isherwood. But it was not to remain so for long. By the end of August 1931, despite the efforts in both England and Australia towards secrecy, it was common knowledge that Accrington had made Bradman an offer, or at least made it through Claude Spencer. At the same time there were suggestions that Bradman would play for Lancashire after a qualifying period of two years in league cricket; but Harry Rylance, the popular Lancashire secretary who was to die so tragically young a few weeks later, said the Lancashire committee, after meeting on 1 September, knew nothing about it. This was confirmed by the Accrington chairman, Herbert Crawshaw, who went out of his way to dispel any notion that Lancashire C.C.C. were supporting the Accrington efforts or in any way were after Bradman. It was Crawshaw's view that 'no cricketer ever before received so munificent an offer'. He said: 'I cannot tell you what our offer is, but I can assure you that, according to my calculations, Bradman would make £1,000 a year by accepting.' Apart from a weekly salary, Bradman was promised £5 for each innings of fifty or over, £5 each time he might take five wickets, as well as newspaper contracts and normal collections on the ground (Learie Constantine at that time had often received collections exceeding £10). Mr Crawshaw also said something about the difficult matter of who approached whom: 'It is not that we sprang a surprise on Bradman by making the offer. The first overtures were from him.'

So far as playing in England was concerned, Bradman was still bound by the terms of the stringent 1930 tour contract, the relevant clause of which read as follows:

> Each and every of the players hereby specifically undertakes and agrees with the board that he will not return to England within two years from the completion of the official tour for the purpose of playing cricket.

The official tour, of course, ended in September 1930, and thus the earliest season for which Bradman could properly accept an English offer was 1933. Any earlier acceptance would almost certainly have entailed excommunication by the Australian Board. Alan Fairfax chose to break this clause of his contract and he never played for Australia again. Accrington wanted Bradman for 1932.

The Professional sub-committee at Accrington was under the chairmanship of the late James Chapman, the Accrington representative on the league committee. His other two members were the club secretary, the late Gideon Holgate, and the assistant-secretary, Jack Isherwood. These three did the negotiating. Accrington at first denied they were negotiating with Bradman at all. Strictly this was true, for they were negotiating with Claude Spencer, who was passing on the details to Bradman. With Accrington's denial, emphatically expressed, speculation turned to other clubs. Nelson let it quickly be known they had already re-engaged Constantine. Rishton were also among the rumours, but they said they could not afford to make an offer even if they wanted to. The Manchester journalists were naturally restless, and one of them sent a cable to Bradman asking him point blank for the truth. Bradman replied and admitted he was considering an offer. The London *Daily Telegraph* asserted 'on good authority' that it was practically certain that Bradman would play for Accrington and that he would be arriving in England about the middle of April 1932.

Accrington's offer, it soon transpired, was a three-year contract at £25 a week, to which Bradman cabled suggesting a two-year contract. It was easy to see he had his eye on the 1934 Australian tour of England, though had he played league cricket in 1932 and 1933 – and thereby broken his contract with the Board – his future prospects of going on tour under the aegis of the Board of Control would have been placed squarely in jeopardy. Bradman played a waiting game, and there was indeed some private correspondence between him and the Board. Accrington were agreeable to a two-year contract – which club would not have been? – and then confidently announced they expected Bradman to play in 1932 and were merely awaiting his confirmation. By the first week of September Bradman was having to read lies in the press – which he greatly resented – that he had actually signed a contract. 'I certainly do not appreciate', said Bradman somewhat hotly in Sydney on 3 September, 'some of the caustic comment which has been made in England about my accepting the Accrington contract, for I have not done so. Should I accept the contract, that will be the time for comment. They are pulling me to pieces before I have done anything.'

Accrington's 1931 pro had been the 44-year-old P. E. Morfee, a little-known bowler who had played a few first-class matches for Kent in 1910–12 and had been a professional in Scotland and in the Lancashire and Central Lancashire Leagues. He gained some small renown by being photographed holding, with no apparent difficulty, as many as six cricket balls in one hand. He had had one year with Nelson and two with Todmorden, but his best days were behind him and his single summer with Accrington was to be his last there. He was an honest toiler. Bradman was the biggest catch on the horizon. Accrington, who could boast C. B. Llewellyn and the pre-Yorkshire Hedley Verity among their former pros, were looking for success[1]: they had last won the league title in 1916 (when sides were considerably weakened) and ironically were not to win it again until 1961, when Wesley Hall carried all before him.

In 1931, however, they were hoping for big things with what seemed to them the imminent capture for the following summer of Donald George Bradman. The course of cricket history would have been changed had they pulled it off. Both Australians and Englishmen were divided over the issue. Bradman's potential defection was viewed with horror by many; while equally his right to exploit his own talents was recognised. Certainly, if his actions had alienated him with the Australian Board, his absence from

[1] They had finished 12th out of 14 in the Lancashire League table in 1931, winning only three of their 26 games. Not a single Accrington name appeared in the top 20 in either the batting or the bowling averages of the League.

Australian Test teams of the '30s would have rendered somewhat less than real the contests between England and Australia. And presumably, as a consequence of that, he would not have made the come-back, partially out of a sense of loyalty, that he did make in 1946–47. The *Observer* (London) of 6 September 1931 wrote:

> No sporting interest would be served by bringing Bradman to Lancashire. He is an ornament to his own country, and in that capacity is always welcome here, but as a salaried run-getter for an English club he would be only a reminder of how money deranges the natural order of things. Lancashire did not begin this business of importing players, let her have the distinction of ending it.

Accrington meanwhile had come right out in the open, and their secretary said they had sent a letter to Bradman summarising his duties: 'Accrington is not the least worried about what Australia may be doing to retain the world-beater. We neither know nor care whether Australia can offer more financial attractions. We have made a good offer and hope to pull it off.' That good offer had now been increased to £30 a week, a minimum guarantee of £300 talent money in 1932, at least £200 'from other sources', and free passage from and back to Australia. In a period of severe economic depression, both in England and Australia, all this was a highly generous inducement. The Accrington secretary telephoned Bradman in Sydney to try to persuade him to accept it, though Bradman refused to be rushed into an answer. Bradman himself has written of the proposal: 'I consider it was a very handsome offer, and I must say I was greatly tempted by it. I don't think anyone could have blamed me if I had then chosen to capitalize my cricket by accepting it. No one would criticize a singer for getting as much as he could for entertaining the public in his particular way.' The offer was in fact by far the best ever made to a cricketer up to that time to join a league club in England.

Bradman delayed still further and Accrington hoped to clinch the issue by sending him the actual written contract for signature. Bradman received this on 26 October 1931, with advice pouring in on him. Away from the public gaze, plans were being carefully laid to keep him in Australia.

With the Australian cricket season already under way, Bradman announced on 30 October that after due consideration he had declined Accrington's offer and that he had accepted a proposed contract – that would take effect from 1 February 1932 – that would keep him in Australia for two years. 1 February 1932 was when his existing contract with Mick Simmons was due to expire. He had cabled Accrington accordingly, in the following terms: 'Regret decline your offer. Appreciate pleasant nature of negotiations. Writing full details.' There were many deep sighs of relief – but not in Accrington. Mr Holgate, the secretary, was disappointed and threw a little more light on the origin of the episode: 'That appears to be the end of the matter. The suggestion that he should play for Accrington did not come in the first place from us. Neither did it come direct from Bradman, but there was a letter written with his full knowledge.' Within 24 hours Accrington's offer of a contract had been communicated to Alan Fairfax, and despite the Australian Board's refusal to give him permission, he duly went, accepting the responsibility for his action, to become Accrington's professional. (Fairfax's fee was £480 for 20 weeks.) In the event, and despite subsequent offers in later years to lure Bradman to league cricket, Bradman never in fact went into the league. Ponsford, it may be recalled, had had a similar offer to join Blackpool, then in the Ribblesdale League, in 1927, with a view also to playing for Lancashire: but public agitation – and public collections – in Melbourne prevented him going. Blackpool was also linked with Archie Jackson's name at the same time as the Bradman negotiations – there was a rumour in Sydney, promptly denied by both Blackpool and Lancashire C.C.C., that Jackson had been offered a large sum of money, as well as £10 as a weekly wage and employment in a solicitor's office. A few weeks later Grimmett denied a rumour that *he* was joining a Lancashire League club – he had already turned down a proposal from Accrington before the Bradman negotiations began – and in early May 1932 Oldfield renewed speculation by saying that Grimmett and Ponsford were likely to follow Fairfax to join English clubs. But the certain fact remained that the deep public concern and national spotlight was reserved exclusively for Bradman's case and he alone among his contemporaries was destined to suffer this perpetual and probing gaze from friend and foe alike.

Bradman of course realised that his acceptance of the Accrington offer would mean the end of his Test career. There was never any *real* prospect of that happening, despite all the ballyhoo which had all but removed the Accrington signing from speculation to a *fait accompli*. Bradman himself never intended it to happen, though he was quite prepared to put his current market value to the test (which could only enhance his future prospects in Australia). 'I didn't want to leave home', he said the day after the offer was declined. 'I am happier than I have been for a long time and I slept well last night.' That day Mick Simmons's premises were stormed by a crowd of visitors who blocked the pavement in front of the store as they rushed to congratulate Bradman.

It was a personal relief to Bradman to have the Accrington affair behind him. Wherever he had gone in the preceding weeks he had been asked the same question, about whether he was or was not going to England. Knowing how readily his words were apt to be quoted, his replies had to be couched in the discreetest terms. The susceptibilities of the Board, too, could not be needlessly irritated. 'Down inside me I wanted to stay in Australia to play my cricket for Australia', confirmed Bradman later on. 'It meant a considerable financial sacrifice, but, on the whole, I am glad I made it.' That financial sacrifice was all the greater as he was about to become engaged to be married: but at the same time the terms that dictated his remaining in Australia were by no means either uncongenial or unsatisfactory.

Those terms – in view of the exhortations that had come from Lancashire –

had to be sensibly attractive, and they took the shape of a combined two-year contract (under which he was reputed to receive £30 a week) with three Sydney business groups: a daily newspaper, a wireless station and a leading store. All three contracted that Bradman was to be given every leave necessary for him to fulfil his commitments in first-class and Test match cricket. The newspaper was the Sydney *Sun*, to which he would be contributing signed articles on cricket; the radio station was 2UE, Sydney (and its affiliates in other States), on which he would give broadcast addresses on cricket[1]; and the store was F. J. Palmer and Son Ltd, on the corner of Park Street and Pitt Street, Sydney, a men's wear store to whose sporting department Bradman was attached and who forthwith made a good trade in 'Don Bradman' Complete Cricket Sets for youths, the handsome presentation box showing Bradman's autograph and including his photograph. He was officially designated Sports Adviser to F. J. Palmer, who thereafter used (to the end of Bradman's association with them) a handsome form of headed notepaper depicting Bradman completing an aggressive drive and bearing the legend, beneath the company's name, 'The Home of Don Bradman'. The young record-breaker's name was one his new employers took a just pride in. (To illustrate, however, that business success could not depend on a single name, however illustrious, the published balance sheets during Bradman's two years with Palmer's showed that although the profits rose to £4,000 in the first year, they dropped to £2,000 in the second.) Bradman thus parted company with Mick Simmons, where he was replaced by Stanley McCabe. However, in solving one problem, another was created, for Bradman's new tripartite agreement turned him into a player-writer, a species of cricketer viewed with a long-standing distaste by the Australian Board and against which they had already legislated. Bradman's new status, before 12 months were to go by, was destined to land him in an administrative furore beside which the Lancashire League issue seemed quite pale. (Lord Hawke, by the way, whose Presidential remarks at every Yorkshire A.G.M. were both bold and to the point, told Yorkshire members at Sheffield in the winter of 1931–32 that he felt confident that no real cricket lover was sorry when Bradman cabled his refusal to play in the Lancashire League. He said he was glad to have the pleasing assurance that 'our red rose county friends' had nothing to do with the attempt to bring Bradman to England. It was Lord Hawke, too, in January 1927, who had criticized the proposed engagement of Ponsford in England.)

Meanwhile Bradman had been showing remarkable form in the new

---

[1] When these broadcasts got under way, they were put out twice a week during the cricket season, normally on Thursday nights at 9.30 and during the peak listening period every Saturday, from 7.30 to 8 p.m. The programme was simply called 'Don Bradman's cricket talk'. Under his contract Bradman received £1,000 for 12 months from Radio 2UE, and if he was away from Sydney and unable to broadcast, he was required to send a letter, which was read for him over the air. Bradman's talks were not sponsored by an advertiser, as were the broadcasts of some others. The manager of station 2UE in due course said that Bradman's engagement was responsible for a big increase in business.

Australian season of 1931-32. Cricket for him began that summer when he left Sydney with A. F. Kippax's side for a whirlwind tour of Southern New South Wales country districts in September 1931. In the side with him was his St George captain, W. F. Ives. Bradman scored four centuries on the tour, all from his favourite number three position – 124 v Parkes, 137 v Forbes, 111 v Young District, and 130 (retired hurt) v Wagga Association at Wagga, where, after a most spectacular display, he was obviously in pain when struck on the chest by a fast rising ball and decided to retire. Fortunately he was not seriously injured. In his 137 at Forbes he scored 26 runs (three 6s, two 4s) off five consecutive balls, one of his hits striking the headlight of a parked car and smashing it comprehensively. Among his other scores were 52 at Lithgow, 63 v Harden at Murrumburrah (when he was sensationally caught at mid-wicket), and 85 not out at Yass. There may just conceivably have been a Bradman among the crowd at this game at Yass, for it was here that Don Bradman's uncle, John Thomas Bradman (his father's elder brother), was last heard of. Altogether the team travelled 1,000 miles, played ten matches and went to ten dances. Bradman's footwork, with or without the ten dances, was in very good order.[1]

On his return to Sydney, and with a month to go before his first Shield match, he was able to play for St George – and in his second grade match of the season he shattered his own first-grade record for the club with a quite brilliant innings of 246 in 205 minutes v Randwick at Coogee Oval. It was to remain the highest innings Bradman ever played for St George, and the victims, Randwick, were the same side against whom he had scored the then-existing St George grade record, his 187 in 1929-30. On an uncertain pitch on which the next highest scorer could make only 39, Bradman's 246 contained only two hard chances, one when 238. In nearly 60 years of competition in Sydney first-grade cricket (since 1921-22) St George has so far never had a higher innings played for the side.

The form Bradman was in around this period was astonishing even for him. On 3 November 1931 he actually scored 100 runs in the course of three overs, by means of ten 6s, nine 4s, a 2 and two singles. He was playing in an exhibition match at Blackheath, New South Wales (in the Blue Mountains, outside Sydney) for a combined Blue Mountains team against the Lithgow Pottery Cricket Club. The game was staged by the Blackheath Council to mark the official opening of their new ground and to test a new malthoid wicket being used for the first time in the Western Districts. The pitch resembled a thick linoleum floor and did away with the need for matting over

---

[1] Although this tour was confined to ten days' cricket, Kippax's side – as always – was so attractive that a profit of £800, wholly for the country centres, resulted. On the much longer tour of Northern Queensland country districts at the end of the 1930-31 season, when Bradman had also been in splendid form, a profit of £3,000 accrued, likewise for the country players. Few cricketers in Australia between the wars did more for the encouragement of country cricketers than Alan Kippax. He was fortunate, of course, in his players – not least in Bradman: but he also had Jackson, McCabe, Fairfax and Wendell Bill, among others, as well as his own graceful self. There was always a banquet of batting on his tours.

the concrete beneath. Bradman, going in on the fall of an early wicket, revelled in it, and raced to 256 including 14 sixes and 29 fours. In the midst of his onslaught he hit 6, 6, 4, 2, 4, 4, 6, 1 off one over of off-breaks from Bill Black, thus retaining the strike. Off the next over, from Horrie Baker, a future Town Clerk of Lithgow, Bradman scored 40, with 6, 4, 4, 6, 6, 4, 6, 4. Black's next over was hit for 1, 6, 6, 1, 1, 4, 4, 6 – the first and fifth balls being hit for singles by O. Wendell Bill, the others by Bradman, who had thus scored 100 out of 102 in three overs. Black was promptly taken off after his two overs! At Blackheath to this day the fully-grown Monterey pines over which Don Bradman sent some of his leg-side sixes that day are still pointed out to visitors. Bradman hit 200 in boundaries alone that day in his 256, which must have been scored in an incredibly short time and it is a great pity that the innings appears not to have been timed.

One of the most delightful anecdotes of Bradman's career concerns that innings at Blackheath, which was actually the second time that season he had faced the slow to medium off-breaks of Bill Black. In the first match of Kippax's tour, on 12 September, Black was playing for Lithgow and surprisingly bowled Bradman for 52. The bowler's umpire, 'Gub' Kirkwood, called out excitedly: 'Bill, you've got him!' Umpires were apt to sacrifice something of their decorum when an event like this happened in a country town in the early 'thirties. And the ball that took the most prized wicket in Australia was mounted, inscribed, and presented to the bowler for proud and permanent retention in his home. Now to the anecdote. When Bradman was about 50 at Blackheath, the same fielding captain who had seen Black do his heroics at Lithgow threw the ball to Black in the hope he might do it again. 'I stood at the bowler's end', recalled Bill Black years later, 'and while I placed my field Bradman was talking to the wicketkeeper, Leo Waters. Later Leo told me this conversation took place.'

Bradman: 'What sort of bowler is this fellow?'
Waters: 'Don't you remember this bloke? He bowled you in the exhibition match at Lithgow a few weeks ago and has been boasting about it ever since at your expense.'

Two overs later Bill Black had to plead with his captain to be taken off, nursing an analysis of 2–0–62–0.

Bradman was reminded what a hard mistress cricket could be when he began the first-class season with a duck at the hands of Eddie Gilbert in Brisbane. The aboriginal's speed that day – whatever may have been the opinions as to his action – was classed by Bradman as the fastest he ever experienced. The duck gave the Queensland wicketkeeper, L. W. Waterman, on his first day ever in Sheffield Shield cricket, a most notable scalp with which to remember his debut, the more so as he had, only a few minutes before, caught Wendell Bill for a duck too. Bradman was actually out to the fifth ball he received, having been in terrible trouble against Gilbert and been struck by him the ball before. It was the first time he had ever faced

Gilbert.[1] In his next seven first-class matches Bradman made seven hundreds! In fact he was to have a dazzling summer of almost unrelieved success, his obvious gifts now fully mature and his daring and certainty at the crease representing a wall of despair for most bowlers to bowl at.

The visitors to Australia that season were the South Africans, whose tour had been in jeopardy until as late as 5 July 1931, because of the adverse rate of exchange and the continuing conditions of economic depression in both countries. There was talk of the tour being reversed, with Australia going to South Africa, which would have seen Bradman on South African wickets, a circumstance fate was never to decree. In the end South Africa decided to send her team to Australia after all – and Bradman gave them as memorable a few months as had Trumper given the only previous South African visitors 21 years before. Bradman absolutely demoralised the South Africans, so much so that they were quite unable to bowl anything like their best when he was at the crease. His successive scores against the South Africans on the tour were as follows:

30 } 135	for New South Wales	at Sydney
226	for Australia (1st Test)	at Brisbane
219	for New South Wales	at Sydney
112	for Australia (2nd Test)	at Sydney
2 } 167	for Australia (3rd Test)	at Melbourne
299*	for Australia (4th Test)	at Adelaide

This gave him an aggregate of 1,190 runs (av. 170) against the South Africans alone, a world record total for a season's runs against a touring side. In the Tests only – injury prevented him batting in the final match – his average was such as to make even the term Bradmanesque seem inadequate:

Innings	N.O.	Runs	H.S.	Av.
5	1	806	299*	201·50

The next best average was 70·16 by Woodfull; and Bradman and Woodfull between them scored more than half the runs made by Australia in the series. So far as the watching public were concerned, Bradman himself considered this his best summer. His average was, and remains, the highest in any Test rubber in the world, dwarfing his own wonderful average of 1930

---

[1] The New South Wales team manager in Brisbane, A. L. Rose, openly accused Gilbert of throwing in a statement to the press at the end of the match. He thought his bowling was 'a blot on the game' and that there was 'not a shadow of doubt' that the majority of Gilbert's deliveries in his opening overs had been throws. He said Gilbert made an 'aunt sally' of Bradman as soon as he came to the wicket. Mr Rose assured Queensland officials that four of the leading players in the New South Wales team were emphatically of the opinion that Gilbert threw his fastest ball. The following month, in Melbourne, Gilbert was no-balled for throwing 11 times in his only three overs. Later on Bradman himself wrote of Gilbert: 'From the pavilion his bowling looked fair to me, but when batting against him it appeared to me that if he did not actually throw the ball he certainly jerked it.'

and more than doubling what was hailed in 1910–11 as the remarkable average of Trumper of 94·42. Prior to Bradman meeting South Africa, Trumper's had been the best average by an Australian in Australia.

If the West Indians the previous year had been let off comparatively lightly by Bradman (only two centuries in ten innings against them), Cameron's side took the sort of punishment that had been meted out to English bowlers in 1930. The South Africans must have been haunted by the chants of 'You'll never get Braddy out!' by the children at the wayside stations as they crossed the vast Nullarbor Plain at the start of the tour. Oddly enough, they actually dismissed him for 30 on their first meeting, and a highly unimpressive 30 it was. Now and again, even in club cricket, Bradman did play a most uncharacteristically unimpressive innings. But such innings were very few and far between, and bowlers who hoped – indeed thought – they had the measure of him were awakened with a rude and shattering subsequent encounter. So it was with the South Africans. Before long Bradman was simply gorging himself at their expense.

Bradman christened the Woolloongabba ground at Brisbane as a Test venue by scoring exactly 200* on its first day in use, passing 2,000 runs in Test cricket in the record number of only 22 innings. If the South Africans could not indeed 'get Braddy out', they had only themselves to blame. On that first morning at Brisbane they dropped him twice in the slips, Vincent (second slip) and Mitchell (first slip) being the culprits at 11 and 15 respectively, both off the left-hander Neville Quinn. His next chance, a stumping one, came when he was 224, two runs before he was out. R. S. Whitington has recorded that when the first chance went down in the slips, 'the normally reticent and dignified Bruce Mitchell was heard to utter a four-letter word for the first time in the memory of men who knew him intimately. When he missed Bradman himself in slips four runs later Bruce was even more profane'. Over 10,000 saw Bradman's first innings for Australia at the Brisbane Cricket Ground and his 226 remains a ground record for a Test match there. A year before, he had also scored a double-century in a day at Brisbane, on the old Exhibition Ground, against the West Indies.

As if this was not enough, Bradman promptly scored yet *another* double-century in a day immediately after the Brisbane Test was over, and again the South Africans were the victims, when they played their return match with New South Wales at Sydney. His form was devastating. This time it was 219 (and he was out well before the close of play) in 234 minutes, going from 150 to 200 in 37 minutes. It was an innings of 'riskless certainty', and except for pulls for four through wide on-side gaps, he did not lift a ball until the one from which he was caught – a skier to deep mid-off. His last three first-class innings now read 135, 226, 219.

He made it four centuries in four innings – all of them against the luckless South Africans – when he scored a chanceless 112 in the Sydney Test in a fraction over 2½ hours, despite a strained leg. This was his third Test at Sydney (excluding his long appearance there as 12th man in '28–29) and was his maiden Test hundred before his home supporters. Melbourne, of course, was well accustomed to a Bradman Test century, and he duly obliged at the next opportunity with the fastest Test hundred of his career in the second innings of the third Test. The majority of his 29 Test hundreds were scored at a healthy pace, and in his 167 against South Africa at Melbourne he reached three figures in 98 minutes, which was actually a minute faster than when he scored his century before lunch at Headingley in 1930. He went from 50 to 100 in only 34 minutes, and once again gave no chance, his 167 taking 183 minutes. This was a really brilliant rate of scoring for Test cricket, but the sort of rate people were now taking for granted from Bradman. It was classic batsmanship at its best. The better his first-innings conqueror, Neville Quinn, bowled, the harder Bradman flailed him. It sent old cricketers into rhapsodies. Despite being 160 behind on the first innings, Australia won at Melbourne very comfortably. The *News Chronicle* in London, viewing this third great innings by Bradman in three Tests, came out with some musings:

> As long as Australia has him she is apparently invincible, for he always seems able to score the number of runs required at any given time. In order to keep alive the competitive spirit of the game the cricket authorities might take a hint from billiards. As soon as a player invents a shot that can produce an unlimited number of points they put a legal limitation upon its use. It is almost time to request a legal limitation on the number of runs Bradman should be permitted to make.

How the South Africans of 1931–32 would have welcomed such a legal limitation! Vic Richardson once said, 'As captain of a team opposing Don I would willingly offer him 100 every time he batted, if he would give his wicket away for that score.' The South Africans would have probably lost anyway under such an arrangement, but their morale would not have been so cruelly frayed. As it was, their cup of woe was filled to overflowing at Adelaide soon after when Bradman flogged them in one of the most technically merciless innings even he ever played. He scored 299 not out – a new record innings for a Test in Australia – with only a single hard chance (at 185) in 6½ hours. The next two highest scores were 82 and 35. When R. M. Cowper, 34 years later, beat Bradman's record for a Test in Australia with 307, he batted for more than 12 hours. The extreme physical fitness that Bradman maintained that summer cannot be better exemplified than by this innings. After fielding through South Africa's 308, he had scored 170* by the close on Saturday night, having then been on the field for all but a few minutes of the match. He added a further 129 on Monday before he ran out of partners. On the intervening Sunday he played a full afternoon of tennis – and, no doubt, if the facts be known, a highly *successful* afternoon of tennis! (The day before his 200 runs in a day in the Brisbane Test, he had a highly effective outing at golf on the Yeerongpilly course.) George Hele stood in all five Tests in that series, and of Bradman's 299* at Adelaide he said in his 1974 book: 'I have watched no batsman of any era so completely in control of an attack. This was one of the greatest innings, in a technical sense, that I have umpired for, or seen. Don really enjoyed himself. His unconcealed delight in his art was often misconstrued by opposing teams, who mistook his smile for gloating. Don was never one to gloat. I always found him most modest. What human being would not have been delighted to have been able to bat as he could? It was just one of those quirks of fate that saw his partner 'Pud' Thurlow run out while scampering for the run that would have given Don his 300.'[1] Sir Donald Bradman himself in due course was to say that the finest innings he watched in Australia was Garfield Sobers' 254 for the Rest of the World v Australia at Melbourne in 1971–72. But he did not of course see his own innings at Adelaide 40 years before.

The poor South Africans, who had never once hit Bradman's stumps in eight attempts on the tour, were now completely battered to submission, and if – in those days of uncovered Test pitches – they had thoughts of a belated and final revenge on Bradman in the fifth Test at Melbourne, completed in less than two days' play on a treacherously difficult Melbourne 'glue-pot', they were to be denied even that. Bradman twisted an ankle when he jumped from a form in the dressing-room just before the start and caught one of his boot sprigs in some matting. 'Skylarking' it was, according to The Australian Cricketer. But Dr Ramsay Mailer, of the Melbourne Cricket Club, ordered him to rest for the day. Though in the Australian XI, he went down on the scorecard at number 11 as 'absent hurt'. The ankle responded to treatment, and he was able to field in the South Africans' second innings.

A. J. ('Sandy') Bell, the tall and powerful in-swinger from Cape Town and one of the best turf-wicket bowlers in South Africa, had an execrable time against Bradman in Australia. He took 23 wickets in the series and 51 altogether in Australia, but never dismissed Bradman in eight attempts. (He dismissed Woodfull and Ponsford seven times between them, four times in single figures.) He fielded right through Bradman's 1,190 runs against the tourists, and his nearest consolation was to induce a false stroke through the slips in the eighth innings, Bradman's 299*. Bell lost six pounds in weight in a single day's bowling while Bradman was scoring 200 on the first day of the series at Brisbane. There was a well-known occasion when Bell was sitting in A. G. Moyes' newspaper office in Sydney when Bradman walked in for a few moments and then left. Looking towards the receding Don, Bell exclaimed, 'That's the first time on this tour that I've seen his back.'

Did the South Africans develop a 'Bradman complex'? Steyn and van der Merwe, at least, denied it when they got back to South Africa but admitted

---

[1] In fact had Thurlow made his ground safely, Bradman's score would still have been on 299, though Hele is in almost universal company in believing that Bradman – who was certainly the striker of the relevant ball – would have got to 300. Thurlow was run out, having been *sent back* by Bradman. In his one and only Test innings, Thurlow had the distinction of being at the other end while Bradman passed R. E. Foster's 287 of 1903–04, the previous highest Test innings on Australian soil. In Thurlow's solitary Test he did not score a run, did not take a wicket and did not make a catch (despite what the score-sheet in *Wisden* records to the contrary).

that undoubtedly Bradman's scores had discouraged the team. He was certainly the biggest single factor in the tour. It was not only Bradman's talent but his confidence that was so marked. On the Saturday afternoon of the third Test at Melbourne, he sat padded up while Woodfull and Ponsford scored easily for the first wicket. 'If I can only get in before five o'clock, I'll make a hundred', remarked Bradman. He went in soon after tea and only narrowly failed to score a century in the session, being 97 not out, at a run a minute, at the close. Louis Duffus, who recorded this little story, said: 'Two or three more batsmen like Bradman in the world and the game of cricket would be ruined. As it was, the little fair-haired player with the nasal voice caused the game to be seen in a new perspective.' Little wonder the South Africans sought some consoling reason to account for Bradman's mastery. They formed the conclusion that he did not sweat.

Bradman was able to play in only half the Sheffield Shield matches of 1931–32, and scored only one century in five innings, with two ducks. Nevertheless New South Wales won the title, albeit very narrowly on the 'averages' principle, South Australia having the same number of points. Between the third and fourth Tests Bradman made 23 and 167 against Victoria at Sydney, hitting Darling in the second innings for 20 in an over. As a curiosity, he made 167 twice in his first-class career, and the two innings happened to come in successive matches. In this Shield match against Victoria, a newspaper claim was put forward that Ironmonger had the measure of Bradman after the left-hander had dismissed him cheaply in the first innings. The article came to Bradman's notice and was the subject of conversation in the New South Wales dressing-room. Bradman was not pleased by the insinuation – and his 167 in the second innings was quite insolent in its execution. Tim Wall, who had once dismissed Bradman for 5 and 2 in a Shield match, gave him a duck to end the season, just as Gilbert had given him one to begin it. (Bradman was *always* dismissed, incidentally, when playing against South Australia, against whom his eventual average of 63·45 and century ratio of four hundreds in 20 innings were infinitely lower than against any other State.) His Shield average in 1931–32 – only 42·60 – was the lowest of his career (excepting his final season, when he played only one innings of 30), and was in stark contrast to his two previous and two following seasons, in all of which he averaged well over 100. Nevertheless, in *all* first-class matches in 1931–32 Bradman averaged 116·91, which easily put him ahead of any other player in the country. After his seven centuries, the next best was three.

He also scored that summer – for the first and only time in his life – most runs in the season in first-grade cricket in Sydney. In three seasons altogether he topped the overall *averages* in Sydney grade cricket, but so often his first-class commitments prevented him having anywhere near the number of innings of others that even *his* prolificness could not compete with the runs of the regular players. His appearances for St George were mostly limited to the beginning and end of each season, and as each match, of course, was spread over two (normally successive) Saturdays, he had to be free of other cricket on *both* Saturdays, under the grade rules prevailing, in order to turn out. It was not possible for him to bat on one Saturday and for his side to field a substitute a week later. In 1931–32 Bradman headed both the averages and aggregate in Sydney cricket, with these figures for St George:

Innings	N.O.	Runs	H.S.	Av.	100s
8	1	785	246	112·14	3

Only one other man in the whole of the 16 clubs in the Sydney first-grade competition averaged even 50! He was L. R. Leabeater, of Central Cumberland, with an average of 62·50 from 14 innings. His form rewarded him with three Shield matches that season (his only season as a first-class player), appearing in the three games in which Bradman could not turn out.

Apart from Bradman's record 246 for St George that season, on 10 October, he scored two further hundreds for the side in April 1932 – 128 in 2½ hours v Paddington at Trumper Park, against some very good bowling and field placing, with one chance at 115 that was too hot to hold; and then, in the next match, a really wonderful 201 against Gordon, with Charlie Macartney fielding through it, before a record crowd of some 3,500 at Chatswood Oval who gave Bradman such an ovation when he left the field that he had to enlist the aid of other players to help him through the mass of admirers and autograph hunters who rushed the gate. Bert Oldfield stumped him that Saturday after Bradman had hit 2 sixes and 28 fours in his 201 in 171 minutes, with only one chance at 189. He scored his third and fourth fifties in 21 minutes and 24 minutes respectively (i.e. his second hundred in three-quarters of an hour) and scored 112 in the session after tea in well under an hour. The South Africans were not the only bowlers to suffer that season! His innings made him the first batsman ever to score two double-centuries in a season of Sydney first-grade cricket. Bradman's aggregate of 785 runs for St George established a new season's record for the club in first-grade matches, the previous record having lasted but a single season (R. J. Louden's 777 runs in 1930–31). It had of course also been Bob Louden's individual innings record that Bradman had surpassed earlier in his career for St George. By a pleasing coincidence, Bradman emerged at the head of the Sydney grade averages on 23 April 1932, which was, of course – appropriately enough in view of the club he was playing for – St George's Day! Bradman's brilliant scores for St George in 1931–32 were achieved, by the way, under the larger wicket which was introduced to grade cricket in Sydney for the first time that season, to follow the practice already in use in Shield matches. There was some small opposition by club cricketers in Sydney to the bigger stumps – but so far as Bradman was concerned, he merely continued to hit the ball in the middle of the bat.

At the end of that summer Don Bradman, at the age of 23, took the biggest, and most satisfying, step of his domestic life when he got married. His bride was Miss Jessie Menzies, a young and pretty brunette, with vivacious blue eyes and wavy hair, who then worked in a Sydney bank, the daughter of Mr and Mrs James Menzies, of Mittagong. Her father was a bank manager. Don Bradman had known her for most of his life and they had been playmates together as schoolchildren in Bowral. As a child she used to stay with the Bradman family in Bowral, and she had watched some of Don's youthful batting feats. She left for Sydney first (with her family) and when Don Bradman followed, the romance ripened. Her father and his mother had been in kindergarten together, and Don Bradman and Jessie Menzies had themselves attended the same school together, but in different classes, Bradman being about 15 months older. (Jessie Menzies had won a gold medal for needlework at Bowral Intermediate High School in 1924.) Like Don Bradman himself, Jessie Menzies was a first-class motorist and was fond of tennis and music – but she did not think cricket a woman's game. Their engagement was announced in the middle of November 1931, where-upon any excuse was found by people to visit the Commonwealth Bank in Sydney to catch a glimpse of the future Mrs Bradman, while endless tele-grams arrived. Her platinum engagement ring, incidentally (set with a large diamond surrounded by smaller ones), had been brought by Bradman from England a year before. The rumour that had linked Bradman's name with a prospective bride in England in 1930 had therefore been so much hogwash. Don Bradman, looking very spruce, and Jessie Menzies, looking very beautiful, were married on 30 April 1932 at St Paul's Church, Burwood, Sydney. The ceremony was performed by the Rev. Canon Ernest Selwyn Hughes, Canon of St Paul's Cathedral, Melbourne, and Vice-President of the Victorian Cricket Association, who travelled from Melbourne to Sydney, and while there took the opportunity of handing over physical possession of the Sheffield Shield to the new holders.[1] Despite Bradman's wish for a quiet wedding, a large crowd naturally congregated outside the church, and the barriers which had been especially erected were broken down by sightseers straining to see the bridal pair. There were many cricketers at the wedding reception, and a cricketing baritone sang to the guests – Bob Nicholson, who had been one of the suffering bowlers during Bradman's devastating 256 at Blackheath, and who later joined the New York Metropolitan Opera House.

'Thus began', said Don Bradman, 'the best partnership of my life.' As a source of inspiration and guidance, Mrs Bradman was to mean a tremend-ous deal to her husband in the years ahead, especially during the many difficult times in the 1930s, when her husband had to combat ill-health as well as detractors. His marriage became a turning point in his career, when

---

[1] Canon Hughes (1860–1942) was a notable lover of cricket who rendered distinguished service to the V.C.A. As first a Vice-President and then President from 1932, he naturally saw many of Don Bradman's finest innings on the Melbourne Cricket Ground. He had played cricket as a young man for East Melbourne and – as an Essendon footballer too – became known as 'the sporting parson'. From 1911 he was President of the East Melbourne (later Hawthorn–East Melbourne) Cricket Club. Don Bradman always held him in the highest regard.

for the first time his life could be filled with something other than cricket. Don Bradman may have enjoyed the pedestal on which cricket had put him, but he was only too alive also to the strain imposed on him as a public idol. The wisdom that his wife offered made him in turn acquire a more mature and philosophic outlook on life. When Mrs Bradman was interviewed in 1933 she made the rather startling statement that cricket was never mentioned in their home. 'That's why we never get tired of it', she added. When Don Bradman, in December 1947, received a presentation at Sydney to mark his 100th hundred in the game, he heard Sydney Smith, jnr, the President of the New South Wales Cricket Association, speak in glowing terms of Mrs Bradman. Don Bradman himself said in reply: 'There have been times when without her I would have found it impossible to carry on.' That was a heartfelt tribute to a most successful marriage, and Lady Bradman remains a source of great strength and wisdom to the present day. Sir Donald is on record as having called his wife: 'My best critic and my best friend.'

Marital status meant a change of home, and Don Bradman said a most grateful thank you to Mr and Mrs Frank Cush in Rockdale after three years of enjoying their residence as his Sydney home. He moved with his wife further north in Sydney, to Bayview Street, North Sydney, across the magnificent new Sydney Harbour Bridge, officially opened on 19 March 1932, by the Premier, Mr Lang, amid pageantry without parallel in Sydney's history. The proud residents of Sydney could now boast of 'our bridge and our Bradman' – the two ultimate highlights they could display to visitors – and many an irreverent parody of the Lord's Prayer was created which might begin:

> Our harbour which art in Heaven,
> Sydney be its name,
> Our bridge be done in 1930 or 1931
> Give us this day our Don Bradman –

and which might end:

> For ours is the harbour, the bridge and the Bradman,
> For ever and ever.

Canon Hughes might not have approved!

It may be as well to pause at this point and consider exactly what sort of phenomenon Bradman was in the world of cricket in April 1932. Many others must have paused for reflection around that time, too – not least England's captain, D. R. Jardine, who in the first week of July was to be named M.C.C.'s captain of the forthcoming tour of Australia. Jardine had, of course, been appointed England captain in 1931: he had plenty of time to ponder on the menace that was Bradman and had no few reminders of it in the Australian summer of '31–32. To say that Bradman was head and shoulders above every other batsman of his period was to recognise his extraordinary skill but not explain it. He was *so far* above all others that comparisons quickly became unreal. He was virtually a complete batting side in himself, and if, in theory, his ten colleagues did not score a single run, the side's total would still be a good enough one simply from Bradman's contribution. If Australia had been all out for 226 (Bradman's score) in the first Test against South Africa at Brisbane, they would not have won by an innings but would have been in no jeopardy at all. Whereas all other batsmen in the world seemed to *work* for their runs, Bradman just stood there – or rather moved his feet with lightning speed – and pulverised any attack. The prognostications of those who saw him score 236 at Worcester in 1930 had been justified with a vengeance. Somebody who watched that innings, the first played by Bradman on an English pitch, said of him 'That philosophic young man, it seems, could go and get a century in Iceland or in the Sahara, were cricket played there, for all the difference that a change of conditions makes to him.' 'Plum' Warner said the tramlines of Vauxhall Bridge Road would not be a bar to a Bradman hundred.

In all matches in Australia in 1931–32 Bradman's aggregate soared well beyond 3,000, at an average of over 120, with at least 16 centuries, six of them double-centuries. His very presence was all but a guarantee against defeat. His occasional failures emphasised he was no machine – a derogatory dismissal of someone with superb individual powers. To find the right adjectives to describe his skill and his impact is no more easy today in the quietude of one's home than it was in the hurriedness of the press-boxes of the early '30s. The adjectives that were applied to all others seemed woefully tepid for Bradman. The other brilliant batsmen in the land seemed more often to be brilliantly erratic. Bradman's consistency was terrifying to any potential opponent. He was master of all occasions, whether in a picnic match at Callan Park or in a Test match at the M.C.G. His technical skill and his temperament were perfectly in harness. His attitude of mind almost certainly was responsible for some portion of his success, just as psychology in other great athletes has put them above their fellows. Bradman's temperament rarely allowed him to adopt a subservient role at the crease. The times he got off the mark first ball (most frequently with a single) make an uncannily long list, and it must be very doubtful indeed whether these occasions can be matched by any other player in history, even those with over 1,000 innings. R. W. E. Wilmot, the old Melbourne University blue and Melbourne journalist, wrote this of Bradman's temperament in September 1932:

> The best illustration of temperament I know is the case of Don Bradman. In him it is developed to the nth degree. It possesses him, radiates from him, raises him above his fellows in the most remarkable way. If Bradman's batting be examined carefully, studied in the light of the accepted standards, much can be found that is not usually associated with a first-class batsman. He does not always play with a straight bat; some of his strokes are almost crude; but he rises superior to these defects; he confounds his critics and exasperates bowlers. For four years he scored centuries with a regularity which had almost become a habit, as he passed on to his second, his third, and even his fourth 100, in a manner which was altogether amazing.

Don Bradman's relentless march through cricket history – the joy of New South Welshmen and of all Australians – was soon to cause a furrow on the brow of D. R. Jardine, if it had not done so already. But before the storm, there was the calm: the calm of an interlude – an American interlude.

During the English summer months of 1932 Don Bradman visited Canada and the United States with a strong Australian side (that would have been stronger still had not Ponsford declined an invitation) gathered together by Arthur Mailey, who managed the side and bowled far too guilefully for North American cricketers, and captained by V. Y. Richardson.[1] A proposal that the team should also visit Jamaica fell through, and it so happened that Bradman never played on a West Indian wicket. A match was also due to be played at Suva, in the Fiji Islands, on 3 June, but rain ruled out play. Mailey had hoped for two games in Philadelphia (where cricket, alas, had sadly fallen away) and perhaps in retrospect it was as well they were not arranged.

The major part of the tour was in Canada, and the promoters there stipulated that Bradman had to be one of the players: on his ability to form one of the team the whole tour depended. Mailey made this plain to Bradman and it was not difficult to understand the point of view of the promoters. Whatever difficulties they might encounter in attracting reasonable audiences to watch the Australians would be multiplied tenfold in the absence of Bradman. For his own part Bradman had some difficulty in obtaining leave of absence from his employers – this was, after all, to be a goodwill tour of relatively minor importance. Most of the negotiations, moreover, took place in the few weeks before Bradman's marriage, and he did not look forward particularly to his married life starting with an almost immediate separation on a tour abroad. Bradman did accept the invitation to tour, but in turn made it a condition of acceptance that he took his wife with him. Exactly 26 days after they were married, Mr and Mrs Bradman sailed from Sydney for North America in the *Niagara* by way of a unique form of honeymoon. Mrs Bradman was the only woman who travelled with the party – and she emerged as the charming life and soul of it. She acted as hostess for the team when it entertained, went with the team to all functions, and in fact 'Jessie' (as she was known to the team) proved the most popular member of the party.

It is amazing to consider that although Mailey arranged the tour privately with North American promoters, the Australian Board of Control at once laid down a stringent set of conditions which had to be accepted before the tour could take place. The power of the Australian Board in the 1930s was

---

[1] The team, for a strenuous tour of 51 matches, was courageously limited to 12 players, namely V. Y. Richardson (captain), A. A. Mailey (organiser–player–manager), D. G. Bradman, P. H. Carney, H. Carter (aged 54, still keeping wicket), L. O'B. Fleetwood-Smith, W. F. Ives, A. F. Kippax, S. J. McCabe, R. N. Nutt, E. F. Rofe and E. K. Tolhurst (with Dr Rowley Pope and his many bags!). All except Carney (a Melbourne cricketer) and Rofe (Manly) were Sheffield Shield players. C. V. Grimmett was originally named as a member of the team, but he did not go. Subject only to Hanson Carter, Bradman was the *smallest* member of the touring side!

quite extraordinary (as Don Bradman had already discovered, and was to discover further in the future). For this private tour – as was to be the case also with Frank Tarrant's private tour to India in 1935–36, arranged for the Maharaja of Patiala – the Board had very nearly as much to say as for an official tour under their aegis, and they would in all probability have banned the presence of Bradman's wife (as they in fact banned other wives) had they not realised that Bradman's absence would mean the cancellation of the entire tour and the subsequent loss of profit that the Board astonishingly stipulated for itself. As it was, the Board laid down virtually all the conditions – e.g. a maximum of six Test players, distribution of profits to charity, payment of players, date of return, and so on. Why private teams allowed themselves to be so utterly dictated to by the Board is explicable only by the undesirable fate that players knew must befall them if they fell foul of the Board. For its own part the Board could (as it could so often) quote authority – its own resolution of 15 September 1927, when it was laid down that no team containing first-class cricketers coming under the jurisdiction of any State association could privately visit any country outside Australia without the Board's consent. Accordingly the following three major conditions specified by the Board for Mailey's tour – *a private tour* – will be of special interest:

i   The Board had to approve the personnel of the team and all the conditions under which the players were to go.
ii The Board had to be furnished with full and detailed accounts of all receipts and expenditure.
iii Out of the profits, the players might receive a sum not exceeding £100. All profits above that amount were to be distributed by the Board as it thought fit.

Three of the team actually paid their own expenses, though Bradman, in common with the other leading players, naturally had his expenses paid. The journey across the Pacific Ocean was via Auckland, Suva and Honolulu, the three stops before reaching Vancouver Island, British Columbia, on 16 June 1932. The tour began next day and Bradman – for him – began moderately enough with scores of 60 and 94 against a Cowichan XVIII at Duncan and XV of Vancouver Island at Victoria respectively. Within a few days he had really announced himself with 110 (retired) v a British Columbia all-mainland XI and 180 (in two hours) against a selected mainland XV at Vancouver.

None of the matches in either Canada or the United States was, of course, first-class, and more than half were against odds, but Bradman, as usual, had an outstanding tour. In 51 innings (14 not outs) spread over ten weeks, from mid-June to the end of August, he amassed 3,782 runs at an average of 102·21, scoring 15 centuries in Canada and a further three in the United States. (His 18 centuries on the tour quite overshadowed the next best – eight by McCabe and four by Kippax.) In exactly 60 days from the start of the tour – including many days on which there was no cricket – Bradman reached an aggregate of 3,000 runs, an extraordinary performance in any class of cricket. He normally batted in his usual position of number three, but often opened as well, and there were naturally some remarkable feats from his bat. Against XVIII of Western Ontario at Guelph on 4 July, going in soon after the start of the innings when one of the openers was out for 1, he played an innings of 260 before he was caught and bowled by a player named Kelly: this remains the highest score ever made in Canada, and four days later Bradman scored 200 not out against XV of Montreal at Quebec. The team played two matches in Ottawa, on the beautiful Rideau Hall grounds (the residence of the Governor-General of Canada, then Lord Bessborough, great-nephew of one of the founders of I Zingari), and Bradman scored hundreds in both. At one stage at the beginning of August he scored four centuries on successive days, the start of a spell which brought him ten centuries in 16 innings. One of them was a score of 159 not out against a selected Edmonton XVIII, the result of unmerciful flogging of the bowling which included 50 in his first 15 minutes. On the very first day of the tour, in the match against a Cowichan XVIII at Duncan, Bradman and Richardson at one stage put on 50 in 7 minutes, and a whirlwind partnership with E. K. Tolhurst in San Francisco produced 168 in 34 minutes. Bradman's 18 centuries in 51 innings, be it noted, was almost exactly the ratio of hundreds that he scored in first-class cricket over his career.

With the ball Bradman took 26 wickets on the entire tour in only 52 overs – an astonishing rate of striking. On the second day of the tour he took six wickets in one eight-ball over against XV of Vancouver Island on matting at Victoria, his wickets coming with the first, second, fourth, fifth, seventh and eighth balls – thus adroitly avoiding the hat-trick![1] When this match ended the home side's second innings stood at 99 for seven – all seven taken by Bradman (who had also scored 94). Towards the end of the tour, when the team returned to British Columbia, Bradman took six for 25 against a team of British Columbia colts at Vancouver, in addition to scoring 125 not out. When everything was totted up, the promoters who insisted on Bradman's presence could have found little cause for complaint.

Bradman himself, needless to say, was the centre of attraction wherever the tourists went. His record-breaking feats over the previous two years or so had filtered through to the sports pages of some American papers, where cricket had never previously been featured. He had become an object of curiosity there, if nothing else. Pressmen were always striving to interview him and they took the precaution of arranging to meet Bradman aboard the tourists' train several miles out of New York, as they feared Bradman would be lost – and likewise their coveted interviews – in the crush and excitement at Grand Central Station.

One extraordinary performance by Bradman on the tour does not seem to

---

[1] Cables at the time alleged that Bradman's six wickets were taken with consecutive balls, but this was not the case.

12 Don Bradman, left, shakes hands with 'Babe' Ruth, the celebrated baseball star, at the Yankee Stadium, New York, during the Australian cricketers' tour of North America in 1932.

13 Don Bradman and his wife at Wellington, New Zealand, on their way home to Sydney in October 1932 after the private tour of Canada and the United States with Arthur Mailey's side. At some stages on this tour Bradman was scoring at the rate of more than 400 runs a week.

14 Don Bradman at Marrickville Oval, Sydney, in December 1933, as 'father' to the 'Sun-Palmer' colts. The boys in the above picture who gained the greatest renown are Len Livingston, kneeling, immediately in front of Bradman, and Keith Carmody, in cap, beside Bradman.

W. A. Brown   A. G. Chipperfield   C. J. Hill

R. Rowe   D. G. Bradman

15 New South Wales v Victoria, January 1934 – Bradman's farewell match for his native NSW. Thereafter he played in Sydney as a visitor from his new State of South Australia. In the above match he said goodbye in the most devastating manner, hitting four huge sixes in an innings of 128 in only 96 minutes.

...k   W. J. O'Reilly   O. W. Bill   W. A. Oldfield

J. H. Fingleton   H. C. Chilvers

16 D. G. Bradman, right, and S. J. McCabe at the start of the second day's play against Worcestershire at New Road in 1934. Bradman took his overnight score of 112 to 206 that morning.

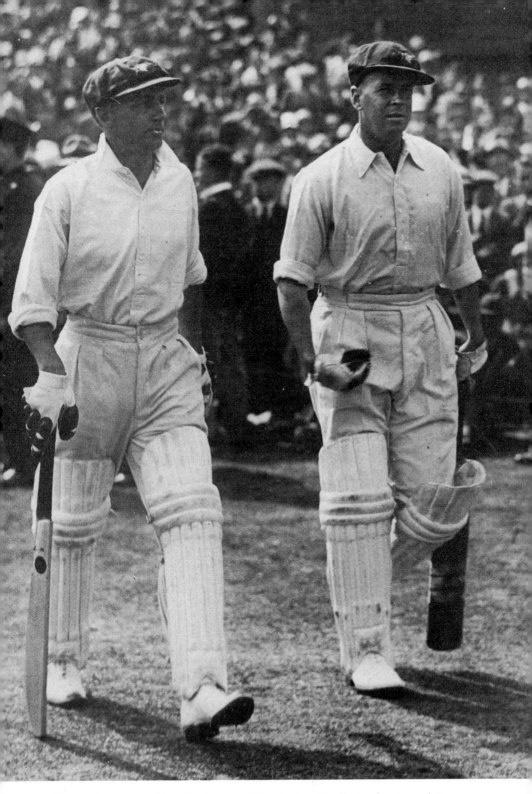

17 The mighty partnership – Bradman and Ponsford at Headingley in 1934, when they shared a stand of 388. They remain the only Australians in history to score a quadruple-century in first-class cricket.

18 One of the Headingley triumphs – Don Bradman returns after his innings of
304 against England in 1934. It was his second triple-century in successive Test
innings at Leeds.

have been previously recorded. It did not take place in a match proper, but in an exhibition put on by Bradman, at his own request, after the second of two matches against a picked California team in August at the capacious Kezar Stadium in San Francisco (normally used for American football, attended by huge crowds – though only a handful came for the cricket). Bradman himself had just scored there his 17th century of the tour, a whirl-wind 122 which was his ninth century in his last 14 innings (giving him an average over those 14 innings of 204·28!). He requested that he should be bowled against with a field consisting of a wicketkeeper, three slips and a deep third man, plus of course the bowler. Bradman stated that he would allow the ball to hit his glove and then on to his bat while he would specify the intended direction of the ball as he played it – either between the 'keeper and first slip, first slip and second slip, or second and third slips. The ball was first dipped in whitewash and allowed to dry, in order to produce a white ball which would leave a mark on the glove and bat. On a matting pitch, the local bowlers bowled a good length outside the off stump, mainly Arthur Trenholm, an Englishman, who bowled medium-pace, and Alan V. Percival, also an Englishman (indeed a Yorkshireman), who has kindly related this episode, and who also bowled medium-pace. (Percival, in fact, earlier in the day had had the distinction of bowling Alan Kippax for a duck.) Bradman unerringly for some 15 minutes nominated where he would play the ball, and quite astonished the few participants in this unusual exercise. Bradman alone out of the entire Australian party gave this exhibi-tion: and it is almost certain that only he could have possessed the skill to have done so.

The true merit of the performances in North America cannot, of course, be readily judged, for a great many of the matches were of a very minor importance and seldom approached the standard of cricket to which Bradman was accustomed. But the presence of Bradman and other Australian stars gave North American cricket centres a series of experiences that are still spoken of with reverence and gusto to this day.

Bradman saw the visit as 'one of the sporting features of the year' in America, as he put it when the side returned to Sydney on 23 September in the *Monowai* from San Francisco, via New Zealand. The following night Bradman gave a broadcast address on radio 2UE describing the highlights of the whirlwind tour and revealing all the marvellous statistics, not least being the incredible all-round performance of McCabe, who scored 2,361 runs (av. 54·90) and took 189 wickets at only 6 apiece. Fleetwood-Smith (aged 22) and Arthur Mailey (aged 46) both exceeded 200 wickets. The man under whom Bradman had played most of his cricket for St George, W. F. ('Big Bill') Ives, took 92 wickets at 7·51. The end of the tour had been at Hollywood, where Bradman played against Boris Karloff ('They hid me in the slips'), C. Aubrey Smith (in his 70th year), H. B. Warner, Desmond Roberts, Murray Kinnell and Claude King. In one match, for 17 British-born film stars, Aubrey Smith (probably the oldest player and certainly the only Test player the Australians encountered on the tour) made top score of 24 and fielded through a half-century (52) by Bradman. Bradman rounded the tour off with an undefeated 83 against 20 of Hollywood which raised his average beyond the 100 mark. Had he not played in that final match it would have been only 99·97! He also visited the Metro-Goldwyn-Mayer studios and met, and was photographed with, stars like Jean Harlow, Clark Gable, Mary Astor and Myrna Loy. An evening at dinner was spent with Leslie Howard and his wife.

Altogether, for all the fun, the tour had inevitably been something of a strain, even for a fit man like Bradman. Well over 6,000 miles were travelled (excluding the sea journeys) and 51 matches played – and Bradman played in 49 of them. From 29 June to 30 July alone, the team played on 26 out of 32 consecutive days, Bradman having only one of those days off. There were banquets and receptions, good hotels and poor hotels, good conditions at grounds and occasionally bad conditions, and of course an almost ceaseless programme of matches. Bradman's fame had preceded him, and he was variously called 'the antipodean slugger' and 'the Babe Ruth of cricket'. He actually met 'Babe' Ruth, then nursing an injury, in New York at a baseball game at the Yankee Stadium – known as 'the House that Ruth Built' – but neither ever saw the other play his respective sport.[1] An attempt was made to get Ruth to play against the Australians for one of the selected New York sides, but his injury prevented it.

Between September 1931 and August 1932, Don Bradman actually scored the staggering number of well over 7,000 runs at an average of over 100. Most of these were obtained in non-first-class cricket, but such an aggregate is by no means a disrespectful one for a whole *career*, let alone a 12-month period. No cricketer at any time can surely have rivalled such a truly mammoth accumulation of runs in so short a time.

While America was celebrating Independence Day on the 4th of July, two other independent acts were happening elsewhere that seemed strangely to be symbolic in their coinciding. Don Bradman was creating a batting record (with his 260, the highest innings on Canadian soil); and Douglas Jardine was named as captain to lead the England side in Australia that winter. Neither man that day knew of the other's distinction. But they were to be brought together in a fearful confrontation before very long that was to shake the very foundations of cricket's councils.

---

[1] 'Babe' Ruth – actually George Herman Ruth (1895–1948) – was supposed to have been monumentally ignorant of cricket, allegedly not knowing whether the ball was struck with the flat or the humped side of the bat. But he was one of the world's experts at earning money. Compared to the Australian Board's maximum of £100 allowed to any player on the North American tour – and the ten shillings a day Bradman had received for touring Queensland the year before! – Ruth in 1930 and 1931 earned $75,000 a season under contract and $70,000 in 1932, his total earnings being nearer $80,000 with 'win' money and endorsements. But Bradman said he would dearly love to have seen him face Fleetwood-Smith! (Even in the Test matches against South Africa in 1931–32, the Australian players had received no more than £25 per match – and this indeed had been reduced from the £30 per match they had been paid against the West Indies in 1930–31.)

6 Under Fire

Three possessions lie nearest to the true Sydneyite's heart – 'our 'arbour, our bridge, our Bradman' – and maybe I have placed the order wrong. When there is cricket about Bradman becomes number one.

Bruce Harris in 1933

At the approach of the 1932–33 series in Australia, it was clear that Bradman was a better player than ever. He had, if anything, more strokes than before – Jack Hobbs confirmed that by the end of the tour – and he had more experience and the confidence that comes from having had two superlatively successful home seasons against Test opposition. There was also the shining memory of his last encounter with English bowling – in 1930.

Volumes – a library shelf of them – have already been written on the acrimony of 1932–33. Test cricket between England and Australia was never the same game for the participants thereafter. If it became less enjoyable to play, the reasons made that explicable enough. England won a series but – as anticipated by Rockley Wilson, Jardine's cricket master at Winchester – all but lost an empire.

Without Bradman there would have been no bodyline. Without Jardine there would have been no bodyline. The historical coinciding of the relentless batsmanship of the one and the relentless captaincy of the other touched off a formula that no alchemist could have devised. The term 'bodyline bowling', coined by the Australian press and used by the Australian Board in its initial cable to the M.C.C., was an altogether more aggressive term than 'leg-theory bowling'. The two styles were only very distant cousins. Leg-theory was to bodyline as a lizard is to an alligator. Leg-theory was nothing new. It had been bowled occasionally, as by Warwick Armstrong in 1905, or frequently, as by Jaques of Hampshire and Frank Foster of Warwickshire before the war and Fred Root after it. It was dull and made for dull play, designed of course to restrict a batsman's strokes to the leg. Just as there was nothing in the laws to prevent leg-theory, so there was nothing to prevent bodyline.

It was the double-hundreds of Bradman that must have been a nightmare on Jardine's horizon as he contemplated his first tour abroad as captain of England. In prime form Bradman could annihilate any attack in the world. In October 1932 Hanson Carter, the old Australian 'keeper who had been with Bradman on the North American tour, was of the firm view that Bradman had improved since 1930 and was placing the ball more skilfully. If he was an improved player – and why should he not be? – he was no more than reaping the benefit, as countless players had done before him, of his years in the game between the ages of 21 and 24. The Australian public by then certainly saw him as a greater attraction than ever. To them Bradman was king, to be hero-worshipped as no games-player had ever been idolised before in Australia.

It came then as a shock to Australians to learn in September 1932, with Jardine's team still on the *Orontes* with a fortnight's sailing time yet to Colombo, that Bradman might not play against England in the Tests of 1932–33. The news hit Australia like a bombshell and predictably caused a sensation in cricket circles. It arose out of a further clash with the Australian Board of Control – a determined body, as Bradman was a determined man.

In October 1931 Bradman had intimated his willingness to enter into his two-year contract with the three Sydney business organisations, which included of course a daily newspaper. It was known then that Bradman's contributing to a Sydney paper (the *Sun*) would fall foul of the Board of Control's regulations, for at the Board's meeting on 11 September 1931, the player-writer issue was fully discussed and the Board's publicly announced attitude was made unambiguously clear. The Board said then that it would not approve the selection of any player for any Australian Test side who, during the relevant cricket season, wrote or contributed any article for the Press which, in the opinion of the Board, commented upon play in any first-class match or upon the prospects of selection of any cricketer for such match. (This of course left precious little scope for any worthwhile writing on the current scene if the Board's strictures were to be avoided.) The one proviso that the Board laid down was that, when a cricketer's *sole occupation* was journalism, such a player would, after first having obtained written permission from the Board chairman, be allowed to publish articles commenting on the play in first-class matches. It is true that all this related to the 1931–32 series with South Africa, but on 23 September 1932 – the day Bradman arrived back in Sydney from North America – the Board reaffirmed its attitude on player-writers and again adopted a resolution that the only players who might contribute to newspapers were those solely engaged in journalism. In fact for the Tests of 1932–33 the Board's resolution was practically identical with that of 1931–32. The Board's policy on this issue had actually not been altered during the previous four years.

Bradman, of course, was only partly employed in journalism, so was directly affected by the ruling. But the Board's resolution was not new, and Bradman must have known of it (for it was certainly in the Sydney papers) before he signed his contract in 1931. That contract contained no provision for releasing Bradman from his writing obligations to comply with any rulings of the Board.

On his return to Sydney, Bradman made it plain that he was prepared to remain loyal to his contract even at the cost of giving up cricket. 'If the Board has said its last word, I shall not be available for the Test matches', Bradman declared on 23 September. 'I have signed a contract to write newspaper articles, and I intend to carry it out. I must earn my living, and if cricket interferes with my living then I must give up cricket.' This was quite some first day back on Australian soil!

With Bradman's fame as it was, such a statement all but stunned Australia. England, for their part, could not have taken much pride had they beaten Australia less her star performer. 'Bradman Bombshell' shouted the lunch-time newspaper posters in London when the news first broke, and naturally the story was on every front page. While all were hoping it would prove a storm in an administrative teacup, the controversy continued to rage more fiercely than ever. Bradman and his newspaper took care that he should not that season actually begin writing articles, the cessation of which might disappoint the public, and accordingly he did not jeopardise his place in the Combined XI side to meet M.C.C. in Perth. With the matter still unresolved, and with Bradman still carefully refraining from doing any writing, he was named also in the Australian XI to meet M.C.C. in Melbourne, and those who knew Bradman best were saying he was very unlikely to write without the necessary permission. Ponsford, when he was on the staff of the Melbourne *Herald*, had not been allowed by the Board to comment on the 1928-29 Tests, though his criticisms of Chapman's side duly appeared before the arrival of the team, and – especially his remarks on Larwood – caused a certain ill-feeling. (In September 1932 Ponsford, having left the Melbourne *Herald*, his contract having expired in March that year, became employed as pavilion clerk by the Melbourne Cricket Club.) In any event, it was overwhelmingly unlikely that the Board would relent in the case of Bradman, for their repugnance towards the player-writer was deep-rooted and many Board members had never forgotten the distasteful days of 1920-21, when the writings of P. G. H. Fender and Rockley Wilson that were cabled to England – and duly cabled back to Australia – caused such unpleasantness and even bitterness. On the M.C.C. tour of 1928-29 not only Ponsford's but also Hendry's printed remarks had caused annoyance among the English team. As many as four of the Australian side in the first Test at Brisbane on that tour had forecast in the press the composition of their own side, and each had included his own name and left out others who were eventually chosen. It may not be widely known that in Brisbane on that occasion there were quarrels among the Australians, in one case leading to blows. One member of the side left the hotel in which the rest of the team were staying. This was, of course, Don Bradman's debut in Test cricket – and he was indeed one of the victims of this press criticism. Ponsford, for example, for one, omitted the name of Bradman from his pre-Test team. In the dressing-room certain members remained aloof from others, and Don Bradman, young and inexperienced as he was, could not have failed to notice this. It did little for team spirit. Australia lost by a record margin. There was also the Board's fine and vote of censure against Bradman himself for his writings in England in 1930. The whole principle of the player-writer was repellent to the Australian Board and to reverse that principle for an individual would in addition have meant paying the price of complete loss of authority. The power of the Australian Board in the 1930s was not to be tampered with. The game was *always* greater than the individual.

Bradman in 1932 saw nothing wrong with the player-writer creature. That, it might be said, was natural enough in view of his contract. However, his view is still the same today. In 1975 he wrote: 'Though I am aware that there are very mixed feelings about current players writing in the press, some of the most reasoned, best informed and best expressed comments in 1974–75 came from a current player.' (Sir Donald probably had in mind Ian Chappell's writings for the Melbourne *Age*, composed with much assistance from a 'ghost': but whoever he had in mind, his attitude is clear.)

When the fresh Board v Bradman controversy broke in 1932, Bradman formally applied to the Board for permission to write about the forthcoming Tests, claiming at the same time the right to earn his living by writing. The situation had some strange elements. The circumstances which led to Bradman's contract were known to the Board – indeed the whole affair was public knowledge, and could hardly have been otherwise – and the Board members must have given as substantial a sigh of relief as the cricketing populace of Australia when the Accrington overtures were rejected in 1931. The means of their rejection took the form of the Bradman contract. The Board remained silent, content for the time being that Bradman was safely harboured within Australia – but knowing well enough the prickly hazards that would inescapably emerge. The Board was content to rest on its powers, knowing the iron control it could exercise. If matters were to be brought to a somewhat disagreeable public pass, the Board would then stir itself into activity.

The Board indeed refused to acknowledge that there was any sort of dispute at all. It would only arise, they said, if Bradman began writing. But this was nothing more than brinkmanship diplomacy. There *was* a dispute and it was real enough: and no one can have been more conscious than the members of the Board that the forthcoming Tests without Bradman would be the most classic case they were ever likely to encounter of *Hamlet* without the Prince. All sorts of rumours flew about – that Bradman had formally told the Board he would not be writing for the press, that the Board and Bradman had come to a decision allowing Bradman to play in the Tests *and* to write for the press – but they remained rumours and nothing more. The M.C.C. team, still on the *Orontes*, looked on it as a 'publicity stunt'. Dr Robertson, the Board chairman, announced at the beginning of October that the Board had asked Bradman for an assurance that he was employed solely as a journalist, and Bradman had not yet given that assurance. Of course he had not given it: he *could* not.

If a soothsayer were able at that point to positively state with certainty that Bradman *would not* be playing in the first Test against England, the conclusion must only have been that the player-writer impasse was to triumph, at least temporarily. That was not in fact to be so, although Bradman did *not* play in the first Test. Ironically he was kept out not by the administrators but by illness.

All this furore raged before Bradman had even taken the field in the new season. But if his scores are any indication of his state of mind, he was not at all perturbed – for he promptly began in classic Bradmanesque style with three hundreds in his first three innings! They were not first-class matches, to be sure, but that was only because the first-class programme had not yet begun. He scored 108* in his first Sydney grade innings of the season, for St George v Gordon, reaching his century in only 64 minutes; 105* in exactly two hours for St George v Mosman in his second grade innings of the season; and then a most brilliant 145 in one of the New South Wales trial matches for his own team v H. S. B. Love's team at the Sydney Cricket Ground No. 1, when he reached 50 in an hour, scored his second 50 in 28 minutes (despite a slow outfield) and his final 145 (2 sixes, 23 fours) in 105 minutes before he threw his wicket away. Against the not inconsiderable bowling on display to assist the New South Wales selectors, he actually scored his last 95 runs in 45 minutes. How could Australia really contrive to do without him? It should be remembered that these innings followed his great run-accumulation in North America, when at some stages he was scoring at the rate of more than 400 runs a week. If some cricketers might have suffered the reaction of going stale after such an exercise, that was not to be the lot of Bradman.

Whether Douglas Jardine heard of these scores – the third of them was made three days before the M.C.C. docked at Fremantle – is not certain, though with his special gift for sniffing out detail, it is not at all unlikely. But he had certain plans for Mr Bradman most methodically hatched in his mind. It is doubtful if he paid much attention to the speculation that appeared in *The People* in London on 2 October:

> An Australian Test team without Bradman is almost inconceivable. If the deadlock is not overcome England will battle for the Ashes in almost farcical circumstances. Our selectors puzzled their brains to select a side sufficiently strong in bowlers to cause trouble to the 'bogey batsman'. It now appears that the bogey man has been laid with never a ball bowled.

Things were not going to be as easy as this. Indeed, it is certain that Jardine would not have *chosen* them to be as easy as this.

During the closing days of September, virtually the whole of the major Australian press – and a good many papers in Fleet Street too – were trying to get in touch with Bradman for *some* sort of quote on the administrative predicament. He was not able to be contacted on the telephone and the local police stated that he had been so inundated with inquiries that he had left his home for an 'unknown destination'. On 3 October matters took a fresh twist when a big Australian company offered to buy Bradman's newspaper contract, pay him the same fee as he would receive for writing, and allow him to concentrate on cricket. The newspaper offered to release him: but Bradman refused both offers.

The player-writer crisis removed itself from the front pages – but was not an inch nearer being solved. The New South Wales Cricket Association refused to involve itself in the dilemma. It was a matter for the Board. One of the Board's members was interviewed in Melbourne in the second week of October and with typical forthrightness – though with absolute accuracy – said: 'If Bradman wants to write about the game at all his first duty is to ask the chairman for permission. He has done that, and as he could not say he was a full-time journalist, permission could not be given. Until he does write he is in the same position as the other players.' In other words, he was still eligible for selection for all sides – including Australia's Test sides.

Maurice Tate – as ever – was ready with a comment on Don Bradman. He did not travel with the rest of the side to Australia, leaving late after recovering from a nervous breakdown. On the day before he left, he was telephoned at his Brighton home by an Australian newspaperman, whom he told: 'So far as I am concerned, I am willing to bet Don Bradman plays in the first Test match and will probably make a hundred. I hope to knock his "castle" over several times during the next few months.' Poor Tate, through no fault of his own, was wrong again: and the Bradman 'castle' fell to him only once that Australian summer. When the rest of the English team stepped off the *Orontes* on 18 October, the serious part of 1932–33 could be said to be starting. That night P. F. Warner made a broadcast from Perth – which was relayed to Sydney – in which he said he did not intend to discuss the Bradman dispute, but added: 'All I would say is that cricket as a game would lose much if Mr Bradman should not play. I sincerely hope he will.'

Bradman's status in the eyes of the Australian public at this point was probably greater than at any other moment in history. It needed no great cricket credentials to appreciate what he could do. Every time he stepped on the field he was liable to reduce his opponents to impotence. Bowlers in Sydney, at least, virtually gave up trying to keep him quiet – and simply waited for the moment he was prepared to give his wicket away. Bradman seemed immune from the ordinary laws of batsmanship, in which a generous ration of failure was intermingled with success. Provided he was not caught on a sticky wicket, he could all but do just as he chose – and do it ruthlessly, quickly, and almost clinically. He knew no fear or nervousness. Small occasions and great occasions had no terrors for him. President Wilson, when he was formulating American policy, had once said of himself that he had 'a single-track mind with no sidings', and Don Bradman could claim precisely that when he was at the crease. A foolish effort was even made at that time to induce Bradman to travel from one end of Australia to the other and back again, purely as a drawcard – turning him into some sort of circus exhibit – a folly duly condemned by Dr E. P. Barbour, one of the New South Wales selectors, in the *Sydney Mail*, where he deplored the sacrificing of Australian players on 'the altar of the treasury'. At least it was not intended that Bradman should do the long journey walking on his hands!

Small wonder that Bradman's journey across Australia, from Sydney to Perth, to play for the Combined Australian XI against M.C.C., was one long tale of wild enthusiasm at every stop along the line. The most elaborate preparations were made in Perth for his arrival. The railway station was barricaded and a special posse of police instructed to deal with the vast throng expected to meet him. When he in fact arrived, there were indeed thousands awaiting him and he was given a welcome as no man had been given in Perth since the visit to Australia of the Prince of Wales in 1920. 'Bradman Must Play' was inscribed on lapel buttons worn by enthusiasts, and the Palace Hotel proved no sanctuary from the attentions of a cricket-mad populace. It was expected that a record crowd of some 15,000 would turn up to see Bradman bat. In fact 20,000 turned up, many having travelled hundreds of miles. They had descended on Perth not to see Hammond or Jardine, but to feast themselves on Bradman. They were hoping for a century – or perhaps a double one. What they saw appalled them and disappointed them. On a rain-damaged pitch, Bradman was out twice in a day, for 3 and 10. He lasted seven and 22 minutes respectively. He had characteristically hooked his first ball of the season in first-class cricket (from Mitchell) for 2, but he could not score at all off Verity, who had him brilliantly caught wide at second slip almost at once. Later in the day he was well caught at short-leg off Allen – the one and only occasion in Bradman's life that he was out twice in a single day in a first-class match. His previous three innings had been three centuries. The peaks and the abysses lie close together in cricket.

When he had gone through Melbourne on his way to Perth, Bradman – together with Fingleton and McCabe – had lunched with Dr Robertson, chairman of the Australian Board. Everyone jumped to the conclusion that the luncheon had been engineered to resolve the player-writer controversy. But Dr Robertson *always* entertained visiting first-class cricketers to lunch, and the only point worth talking about would be if he had not on this occasion. It is true, however, that when Bradman got to Perth – against a background of prospective cricket strikes and boycotts if the Board banned him – he publicly declared that he *had* decided to play in the first Test, if selected (!) and he had promised not to write any articles until a meeting of the Board just before the second Test, when he hoped something would be agreed to 'put him right' for all the Tests.

In the midst of all the uncertainty Bradman received several extremely lucrative offers from English newspapers to write on the 1932–33 series on their behalf. One of these offers was £3,000 – about £120 a day, a fee that would enable him to earn *in a single day* very nearly what he would get from the Board of Control for the entire five-match series. There is no doubt that Bradman was capable of doing the job, and of doing it without a 'ghost'. A blank sheet of paper did not frighten him, and he could express himself concisely, clearly and interestingly. His powers of observation, of course, could hardly be doubted. But of course if he were going to write at all, it would be for his contractual employers, Associated Newspapers of Sydney, owners of the *Sun*. They in fact in due course were to take the matter out of Bradman's hands and to settle the whole controversy. Their managing

director, Sir Hugh Denison – after the New South Wales members of the
Australian Board had seen the editorial head of the company – announced
that the *Sun* would release Bradman from his contract that summer and make
him available to play. It was a victory to the Board, or perhaps to the persuasive powers of Messrs R. A. Oxlade, W. C. Bull and F. M. Cush in the
Sydney *Sun* offices. But throughout it all Bradman had maintained a dignity
and – as important – a loyalty to his contract that might, in different circumstances, easily have seen him stand down as a Test cricketer in 1932–33.

Despite his 'unlucky 13' aggregate in Perth, Bradman was soon to prove
he was still the best batsman in the world. Exactly a week after his sombre
Saturday in Western Australia, he walked out to bat in New South Wales'
first Shield match of the season and his first first-class innings in Sydney since
his marriage. He scored a most breathtakingly wonderful 238 in 200 merciless
minutes against Victoria. A fortunate crowd of 24,658 saw it. It was considered perhaps Bradman's greatest innings in Australia up to that date – a
tremendous claim in view of his record. In half an hour he was 50; and in
73 minutes had reached his century, treating the bowlers with the nearest
thing to contempt seen on a cricket field – the bowlers including Fleetwood-
Smith, Ironmonger, Blackie and Alexander, who were either actual or future
Test match bowlers. Woodfull just could not place a field for him. He scored
all his runs in a single day (indeed, he did not go in until after lunch) and hit
32 fours with absolute mastery. At the close of the day, Fleetwood-Smith's
13 overs had cost him 110 runs. It was the sort of innings that, had it been
played by any other cricketer, would have been forever remembered as the
great highlight of his career. With Bradman, it simply fell into the great
galaxy of memorable innings he produced at regular intervals. It does not
get the briefest reference in his book, *My Cricketing Life* (1938); and is dismissed in but three modest lines in *Farewell to Cricket*. In the second innings
Fingleton and Bradman shared an unbroken stand of 63 which won the
match, of which Bradman made 52 – altogether 290 out of 402 in the match,
or 72 % of the runs while at the crease. The sadly overshadowed Ponsford
suffered again in this match. On the second day he took his score to 200 and
was once more – together with Bradman – the leading double-centurion on
Australian soil: he was to hold the distinction for but a few hours, as Bradman
scored his 238 later that same day. It was the only match in which Bradman
and Ponsford each fielded out to a double-century by the other. Bradman
had by far the longer spell in the field!

That 238 (which was to prove the highest innings of the Australian first-
class season) was made while Douglas Jardine was in Adelaide – he was
making a far less spectacular century himself that day. He had the whole of
Sunday to contemplate the Bradman menace afresh, and he was to have two
further opportunities of meeting him before the date of the first Test. In those
two matches Bradman was to have a very lean time, falling to Larwood for
36 and 13 for an Australian XI at Melbourne and, despite Larwood's
absence, making only 18 and 23 for New South Wales. His average against

the M.C.C. side in six innings was thus the unbelievably low one of 17·16, though during the Melbourne match his name was naturally announced among Australia's 13 for the first Test.

It was at Melbourne, during his innings of 36 on 19 November, that Bradman first encountered the shock tactics of the short, bumping ball and distinctive field placing that was to become known as bodyline, operated by Larwood in particular, and also by Voce, with a strong cordon of leg fielders for a mis-hit. Actually Jardine was not on the field as captain, Wyatt leading the side. Jardine had gone trout-fishing, but he knew precisely what his bowlers were going to do. He explained the leg-side attack later by saying he had noticed at Perth 'an almost totally unsuspected weakness' on the leg stump in several of the Australian batsmen, and Bradman in particular. At Perth, Bradman had found Larwood, Voce and Bowes kept out of the side. At Melbourne he encountered all three of them for the first time on the tour. 'Hunter' Hendry was still writing cricket, now no longer a Test player, and he said, after watching the M.C.C. tactics: 'Larwood placed his field in a manner that left no doubts about his intention to "bowl at the man". It's no use trying to evade that plain fact.' And a line or two before: 'It is still more undeniably fact that England's shock attack of last weekend was put on especially for the "benefit" of the unfortunate Mr Bradman. It was the Englishmen's policy to break Don's morale at any price. They realized what a menace he constituted to their Test hopes – and likewise Woodfull too – and adopted the tactics of "if you can't bowl 'em out, well, knock 'em out"!'[1]

Bradman batted altogether in that Melbourne match for just over an hour, and Larwood always remembered what a refreshing sight it was to him 'to see Bradman clumsily waving his bat in the air'. Jack Hobbs, in his cable home to *The Star* on the last day of the match, remarked that 'it was something to make Bradman duck away, wonderful player that he is. It gives a certain satisfaction to know that Don is only human after all, having the same dislike for lightning bumpers as all other batsmen'. But Hobbs had his reservations. He said also that day:

> I felt a lot safer in the press box, for the bowling looked very dangerous stuff.
> I found it amusing, your feelings are different when just watching.
> The newspapers will have very unpleasant things to say about these undoubted shock tactics and attacking methods England evidently intends to adopt.

Not only Hobbs found it 'amusing'. The crowd did so too, for they, like many people, could not assess what it meant. Bradman himself, however, was in the middle long enough to know at once. 'Its purport was obvious to

[1] Bradman played in the Australian XI match at Melbourne at the expense of the Sheffield Shield fixture at Brisbane. There would not have been adequate time, had the Shield match at Brisbane run its full course, for Bradman to have made the journey to Melbourne. His primary allegiance being to his State, he asked the New South Wales Cricket Association which match he should play in, and they told him the M.C.C. match was the more important. After his dismal few minutes against the Englishmen at Perth, he was doubtless happy to take this fresh chance of assessing them – without knowing what was in store.

me', he later wrote. 'I promptly confided to responsible officials my predictions regarding the future, but found little sympathy for my views.' Perhaps those officials thought nothing beyond that the tactics happened to be employed simply because that Melbourne wicket happened to be a lively one.

As for Larwood, he said in his autobiography: 'I knew I had Don on the run. I had upset his equilibrium and put him right off his game. Leg theory had succeeded far better than I expected. Don, caught in two minds by the leg trap, had jumped out of the way to avoid rising balls over the leg stump, at times using his bat with a clubbing action that would have done credit to a wood-chopper.' Not the most complimentary language to use of a formidable opponent.

Don Bradman was clearly unhappy after his experience, but he arrived back in Sydney with all his old, perky confidence – outwardly, at least. He grinned broadly at the suggestion of a Larwood 'hoodoo', and said the Englishmen should not forget his score at Leeds in 1930. 'Don't worry about the shock bowlers', he said. 'We shall be as right as pie.'

Bradman himself, however, was not 'right as pie'. A few days later he was taken ill, during the New South Wales match against M.C.C. Here again the fast bowling shook him. 'Poor Don', said Jack Hobbs, after his first innings of 18. 'I am afraid that to-day Bradman descended from his throne in the minds of his admirers. I never remember him scratching for runs on a dry wicket as he did to-day.' He was thereafter confined to bed with a chill and sore throat, but pluckily went to the Sydney Cricket Ground on the final day to take his second innings – and some further unwanted medicine, as it turned out. He looked very pale, and went in at number six to face some short-pitched bowling from Voce. Eventually, expecting a bumper, Bradman walked right away to the off, only to see the ball keep unexpectedly low and bowl him middle stump. He then returned home to bed. His suspected influenza, caught playing golf on the Sunday of the M.C.C. match, was only part of his medical worries.

By this stage some critics were gleefully saying Bradman was not worth his place in the Test side. The one-time remark of a Yorkshire and England cricketer on Bradman was recalled: 'Rockets go up – but they have to come down.' It is true that all the leading England bowlers, except Bowes, had got his wicket – Larwood twice, and Verity, Allen, Tate and Voce once each. And his top score in six innings against them was 36. His previous six innings against the best of English bowling, in 1930, was a telling contrast. Was his largely self-taught technique equal to the challenges before him?

Among those who were moved to go into print on his behalf, he had one unexpected but fervent supporter of quite hippopotamic proportions on the other side of the world in Oscar Asche, cricket-lover and actor-manager (and Australian by birth!) and just about as bad a batsman as Bradman was good. Not long after appearing as Casca in *Julius Caesar* in London, he admitted with theatrical panache that 'the downfall of Bradman has shaken the cricketing world as the fall of Caesar shook and moved the mob of Rome'.

But at the same time he published some fiery verse denouncing those who had labelled Bradman a fallen idol. The last two lines read:

> Come, Bradman, rise, strike out, belittlers stun;
> By fresh deeds prove you are still Don – not done.

The fresh deeds had to wait a while as doctors Aspinall and Holmes a'Court examined Bradman in Sydney at the instance of the Board of Control the day before the first Test was due to begin. They promptly pronounced him unfit to play – he was in a seriously run-down condition. Dr Dolling, a selector, announced the news which stunned Sydney in particular that Thursday. 'It might have been the fall of an Empire', said Reuter's man on the spot. 'Bulletins were posted in the shop windows, and no one could talk, think, or speak of anything else.' Could anyone have imagined bulletins being posted in the shops, say, in Oxford Street if Walter Hammond or Hendren had been unable to play in a Test match at Lord's?

By this time the fickle Australian public had circulated all sorts of wild rumours about him. But they still regarded him as the most noteworthy individual in Australia. Reports came out that his cricket career was finished, but Bradman scoffed at them, admitting only that he was badly run down. He still could not move a yard without being mobbed. So many people telephoned his home that he was forced to instal a blind telephone. No cricketer had ever before been obliged to pay the penalty of fame like Bradman.

It was fortunate that Bradman was seriously run down and nothing more. Fears that he was suffering from some form of anaemia proved unfounded a few days later, following a satisfactory blood test. But he was advised to rest for two to three weeks.[1] He actually watched the first Test at Sydney and visited the broadcasting station to broadcast his impressions of the play – the Australian Board, strangely, at that time saw nothing wrong with a cricketer disseminating his views over the air, though he could not do so in print. Sydney, by the way, had still yet to see Bradman play in a Test against England, for in Sydney's only match of the previous tour Bradman had been twelfth man. It is an unusual fact that Bradman actually scored as many as 1,719 runs in Test cricket against England before he was to score his first run against England on his home ground, later in 1932–33.

Jack Hobbs saw Bradman in the pavilion on that first day of the series. And he cabled the following home to *The Star*:

---

[1] With a sad irresponsibility, one Sydney newspaper carried a huge 'scare' story, published without any sort of professional confirmation, that Bradman was suffering from pernicious anaemia. The New South Wales Cricket Association, innocent of such things, was frightened into arranging an immediate medical examination and blood test. Had the story been true, it would have meant of course the end of Bradman's cricket career. The disease is rare in someone as young as Bradman then was, and in its worst form – especially in 1932, comparatively early days of curative knowledge – rarely yielded to treatment. One London newspaper – which shall be nameless, but which owed something to Bradman – wrote what was virtually an obituary notice of him (or at least of his career), so grave a view did it take of the report. The paper's Sydney correspondent seemed quite satisfied that Bradman's career was over.

I talked to Don for a few minutes. He does not look well, and has a drawn look.

I can quite understand his feelings, for he has been living for a long time in a state of continual upset.

Things he has never said have been attributed to him in some of the papers.

The public is fickle, and Don has found that the higher pedestal you stand on the greater the fall.

Bradman said wistfully: 'I would like to be out there, Jack, and not sitting here watching.'

Somehow I felt he has not had a square deal.

The Australian public seems to forget its favourites sooner than our public does.

Lots of people here appear to ignore the fact that Bradman has had nasty wickets, and not much luck other ways.

Of course, by the same rule, a big score or two will put Don back in the public favour.

I hope that as he sat in the pavilion he realised it.

What was realised most abundantly at Sydney – Bradman or no Bradman on the field – was that the arguments about leg-theory bowling, with the leg side packed with fielders, were growing more and more intense. Australia's batsmen were using three body-pads.

In Bradman's absence Australia lost by ten wickets – the fourth innings, which lasted 15 seconds, being the shortest in the history of Test cricket. Bradman then took himself off, with his wife, for a holiday on the south coast of New South Wales to comply with his doctors' orders. For more than a week he stayed at the property of Mr T. A. Langridge, who was the official masseur to the New South Wales Cricket Association and who had attended virtually every touring team to Australia for many years. While Bradman was recovering his health, he had naturally to ponder too over the new bowling tactics of England in Australia. If the Sydney *Referee* of 14 December 1932 reached him, he could have read in that notable sporting paper's first Test post mortem its most vehement attack on 'the pernicious body battering attack by England's fast bowlers, an attack utterly foreign to our batsmen, because it is utterly foreign to true cricket'. The article went on:

> This method of attack is not only ruinous to cricket, but is a direct and emphatic negation of the principles and traditions of the game, and, in addition, is an alarming danger to the batsmen who are called upon to face it.

The writer added – and it was his view only, of course – that the most amazing thing was that the M.C.C. must have known what was being done, and suggested that the authorities should intervene 'before serious injury, and perhaps a fatality, occurs, before friendly rivalry changes to hatred, and before cricket degenerates into a brawl'. These were strong words for a strong situation. And the *Referee* was far from alone in its condemnation.

Poor Pelham Warner, managing the M.C.C. side, saw all his old ideals in danger of crumbling as he contemplated the consequences of what was happening. 'Personally I am terrified of some *horrible accident*', he confided privately in a letter home five days after the first Test ended. He also acknowledged privately, if not publicly, the strength of Australian feeling against the new bowling. Later on he very much defended the Australians and their objection to bodyline.

Jardine broke his silence on the controversy when his team arrived in Tasmania between the first and second Tests. His words followed hot on the heels of the Sydney *Referee*'s eruption. 'The leg theory originated in the Australian newspapers', retorted Jardine in Launceston. 'It is exactly the same type of attack on the leg stump that has been tried times without number from village cricket to Tests. The only difference is that we place the field differently to that usually adopted.'

That 'only difference' was a highly significant one, of course: indeed, it was at the very root of the entire controversy. 'There is nothing new and nothing dangerous in it', continued Jardine, 'and we hope to go on being successful with the same methods.'

This was a declaration of intention in the clearest possible terms, and though Bradman's health, after his coastal holiday, was now very much improved, his reception of Jardine's words could hardly have been a comfort. He returned to Sydney and then went with his wife on a motor trip to Melbourne. When he got back home, he said: 'I am as fit as a fiddle', and his bronzed, fresh appearance certainly confirmed it, as did the two specialists who examined him and pronounced his condition as 'entirely satisfactory'. Bradman said he would like to play against Victoria at Melbourne.

In his first innings after his indisposition, Bradman scored 157 in 199 minutes, without a chance, against Victoria on Boxing Day, 1932, his last 50 in under half an hour. He received a remarkable ovation when he went out – there were 21,187 present – and he proved himself worthy of it. He strained a leg while batting, but was very soon perfectly fit – and in good form. The New Year Test had almost arrived, and Bradman stayed on for it in Melbourne.

Sir Edward Cook, that most percipient of journalists, once pointed out to the undergraduates of New College – when Don Bradman was a little boy of five – that in biography, as in the novel or the drama, contrasts and foils are often useful. The hero demands a villain. For Mr Gladstone the villain was ready-made in Mr Disraeli, and vice versa. These things cannot be ordered, and Sir Edward Cook did not live to hear of bodyline. But for D. G. Bradman the villain was ready-made in D. R. Jardine. Bradman at 24 would not have chosen that a villain should walk on the stage at all, not even for the sake of a future biographer. But walk on he did, wearing a Harlequin cap and with all the malevolence of Beerbohm Tree playing Svengali.

Jardine knew as well as any man in the world of what Bradman was capable. If there had seemed no answer to his batting in 1930, the intervening two years had given bowlers an equal absence of hope. Bradman was, by that time, as R. S. Whitington was later to put it, 'Alexander the Great, Samson, Horatio Nelson, and Houdini combined, in the eyes of his compatriot Australians – and deserved to be'. Larwood remembered that in 1930

Bradman 'did all the things you didn't want him to. You could bowl on the off trying to get him to lift one or give a catch behind and he'd pull you hard to the leg fence. He had the quickest eye of any batsman I ever met. There seemed only one way to get him out – tire him out. But he never seemed to tire. His stamina and concentration were extraordinary'.

The stories are well known of how Jardine visited Frank Foster's flat in London to discuss field placings for leg-theory before he left for Australia – the gory details in due course appeared under Foster's name in *Smith's Weekly*, admittedly not the most 'pure' reading matter in Australia in those days; and of how Jardine, Larwood, Voce and Arthur Carr met in the Piccadilly Hotel not just to dine but to talk deeply about leg-theory. 'I could see what they had in mind', said Larwood. 'Bradman was the big problem. He was the key man in Australia and Jardine wanted to curb his run-getting.'

Larwood had bowled some leg-theory occasionally in Australia in 1928–29. He used it against both Bradman and Jackson in the Adelaide Test that season, with five or six men on the leg side. 'I bowled rising balls on the leg stump', he recalled. 'It was a desperation move to dislodge the batsmen who were on top in hot and exhausting conditions. They both seemed to play it well enough.' But at the little dinner gathering in the Piccadilly Hotel, it was the Oval, 1930, that was most freely discussed – and Larwood told Jardine that he thought Bradman had flinched from his fast-rising balls on the leg stump. Jardine said he knew that; and before long, in that grill room, according to Larwood, 'Jardine asked me if I thought I could bowl on the leg stump making the ball come up into the body all the time so that Bradman had to play his shots to leg'. The decision to bowl the new version of leg-theory to Bradman was then conclusively taken. Jardine's tactical objective, in simple terms, was to discomfort Bradman to the extent that he would no longer be in control of his stroke-play. If all his shots had to be played to the leg all the time, he would assuredly give a catch to one of the fielders.

The menace of Bradman was the only reason for Jardine bringing together Larwood and Voce, and their county captain, in the mellow surroundings of a West End grill room. The hard Australian wickets, the blazing sun AND Bradman did not present a pleasing prospect. Larwood and Voce were professionals. It is unlikely that either of them could really have refused Jardine's bidding, the more so in their own captain's presence. (G. O. Allen was later to do so, in Australia, but he was an amateur.) In any event, conventional bowling had already seen Larwood take a terrible battering from Bradman's bat, and as Larwood himself put it of leg-theory, 'I could see it might give me a chance'. The food and the wine and the professionally persuasive tongue of Jardine the lawyer combined to settle the issue. No other Australian batsman, from what one can gather, was seriously mentioned at the dinner: except that Jardine did observe that, if leg-theory unsettled Bradman and succeeded against him, it might well succeed against others.

Then followed the visits to Foster in St. James's, and the detailed discussions on board the *Orontes* on the way out. Bradman and the entire world was innocent of what had been hatched. At the time of the casting of the die, Bradman was on his cricket-cum-honeymoon trip in North America. A few cricketers in England were in the know, but very few even of them. In case it should still be believed that bodyline (in intention, if not yet in name) was not conceived until *after* Jardine's team left England – and Jardine himself gave never a clue that it was conceived in England – A. W. Carr, in *Cricket With the Lid Off*, may be fairly quoted:

> I may here say that I discussed that new form of bowling technique – leg theory, or whatever you like to call it – with a number of cricketers before Larwood went to Australia with Douglas Jardine's team. My own idea was that it would succeed if bowled by a bowler of Larwood's accuracy after the shine was off the ball (which happens after a few overs on Australian wickets). But at least two cricketers with first-hand experience and knowledge of Australia did not agree with me.'

It is not very relevant that the two who disagreed were Ernest Tyldesley and George Duckworth: it is relevant that Carr was in a position to discuss it with them at all.

The supreme irony – and easily the most piquant aspect of the whole situation – was that Jardine very nearly did not go to Australia at all as captain in '32–33. According to Jardine's cousin, he changed his mind after his appointment and informed P. F. Warner that he would not be available. In some perturbation, Warner turned for aid to a fellow-Oxonian blue, Jardine's father, M. R. Jardine, then living at Walton-on-Thames. They were on first-name terms, and Malcolm Jardine, former Advocate-General of Bombay, is alleged to have said: 'I'll have a word with the boy.' And have a word with the boy he did – and 'the boy', of course, duly went to Australia.

In Australia there was a conspiracy of silence by the M.C.C. team – duly ordered by Jardine – so that Bradman in particular should be taken by surprise by the new tactics. When Bradman experienced them for the first time, in the Australian XI match at Melbourne, he had indeed not had an inkling that they were to be unleashed on him. If Bradman's immediate view – that there would be serious trouble unless this type of bowling were dealt with quickly – had been acted upon, or even heeded, by the administrators to whom he spoke promptly and in confidence, much of the bitterness of 1932–33 might have been avoided. That cannot be certain, for Jardine was a man of iron resolve. Before the end of the tour, the quiet Englishman who had read Chaucer in a corner on the boat to Australia, had become by far the most hated antagonist among all the cricketers who had ever visited that land.

Though there cannot be the smallest doubt in the world that bodyline was conceived to impose a technical strait-jacket on Bradman's runaway scoring propensities, the fact remains that bodyline was nevertheless used in Bradman's absence in the first Test at Sydney. He was present at the ground from beginning to end, however, observing most shrewdly, and it is umpire George Hele's view that 'it was used in the Sydney Test because the Englishmen knew Don was watching and wanted to show him what he would receive if he rejoined the Australian ranks'.

When Jardine had made his unequivocal declaration of intent in Tasmania on 15 December, the President of the Northern Tasmanian Cricket Association, General W. Martin, an old opponent on the field of English sides in Tasmania, was one of those (and he was not alone) who sided with Jardine. Whether or not it was out of courtesy to a visitor to his island, General Martin nevertheless said in welcoming Jardine and his team: 'The Englishmen have a perfect right to bowl in any way they like. The Australians should be able to overcome the leg theory as McCabe and Fingleton have done. The Australians also have a perfect right to bowl the same theory.' Perhaps General Martin had got Jardine's word that it was to be used only on the mainland! The innocent use of the term 'leg-theory' was still being used – and not least by Jardine – to describe the new bowling. Even Arthur Carr, already quoted, was merely to describe it as 'leg theory, or whatever you like to call it'. What Australians very quickly liked to call it was 'bodyline'.

Thus it was that Bradman knew well enough what he could expect when he made his bow in the Test series of 1932–33. The Australian Board, not deaf to Jardine's words from Launceston, knew also what the future held, and two days before the second Test at Melbourne it was known that bodyline bowling and its packed leg-side field would be officially discussed by the Board on the morrow. The Australian Board at that time could hardly be accused of living in a Disneyland of administrative chaos, but there is no doubt that bodyline caught them unprepared. They chose to keep their peace. And they continued to keep their peace for too long.

It was one of the great ironies of 1932–33 that in his first innings of the series, the very man for whom the bodyline plot had been so carefully hatched did not face any bodyline bowling at all. Indeed, what bowling he did face amounted to a solitary ball. The occasion has high claims to be the most dramatic moment ever experienced by Don Bradman on a cricket field. The crowd was the then world record one of 63,993, watching in hot sunshine on the huge Melbourne ground. When Bradman came to the crease on the first afternoon, with two wickets down for 67, they gave him the sort of wild and prolonged acclamation that even the greatest player experiences only once in a lifetime. He was still 'king', and if England had won at Sydney in his absence, his return now was all that Australians needed to be sure of the tables being turned. As usual, he walked slowly to the wicket, each step clapped and cheered. He walked in a semicircle, perhaps both to allow the crowd to quieten itself and to accustom his eyes to the light. He asked for 'two legs' and as Bradman took his stance, motionless, to await Bill Bowes, the crowd turned to silence – 'as I imagine', said the bowler's umpire, George Hele, 'men await a hanging or the volley of rifle fire at a military execution'. It was 2.57 p.m.

The 'impossible' then happened. Here is how Hele saw it from 22 yards:

Bowes' first ball to him was short and well outside the off stump. Crouching a little Bradman stepped back a foot or more outside the off stump, his right leg bent almost at right angle as he pivoted almost square-on to the ball, now approaching his left shoulder. Swinging his bat horizontally and over the ball, he contacted it with the bat's lower edge and dragged it on to the base of his leg stump before he followed through.[1]

The crowd was shocked into silent disappointment, 'a silence that would have been a theatrical producer's triumph', recalled Bowes. 'It was as though they expected the skies to fall', said Hobbs. Jack Fingleton, at the other end, was surprised to see Bradman move across the wicket before Bowes had bowled the ball. 'A hush fell on the ground, an unbelievable hush of calamity for men refused to believe what their eyes had seen. Bradman left the wickets in silence.' A few cheers of sympathy broke out as the sad figure approached the pavilion. Bradman's own verdict was that it was 'a rotten shot – and that's all that can be said about it'. It was the one and only Test wicket that Bill Bowes ever took on Australian soil. It was also the first ball he had ever bowled to Don Bradman in a Test.

Bill Bowes – whom would he not rather have chosen, out of all the batsmen on parade, to give a first-ball duck on his debut against Australia? – was extremely pleased and extremely proud, and pardonably so. And what of Jardine? Bowes has provided the answer: 'It was then that I noticed Jardine. Jardine, the sphinx, had forgotten himself for the one and only time in his cricketing life. In his sheer delight at this unexpected stroke of luck he had clasped both his hands above his head and was jigging around like an Indian doing a war dance.' Jardine later described the shot as 'very daring', but of course had it gone to square-leg for four, as Bradman intended, that same daring would have been applauded as brilliance. George Hele was to write: 'Knowing Bradman's genius, I am confident he could have directed that delivery of Bowes anywhere he wished on the off side of the wicket through the virtually vacant field for four. But that is cricket and that ball and stroke will remain immortal.'

There is a pleasing story – a true one, incidentally – how this duck by Bradman almost certainly saved the lives of three young children in Tasmania. Listening to the progress of the Test on the radio in a hotel in Launceston, a Mr P. Hancock stood up and walked out in disgust at Bradman's failure. His brief walk took him past a nearby river, on whose bank three children – the youngest only 2½ – were playing and accidentally fell in. Mr Hancock promptly dived in fully clothed to rescue them – and one

---

[1] Hele says that the bail on the middle and off stumps did not fall. He is wrong, however, as the film and many photographs of the incident incontrovertibly confirm. Both bails fell. Hele, recalling the dismissal more than 40 years after the event, almost certainly based his assertion on a photograph published in his book (and elsewhere). Within the merest fraction of time of the taking of that picture, the off bail fell. It is a good example of how the camera, while not actually lying, can sometimes mislead.

would like to think that all three (and the gallant gentleman too) are still thriving healthily and fully cognisant of the miraculous powers of a Test match duck.

The whole drama of this immortal stroke is preserved for posterity on the newsreels of British Movietone News, who covered that Melbourne Test particularly well, and is held at the Rank laboratories at Denham. Occasionally television producers make use of it to remind their viewers that Bradman was no robot. It never fails to strike awe into those both familiar with it and fresh to the view. It was the one indispensable piece of film that formed part of the story of England–Australia cricket put out by the B.B.C. in London to mark the centenary of Test cricket between the two countries in March 1977. That ball always remained the most memorable ball of Bowes's career.

Johnnie Moyes years later revealed that Bradman had gone into that Melbourne Test having scrupulously worked out his tactics to counter the new English bowling methods. He had thought out his answer in the peace of Tom Langridge's cottage on the New South Wales coast and on his return to Sydney put the details to Moyes in his office at the Sydney *Sun*. Moyes, who had been one of the selectors to give Bradman his first chance on the road to fame and who had always been regarded by Bradman as most fair-minded and intelligent, was then Bradman's sports editor on the *Sun*. Throughout his career Bradman nearly always consulted him with his cricket problems. Moyes, the father-confessor, thus recorded the Bradman plan:

> He would walk away from his wicket and try to hit the ball through the off-side field. If he succeeded it would put the bowler off his balance, and would force him to weaken the leg field and strengthen the off field. Then he could revert to normal batsmanship. His plan was, in effect, to meet unorthodoxy with unorthodoxy: he must make runs.

Bradman listened to Moyes's doubts, and duly rejected them. No one knew better than Bradman that the canons of batsmanship would be disgracefully flouted, but no one knew better than Bradman too that his public would demand runs from his bat and not a mere weaving out of the path of difficult balls. In due course in the series he was to play some incredible strokes of his own invention, which both brought him many runs and cost him his wicket. Larwood was certainly his enemy and tormentor throughout, and even when Bradman twice lost his wicket to Verity, it was Verity reaping the reward of Larwood's efforts.

Just as Bradman's first-innings nought at Melbourne was perhaps the most spectacular failure of his career, so his second-innings century at Melbourne was perhaps his greatest triumph. Here he put into practice his plans to combat bodyline, and while his colleagues were falling all around him, he stayed with ever-increasing certainty to make 103 not out – the only century of the match – in a total of only 191. Arthur Mailey called the innings the greatest he had ever seen Bradman play. George Hele, who had witnessed all in his white jacket, in 1974 described it as 'one of the greatest innings I myself ever watched'. Even Jardine admitted that not only was Bradman always at ease against the fast bowlers but that 'he obtained the complete mastery which so many Australians associate with his batting'. Larwood himself acknowledged that Bradman played him better than at any other time on the tour, and the innings, he said, 'must rank as one of the greatest of his life'. The moving to leg to hit Larwood to the off was successful, and while Larwood's field was set as it was, he was obliged to bowl to it. 'Although he was obviously put off his normal game he played well enough to make me think he might yet tame bodyline.' Thus said Larwood years later. '*Bradman was a good one, all right*', he added.

A world record cricket crowd of 63,993 had come to see Bradman on the first day. A new record was established on the third day, Monday, when 68,188 watched[1] – primarily Bradman. According to Mailey, they 'packed like sardines, hanging on to balcony, railing posts, trees, and every other vacant spot, forgot their discomfort for a while, and looked forward to seeing the young champion stop the rot'. The young champion dominated the day. 'Bradman first: Rest nowhere', said a headline. Bradman had to fight not only bodyline but his many critics who believed this bowling had beaten him. He went in when Australia were only 86 ahead with two second-innings wickets down. In the end, everything depended on him. He scored half his runs (52) off Larwood and Voce, and even if he retreated to leg – deliberately, of course – his footwork had the crowd roaring with delight. Jardine was very reluctant to put on Bowes against Bradman. He had got off the mark – most bravely – hooking Bowes for four between short-leg and mid-on, from a ball very similar to that which dismissed him in the first innings. But altogether in his innings of 185 minutes, Bradman received only six balls from Bowes. More than half (83 out of 146 balls in all) came from Larwood and Voce. It was not all, however, bodyline, but a generous, and disconcerting, mixture of the orthodox and unorthodox, though Bradman never spurned to play – and to hit – the bodyline balls into the vacant off-side field. Bradman's temperament throughout was imperturbable, and he never gave anything approaching a chance. The all-out total of 191 is the lowest in the history of England–Australia cricket to contain a century innings. (Colin Cowdrey, in 1954–55, also in the New Year Test at Melbourne, equalled the feat.)

Jack Hobbs cabled home to England that day: 'Bradman certainly answered his critics, some of whom have not even realised that to err is only human. They don't realise the difficulties of batsmanship or the quality of the bowling.' Hobbs said, as did all the critics, that Bradman never looked

[1] The ground record for any crowd at that time at the Melbourne Cricket Ground, however, still remained unbroken at 69,724 at the League football grand final between Richmond and Carlton the previous season.

in difficulty; and interestingly observed that he considered then that Bradman had 'more scoring strokes than when he was in England'. Any captain's problem, in 'normal' conditions, could thus readily be appreciated. Mailey's verdict on Bradman's innings was that it 'stood out from those of his team mates like a diamond set in pieces of glass'. When he was 98, the ninth wicket fell and one of the worst batsmen in Australia came out to join him – and due to take strike. Bert Ironmonger's greeting to Bradman was: 'Don't worry, son, I won't let you down.' And he did not. (Ironmonger's Sheffield Shield record at that point that season was five runs in five innings.) At that moment, wrote Mailey, 'people could hardly restrain their anxiety. Barmen, gatekeepers, waitresses, groundsmen, cashiers, policemen joined the big crowd which was waiting to burst into one mighty cheer'. Were they to suffer galling disappointment from watching Bradman for the second time in three days? When Bradman hit Voce for three to leg to put up his century, thousands rose and cheered him. 'Hats, caps, and coats were flung in the air', said one message, 'and it was some minutes before the cheering died down.' He was 101 out of 162 since he had come in, and two runs later Ironmonger was run out. Then the air was black with the hurled-up caps of the record crowd, with a happy smile on Bradman's face:

> A scene of hero worship marked his return bare-headed to the pavilion from his great innings: women threw their arms round him and kissed him; the cheering was sufficient to shake the foundations of England's faith in themselves.
>
> And later in the day a shilling fund was opened by the Melbourne Cricket Club committee for the purpose of presenting to Mrs Bradman a memento of her husband's remarkable performance. But Bradman would probably deny that it was remarkable. It was just Bradman back to normal again.

Certainly he was back on his pedestal again. The innings was his seventh Test hundred against England, a new Australian record at that time, surpassing the six hundreds of Trumper and Woodfull. It was the only century made for Australia in any of the four Tests in which Bradman appeared in 1932–33. It went a long way to winning Australia's only Test of that rubber. By the end of the match there had still not been the smallest official whisper from the Australian Board on the subject of bodyline bowling. But the fact that they had discussed it was quite certain.

Bradman's hundred in the Melbourne Test was all the more remarkable because of the several influences that had been disturbing his mind – not just bodyline, but his health and the continuing saga of the player-writer. He almost did not play at all at Melbourne, for on the very day before the Test began the Australian Board presented him with an ultimatum – that he either writes or plays, but he cannot do both. A New South Wales motion on Bradman's behalf urging that the player-writer rule be altered was put to the vote and defeated. Bradman had to give way if he wanted to play. He *did* want to play, and at the same time did not wish to defy his newspaper contract. It was then that his newspaper settled the issue and specifically asked him to play, the Board confirming itself as immovable. Bradman and all Australia were no doubt duly grateful, but Bradman did not allow the occasion to pass without revealing his own feelings on the matter and issuing his own statement, which he released with some dramatic impact on the very morning of the first day at Melbourne. The text of it was as follows:

Through the generosity of the Associated Newspapers of Australia, who requested me to play for Australia instead of occupying a seat in the press box, I have been enabled to play in the second Test. To the great cricket-loving public of Australia, may I express my extreme pleasure at being thus able to represent my country once more.

Even though the Board of Control continues to prevent me from earning an honourable and permanent living from journalism, it allows other members of the Australian eleven to broadcast comments freely, despite the fact that broadcasting to them is only a temporary occupation.

Again, the difference between journalism and radio work is so small to make any distinction appear ridiculous.

The Board had all the facts before them at their meeting, and their legislation means that they are able to dictate to players the means by which they shall earn their living.

If any player wishes to make a living in a channel which is not acceptable to the Board, he is not going to be allowed to play for his country.

Only through the generosity of my employers am I enabled to play to-day. While doing so, I most emphatically protest against the Board's being allowed to interfere with the permanent occupation of any player. To my mind the Board was never meant to have powers directing the business activities of players.

It is certainly no encouragement to any player to remain in Australia when such restrictions are brought in.

This public rebuke of the Board was one that would have been made by no other player but Bradman, and even he would not have made it but for a strong sense of loyalty to his newspaper. Bradman never was afraid of putting his cards on the table – no one who acts honourably ever is – and he did so on this occasion in firm and almost judicial tones, but tones which could not have endeared him to the members of the Board. Some of them might not have been altogether displeased at the retributive duck that the day was to bring. A newspaperman tracked Bradman down that morning at the home of a friend in a Melbourne suburb and caught him in his dressing-gown before breakfast. 'What would you do if Accrington offered you a job in England?' he asked Bradman. Bradman just grinned and shrugged his shoulders: 'I really don't know', he said – and was then allowed to eat his breakfast in peace. It is strange that even the words 'I really don't know', so long as they were uttered by D. G. Bradman, were enough to make news in 1932, and were sent across the world at no inconsiderable expense and eagerly printed by news-conscious editors. During the tea interval on that first day in Melbourne, a rumour was rife that Bradman had actually accepted a job in England. Accrington was mentioned. But an official of the club, when asked, said with some disdain: 'We are not interested in Bradman. We already have Fairfax.'

In fact another Lancashire League club had put out a feeler, which had been the source of the rumour. The club was Ramsbottom: but it was only a feeler and no offer was made. Ramsbottom were the only Lancashire League side which had not yet fixed up a professional for 1933 and Bradman had been asked indirectly if he was now prepared to come into the league.[1] The news got out on the second day of the Melbourne Test, but before the game began Bradman had already cabled as follows: 'Present Australian contract binds me until 1 February 1934. Cannot consider Lancashire before then. – Bradman.' The vice-chairman of Ramsbottom, Mr Foster, was asked if he thought Bradman would be a paying proposition in a small town like Ramsbottom. 'I do', he replied. 'Our gate receipts were only £134 last season. Our season's gate would certainly be well over £1,000 if Bradman came.' Bradman, of course, could not come to Ramsbottom, but instead his New South Wales colleague, S. F. Hird, went in 1933 and stayed for all seven seasons up to the war.

When the terms of Bradman's cable became known, yet another club, Rochdale – this time in the Central Lancashire League – cabled terms to Bradman to be their professional when he would be free to leave Australia in 1934. Rochdale, an ancient club which had won the League title far more often than any of its rivals, was commonly regarded as the richest club in the League. They were said to be prepared to give Bradman a contract worth four figures. Rochdale, famous not only for fish and chips and Gracie Fields, had already signed since the First World War – and at handsome salaries – such Test players as Cecil Parkin, S. F. Barnes and J. M. Blanckenberg. Bradman of course knew that 1934 was an Australian tour year to England, but Rochdale did not give up easily and their efforts to succeed where the Lancashire League had failed went on for weeks. Bradman wrote the club a long letter during the second Test at Melbourne. It was a private letter, but two months later (a week after the close of the series), much to Bradman's surprise, the contents were made public. Bradman had pointed out to Rochdale that, while his contract would keep him in Australia during the 1933 cricket season, he might be free to go to England in 1934. He said in his letter that he did not want to leave Australia, but if the prospects there were bad and not to be compared with what he might expect in England, he would have no hesitation in going to England. 'At present I cannot accept your offer', he wrote to Rochdale, 'but by 1 January 1934, I may be able to do so, or else will not be interested at all. If you care to withhold your plans and communicate with me then, I will give you a definite "Yes" or "No".' The letter went on to reveal Bradman's (as yet private) thoughts on bodyline, written well before the Adelaide explosion and well before the Board began

---

[1] Ramsbottom finished one from bottom in the 1932 table. The player who headed their batting (an amateur) sported an average for the season of 17·68. And that was a very long way ahead of the second man in the batting!

to draft its first cable to Lord's. Bradman told Rochdale:

> When my present contract expires, though, I cannot say with any certainty that I shall receive any further offers to remain in Australia. In view of recent happenings, there is nothing definite as to the future of cricket.
>
> The Australian team in 1934 may not eventuate if conflicts continue or bodyline bowling may kill all cricket under M.C.C. control unless they ban it.
>
> Also, I informed the Accrington Club I would give them first refusal of my services in the future should I be available for Lancashire.[1]

The letter was not received by Rochdale until 6 March, and on the following day their secretary, Mr Harvey Sutcliffe, cabled Bradman in reply as follows: 'Letter appreciated. Can you accept offer definitely not later than 30 June 1933? Hearty welcome awaits you.' In Rochdale, the club's president, Mr G. A. Close, confirmed that day it was imperative that Bradman reply before 30 June. 'We cannot afford to wait until next January', he said, 'because it would be too late then to fix up with any other player should Bradman refuse the offer. Besides, it would be very unfair to our present professional, Blanckenberg, the South African player. Bradman says he cannot commit himself so far ahead, but we must know by June if he is coming or not. It would be better for him to come to Rochdale rather than Accrington. We are members of the Central Lancashire League, and Bradman would be a bigger star with us than in the more powerful Lancashire League. We are now waiting for the reply from Bradman.'

In Australia Bradman said he was not going to make up his mind at present what to do, but if an Australian team visited England in 1934 he would like to go as a player. In the event Rochdale, like Accrington and Ramsbottom, failed. Don Bradman in the 1930s was of course by far the biggest fish in the ocean for either the Lancashire League or the Central Lancashire League to seek. Both these leagues went for the best, though they have been less able to do so since the introduction of special registrations in county cricket, whereby league clubs have been unable to match the offers of the counties. But in former days their offers were tempting indeed, and only Don Bradman and later Keith Miller withstood them.[2]

Despite Australia's victory in the second Test at Melbourne, her batsmen were no nearer to solving the bodyline problem than at Sydney. Bradman

---

[1] Don Bradman's forebodings on the future of England–Australia cricket were not as gloomily unjustified as they may now appear. Later in 1933 the decision of the M.C.C. committee that the Australian tour of 1934 should be proceeded with was passed by the comparatively delicate margin of eight votes to five.
[2] Despite Bradman's continued rejections of offers from the leagues, there were still people in 1933 who firmly believed he would end his cricketing days in England. In fact more offers were made to him that were publicly announced. A sports-salesman post, for example, was offered him that would have permitted him to engage in club games in England.
In August 1933, Rochdale signed Ellis Achong, the West Indian slow bowler, to be their professional for 1934 in succession to J. M. Blanckenberg. Achong was to have a most distinguished career in the Central Lancashire League, and had taken over 1,000 wickets when he finished his professional career in that league with Walsden in 1951.

himself might have felt satisfied at getting a hundred, but he played the bowling at Melbourne better than he was to at any later time in the series. The pitch there was not the usual Melbourne pitch, with a touch of fire, but was easy paced and not of great assistance to the fast men. The Adelaide wicket, for the third Test, however, certainly *was* fiery, but became progressively easier as the game went on. Although the Adelaide crowd had not often been known as demonstrative, its temper reached the point of hostility in this match as the bodyline tactics continued with unabated fervour. The Australian Board's first cable went off to the M.C.C. This had been the Test, incidentally, in which Jardine, after all the criticism poured on him, offered to stand down. It was also the Test which gave rise to the rumour – not substantiated, as it turned out – that Jardine would ban bodyline bowling pending a reply from the M.C.C. to the Australian Board's cable. In the meantime the Australian Board had telegraphed to all its members for their opinions on the English tactics.

Bradman scored a stirring 66 in the second innings at Adelaide, out of 88 in only 73 minutes, not all of it by any means off bodyline, but he gave the certain impression that he intended his life to be a short and merry one. Against the conventional bowling he played hectically but brilliantly. While Larwood bowled at the wicket, Bradman made him look simple and took his fours cleanly and nonchalantly; but when the leg field was put in position, he swung wildly at nearly every ball. At the other end, hoping to gather runs while he could, he on-drove Verity for a beautiful six – the first he had ever hit in a Test match, and his first ever in any first-class match in Australia. It was not a typical Bradman stroke, and the cheering for it had hardly died down when Verity caught and bowled him off the very next ball. His feverish tactics brought much criticism on him, and as Jardine later observed, 'he made the pace so hot that somehow one felt that it simply could not last'. However electrifying had been his play, it could not be termed sound. Woodfull was alleged even to have favoured dropping him after it. Bradman had fallen into Larwood's leg-trap for only 8 in the first innings, attempting to play orthodoxly – only a shadow of his real self – and he reverted to his own pre-conceived plan thereafter. At the end of his 66 Hobbs wrote: 'I am satisfied that only leg theory can stop Bradman. The power he gets in his strokes, and their very wide range alike, are wonderful. He hits freely where others would just defend.'

Bradman passed 70 in both the fourth Test at Brisbane and the fifth Test at Sydney, making strokes off Larwood's fastest deliveries in both these games 'which no other living batsman could have made', said Kippax. He was still drawing away to leg to crack Larwood to the off. When he was out for 76 in the first England–Australia Test staged on the Woolloongabba ground, he was trying to cut a ball on the leg stump from Larwood, the previous ball having gone just over the wicket as Bradman ducked to the off side. 'This proves what I have said before about leg theory', cabled Hobbs, '– it forces you into making strokes you never would dream of doing in the ordinary way. If a schoolboy tried to cut a ball on the leg stick you would smack his head, yet here Bradman was doing it.' Bradman had played well enough on the first day to be 71 not out, with people cautiously saying that bodyline had been mastered. Next morning, when Larwood began at once with body-line, Bradman was at his unhappiest, showing extreme discomfort while adding five in 31 minutes. He drew away once too often, to see his leg stump knocked back. Warwick Armstrong's blunt verdict was: 'I have to say can-didly that Bradman showed unmistakable signs of fright when facing every ball from Larwood to-day and that his last shot was shockingly bad.' But he was still second top scorer in the innings, and if his last shot was indeed bad there were a good many earlier in the 76 that were admirable and safe. He had, incidentally, in the meantime made 1 and 71 in M.C.C.'s return match with New South Wales, and after his three minutes' innings of 1 (deceived by the spin of Mitchell), his old fervent supporter of 1930, Trevor Wignall, sitting in Fleet Street, asked: 'Have his prodigy days disappeared, and is he now destined to sink back to mediocrity? I cannot believe that is possible, but that is precisely what some folk are saying.'

The troubles of 1932–33 provided indeed the only occasion in Don Bradman's distinguished career when people were seriously able to ask them-selves whether he was 'sinking back to mediocrity'. Even in that season, be it remembered, he passed 1,000 runs in all first-class cricket – the only Australian to do so – and his average of 61·63 was likewise the best of any Australian. His failure, if that be the correct term, was only comparative, following upon the stupendous standards he had set. His innings of 48 and 71 (top score) in the final Test put him easily at the head of Australia's Test averages that season, with 56·57, a better average than Sutcliffe or Hammond, who had no bodyline to face. He reached fifty in one innings or other of all four Tests in which he played, and no other Australian managed this. It was a remarkable tribute to him that he headed the averages despite playing so unnaturally and so often with a horizontal or diagonal bat. Bradman did not dominate the Test series, as he almost certainly would have done without bodyline and as he had done against England in 1930, against the West Indies in 1930–31 and South Africa in 1931–32. The double-centuries that he was capable of scoring were effectively scotched. So bodyline, to the extent that it subdued the man it was fashioned for, succeeded. But at what cost? On the Sydney Domain, a junior match ended in a brawl after 15 minutes when one team introduced bodyline; an Adelaide match was abandoned after ten minutes with another brawl; at Centennial Park, Sydney, the casualty list of junior cricketers with head injuries multiplied appallingly and alarmingly. In some horribly perverse way, the dazzling genius of Bradman had been the cause of it.

Bradman gambled when he devised his method to play bodyline, though his constant drawing away to leg left his wicket dangerously unprotected time after time. But he also audaciously hit a good many of Larwood's leg balls on to the off, and frequently pierced the leg cordon too. Larwood dismissed him four times in the series, but Bradman scored more runs off him than any other Australian, even those like Woodfull, McCabe and Richardson, who played in all five Tests. In the 1932–33 series Bradman scored his 396 runs as follows:

	Balls received	Runs scored
Off Larwood	151	115
Off Voce	64	42
Off Bowes	7	9
Off Allen	131	109
Off Hammond	93	71
Off Verity	73	44
Off Mitchell	10	6
	529	396

His ratio of runs scored to balls received – 75 runs per 100 balls – was superior to any other Australian in the series apart from the bowlers P. K. Lee and H. H. Alexander, who both played in only the final Test. It was superior to *every* English player. Surely that must be some strong justification for Bradman's methods.[1]

Bradman lived dangerously, to be sure, in 1932–33 – in more senses than one. Larwood and Voce bowled the ball shoulder or head high in every Test without exception. But Bradman's method virtually obviated the prospect of injury, and he was hit only once during his eight ventures to the crease – on the left arm above the elbow by Larwood in the final innings of the series. As has been emphasised, Bradman's pulling away to leg was a deliberate ploy. It was also novel, however, and led Warwick Armstrong at least to believe, and to say more than once, that Bradman was frightened by Larwood. When Bradman was out for 24 in the second innings of the fourth Test at Brisbane, Armstrong cabled to the London *Evening News*:

Bradman started off by cutting Larwood for two fours off his wicket after pulling away. There was no doubt whatever in my mind that Bradman was scared of Larwood. As in previous matches, he played him badly.

---

[1] The leading Australian batsmen in the 1932–33 series finished with scoring rates as follows off the England bowlers:

Bradman	–	74·85 runs per 100 balls
Darling	–	60·90 ,, ,, ,, ,,
McCabe	–	59·59 ,, ,, ,, ,,
O'Brien	–	51·78 ,, ,, ,, ,,
Richardson	–	46·73 ,, ,, ,, ,,
Kippax	–	43·54 ,, ,, ,, ,,
Bromley	–	40·24 ,, ,, ,, ,,
Ponsford	–	39·60 ,, ,, ,, ,,
Fingleton	–	32·96 ,, ,, ,, ,,
Woodfull	–	30·68 ,, ,, ,, ,,

Bearing in mind the vastly different circumstances of the two series, Bradman's figure of 74·85 runs per 100 balls may be contrasted with his figure of 61·64 runs per 100 balls in 1930. His far more hectic approach in 1932–33 is quickly apparent.

Eventually he pulled right away from his wicket and cut a ball from Larwood straight to Mitchell at point. And Mitchell held it.

The plain truth about Bradman is that he is a class bat, but can never be described as a champion while Larwood is bowling to him. I also feel that he must learn to play for his side instead of for himself.

On the form shown in this series of Tests Bradman is nothing more than a cricket cocktail.

In Larwood's own book on the tour, published four months later, he took Armstrong to task for this 'rather uncouth sneer' and said of Bradman: 'Let me assure my readers that when bowling to him my share of the battle was certainly not one of brute force and something ignorance. The bowler who is confronted by Bradman and doesn't think doesn't bowl for long. Mere getting rid of the ball, leg-side bumpers for example, cuts very little ice when in opposition to such a cool and practised player as Don. That fellow is a very long way from being the "cocktail cricketer" which Warwick Armstrong in a rather uncouth sneer styled him last season. Apart from his wonderful eye and wrists Don has a very quick thinking brain. To him leg-side bumpers would be mere gift fours as often as any bowler was fool enough, and incompetent enough, to serve them up.'

For all that, on the day after his above-recorded sneer, Armstrong further accused Bradman of 'fiddling with a few spectacular and dangerous shots' instead of steeling himself to play 'the right type of innings for his side' and revealed that Woodfull and the rest of the team were 'very dissatisfied' with Bradman's tactics. However dissatisfied they may have been, their own tactics were hardly more markedly successful. To show he was not perhaps blinded by a little inherent State prejudice, Armstrong was direct enough to include three Victorians in this interesting surmise when the series was decided at Brisbane: 'To those whose Test career is virtually finished I must now regretfully add the names of Ponsford, Woodfull, and Ironmonger, and while bodyline continues, Bradman.' Although the proviso attached to Bradman, three of those four – including of course Don Bradman – were still to have a part to play in the future of Australian cricket. Australia lost the bodyline series by four matches to one, of course: and let the bold Armstrong be quoted for a final time from Sydney on the very last day of the rubber:

Had Bradman been built with more backbone, it is possible the whole story might have been different. The rubber hinged largely on Bradman and Larwood, and Larwood conquered him.

Those must not, however, be the final words of all. Larwood undoubtedly made Bradman change his game in 1932–33, for the method of attack was something new and Larwood was indisputably a great fast bowler. It was only natural that he should cause some consternation even to a talent such as Bradman's. But, as Jack Hobbs put it in his review of the tour: 'It was not ordinary fast bowling, even of the Larwood or super type, that reduced Bradman and Australia. That was done by bodyline bowling – leg-theory, with short balls interspersed, plus Larwood's great pace and accuracy, together with exceptionally clever setting of the field. More than enough, I think you will agree, to make any batsman think. Shortly, I considered it bowling the purpose of which was to intimidate the batsmen.'

It was not only Bradman who was subdued – indeed he was subdued far less than the others. But, as Hobbs again observed, the later Australian batsmen seemed to think, 'Well, if Don can't do it I can't.' When it is remembered to what extent Australia relied on Bradman, the result of the rubber is not surprising. Bradman was satisfied, rightly or wrongly, that there was no truly orthodox answer to bodyline. He studiously sought out his own answer, and with much moral courage ignored his detractors to see it through. He saw in his method the one certain way of not surrendering to Larwood. 'Had he batted normally', George Hele has observed, 'I believe his Test average would have been in the thirties, not in the fifties.'

Bradman's view of bodyline in 1932 was the straightforward view he has held ever since – that it would have killed cricket had it been allowed to be regularly practised, for within a matter of years there would have been no batsmen left in the game prepared to tolerate it, or rather prepared to tolerate its dangers. He said this from almost the first day he saw bodyline in operation. If he had had the smallest doubt in 1932 whether or not bodyline had been concocted for him – and he was shrewd enough to know that it *must* have been, although modest enough never to say so – he and the whole world were to be unambiguously informed of the truth in due course, by the principal actor himself, in *The Larwood Story*, where Bradman was confirmed as 'the human catalyst for whom the sharp prong of bodyline was shaped'. Larwood wrote in that 1965 book (and the italics are his):

> And here let me confirm what so many people have always believed and about which I have remained silent for more than thirty years – *bodyline was devised to stifle Bradman's batting genius.*
>
> They said I was a killer with the ball without taking into account that Bradman with the bat was the greatest killer of all.

When Larwood paid his second visit to England in 1977 since emigrating to Australia, he was interviewed for television before the start of the fourth day's play in the Test at Trent Bridge. Peter West asked him about 1932–33. 'We realised there was only one man to beat', said Larwood, 'and that was Bradman. Bradman we knew he was the danger. He was terrific.'

Larwood had an immense respect for Bradman's skill, and so of course did Jardine. It was the sheer immensity of the respect that turned it to fear. '*Something* had to be done to curb Bradman', said Larwood. 'The answer was found in bodyline. Bodyline *was* a plot and I was involved in it having been given the job of spear-heading the attack to put the brake on Bradman.' This plot was diagnosed pretty quickly in Australia in the closing weeks of 1932, and as a plot it was perfectly legitimate within the laws of cricket as they then stood. This is what made the problem so difficult and this is what divided the professional observers so dramatically. What did M. A. Noble say of Larwood in *The Australian Cricketer*? 'It is all humbug to say that his tactics were unfair, or that he bowled at the man, instead of the wicket. He didn't.' What did J. W. Trumble say in the Melbourne *Argus*? 'I disagree with the popular view of the leg-theory attack. I consider it quite legitimate and justifiable in Test cricket.' What did Archie Jackson, with the shadow of death above him, say in the Brisbane *Mail*? 'For the sake of Australia's sporting traditions, may it be left to the cricketers themselves to furnish the only answer to the legitimate tactics employed by the Englishmen.' What did Jack Ryder say in the Melbourne *Sporting Globe*? 'Slow and medium-pace bowlers can exploit it, so why not fast bowlers? . . . A captain can place the field where he desires.' There was also, needless to say, a powerful corpus of opinion to the contrary.

As Larwood contemplated the Australian tour, he could not help remembering the three Tests he and Bradman had played in together in 1930 – and Bradman's scores in them of 131, 334 and 232. At Leeds and the Oval, Bradman had hit Larwood unmercifully. 'Bowling to Australia's batsmen was rather like potting pheasants on the wing', recalled Larwood through his literary collaborator, 'but with Bradman it was like trying to trap a wild duck, his movements were so swift.' In fact in 1930, of the 292 runs Larwood had conceded in the series, Bradman had scored 137 of them, and the other 12 Australians to whom Larwood bowled made the other 155 runs between them. Never in his entire career was Larwood punished by an individual batsman to the extent that Bradman punished him in 1930.

When the Jardine tour was over, Larwood, perhaps unwisely, yielded to the implorations of Fleet Street. He had not gone on to New Zealand but returned home early after he hurt his foot in the final Test. The London morning, evening and Sunday papers vied for his revelations. Eventually, on the first Sunday of May, the new season having just started, the *Sunday Express* carried a huge story from Larwood's lips: 'You ask why Woodfull and Bradman could not stand up to my fast leg theory bowling. These are the true reasons. Woodfull was too slow and Bradman was too frightened. *Yes, frightened is the word.* Bradman just would not have it. He was scared of my bowling. I knew it, as everybody did. Time after time he drew away from the ball.'

All this – and there were columnfuls more – was undignified, provocative and embarrassing. It naturally brought swift condemnation as offensive comment from Australia. The impugning of Bradman's courage by the outright allegation of cowardice made no doubt splendid Sunday reading in some English households. After all, who was in a better position to see, and to judge, than Larwood? And had not Warwick Armstrong, an Australian, said much the same a few weeks before? Larwood's tirade that Sunday was unworthy, if not unpardonable. It was closer to abuse than to argument. Larwood himself had been attacked with great vehemence in the Australian press in the course of the tour, and here was a chance to retaliate in print.

He might surely have more wisely reflected that only one man can be held responsible for the tactics of a cricket side on the field – the captain. Bradman was obliged to emphatically deny the accusation of cowardice. He could not allow it to pass by default. He did not say much, but he reserved a word for bodyline: 'Larwood is entitled to his opinions as to my shortcomings with the bat, but by expressing them he is not entitled to suggest they offer an argument in favour of this theory. Whether I can play bodyline bowling, successfully or otherwise, is entirely irrelevant.'

Larwood defended himself fully, as well as the tactics of 1932–33, in his book on the tour, *Body-Line?*, published in June 1933, which carried an approving foreword 'from a very grateful and admiring' Douglas Jardine. Bradman by now, in the Australian winter, was free to write in the Sydney *Sun*, and when some of the early Larwood chapters were published, Bradman replied in print, in a reasoned and judicial way. Larwood included Noble's quotation from *The Australian Cricketer* in his book, which prompted Bradman to remind his readers thus: 'We may as well complete quoting Noble's comments. He stated that Larwood's tactics represented "preventable brutality". But that is not quoted in Larwood's book.' When distortions in Larwood's book became too obvious, Bradman ceased to bother to reply. Like other Australian cricketers, he did not consider it necessary to contradict the more excessive outbursts, and treated with a silent contempt the passages of personal animosity that Larwood penned about him.

Although Bradman had of course been prevented from writing during the series itself, he – in common with all other Australian players – had been permitted to broadcast at the close of each day's play. Bradman, Woodfull and McCabe regularly gave their impressions over the air, and Ponsford, Richardson and Rigg occasionally, while Kippax provided material for broadcasting to Europe. Bradman himself was always scrupulously careful while on the air in this series to speak generously of his opponents and not to succumb to the provocations of bodyline. He never disparaged Larwood or Jardine, and, like Woodfull, never betrayed a trace of bitterness. This was not so much a desire to stand aside from controversy as a simple exercise in sportsmanship. He was generous to his team-mates, too. On the evening that he scored his century at Melbourne, he paid tribute to the tail-enders who stayed with him while he scored runs. He interestingly expressed the opinion that Hammond had been the best English bowler that day. He also thanked the crowd: 'Only those who have played in a Test match can realise what an incentive it is to know that the thousands of cricket lovers at the ground are hoping for one's success.' Bradman's broadcasts normally consisted of a summary of the day's play, details of the scores, and, often, a humorous story about a team-mate or a barracker. He may have disappointed some listeners, but he always kept his calm.

Larwood's press and book allegations against Bradman were only a small part of the seething discussion that the events of 1932–33 had engendered. At the highest level the cables continued to pass between Australia and

England. As far on as 12 June 1933, the M.C.C. committee – if their cable of that date is any evidence – still could not properly distinguish between bodyline and leg-theory: or at least, if they could, they refused to believe that bodyline had been bowled by any English bowler in Australia. Bradman, in the Sydney *Sun*, quickly dubbed this M.C.C. cable as 'astounding' and said it appeared necessary for the Australian Board to send an ambassador to London to place the facts before the M.C.C. He suggested that Woodfull should be sent. 'Meanwhile, what a wonderful opportunity the M.C.C. has of arranging a demonstration of "bodyline" bowling with the West Indies on a fiery wicket at Lord's', wrote Bradman. Barracking had been roundly condemned by the M.C.C. in its cable, and Bradman commented briefly on that by asking what methods could be adopted to prevent it when 50,000 people combined to protest against the methods of the bowler. Bradman's writing was as direct as his batting – he knew what he wanted to say, and if he believed his point to be a good one, he presented it unambiguously and with a ruthless candour. He never chose to beat about bushes on a cricket issue, either at that time or at any time since.

The allegations of cowardice against Bradman that Larwood had made in the *Sunday Express* were no doubt recognised patently enough, by those with an understanding of these things, to be no more than a succulent journalistic morsel and probably not even Larwood's words anyway. (The offending piece was actually written up by another person, though Larwood did sign the proof.) When Larwood, at the age of 70 – during the 1974–75 M.C.C. tour of Australia – was asked by the Derbyshire journalist, Michael Carey, to look back at 1932–33, he admitted Bradman was not frightened:

> There was only one man we were after – Bradman. There'll never be another like him. I've never seen such quick footwork.
>
> We'd noticed that Bradman showed signs of distress at dealing with the short-pitched ball and flinched a bit. You couldn't afford to bowl at his off stump or he'd have smashed you all over the place.
>
> So, although I started out with an orthodox field, after a few overs all the slips would move over to the leg side. I used to bowl with no slips, a short gully, a silly point and three or four short legs.
>
> Bradman tried all roads to play me. He used to back away, not because he was scared, but to make room to try to hit me through the off side.[1]

That reason given by Larwood for Bradman's backing away was not only the accurate one, but precisely the preconceived pattern devised, of course, by Bradman himself. It illustrates conclusively enough both the falsity and the luridness of that old *Sunday Express* allegation.

Joe Darling, incidentally, in 1933, in rejecting the term 'leg-theory', said that as the bowling had been devised with one obvious purpose above all others, it should have been called 'The Bradman Theory'.

Sir Donald Bradman himself, in the years since bodyline, has never been

---

[1] *The Observer*, 26 January 1975.

anxious to resurrect the old controversies. He has never, on the other hand, wavered from his initial revulsion towards it – not because he, unwittingly, was its principal target but because he saw what the effect on the game might be of the short-pitched bumper, the purposely set field and the ever-present consideration of the risk of serious physical injury. He himself was aware that other players were threatening to give up cricket unless it was eradicated from the game. 'Those who are in charge of the welfare of cricket', reflected Bradman in 1938, 'must preserve its traditional beauty by confining the rivalry to bat and ball.'

When the great galaxy of former Test players converged on Melbourne for the Centenary Test in March 1977, Harold Larwood spoke of 1932–33: 'I still have no regrets about the tactic. Bradman had given me a hammering two years earlier. Attacking his leg stump was the only way to combat him.' Sir Donald Bradman refused to be interviewed.

The fact that Bradman averaged only 56·57 in the Test series of 1932–33 did not mean he was any less a batsman than he had been. He was still the best batsman in the world, or, if 'best' be open to opinion, certainly still the most prolific. His Sheffield Shield average that summer was 150 – not the highest of his career, but high enough to be the best ever for New South Wales to that date. In all matches for New South Wales, including two against the M.C.C., he made 713 runs at 89·12. He passed 1,000 first-class runs for the fifth successive season in Australia. He also passed 10,000 runs in his career, at the age of 24 years and four months (a world record at that time) – and did it, of course, in fewer innings (126) than any man before or since.[1] A few days later he reached a career aggregate in *all* matches, first-class and minor, of 25,000 runs, at an average just bordering on 90.

For St George in first-grade cricket his average was 170·66, and he performed for them the wonderful feat of scoring four centuries in four consecutive innings – all of them, incidentally, on different grounds. This was to be his final season with St George, and he gave, as usual, tremendous value whenever he played. His first-class commitments and ill-health restricted him to only five innings, but these are set out below, with their respective dates, so that his skill in relation to the incidence of bodyline elsewhere in his life may be gauged:

108*	St George v Gordon	at Hurstville Oval	on 3 October 1932
105*	St George v Mosman	at Rawson Park	on 8 October 1932
112	St George v Manly	at Manly Oval	on 4 March 1933
134	St George v Balmain	at Birchgrove Oval	on 25 March 1933
53	St George v Waverley	at Hurstville Oval	on 1 and 8 April 1933

[1] Bradman's average at the end of the innings in which he passed 10,000 first-class runs was 91·99. Among batsmen in the whole world, either contemporary or retired, the previous best average at that moment for anyone with 10,000 runs was 67·29 by Woodfull. Bradman was the 14th Australian in history to reach 10,000 runs in first-class cricket. He actually beat to that landmark Jack Ryder – who had been playing first-class cricket since Bradman was aged four!

The first two of these innings have been mentioned earlier in this chapter. His 112 against Manly was a dashing display of only 85 minutes, though he did escape being stumped first ball! Manly Oval had its largest crowd for many years, and Bradman gave his wicket away after his hundred. Another large crowd turned up to see him against Balmain, when he was dropped in the slips by Arthur Mailey when 2, but gave no other chance in his 134. (Mailey, tempted to make one of his very rare appearances now for Balmain, tried hard to dismiss him, but ended with nought for 76.) On his home ground at Hurstville Oval, Bradman ended the Sydney grade season with a bright 53 against Waverley, reaching a 3,000-run aggregate for St George (excluding friendly matches) and yet another large attendance watched him, though as soon as Bradman got out the public went home. This was, and was to remain, the pattern on many grounds, not just at Hurstville Oval.

Before his final innings in first-grade cricket for St George, Bradman had scored 2,969 runs in his career for them, for 32 dismissals – a state of affairs strangely similar to and reminiscent of his composite figures in first-class matches in England in 1930: 2,960 runs for 30 dismissals. When his over-whelming success in England that year is considered, his equally shattering dominance in St George matches is put speedily in perspective. His fielding for St George, too, was always quite outstanding – both the accuracy of his throwing from the outfield and his catching: memorable catches by him at Hurstville Oval are still vividly remembered by spectators of those years. He also captained St George on several occasions, both at home and away, was not afraid to put his opponents in when he deemed it proper, and gained his first experience of captaincy in competitive cricket. (He captained the side whenever he was available in his last two seasons.) He took a few wickets for the club, too, with his leg-breaks, especially in his earlier years. The St George finances were, in addition, handsomely bolstered by his presence. St George, and the other Sydney clubs, made a modest admission charge to the public for first-grade matches, and Bradman's magnetism attracted unusually large crowds whenever he played, besides enhancing the prestige of St George among Sydney clubs.

Here are Bradman's season-by-season batting figures in first-grade cricket for St George:

	Innings	N.O.	Runs	H.S.	Av.	100s
1926–27	7	1	289	110	48·16	1
1927–28	10	3	411	130*	58·71	1
1928–29	4	0	261	107	65·25	1
1929–30	7	2	549	187	109·80	2
1930–31	3	2	215	116*	215·00	1
1931–32	8	1	785	246	112·14	3
1932–33	5	2	512	134	170·66	4
	44	11	3,022	246	91·57	13

(*Note:* He never played in second-grade or third-grade cricket for St George. On occasions he appeared for the club in non-competitive matches in aid of local hospitals and similar causes, or on tour in New South Wales, but the above figures are confined to his first-grade appearances.)

When Bradman reached 3,000 runs for St George in 1932–33, only one player had previously reached this aggregate in first-grade matches for the club – R. J. Louden (debut 1924–25), who had played many more innings than Bradman. Louden reached 3,000 runs in 1930–31.

Bradman's 13 centuries in first-grade cricket constituted a record for St George at the time. Since then B. C. Booth, W. J. Saunders and W. J. Watson have all exceeded this figure for the club, and A. R. Morris has equalled it, but all in many more innings than Bradman. Bradman's average of 91·57 remains unrivalled, the next best average for St George in first-grade matches being 61·57 by N. C. O'Neill (3,879 runs).

Bradman's other minor cricket in 1932–33 proved further that bodyline had had no effect on either his temperament or his capacity for making runs against 'normal' bowling. On 8 March 1933, at the Sydney Cricket Ground No. 2, he went in first wicket down and hit a furious 148 in 85 minutes for a N.S.W.C.A. Coaching Team v Northern Suburbs Junior Association: he reached his hundred in 65 minutes and scored his last 48 in 20 minutes, including 22 in one over – altogether he hit 5 sixes (all of them after passing his century, including one on to the tramline) and 22 fours. On 21 March he took part in a match for the Archie Jackson Memorial Fund (which benefited by £182) when he made top score for New South Wales against a team of ex-internationals at the Sydney Cricket Ground No. 1: his dismissal took the distinguished form of c Macartney b Mailey 98. It was scored in only 54 minutes, and New South Wales' total of 289 for five took only 109 minutes. Bradman had earlier in the match bowled Tommy Andrews for 77 and caught Macartney for 64; and had caused the biggest laugh of the day when, just before the veterans' innings closed, he packed a full leg-theory field for G. L. Garnsey, the esteemed N.S.W.C.A. coach, known to be bitterly opposed to bodyline bowling, and tried to emulate Larwood: the ball bounced four times, but Garnsey failed to hit it!

Over Easter week-end, 1933, Bradman went back to old pastures when he toured Moss Vale and Bowral with a St George team led by his former Sydney guardian, Frank Cush. On Good Friday Bradman played at Moss Vale for the first time since his record score there as a youth in May 1927, and several players who appeared in that game now opposed him again: Bradman scored 152. On Easter Saturday he scored a hurricane 71 v a Berrima District XI at Loseby Park, Bowral (a little to the south of Glebe Park, but still very close to his parents' home), his brother Victor and his old friend, Sid Cupitt, opposing him, with Alf Stephens, another old friend, as captain. And on Easter Monday, again at Loseby Park, St George met a combined team of district and visiting cricketers, and Bradman gave a most brilliant display by hitting 11 sixes and 14 fours in 159. In his three innings on the short tour, Bradman had reminded his old friends in the most practical way of his glittering prowess, undiminished by the experiences of bodyline. They must have been very grateful to see him in such form – and grateful, too, that he was no longer in their regular midst to punish them and plunder them as of yore. This was the last time he ever played cricket in Bowral.

In all matches in Australia in 1932–33, Don Bradman scored about 2,500 runs at an average of about 90. D. R. Jardine had tried his best to clip his wings, but at the end of the season he was still as great a force as he had been at the beginning.

One final – but not unimportant – fact about Bradman in 1932–33 should be recorded. Bradman himself later said privately that any success he encountered that season was due to the devotion of his wife. 'If it had not been for her I could not have played in a single Test match that season.' Not only did she attend him everywhere, but she also watched every ball in the matches and prepared the skeletons for his writings and broadcasts. She did his secretarial work and saved him from the tender mercies of countless idol-worshippers. What was in any event a very strenuous and emotional season would have been more strenuous and emotional still without Mrs Bradman.

7 Farewell to Sydney

On and on and on he seemed to go, batting into cricket eternity.
Jack Fingleton on D. G. Bradman

At the close of the 1932–33 season – a season that was to leave a more than ordinary impression on those who took part in it – Donald Bradman decided to make a thorough study of the laws of cricket. He was spending his first winter at home with his wife in Sydney. His decision to study the laws was with a view to sitting the examination of the New South Wales Cricket Umpires' Association. (This body, constituted on the day after Bradman's fifth birthday in 1913, did yeoman work for the game – as it still does – in both city and country. Before its formation, cricketers were obliged to accept umpires who, frankly, often had little knowledge of the laws of the game.) Bradman's decision was, paradoxically, surprising and typical at the same time – surprising in that the endless day-to-day cricket involvement to which his job in Sydney subjected him should prompt him to devote even more time (and concentrated time) to off-the-field engrossment in cricket; and typical in that he did not consider himself a complete cricketer until he had thoroughly understood the laws and their interpretation. The study was intended to improve him as a cricketer and to fit himself as a knowledgeable future captain: there was never envisaged any ultimate career as an umpire. After three months of study, Bradman passed the Association's examination 'with great credit', at the first attempt, on 1 August 1933 – one of the rare instances of a first-class cricketer in his prime, and a Test cricketer at that, sitting for and passing the Association's examination. (Sir Donald was lucky, for today – and since the war – no one is allowed to take this examination without a view to a bona fide umpiring appointment. When, in his early twenties, Richie Benaud likewise concluded a study of the laws and sought to take the Association's examination, he was turned away, in spite of pleading the Bradman precedent. Even so, during the 'permissible' era, very few first-class players bothered with such things: apart from Bradman, only F. A. Easton, the New South Wales wicketkeeper of the '30s, entered for this examination.)

Sir Donald Bradman has never regretted the study of the laws he made as a young man of 24. Though his contribution on the field was, and was to continue to be, as a player, his theoretical knowledge of the intricacies of cricket law – added of course to his constant observation of the laws being applied in practice – fitted him admirably as a voice of authority in discussing administrative and legal problems. And he always, and even more so after his early studies, maintained a most healthy respect for umpires, both on the field and in committee. More than 30 years after his examination success, and very nearly the same period as an exile from his native State, Donald Bradman – by now knighted and a senior statesman of the game – accepted the invitation of the New South Wales Cricket Umpires' Association to be their Guest of Honour at their 50th anniversary dinner at the Cricketers' Club in Sydney, held on the Saturday of the fifth Test between Australia and South Africa in February 1964. Sir Donald's outstanding address is still vividly remembered as the highlight of the evening.

While he had been studying the laws, Don Bradman also put himself into the hands of his dentist and had a number of teeth taken out, so that his general health greatly improved as a result. Bradman's health had begun to give him concern from the 1932–33 season and he was never altogether at his best right through to 1934, at the end of which season he was taken so desperately ill. That he was able to amass during that period so many big scores is testimony not only to his skill but to the great strength of his will in overcoming physical indisposition.

When Don Bradman married, he left the Hurstville district of Sydney to live further north in the city – and thereby lost his qualification to continue to play for St George. The members of the club formally learned the news of the loss of his services at their annual general meeting on 5 July 1933. His new club for the forthcoming season was to be North Sydney, a strong side[1] with O'Reilly in its ranks and who had won the first-grade competition in 1931–32 and come fifth in 1932–33 – in each case better than St George. In both those seasons O'Reilly had finished with the best bowling average in the entire Sydney first-grade competition: 54 wickets at 7·88 and 31 wickets at 8·38 respectively. Now the club was to annex the greatest run-getter in Australia.

Before the start of the new Australian season of 1933–34 Bradman turned 25, with, it need hardly now be emphasised, a staggering wealth of achievement behind him. 'Twenty to twenty-five! Those are the years!' said Winston Churchill, and in that five-year span Donald Bradman amassed 10,232 runs in first-class matches at an average of 92·18. The spark was still thrillingly vital, and if anyone supposed that the rigours of bodyline had either changed Bradman the run-getter or altered his basic approach to the bowler, they were to be set wise in this new season of almost unrelieved triumph. This was the season, more perhaps than in any other, when run-making was made by him to appear simpler than shelling the proverbial peas. It seemed that he was even bored by the apparent ease of it all, and therefore indulged himself in dazzling displays of pyrotechnics at the crease, the orthodox yielding to the exotic, sixes flowing where they had previously been eschewed, and his scoring-rate rising higher than ever before. The runs still poured forth,

---

[1] And a rich one too. On 16 March 1929, the club opened its new pavilion at North Sydney Oval – at a cost of about £11,000.

whatever his methods: and it would have required a brave man – or a foolish one – to criticise a batsman who could twice score a double-century at more than a run a minute and end up with a Sheffield Shield average of 184. His Brobdingnagian achievements once again quite overshadowed the Australian summer.

Bradman was still employed, under his three-tier contract, with F. J. Palmer, in their Sydney sports outfitting department; and he was still doing his local writing and broadcasting. For the first time in four years there were no Test matches in Australia, but the domestic season naturally was to have its significance with a tour to England following at once. Bradman had no brushes with the Board of Control – and what a difference to his cricket this made – and indeed ended the season very high in the Board's good books, clearly earmarked as a future captain of Australia. Although his triple contract was due to expire in February 1934, the Board had by then named him as vice-captain for the tour of England: and thus any possible defection from Australian cricket that a tempting offer might prove could be treated as effectively scotched.

Bradman's employers provided him with a novel way of getting the season under way. He and McCabe (employed by Mick Simmons) accompanied some 200 schoolboys on a holiday tour of northern New South Wales in early September 1933, the two Test players being responsible for coaching and the organising of some matches. Bradman's role as 'father' on this venture is still remembered by many of those boys, not least by 'Jock' Livingston, then aged 13, whose ambition was duly fired and who – like several others among those boys, including Keith Carmody, Ron James, Jim Minter and George Powell – went on to play for New South Wales. Bradman, characteristically, went to immense pains prior to the tour to ensure that each of the many boys for whom he was responsible was properly briefed and properly equipped. He did not merely sit back and await the arrival of the tour to begin his duties. He wrote a vast number of detailed letters, all in good time to avoid last-minute hitches. 'Please don't be afraid to treat me as a friend and adviser', he wrote to the boys. However minor this six-day goodwill tour by schoolboys may have been in the context of the wider history of cricket, Don Bradman at least treated it with something like military precision. It was in fact his first venture outside Sydney as captain of a team. At Wangi Wangi, Lake Macquarie, Bradman gave a 15-minute exhibition of batting in his street clothes; and in one of the organised matches, at Lismore, Bradman scored 71 in 30 minutes for the 'Sun'–Palmer Colts, as his team was called, and which of course he captained, against Mick Simmons' Radio Club, captained by McCabe. In this innings Bradman showed the boys something to remember, scoring 34 in a single over (3 sixes and 4 fours) and scoring his last 49 in ten minutes!

Bradman had always been able to hit sixes *if he had wished it*, but his methods in the first-class game (where in any event he encountered larger arenas) had hitherto virtually eliminated them. He had never, for example, hit a six in a

Sheffield Shield match when the 1933–34 season opened, and altogether in 102 innings at that time on Australian soil (yielding 7,688 runs) he had struck but a solitary six, and that was in the Test match at Adelaide the previous summer when he was batting somewhat hectically against England. He had actually scored over 8,700 runs in first-class cricket in Australia before he hit his second six there, and then he hit *eight* sixes within two innings!

After he returned to Sydney from his 'Sun'–Palmer venture, he left almost at once for a pre-season country tour with a New South Wales Cricket Association team, under his State captain, Kippax, and managed by one of his early St George captains, E. W. ('Ted') Adams. Bradman had a fine tour, playing in all the eight matches and passing 500 runs. Before the largest crowd ever seen at a cricket match at Mudgee, where the tour opened, he hit 87 on a non-turf wicket; he scored exactly 100 in 45 minutes v Dubbo; 49 in 42 minutes v Cowra; 58 v XV of Holbrook and District; 109 – 88 in boundaries – in slightly over an hour v XV of Albury, when Fingleton and McCabe were both dismissed for ducks in the same over, and when the other batsmen made only 30 while Bradman was at the wicket; a bright 51 before a record crowd on the Saturday at Albury in the second match against the local XV; 48 at Leeton, where international cricketers were playing for the first time; and at Wade Park, Orange, before a crowd of 2,000, Bradman ended the tour by actually being bowled for 6! But earlier in the day he had taken seven for 21 with the ball – Orange batted 15 men – though doubtless there were many who complained at the end that they had not come to see Bradman bowl! The team had travelled 1,300 miles in 16 days through the western and Riverina sections of New South Wales, and as in previous seasons Bradman had already got himself into good form before the approach of more serious things.

The new grade season in Sydney began under a minor cloud of controversy for Bradman, though not through his doing. He was now with North Sydney, of course, and before the season began the club had reappointed as captain Albert Vincent, one of the most experienced club cricketers in Sydney and a man absolutely devoted in his allegiance to the North Sydney club. Bradman's arrival immediately created a strong group of supporters who declared that he – Bradman – should captain the side (as he had done St George the season before) and indeed that he should have every opportunity possible to act as captain, being a potential candidate in due course for the captaincy of New South Wales. (This was never to come about, though his supporters could not anticipate that at the time.) A. H. Vincent, incidentally – he was also one of the club's two delegates to the New South Wales Cricket Association and was a delegate in all for a quarter of a century, as well as, in due course, a State selector – had captained the side which won the first-grade championship in 1931–32, and had also been captain in '32–33. He was now very upset by the criticism of his fresh appointment as captain and promptly resigned the first-team leadership. The club appointed Bradman in his place. It was an unpleasant episode, though when Vincent stood down he made it clear that he did not blame Bradman in any way 'for any unpleasantness that has occurred'. Nevertheless, it was not the start of a new relationship that Bradman would have chosen himself. (Sixteen seasons later Bradman and Vincent were to serve together as Australian selectors for the 1949–50 side to tour New Zealand.)

In the event, and somewhat ironically, in this his first – and only – season with North Sydney, Bradman was to play only three innings for them in the first-grade competition, and Albert Vincent was fairly rapidly back in command as captain. Bradman's proposed debut, on the last day of September 1933, saw not a ball bowled through rain. His first innings for his new club was played two days later, against Waverley on a wet wicket at Waverley Oval, where he was given a fine reception by the crowd but was out, in a low-scoring match, for only 19, caught by Jack Fingleton. Then on the Saturday of that week, he met all expectations by scoring his first century for North Sydney – a brilliant 127 v Western Suburbs at North Sydney Oval, reaching his century in just over 90 minutes, then hitting two fine sixes (the second clean out of the ground) before being stumped trying for a third. Thus in his first innings on his new club's home ground, he had reached three figures.

One of the features of Bradman's cricket in Sydney in all the years he had been living there – both before and after his marriage – had been his eagerness to play in as many matches as he could, of whatever kind. His fitness was never in doubt and his appetite for runs was never in doubt. He did not willingly give up his wicket, however minor the engagement. His dash and genius with the bat were equally evident wherever he played. If he could play in three one-day matches on successive days, he would do so – and if in the process he could notch up three hundreds, he would willingly do that too. Scoring runs was almost certainly an easier exercise for D. G. Bradman in the early '30s than for any other man in the world. In the 1933–34 season the first signs that his stamina was not what it had been began to make themselves manifest. 'I felt', Sir Donald himself has said, 'that the runs had to be obtained quickly before fatigue intervened.' This was not a welcome discovery for a man of 25: but the fact remains that he was never thereafter the same fit and ebullient Don Bradman that he had been before.

The increasingly rare, though still welcome, sight of Bradman and Macartney at the crease together occurred at the North Sydney Oval on 11 October 1933, when they played together for Bradman's XI v North Sydney Boys' High School Past and Present. Macartney scored a most sparkling 71 in an hour as an opener, while Bradman, at number three, made 37. A fortnight later the pair shared a good stand again when Bradman's XI played Oldfield's XI at Chatswood Oval in aid of the funds of the Young Citizens' League. Macartney had begun the day by taking three for 26, and when his turn came to bat, Bradman gave him the number three position, going in at number four himself. Macartney scored 30 and Bradman 144 – on a wicket soft after rain. Bradman hit seven sixes, admittedly not on a large ground, most of them after reaching his century, when the small boys collecting autographs from the many Test players present forgot them temporarily to watch these soaring sixes. Apart from Bradman's 144, the highest innings of the day was Wendell Bill's 33. A. G. Moyes was playing in this match, and he has told the extraordinary story of Bradman asking: 'What would you like me to do with the next one?' 'We suggested a six over the head of point', recorded Moyes. 'Bradman pivoted on his feet and lifted the ball over the fence. We called it a fluke, so he repeated it.'

Bradman began the first-class portion of the season with a Shield match at Brisbane. The last time he had played a Shield match at Brisbane he made 0. This time he made 200. Bradman had lost a certain amount of popularity in Queensland over his stand with the Board of Control on the player-writer controversy. His tactics in that dispute left the Queensland public – as well as the Queensland Cricket Association – out of favour with him. There may still, too, have been some lingering regrets that he had not thrown in his lot with Queensland at the very beginning of his Test career, as Brisbane folk had heard rumoured. How their side could have done with him in those years! This was now his first appearance for New South Wales in Brisbane since the player-writer episode. He treated – or punished – the crowd in the most positive manner, with batting of a perfection said to have been 'never previously seen in Brisbane'. He reached 100 in 92 minutes, 150 in 160 minutes – and then scored his last 50 in 24 minutes without the aid of a single six or a single chance. Not only had he scored a double-century in a day, but had not made use of $2\frac{1}{2}$ hours of that day! It was his highest Shield score in Brisbane. 'At times', said one writer, 'his daring made one gasp with astonishment, but his execution and timing never erred.' If Queenslanders did not relish Don Bradman as New South Welshmen did, he was to give them a further, and even more potent, sample of his savagery before the season was out. (In Brisbane, by the way, his wicket was captured by the Queensland captain, R. M. Levy, once prominent in Sydney cricket as a former colleague of Kippax's in the Waverley side. It was his only wicket of the season and the first of his career. He bowled only one over in the match!)

Before leaving the fixture against Queensland, it should be mentioned that Bradman shared there his highest ever partnership at Brisbane, a second-wicket stand of 294 in 171 minutes with W. A. Brown – the last 94 in 41 minutes. Although Brown had opened the innings and shared a century first-wicket partnership with Fingleton, and though he had a start over Bradman of $2\frac{1}{2}$ hours, Bradman at number three overhauled Brown's score most comfortably while they were together – and Brown learnt a great deal from the experience! In this match Bradman actually scored his 1,000th run against Queensland in only his sixth game against them!

On their way back from Brisbane, the Sheffield Shield team played a two-day match at Newcastle, and Bradman confirmed his dazzling form with his best ever score at Newcastle – a beautifully compiled 183, in which he reached his century in 85 minutes on the first evening, and then gave the

Saturday crowd another treat (as he had done at the Sports Ground at Newcastle four years before) by adding a further 74 on the second day before being caught on the boundary, with a six and 20 fours to his name. He and McCabe (98) added 231 for the third wicket.

Two Test Trials were held that month (really benefit matches for distinguished players), and the very man the Australian selectors needed least evidence from – D. G. Bradman – duly scored most runs. He made 55 and 101 at Melbourne, and 22 and 92 at Sydney. His 55 was scored out of a second-wicket stand with Fingleton of 79 in 61 minutes. At Sydney he was dismissed in the 90s for only the second time since he had returned from England in 1930. In that period he had got to 90 in first-class matches on 19 occasions – and gone on to three figures in 17 of them.

New South Wales lost their first Shield fixture since two seasons before when they went down by ten wickets in the Ernie Jones testimonial match against South Australia at Adelaide just before Christmas. Grimmett did not bowl against Bradman (1) in the first innings, but gave him a torrid time in the second, inducing several chances from the Bradman bat and eventually dismissing him for 76. No one took more wickets in that Australian summer than Grimmett. In the traditional Christmas fixture against Victoria in Melbourne, Bradman – despite a strained back – was at his very best with two chanceless innings of 187* and 77*, never giving a hint of getting out in his whole six and a half hours. In the first innings he scored 79 of his side's last 96 (i.e. 82%) and 37 out of 39 for the tenth wicket with W. Howell. It was his fourth hundred in his last four matches in Melbourne – a sequence that was to be extended, incredibly, to eight hundreds on that ground in eight successive matches.

One of the highlights of the Australian season followed at once – and Bradman reserved his highest score of the summer, and his most glittering spectacle, for the luckless Queenslanders. For the second time within two months he thrashed them for a double-century, once again reaching three figures at better than a run a minute (this time in only 86 minutes) and scoring in all 253 in under 3½ hours. He scored a century in a session twice in this innings – in the post-tea session on the second day and before lunch on the third. This match was played on the Sydney Cricket Ground, where Bradman had never before hit a six in a first-class match. Now he hit four, all of them while scoring his last 53 in 19 minutes, and all of them off R. M. Levy, to whom Bradman had fallen in Brisbane and who was now tempting Bradman in the hope of getting him caught: he conceded 25 runs in one over, including two sixes by Bradman, and 22 in his next over, including two more sixes by Bradman. Bradman had actually gone from 200 to 250 in 16 minutes, and threw his wicket away in the end, satiated with runs – and with a career average against Queensland on the Sydney Cricket Ground alone of 180·25!

In this match Bradman shared in his highest ever partnership in a Sheffield Shield match, he and Kippax adding 363 for the third wicket in only 172 minutes (126 runs an hour) – still a Sheffield Shield record for this wicket for any State. Kippax scored 125 of the runs, but Bradman outscored him by more than 100 while they were together. They added their last 190 in 92 minutes on the third morning, their final 63 in 17 minutes, and at one time making 50 in only 14 minutes. No wonder the New South Wales treasurer wept tears of grief when he was to learn very soon that Don Bradman was leaving the State to play elsewhere.

In the course of 11 days (and six days' actual cricket) Bradman had scored 517 runs before being dimissed – and even then he gave up his wicket. This fine spell at that time had only been exceeded by 'Patsy' Hendren's 630 runs before being dismissed while on tour in the West Indies in 1929–30, though other batsmen have since had even better spells. Bradman, for the fourth time in the last six Australian seasons, made the highest score in Shield matches (his 253), though outside the Shield C. L. Badcock had just scored 274 for Tasmania and a month later I. S. Lee was to make 258 for Victoria against Tasmania.

Bradman's back trouble in 1933–34 – the first time it had manifested itself – kept him out of the North Sydney side and the State side in the very season when he might otherwise have played regularly without the intervention of Test cricket. After 3 January he played only one further first-class match and no Sydney grade cricket at all. (In fact, due to his first-class commitments and then his back trouble and subsequent departure from Sydney, his last innings for North Sydney was played on 14 October – 62 v Petersham – so that he finished with an average of 69·33 from his only three innings with the club.)

While the selectors were putting the final touches to their deliberations for the side to tour England in 1934, Bradman played in his final first-class match of the season, against Victoria at Sydney. It was to prove his last Sheffield Shield appearance at Sydney as a member of the home team. If his public did not know that, he certainly did, for within a few days he was no longer even a resident of New South Wales. He made his farewell innings a memorable one. Not many batsmen can play a final innings of the season of 128 and yet see their first-class average reduced, but that is what happened to Bradman. He scored his fifth century in seven matches, his 128 (out of 192) taking only 96 minutes, his last 78 in 39 minutes. Although he batted at number three, he went in with the score at 148 for none, when Fingleton retired with cramp, Bradman then helping Brown add a further 192 before the first wicket – that of Bradman – fell at 340. It was the highest partnership for the first wicket in which Bradman ever took part in his first-class career.[1] At 80 runs an hour off his own bat, his 128 was also the fastest century innings of his career so far. He hit four sixes, all of them off Fleetwood-Smith. The first was judged to have been one of the mightiest seen at the ground for

---

[1] It was W. A. Brown, Bradman's last partner in cricket for New South Wales, who succeeded Bradman in the sporting department of F. J. Palmer and Son Ltd. Brown began with the firm the day after the match with Victoria ended, on 31 January 1934.

many years: hitting with the breeze from the southern end, Bradman drove the ball to the roof of the small northern stand, close to the sight-board. He then really set about Fleetwood-Smith, and with the total already past 300 without a wicket down, he proceeded to hit him for three sixes in an over while the crowd were in a frenzy of delight. In the same over he was caught in the deep, content to give his wicket away. It was a memorable end to his career with New South Wales. It might so nearly, too, have been the last time an Australian crowd was ever to see him, for before he played again in his native land he was to hover at death's door as closely as has any man who has come through and survived.

The 1st of February 1934 saw the contractual end of Don Bradman's two-year agreement with F. J. Palmer, the Sydney *Sun* and Radio 2UE. Their combining together had, of course, made it possible for Bradman to resist the tempting overtures to leave Australia for England. The terms had also, how-ever, carried their problems, not least with the Australian Board. The antici-pated expiration of this contract naturally caused Bradman to think afresh about his future. He was not a man of independent means any more now than he had been at the time of the Accrington negotiations. But if the truth be known, he had found the terms of his contract something of a strain when they were added to his playing commitments. As a medical man was later to point out, Bradman played cricket, wrote cricket, talked cricket, thought cricket, and lived cricket. This was not good for any man. And Bradman realised that, even if others were reluctant to. He probably did not know that Bernard Shaw had regularly welcomed the opportunity for a walking holiday with the Webbs, for he could then switch wholly to non-theatrical matters: but Bradman would have appreciated the point better than most. As the end of his contract came in sight, Bradman frankly did not relish a renewal of a life of travelling in sports goods, rushing to broadcasting studios at the close of a day's cricket and the possibility of further skirmishes with the Board of Control over his ventures in journalism. He had had his full share of this life, and had concluded that it could not be indefinitely reconciled to the considerable demands of first-class and Test match cricket.

Bradman had never really wished to leave Australia to take a league appointment in England, and when the time came to settle the future, league offers were discounted. In any event, that would merely have taken him from one cricket milieu to another. The Sydney *Sun* were reluctant to lose him – his exclusive writing was a handsome feature of their cricket coverage – and made him a good offer to join the staff full-time. He considered it, but turned it down. In the interim – actually at the end of September 1933 – Bradman had indeed had visions of becoming the independent business man who could control his own destiny. It was then that he entered into a five-year contract as a director of Don Bradman Ltd, a new company which was being formed with a nominal capital of £35,000 to carry on business as tailors and dealers in sporting goods. (Also a director of the new company was to be F. T. Smith, formerly general manager of Palmer's Emporium, where

Bradman was employed.) But Bradman's visions were quickly to come to naught. When a proposed issue of 25,000 £1 shares was announced simultaneously in Sydney and Melbourne and a prospectus issued, only about 8,000 were taken up. The promotion of the company was suspended, and by the first week of December the episode had been relegated into history. The failure to launch this company disappointed Bradman, and he was back in the market again to receive offers from others. While the matter was still in the balance, he had frightened his fervent supporters – who never again hoped to hear talk of defection to England – with the statement: 'If the new enterprise fails to provide me with a livelihood I will have to seek other employment, either in Australia or England.'

The offer that interested him most came from outside the State – from Adelaide. Running a stock-broking business there was H. W. Hodgetts, one of South Australia's long-standing members on the Board of Control and a former secretary of the Adelaide Stock Exchange. He was, incidentally, also a devoted admirer of Don Bradman. It was he who gave Bradman the important opportunity to separate completely his cricket from his daily work. It was not the ideal solution for Bradman to leave New South Wales – his family were there and his wife's family were there. They both thought very deeply about the Adelaide offer. They realised at the same time that what Sydney could offer instead *always* insisted on exploiting Don Bradman's name as a cricketer.

Bradman travelled from Sydney to Adelaide to talk the matter over. He travelled incognito. Harry Hodgetts invited him to join his staff on his return from England in 1934. He would also in these new circumstances play for South Australia. Bradman accepted the offer, and he and his wife moved to Adelaide in February 1934, to qualify by three months' residence to play for his new State. It was announced to the world – and to a saddened New South Wales in particular – on 12 February that Bradman was joining Hodgetts in his Adelaide business after the 1934 tour. It was intended that he should start playing for South Australia in 1934–35. (It is a strange, and little known, fact that South Australia tried to get Macartney in 1914 to move to Adelaide and to play for that State, but of course without success.)

Meanwhile the Australian Board – on 31 January – had announced their side to visit England in 1934. Don Bradman was named as vice-captain, even though Kippax was in the side. It was a sure sign that any old feuds he had had with the Board were at an end. It was a sign also that he was destined to succeed Woodfull as captain of Australia at the appropriate time. He was now recognised by authority – as he had long been recognised by his cricketing opponents – to possess cricketing wits as quick as his bat. His judgment was sound and his understanding of every aspect of the game's tactics absolutely thorough. Only the experience of leadership at first-class level, which had never yet come his way, was necessary to fit him for the role of strategist. The 1934 vice-captaincy was the first position of 'rank' he had occupied in the first-class game – the first of a great succession of positions that were to come his way in the near and distant future. During the tour of England itself in 1934 he was one of the Australian team selectors along with Woodfull and Kippax.

The Australian selectors themselves for the 1934 tour of England were Dr C. E. Dolling (South Australia) – the only survivor of the 1930 tour selectors – E. A. Dwyer (New South Wales) and, for the first time, W. M. Woodfull (Victoria). They clearly had as little trouble selecting Bradman's name now as had had their predecessors four years before. In 1930 Bradman's average for the season had been 127·27 when the team was announced. In 1934 it was 132·44.

Percy Fender went into print on that last day of January with a much sounder forecast of Bradman's potentiality in England than had been the case before 1930:

> It seems odd to see Bradman as vice-captain, while seniors such as Ponsford, Kippax and Oldfield are in the side.
>
> That he is the greatest batsman whom Australia have is beyond doubt, as also is he their greatest fielder anywhere except in the slips.
>
> There should be no reason to think that he has done anything else than improve since his last visit, though many say that is hardly possible.
>
> His feats in 1930 would excuse us from thinking of such a possibility, but he is four years older, and has had that much more experience, and it would seem to me that if anything is certain about the tour it is that Bradman will be found to be better than ever.
>
> Bradman is capable of winning almost any match off his own bat, and that is something which will never be forgotten by our players, no matter what the state of the game.

There was no critic in the world, English or Australian, Fender or otherwise, who dared now forecast other than success for Bradman. Even those who knew – and there were very few who did – of his health worries and of his problems about settling his future, would not be prepared to count them as factors so far as his batting was concerned. J. C. Davis, the considerable authority on Australian cricket and editor of the Sydney *Referee*, cabled to the London *Evening News* the following view of Australia's new vice-captain on the day the team was announced:

> Bradman looks better than ever, though to Englishmen this may sound like a bit of romancing. When fighting for runs he still plays the type of game England knows so well, faultlessly and brilliantly.
>
> Recently he has developed powers of big hitting that were hardly suspected, and in the last two Sheffield Shield matches hit eight sixes, all very big hits.
>
> Bradman may try this big hitting against the English counties if he reaches the century mark. But one scarcely expects him to adopt a Jessop role in Test matches. He has gone in for his big hitting here only when looking anxious to get out. The suggestion that he is up against the Board of Control has no foundation.

'Dick' Jones, though no longer a State or national selector, was still very delighted that day, and he can have been forgiven a little nostalgic pride at the news: 'I am naturally very pleased to see that Bradman has been appointed vice-captain. I had previously predicted that one day he would lead Australia; and it looks as if my prophecy will come true.'

At this stage Bradman's impending departure for Adelaide was still not public knowledge. In retrospect it seems that his four sixes against Victoria – and a phenomenal New South Wales scoring rate of 120 an hour while he was at the crease – was Bradman's method of giving his loyal Sydney supporters something by which to remember him. In truth they had had six full seasons of the sheerest magic, when connoisseurs flocked to the cricket ground to see him bat and when those who knew nothing about cricket flocked likewise to the ground to see him bat – and to go back home at once the moment he was out. In Sydney when Don Bradman was playing it was a social obligation to go to the cricket, for males and females and young and old. He was applauded and worshipped irrespective of style: just the domination, the accumulation, and the spirit of 'gamin' was enough. There was cause for administrative congratulation if he were not out at an interval or overnight. A New South Wales v Victoria match would attract 35,000 when Bradman was playing. Only a fifth of that number would turn up when he was no longer with New South Wales.

It may be considered strange that Bradman was never offered any administrative or official post while with New South Wales. It was, however, nothing more than the pattern of New South Wales cricket of the time. Don Bradman was a very young man, and very young men were not suitable material for the reposing of confidences or the seeking of advice. Their skill and experience at the highest level counted for nothing. There was never, for example, one chance in a hundred that Bradman would be a St George delegate on the N.S.W.C.A. – or at least not unless he put away his bat or had played a dozen or more seasons in Sydney cricket. It was not quite impossible to find a first-class cricketer among these club delegates, but they were *rarae aves*, as indeed they were on the Australian Board itself. When Bradman found himself in the New South Wales side against South Australia at Sydney in February 1933, with Kippax absent, it was not the 24-year-old Bradman (with 21 Test matches behind him) who was made captain, but the 37-year-old 'Hammy' Love (with no Test matches behind him). Some considered this a deliberate snub to Bradman and felt it was a sad pointer to his chances of succeeding to the State captaincy. (Not too much should be read into it, however, for Love had just captained New South Wales in their previous Shield match, with Kippax, Bradman and Oldfield away, so it was not very improper to retain him as emergency leader.)

Whether it was reaction to the strain of securing his livelihood, or the physical upheaval of moving from Sydney to Adelaide, Don Bradman's health gave him further cause for concern as soon as he arrived in Adelaide in February 1934. Far from keeping himself physically in shape for the forthcoming tour of England, he was able to play no cricket at all. The absence of practice might not have meant much where an exceptional skill such as Bradman's was involved, but a decline in general health, away from familiar surroundings, meant an unwelcome period of stress on the eve of an important tour. He consulted two specialists in Adelaide. He was found to be extremely run down. They told him he must not play again before arriving in England and that he must take the fullest advantage of the rest on the boat journey across. Thus he did not play in the touring party's traditional pre-departure matches against Tasmania at Launceston and Hobart in the middle of March or against Western Australia at Perth. Bradman in fact did not make the trip to Tasmania. Nor did he play in the one-day match against Ceylon on 4 April when the Australians stopped off at Colombo on their way to England: the Ceylonese desperately wished to see him, and calls of Brad-man's name came forth at the fall of each wicket.

For all his health anxieties, Bradman had nevertheless ended the 1933–34 season as the best batsman in Australia, with all the confidence and certainty he had displayed before the temporary intrusion of bodyline. For the sixth season in succession he passed 1,000 runs. He scored a greater percentage of his side's runs than in any season hitherto. He also scored faster than in any season so far. His average of 132·44 was also the highest of his career so far. In Sheffield Shield matches alone he played innings of 200, 1, 76, 187*, 77*, 253, 128: to give him 922 runs (a new record for New South Wales) at an average of 184·40 – another record at that time for *any* State. In nine of his 11 innings in first-class cricket he passed fifty, including five centuries. His figures provided yet again the yardstick of his domination of first-class cricket, a domination that had started in 1928–29 and had had only an interim setback in 1932–33.

8 England and Adelaide

I wish I could have used my bat like Don. He's a gem of a batsman. I just love
his finished technique and inevitable surety. How he must enjoy getting his runs.
C. B. Fry on his first sight of D. G. Bradman, 1934

When Trevor Wignall, of the *Daily Express*, went out to Ceylon to accompany
the 1934 Australians on the *Orford* for the rest of their trip to England, he
naturally had a chance to see his old friend of 1930 – and tormentor of his
phrase-book – Don Bradman. He sailed with him from Colombo to Southampton. When he got back to Fleet Street he reported to his readers on
Bradman that 'when I first spoke to him in Colombo his tired, much-older-
than-his-years look genuinely astonished me, but in the boat coming home
I saw him improve every day'.

There is no question but that the long sea voyage did him a power of good.
 It can be stated now without offence to anybody that for several months before
sailing Bradman was very worried about his future.
 It was that, I fancy, that so changed him, but I am happy to record that to-day
he is nearly back to his old self.
 He will never again be the dashing young record-breaker of four years ago, but
I am willing to stake my existence that he will pile up many another century before
September arrives.

On the boat coming across – it was the same ship, the *Orford*, used by the
Australians in 1930 – Bradman again proved himself especially skilful in the
deck games, playing his full part in the tennis and deck quoits. The Australian
Davis Cup team were on board, but they mercifully did not enter for the
tennis event! But their manager, Mr S. R. Youdale, *did* compete, and it was
he who knocked out Bradman in the deck tennis, to prevent him repeating
his 1930 *Orford* finals win. Bradman also got through several rounds of the
bridge tournament.
 There was no camel-riding in Egypt for Bradman this time – he left that
to his more intrepid colleagues. Nor did Bradman join that group of the
Australian team that went on a continental tour before going on to England.
On arrival at Gibraltar, those Australians still on the *Orford* were invited to
lunch at Government House with the Governor, General Sir Charles
Harington (M.C.C., I Zingari and Free Foresters), remembered not only as
a distinguished soldier but as one of the few men ever to decline the invitation
to become President of the M.C.C. It was on that day that Bradman said:
'After this long rest, I am a different man. . . . I am feeling as fit as ever.'
Bradman disembarked at Southampton on Anzac Day, 25 April, and

travelled by train to London. He had put on 7 lbs in weight and outwardly, at least, seemed in good health. Before the team left London for Worcester, Bradman raced Brown round Lord's, and his breathing at the end was reported to be 'practically as sound as when he started'.

The first of the centuries predicted by Wignall duly arrived – with the inevitability of clockwork, it seems in retrospect – on the opening day of the tour on the New Road ground at Worcester. It was not, however, *quite* so inevitable: and nearly did not happen. Bradman, despite appearances, was still not feeling fit, and rumours about his indifferent health had been circulating before his arrival. But Woodfull persuaded him to play in order not to let those stories get out of hand. Bradman responded by adding to his 236 at Worcester in 1930 an innings this time of 206, made without practice (beyond two brief nets at Lord's), in only 3½ hours, playing every known stroke in the game before deliberately giving his wicket away. He had given one stumping chance when 102, and scored 94 before lunch on the second day, being out well before the interval. At virtually a run a minute, it was a faster innings than his double-century on the ground in 1930. The Australians' scoring rate while Bradman was at the crease was 94 an hour. His scimitar-like strokes – he hit 24 boundaries and three all-run fours – brought the verdict from the ring of 'better than ever'. But as in the Australian summer just ended, there was a brilliance allied to a looseness or jauntiness – more strokes were in the air in three hours at Worcester than had been in three weeks in England in 1930. Nevertheless his 206 was only a single run short of the combined two innings totals of his opponents.

Watching that innings of 206, as one of the umpires, was T. W. Oates, the old Nottinghamshire 'keeper. He seems to have been something of a lucky mascot for Bradman, for he had also been standing at Worcester in 1930. Not only that, he was one of the 1930 umpires, too, when Bradman made his Test scores of 254 at Lord's and 334 at Leeds!

Bradman went on to play in 1934 immediately against Leicestershire (the wooden spoonists of the previous season) at Leicester – Aylestone Road's first match of the season. It was an important match for Bradman, for it marked his first game as captain in first-class cricket, and he received the congratulations of his colleagues accordingly. He was now leading, among others, Alan Kippax, under whom he had played virtually his entire cricket for New South Wales. His first opposing captain was A. G. Hazlerigg, and Bradman called wrongly to his toss.[1] On his first day in the field as a first-class captain, Bradman saw his club and State colleague of the past Australian

---

[1] The opposing captains in this match – without either of them knowing it – were thus a future knight (Sir Donald Bradman) and a future peer (the second Baron Hazlerigg). It happened, by coincidence, to be Hazlerigg's first game as appointed captain of Leicestershire (though not his initial experience of first-class captaincy). Bradman, at 25, and Hazlerigg, at 24, made one of the youngest pairs of captains, outside the University captains, in first-class cricket that summer, slightly younger than Bradman and Alan Melville (also 24) in the Sussex match at Hove in August.

season, W. J. O'Reilly, take all the first seven wickets to fall. The match was drawn, in the Australians' favour, and Bradman scored a forceful 65 (his lowest score ever against Leicestershire) out of 93. It was scarcely noted at the time, but the innings put the seal on a new world record, and one that still stands – it was the 16th match in succession in which Bradman made a score of at least 50 in one or other innings. His average over those 16 matches was 97·43!

What appeared to be growing into an ominous renewal of the Bradman march of triumph of 1930 was halted suddenly and unexpectedly on a beautiful Wednesday morning at Fenner's following the Leicestershire match. On this pitch of celebrated batting perfection, and which had been carefully protected from the recent rain that had fallen on Cambridge, some tall Australian scoring could be anticipated. It duly came – Ponsford scoring 229 not out and Brown getting his first hundred in England – but the number three batsman in the Australian order went down on the scorecard thus:

D. G. Bradman b J. G. W. Davies   0

To say this was a surprise is a feeble assertion. It was a minor sensation. Davies had no great claims to bowling skill, though as a batsman and cover fieldsman he was outstanding. His 1934 figures for Cambridge prior to the University Match were eight wickets at 44·25 each. He bowled slow off-breaks, and with his fourth ball to Bradman he struck his off stump to give the great man his first duck in England. It dramatically reduced his average from 135·50 to 90·33! The Cricket Correspondent of *The Times*, much as he may have thought it not wholly desirable to either single Bradman out for special descriptive treatment or, worse still, to analyse a run-less innings, found himself compelled to write as follows: 'Davies bowled a ball which floated across from leg and which Bradman expected to break back. He was wrong. It went on and, as he had not quite got across, it hit the off stump. That was what happened, but I do not propose to give an analysis of every ball that bowls Bradman in future.' There was an immense crowd of under-graduates and others, and Beau Vincent went on: 'The immediate effect of Davies's indiscretion was absurd and rather sad. The bowler seemed a shade ashamed; the crowd remained stricken in silence before they rewarded a fine ball with the acclamation it deserved.' To clean-bowl Bradman for 0 was a distinction no other English bowler could claim until Bedser and Hollies did it after the war. (When Bowes dismissed him for 0 in 1932–33, Bradman dragged the ball into his wicket from outside the off stump.) The circumstance, gratifying as it must have been momentarily for Davies, nevertheless served to obscure in the public eye a subsequent sporting career of notable all-round service to Kent. As far on as September 1976, when Davies's appointment to the treasurership of M.C.C. was announced, he was still inextricably linked with that one ball he sent down in 1934. His identity was disclosed by one morning newspaper as follows: 'Former Kent and Cambridge University bowler Jack Davies, who once bowled Sir Donald Bradman, is to succeed "Gubby" Allen as treasurer of M.C.C. on 30 September.' Rather like 'the boy Collins', it may be that Jack Davies later wished he had never done it.

The 1934 tour, despite the start at Worcester, was never destined to be anything like *le grand succès* of four years before. Bradman was still a great batsman, of course – a very great batsman, with, if anything, an increased range of stroke. And he was still able to play his dominating, awesome innings. That he played them less regularly in 1934 can be attributed partly to the fact that his health was affecting his form and imposing, at times, on his batting a strange look of carelessness; and partly to his pre-conceived batting plan aimed at giving himself less strain at the crease than formerly on occasions when big scores from him were not essential. He was more fallible in 1934 than on any of his other tours of England. He had more prolonged spells of ordinariness than at any other time in his career. He was off colour right through the 1934 tour of England with an undefined ailment that stretched back to the preceding season in Australia and indeed back to 1932–33. It was, as has already been said, a noble tribute to his skill and will that he was able to play some of the fine innings he did play – most especially in the Leeds and Oval Tests – while the seed of illness was lurking disconcertingly. His 'curious' season was remarked on by Sydney Southerton in *Wisden*: 'It was noticeable that in many innings Bradman lifted the ball to a far greater extent than when he came here first and there were many occasions on which he was out to wild strokes. Indeed at one period he created the impression that, to some extent, he had lost control of himself and went in to bat with an almost complete disregard for anything in the shape of a defensive stroke.' That this was an unnatural aberration, explicable only by the subsequent facts about his health, was indicated by Southerton's high assessment of Bradman's batting in '34 outside his 'careless' patches: 'To those, however, who watched him closely in his big innings it was obvious that in the course of four years he had improved his technique almost out of knowledge. He was much more interesting to look at because of the wider range of his scoring strokes. At his best he was probably harder to get out than ever and at times so marvellous was his footwork and power of execution that all bowlers were at a complete loss as to where they should pitch the ball. An amazingly brilliant batsman, he retained that faculty, given to most really great players, of delaying his stroke until the last possible moment.'

When Bradman went to Lord's to play against M.C.C., he lasted only six minutes (caught and bowled by Freddie Brown for 5); and at Oxford, on the Christ Church ground, he won his first match as captain in first-class cricket when the Australians beat the University by an innings, Bradman making a somewhat ordinary 37. Then, against Hampshire at Southampton, he made his second duck of the month – a quicker one even than at Fenner's. Giles Baring (who was to take 0 for 113 for the Gentlemen v Players later that season) was bowling very fast and had just dismissed Brown for a duck when

Bradman came in – to be caught second ball trying to cut an out-swinger. The ball went to Mead at first slip, who clutched it with a desperate (but not too certain) embrace to his bosom, at which several Hampshire voices from the field cried urgently to Mead: 'Don't move!' Mead duly did not move and Bradman walked without the slightest hesitation – and it was then that John Arnold discreetly and gently removed the ball from the trembling Mead for fear that it should fall! (Mead had caught Bradman on the same ground in 1930 – for 191!)

Thus it was that by 25 May Bradman had scored only 313 runs for six dismissals (av. 52·16), and 206 of those runs had come in a single innings. By the same date on the tour of 1930 he had scored 922 runs at an average of 153·66, likewise for six dismissals. Now, in 1934, he returned to London lying uncharacteristically sixth in the averages, with a match against Middlesex at Lord's on the morrow.

Those lucky enough to have been at Lord's on Saturday, 26 May 1934, saw Don Bradman play one of the greatest innings of his life. Many who have watched cricket for several decades still class it as the finest innings of their experience. When he first saw 'Patsy' Hendren after his arrival in England in 1934, Bradman told him he had now reached the stage when he had definitely made up his mind to enjoy his cricket. Hendren saw that enjoyment flower in its fullest glory against Middlesex. Bradman went in at 5.13 p.m. on the Saturday evening, with 77 minutes to go before close of play. Woodfull had just been out to 'Big' Jim Smith for 0; Ponsford was out to Smith for 0 soon after. At one stage Bradman scored 25 out of 26 in three overs. He took 27 in three overs off Robins and 18 in two off Peebles. He scored 55 off the last ten overs, which included a maiden to Darling. He reached his half-century in 49 minutes, and as the time was already two minutes past six, it seemed a mere fancy to expect him to reach his hundred that night. But 28 minutes later he did so. Off the last ball of the day Bradman ran a quick single off Peebles just wide of mid-on to reach his century, out of a total of 135 for two. He had been absolutely brilliant, and the Middlesex bowlers quite helpless to stop him. Robins, Peebles, Smith, Enthoven and Judge were all hit – off good-length balls or otherwise – for exhilarating fours (there were 19 in the century). The occasion prompted Fergie to exceed his duty as scorer and enter on his scoring-sheet that evening, 'great innings'. Jim Smith still remembers the occasion most vividly: 'As soon as Don came in he tried to cut me three times and missed them all. Then he did cut me for a single off the last ball of the over, to get off the mark. When he came down to my end, he said: "Hard luck, Jim. My luck's in now." He then set about Judge, and all the rest of us, and didn't need any more luck.' Apart from those dangerous swishes at Smith, Bradman proceeded chancelessly, never lifting the ball from the ground, adding faultless timing to extra-ordinary strokes. 'All the shots were his,' wrote William Pollock, 'the whole field his kingdom.' His eye, wrists and footwork had been proved every bit as good as in 1930. 'All his defensive strokes seemed to be attacking strokes', recalls one spectator. After he retired Sir Donald ranked this innings as probably the most attractive of his career from a spectators' point of view. Beau Vincent wrote after that 77-minute century: 'Bradman has had a bad spell lately, but he is now a greater cricketer than he was in 1930. A more certain run-maker he could not be expected to be, but there is a self-pleasure, relieved of anxiety, in his batsmanship which now makes him every bit as dear to an English crowd as were Macartney and Trumper.' The words, if Don Bradman read them, must surely have pleased as well as inspired him. On the Monday morning he scored a further 60 out of 90 in 47 minutes before Joe Hulme held a magnificent catch from a hard drive at long-on, stumbling backwards up the grass slope in front of the pavilion. If ever first-class bowlers looked as if they could not bowl, this was the occasion.[1] Sir Pelham Warner was fond of telling of the Hon. R. H. Lyttelton's reaction to Bradman's score. 'Bob' Lyttelton's absolute limit was one glass of port after dinner, but 'last night I had to have another in honour of that innings'. There was very little use of the pads by way of defence that day to upset 'Bob' Lyttelton!

This innings of 160 was like a great flash of summer lightning across the 1934 sky. It was only two hours out of the whole season, but two hours of which no other batsman – not even Hammond – could have been capable. All the old adjectives of four years before were pulled out, and for 20,000 on the Saturday the display had been breathtaking magic. 'Set a field for Bradman?' commented the Middlesex captain, H. J. Enthoven, shortly afterwards. 'Twenty-two men would not have been enough to plug all the holes he found in our run-saving barbed-wire entanglements during his masterpiece. . . . As a brilliant demonstration of scientific hitting I have never seen it remotely approached.' At the Carpenters' Hall the following Thursday, Sir James Barrie alluded to the innings in toasting the Australians at the Surrey dinner to the tourists and distinguished Bradman's clinical precision of 1930 from his new-found exuberance of 1934: 'Bradman, when you were here before, we knew that another prodigy had arisen in the land of cricket; you won every garland batting can claim except one only, yours did not seem to issue sufficiently out of excess of joy and gaiety to win the love of greybeards, but the other day at Lord's you did enter into our love.'

It was now clear that although Bradman's batsmanship could be as wonderful as ever, he was not the acquisitive menace to English bowlers that he had been in 1930. This was as much a state of mind as anything else. By the end of May he had scored 550 runs at an average of 68·75 – at the same moment Ponsford was averaging 122 and McCabe 110·33. Bradman's figures

---

[1] The 1934 season was the first in which the Lawrence Trophy was awarded for the fastest century of the season. Bradman's century against Middlesex in 77 minutes, though his fastest up to that time in England, was strangely not even a contender, for four days before Ian Akers-Douglas had reached three figures in 65 minutes for Kent. The eventual winner that year was Frank Woolley (63 minutes). Bradman had led the field for only a brief time with his century in 104 minutes at Worcester on 2 May.

were the same when he entered the first Test on 8 June, considerably less than half the runs he had amassed at the same stage in 1930.

Bradman's innings in the first three Tests of 1934 were so ordinary that the figures have failed to impress themselves on any minds. After Old Trafford his average in the series was 26·60, and he had behind him his experiences in Verity's match at Lord's to live down. His efforts outside the Tests in this period were not much better, and he experienced the worst spell of his entire career by going 13 consecutive innings without recording a century. This was bad, of course, only in the context of the career of Don Bradman. No cricketer who has played any appreciable first-class cricket can claim such a low figure as 13 innings for his worst spell without a hundred. So good a batsman as Charles Barnett, who was played 20 times for England for his batting, once went 226 innings without a century. And there is a long enough list – too long, some of those included on it will say! – of outstanding batsmen who have played more than a hundred innings in succession without reaching three figures.

Bradman, or indeed any of the Australians, did not play against either Jardine or Larwood all summer in 1934. Jardine was now one of the gentlemen of the press, playing no first-class cricket and writing on the Tests for the *Evening Standard*. Larwood was surrounded by rumour and counter-rumour until, with a certain truculence, he excommunicated himself in June by bursting into print that he would never play against the Australians again. In fact after 1932–33 neither of those two principal actors in the body-line drama ever appeared against an Australian side again.

Bradman was reported to have been most anxious to make another of his tremendous scores in the first Test at Trent Bridge. It was feared – and rumoured – that the Nottingham crowd, resentful at Larwood's absence, would prove hostile to him and that groups of miners (supporters of Larwood) had determined to be unfriendly to Bradman.[1] All these stories proved false, and on his appearance Bradman was cheered. But he played a rash and hectic innings of 29 – in accordance with his new policy of 'enjoyment' – which caused his old admirer, Trevor Wignall, to write: 'I have never seen Bradman like this before. He was reckless in the extreme, especially in his calls for singles. Instead of walking to the pitch in slow time, as was his invariable custom four years ago, he practically ran to it. But what caused Bradman to open his innings in a fashion that would have lost many a boy his place in his school side?' It was one critic's view that 'Bradman began as if he had about five minutes in which to catch a train'. He made a very sketchy 25 in

---

[1] Earlier in the tour Bradman received a disconcertingly large mail of abusive and threatening letters, questioning his sportsmanship and threatening personal violence. This was the aftermath of 1932–33. Some of the letters carried a Nottingham postmark. Bradman could make no public pronouncement on this situation, being prohibited by his contract, but his old friends in Bouverie Street, *The Star*, spoke out on his behalf and pointed out the absurdity of these insults. They made a public appeal to the letter-writers to give Bradman a 'good break'.

three-quarters of an hour in the second innings, so that Australia's victory by 238 runs owed unusually little to his efforts.

The story of Bradman and the Nottinghamshire miner is one that leaked out only by accident, but it is proper that it should be recorded in these pages. On his way to the ground on the second morning, Bradman saw an unemployed miner outside the ground looking wistfully – and glumly – through the gate at the crowd going in, and quite clearly in somewhat dire straits. Bradman invited him to come in, paid for his admission to the ground and also for a stand seat, and gave him a few shillings. It was found that the man had a wife and eight children, and Bradman and various cricketers and friends there and then raised a subscription for him amounting to several pounds. Bradman himself headed the list with a substantial subscription. It was rough justice that at the very end of the match, Bradman, in hurrying off the field, should trip over a boundary rope obscured by the crowd. He suffered a painful ligament strain in the thigh, and though limping badly, captained the Australians at Northampton (batting twice with a runner) because Woodfull had to return to London. When Bradman himself got back to London he was ordered to spend a night in a nursing home so that the thigh could be treated before the second Test.

As at Lord's in 1930, Bradman went in in the Lord's Test of 1934 before a Saturday crowd (and a huge one of over 30,000, on whom the gates had been closed). His style of batting by that stage of the tour had become so 'predictably unpredictable' as to cause P. G. H. Fender to speculate for his evening newspaper readers before Bradman's arrival on that Saturday afternoon thus:

> One of the things for which I shall hope is that we may get a wicket early enough to force Bradman to face the new ball. He is such a very queer proposition as a batsman these days that one never feels certain of the trend of events until he has been disposed of.
> One day he may take command through sheer brilliance and on another the reverse may happen, but I do feel that the more he can be made to face the fast bowlers when they are fresh, the better the chance England will have of subduing him.
> It does not necessarily follow that a fast bowler will get him out, but it is certain that a fast bowler, if one can be kept on all the time he is at the wicket, has an unsettling effect on him.

Bradman went in just after tea, and at once went bald-headed for the bowling, even more so than was the case at Trent Bridge. He hit 14 in an over off Farnes and reached 20 in as many minutes. He hit the first three balls of a Verity over for four apiece: but with 36 off 37 balls, Verity caught and bowled him – a now typically short life and a merry one. He played brilliantly and creatively – with 'the fire of genius', said Cardus – but perhaps too much so. B. J. T. Bosanquet reflected as follows: 'What a difference when Bradman came in – "vin ordinaire" at one end and champagne at the other. Practically every ball bowled to Bradman was played hard enough for four runs.' In three-quarters of an hour Bradman had beaten the field to a frazzle. But were dazzling pyrotechnics going to aid Australia in the score-book? One purist termed the innings as 'clowning'.

Verity's 14 wickets on the final day at Lord's – on a wicket (after rain) on which the Australians had had virtually no practice – gave England their first victory over Australia at Lord's since 1896. It was the first time Australia followed on in a Test in England since Old Trafford, 1905. Whatever Bradman's style in this innings, it was unlikely to save the match for his side. He was in fact far more restrained than usual – until his patience gave out. He hit wildly against Verity's spin and sent the ball so high and so straight up between the wickets that, incredibly, any one of *seven* fielders, including Verity himself, could have taken the catch. Ames, with the gloves, actually held it. William Pollock humorously wrote: 'The ball was so long in the air that the whole of the England selectors might almost have issued from the pavilion and been in time to go into committee as to whose catch it was to be.' Bradman made 13 out of 14 in 28 minutes – but they were 28 minutes, mainly against Verity, that were remembered for years and years. The stroke off which he was caught made a most awful recollection. P. F. Warner, now in his second year with the *Daily Telegraph*, called it, with even a hint of generosity, 'a most unguarded stroke at a critical time'. Neville Cardus recalled that as Ames came forward from behind the stumps, 'Bradman stood aside, exposed in momentary embarrassment like a detected schoolboy'. The series was level, and Bradman's average in it was 25·75.

To add to Bradman's Test match woes by way of low scores came further anxiety about his physical condition. During the third Test at Old Trafford, and before he went in to bat, he suffered an affection of the throat, recurring abdominal pains, and his body broke out in spots. Bradman had actually reported sick the night before the Test began. On the Wednesday he had been to Wimbledon, and Fred Perry, Bunny Austin and several other tennis stars suffered a similar malady as Bradman. The throat trouble was common to several members of the team. Bradman retired from the field at lunch on the first day, was taken back to his hotel, sent to bed and a doctor called. On the second day he was not allowed out of his hotel room at all, but bravely said he was quite prepared to leave his bed to help his side if needed. Over the week-end the suggestion was made that Bradman had been perilously near to a nervous breakdown almost from the moment of his arrival in England. When he batted on the Monday afternoon he was subdued and made only 30. His cheeks were very drawn, Trevor Wignall observed from the press-box, 'and never before have I seen him look so thin. . . . I felt that I was pulling for him as he vainly strove to overcome insuperable obstacles. He was but the wraith of the greatness we once knew.' Perhaps he might have been better advised not to bat.

Soon after this came foolish rumours – cabled, naturally, to Australia, where they were read by Mrs Bradman – that Don Bradman would have to visit a London heart specialist. Whatever else may have been troubling

Bradman in 1934, the one thing he did not have was heart trouble. His wife sent a most anxious cable of enquiry. Bradman cabled in reply that she must not believe such reports, and added – most ominously – that if she waited till the Test match at Leeds he would 'show them'. It would seem in retrospect that it could well have been this incident, together with his wife's cable in reply of 'Go to it, Don. I believe in you', that brought about the dramatic change in Bradman's mental approach to batting in the middle of 1934. One cannot be sure, but he did of course 'show them' effectively enough at Leeds. His physical energy throughout a full day at the crease there made any suggestion of heart trouble seem farcical.

Actually Bradman did not rest after the third Test at Manchester, but played at once in the Australians' following two games immediately before the Headingley Test. Not at his best, he made the top score of the match – 71 – against Derbyshire at Chesterfield. And then against Yorkshire at Bramall Lane he scored his first century for nearly two months, with a really brilliant innings reminiscent of his hundred against Middlesex in May. In front of a 12,000 crowd, and against bowlers including Bowes, Macaulay and Verity, he went in *after* lunch and was out *before* tea for 140. He scored his second fifty in 26 minutes, and his last 40 in 20. Two sixes and 22 fours (i.e. 100 runs in boundaries) were hit in the single session by Bradman, who went from 50 to 100 by means of one six, ten fours and four singles. His final 90 runs, in only 46 minutes, were made up as follows, at one stage 46 out of 47 coming from boundaries:

4441644444441114421644412444.

It was clear that when Bradman *was* able to score hundreds, he wasted no time over them. In fact at this point his last five centuries in first-class cricket had been reached in the following splendid times:

86 mins.	253 v Queensland, Sydney	1933–34
87 mins.	128 v Victoria, Sydney	1933–34
104 mins.	206 v Worcestershire, Worcester	1934
77 mins.	160 v Middlesex, Lord's	1934
100 mins.	140 v Yorkshire, Sheffield	1934

Thus the stage was set for Bradman to appear again at Leeds, where in the only previous innings of his life he had scored 334. Hitherto, the style of play he had adopted in the Tests – deliberately, one must assume – had brought poor results and much criticism. 'He almost gave the impression of having made up his mind that a rate of scoring of anything less than eight runs an over was beneath his dignity', said Douglas Jardine. 'Fortunately for his captain, his side and himself, he ultimately abandoned this creed. The instantaneous success which rewarded his return to his more normal methods at Leeds, served not only to place him on his former pinnacle, but to convince him himself of the error of his previous ways.' Jardine could well have reflected on the ironies of life. In a scrupulously prepared – and bitterly carried out – programme against Bradman in 1932–33, after three Tests Bradman's average was in the 50s. Now, with no special plan against him by England, after three Tests his average was in the 20s.

That average could hardly have prepared Headingley spectators for a second triple-century from Bradman's bat, though people were inevitably saying that one of these days Bradman would make another of his mammoth Test scores. 'We will make a big error if we indulge in pleasant fancies that Bradman is a spent force.' So C. B. Fry had written at the beginning of July, just before the Old Trafford Test. He had not been right on that occasion, but he was to be so now. And what had R. C. Robertson-Glasgow said after Bradman's second innings at Lord's? 'He is still rather inexplicable, but I still fear him.' When the second day of the fourth Test began, Australia were 39 for three (in reply to England's total of 200), with two balls of an uncompleted over by Bowes to be bowled. Bradman had not gone in over-night. That was the night that Neville Cardus invited Bradman to have dinner with him in his hotel. Bradman declined, wishing to go to bed early. 'Thanks', he said, 'but I've got to make 200 tomorrow – *at least*.' Cardus could not resist the reminder that in his last Test innings at Leeds he had passed 300. 'The law of averages is against your getting anywhere near 200 again.' Firmly enough Bradman replied: 'I don't believe in the law of averages.' Here was not only unshakeable confidence but positive evidence indeed of the new Bradman mentality of 1934.

A quarter of an hour before the resumption on Saturday morning, Bradman had a few minutes' practice against the boundary posts just inside the playing area in front of the old dressing-rooms. He then went out to resume the proceedings with Ponsford. The two balls of Bowes's overnight over were both driven by Bradman past the bowler for four. 'I knew he had got me', was the reaction, later freely admitted, of Bowes. And the day was certainly to be Bradman's. The runs flowed just as they had from the real Bradman of 1930. The 'playboy' cricket of earlier in the season was gone. The old relentless and merciless mastery was back. The more orthodox that was Bradman's cricket, the more likely he looked to make runs. He was 271* by the close on Saturday night, with Verity's analysis this time standing at one for 100. That one was Ponsford, who had shared with Bradman a titanic fourth-wicket stand of 388 at 68 an hour between 11 o'clock and 5.51 p.m., setting a new record for any wicket in Test cricket. The two Australians – and it was the ultimate fear that at last engulfed England – simply wore out and devoured the England bowling. It was the day that the stentorian voice of a spectator cried out: 'Put on Dolphin!' (He was one of the umpires.) It was the day that J. C. Laker, aged 12, had his first sight at the crease of Don Bradman, to whom of course he was to bowl on that very ground in Test cricket 14 years, almost to the day, later. It was the day that Bradman made 76 before lunch, 93 between lunch and tea, and 102 between tea and the close. It was the day that J. M. Kilburn, in the *Yorkshire Post*, described him as 'the champion of champions . . . He is a text-book of batting come to life with never a mis-print or erratum.' When stumps were drawn the Yorkshire police had to race to the middle to protect Bradman from the hysterical crowd. 'What they would have done to him', said Kilburn, 'I really do not know (the policemen won the race) but no honour could have been too high for the incredible cricketer.'

At the Prince of Wales Hotel, Harrogate, that Saturday night, Bradman told Tom Clarke (who was accompanying the Australians for the *Daily Mail*) that when he got back to the Australian dressing-room after his undefeated 271, the whole Australian team gathered round him with a bottle and a toast 'To Don'. It was perhaps an act of relief as well as of homage. But Bradman would not have it. 'I am listening to one toast', he told them, 'and that is "To a victory".' 'I am not out to make personal records', he told Clarke. 'My side required the runs. I am not going out on Monday with the intention of breaking my former record. I am going out in the spirit that we Australians want to win this match.'

Bradman went on to 304 on Monday morning before his leg stump was knocked out of the ground by Bowes. The last time Bowes had dismissed Bradman in a Test it was for o! Bradman left the field wreathed in smiles, his side's score 550 for six, and cheered every step of the way back. During the innings he had exceeded Clem Hill's record 3,412 runs by an Australian in Test cricket. He had batted for seven hours and ten minutes and hit two sixes and 43 fours. Ferguson's scoring chart showed hardly a spot on the Headingley field to which he had not sent the ball. He was back again on top of the Test averages, for either side.[1]

Bradman still remains the only cricketer in the world who has twice scored a triple-century in Test cricket (and he was only a single run short of another such score in 1931–32). Both his triple-centuries, moreover, were scored in matches limited to four days, and were compiled respectively at 52 an hour and 42 an hour off his own bat. (Every later triple-centurion in Test cricket, without exception, has not been so enterprising: Hutton's 364 was made at 27·40 an hour; Hanif Mohammed's 337 at 20·84; Sobers' 365* at 35·66; Simpson's 311 at 24·48; Edrich's 310* at 34·96; Cowper's 307 at 25·33; and Rowe's 302 at 29·60. The two remaining triple-centuries are Sandham's 325 at 32·50 an hour and Hammond's 336* at 63·39 an hour – which puts Bradman's two scores into second and third place in the table of runs per hour. No one would pretend, however, that Hammond's innings at Auckland in 1932–33 was scored against a particularly potent attack.)

Bradman's 304 at Leeds was a full five hours longer than any innings he had played since his 206 at Worcester at the very start of May: and in fact it

[1] After his 271 runs in the day, Bradman – now vice-captain and perhaps sensitive to the criticism of four years before, when he could not be seen on the evening of his great Headingley triumph – was in convivial mood, dining that Saturday night with a large party of his fellow-cricketers and friends, and allowing himself the rare luxury of a sip of champagne. These moments of good cheer are rarely recounted in the Bradman saga. Too often the choice of emphasis is on Bradman's unsociability.

was even twice as long as that innings. His muscles reacted, and he has himself recorded that his team-mates had to undress him and carry him to the massage table. Then, just after five o'clock on the third day, Bradman, at full stretch at extra cover, strained his right thigh while stopping with his left foot an off-drive by Hendren, and had to limp off the field. The injury – a badly pulled muscle – kept him out of the Australians' next six matches. He entered the Park Lane nursing home of Sir Douglas Shields at once, and although ten days had been the estimated time of his indisposition, he did not play again for three weeks. His wrenched thigh got better, but his general health remained dubious. Sir Douglas Shields took a personal as well as a professional interest in him, and took Bradman off for a period of recuperation in August to his and Lady Shields' charming country residence at Colinswood, Farnham Common, Bucks, on the edge of Burnham Beeches.

He tried himself out – without having had even a net since his injury – in the one-day match against the Army on the Aldershot Garrison ground three days before the deciding fifth Test at the Oval. On a sunny day and on a good pitch, he scored 79, ending with a flurry of boundaries, before giving his wicket away. He felt fit for the Oval, and the rest had done him much good. He turned up for net practice with his old smile and jauntiness.

The pitch for the Test at the Oval, tended with loving care by 'Bosser' Martin, had not been used since Surrey had made 560 for six on it against Yorkshire in August 1933. It now looked absolutely perfect. Bradman and his captain inspected it closely for a long time on the eve of the Test and pronounced it 'a beauty'. So it proved. Australia ended the first day at 475 for two and Bradman had absolutely butchered the England attack. He played again in his Headingley manner, and once again he and Ponsford shared an enormous partnership, this time adding 451 for the second wicket (a new world record for that wicket and beating their 388 at Leeds as a record for any Test wicket). It was the biggest partnership of Bradman's career. Ponsford, as at Leeds, was the perfect foil for Bradman – the solid imperturbability and the manifest brilliance. This time the prolific pair scored at 85 an hour between 12 noon and 6.23 p.m., when Bradman was out for 244. Ponsford was 205* at the close. When the stand had passed 300, Herbert Sutcliffe went to collect a ball hit by Bradman that bounced into the crowd. He put his hand on the boundary rails and said with a smile: 'Anyone got any suggestions?' A. W. Carr had some suggestions in the press-box – that Jardine, Larwood and Voce should have been on the field. 'I wish I had been in the field, too', was Jardine's recorded comment to Carr. Abe Waddington, the old Yorkshire bowler, was at the Oval that day and when Don Bradman was in the 30s remarked: 'Yon little chap's going to get some today. He's digging in.' The match was a 'timeless' Test, but Bradman's 'digging in' did not prevent him scoring at 46 an hour off his own bat and at very nearly a run every ball he received. In the most comprehensive manner possible he proved utterly groundless those critics' fears that a 'timeless' Test would see doggedly slow batting on the opening day. His timing, judgment and stroke-play were all equally faultless. In 5¼ hours he lifted the ball in the air only twice – once to hit a six off Verity and once to try for a six off a no-ball. It was one of his most brilliant innings, and quite free of any hint of a chance. 'He never seemed to let himself get out of control for a minute', observed Fender. Douglas Jardine, for his part, wrote that Bradman's innings was 'at least as good as any of his past prolific efforts with the bat, and that is saying a great deal'. It was indeed.

So perfect an innings as that 244 can merit a further few lines of comment. With absolutely clinical impartiality, Bradman scored 122 runs from the pavilion end wicket and 122 runs from the Vauxhall end. In those days there was no sightscreen to aid batsmanship from the Vauxhall wicket, but on the evidence of this strange coincidence such a deprivation hardly worried the Don. As many as 70% of his runs that day came in front of the wicket (or square of it) and he distributed his stroke-play with more or less equal largesse to the off side (128 runs) and the leg side (116).

It was not to be for another 42 years – the August of 1976 – that a touring batsman was to make 200 runs in a day in a Test on the wide expanses of the Oval. And then it was *exactly* 200 runs (as opposed to Bradman's 244) by Vivian Richards, for the West Indies, on a parched and exceedingly fast Oval outfield during a summer of unprecedented drought. Richards also scored his runs on the opening day. Lest it be alleged that the over rate in 1934 was infinitely quicker than that of 1976, let it speedily be recorded that *100* overs were bowled on the first day at the Oval in 1934, and *102* overs on the first day at the Oval in 1976. Moreover, Bradman did not begin his innings until 30 minutes after the start and was out at 6.23; while Richards began 14 minutes after the start and batted through to close of play. The cascade of superlatives that was – quite deservedly – showered on the batting of Richards that day served to emphasise the sort of thing Bradman, too, could do in his prime – and do frequently.[1] Bradman's innings – and Richards' – can be set in some sort of perspective when it is remembered that Bradman scored 201 after lunch in 226 minutes, while Richards scored 140 after lunch in 241 minutes. Let it further be remembered that the bowlers Bradman faced were Bowes, Allen, Clark, Hammond, Verity, Wyatt and Leyland: and the bowlers Richards faced were Willis, Selvey, Underwood, Woolmer, Miller, Balderstone, Greig, Willey and Steele – only Amiss, Knott and the two umpires were not given a turn!

On that Saturday night in 1934, with his 244 runs tucked safely in the book, Bradman went to a London theatre, after which he took a stroll, with another member of the team, along the Thames Embankment. He there had his first experience of London's 'down-and-outs', a sight that affected him profoundly. Before he returned to his hotel, Bradman practically bought up

---

[1] In his very preceding innings in first-class cricket he had of course scored no fewer than 271 in a day, also in a Test against England. What other players achieved once in a lifetime, Bradman turned almost into the commonplace.

a coffee-stall which was soon the centre of a hungry and thirsty crowd of 'homeless'. Bradman urged them on to eat and drink. 'Who are yer?' asked one poor, famished man. And Bradman answered him by pushing a half-crown into the man's palm.

Back at the Oval Bradman added a chanceless 77 to his 244 of the first innings as his contribution to Australia's victory by 562 runs. In the last two Tests alone, he thus scored 625 runs. It was no doubt principally of these two Tests, and of those 625 runs, that Bill Bowes was thinking when he said of Bradman, after they had both retired: 'He hit your bad 'uns for four, and many of your good 'uns, too!' Bowes actually dismissed him at Leeds and in both innings at the Oval, but before he did so Bradman occupied the crease altogether for just short of 14½ hours – and in the whole of that time gave only two unaccepted chances. When Bill Bowes came to draw up his list of best cricketers in the world – best all-rounder, hardest hitter, best captain, best bowler, and so on – he headed his list with the words: 'Greatest cricketer of all . . . Don Bradman.'

Why Bradman had deserted his old methods in the first three Tests of 1934 was a matter of temperament and choice. When he returned to them in the last two Tests he was as formidable and heartbreaking as ever. He averaged 94·75 in the series (fractionally behind Ponsford) and his aggregate for the series of 758 was far and away the best on either side. (One of those splendid little arithmetical posers – which cricket has a regular habit of throwing up – presented itself with regard to the final Test averages of the series. Before the Oval match began, Bradman had a slight lead over Ponsford in the averages (72·83 to 70·25). In the Oval Test Bradman scored 321 runs for two completed innings and Ponsford scored 288 for two completed innings. And yet Ponsford finished on top! Such are the ways of cricket mathematics!)

When Bradman went to Canterbury two days after his 26th birthday, his repute was such that 'Punter' Humphreys, the Kent coach, ordered all the young professionals on the staff out of their hiding-places in the pavilion and elsewhere on the ground to watch Bradman in action. But the match was so sadly ruined by rain that on the fall of the first wicket, instead of Bradman coming in, he declared. And the young professionals had to take his skill on trust.

Such was Bradman's form in the closing portion of the tour that he ended up easily at the top of the tour averages – something that had seemed very unlikely even as far on as the middle of July. His average of 84·16 was actually the best in the whole country. His two festival matches in September were quite extraordinary affairs. At Folkestone, against an England XI, he scored the 50th century of his career – and what a century it was. He got to three figures in 87 minutes and then hit 30 in an over (466464) off A. P. Freeman, actually scoring 31 in a spell of seven minutes. Those 30 runs off a six-ball over constituted yet another world record at the time, though it has been exceeded several times since. He scored 149* in all, the last 49 in 17 minutes. He hit four sixes that afternoon, one of his hits off Freeman landing in the guttering on top of the grandstand. Bradman played that innings, as indeed he was to play his next, with a large blood clot on the muscle of his right thumb, formed after his 244 at the Oval. Then the first-class programme ended at Scarborough, where Bradman proceeded to score 132 out of 182 in 90 minutes against H. D. G. Leveson Gower's XI, and was back in the pavilion some ten minutes before the luncheon break. This time he had a spell of 31 runs in five minutes, including 19 in an over off Verity. Every known stroke was played, and 'if the ball ever missed the middle of the bat', wrote J. M. Kilburn, 'memory has no record of the mishap'. Nichols, Farnes and Bowes were other bowlers who were simply sunk without trace that morning. 'I know I enjoyed myself in those ninety minutes', recalled Bradman. The Special Correspondent of *The Times* said: 'To describe his strokes would be impossible. He hit the ball in every conceivable kind of way to every conceivable corner of the field.' Over 10,000 gave him a superb ovation when he was out. He had been glamorous, ferocious and irrepressible. No change in field-placing could stop him. Surely not even W. G. Grace in his prime can have been a greater attraction.

Once again Bradman had delighted a Yorkshire crowd with an innings to remember. He scored a hundred every time he batted in Yorkshire in 1934. Scarborough always saw him score runs – the lowest of the three innings of his career there was 96 – and at the senior of Yorkshire's grounds, at Heading-ley alone (where he played exclusively in Tests), he scored nearly 1,000 runs in only four matches. No wonder an honorary life membership was bestowed on him by the Yorkshire C.C.C. after his final tour of England. He remains the only overseas cricketer – or, for that matter, non-cricketer – ever to enjoy this distinction. Bradman's prowess on Yorkshire grounds may conveniently be set out at this point. Outside London, Yorkshire saw him more often than any other part of England. His only real failure there was at Park Avenue in 1930, the match in which 'Ahr Emmott shifted 'im' for 1. His record in Yorkshire, embracing his four tours of England, was as follows:

	Matches	Inns.	N.O.	Runs	H.S.	Av.	100s	50s	0s	Mins. Batted	Runs per Hour
Headingley	4	6	1	963	334	192·60	4	0	0	1,340	43·11
Scarborough	3	3	0	381	153	127·00	2	1	0	434	52·67
Sheffield	4	6	0	459	140	76·50	1	4	0	693	39·74
Bradford	1	1	0	1	1	1·00	0	0	0	8	—
	12	16	1	1,804	334	120·26	7	5	0	2,475	43·73

He was never on the losing side on Yorkshire soil. The only time he *might* have been – when H. D. G. Leveson Gower's XI, with ten Test cricketers in the side, defeated the 1938 Australians in the Scarborough Festival – his injured ankle saw him *hors de combat*.

Whatever else may be said about Bradman's batting in 1934, he was still a wonderful entertainer – and he *still* scored more runs in all matches, including minor ones, than any other member of the side.[1] He scored off his own bat at the rate of 50·22 an hour (his highest scoring rate ever in England) and many of his partnerships that year were scored at such a fast pace that some of them deserve to be set out separately. Throughout his career the stands in which he participated often came at a handsome rate, but the following are among those for the tour of 1934 alone:

54	for 4th wkt. in 25 mins. with Brown	v England XI, Folkestone
73	for 6th wkt. in 33 mins. with Kippax	v Sussex, Hove
73	for 4th wkt. in 40 mins. with Darling	v Surrey, Oval
73	for 2nd wkt. in 46 mins. with Brown	v England, Lord's
84	for 4th wkt. in 35 mins. with Kippax	v Middlesex, Lord's
90	for 5th wkt. in 61 mins. with McCabe	v England, Headingley
111	for 5th wkt. in 63 mins. with Bromley	v Worcs, Worcester
130	for 2nd wkt. in 73 mins. with McCabe	v Surrey, Oval
150	for 3rd wkt. in 94 mins. with McCabe	v England, Oval
180*	for 5th wkt. in 77 mins. with Woodfull	v England XI, Folkestone
182	for 2nd wkt. in 90 mins. with Ponsford	v H. D. G. Leveson Gower's XI, Scarborough
189	for 2nd wkt. in 120 mins. with Woodfull	v Yorks, Sheffield
388	for 4th wkt. in 341 mins. with Ponsford	v England, Headingley
451	for 2nd wkt. in 316 mins. with Ponsford	v England, Oval

Were these the performances of a sick man? It does not seem so, but at the same time it is an inescapable fact that Bradman laboured through the 1934 season with the shadow of illness never hovering far from him, and he drove himself, with a conscious effort of will, both to entertain spectators and to pull his weight in the side. Outwardly, his physical fitness could at times be staggering. Towards the close of play on the Saturday of the Headingley Test, as he was advancing towards 271 runs in the day, he was sufficiently energetic to help in gathering newspapers blowing round the pitch, and while Ponsford was becoming weary after tea, Bradman was still sprinting freshly. But he was not the same physical specimen of 1930. He had not needed his team-mates to carry him to the massage table that year, and his muscles then were altogether more highly tuned.

It was nevertheless a considerable compliment to Bradman's extraordinary performances over the previous four or five years that such consistent surprise and comment should have been forthcoming over his run of low scores in the middle of 1934. Such a run was as unexpected in Bradman as it was natural in others. Maurice Leyland scored only one century in the County Championship that year, but there was no comment and he still played in all five Tests. Bradman had been too successful for his own good. Truly has it been said that uneasy lies the head that wears a crown. Bradman had come to England

---

[1] In all scheduled fixtures on the tour, first-class and minor, Bradman scored 2,106 runs at an average of 81·00 (top of the overall averages), while McCabe scored 2,094 runs. If the exhibition match at Forres on the last playing day of the tour be included, Bradman's aggregate advances to 2,108 and McCabe's to 2,104.

after a season in which he had become the most dazzling stroke-maker in the game. He continued in that vein in England – producing batting that was brilliant but unreliable. Then, at precisely the time when his side most needed it, he turned himself into the old inexorable match-winner, starting with the great responsibility he had to carry at Leeds. Having had his first experience since his debut in 1927–28 of knowing what it was to lose touch with form, he revised his tactics, as it were, in the interests of his captain and his side. By the time September came, Bradman was the great hero once more. As a statistical curiosity that illustrates Bradman's striking superiority, it may be remarked that although Ponsford made his first-class debut in 1920–21 and Woodfull in 1921–22, by the end of the 1934 tour of England Bradman had overhauled both their aggregates.

The 1934 tour ended at Forres, the most northerly spot in the world where Don Bradman has played cricket, and where Bradman captained the Australians against the North of Scotland, who were beaten in a day. An exhibition match between the same sides was played next day for the sake of the Saturday crowd. Bradman had made a pledge before the 1934 visit to England that he would not bowl on the tour, and a minute perusal of every match in *Wisden* would indicate that he kept it. In fact he broke his pledge at Forres on 15 September (the solitary match not set out in *Wisden*), when all the Australians bowled except Kippax, who kept wicket, and Bradman dismissed the number 11 batsman, J. I. Kemp, for an analysis of 3.5–0–20–1 – the most expensive Australian bowler of the day! It was the very last of the 559 wickets that fell to the Australians on the tour.

One further wicket very nearly fell that September – but not on the field of play. Don Bradman was taken desperately ill and very nearly died. It all happened very suddenly. He was feeling jubilant, he himself had recalled, that his health had stood up as well as it had to the end of the tour. Bradman and several others of the Australian side were due to leave England for home on 29 September. Exactly a week before, on Saturday the 22nd, the symptoms of something serious revealed themselves when Bradman complained of feeling unwell. He was then in the team's London hotel – the Langham Hotel in Portland Place. He spent the Sunday packing, but with increasing internal pain. On Monday morning, 24 September, he felt worse: and it was quickly realised that he was ill. It was something far worse than anything he had previously experienced. He had been looking forward to going to the theatre that evening with Arthur Chipperfield. But now Bradman was removed at once on that Monday afternoon by ambulance from the Langham Hotel to Sir Douglas Shields' nursing-home at 17 Park Lane, less than a mile away. The diagnosis was acute appendicitis, and an emergency operation was performed within an hour of Bradman being admitted. Sir Douglas Shields, who performed the operation, was an eminent Melbourne surgeon who was Administrator and Surgeon-in-Chief at the nursing-home. He already, of course, knew Don Bradman from earlier in the summer, both as a patient and friend. Now he was fighting to save his life.

There was great anxiety in the period immediately following the operation. Sir Douglas Shields did not pretend to hide the fact. The appendix had been practically gangrenous. In addition, there was a successful fight against impending peritonitis, which would have resulted had the operation been left even a few hours. It was what is called a 'thunderstorm appendicitis' – one in which no time is given for adhesions to form and shut off the danger to one corner. The condition was complicated by the appendix having slipped round, away from its normal position. Bradman was seriously ill and all visitors were forbidden, with the sole exception of the Australian manager, Harold Bushby, and even he was allowed to see Bradman for only a few seconds.

'That there is something very much the matter with him is palpable, and the sooner the tension on the lad is reduced the better it will be for all concerned.' Those words were written at Old Trafford on 9 July by Trevor Wignall who, like many at the ground that day, could hardly recognise the sick face of Bradman. When Wignall had met the Australians in Colombo at the beginning of April, he had quickly sensed that all was not well with Bradman: 'There is an amazing change in Bradman, who is obviously in indifferent health, and looks 20 years older than his age. He consulted the doctor before he smoked a cigarette. Bradman will have to be much healthier before he can play in the Tests.'[1] The voyage on the *Orford* did of course bring about an improvement. The tendency to facial pallor that had been with him for something like the previous two years disappeared. But Bradman later said he had pains in the back almost throughout the 1934 summer, before the appendicitis symptoms appeared. He himself suspected in mid-tour that something might happen and went so far, indeed, to confide this to a team-mate with whom he left addresses to find his wife by cable in emergency. He even wrote to his wife from England asking her not to go on a holiday to the Solomon Islands that she was proposing to take in September – she would have been there precisely at the time of the operation. Bradman had in fact been playing cricket for two months when he should have been in bed. He had been carrying on by will-power.

In the event, of course, he saw the tour out and finished it indeed in a blaze of dazzling glory, with an innings of sheer genius at Scarborough. It was the sort of batting seen only once in a whole era of cricket. It was as if he had reached the very acme of all possible glory in batsmanship, with not a trace of imperfection – and the gods then chose to cry 'Enough'. It was, to put it another way, as if the words of Morell in *Candida* were being whispered to him: 'Man can climb to the highest summits, but he cannot dwell there long.'

Bradman had lost a lot of blood and was weak. Even when he had had a

---

[1] Wignall got into a lot of private hot water for daring to say that Bradman looked older than his years and that he was out of health. 'It would have been a lesser sin if I had set a cathedral on fire', he remarked a couple of years later. But Wignall of course was right.

tooth extracted in the past, he had lost more blood than is usually the case. Arrangements were now made for a blood transfusion, if necessary: and many unknown persons (as well as personal friends of Bradman's) offered their blood in the emergency. Meanwhile his pulse became weaker. King George and Queen Mary telephoned from Balmoral to send their wishes for his recovery. It was the King's express desire that he be kept in constant touch with Bradman's progress. 'I want to know everything', the King said. In fact so overwhelming were the telephone calls that the nursing-home was thrown into chaos and they had to be banned in favour of bulletins. There were as many as five official bulletins a day when the crisis was at its worst.

Clarrie Grimmett had stayed behind in London for a few days after the rest of the team left, and his name was added to Harold Bushby's in being allowed to see Bradman each day. Otherwise, in the early anxious days of the illness, Bradman was protected from visitors, however eminent. J. H. Thomas, Secretary for the Dominions, called at the nursing-home, but his enquiries were answered without allowing him into Bradman's room. P. F. Warner called. He was accorded 20 minutes with Sir Douglas Shields but was not allowed to see Bradman. It was not until the patient's temperature became lower and his pulse stronger, and when he began to take nourishment, that visitors were allowed in. These included Jack Hobbs, Oscar Asche, Sir James Barrie and Lord Hailsham. Jack Hobbs, who himself had been operated on for appendicitis 13 years before, was a great comfort. 'You'll forget it, once you're better', he told Bradman. Bradman's new employer in Adelaide, H. W. Hodgetts, who had been expecting Don Bradman to commence his new job in his stockbroking office in October, spoke on the telephone from Adelaide to Sir Douglas Shields. Bradman was in a third-floor room at the nursing-home, his window adorned with Australian wattle flowers. The corridor outside was 'like a florist's shop'. The interior of his room was a whole mass of flowers and fruit and he had a virtual library of books, sent to him by friends.

In Australia, Don Bradman's wife had watched the progress of the 1934 tour with some anxiety – anxiety about the recurring reports since April of her husband's health and a lesser anxiety about his poor run of scores in the early Tests. While Bradman was playing his great innings of 304 at Leeds, he had in his pocket, crumpled but treasured, that inspiring telegram from his wife, already mentioned, which read: 'Go to it, Don. I believe in you.' The innings marked the crucial turning-point in his own and Australia's fortunes. On the morning that the fifth Test started at the Oval, a surprise awaited Don Bradman in the form of a beautiful photographic enlargement of Mrs Bradman's smiling face, brought 12,000 miles by Mr T. G. Victor Lewis, a Brisbane omnibus proprietor, and presented to Bradman on behalf of Brisbane admirers. (Mrs Bradman had just spent a very happy holiday in Queensland.) Later that day the Don scored 244.

Now Mrs Bradman's face had fewer smiles as she heard of the serious condition of her husband in London. She received the sudden news of the operation when she was in the country, 80 miles from Sydney, on 25 September. It was followed by a cable from her husband asking her to catch the next steamer for England. That cable had been Bradman's final message before he went under the anaesthetic, and he had asked Sir Douglas Shields to send it off at once if he came through. 'I must go to him', was her instant reaction. Johnnie Moyes in Sydney very kindly made immediate arrangements to get her to England, and an emergency booking on the P. and O. liner *Maloja*, which had already sailed from Sydney, was made. 'My luggage was in an awful muddle', she later recalled. 'I had neither heart nor time to think about picking frocks.' Mrs Bradman sped across Australia to board the ship at Fremantle on 1 October. The P. and O. very generously offered her, in these sad circumstances, a complimentary ticket to London.

Meanwhile a rumour spread, as rumours do, like wildfire across Australia that Bradman was dead. It originated in Sydney, on the radio. It was not true, of course, and was quickly denied in the newspapers: and Mrs Bradman, on reaching Melbourne, confirmed the falsity by telephoning the nursing-home in London. She also received a cable from a friend in London urging her to 'disregard wild rumours' about her husband's condition. But the obituarists, in both Australia and England, were ready in their newspaper offices for the worst. At *The Times* in Printing House Square, the Cricket Correspondent went into galley proof in measured phrases that would not be proper here to quote. In the *Daily Telegraph* office in Fleet Street, the Australian-born critic and playwright, Campbell Dixon, wrote his fellow-countryman's obituary, which was quickly put into type. At 19 Bouverie Street – where the *Star* sports room had had a special affinity with Bradman since first carrying his life story four years before – they could hardly comprehend the possibility of his death. 'Don Bradman gone!' their obituarist began. 'It is unbelievable.' But mercifully the obituaries were not needed. The skill and care of Sir Douglas Shields saw Bradman through.[1] But it had certainly been the hardest innings of his career.

After a 31-day journey from New South Wales, covering 13,000 miles, Mrs Bradman arrived in England, via Paris, on 27 October. Outwardly she was extraordinarily self-possessed. Her husband was allowed out of the nursing-home for the first time three days before, and he was motored down to Dover to meet her. The reunion, in a private room at the Lord Warden Hotel, was naturally an affectionate one. At the time when the happily-false rumour as to Bradman's death had been denied, the *Sydney Morning Herald* leader-writer said: 'Bradman has been idolised for his maintained brilliance and his almost superhuman skill. All hearts will go out to him the more because his admirers realise at last that he is not superhuman at all, and that

---

[1] Those who attach significance to coincidences may note that Sir Douglas Shields' birthday was on 21 July, the very day that happened to be the turning-point of Bradman's whole 1934 season so far as his return to his 'old' style of batsmanship was concerned. He scored 271* that day in the Headingley Test, on his way to his 304.

in the cause of satisfying public demands upon him he has exceeded the limits of what was fair to his own physical capacity.' He very nearly indeed paid the final penalty for his supreme pre-eminence on the cricket field.

Mr and Mrs Bradman spent a long holiday in England and Scotland, including two days with the Duke of Portland (the President of Notts) at Welbeck Abbey – the Duke and Duchess had entertained the Australians on the Sunday of the Trent Bridge Test – and also had stays in Edinburgh and Perth, then going south to Devon, for a stay at Budleigh Salterton, before returning to London. Bradman's first public appearance after his illness – and his only public appearance before he left England – was at a charity function on 15 December at the Battersea Hospital, where the superintendent was Dr John R. Lee, an Australian, who was one of the consultants during his illness. Bradman took the dance floor with his wife and Dr Lee took the opportunity of revealing that 'Bradman might not be here today but for Mrs Bradman. Her cablegram, "It's all right, Don, I'm coming", meant a great deal to the patient at a critical stage.' Dr Lee and Sir Douglas Shields himself were in due course warmly thanked by the Australian Board of Control for their services towards Australia's vice-captain.

Bradman was weak after his illness and Sir Douglas Shields had ordered him to have a complete rest in the winter of 1934–35. There was to be no question of cricket that season in Australia of any kind. For a short time his eyes began to give him trouble and he had to wear glasses, but he was assured this would be only temporary, and so it proved. He and his wife left England for Paris (via the Calais boat-train from Victoria) on 18 December and were bade farewell at Victoria Station by the secretary and assistant-secretary of M.C.C., Messrs W. Findlay and R. Aird. Winston Churchill happened to be on the platform, seeing his wife off, and there was an intriguing little episode concerning two of the most prominent public figures of the day – whose paths had never crossed before. Wishing Bradman farewell, too, was the late Tom Clarke, a major name in Fleet Street journalism, who had been one of Northcliffe's shining stars and a one-time news editor of the *Daily Mail* and, until 1933, editor of the *News Chronicle*. He travelled with the Australian touring team of 1934 for the *Daily Mail*, and, through his wide political contacts, knew Winston Churchill. Churchill called him to his side on the platform and whispered: 'Isn't that Bradman you are with? I'd like to be introduced.' Tom Clarke himself later recalled: 'Don, in shy embarrassment, threatened to become "difficult". He protested he was "only a cricketer", and would like to go where nobody would know him. Most reluctantly he was coaxed across the platform to meet the future Prime Minister.' The two men actually posed at a carriage door and were photographed together.

After a brief visit to Switzerland, the Bradmans spent Christmas on the Riviera before they at length sailed for home on the *Otranto* from Toulon on 28 December.

They reached Australia, on the *Otranto*, on 22 January 1935, bound for their new home in Adelaide. On his arrival that day, Bradman said: 'Acting under doctor's orders, I will not play any cricket this season. When I start I will play with Kensington.' Kensington was to be his club side in Australia until the end of his career, and his home also was to be in the same district – 2 Holden Street, Kensington Park. (Actually for a short period he lived opposite, while his new home was being built.) The *Otranto* made its way round the coast from Fremantle to Adelaide, where the Bradmans at length arrived on 26 January, to be welcomed by H. W. Hodgetts, W. H. Jeanes (the Board secretary), and Mr and Mrs Tim Wall. (The Walls have always been close friends of the Bradmans.) They stayed with the Hodgetts family at Kensington Park for a few days and then left for Bowral, where, for the first three months after his return to Australia, Bradman had a long and quiet holiday, playing a little tennis and a little golf, but otherwise taking life gently. 'One does not recover in a week or so from an experience such as mine', he remarked at the time. Even at the end of his Bowral rest, it was obvious he had not fully recovered from the effects of his desperate illness. South Australia had expected him to be in their ranks at that time (together with C. L. Badcock in his first year with the State) but of course they had to see through their Shield programme without him. Bradman may have noted with satisfaction, however, that Grimmett headed the South Australian bowling for the 11th successive season and took more wickets for the State than ever before. He might also have noted that in five out of the six Sheffield Shield matches played by South Australia, no century was recorded for the side. Such a state of affairs was never to obtain when Bradman was in their ranks. Another match Bradman had had to miss was the Woodfull–Ponsford Testimonial match at Melbourne.

Meanwhile, at the same time, New South Wales too had had to go through their first season without Bradman since he had burst on the scene. His absence was all but catastrophic to the State's finances. The crowds were no longer there and the glamour was no longer there. Bradman had almost proved that the individual was greater than the game. To that extent he had not been good for cricket. But it had not been his fault. It had been the fault of those who chose to worship the cult of personality. (It was Jack Fingleton who observed that at one period 'it almost seemed that the game of cricket was subservient to the individual Bradman. His colleagues frequently felt that they were mere lay figures or items of scenery to be arranged to provide a background for the principal actor'.) The New South Wales accounts for the year ending 30 June 1935 included receipts of £6,000 as the State's share of the 1934 tour profits of England. This enabled them to show a surplus of £577.6.9d. Without that tour bonus, the loss would have been the crippling one of £5,422.[1] The Sheffield Shield matches in Sydney for 1934–35 pro-

---

[1] The New South Wales accounts for the year ending 30 June 1934, embracing Bradman's last season with the State (and which of course included no tour revenue), had shown a surplus of £3,167.

duced a revenue of only £1,854, compared with £4,172 in 1933–34. Here were the sad comparisons that confronted the New South Wales treasurer:

		1933–34 matches (last Bradman season)	1934–35 matches (first post-Bradman season)
v Victoria	at Sydney	£2,480.11. 7	£1,287.11. 9
v South Australia	at Sydney	627.17.11*	96.11. 7
v Queensland	at Sydney	1,063.18. 1	470.15. 6
		£4,172. 7. 7	£1,854.18.10

* Bradman had not played in this match through back trouble.

The financial future without Bradman was bleak, and when the above figures were known, the New South Wales treasurer, E. A. Tyler, estimated a loss for the next year of over £3,500. This was not just rank pessimism. It turned out to be £3,460. When the finances of the N.S.W.C.A. were discussed in committee, great hopes were pinned on Bradman coming to Sydney with the South Australian team – and equally great hopes on the Saturday of the match not being wet. New South Wales, after their first Bradman-less season in 1934–35, were so keenly aware of their loss of income through Bradman's departure that they reached a partial state of panic by reducing payments to umpires in grade and municipal and shire cricket from 10/– to 8/– for a Saturday afternoon in 1935–36.

This is how receipts in Sydney for the major fixture against Victoria steadily declined after Bradman's departure:

	Revenue to N.S.W.
1933–34 (Bradman playing)	£2,480.11. 7
1934–35	1,287.11. 9
1935–36	498.12. 3
1936–37	98.15. 0
1937–38	130. 0. 4

Poor Ted Tyler, the hon. treasurer, died on 24 October 1937, after 22 years of continuous service. He might well have been heart-broken at some of the above figures.

During his absence in England in 1934, the Board of Control, at their annual meeting in September (and before Bradman had been taken ill) appointed Bradman a national selector for the first time. He was now, of course, very much on the Board's good side and their undoubted nominee as future captain of Australia in succession to Woodfull. He was appointed one of the selectors for the forthcoming (1935–36) Australian tour to South Africa. His illness, however, changed everything, and when it became obvious that he would be unable to perform any ordinary functions of a selector in the season of 1934–35 – he would be neither playing nor watching and the team was to be selected exclusively on the performance of that season – he sent in his resignation, adding also that he would be unavailable for the South African tour as a player. The Board, at their December 1934 meeting, noted the resignation and appointed V. Y. Richardson as a selector in Bradman's place. It was Richardson who eventually captained the side to South Africa. Bradman's 1934 appointment, abortive though it in fact became, showed an unusual departure by the Board of Control. They had never in their history appointed a selector so young – Bradman was just 26 – and they had only rarely considered contemporary first-class players. Woodfull, at the successful end of a distinguished career and a reigning Australian selector, was considered to be well in the running, and there was disappointment, especially in Melbourne, when his name was missing. Bradman was to have joined E. A. Dwyer (New South Wales) and W. J. Johnson (Victoria) in picking the side for South Africa.

After his salubrious holiday in Bowral, Bradman returned to Adelaide on 24 April 1935, the day before Anzac Day – almost exactly a year to the day after he had landed in England with the Australian cricket team. Much unexpected water had since flown under the bridge. He was now busy moving into his new home in Holden Street, and he formally began his new occupation in the stockbroking business of H. W. Hodgetts at 23 Grenfell Street, Adelaide, on 29 April 1935. Bradman had played no cricket at all since 15 September 1934. He gave himself the physical benefits of golf in the Australian winter of 1935 with the Mount Osmond Country Club, near Adelaide, where he was to play a good deal of golf, and with much enjoyment, in the years to come. He actually entered for the club championship, and perhaps not surprisingly to those who knew Don Bradman well, he won it.

In May 1935 Bradman was revealed again in the role of author. The London *Daily Mail* heralded the new English season by publishing a series of articles by him (commencing on 13 May) under the general title 'How to Play Cricket'. These articles contained specially posed slow-motion pictures illustrating every stroke described by Bradman in the text. He himself arranged those pictures and posed for all the close-up illustrations of batting and bowling grips. The series was a success, and the *Daily Mail* put it out in book form in paper covers – 95 pages for a shilling. After the war, several other editions were brought out, both in England and Australia.

Meanwhile, Adelaide's newly acquired citizen had been occupying himself with stocks and shares. There is no doubt that Bradman did himself a very good turn in joining the firm of Mr Hodgetts. Not only did it provide the platform for a secure income from the world of business once the days of cricket were over but it served the more immediate purpose of effectively divorcing Bradman from the endless, all-the-year-round cricket routine that Sydney imposed on him and from which, while he remained in Sydney, there appeared little prospect of escape. Sydney, of course, its public and its business houses, had demanded more and more of Bradman as his great career unfolded: Adelaide, where life was less hurried, promised greater serenity – and for the first time in his life Bradman could go into work without cricket, in any shape or form, being on the agenda. Bradman was an employee in Mr Hodgetts' firm and, while there, always remained one, so none of the responsibilities of a principal were thrust on him. At the same time he carefully learnt and eventually thoroughly mastered the art and practice of stock and share broking which was to enable him later to gain a place on the Adelaide Stock Exchange. Bradman dealt with clients in the same way as anyone similarly employed would do, but he dealt with them as Don Bradman qua business employee and not as Don Bradman qua cricketer.

However, as each fresh summer came round, cricket came with it. Harry Hodgetts, by virtue of his positions with the South Australian Cricket Association and the Australian Board of Control, was a very influential man. In the councils of South Australia, in particular, his voice was very strong – somewhat akin, in fact, to the sort of voice to be possessed in the same councils by the future Sir Donald Bradman. Harry Hodgetts – again like the future Sir Donald – also liked to get his own way, though he saw that way allied to the best interests in South Australian and Australian cricket. To those respective ends, he had from the start envisaged Don Bradman (Woodfull's vice-captain in England in 1934) as both State captain and captain of the Australian XI. Both positions suited the ambition of Bradman himself. And so far as the South Australian captaincy was concerned, Henry Warburton Hodgetts lost no time in implementing that first prong of the fork.

Don Bradman, his illness and days of recuperation behind him, was fit enough to resume cricket at the start of the 1935–36 season. He was, for the first time, appointed a South Australian selector, thus at once becoming privy to the intimacies of cricket in Adelaide.[1] On medical advice he had of course said he would not be available for the tour to South Africa, and in fact never played in that country in his life. Bradman was not actually ill when the Australian side was due to leave for South Africa and could, at a pinch, have gone – and would, no doubt, have scored heavily there, where the tour arrangements were for covered wickets throughout. It would, however, have meant an inevitably more strenuous season than one conducted from his base in Adelaide; and his doctor's injunction to take things quietly settled the issue.

When Bradman withdrew from the selection panel for the South African tour, his place had – in accordance with Australian cricket politics – to go to another South Australian, and it went, as has been related, to the popular State captain, V. Y. Richardson. Richardson, in the absence of contenders, was also appointed captain of the touring side – thus leaving vacant the South Australian captaincy for the Sheffield Shield season of 1935–36, a vacancy duly filled by D. G. Bradman. Those who appointed Bradman did

---

[1] His first fellow-selectors at first-class level were Dr C. E. Dolling and H. H. M. Bridgman. They were appointed as the South Australian State selectors for 1935–36 on 18 September 1935. Bradman had been one of the team selectors during the course of the 1934 tour of England, but of course had had no say in the original composition of the team.

not intend the captaincy to be taken from him on Richardson's return – not least the power behind the South Australian Cricket Association, Harry Hodgetts, business employer of Donald Bradman. R. S. Whitington has related how, at a farewell function in Adelaide to Richardson and Grimmett, just before they left for South Africa in 1935, Hodgetts declared what a fitting tribute it was that Richardson be appointed captain of Australia 'at the end of his career' – at which Clem Hill, bristling with anger and indignation, jumped up to exclaim: 'End of his career! Bunkum!'

The truth was that by then Richardson had already been approached by certain members of the South Australian committee to retire after the tour of South Africa, having held the State captaincy for more than a dozen years (since 1921–22). They wanted Bradman to be captain in 1936–37 so that he might also be captain in the Test series that summer – it was only an outside chance that the Board would appoint their Test captain from outside the ranks of the State captains. Thus, with an almost indecent haste, Bradman, in his mid-twenties, was being led to the very top.

As it happened, Richardson led the Australians on an undefeated tour of South Africa, winning 13 and drawing three of their first-class matches. Richardson captained brilliantly, as shrewdly and astutely as ever. He was always regarded as an outstanding tactician. He was also a great public favourite in Adelaide. But South Australia, predictably perhaps, deposed Victor Richardson, now in his early forties, and confirmed D. G. Bradman, aged 28, as State captain for 1936–37.

Meanwhile, Bradman had tasted his first cricket season in Adelaide, playing Saturday matches for his new club, Kensington, and a full season of Sheffield Shield matches, three at home and three away.

He returned to first-class cricket on 8 November 1935, captaining a first-class side for the first time on Australian soil. It also, of course, marked his debut for South Australia. It was a match against Errol Holmes' M.C.C. side on its way through Australia to New Zealand. Bradman scored modestly – 15 and 50 – and lost a match for the first time as captain at first-class level. It was also his first sight of Joe Hardstaff at the crease (he made 90, top score of the match) and Bradman was to see much of him in the future, not least at the Oval in 1938.

When Bradman took over the captaincy of South Australia in 1935–36, his career average was 90·58 and his Sheffield Shield average 107·74 – figures naturally unapproached by any other player on a transfer from one first-class team to another. (Both his career average and Sheffield Shield average were to be bettered by the time his career with his new State was over.) So he did not exactly need to prove himself, though in the art of captaincy his Sheffield Shield experience was nil. The captains under whom he had played his major cricket hitherto had been Kippax (for New South Wales) and Woodfull and Richardson in England, though of course Bradman himself had been Woodfull's vice-captain in 1934. His cricket for St George had been with several captains, but mainly under W. F. ('Bill') Ives, a fine all-rounder who played four times for New South Wales, though Bradman himself captained St George in some matches in 1931–32 and was the appointed captain in 1932–33. Though Bradman had led the Australians in six first-class matches in England in 1934, he was not of course responsible for the team in the sense that an appointed captain is. It would seem, if comment from such a distance may be allowed, that he might profitably have been given more than those six matches in 1934, especially as Woodfull had made it publicly known before the start of the tour that he was to retire from the game at the end of that season.[1] Bradman did nothing unorthodox as captain in England in 1934 – even putting Kent in at Canterbury was considered the only thing on such a pitch, but Bradman *did* use O'Reilly as one of his opening bowlers on that occasion. Actually he had O'Reilly at his command in four of the six games – a considerable comfort – and Fleetwood-Smith in all six. After the sudden victory, under Bradman's captaincy, over Sussex at Hove in August, C. B. Fry wrote of him as follows in the *Evening Standard*: 'Bradman is an extremely intelligent, observant, and quick-witted captain. In the field he bowls every ball with the bowlers, and fields every stroke with the fielders. No fielder is allowed to stray an inch from his allotted blade of grass, or to lapse into independence of what Don considers exactly right.' A. G. Hazlerigg (now Lord Hazlerigg), the 1932 captain of Cambridge and 1934 captain of Leicestershire, and Bradman's first opponent as a captain on the first-class field, was not so certain of Bradman the captain. Of the 1934 match at Aylestone Road, he has recently said: 'I can remember thinking at the time, and have often said since, that his captaincy left a great deal to be desired. In fact there was really very little which he did right as a captain in that match and we all commented how extremely inexperienced he seemed to be.' Bradman was a very fast learner, but for all C. B. Fry's bepraisement, it must be remembered that Bradman's only experience as a duly appointed captain – before assuming the captaincy of South Australia – had been in club matches with St George and with North Sydney.

Bradman took to the South Australian captaincy with much gusto. Leadership suited his temperament. If he lost a match at the first time of asking (v M.C.C. at Adelaide), the Sheffield Shield itself was a different matter. It was not until his tenth match as captain of a Shield side that he lost for the first time. And in his initial season of 1935–36, he did not lose at all, and South Australia won the Sheffield Shield – as Harry Hodgetts had no doubt intended should be the case – for the first time for nine years and for only the second time since the First World War. The best Australian players, it is true, were away, either in South Africa or with the lesser touring side in India. But even so, the standard of Shield cricket at that time could hardly be termed weak. 'I can never remember taking the field in any match

---

[1] Of the 30 first-class matches on the 1934 tour of England, Woodfull was captain in 22, Bradman in six, and Kippax in two. When Kippax captained the side, Bradman was unfit. In addition, Bradman led the side in the minor matches at Aldershot and Forres.

without setting out to win', said Sir Donald after his career was over. He was as positive in this respect as he was confident with regard to his own batting.

That Bradman could still hit a cricket ball with the same certainty – and ruthlessness – as before his illness was proved by his first three Shield innings of '35–36. They yielded scores of 117, 233, and 357, and the respective victims were New South Wales, Queensland (inevitably), and Victoria. As in December 1927, when he scored a century in his first Shield innings for New South Wales, so now in December 1935, he scored a century in his first Shield innings for South Australia: it was, of course, the first time he had played against his native New South Wales. His 233 v Queensland all came in one day – indeed in just over three hours – and, as his eighth double-century in the Sheffield Shield, created a new record for that competition. (Eventually he ended with 13.) His 357 v Victoria was on his favourite Melbourne ground, though against an ordinary attack. (No Victorian bowler averaged better than 31·11 in the Shield that season.) He scored his first 229 on the first day, added 109 before lunch on the second, and his whole innings contained not a single chance. Yet another world record came with it – it was Bradman's fifth triple-century of his career. It also surpassed Warren Bardsley's previous Australian record of 53 centuries in a first-class career. It is said that someone in the Victorian side had upset Bradman before that match – a rash thing to have done and for which the fullest penalty was exacted. Warren Bardsley's previous record for an Australian of 53 centuries in first-class cricket had for a long time been regarded by his countrymen as a phenomenal achievement, in view of the limited number of first-class fixtures available. Bradman, neither for the first nor the last time, was to upset the conventional understanding of phenomenal and to replace it with his own unique standards of arithmetic.

Bradman then had a poor run, with 31 against Queensland at Brisbane, and – on his first visit to Sydney as an opposition player – a duck. Was this some retribution for his defection? We shall never know, but he did little better on his return to Adelaide. Here, against Victoria, a South Australian batsman registered a triple-century: and if, before the start of the game, that fact could have been stated by a seer, only a fool would have discounted Bradman's name as the performer. In fact it was Badcock who scored 325 – and Bradman 1! He was caught in his first over at the crease by second slip off Hans Ebeling, Jack Ledward throwing the ball in the air in joy several times.

His repute, needless to say, was hardly affected by these temporary aberrations. When the chief inspector of schools in New South Wales, Mr B. C. Harkness, visited a little school in Cooma towards the end of January 1936, he put a sudden question to one class: 'Who is the greatest man alive today?' 'Don Bradman', answered one boy at once. 'Stand up all who had that answer', ordered the inspector. And all the children but one rose.

If his single against Victoria was a grave disappointment for his new Adelaide supporters, he was to redress the balance more than sufficiently within a mere few days. He played an absolutely shattering innings of 369 for South Australia v Tasmania on the Adelaide Oval on 2 and 3 March 1936, quite engulfing the poor Tasmanians. He reached the fastest century of his first-class career (in 70 minutes); added 356 with Hamence for the third wicket in only 181 minutes; scored his last 168 in 80 minutes; and scored more runs in fours and sixes than ever in his life – four sixes and 46 fours. His 369 in 253 minutes (i.e. 87·50 an hour off his own bat, while his side's scoring rate was 125 an hour) was a new record score, as it still remains, for South Australia, and likewise a record for the Adelaide Oval – surpassing Clem Hill's 365* there for South Australia in December 1900. It was from Clem Hill that a telegram came: 'Congratulations you little devil for breaking my record.'[1]

The season had shown several things – that Bradman's health was again back to normal; that his form was not in question; that his old concentration and stamina were no less than they were; and that he was a tremendous asset to South Australia. How Harry Hodgetts must have congratulated himself! Bradman averaged 130·33 in all first-class matches in 1935–36, which was the best, by a big margin, in Australia, as was his total of 1,173 runs. He had scored all but two-thirds of the runs while he was at the crease (actually 65·97%, including extras) – the best proportion of his career. When extras are taken into consideration, he scored twice as fast as his South Australian colleagues throughout the season. In addition he had captained a young team with much discernment in every department of the game and had re-invigorated cricket in Adelaide, gaining for himself at the same time as high a degree of popularity as any of the old South Australian heroes. He handled the young players in his side especially well, and was to continue to do so – in contradistinction to his predecessor, V. Y. Richardson – to the end of his reign as State captain.

In Adelaide district cricket for his new club, Kensington, he was naturally a tower of strength when his first-class commitments allowed him to turn out. His best innings was 194 in 131 minutes – including one six and 28 fours – for Kensington v Port Adelaide on 28 March 1936, an innings compiled with a steel-shafted bat. Earlier in the season there had been an allegation that Bradman had been using such a bat: it was wholly untrue – but it provided the idea for him to try one out, and early in March he duly sent one of his favourite bats to Sydney to be fitted with a steel-shafted handle. Two flat strips of steel were inserted, extending some six inches up the blade of the bat, the handle then being covered with a cork and rubber compound. The bat had its first official trial at the Sydney Cricket Ground and it was claimed that the new handle gave greater power and smoothness to stroke-

---

[1] The South Australia v Tasmania match was the only time in Bradman's first-class career that he scored a triple-century in a three-day match. His side won comfortably (by an innings and 349 runs). His next best innings in a three-day match was his 278 for the Australians v M.C.C. at Lord's in 1938.

19 Don Bradman and his wife at a hotel in Dover on the day Mrs Bradman arrived from Australia after learning of her husband's desperate illness in England in 1934.

20 Bradman's first public appearance after his desperate illness of 1934. He dances with his wife at a charity function in aid of Battersea Hospital three days before leaving England for home in December that year.

21 Two giant personalities of the twentieth century – Winston Churchill and Donald Bradman, who found themselves by chance on the same platform at Victoria Station on 18 December 1934, when Bradman was leaving England after his desperate illness.

22 Don Bradman, in his first season as a Test selector, at the Sydney Cricket Ground during the second Test v England in December 1936. With him are his fellow selectors, W. J. Johnson (Victoria), left, and E. A. Dwyer (New South Wales), hat in hand.

23 Cricketers at play. A card session on the train when the Australians left London for Nottingham before the first Test of 1938. Left to right, E. S. White, D. G. Bradman, B. A. Barnett.

24 An informal picture of Australia's captain playing deck quoits on board the *Orontes* on the way to England in 1938.

25 Testing the pitch on the first morning of the 1938 series in England. Left to right, A. G. Chipperfield, S. G. Barnes and D. G. Bradman at Trent Bridge. The match produced 1,496 runs in four days at an average of 62·33 per wicket. Bradman scored 51 and 144 not out.

26 A moment of practice, without pads. Bradman keeps his eye firmly on the ball at the New Road ground, Worcester, in 1938.

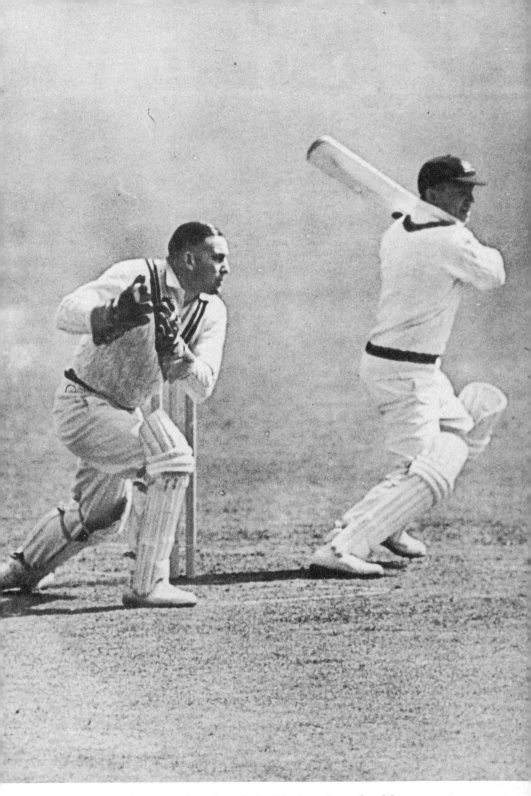

27 Don Bradman hits one of his 33 fours during his chanceless 258 at Worcester on 30 April 1938. J. S. Buller is the wicketkeeper.

28 The Oval, 1938, when Bradman fractured his right ankle during one of his rare spells of bowling. He is assisted from the field by E. S. White, left, and L. O'B. Fleetwood-Smith. England's score at the time was 887 for seven, and eventually ended at 903 for seven declared. The injury put Bradman out of the remainder of the tour.

play, with a 'springy' effect. When Bradman himself tried out the weapon for the first time in March, he made 155 with it for the South Australian State team against a country side at Adelaide – and a few days later his 194! There was a suggestion – a quite foolish one, of course – that the M.C.C. might have to be approached as to its legality. Then, as now, there was nothing in the laws of cricket whatsoever to prevent a bat comprising *any* substance, provided the width and length were not violated.

There was a certain amount of cynical criticism – and criticism that has subsisted to this day – that Bradman did not feel able to go with the Australian side to South Africa in 1935–36, while in the same season he was able to make such scores as 233, 357 and 369 in Australia. It is profitless to pursue the matter. The decision to avoid the South African tour, while in the final analysis Bradman's, had virtually been dictated to him. He had been told firmly enough by Sir Douglas Shields that his programme on returning to Australia after his 1934 illness was firstly three months of complete rest (which he duly had) and then to take things very quietly for at least a year. The team for South Africa was selected at the end of April 1935, a matter of days only after Bradman's Bowral recuperation ended. There were rumours saying Bradman would certainly be available for the tour, but the day after he arrived in Adelaide to start his new work he promptly scotched them. He would *not* be available. To have left for South Africa in October 1935, with all the prospective strain of a four-month tour in a strange country, would have been a direct and dangerous violation of his doctor's instructions. Moreover Bradman, had he gone, would almost certainly have been either captain or vice-captain: but even as an ordinary player, it would certainly have been a most incautious undertaking. South Africa, in the event, conceded 45·31 per wicket during the Test series: so their bowlers at least must have sighed gratefully to see Bradman absent.

By the mid-1930s Don Bradman was of course many things to many people. To the bowler, he was cricket's greatest menace; to the spectator, he was cricket's greatest spectacle; and to the game's treasurers he was undoubtedly – for he proved it time and again – cricket's greatest money-spinner. In the 1935–36 season three Sheffield Shield matches were played at Melbourne. There were 12 days of play. The total attendances and receipts were 75,019 and £2,957. Bradman batted for the greater part of one day at Melbourne and for a little under two hours the next. Yet *for those two days* the attendance was 40,000 and receipts £1,890.

9 Captain of Australia

There is no trick to being a captain as long as the sea is quiet.
Park Benjamin II

The acme of cricketing ambition came to Don Bradman in 1936–37, when he was appointed captain of Australia. It is not true, of course, that all things come to those who wait. Many have waited a long time for the captaincy of their country, and have waited in vain. Don Bradman waited a lesser time than most, but there is no doubt he was the fittest man for the post in Australia when the time came.

With his huge scores of the preceding season – including two merciless triple-hundreds – he was back at the very forefront again of public worship. In Australia in 1936–37 Bradman was the staple topic of conversation. 'Australia is Bradman mad', wrote William Pollock after but a mere few weeks of that summer. 'You hear his name all day long in the mouths of men, women and children. Everything he says or does – or is supposed to say or do – is seized upon. . . . There are rather fewer people in the whole of Australia than there are in London, and most of them idolise the little champion of cricket.'

There was, of course, beneath it all the most profound relief that Bradman was back again, fit and able to do battle in the Test arena, after the terrible anxiety of 1934. The public idol, in whatever sphere, has always been in a class of his own. As Sir Joynton Smith said in the Sydney *Referee* at the time of Bradman's serious illness: 'He has won a place in the thoughts and affections of all classes of the community, which is but rarely achieved by prime ministers, or even by monarchs, who stand high in the regard of the people.'

The new season of 1936–37 saw another visit from M.C.C. – the peacemaking tour led by G. O. Allen, to follow the near-warfare of four years before. For the first time Bradman was appointed an effective Australian selector, with one season of State selectorship behind him. The Board of Control appointment came at their Adelaide meeting on 10 September 1936 – a few days after Bradman's 28th birthday – and he joined E. A. Dwyer (New South Wales) and W. J. Johnson (Victoria), Bradman being the only newcomer to national selectorship. Though he had not yet been appointed captain, it was generally assumed he would be. When, in the July of 1936, Allen's name had been announced as leader of the M.C.C., it was Bradman – then neither an Australian selector nor of course captain – who publicly commented on the news and said Australia would be delighted to welcome him. Bradman's comments were sought exactly as though he were already captain.

As Allen's side landed at Fremantle in October 1936, the stentorian tones of a tugboatman shouted: 'Have you heard Bradman's latest score? It's 212.' That was correct – his first century in Sydney since he left there, in the Bardsley–Gregory testimonial match, and was made in only 202 minutes, his last 112 in 72 minutes. This was the long-awaited first confrontation at first-class level between Bradman and O'Reilly. There was no doubt who was the victor. O'Reilly's leg-trap Bradman demoralised and pulverised. No matter where the field was placed Bradman pierced it. His shots were masterpieces of timing and judgment. Against O'Reilly at his best Bradman scored his second century in 61 minutes. And the statisticians noted with a mixture of amazement and glee that his last seven innings in first-class cricket had now been 233, 357, 31, 0, 1, 369, 212. If it had been alleged that Bradman's big scores of the previous season had been made while the best bowlers were out of the country, that could not be said now: every one of the players he opposed in his 212 had been with Richardson's side to South Africa.

'As great with the bat as ever, if not even greater', was the verdict of J. C. Davis of the *Referee* as the prospects for the season were considered. Bradman was now the mature master, an untameable legend. Australians pinned an unshakeable faith on him. 'The Tests would be fair if it wasn't for Don', people were saying a week before the series began. 'He's a team in himself.' It was alleged – and all three have, alas, now passed on, so it cannot be confirmed – that Farnes, Copson and Sims had nightmares about him. His batting, at the very least, was calculated to upset many a breakfast table in England in 1936–37.

But first there was a personal tragedy for Don Bradman and his wife to face. On 29 October their day-old baby son – their first child – died. It was a terrible blow. It was the day before South Australia were due to play M.C.C. In the circumstances Bradman felt he could not face the crowd. The decision was left to him, and G. O. Allen sportingly agreed to leave his place open when he tossed up with Victor Richardson, who deputised as captain. But Bradman did not turn out; and the flags at the Adelaide Oval flew at half mast. He attended the ground on the Saturday. As Johnnie Moyes put it: 'He rose above his grief to pay his respects to the visitors.' By a strange, and sad, coincidence, during the previous Australian winter Stanley McCabe had likewise suffered the anguish of the death of his infant son, also his first-born.

A fortnight later Bradman took the field again for South Australia and played another of those astonishing innings – he played them at least once and often several times in the course of each season – that most batsmen would be proud, and satisfied, to claim on just a single occasion in their careers. In none of his books does Don Bradman give it the smallest mention. But, despite being taken ill on the eve of the match with ptomaine poisoning, he hit 192 in exactly three hours against Victoria at Melbourne, making his last 89 in 46 minutes with such ferocious hitting that the fielders were quite helpless while the spectators roared with delight. He went from 103 to 150 in 30 minutes – and then scored his last 42 in 16! Towards the end he hit 14, 13 and 19 off different overs. With R. A. Hamence he added 108 for the fifth wicket – Bradman 99 of them, and Hamence 9!

The visiting Englishmen, however, were the real objective of the season. And so far as Australian crowds were concerned, the real objective was Bradman. In the pre-Test period on the '36–37 tour, there were two fixtures from which Bradman was absent but in which he had appeared four years before. The respective receipts make an instructive comparison:

	1932–33 gross receipts (Bradman present)	1936–37 gross receipts (Bradman absent)
M.C.C. v Combined XI, Perth	£3,345	£1,846
M.C.C. v N.S.W., Sydney	£5,080	£3,134
	£8,425	£4,980

Sydney now had only one half of its famous boast of 'our Bridge and our Bradman'; and thousands upon thousands fewer spectators turned up at the S.C.G. – Test match time excluded, of course – as a result. It may here be mentioned that during the 1936–37 tour of Australia it was discovered as a fact that if Bradman was dismissed cheaply in the morning, the expected receipts in the afternoon fell by some £2,000.

Bradman and his co-selectors announced their 12 for the first Test – with Bradman as captain – on 25 November. The captaincy nomination, if reasonable enough (there being no other candidate for the captaincy in the 12), was strictly premature, for it was the Board of Control that made that appointment, not the selectors. Five days later the appointment was made *officially* – it was Bradman, of course, with McCabe as his vice-captain. At Adelaide earlier in the tour Bradman had told Neville Cardus he did not intend to score 'any more two-hundreds in Test matches'. As in 1934, he wanted to enjoy himself. As in 1934, he began the new series with bad scores – until the crisis came, and Australia *had* to have two-hundreds from him to stem disaster.

At Brisbane, where there had been no rain since Easter, Bradman captained Australia for the first time. It proved a joyless experience. He lost the toss, scored only 38 and 0, and saw his side lose by 322 runs. Rain before the fifth day condemned Australia to bat on a horrible wicket. They made 58 in 71 minutes, and Bradman was out second ball. It was all an enormous disappointment for the thousands who had come hundreds of miles to see Bradman. They had come by road, rail and air. In the first innings Cardus recorded that 'Bradman was heralded with trumpets and trombones of acclamation as he walked to the wicket'. The stroke that gave him his 0 he called 'as purposeless as a man flicking at the gyrations of a wasp or mosquito'. All Australia was stunned. In addition Bradman's captaincy was criticised. Gubby Allen wrote privately: 'Don Bradman seems very jumpy, and, I should say, was not at all well, and, if we can keep him in that frame of mind, we ought to win the rubber.' Disguised in black sun-glasses, Bradman left the Woolloongabba ground pondering on his fate.

Worse was to follow at Sydney. This time Australia were all out for 80 in 107 minutes on another sticky wicket – and Bradman got a duck again, caught off a 'sitter' at short-leg first ball, 'an amiable Christmas present to Allen'. Cardus cabled home: 'Bradman's stroke to-day was not fit for public view.' Vic Richardson did not consider the wicket really difficult. Most of the batsmen, he thought, 'got themselves out during the storm in the night'. All this followed England's declared total of 426 for six. Bradman made a somewhat lucky 82 on a much surer pitch in the second innings in nearly three hours, but his dismissal – bowled by a slow long-hop by Verity, attempting to hook with his head in the air – caused C. B. Fry almost to weep: 'The greatest run-getter in the history of cricket has made the worst stroke in the history of cricket. A wild hook with his eye off the ball. So Hedley Verity finished this Test match . . .' Australia lost by an innings. Allen was jubilant. Don Bradman had nothing to say.

Then came the public repercussion. The critics were urging that Bradman should be deposed from the captaincy. Not only were Australia two down but the position would probably have been the same even without rain. There were stories of differences among the players; that some of them were staying up too late; that Bradman was unable to reconcile the triple role of selector, captain and senior run-getter. 'I heard people say that Bradman's popularity was in the balance at this time', wrote William Pollock. 'I didn't believe it. I should say that quite ninety per cent of those who follow cricket in Australia – which is approximately ninety-nine per cent of the total population – were with him.' Bradman himself knew his experience of captaincy was limited, but there was simply no other cricketer good enough to take over. (The selectors had not considered Richardson as a candidate for the Test side.) It would have been, as Bradman himself put it, 'sheer cowardice' to abandon what appeared to be a sinking ship.

Bradman's position was not eased by the sensational paragraphs that appeared in the Sydney *Daily Telegraph* on the morning after the second Test defeat:

> Selectors and the Board of Control are disturbed at the suggestion that the Test teams are not pulling together, and that Bradman has not had the support generally given to an Australian captain.
>
> There is an important section of the team that has not seen eye to eye with Bradman, either on or off the field.

McCabe (the vice-captain) repudiated it; and Bradman himself repudiated it. But the murmurings of dissent continued, and it is probable if there was some smoke there was reason for it. One cause of the trouble stated at the time was that some players (not McCabe) thought that McCabe should have been captain. McCabe was vice-captain in South Africa and some considered he should have been given his chance against England. But McCabe most positively did not lead any cabal against Bradman. The criticism against Bradman as captain after the second Test defeat was described as 'entirely sympathetic and in the hope that the Board would relieve him of a great responsibility'. Then immediately the third Test ended – on the very same day – four of Australia's players (McCabe, O'Reilly, Fleetwood-Smith and O'Brien) appeared before a special meeting of the Board of Control at Melbourne at the instigation, it was reported, of Bradman. The news came through to England thus: 'Bradman complained to a meeting of the emergency committee of the Australian Board of Control of the behaviour, off the field, of the four. . . . All the men brought before the Board denied the complaints made against them by Bradman.' The fact that Fleetwood-Smith was among them would indicate that any matters of complaint did not arise exclusively from the first two Tests. Bradman was not invited to the meeting – which seems in retrospect a mistake by the Board – and no statement was issued, beyond that all the parties parted on the best of terms. Australia had then just won the Melbourne Test, though the players had been summoned before that result was known. In the euphoria of victory, the Board decided to take no action. It was effectively the end of the matter, but the following week Alan Fairfax arrived in London from Australia to attend to his cricket school, having met Bradman and most of the Australian players before he departed. He summed up the position to a *Daily Express* staff reporter:

> The boys in the Australian team feel that they are not getting a fair break from the crowd.
> Bradman, Bradman, all is Bradman. Well, the boys know he is a cricket genius, but that does not mean that the other players should be left right in the cold.
> Some of the trouble is caused by Bradman being captain. Now a man as successful as Don must concentrate on his own cricket. He can't give the time to the other players. He hasn't a chance to study their temperaments.
> You have to mother a cricket team, and Bradman is no mother. He is too brilliantly individual.
> Armstrong, Woodfull – they were the skippers to study the players' interests and get the best out of them. Don simply does not come up to that. He is a pleasant little chap, hard-headed, shrewd. I played with him for ten years.

That, at least, was the version that *seemed* to be the case at the time. Fairfax had given no more than a general view of minor dissatisfaction, not amounting to dissent. He knew nothing of the special meeting of the emergency committee of the Board. As to that special meeting, Don Bradman at the time denied categorically that he had been responsible for the complaints. He denied it with equal firmness in *Farewell to Cricket* in 1950. Sir Donald Bradman is, and always has been, an honourable man. His denial certainly is consistent with his absence from the emergency meeting, but as captain the Board *still* might have been wiser to have had him there. Newspapermen in Melbourne in January 1937 certainly had no doubt that Bradman had instigated the action, and stated it as a plain fact. Newspapermen, of course, must rely on their sources. O'Reilly in 1970 gave his account of the affair and of the moment before the four players left to attend the V.C.A. rooms in Melbourne: 'We asked Bradman if he knew what was transpiring. Don said he knew nothing and that he hadn't been invited to the get-together.' O'Reilly makes no further reference to Bradman, but says the complaints concerned 'indulging in too much alcohol and making no effort to get into top physical condition'. The complaints had been read from typed foolscap paper.

After the two–nil position brought about by Brisbane and Sydney, Bradman was sportsman enough to respond to the criticism by saying that not enough credit had been given to the part the Englishmen had played in the matter. Allen himself had said at the time that his respect and liking for Bradman had increased because he had proved himself a good loser. Privately Allen went further and said he was one of the best losers he had ever met. But Bradman, perhaps out of the optimism of despair, told Allen that his side would make a better show in the third Test at Melbourne. That proved very much indeed to be the case.

It was Maurice Leyland, after the two successive ducks perpetrated on Bradman, who remarked that someone was bound very soon to suffer as a result. Those who spoke with Bradman after the defeats in the first two Tests said his manner in conversation was far from downhearted or resentful. On Christmas Eve, Neville Cardus wrote, 'we all gave presents to Allen and congratulated him "in advance", though there was always the thought of Bradman in our minds'. There might also have been the thought of Bradman in 1934, who in mid-series produced all his awesome greatness to confound England. Small scores from Bradman presaged a swift retribution. On such occasions he was apt to treat bowlers, in the simile of A. A. Thomson, as the late Mr Justice Avory treated criminals: with justice but without mercy.

In *The Wild Duck* by Ibsen we are reminded that there are people in the world who sink to the bottom the moment they get a couple of shot in their body, and never come to the surface again. Don Bradman, by upbringing and by temperament, was most emphatically not one of those people. Bradman turned the tables astonishingly and heroically in the last three Tests, with epic innings of 270, 212, and 169. He batted in all for nearly 19 hours – chanceless and awe-inspiring hours – for these three scores, decisively dispelling all suggestion that captaincy was affecting his batting. The three innings placed him again at the very top of the pedestal from which some had chosen to remove him. Each innings contributed to a huge Australian victory, to give them the rubber by three matches to two – the only instance in history of a side emerging triumphant after being two–nought down. And this on Bradman's debut as a Test captain.

The sheer relentless application of Bradman in these crucial innings made

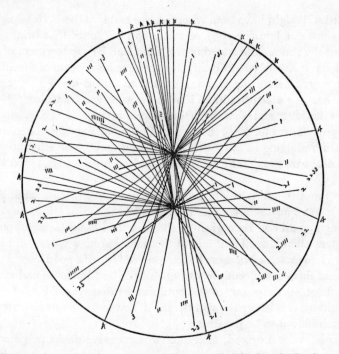

W. H. Ferguson's scoring chart of one of the most vital innings in Bradman's Test career – his 270 in over 7½ hours against England at Melbourne in the third Test of 1936–37. When this Test began, England were leading in the series 2–0. Australia finished winners of the series 3–2. The above innings contained as many as 110 singles, as well as 22 fours, 8 threes and 24 twos.

those voices – and they were strongly opinionated voices – look silly when they said Bradman was on the decline after the second Test. 'Once he had got over the difficulties which beset him at the beginning of the tour', said Cardus, 'his confidence in himself was terrifying in its quiet modesty.' The situation called for nerve, skill and unflinching resolution. Bradman provided them all, and here is the evidence:

> 270 in 3rd Test at Melbourne in 7 hrs. 38 mins.   No chance.
> 212 in 4th Test at Adelaide   in 7 hrs. 21 mins.   No chance.
> 169 in 5th Test at Melbourne in 3 hrs. 43 mins.   No chance.

Not only did he give no chance, but scarcely took a single risk or lifted the ball off the ground. He had planned to win the rubber and he did so. He was one of a team, of course, but now its unquestioned leader and inspirer. At the end of the series Australians might have been forgiven for applying to Bradman the words of Bizet on Beethoven: 'He is not a man, but a god.'

But there was nothing of the insufferable young hero with a swollen head about Bradman. There never had been before, and there was certainly never to be in the future. He coped with the fortunes and misfortunes of 1936–37 with the same level head he had always possessed. Some of the criticism that season was in fact particularly virulent. He was castigated when Australia were losing, and castigated when Australia were winning – in the latter case for hogging the crease and adding to his personal pile of records. He was charged with changing cricket from a team game to an individual game. He was certainly the star so far as crowd-attraction was concerned, perhaps the only real star in this respect in the entire series. People who knew nothing about cricket went to see him bat, especially women. There are thousands of them all over Australia to this day who are not ashamed to make that confession. (Bert Oldfield at the end of the tour said that 60 per cent of the record attendance at Melbourne were women.) But Bradman was, after all, something outstanding. Would Australia – and even his most persistent critics – have preferred him to stand down from the Test arena, making way for another batsman, while he perhaps penned his observations from the press-box? In such an event it is certain that those same detractors would have assailed him for deserting the cause of Australian cricket and for taking a sordid financial advantage of his association with the game. If a man has determined critics, they will stay determined critics.

Woodfull had been right, of course, when he said of Bradman before the series began: 'If I were a selector I should count him as two batsmen if he was playing in form. I mean that literally.' In other words Bradman in form (his usual condition) would make way for an extra bowler of all-rounder in the side. The real selectors did not follow that precept, but Woodfull's view was not all that fanciful a one. Actually Bradman scored 810 runs in the series, against the next best (on either side) of 491 by McCabe. Fingleton, in the same number of innings, was third among the Australians with 398, and no other Australian reached 200. Bradman was Australia's spinal column.

A few brief details should be recorded before those epic innings of 1936–37 are left behind. In the New Year Test at Melbourne, Bradman won the toss for the first time in Test cricket. This was the match when heavy rain so affected the wicket that Bradman's captaincy was put to the test in a crucial crisis. After Allen declared, Bradman upturned his batting order in the second innings when the pitch was still fearsome. He himself went in at number seven, to join Fingleton at 97 for five. They added – on a gradually improving wicket – 346 for the sixth wicket in just over six hours, still a record for the sixth wicket in Tests between any countries. England had devised a scheme, with a widely dispersed field, to make Bradman run as many singles as possible, on the premise that even Bradman could not run two hundred singles. He didn't, but he did run 110 of them (apart from those of his partners) and chose to bat for his 270 for the longest period of his life in a Test match: seven hours 38 minutes, spread over three days, partly with a heavy cold, and just when his presence was most needed. It seemed hopeless to try to get him out. He played, by the way, on the third day, Monday (when he made the first 56 of his great score) before the biggest crowd of his life – an official attendance of 87,798. When, at the close of the fourth day, he was 248*, the Melbourne *Sun* expressed the feelings of the nation with a grateful headline that stretched across the entire width of its cricket page: 'Master Batsman Back On His Throne'. The narrative began with just what the readers wanted to see: 'A day of Bradman and a day of broken Test records – the terms have again become synonymous.' Australia's great fortune was England's misfortune.

At Adelaide, the hot weather city of Australia, Neville Cardus anticipated '100 in the shade, and Bradman 300 in the sun'. Well, it wasn't quite either: but the temperature climbed into the 90s and Bradman got 212, so the forecast wasn't dramatically awry. For the second Test in succession Bradman batted for three days – a tense innings, for had he failed, the rubber would almost certainly have been England's. The third day was a public holiday: the fourth day – which was not – saw the attendance up by 7,000, for Bradman was not out overnight. As he progressed – with 'most fell purpose' – towards his second hundred, Cardus wrote: 'Bradman's fires blazed forth, threatening to consume England; there is no argument about the name of the game's greatest match-winning stroke-player when Bradman is Bradman. He has emerged royally from the difficult state of a few weeks ago, and once more he is the master.' This was England's 13th Test at Adelaide, and they suffered their worst defeat there since 1907–08. Once again Bradman batted more than seven hours. Once again he gave no chance. C. B. Fry called him the eighth wonder of the world.

After that 212 Bradman said it was 'no good' to him to play like that – strictly orthodox, eschewing the hook stroke, playing relentlessly up and down the line of the ball. He had played like that also for his 270 at Melbourne. There was no hint of a cross bat in either innings. It was nothing like the Bradman of Headingley or the Oval. 'I cannot call to mind any innings in which he played such orthodox strokes', said Oldfield of the 270. This method may not have pleased Don Bradman, but it happened to win two Tests.

In the final Test at Melbourne, which marked the Diamond Jubilee of Test cricket between England and Australia, Bradman won the toss for the third time, and his 169 was a quite perfect, as well as a quite different, innings. His self-discipline now was replaced by all his old brilliance. He faced only 191 balls. 'What are we to do about him?' sighed C. B. Fry this time. This was actually his eighth hundred in his last eight matches on the Melbourne ground, a staggering sequence. Allen, Farnes, Voce, Verity and Hammond were as nothing to Bradman. He made the fastest bowling appear medium-pace. 'I wonder', mused Cardus, 'if Bradman ever grows tired of his own mastery and sighs for new worlds to conquer, new reaches of achievement outside the great capacity of his skill. Or is he satisfied to go on being humanly acquisitive? To-day he caused batting to appear as easy and as natural as breathing, walking, or eating.'

G. O. Allen, in a private letter home, had expressed the view between the third and fourth Tests that the Australian XI was 'simply Bradman and no one else'. That view must have been enhanced by the end of the series. Three marvellous innings by Bradman and the rubber to Australia. Bradman received, on behalf of the team, a telegram of congratulation from the King. It was all highly satisfying. The critics had been silenced; and in the five Tests Bradman had averaged 90. He and Gubby Allen had fought a series in splendid spirit. When the last ball was bowled, Allen told the crowd out-side the pavilion: 'If I were in Bradman's position and had his ability, I should be very glad to be standing here. . . . Australia owes a great deal to a captain who has shown magnificent form first with the bat and then with that infernal coin . . . I'll only say that though we lost we live to fight again.' It was all very different from 1932–33.

Thus in the course of a single summer Bradman experienced the private grief of a lost first-born child and the public joy of the winning of the Ashes. Fate did not give him any choice in the matter.

The sheer personal effort that Bradman brought to bear on reversing a two–nil situation against Australia was one of the monumental feats in a career that could boast many peaks. Apart from the captaincy aspect, it might be said that the batting of Hammond or Grace or Trumper might have done the same. But the fact is they did not do it. Bradman did. It was no doubt Bradman's batting in this series that prompted R. C. Robertson-Glasgow a few years later to say: 'In certain aspects Bradman is the most wonderful batsman that the game has known. For he introduced a new conception of what a batsman could do in physical endurance and mental concentration.' It was in fact also the most obdurate self-discipline, allied to the most indomitable will in cricket.

Before he put his bat away that season, Don Bradman satisfied his resolve to enjoy himself. He turned out for his club side, Kensington, and played an innings of 127 in 88 minutes. He scored the last 27 in seven minutes. By then he was back at work in Grenfell Street among his stocks and shares.

Bradman had now passed 4,000 runs in Test cricket, with 18 centuries, at an average of 97·06. Against England alone he had passed 3,000 runs at 89·63. Both aggregates were easily a record for an Australian (and both averages were to be slightly improved upon before the end of his career). It might seem somewhat comic – even comically impudent – that at this juncture of Bradman's career the universal panacea for tackling him should be enunciated in full earnestness by none other than Douglas Jardine, who was not in Australia that winter. But for his *Evening Standard* readers in London in March 1937 he had the final answer:

> Bradman, after a most unpromising start, has reinstated himself as the bowler's greatest problem. In three or four-day matches he may well represent an almost insoluble problem. In the timeless Tests, however, one may venture the suggestion that a more methodical strategy than that to which he was subjected might reduce this menace, and would in any case prove an exceedingly interesting experiment.
>
> To carry this out the first essential would be to deprive him of the strike as much as possible right from the start of his innings; treating his partner, however good,

as if he were a rabbit who should be manœuvred into getting all the bowling possible.

This would entail setting two radically different fields to which the bowlers would have to bowl with faithful accuracy. In Bradman's case the field would be set so deep as to make it very easy for him to score a single early in the over – and thus deprive himself of the strike – and exceedingly difficult for him to score a two or a four.

Bradman's partner would be faced with an inner and an outer ring of fieldsmen which, while saving the ones and threes, would necessarily have to concede the twos and fours. In Bradman's case, save when the ball was new, the bowlers would hardly attack the wicket, but make him 'stretch for his runs' with big doses of off theory to a packed off-side field.

It may be argued that this would not get Bradman out. It would, however, reduce his rate of scoring annoyingly and materially. 'Even Apollo sometimes nods', and the chances of Bradman getting himself out must often be as good as the bowler's chance of getting him out.

It might have made interesting reading, but cricket strategy, even from one such as Jardine, was not a matter of paperwork. In fact Allen had tried something like it in the Melbourne Test in January, and Bradman scored 270. He was all but exhausted at the end, but he still scored 270. The truth was that Bradman's performances could scarcely be discussed in terms of ordinary batsmanship.

One of those who *had* seen every ball bowled to Don Bradman on Allen's tour was William Pollock, the *Daily Express* man, who wrote most entertainingly and without the smallest hint of uncharitableness. After 1932–33, when Fleet Street was very thinly indeed represented by its own writers in Australia, London newspapers were never to be caught on the hop again, and the '36–37 tour showed the way for the formidable posse of journalists that have always since covered an England visit to Australia. Pollock, in Australia for the first time, got to know Bradman reasonably well, an association that was to be to their mutual advantage. 'People told me', said Pollock, 'that he was a go-getter and not a good mixer, but even if this was true there were things in him that interested me. I could see that he was intelligent, and, I thought, shy. I nearly always come to like shy people; there is usually a lot in them.' Pollock did find a lot in Bradman, for the upshot of their association was that Pollock went back to Australia the following winter to collaborate with Bradman in the writing of his life story. He had put it to Bradman towards the end of Allen's tour. 'We got together in his house in Kensington, outside Adelaide, where he has dogs, and canaries in open cages, and a grand piano – which he plays – and a charming wife. Before I left his house we had made a verbal "gentlemen's agreement" that I should have an option to find a market for his story and help to write it, the option to hold good for two months after I had got back to London.'

The *News of the World* accepted Pollock's proposal with alacrity and gave him £1,000 to go back to Australia in 1937–38 to do the writing. Characteristically, when he arrived in Adelaide he was handed a sheaf of typescript by Bradman. 'I thought I had better write as much as I could before you landed', he said. And Bradman had indeed, in his methodical way, written sufficient to get the book truly under way. In the event, it took only two months to write. It came out, of course, in 1938 as *My Cricketing Life*, published in July that year by Stanley Paul at the bargain price of 3/6d – a happy, uninhibited book, utterly frank, and showing unmistakably the controlling hand of Bradman on every page, whatever may have been Pollock's contribution. 'What Don got out of the newspaper serial and the book rights is none of my business to tell', said Pollock afterwards. 'But it was a lot more than I did. And quite right, too.' The book was exclusively – and imposingly – serialised in the *News of the World*, commencing on 29 May 1938.

Meanwhile the 1937–38 season saw Bradman add both to his records and to his reputation. There were no ducks, no minor loss of form – just a relentless progress to a Sheffield Shield average of 98·30 and an overall total of seven centuries in his 12 first-class matches. His first innings for Kensington was a brilliant 116 in just over two hours, his century coming in 96 minutes. He played against a New Zealand side for the first and only time in his life when M. L. Page's team played three of the Australian States on their way home after their 1937 tour of England. The fact that Bradman was out for 11 against them at Adelaide, first thing on the second morning, was held largely responsible for the loss suffered on the New Zealanders' tour. His influence on gate receipts was so enormous that any pre-lunch dismissal was a huge financial setback. If this was a matter for concern among Australian administrators, there was nothing they could do about it.

A financial hazard of another kind accompanied Bradman's dismissal for 17 in the joint Richardson–Grimmett testimonial match at Adelaide. The clock was turned back ten years and, as on Bradman's first appearance in first-class cricket, he was out 'b. C. V. Grimmett' – and thereby hangs a tale. Bradman and Grimmett were now both members of the same Sheffield Shield side, so a duel between them at first-class level was a rarity confined to a special fixture. As Grimmett's captain for South Australia, Bradman had been observing an increased use by Grimmett of the 'flipper' instead of the basic leg-break. 'I don't think you *can* bowl a leg-break any longer', said Bradman to Grimmett in due course – meaning a leg-break that would turn effectively on Australian pitches. In the testimonial match at Adelaide Grimmett bowled Bradman with a quite perfect leg-break after half an hour, and joyfully informed his co-beneficiary: 'That will teach the little beggar I can still bowl a leg-break.' To which Victor Richardson's rueful reply was: 'I suppose you know you've bowled us out of a thousand pounds.' It was later in that season that there was an alleged dressing-room contretemps between Bradman and Grimmett, in which Grimmett accused Bradman of playing for himself instead of the side – an exchange that perhaps shut the door on the 1938 tour of England for Grimmett.

After the tour of 1936–37 – and especially after the almost miraculous way in which Bradman's batting had turned the tables on Allen's side in the

Tests – many Englishmen considered that such was Bradman's personal mastery and effect on a game of cricket that no side for which he batted twice on a good pitch could be beaten. This was not true of course – and Sheffield Shield bowlers *dared* not think it true. O'Reilly, for one, would never accept it: and when the pair were next in contention in a Shield match (at Adelaide in December 1937) O'Reilly duly proved it false by seeing South Australia beaten by 33 runs in spite of innings of 91 and 62 by the Don. O'Reilly, who headed the Shield bowling averages that summer, had his best-ever figures for New South Wales in that match – nine for 41 in the first innings. His 14 wickets in the match – great bowler though he was, he never in his life managed 15 – included Bradman twice: and the Don's match aggregate of 153 took nearly $5\frac{1}{2}$ hours, an untypical and telling rate of only 28 an hour. This was marvellous cricket, however – the brilliant facing the brilliant. But Bradman's side lost! On a blameless wicket, Bradman felt his way slowly to 91, with only four fours, before allowing himself the luxury of his first aggressive stroke against O'Reilly. He was at once out to it, caught off a skier to square-leg.

Queensland paid their usual Christmas-time visit to Adelaide in December 1937, but as usual the presence of Don Bradman made the occasion anything but a festive one for the visiting bowlers. For the fifth time in his life (and not the last!) he took a double-century off them. This time it was 246, the highest score of the Australian summer. Whilst he was with South Australia, Bradman played only four Shield matches against Queensland at Adelaide (always over Christmas) and played a masterful innings each time:

December 1935 – 233 v Queensland, Adelaide (Chances at 191 and 219)
December 1937 – 246 v Queensland, Adelaide (No chance)
December 1938 – 225 v Queensland, Adelaide (Chance at 147)
December 1939 – 138 v Queensland, Adelaide (No chance)

Adding a second innings of 39* in the second of the above matches, his average for this little collection of innings becomes 220·25!

The last day of 1937 saw the relentless Bradman bat create two more records, and worthy ones at that. In a modest innings of 54 at Melbourne, he became the highest Sheffield Shield scorer of all time, surpassing the previous record aggregate of Clem Hill. Hill had retired before the war, coming back to play one Shield match – the George Giffen testimonial game – in February 1923. In that, he took his final Shield total to 6,270 runs. Like Bradman who was to follow him, he was a star of his own age and a great number three batsman. Now, in 1937, he was a South Australian representative on the Board of Control, no doubt discussing frequently enough the 'little devil' named Bradman. On the night of 31 December 1937, the two highest scorers in the history of the Sheffield Shield had figures as follows:

	Matches	Inns.	N.O.	Runs	H.S.	Av.	100s	50s	0s
D. G. Bradman	44	69	11	6,280	452*	108·27	23	15	4
C. Hill	68	126	6	6,270	365*	52·25	18	27	5

On the same day Clem Hill – who must have been blissfully unaware of the fact, for records rarely entered into his thinking – was demoted from another landmark when Bradman passed his 17,160 runs to become the highest first-class scorer among Australian cricketers. He did it in more than 200 fewer innings than Hill. If it was any consolation to the former hero, who a few years before had remarked that cricket was a national pastime not a national business, he could claim that all *his* runs were scored on uncovered wickets. He was, and is, one of Adelaide's great sons.

This particular New Year match against Victoria saw L. O'B. Fleetwood-Smith take nine for 135 in the first innings. The one wicket perhaps that would have meant more to him than all the other nine eluded him – Don Bradman. Despite many attempts, Fleetwood-Smith had never yet, before his home crowd at Melbourne, managed to dismiss the Don: and he was to do so there only once in his career – after Bradman made 267 on 1 January 1940. For all that, Bradman had the highest opinion of Fleetwood-Smith's spin, though his lack of control at times made him expensive. The New Year match against Victoria of 1937–38 was also the first time Bradman failed to score a century at Melbourne in any match since the 1932–33 season.

The calendar year 1938 was to prove one of superb consistency, even by Bradman's own standards. From Melbourne, South Australia travelled up to Brisbane, and Bradman made the two top scores of the match – 107 and 113, to make his aggregate in two matches against Queensland that season 505! The side, still on tour, went on to Sydney, where Bradman reminded his old supporters (and not least the new treasurer of New South Wales, Frank Cush) of his continuing skill with his first Shield century on the Sydney Cricket Ground since his defection, and showed them also what they had not seen before – Bradman the wicketkeeper. When Walker was injured, Bradman kept wicket in both New South Wales innings – ignoring the possibility of injury to himself before the forthcoming tour of England – making three catches and a stumping and allowing only eight byes. The match provided a further curiosity in that it was the first time for nearly eight years (since the Trent Bridge Test of 1930) that Don Bradman scored a century in a first-class match and was on the losing side. In the intervening period he had scored 46 first-class hundreds, every one of which had either helped his side to victory or at least kept it immune from defeat. A Bradman century usually was a guarantee against defeat, and of the 117 centuries that he scored in his first-class career, only eight were for a side that lost (including two in the same match, so only seven matches were actually involved). The other 109 – or 93 per cent – helped materially towards keeping defeat away. His batting, it is commonplace to say, had a tremendous effect on the course of a match. Bradman's Test opponents in particular could reflect that there were only two occasions in history that a hundred by Bradman coincided with defeat for Australia, and they were at the very beginning of the Bradman era. The last 26 centuries he made in Test cricket (including a century in each innings) were made in 25 matches, which resulted in 21 wins for

Australia and four draws. In two of those draws – the two occasions of Bradman's triple-hundreds at Leeds – rain saved England from probable defeat.

Having been through the fire of Test captaincy in 1936–37, Bradman matured quickly as a strategist who was never to lose a Test series in his life. Indeed, after those two initial reverses at the hands of G. O. Allen, he lost only one of the final 22 Tests in which he led Australia. Even if he had lost the series against Allen's side, it is almost certain he would have been captain in England in 1938, for there was no effective rival and Bradman was still potentially the best match-winning batsman in the world. As it was, the Board of Control inevitably picked him to lead the 1938 side, and at the age of 29 he became the youngest Australian captain in England since Joe Darling in 1899. The side, of course, was also the first touring side in which Bradman himself had a hand as a selector: Messrs Dwyer and Johnson completed the trio of selectors, as was the case in '36–37. The selectors, precisely as in 1934, opted for a team of experience and freshness – eight had been to England before and eight had not. For Bradman it was the highest honour that can come the way of any cricketer – leading his country overseas on a mission for the Ashes.

The packing done and the farewells made, the Australians played their usual pre-departure matches in Tasmania and Perth. The Rev. R. A. Coogan, now of Hampstead, London, remembers going to see the Australians, as a boy of eight, on the pleasant little ground at Launceston, and watching the touring team practise at the nets. Bradman was kind enough to play with some of the boys and invited them to send down a few balls to him – an invitation keenly taken up before the game began on the Saturday morning. He then rewarded the schoolboys with his autograph. Bradman's health had prevented him going to Tasmania in 1934, but this time he looked very fit and well. He made 79 at Launceston and 144 a few days later at Hobart, giving his wicket away both times. His 144 came in only 98 minutes and included – for the only time in his life in a first-class match – three sixes off successive balls, off the leg-spinner S. W. L. Putman. Bradman and Badcock that afternoon put on 241 at 147 an hour! Then at Perth, Bradman scored 102 in two hours and sailed off with his side on the *Orontes*. The two leaders in the Australian averages that season had been Bradman (89·81) and Lindsay Hassett (53·30).

The domestic accounts for the 1937–38 season had still to be audited, but when they were published they were to show once again what a terrifying effect the presence of Bradman had in swelling State profits. Virtually 72% of Shield revenue in Sydney in the two seasons 1936–37 and 1937–38 came from South Australia's visits under Bradman. In 1936–37 the South Australia match actually formed 84% of Sydney's Shield revenue. The ancient New South Wales rivalry with Victoria was utterly supplanted as a public spectacle by Bradman's South Australia, as the following small table shows:

At Sydney	Revenue to N.S.W.C.A.	
	1936–37	1937–38
v South Australia	£1,162.12.6	£1,539. 8.6
v Victoria	£ 98.15.0	£ 130. 0.4

What greater pointer could there be to the magic appeal of Bradman?

South Australia themselves, it need hardly be said, were basking in financial bliss since the arrival of Bradman. A typical balance sheet – one published in October 1937 – showed a profit of £7,080 (even after the spending of £2,269 on permanent building improvements). The South Australian membership at the same time had risen to 3,519 – a record. Bradman's drawing-power was in keeping with his status as a world figure. And he was still not yet 30 years of age!

10 Captain in England and War

There are those who say that he cannot get any better, but when a genius or phenomenon of this nature crops up there is no telling what he may do.
'Second Slip' (Frank Mitchell) on D. G. Bradman in
The Cricketer, 1930

The leisurely journey of Bradman's Australians to England in 1938 followed close in the wake of Germany's annexation of Austria and coincided with the detailed plans for the taking of refugees from Germany, and heavy Japanese bombing of Canton. The world was not what it was. The usual match in Ceylon was played on the way, on 30 March, though Bradman himself did not turn out because of a cold. His name, however, was on the scorecard, and when Hassett scored 116 the crowd *thought* it was Bradman – and were delirious with delight! When the *Orontes* was at Port Said in April, the five-year-old Colin Cowdrey was on another ship, going from India to start school in England. He has told of the intense excitement when his father lifted him in his arms and pointed solemnly to the *Orontes*: 'Don Bradman is on board that ship', he said. 'He's bringing the Australian team to try to beat England.' And more than 30 years afterwards, Colin Cowdrey remembered the incident vividly and remembered his father's tone: 'Clearly the Australians excited him, but Bradman was God, or that was the impression he gave me.'

In the fancy-dress ball on board the *Orontes*, Bradman appeared festooned with bottles to represent 'departed spirits'. There was a little interlude at Nice, where there was much bustling to get Bradman to a tennis tournament (to watch, not to play!). There was another meeting at Gibraltar with Sir Charles Harington, who took the salute at the march past of the King's Regiment after a church service, while Bradman, also at the salute, stood by his side. After the ceremony Sir Charles remarked: 'Although I was taking the salute, not one man looked at me.' There was, in a more serious vein, the captain's woe of knowing that one of his leading batsmen, Sidney Barnes, had injured his left wrist on deck. And then England and a fresh tour. The *Orontes* docked at Southampton on 20 April. Almost the first act that Don Bradman did on arrival – on his first night in London – was to pay his respects to Sir Douglas Shields, but for whom he might not have been in England at all in 1938.

Don Bradman played in fewer matches in 1938 (and played fewer innings) than on any of his four tours of England, injury in the Oval Test cutting him off from the final portion of the tour. But in his 20 matches he became the first batsman in history to average more than 100 in an English season, and his final average that summer of 115·66 is still the highest on record for an English season. At 29 he could not be expected to be what he was at 21, in 1930: but he was no less a difficult problem for English bowlers. If anything he was more difficult to get out (as his 13 centuries in 26 innings indicated) for as his audaciousness lessened his impregnability increased. 'One did not detect any waning of his powers', said the editor of *Wisden*. 'Judged by the standard he set himself, he was perhaps a shade better.' It was the season when Neville Cardus asked Voce – who saw Bradman score 56 and 144 against Notts – which ball did he consider the best to bowl at Bradman. 'There's no ruddy best ball to bowl at him', replied Voce from the heart.

The Worcestershire bowlers had known the truth of that from painful experience. Now, for the third successive time – a unique performance – Bradman began a tour of England with a double-century against them, scoring 258 on the opening day of the season. In both 1930 and 1934 he had given a solitary chance in his Worcester 200s: but in 1938 he was faultless, despite a personal scoring-rate of 52·83 an hour. While he was at the crease – just short of five hours – the Australians' total advanced at almost 86 an hour. No one has ever made a score remotely approaching 258 on the opening day of an English season – and Bradman was more than a quarter of the way towards 1,000 by the end of May before May had even begun! (The B.B.C., incidentally, who provided live commentary on the Worcester match, instilled some momentary, if false, hope in English breasts when their commentator portentously announced that Bradman had been 'scratching around' and was out for 34. Later listeners were informed that he was 150 and then 200. It had been McCabe who was out for 34!)

As had now become nothing more than ordinary in the terminology of Bradman, he proceeded to dwarf all precedent by reaching his 1,000 before the end of May for the second time. No other cricketer has ever done this twice. As in 1930, he reached the target against Hampshire at Southampton; and by reaching it on 27 May he set a record which still stands as the earliest date to the landmark. He also reached it in seven innings, another record for an English season. Those innings included five centuries, the fifth of them recorded on 27 May. So good a sextet of batsmen as Compton, Leyland, Sutcliffe, Washbrook, John Langridge and Worthington all scored exactly five centuries apiece in 1938, but none of them got to that mark earlier than 20 August. Previously known values were once again turned upside down by Bradman. As A. G. Gardiner wrote of him that May: 'He has upset the balance of the game as it has never been upset before by the genius of a single player.'

An illustration of the quiet confidence of Don Bradman is related by Hampshire's 12th man at Southampton, Lloyd Budd. On the final day of the match, with Bradman needing a further 53 to reach his 1,000, the Australian captain quietly remarked: 'I'll get these today.' And get them he did. His average on the night of 27 May, as the Australians left Southampton, was 170·16 (from 1,021 runs). Ten days before, it had actually been 182·75, after his brilliant 278 against M.C.C. at Lord's (his highest-ever score on that ground), when 32,000 packed the ground on the Saturday, with many more unable to get in, while Bradman rewarded them with a chanceless 257* by close of play. R. W. V. Robins, M.C.C.'s captain, cemented in this match his firm friendship with Bradman which had grown on Gubby Allen's tour, and the friendship was to prosper even more strongly in the future. (Bradman in 1945 was to become godfather to one of Robins' sons after opening his home to some of the Robins family during the war.)

Among the many unique records set up by Don Bradman, one that he established in 1938 deserves special mention. He is the only cricketer to reach 1,000 runs before the end of May *without being bowled*. He scored 1,486 runs that season before he was bowled for the first time (on 25 June) and had taken his aggregate to 2,127 before he was bowled for the second time (on 23 July). On the first occasion he was out 'bowled', he actually dragged a ball from Hedley Verity on to his wicket, so he was not in fact *clean* bowled until well past his 2,000 for the season. (Such good batsmen in 1938 as Fingleton and Leyland were each out 'bowled' as many as five times before May was out.)

There was one other quite astonishing feature of Bradman's 1,000 runs before the end of May in 1938. When he reached the target, he had given *not a single chance* thus far in the entire season (beyond, of course, his actual dismissals). No single fact could have been a more ominous one on the verge of a Test series.

Bradman actually had one further match in May after reaching his 1,000 and in it (against Middlesex) he raised his aggregate by the end of the month to 1,056, second only to Tom Hayward's 1900 record of 1,074 by 31 May. Bradman's average at that point of 150·85 remains the best on record of those instances of 1,000 runs before June, just as his 1930 average of 143·00 remains the second best. He could almost certainly have beaten Tom Hayward's record had he not (when 30*) declared 21 minutes from the close of the match against Middlesex, knowing that Bill Edrich, one of the fielding side, at that point had 990 runs to his name. This is how Edrich himself has put it: 'And then, Don Bradman – grim-faced, unsmiling, the man they say is a cricketer without a heart and never gives an opponent a chance – declared their innings closed, for the sole purpose of letting a miserable youngster who had thrown away his own golden chances get his 1,000 runs before the end of May.' Edrich duly reached the magic landmark, and Bradman's hand was the first to congratulate him. It had been a generous gesture by Bradman, and Edrich has never forgotten it.

Bradman rested a troublesome back in the week prior to the first Test, and therefore entered the series with his season's average on that same lofty pinnacle of 150·85. It quite swamped the best by any Englishman, Test player or otherwise – Walter Hammond's 86·00, outstanding as that was. Time and again, of course, throughout his career Bradman not only exceeded the averages of those around him but exceeded them by almost inhuman margins. W.G. had done the same in his high noon, and there was, and is, no greater indication of a player's superiority over his contemporaries. The sheer moral effect both on Bradman's own team and on his opponents achieved by his presence and by his figures was no less real for being immeasurable. As the first Test was about to begin, the Special Correspondent of *The Times* (who for that match was Dudley Carew) said this of the Australian side: 'Also they will have Bradman, and the influence Bradman has on the side is not to be assessed by the virtue of his office or of the splendour of his thousand runs. The team seem to take their cue from him as an orchestra takes it from an inspired and trusted conductor.' If there had been any earlier reservations about his captaincy prowess, these had dissolved by 1938. Had not Jack Ryder said Bradman was the quickest learner in the game? He was now a Test match captain to be feared as much as he was overwhelmingly a Test match batsman to be feared. Walter Hammond, his opposing captain, had never led a Test side in his life. He was not even captaining Gloucestershire.

Bradman had stayed behind in London when the Australians went to play a Hammond-less Gloucestershire at Bristol. Hammond was also in London, captaining England v the Rest in the Test Trial at Lord's. Bradman watched part of the game, thus seeing for the first time Hammond in the role of captain. He also saw, for the first time in his life, Douglas Wright bowling, and saw him bowl uncommonly well. Don Bradman, on his own subsequent admission, never watched a day's cricket in his life without learning something, and there is no doubt that this pre-Test view of Wright was used to his own and his side's advantage in the subsequent Tests. (In a radio talk in Australia in November 1938, Bradman called Wright 'the discovery of the year'.)

At Trent Bridge, although Bradman scored his 13th century against England (thus exceeding Hobbs's record of 12 centuries in England–Australia games), the innings of the match – indeed the innings of the season – was McCabe's 232, which Bradman has always held to be the finest innings he has ever witnessed. As McCabe's stroke-play reached a glorious crescendo, Bradman from the balcony called to his team in the dressing-room: 'Come and look at this. You may never see anything like it again.' That was spontaneous praise indeed, and it was merited. 'Towards the end I could scarcely watch the play', said Bradman later. 'My eyes were filled as I drank in the glory of his shots.' When McCabe returned to the dressing-room, Bradman told him: 'I would give a great deal to be able to play an innings like that.' But Australia still had to follow on, and on a wearing wicket all Bradman's defensive skills were required to effect a draw on the final day. Early that morning he was writing a letter in the hotel lounge. Neville Cardus says that Bradman called him over, saying: 'I'm just telling my wife in Adelaide that we're in a spot of trouble, but I've reassured her that I'll fix everything all right this afternoon.' Bradman defended as he had never done before. In over six hours he hit only five boundaries. It was the slowest century of his life, reached in 253 minutes – the *only one* of his 117 first-class hundreds to take as long as four hours (and almost certainly the only one of his 211 centuries in all classes of cricket). When he reached his fifty (in 2½ hours – his slowest ever on English soil and his slowest in any Test) he had hit only one four. And when he reached his century he had hit only two. On three occasions towards the end the crowd barracked him – one of only two known instances in England, at any rate – and each time he stood aside, resting on his bat, until they stopped. His chanceless 144* at 23·67 runs an hour was one of his most valuable innings for Australia. He had to hold the side together and that is what he did: the end fully justified the means. Bradman and Brown, each as grimly watchful as the other, by adding 170 in over three hours, against long spells by Verity and Wright, effectively denied England any chance. Bradman declared at 6.15 p.m. on the last day, and it was not worth asking England to bat for five minutes. It is an interesting reflection that if he had not declared, but simply played through those final 15 minutes, he would almost certainly have scored those four runs (at least) by which his final Test average fell short of 100. He was not to know that, of course, in 1938 – and, in any event, he might also have been out!

One of the best extant films of Don Bradman batting in Test match cricket is of his two innings of 51 and 144* in this Trent Bridge Test. The film, rediscovered in the mid-1970s and now in the possession of the Nottinghamshire C.C.C., was taken with much professional skill by a local amateur photographer, a Mr Stevens. (At a time of fierce competition among the leading photographic agencies, there were stringent rights of exclusivity as to the taking of photographs at Test matches in those days: and presumably Mr Stevens, who operated in full view of all, undertook not to make commercial use of his pictures and none, indeed, so far as is known, ever appeared in the press. But as a fine record of the match, his work deserves much commendation.) Don Bradman is on view on both innings in this film. This was not, of course, the dashing and irrepressible Bradman, but splendid close-ups reveal his beautiful stance and footwork and show the bat, however it may be picked up, to be absolutely straight when it comes into contact with the ball. Bradman's overwhelming sense of certainty and serenity at the crease is potently displayed in this film, where his demeanour especially is revealed at close quarters. His remarkable technique and concentration, at least in defence, is awesomely impressive. His sheer impregnability is frightening. One is reminded of his own remark that he was alleged to say to himself each time he confronted a bowler: 'Only one of us can come out of this on top and it's got to be me!'

Bradman figured in two minor pieces of history at Trent Bridge. He announced his chosen side before going to breakfast on the first morning, which was certainly unusual. But if that was not unique (though it may have been), the distinction accorded him by a Nottingham firm of rose-growers certainly was. They produced a new pink hybrid tea rose which they named 'Don Bradman', and on the Saturday morning Bradman was presented with a bloom for each member of his team. Another unique event in Don Bradman's life occurred on the following day, Sunday, when the Australians were entertained by the former President of Notts, Lord Belper, at Kingston Hall, Derby, where, by request, Bradman actually autographed nothing other than three prayer books! That day he also proved himself a fair hand on the bowling green, only just being beaten by the vastly more experienced Colonel Christopher Heseltine, former Hampshire and England fast bowler and at that time President of Hants.

Bradman was reported to have had a strained leg during his great last-day defiance at Trent Bridge, but it could not have been too bad for within 24 hours he had come down to London and knocked up 104 out of 177 in less than two hours against the Gentlemen of England at Lord's. R. J. O. Meyer, who was playing very little serious cricket at that time, was one of the very few bowlers in 1938 who proved capable of keeping Bradman on the defensive against his will: and he eventually trapped Bradman into giving a catch at long-leg. Bradman did not rest before the second Test at Lord's, but scored another dashing hundred – they had now become too commonplace to arouse too much excitement – this time against Lancashire at Old Trafford (where he had never previously got beyond 38 in four innings), reaching his fastest century ever in England, in only 73 minutes. He actually scored his innings of 101* out of 131 while at the crease. He was then in the lead for the Lawrence Trophy, eventually won at the end of August by Hugh Bartlett with a hundred (against the Australians) in 57 minutes.

On his return from Manchester to London, and on the eve of the Lord's Test, Bradman was made one of those sensational financial offers that the continuing glamour of his name and personality periodically prompted rich business folk to proffer. He was approached by a London firm of bookmakers, the Sports Investors Society Ltd, of Regent Street, to become chairman of an advisory committee to the Society at a salary of £2,500 a year, though acceptance of the post would have entailed Bradman remaining in England more or less permanently. He had first been approached by the company when he arrived in England in April. 'Obviously, we consider that Mr Bradman, with his knowledge of sport and his own tremendous sporting public, would be a considerable asset to our firm', said one of the directors. 'We are not, however, making the offer purely from a business standpoint. We feel that if Mr Bradman could be induced to accept a job in this country he might eventually play here for one of the counties, perhaps for Middlesex, the club which I've always followed. If Mr Bradman were playing in this country regularly young English players could not fail to learn much from him, and I believe his permanent presence in cricket here would instil fresh life-blood into our summer game. We feel sure that our action will be warmly endorsed by all our sporting members.' That may have been so, but the offer came to nothing. Neither Don Bradman nor Mrs Bradman had any desire to take up permanent residence in England.

The British public's belief that the (almost) superhuman Bradman could not be on the losing side in a Test had nearly been proved wrong at Trent Bridge. At Lord's Bradman went out to toss in his blue suit and trilby hat, sporting a seasonal average of 146·80. Walter Hammond first gave him a considerable fright with an innings of 240, 'as beautiful as the Venus of Medici'; and then Hedley Verity gave him another by causing him to chop a ball a foot outside his off stump on to his wicket for 18. It was not a difficult ball. Bradman looked startled, but the roar echoed round St John's Wood. As Neville Cardus remarked, 'it is good for cricket that accidents should occasionally happen even to Bradman'. William Pollock, whose literary labours on behalf of his friend Don Bradman were now confined to the *Daily Express*, recorded one of his neatest phrases about that Bradman dismissal: 'When he was out, changed, and on his way to the Australian enclosure we chanced to meet. Don was looking pensive then. Thinking about one of the eternal Veritys, perhaps.'

Hedley Verity bowled more balls to Bradman than any other bowler sent down to him in his entire career between December 1927 and March 1949, and this was the tenth and last time he dismissed him,·and the eighth time in Tests. No other bowler was ever so successful against Bradman in Tests, but Grimmett (with fewer opportunities, but in less exacting circumstances) also dismissed Bradman ten times in first-class games. In a tribute to Verity in 1943, after the Yorkshireman's death in the war, Don Bradman said: 'Although opposed to him in many Tests, I could never claim to have completely fathomed his strategy, for it was never static nor mechanical . . . Verity was the foundation stone of England's bowling in both countries during his era.'

No one at all dismissed Bradman in the second innings at Lord's, when he made his ninth hundred of the summer, in only his 12th match. He came out on the last afternoon to a round of 'cooees' from the Australian enclosure, and saw his side safely through to a draw. He drove and hooked both Farnes and Wellard, and of the 63 put on for the second wicket, Brown made 9 and Bradman 49. Hobbs' aggregate of 3,636 runs in England–Australia Tests was duly passed by Bradman (in 27 fewer innings), and to this day no one has reached the total of either of that pair. Five minutes before the end, Bradman arrived at a magnificent century, chanceless and all but inevitable. The players themselves, in the habit of the time, drew stumps at the close, and Bradman annexed one stump by which to remember – if he troubled to keep it, which is doubtful – his last Test hundred at Lord's. Somewhat incredibly he had now exceeded 1,000 runs in his last five Tests – actually 1,005 runs at an average of 143·57. That night the Australians left King's Cross to go north, with the series still level at two drawn Tests.

It was while Bradman and his team were at their picturesque Derbyshire country retreat at Grindleford for their Chesterfield and Sheffield games that matters came to the boil concerning a request by Bradman that his wife be allowed to join him in England at the conclusion of the tour. This was forbidden under the players' contract, and the Australian Board formally refused the fresh request. Mrs Bradman, who was staying with Mrs McCabe in Sydney, said she was 'bitterly disappointed' at the Board's decision but she did not propose to approach the Board herself. Bradman had the support of his team (both the married and unmarried members) in this matter and they, as well as he, were fully aware of the continuing pressure of captaincy, both on the field and off it. If the Board's refusal might have been predicted, what the Board itself did not predict was Bradman's reaction. If the refusal was expected, Bradman was no less disappointed. The players jointly asked the manager to cable a further request. Meanwhile, Bradman's disappointment turned to anger and he went so far as to prepare a draft retirement notice, announcing his secession from Test cricket after 1938. Happily it did not have to be issued, for the Board swiftly sensed the danger implicit in W. H. Jeanes' cable and relented at once. They refused, however, to allow Bradman any special treatment. They permitted *all* players' wives who so wished to travel to England to arrive when the last match was over and at their own expense. Mrs Bradman duly came to England to join her husband in mid-September, in the company of Mrs McCabe and Mrs Fleetwood-Smith.

Bradman had a further worry at Sheffield in meeting a superlative Yorkshire side, the county champions, who might well have caused the tourists their first defeat but for rain. At least, most of the huge crowd thought so. Bradman, for his part, played heroically on two rain-affected wickets and silenced his many critics who had written him off on such pitches. Bowes certainly worried him, but not so much this time Verity (or so it seemed from the ring). Bradman struggled but conquered. He scored 59 and 42. And Verity, for one, knew it was henceforth rubbish to say that Bradman could not play on sticky wickets if he set his mind to the task.

On all Bradman's four tours of England, only one match was abandoned without a ball being bowled. That was the third Test at Old Trafford in 1938. It was too wet for the teams to practise and too wet for the teams to begin. On the second scheduled day the two captains disagreed. Hammond considered play might be possible after tea, but Bradman disagreed – and the umpires thought likewise. The Playing Conditions for the 1938 Tests provided for the pitch to be protected from rain for 24 hours before play was due to start, and it was accordingly thus protected. But by that time it had been truly soaked by earlier rain, and it is intriguing to reflect that if the game *had* been able to get under way, the pitch would almost certainly have been a wet and slow one – and Bradman's technique, so recently displayed at Bramall Lane, would now have been even more highly interesting to observe than ever. Alas, it was not to be. On the Sunday Bradman took himself off to play some squash at Buxton – squash having taken on an increased appeal for him since playing with Gubby Allen on the '36–37 tour of Australia.[1]

---

[1] Allen (at least in 1936–37) was much the better player, but Bradman – who had first taken up the game when he moved to Adelaide – made such firm progress that he beat Don Turnbull, the Davis Cup player, in the final of the South Australian championship in 1939.

Hundreds came so thick and fast to Bradman in 1938 that the prospect of one even on a doubtful Old Trafford wicket could not be wholly ruled out. Who indeed would ever, in the 1930s, be prepared to rule out a century by Bradman when he batted? In his next two matches, between the rains of Manchester and the next Test at Leeds, he did indeed score two more centuries, the first of them on a soft pitch at Edgbaston on which the Warwickshire batsmen could do very little, while Bradman made 135, his last 85 in 61 minutes. This was the match that the Warwickshire committee desperately hoped Bradman would play in, in such a parlous state were their finances. The club sought to insure against Bradman not taking part in the match, but in the end they were not able to obtain a quotation to cover the risk. They happened to save themselves the cost of a premium, but it was just as well that Hollies, on his first meeting with the great man, did not choose to bowl him second ball!

Bradman could do no wrong at this stage of the season. Against Nottinghamshire he scored 144 after being surprisingly out for 56 in the first innings. He reached 2,000 runs for the season – once again, as in 1930, being the first in the country to do so. It was only his 21st innings of the summer, another record. A few minutes before, he had taken his career total past 20,000 runs in first-class cricket, an aggregate among Australians achieved by no one before and by only R. N. Harvey since that time.[1] Bradman's career average as he left Trent Bridge to go to the Australians' Yorkshire Test hotel at Harrogate was 94·55. His average for the 1938 summer alone was 126·50!

With such a run of superlative form behind him, Bradman was due for a failure at Headingley. Moreover, his last two innings on the ground had both passed 300. But for the man who did not believe in the law of averages, failure was a fate for others. For the third time in the series, Bradman at Headingley carried Australia valiantly through troublesome waters. He made his sixth century in six successive Tests, and it was one of the great performances of his life. It was not a triple-century this time, but a modest score of 103, a mere third of what he once scored in a single day on that ground, but now made on a dampish, difficult pitch. The score was a modest one only on paper. In the context of the match – in which the average per wicket was only 19 – it was heroic and monumental. It shone forth like a beacon in a cave. It very nearly did so literally too, for much of it was played in a light as sepulchral as Test cricket has ever been staged in England. The 103 – chanceless – was made out of 153, and in mid-afternoon on the Saturday, while Bradman was fighting an all but lone cause, Neville Cardus likened the Australians to 'lost souls in a November fog – being led about by Bradman and his torch'. There was a tense struggle to keep him away from the bowling, but Bradman likewise struggled, with considerable success, to keep it, and he could never be kept really quiet. At one stage his seventh-wicket partner, Waite, received only five balls in five overs, and Waite's share of a stand of

---

[1] R. B. Simpson has reached that aggregate while these pages were going through the press.

37 was only three. 'I have never seen a man nurse his partners so deliberately and so successfully', said one who was watching at Headingley that day.

Jack Hobbs was also watching the match, as he did once again the entire series, for the London *Star*, and after observing that 'it looked as if the great little man was after them again to-day', he peered through the gathering gloom and said: 'Bradman is in such form that he could have played by candlelight.' Sir Pelham Warner went even further: 'I believe he would make a hundred in the black-out!' To make matters that much worse, there was no screen at one end in those days. (What a sadness, by the way, that Harrap had by then stopped their 'Fight for the Ashes' series – ended at just the moment that Bradman became captain of Australia. Another volume by Hobbs or Warner would have been highly acceptable. Fender, too, wrote lengthily, and with his usual perception, on the whole of the 1938 series without, unfortunately, going into book form.)

The hallmark of genius that so abundantly stamped Bradman's 103 threw a long way into the background the several records it established. He exceeded Trumper's record of 1902 of 11 centuries by an Australian on a single tour of England. (He had already, in the previous match, broken Warren Bardsley's record of 27 hundreds on all tours of England.) He passed 5,000 runs in Test cricket in the fewest ever innings (56) and at – still – the youngest ever age (29). But few Yorkshiremen that day were aware of these things. They congratulated themselves on having seen three hours of Ajax-like defiance, and most especially on their own Bill Bowes removing Bradman's middle stump for 'only' 103. Bradman had been the pivotal calm among the falling wickets, and when he was eighth out at 240 the innings quickly ended for 242. The first innings lead was a narrow one of 19.

Australia won that Leeds Test in a thrilling fourth innings fight to get 105 runs, which showed the abnormal value of Bradman's century. By common consent, even a further 50 might have been beyond Australia. In that last innings, Bradman's dead-bat defence against balls which lifted off the worn pitch was masterly. The light again was bad and a storm was in the air. He scored only 16, but they were immensely precious. He was out chopping Wright low into the slips, where the catch was held by a Yorkshireman, Verity, to a deafening roar from 36,000, some of them perilously perched on roofs and walls – with an estimated further 12,000 shut out. It was one of the best Test matches of the decade. And it meant, for Bradman and his team, the retention of the Ashes. There was a private celebratory dinner that night. Without Bill O'Reilly's ten wickets England would have won, and without Bradman's century England would have won. In retrospect it was perhaps his greatest innings of the tour.

One minor oddity for those still with an eye for Percy Fender's literary proclivities. He did a typically shrewd overall summary of the match for the *Evening News*, but his 1,300 words managed to name Bradman only once – and that was to give credit to Wright for earning his wicket! Perhaps Bradman's repute had descended in like proportion to the dramatic decline in his batting average on the Headingley ground, which now stood at a mere 189·25!

Before the first match of the 1938 tour was played, Ernest Brown, the Minister of Labour – who, incidentally, shared a birthday with Bradman – in proposing the toast of the Institute of Journalists at a luncheon to the Australians, reminded the visiting cricketers that it was the abnormal that was news. When Don Bradman made a century, that was not news, he said. If they could put one headline 'Bradman, o', that would be abnormal and news! On that basis, it might have been whispered to Mr Brown, there was destined to be precious little news in 1938 – in fact, as it was to turn out, none! (The tour of 1938, like that of 1930, saw no duck by Bradman. In fact, after his o on the sticky wicket at Sydney in the Test match of December 1936, his next duck did not come until 70 innings later, in January 1940.)

With the Ashes now secure in 1938, Bradman let himself go to the extent of 202 at 53 an hour in his next innings against Somerset at Taunton, all scored in well under a day and including 32 fours. Facing Bradman in his 1938 form, it was a considerable feather in the cap of Bill Andrews to induce some false strokes (but no actual chances) early on against the swinging ball. But Bradman quickly corrected himself and was soon hitting Andrews and everyone else exactly where he wished. Poor Bertie Buse, apparently, was almost reduced to tears. Bradman scored his first 72 before lunch and then his last 130 in the single session between lunch and tea. The huge crowd revelled in it. In the end, just before four o'clock, Bradman gave his wicket away, allowing Andrews to bowl him. Since that July afternoon 40 years ago, Andrews has invariably used the same greeting on meeting new folk: 'Shake the hand that bowled Bradman . . .' And of course he had no difficulty in finding a title for his book of memories in 1973. On that day at Taunton Bradman actually scored more fours before the tea interval than he did on his magical day at Headingley in 1930 (when, against a Test match attack of course on that occasion, he had passed 300 in the day, with 31 fours at tea). Had Bradman not chosen to give his wicket away against Somerset, with an imminent declaration in mind, he could in all probability have become the first and only batsman in the world to score 300 in a single day twice. He was not chasing triple-hundreds at that stage of his career, however, though in fact he was to score one for his club side in Adelaide within less than two years. That fixture at Taunton in 1938 was the fourth consecutive match in which Bradman had been top scorer (for either side); it was his 15th century in his last 19 matches; and he had now played an innings of 50 or more in 25 of his last 27 games!

The traditional August Bank Holiday encounter with Glamorgan at Swansea should not really have seen Bradman or any other Australian at the crease, such were the conditions after rain. Bradman, on the wettest wicket he played on all tour, batted a full hour before John Clay had him easily stumped. He had gathered 17 somewhat painful runs. Bradman did not accompany his side for their two Scottish matches at Forthill and at Hamilton

Crescent, Glasgow. He had been unable to go to Scotland in 1934, after his injury in the Leeds Test, and so his further absence in 1938 was a great disappointment, for, as Alfred O'Neil recorded, the satisfactory attendances in both matches were largely due to the expectation of seeing him play. He actually travelled to Scotland and took a short rest away from the cricket. Scotland, for the moment, had to make do with the memory of his hundred before lunch at Hamilton Crescent in 1930.

Bradman had ten days off from cricket altogether before playing what proved to be his last innings in England for ten years. This was against Kent at Canterbury before a very large Saturday crowd on 13 August 1938, when, with some severe driving, he hit 67 before lunch in 90 minutes and was caught at cover-point. It was the day that great numbers of reservists were joining the colours in all parts of Germany for the large-scale autumn manoeuvres. The St Lawrence crowd could never have guessed what up-heavals would take place before Don Bradman would be seen with a bat again on an English ground. On the Monday afternoon Frank Woolley, aged 51, stole every honour till Bradman caught him for a brilliant 81 in 66 minutes, and there was a most pleasing scene when Bradman went into the Kent dressing-room to congratulate the great veteran not only on a super-lative innings but on a superlative career. Don Bradman had first seen Frank Woolley at Sydney in February 1921, when he was 12 years old; and now he fielded through his last great innings.

Though Canterbury had seen Bradman's last innings, it was not quite his last match. There was one other, in which he was not destined to bat. It was the fifth and final Test at the Oval, the fourth actually played that summer, and a 'timeless' affair. Everything that could go wrong went wrong for Bradman. For the fourth time in four calls he lost the toss – well might he have smiled at those with boundless faith in the law of averages. He fielded through the biggest innings of his life – by both a team and an individual – and, as a captain, lost by the heaviest margin of his life. In fact Australia's defeat, by an innings and 579 runs, was, and remains, the biggest in the history of Test cricket. Two of Australia's leading batsmen could not bat, both suffering injury – Jack Fingleton and, worst of all, Bradman himself.

'Bosser' Martin had said – but how many would have chosen to applaud him for it? – that his wicket would 'last till Christmas'; and all that the cricketing populace of London required for this endless prospect was their three shillings a day to get into the Oval. As relentlessly as Hammond had won the toss in 1938, so equally relentlessly had Bradman scored a century. Bradman called 'heads' four times and lost four times. At Leeds he had changed into flannels to toss; at the Oval he stayed in his suit and trilby. The result was the same. The Australians pulled his leg in the dressing-room. The manager, Mr Jeanes, brought along a mascot kangaroo – but it seemed devoid of all good fortune.

Neville Cardus, on the morning of the match, thought there was no reason why England should not win at the Oval. 'At least, there is only one reason

– Bradman, and surely he must fail in a Test match at last. On the other hand, there is this disturbing thought: he never goes through a rubber without scoring one double-century. So far, in the present rubber, he has stopped at a single century. He has each time been compelled to begin his innings under conditions threatening to Australia. If he wins the toss this morning . . .' That must remain one of the 'ifs' of history. Cardus observed that England had nearly won three times in the rubber, only to throw away rare advantages. 'Again the matter boils down to Bradman. O'Reilly is a great bowler, the only living great bowler, but he could not have saved his side. Bradman, always Bradman.'

Bradman's record of 334 in England–Australia Test cricket, watched by young Leonard Hutton in the crowd in 1930, was, of course, surpassed by Hutton on the third day at the Oval, and Bradman was the first to rush over and congratulate him. At that point Hutton had batted for 12 hours 19 minutes, compared with Bradman's six hours 23 minutes. It was the first triple-century of his life through which Bradman had fielded – and the last! The nearer Hutton got to the record, the nearer Bradman fielded to him, until he was only a few yards from Hutton's bat at silly mid-off. O'Reilly strove valiantly to leave the record with Bradman, but to no avail. Hutton quickly passed Hammond's world Test record of 336*, and at lunch England were 758 for five. The butchery continued afterwards. Never had Bradman's captaincy been so severely tried. During the mammoth England scoring at Trent Bridge in June, Neville Cardus had suggested that Bradman send a cable forthwith to Grimmett, 'Come home at once, all is forgiven.' The normally cautious Ponsford, by the way, had described Grimmett's omission when the side was announced as 'a kind of late summer lunacy'. Now at the Oval there was still no Grimmett and it was too late to send a cable. Even in a Test that might last 'till Christmas', Grimmett would not be allowed to bowl. (Was Grimmett, incidentally, spared the ignominy of a lifetime by not being on the tour?)

One cable that *was* actually sent was by Herbert Sutcliffe to Hutton at the close of the second day, when Hutton was 300 not out. After leaving Trent Bridge, where Yorkshire were playing, Sutcliffe wired: 'Hearty congratulations. No one more delighted than I. Go for Bradman's 452 record. Congratulations also to Maurice.'[1] How Bradman would have felt if Hutton had chosen to follow that advice can only be imagined. It was a novel enough experience as it was to have *one* record removed from the Bradman inventory!

Throughout it all at the Oval, Bradman remained an inspirer. Neville Cardus, in the *Manchester Guardian* next morning, wrote:

---

[1] Maurice, of course, was Maurice Leyland (or, strictly, as C. R. Williamson, the cricketing sage of Bradford, has correctly pointed out, *Morris* Leyland at birth). His stand of 382 for the second wicket with Hutton at the Oval in 1938 was by a long way (actually by 120 runs) the biggest partnership through which Bradman ever fielded in Test cricket. It was also the biggest through which he fielded in *any* first-class match in his career, the only other triple-century stand being 333 for the fourth wicket by Hammond and Hendren for M.C.C. v New South Wales at Sydney in 1928–29. The Hutton–Leyland stand, lasting six hours 21 minutes, was also the *longest* through which Bradman ever fielded in his life.

Bradman's fielding and his eager and sensible captaincy throughout a fearful ordeal were beyond praise; he nursed his bowlers, talked to them, put his arm in theirs between overs, and cheered them up; he was not only the team's captain but the father-confessor and philosopher.

England's captain himself later recorded that 'it was a fight every inch of the way, and Bradman is to be congratulated on the magnificent way he heartened his men in the grim struggle'. H. S. Altham also was full of praise: 'I do not think I have ever admired anything on the cricket field so much as his leadership through those heartbreaking days at the Oval in August: his own fielding was an inspiration in itself, and as hour succeeded hour with nothing going right and the prospect of the rubber receding over a hopeless horizon, it was, one felt, his courage and gaiety that alone sustained his side. And when the tragic accident came, the game was over, the balloon was pricked and his team was a team no more.'

Bradman had – prophetically? – done some bowling in the nets at the Oval on the day before the Test began. But he hadn't bowled in a match all tour. In fact he hadn't bowled in a first-class match in England since 1930. After Hutton was out for 364 and with the total at 798 (shortly before three o'clock, after some 13¾ hours), Bradman put himself on to bowl – and began with a maiden to Hardstaff amid loud applause! After two overs of slow leg-breaks, he took himself off. Then, as tea approached, he bowled again, and at 4.15 p.m., and the score 887 for seven, with Hardstaff receiving, he twisted his right ankle in a worn foothole at the Vauxhall end while delivering his second ball. He dropped to the ground, his team crowded around him and removed his boot and sock, and then he was carried from the field by White and Fleetwood-Smith while the crowd stood in silence. It was a moment of tragedy for Australia, their plight now desperate beyond repair. He was carried to the dressing-room and watched the remaining two hours of play from there. Soon after the close of play he was lifted into a car and driven to his hotel. In his hotel bed (in Room 147 at the Hotel Victoria in Northumberland Avenue) an X-ray was taken of his leg, and that night the leg was put in plaster. A pair of crutches were ordered. Hammond had declared at tea in the knowledge that Bradman's ankle, badly swollen up, would prevent him upsetting any calculations. Otherwise, in a 'timeless' Test, he might well have played the innings out. Bradman was found to have fractured a bone in his ankle: it was actually what is known as a feather flake fracture of the right ankle. He was out of the match and the tour.

It was a sad exit from the pre-war Test scene for Bradman. With or without him, England would have won at the Oval. But without him Australia chose not to fight. Batting nine men, they followed on 702 runs behind. P. G. H. Fender wrote, presumably with tongue in cheek: 'I understand that there is no truth in the rumour that Hammond's *only* reason for making Australia follow on is that he feared that, if England batted again, the invalids might have recovered before he had finished.' Fleetwood-Smith, in the final scramble for stumps, got two – one for himself and one for Don Bradman. But it is unlikely that his captain wanted a tangible reminder of the occasion.

England had won the toss at the Oval. But what if Australia had done so? On that most perfect of pitches, would Don Bradman have made one of his 300s? Or would he, as Eddie Paynter did, contrive to be out for a duck? His mishap reduced the match to unreality, but it would have been a fascinating spectacle to see by what methods Bradman would have applied himself in the face of a total of more than 900. That was something quite novel in the career of Don Bradman. But no one dared forget, Hutton or no Hutton, that Bradman was still the greatest run-getter in the world. And no one dared underestimate the ambition of Bradman when confronted with a fresh challenge. It would not have been quite like playing against Somerset, with all respect, when he was perfectly happy to give his wicket away in the over he reached his 200.

So, for the second tour of England in succession, Bradman ended up in the hands of the doctors, but his new plight was a minor one, of course, compared with 1934. With Bradman hobbling on crutches, McCabe took over the captaincy of the team and it was a relief for Bradman that he did not have to remain in hospital. It was hoped that he might still be able to accompany his side as a spectator, but that did not prove practicable and Bradman stayed for a few weeks with R. W. V. Robins and his wife at their home at Burnham, near Maidenhead. Mrs Bradman arrived to help nurse the invalid back to recovery. He was effectively in hiding in the country, resting quietly – but not idly! With his right foot in a red leather slipper, his routine was to breakfast at nine o'clock on the verandah of the Robins' two-storey, gabled, red-brick house, and then settle down to answer the great pile of letters of sympathy from all over the world. These he answered on his portable typewriter – on which he could manage 60 words a minute – and would get through 60 letters at a sitting. After lunch he would take a nap, followed by daily massage for the ankle. The rest of the time he played bridge, the piano, or read. If the Sports Investors Society still entertained any hopes of inducing Bradman to stay in England with their business offer, these were finally scotched when Walter Robins announced that Bradman would definitely be returning to Australia – and, by the time he got there, according to his doctor's promise, he would be able to play cricket again. Bradman made periodic visits to London by car to see his doctor, and the ankle progressed well. Before long he was nearly his old self. Bradman's injury prevented him going with the Australian team to Ireland, a country he has never visited. The teams of 1930, 1934 and 1948 did not include Ireland in their itineraries, and Sir Donald has never found occasion to visit the country in a private capacity.

Apart from the injury and the mortification of the Oval result, the tour for Bradman – on the field, at least – had been a staggering run of triumph. Even when he was judged by the standard he himself had set, he was still a staggering success. His concentration was as incredible as ever, and his bat still very much a weapon of massacre. There were not all that many records left for him to smash, but one that he did smash most triumphantly was one of the most coveted – the record average for a summer in England. He averaged 115·60 in all matches and 108·50 in Test matches. This was the second time (following 1930) he had a century average in an England–Australia series – no one else has ever done that twice. He exceeded 2,000 runs for the third time in three tours; and he scored 13 centuries in the 19 matches in which he batted. If less spectacular than of old, he was more inevitable. And his fielding was quite outstanding throughout the tour, not least during the marathon Oval ordeal.

Off the field he played the role of captain with much good humour, but the stresses of making speeches – utterly delightful as they turned out to be – were greater than most people knew. Those who had heard Don Bradman's response to the toast of the Australian cricket team at the Institute of Journalists' luncheon at the Café Royal on 22 April, before a company of nearly 400, knew at once what a highly skilled speaker he was. They knew, too, that so skilful indeed were his words that it was clear he had worked very hard to perfect them. So it was also at the M.C.C. dinner to the Australians in May, and at many other dinners and functions. The responsibility for the side on an important tour Bradman found, at the age of 29, to be 'exacting, even exhausting'. In the 1945 edition of *Wisden*, A. G. Moyes wrote of Bradman that 'it can now be disclosed that he would not have toured England again as captain had there been no war. He told me this during our trip home in 1938, and no argument could move him. Even then, he was feeling the strain of making both centuries and speeches, and he was most definite that he would not be capable again of representing his country in such a capacity, either to his own satisfaction or in the manner expected of him'. This was not known to the public in 1938, but Sir Donald confirmed it in his autobiography after his retirement: 'I am still convinced that in the normal sense, without any break in the continuity of play, 1938 would have been my last tour of England.' Some people suspected it privately in 1938 and spoke among themselves of 'the fearful strain of being a Bradman all the time'. Jack Ingham, the Sports Editor of *The Star* and long-standing 'ghost' for Jack Hobbs, expressed the suspicions publicly before the Oval Test, but feared desperately to seek confirmation lest he might have heard officially it was true. He mused on the endless magic that Bradman still exuded:

> Everybody talks about Bradman. People who don't know one thing from the next in cricket all talk about him. Round this time on Saturday, you will be talking, or thinking, of the little broad-shouldered, slow-speaking Australian.
>
>   It is strange, but I think true, that all the time, day and night, somewhere in the world somebody is talking about Bradman.

Of how many other individuals in the world of 1938 could those words have been seriously written?

Bradman's prevailing mood as to his playing future in 1938 is reflected also in the episode concerning the secretaryship of the Melbourne Cricket

Club. The long-standing popular and able secretary, Hugh Trumble, died
on 14 August 1938, while Bradman was in England. Before the end of the
year, it was known that Bradman was a candidate for the £1,000-a-year post,
a full-time position that would almost certainly have seen the end of him as a
regular first-class player and would also have severed his active stockbroking
career in Adelaide (where he had not yet, incidentally, been elected a member of the Stock Exchange). Whatever cricket he might have played – and
he would not, presumably, have ceased playing entirely at the age of 30 –
would clearly not have involved any future tours of England. The Melbourne
secretaryship was, and is, one of the most attractive posts in Australian
cricket, and would have preserved for many, many years Bradman's contact
with the game. He was not then a member of the Board of Control – he was
still precociously young for that privilege – but there were many who would
class the Melbourne job as more desirable, and it was a paid position. A
Melbourne Cricket Club committee member approached Bradman and
asked him to stand for the secretaryship. Bradman himself had not, to be fair,
expressed either interest or enthusiasm but was persuaded by this gentleman
to apply largely on the grounds that, not only did the Melbourne club want
him, but that his election was a foregone conclusion if he applied. In fact
there were more than 150 applicants for the position and for weeks a sub-
committee considered their claims. At length the candidates were narrowed
down, and the committee proper of the Melbourne club sat for 3½ hours in
deliberation on 18 January 1939. In the event the voting was equal, Bradman
being one of the two in top place. Vernon Ransford, the old Victorian Test
player, then a member of a firm of shipping agents, who had taken a large
part in the administration of the game as a member himself of the Melbourne
C.C. committee, was appointed on the casting vote of the chairman. (Ransford was absent from the deliberations.) On this casting vote was the future
of Don Bradman decided. There were those no doubt who thought it most
proper that a Melbourne man should get the job, and Ransford held the
appointment with much distinction until a few months before he died in
1958. Had the casting vote gone in favour of Bradman, and had he then
accepted the post, the one thing that is certain above all else is that he would
not have captained Australia in England in 1948. Bradman naturally offered
Ransford his congratulations, and when asked if he intended to remain in
Adelaide, replied: 'Oh, yes. I am quite happy in Adelaide.'

By the end of the 1938 tour of England, however, a fresh distinction did
come Don Bradman's way – he was considered a fit subject for inclusion in
Who's Who (the English version that is), and he duly made his debut within
its celebrated pages – where he has, of course, remained ever since – at the
age of 30 in the 1939 edition where, described as a stock- and share-broker,
he occupied 21 lines in the midst of the most formidable gathering of human
eminence. His recreations were listed as cricket, golf, tennis, billiards and
squash – at all of which, of course, he was somewhat above average. (Walter
Hammond, by the way, also made his debut in *Who's Who* in that same 1939

edition, having, like Bradman, just captained his country in a Test series for the first time on English soil.)

In the English winter of 1938–39 Bradman, though not of course a member of the Australian Board of Control, was taken into their confidence when he was asked, at the Board's December meeting at Melbourne, to prepare a report for the Board on the playing conditions on the 1938 tour of England. Bradman, a player, was asked to do this, and not the manager, for it followed the decision of five of the leading members of that side – Fingleton, O'Reilly, McCabe, Chipperfield and White – to take a holiday from cricket. Some of them, especially O'Reilly, thought the English tour was too strenuous. Bradman at the same time was asked to attend the Board's next meeting, in September 1939, to confer with them before the playing conditions for the proposed 1942 tour of England were decided. (Although circumstances had kept him *hors de combat* after the Oval Test of 1938, Bradman could hardly have avoided noticing that the Australians had successive first-class fixtures at Hove, Blackpool, Folkestone and Scarborough – and these at precisely that stage of a tour when a touring side was at its most tired. This was not to be the case in 1948.)

Bradman had returned to Australia with his wife via a short trip to the Continent. By the time he reached Adelaide his ankle injury was completely forgotten. But a new season was upon him at once. So far as first-class cricket was concerned, it was a season that neither Bradman's stupendous confidence nor the limitless fervour of his warmest admirers could have quite been prepared to anticipate. But it was only a question of time – and no one could have known it more surely than C. B. Fry himself – before Bradman would score six centuries in succession to equal Fry's world record in first-class cricket. In his relentless and impregnable form of 1938, everything was possible: and that is precisely what Bradman did in Australia in his first six innings of the season of 1938–39. They were successively as follows:

118	D. G. Bradman's XI v K. E. Rigg's XI, Melbourne	10, 12 Dec.
143	South Australia v New South Wales, Adelaide	16 Dec.
225	South Australia v Queensland, Adelaide	24, 26 Dec.
107	South Australia v Victoria, Melbourne	31 Dec.
186	South Australia v Queensland, Brisbane	9, 10 Jan.
135*	South Australia v New South Wales, Sydney	14, 18 Jan.

He nearly lost the chance of the record when in the crucial Sydney game rain washed out play completely on the second and third days, while his score stayed put on 22. Then the skies relented, and he naturally showed more caution in this innings than usual.[1] On a slow outfield he had actually hit only three fours when he reached his century, but hit another four boundaries in his final 35. Cecil Pepper ungraciously alleged that Bradman was

---

[1] He was not, however, as cautious as *Wisden* made him. His time for his innings, given there as five hours 20 minutes, was in fact *three* hours 20 minutes.

caught for 96 in this crucial innings. He was fielding at short square-leg when A. G. Cheetham bowled the ball off which he thought Bradman was caught. 'Did you think Bradman had hit the ball?' he was asked. 'Too right, I did', Pepper replied, according to the Sydney newspaper *Truth*. 'I made a half-hearted appeal, but withdrew it when no other member of the team was with me.' The bowler said that both umpires remarked later that Bradman would have been out if an appeal had been made, but S. G. Sismey, the wicketkeeper, on his Shield debut, thought the ball glanced off Bradman's pads. Bradman equalled the record on a cool and dull day, which followed the two idle ones. New South Wales had experienced considerable misfortune with regard to the weather for their matches against South Australia, led by Bradman, in that and recent years, and their finances, already sorely depleted by Bradman's migration, suffered heavily as a result. After the first four centuries in the sequence, there had also been a fright when Bradman left Melbourne after his 107 and arrived with his side in Sydney (en route for Brisbane) suffering from laryngitis. He recovered in time to play in the return against Queensland to make his fifth successive hundred, but was watchful in reaching it: he hit only three fours in the entire pre-lunch period of 105 minutes while going from 42 to 92 on the third morning, but once he had reached his hundred he made 52 of his last 86 in boundaries.

The six centuries were spread over all four Australian Test grounds, and in the actual periods up to the six respective hundred-marks themselves, *only one positive chance* was offered (when he was 6 in his 107). When Fry had established the record in 1901, he gave chances when 14 and 52 in his fourth innings (105 v Surrey) and when 45 and 80 in his fifth (140 v Kent). But Fry's innings were played on less perfect pitches, two of them damaged by rain. (The pitch at Sydney for Bradman's record-equalling innings was compulsorily protected against rain under the Sheffield Shield rules then obtaining.)

Not even Bradman was able to *exceed* Fry's record, for he was out for 5 in his next innings, against Victoria at Adelaide, caught low down at backward short-leg by Fleetwood-Smith. It was one of only two catches held by Fleetwood-Smith all season. Bradman grinned as he walked back to the pavilion. Some 15,000 had turned up at the Adelaide Oval in the expectation of fresh history, and they may well have complained that they came to see Bradman bat, not Fleetwood-Smith catch. That was the last first-class innings that Don Bradman played before the outbreak of war. It was 25 February 1939, the day London's first steel air-raid shelters were distributed . . .

On that Saturday, when Fleetwood-Smith took his sinful catch, C. B. Fry sent the following cable to Bradman: 'Genuinely sorry. Superlative skill merits absence of bad luck. – Fry.' But Bradman's average for the season was 153·16, so the luck wasn't too bad after all.

On that same day Charles Fry, who could not possibly have seen through the week-end confined to a paltry ten words of congratulation, sent off something much more substantial to Bradman. As something passing between

those two special men at that special moment in history, it is worth reproducing:

Dear Mr. Bradman,
    Hard luck! I genuinely wish you had succeeded.
    Apart from my admiration of the unparalleled command you achieved in the
fine art of batsmanship, simple gratitude would impel me to share with you my
small crown – will wattle do? – for until you began your successful series of centuries, I don't believe my own little old record was remembered by one person in
10,000.
    Hence, besides your other great achievements, you have succeeded in endowing
me with an hour or two of semi-posthumous fame. I wish I could remember myself
as a rival worthy of your competitive blade, but you have added so much to the
novelty and complexity of stroke-play as well as to the standard and size of individual scores that none of us old-timers can regard himself even as a figurative rival.
    I see that some of my supporters argue that I had stronger bowling to play, but
I don't go anything on that, because it is easier to make a mistake against bad
bowling than good. If one can really bat, the better the bowling the better one
plays, don't you think?
    So, for what they are worth, my admiration, respect, and gratitude are sincerely
offered.
                                                    Yours truly,
                                                    C. B. Fry

Thus were linked for posterity the names of the two men who probably
knew more about cricket as a science than any who had ever lived before
them. In 1970–71 M. J. Procter joined Fry and Bradman in jointly holding
that world record, with six centuries in consecutive innings for Rhodesia.
The feat will always remain a prodigious effort of batsmanship, however
many times it may be achieved in the future – which assuredly will not be
too often.

On 31 December 1938, when Bradman scored his 107 at Melbourne, he
put the seal on yet another world record, for it was the 22nd century he had
scored in first-class cricket since 1 January that year. The previous record
had been 19 centuries in a calendar year by Herbert Sutcliffe in 1932. After
the war, in 1947, Denis Compton was also to score 22 hundreds in a calendar
year, but no one else has approached that figure. Bradman's average for the
12 months of 1938 was the wonderful one of 112·88.

South Australia won the Sheffield Shield in 1938–39 for the second time
in four years under Bradman's captaincy, while his former team, New South
Wales, finished a very poor bottom, without winning a match. Bradman's
Shield average was 160·20, a record for South Australia, helped materially
by five successive hundreds, another record for the Sheffield Shield (equalling
his own record of 1933–34 and 1935–36). In 1938–39 it could not be alleged
that the leading Australian players were abroad, as had been the case three
years before, although some of the New South Welshmen were taking a 'rest'.
The only significant absentee against Bradman during his big innings of the

season was W. J. O'Reilly, who did not play for New South Wales at Sydney when Bradman equalled Fry's record.

This was the season that Bradman first became a member of the Cricket Committee of the South Australian Cricket Association, as one of the two delegates from his club, Kensington. This committee had wide jurisdiction over the conduct of local club cricket and was responsible for appointing the State selectors for South Australia's first-class matches. Don Bradman had been annually appointed one of the three State selectors since he assumed the captaincy of South Australia in '35–36, and he continued in that role when he was on the Cricket Committee itself.

At 30 years of age Bradman was still a great force in cricket. He had not gone to Melbourne, as might have been the case, and he was still capable of astounding the world with his prolific batting. As *Wisden* succinctly put it: 'At the crease he was master and the bowler, servant.'

Between the close of Bradman's great season of 1938–39 and the start of the next one, the world had been plunged into war. Australia, as in 1914, unhesitatingly took her stand at the side of Great Britain on 3 September 1939 – Mr Menzies, the Prime Minister, told the people of Australia in a national broadcast that they were at war exactly one hour after Mr Chamberlain told the people of Britain. Despite the impending re-introduction of compulsory military service and the preparations being put in train for the despatch of an Australian Corps overseas, the Australian government – since April 1939 with Mr Menzies at the helm – requested that the Sheffield Shield proceed as normal in an effort to minimise the domestic upheaval that seemed certain. All 12 Sheffield Shield matches were duly played, but it was the last time for seven years. Bradman was 31, and in this season shrouded by the ever-blackening shadow of war, he – as did O'Reilly and the ageless Grimmett – reminded Australians of greatness on the cricket field as they prepared for deeds on sterner fields.

Oddly enough, Bradman had never scored 1,000 runs in a Sheffield Shield season; and now, with the prospect of the future uncertain to the point of imponderability, he emphatically achieved that without missing a match and at the glorious average of 132·75. It was as if the chance might slip away for ever, so better to have this landmark stored neatly in the book. It was a great summer, both for Bradman and for cricket – but for the sight of volunteers flocking to the recruiting centres, workers turning themselves over to the production of war equipment, the rationing of petrol, and the incidence of fear, rumours and strung nerves. The Bradman household, incidentally, by this time had been blessed by the arrival of a son, John Russell Bradman, born on 10 July 1939. There were no complications with the birth, and the sadness of 1936 was replaced by joy.

On 28 October 1939, Bradman declared his mood with a brilliant innings for his club, Kensington, of 188 in 148 minutes, the last 88 being scored in 38 minutes, of which 52 were hit off two overs. In all Bradman hit four sixes and 24 fours. It was an aperitif for another shattering season at first-class level.

A curiosity in the career of Bradman occurred in the opening first-class match of that season – he was run out. A telegraphic error was suspected when the news came through, but it was true! Without attempting to apportion the blame – though it seems that his partner, Tom Klose, was by no means blameless – he was run out quite comfortably, for the only time in his first-class career while captain. Bradman was accustomed to, and expected, instant response from his partners in the matter of running. On this occasion Klose, a newcomer to the side in his first Shield innings, did not move. This was after Bradman had made 76 against Victoria at Adelaide and after he and Klose had added 102 for the fifth wicket in 81 minutes. (Klose, incidentally, could move very fast when he wished to – he was a very brilliant fieldsman and was well known in Adelaide as an Australian Rules footballer.) The further Bradman's career advanced the more certain he became as a runner between wickets, and this instance in November 1939 was the first time in ten years he had been run out in a first-class match – and it was never to happen to him again. Of course Bradman was by nature a shrewd observer on the field, more especially since the cares of captaincy or vice-captaincy came his way. And in the matter of running, as in so much else on the cricket field, he was a firm believer in the mastery of basic principles. In his 338 innings in first-class cricket he was run out only four times – and three of those instances occurred at the beginning of his career, before he visited England. This is understandable enough, for at that time Bradman was not a good runner. Few country cricketers in Australia – provided, like Bradman, they are brought up on non-turf wickets – are good runners when they emerge into the first-class game. The basic principles of turf-wicket running, especially the sliding of the bat, cannot be practised on country surfaces. Bradman was aware of his faults (and if he wasn't he was certainly told of them in Sydney) as well as of his poor judgment and calling in his early days. On a minor tour of New South Wales country districts, Bradman was taken in hand by Tommy Andrews, whose brief was to educate the young Bradman in the arts of calling and running. As might be expected, the instruction was not in vain. T. J. E. Andrews might have had the modest average of 26·90 in his 16 Test matches for Australia (in the course of which, in 23 innings, neither he nor any of his partners was ever run out) but he unobtrusively played his part in helping Bradman's average rise so handsomely. In 1928–29 Bradman was still a bad runner – his great innings of 340* against Victoria that season should have been ended three times by a run out, twice before his century. By the time he left for England, that was one of several crudities in his play he had all but eliminated. In his world record against Queensland in January 1930 his running between wickets was faultless, and one report then said of him: 'Bradman is showing vast improvement in this sphere of the game.' It was not yet *entirely* faultless, however, for in his first match after his return to Australia in 1930, though he scored 121, it was written: 'Observation of Bradman's methods leads to the hope that he will devote his mentality to the study of running between wickets. He has something to learn.' Later that season, in the fourth Test at Melbourne, Woodfull called Bradman for a run, but Bradman was watching the ball, which was behind the wicket, instead of his partner, and Woodfull was easily run out. On that same morning another misunderstanding saw McCabe run out.

As a result of the fixture list in the 1939–40 season, Bradman began the summer by playing three consecutive Shield matches in Adelaide, for the only time in his career while living in the city. So he did not need to leave home in those early months of war until after Christmas, when he had three matches in quick succession at Melbourne, Brisbane and Sydney. The three Adelaide matches were won: none of those away from home was – and as a result South Australia were narrowly deposed as holders of the Sheffield Shield. Adelaide saw him at his best, and by Christmas his average there (and for the season) was 206·33. He improved on this when he went to Melbourne, raising his average to 221·50, but it thereafter fell to more modest Bradmanesque proportions.

That pre-Christmas average at Adelaide soaring past the 200-mark did not include a quite dazzling triple-century by Bradman for his club side, Kensington, which turned out to be his highest-ever score in club cricket either in Sydney or Adelaide. It was a district match against Glenelg played on Saturday, 25 November, and out of Kensington's 439 for five, Bradman made 303 in 222 minutes – his first hundred in 101 minutes, his second in 86 minutes, and his third in the marvellous time of 35 minutes. If the Glenelg fielders did not yet know what the penalties were for giving Bradman a chance, they never thereafter forgot – for he was missed when only 7! One of Bradman's colleagues in the 1938 side in England, and in the South Australian XI, Mervyn Waite, was captaining the Glenelg side that day – and it was Waite who was the holder (as he is to this day) of the existing record score in district cricket in Adelaide, an innings of 339 made in March 1936. It was one of the few records not annexed by the inexorable Bradman bat. But he averaged 105.42 for Kensington that season.

In fact Bradman had some truly wonderful innings that summer, in what was to prove the last season spectators were to see the 'old' Bradman. His mastery was as formidable as ever, against even the best bowlers. O'Reilly could do nothing – not even to the extent of inducing a chance – to prevent him scoring 251 and 90, both not out, against New South Wales at Adelaide. It must always be terribly difficult in a career with as many glittering moments as Bradman's to pick out the finest performances of them all, but so far as Sheffield Shield matches are concerned, Sir Donald himself rates these two innings against O'Reilly at the top.[1]

---

[1] O'Reilly took most wickets in the Sheffield Shield that season (52). But in *all* first-class matches, O'Reilly took 55 – and Grimmett 73! This was a record haul from a purely domestic season. Grimmett week by week, for both Kensington and South Australia, was reminding Bradman that he had not really been too old to tour England in '38!

Four days later Bradman reached a century in 80 minutes against Queensland, and followed at once with a masterly 267 (despite a heavy cold) against Victoria on his traditionally prolific Melbourne ground, showing such little concern for the 'nervous nineties' (never nervous for the nerveless Bradman) that he received *only three balls* in the 90s, advancing from 88 to 100 with three fours in four balls from Ring. This little effort gave him 13 fifties in 14 innings – another world record. (Of those innings, nine had actually been centuries.) The nearest approach to this is Ernest Tyldesley's excellent spell of 12 fifties in 13 innings in England in 1926. Bradman then took a first ball on going up to Brisbane! It was a little 'accident' that reduced his average to 177·20, and his first duck for more than three years. It was the first ball that the unknown Jack Stackpoole, a tall fast bowler on his debut for Queensland, ever sent down to Bradman. He was then a 23-year-old Brisbane newspaper employee, but who had lived in South Australia for 12 years and learned his cricket there. He was actually holidaying in Adelaide when he received an urgent call to dash to Brisbane – and to instant fame! He had taken 27 wickets in Brisbane club cricket so far that season, and came in for the unfit Ellis. He caused Bradman to poke his first ball into silly mid-on's hands, 'causing stupefaction among the crowd and a step dance by Stackpoole'. The new man of the hour said: 'I don't want to be made a hero at Don's expense, because I am a great admirer of him. But I am definitely pleased about it . . .' The duck, of course, soon became a feature of the weekend news all over Australia – a far greater sensation than any double-century by Bradman! Jack Stackpoole received heaps of telegrams of congratulation. Bradman scored 97 in the second innings, and of Stackpoole very little was heard again.

Bradman's annual visit to Sydney was always keenly anticipated, and no less so in this season with the future so uncertain. Events were getting more grim, and many men feared they may never see a Sheffield Shield match again. Bradman's visit attracted what is still the record attendance at any Shield match in Sydney – 75,765 over the four days, with a record single-day attendance of 30,400 on the opening day.[1] O'Reilly made sure that the Adelaide carnage would not be repeated. On a quite different and more lively pitch, he got Bradman lbw for 39, one of only two occasions that O'Reilly ever got his old antagonist leg before. (Altogether in his career Bradman was lbw in less than 10% of his first-class dismissals.) This Sydney incident of 1940 is preserved on film, and in 1963 was shown in Sir Donald Bradman's home city of Adelaide, at the State Theatre, in the Cinesound Review birthday edition which featured sporting and historical highlights of Australia's history. Despite Bradman's modest scores of 39 and 40 in that match, he said after playing at Sydney (where the centre of the ground had been re-turfed two years before) that the wicket was the nearest approach he had seen to the ideal pitch.

---

[1] Among that number, sitting on the steps of the Sheridan stand, was a future captain of Australia, Richie Benaud, aged nine, having his first sight of Don Bradman.

After the close of the Sheffield Shield programme – in which he averaged 132·75 from 1,062 runs – Bradman had a brief holiday in Sydney, cut short by the calls of business in Adelaide, and was then committed to a promise to lead the South Australian team on its visit to Western Australia. There he played in two three-day matches against the State at Perth (whose citizens had not seen a South Australian side since March 1927, before Don Bradman was a first-class cricketer). In the first match he scored 209* in 161 minutes, all before tea on the third day, out of 281 at the crease – one of the best monopolies in the history of the game. He scored his third fifty in 26 minutes and his fourth in 30 minutes, his progress from 100 to 200 (in 56 minutes) being the fastest of his first-class career. It was a full half an hour faster, be it noted, than he took for his second hundred when he made his 303 in less than a day for Kensington earlier in the season. Had he not declared at Perth at tea (which he really had to do, as South Australia were then 279 ahead), he might once again have scored a triple-century in a day and would almost certainly have beaten the then ground record for Perth of 211 by another number three batsman, C. McKenzie, of Victoria, in 1909–10. In the second match at Perth he scored 135 at slightly under a run a minute – his fifth century in his last 11 innings. It took his aggregate for the season for South Australia to 1,448, one of the few Bradman records for the State to be broken, for B. A. Richards in due course passed it on 23 February 1971. Bradman actually scored all his 1,448 runs without his bails having been disturbed even once.

On 25 February 1940 Bradman's name was announced as captain of the Rest of Australia team to play New South Wales, the Sheffield Shield winners, in a proposed four-day match at the Sydney Cricket Ground in March, to be played for patriotic funds. Bradman's availability for this match had been in doubt and he somewhat cryptically referred enquiries to the South Australian Cricket Association as the proper channel, but Harry Hodgetts, when asked in mid-February, said: 'Don is definitely available for the match.' It was no secret that it was extremely doubtful whether the proposal for the match would have been pursued if Bradman had not been available. He played, of course, and the match yielded nearly £368 to each of the four Sheffield Shield States for distribution to patriotic funds. Although the war was six months old, it was the last sight of the 'pre-war' Bradman – and O'Reilly again gave him a rough passage. It was a great duel, and O'Reilly won. Bradman hit only one four in his 56 minutes at the crease for 25. J. C. Davis (now a septuagenarian and his great days as editor of *The Referee* over, with the demise of that paper) in the Sydney *Sunday Telegraph* gave Bradman's peccadilloes at the crease more space than they deserved, but as the match marked the end of a great era in Bradman's life, the quotation is not without interest:

We seldom see Don Bradman clean beaten by the ball on a good and true wicket. It happened at least twice on Friday. Don played forward to a perfect-length medium-pace O'Reilly ball, pitched on the middle stump, that, turning from the leg, beat the bat and just missed the off stump.

The batsman smiled broadly, no doubt realising that when such a trimmer evades his bat it ought to click something before reposing in the 'keeper's hands.

A little later, after a quiet spell, Don again played forward in defence, and again missed the ball. This time it turned from the off, and dodged the bat, but was intercepted by the pads into which it had turned. Not so dangerous a ball, and yet the great Don was deceived. It is a tribute to his greatness that we are so astonished when any ball evades his bat.

A little later still he touched a faster straight ball just outside the off stump, as he tried to chop it, and was held by Saggers off O'Reilly.

It was fitting that the great bowler should have had this reward, for he has sampled the might and weight of the Bradman bat.

In a season in which he was in such superb batting form, Bradman must have thought even more highly of O'Reilly than ever. It no doubt helped to settle his view that O'Reilly was the greatest bowler he ever batted against. When E. W. Swanton put the question to him in Sydney in March 1947, Bradman said:

To my mind there has never been a bowler to equal O'Reilly. To play with him was an education – to play against him usually a lesson.

From every conceivable angle, theoretical, technical and practical, he stands supreme. Moreover, his figures are a monument to his skill and they were achieved in an era of high scoring and good wickets.

His control of length was marvellous, his direction always designed to use his fieldsmen to the utmost, and his subtle variations of break and flight were so admirably handled as to be constant source of mental hazard to the batsman.

In support of his natural talents was an outstanding cricket brain which enabled him to achieve a perfection beyond that of any contemporary.

Fate conspired to keep Bradman away once again from playing cricket in New Zealand, for it was announced in Christchurch at the end of November 1939 that the war had caused the cancellation of the Australian tour there, due to start in February 1940, which Bradman was to have captained. A Test match at Christchurch was included in the itinerary: but New Zealand alas was never to see Bradman either in a Test or any other game.

For those who had cared to divert their minds from war to cricket, it was plain that Bradman's style of batting in that uncertain summer of '39–40 was markedly different and deliberately freer than it might otherwise have been – a return to his pre-Adelaide days, as if dictated by the knowledge that both for players and spectators this season would be a watershed in their lives. Cricket all over Australia – first-class and club cricket – had those same characteristics that summer, defensive attitudes being consciously put aside in favour of 'one last fling'. It did not require an excess of percipience to know there would be no Sheffield Shield matches in 1940–41, though the formal announcement did not come until 15 July 1940. In the middle of that '39–40 season, just before Christmas, C. G. Macartney, who was now doing a regular column of commentary for the *Sydney Morning Herald*, wrote after Bradman's magnificent batting against New South Wales at Adelaide: 'Bradman's batting showed a return to the dashing methods he employed on every occasion some few years ago, and will be welcomed in future matches this season. For the past few years he was compelled to take little risk owing to dangerous situations, and most of us thought – and not without a certain amount of justification, considering the tremendous trial on his stamina – that he had retired into a steadiness which made him a more difficult proposition for bowlers than ever. However, his brilliance has not departed, and woe betide bowlers who fail in accuracy.'

After his shattering 267 at Melbourne on New Year's Day, Bradman elicited the following tribute from Macartney (who rarely went overboard, but who kept to sound criteria of criticism):

> Bradman's phenomenal consistency continues. He is the supreme test for bowlers, and nothing yet devised by spin or swing, pace or slowness, seems to provide any unpleasant moment for him.
>
> No total by the opposition seems too great for South Australia when Bradman is about; but the eleven contains a solid and aggressive string of batsmen. Bradman is greatly assisted by his openers, who usually tame the first new ball.
>
> What mystifies bowlers when Bradman is batting is the unerring certainty with which he sends the bad ball to the boundary.

Bradman was a greater attraction than ever wherever he played that summer. In domestic cricket his mastery in recent seasons had become so absolute that it was no longer novel to see his big scores. Now, with the possibility that they might never be seen again, the grounds were full to watch him. The New Year Day attendance at Melbourne was 30,567 to see him go from 52* to 267 in 4¼ hours, and the four days of the match attracted 78,029, though everything conspired towards a good gate, with Bradman batting – against a good Victorian total – on both the Saturday and the Monday holiday. When Bradman captained South Australia in Sydney against New South Wales, the gate takings were £4,915.1.6d. – a record at that time for any Shield match in Sydney. Nothing can illustrate better the public's attitude to cricket in the first wartime summer of 1939–40 than the comparison between the aggregate takings for the three Sheffield Shield matches in Sydney *that* summer with the previous summer – £9,115 in 1939–40 (a new record for a Sydney season), and £2,407 from the same three fixtures in 1938–39. This is how Bradman's own appearance in Sydney, for his annual Shield match there, was affected. Even allowing for two washed-out days in the earlier season, the difference is remarkable:

	1938–39		1939–40	
	Attendance	Takings	Attendance	Takings
N.S.W. v S.A., Sydney	12,181	£656.2.9d	75,765	£4,915.1.6d

F. M. Cush, the honorary treasurer of New South Wales, must have smiled appreciatively at the boy who once lodged in his modest home at Rockdale and who was now captain of Australia and the greatest living attraction in the world of cricket.

Events were becoming more grim week by week as the 1939–40 cricket season came to a close. It was the last season of Sheffield Shield cricket until after the war. Likewise there was to be no more Premiership cricket in Adelaide, and while Kensington played a full season in 1939–40, after that there was only a season and a half of limited club games.

Bradman enrolled in the Royal Australian Air Force reserve – for which recruiting had been in full swing – on 28 June 1940, in Adelaide. That day, after passing his medical examination, he was sworn in and assessed as an observer (i.e. an air-crew member, although he was only two months below the age-limit). The Lord Mayor of Adelaide, the then Mr A. G. (later Sir Arthur) Barrett, who had been in the Australian Flying Corps in the First World War, and was chairman of the R.A.A.F. civil recruiting committee, said: 'It should be an inspiration to all sportsmen. Let us hope now that Don will get centuries in the air as readily as he got them on the ground.' Bradman joined up while Europe was still quivering with the shock of France's fall and before the dust of that mighty collapse had had time to settle. On the following day, 29 June, his great friend, C. W. Walker, also was accepted by the R.A.A.F. in Adelaide as an air-crew member. Poor Charlie Walker failed to return from a flight over Germany in 1942.

When the news of Bradman's joining up was made public on 28 June, congratulations began pouring in on him. He was placed on the Air Force reserve and did not expect to be called up for service for another three to four months. In the interim he attended special training classes. One of the weaknesses of the recruitment campaign (a highly successful one) was that an overwhelming number of applicants joined the R.A.A.F. but were frustrated by being kept waiting for their actual call-up. It was a widespread complaint. (By the first week of July nearly 120,000 applications had been received to join the R.A.A.F., but it had by then been possible to enlist only 5,463 air-crew personnel and 18,211 ground staff.)

While Bradman was thus awaiting his formal call-up, he became un-wittingly involved in a national controversy in the middle of July when it became known that he had written to Canon E. S. Hughes, President of the Victorian Cricket Association and a long-standing friend of Bradman's who had performed his wedding ceremony, saying that all sport should be for-gotten in Australia in wartime. Mr A. G. Cameron, the Minister of Navy and Commerce, agreed and praised the action of Bradman. Sir Frederick Stewart, however, the Minister of Supply, steadily opposed any move for the abandon-ment of sport. A great debate raged in Parliament. Bradman himself an-nounced that he would not play cricket in the war other than for patriotic purposes. On 26 September he gave a talk over the national radio stations in support of the war savings campaign. 'Unfortunately for us', said Bradman, 'the Italians and Germans don't play cricket. I have heard it said jocularly that our diplomacy failed badly in not teaching them cricket, because they would have been so busy arguing whether bowling was fair or otherwise that they would not have time for war against England. However, instead of looking forward to Test matches, we find ourselves participating in the most serious contest that the world has ever known.' (So far as England–Australia Tests were concerned, series had been scheduled for 1940–41, 1942, 1944–45 and 1946. It is interesting that in spite of the lost war years Bradman still remains comfortably ahead of any Australian in the matter of Test runs.)

Meanwhile, on what is believed to have been representations made by Fleetwood-Smith, negotiations began for Bradman's transfer from the Air Force to the Army. In October 1940, before he had yet entered any Air Force camp (though he had been eagerly awaiting this), he was duly selected for transfer and was released by the R.A.A.F. and was transferred to the Army School of Physical and Recreational Training as a student. He was to be one of the instructors attached to all units of the Army. He entered camp at the Army School of Physical Training at Frankston, Victoria, on the last day of October 1940, with the rank of Lieutenant. Like Fleetwood-Smith, he was to be trained as a P. and R. instructor. It was announced that he would become an instructor in charge of Army recreational training in South Australia, and would remain in Adelaide for six months before going overseas as divisional supervisor of physical training with the Australian Imperial Forces in the Near East.

Within days, literally – certainly within less than a week – of entering camp at Frankston, the pennant sides of Melbourne were chasing Bradman for his services. Both St Kilda and Hawthorn–East Melbourne wanted him. But Bradman said that while he was training at Frankston he would not play in Melbourne, adding that anyway he was without practice. Perhaps their optimism had been aroused by a broadcast on Sydney radio which said that Bradman was expected to be available for all South Australia's games in 1940–41 except the match against Victoria at Adelaide in Christmas week. In fact this turned out to be entirely wrong, and the one and only game he did play that season for South Australia *was* against Victoria at Adelaide in Christmas week. Two weeks before, playing for the Army Physical Training Corps v the Fire Brigade on the Richmond ground, Melbourne, in a one-day match for the Soldiers' Cigarette Fund, he had every incentive to get a good score, for the fund was jointly sponsored by five firms to the extent of 2/6d for each run he made – and he scored 109.

This was a deception, however: for in that very month of December 1940 Bradman's eyes were tested by an eye specialist at Frankston, with results that were surprising – not to Bradman (who suspected something of the sort) but to the specialist. The test was not necessary, but because Bradman was Bradman, the specialist sought it. What more ideal guinea pig could a research oculist desire than the man of whom it had been pronounced that he could make a century in Piccadilly by candlelight? Bradman was freely acknowledged in the 'thirties to have possessed the best cricketing eye in the game, and acknowledged so without rival once Duleepsinhji was forced to give up the game. The Frankston test showed his eyes to be very much below par.[1]

When he played at Adelaide against Victoria, he was out first ball, caught in the slips – a Christmas Day shock to the 6,000 who had turned up. He was very nearly out first ball in the second innings, when he fell over and almost sat on his wicket; but after ten minutes he was bowled for 6. He had obtained special Army leave for this match (played for national funds), as he did for his only further first-class game during the war – a Patriotic Match between his own team and S. J. McCabe's team at Melbourne in the New Year. Again he was out first ball, and scored only 12 in the second innings. Lieutenant Bradman's first-class average for the season was 4·50. He had been unable to focus the ball, and his health was in decline. Shortly afterwards Bradman received attention for inflamed back muscles. Fibrositis had struck him, and by the middle of January 1941 he had been admitted as a patient in the Repatriation General Hospital at Keswick, South Australia. He was expected to be there for two weeks' complete rest. Unfamiliar physical training exertions were thought to have brought on the back trouble. When he came out of hospital he took part in the Australian All-Services Athletics meeting at Melbourne on 14 February, when he led the winning team and won his own race and also led the Army team of athletes in the formal march past. But his muscular troubles were worsening. In fact he had three spells in all in hospital before, on 1 May in Adelaide, came the announcement that Bradman had been recommended for discharge from the Army on medical grounds, his health having been indifferent for some months. The medical view was that fibrositis of the muscles of the back, from which he was suffering, and which had proved most painful and persistent, made it impossible for him to carry out any further military duties. He was formally invalided out of the Army in June 1941. A statement was attributed to Bradman (but falsely so) that he would never play Test cricket again. In 1941, however, such an assessment could not have appeared desperately wide of the mark.

For his recuperation he went, once again, to the invigorating New South Wales country, near Bowral. 'I am quite certain', he later concluded, 'that the over-exertion of my earlier cricketing days was exacting retribution in full measure.' Though he was now nominally back in his civil occupation with H. W. Hodgetts' stockbroking firm, he was very unfit indeed in the second half of 1941 and has described how he could not lift his right arm even to comb his hair. His wife had to shave him – as well as look after the newest arrival in the Bradman family, their daughter Shirley June, born in

---

[1] A great deal was made during Bradman's career of his exceptional eyesight, which allegedly enabled him to see the ball early and react quickly. Undoubtedly, he *did* have superb eyesight. A professor of physics at Adelaide University, however, on testing Bradman once, found his reaction to be minutely slower than the average university student's. But those students couldn't get the runs that Bradman got!

Adelaide on 17 April 1941. Eventually Bradman improved to be able to perform his stockbroking work and community work. He played no cricket at all in 1941–42, or in the two following seasons, but in the Australian summer of '42–43 he enjoyed a little regular golf and some tennis in Adelaide. That emergence from the shadows prompted an invitation to be sent to him to captain a Services side against New South Wales in a two-day match at Sydney at the end of December 1942, but his fibrositis prevented him accepting. His recovery was slow, and in any event he was without practice of any kind, playing not even in the most minor kind of cricket. On 11 May 1943, he was elected a member of the Adelaide Stock Exchange – thus following in the steps of Clem Hill, who had been elected a member of the same Stock Exchange early in 1908. As a committee member and later President of the Commonwealth Club of Adelaide, Bradman rendered fine community service in his home city during the war.

Bradman's international renown even came to be used symbolically during the war as an illustration of the sheer might of human effort. On the downfall of Mussolini in the summer of 1943, an M.P. at Westminster declared: 'We have got Ponsford out cheaply, but Bradman is still batting.' Adolf Hitler might not have been impressed – or even have understood – the phraseology, and it was doubtless too great a compliment to him anyway: but that particular 'Bradman' was in due course bowled comprehensively after an uncomfortable innings that lasted a little too long.

On 14 March 1944, the long-awaited signal that was sent to initiate the second assault on the Monte Cassino monastery in Italy read as follows: 'Bradman will be batting tomorrow.' The signal was in that form of 'code' so that, if intercepted by the Germans, they would not understand its meaning (or at least not quickly enough to act on it). It indicated, of course, the start on the morrow of a massive assault on the opposition, and the signal went via the usual Army chain of command and communications down to every unit, until every single soldier knew of it. The British and New Zealand troops there understood its meaning well enough.

Coincidentally, on that very same day Bradman was in the news again. According to a friend in London who had received a letter from him, Bradman was alleged to have said that he hoped his next visit to England would be as manager of the first Australian team in England after the war, and that he had 'said goodbye to cricket, even club cricket'. The news was quickly cabled to Australia and Bradman was sought out in Adelaide to confirm it. Far from confirming it, however, he was angered by it: 'This is another case in which I have been clearly misrepresented. The question whether I might ever become manager of an Australian cricket team has not entered my head, and it is most unlikely that I will ever consider such a proposal, even if it became a practical possibility.'

In 1945 the future looked more prosperous. Events were heralding the final defeat of Germany, and though Japan was still to be dealt with, drastic plans

were being carefully hatched to that end. Bradman's health was still uncertain, though it was vastly improved on its mid-war state. Just at the time
when he might take the reins again and try to lead the life he had led before
the war, a personal tragedy struck him. The stockbroking firm of H. W.
Hodgetts, where Bradman earned his livelihood, collapsed. It was all a very
sad business which resulted in criminal proceedings against Mr Hodgetts. An
affidavit filed in the Adelaide Bankruptcy Court in July 1945 showed his
deficiencies at £82,854. There were 238 unsecured creditors named, with
debts totalling £102,926; and £762 was owing to Don Bradman, by now
described as a 'former' employee. Bradman himself was not implicated, but
it was a blow to his security and peace of mind. He was now well versed in
matters of stocks and shares, with a seat on the Stock Exchange. With advice
and with courage, he decided to open his own firm, also in Grenfell Street –
in fact in the same building – under his own name. Thus Don Bradman and
Co. became a feature of the business life of Adelaide and was to remain so
for nine years.

A major administrative landmark in Bradman's career came on 13 August
1945, when the South Australian Cricket Association elected him one of their
three representatives to the Australian Board of Control, together with
R. F. Middleton and C. B. Jennings, both pre-war Board members – indeed
Middleton had been on the Board when Bradman was fined £50 after the
1930 tour of England. Bradman actually filled the South Australian vacancy
caused by the absence of Henry Hodgetts, and attended his first meeting on
6 September. He was an unusually young representative, at 37, to join a
conventionally staid and middle-aged assemblage. The photograph of the
Board members in 1945, at Bradman's first meeting as a member, emphasises
how distant he was from nearly all of them in age. How distant was he from
them in spirit? Bradman had not been exactly in love with the Board in the
1930s, and even now the Board did not actually seek him – he was sent to
them by his State. As the reigning captain of Australia, whatever his cricketing
future might be, he doubtless saw that his relations with the Board would be
to the advantage of Australian cricket if he were in concert with the Board
rather than otherwise. The number of Test cricketers who had hitherto
served as members of the Board could literally be counted on the fingers of
one hand – there had been five of them only in the Board's whole history.
South Australia, strangely, had provided three of that number in Joe Darling
(who later also represented Tasmania), Clem Hill and Claude Jennings. New
South Wales (and, indeed, Victoria) had provided none: so in that particular
respect Don Bradman's prospects had been considerably enhanced by his
migration from Sydney to Adelaide. Had he, incidentally, become secretary
of the Melbourne Cricket Club after Hugh Trumble's death, he would
certainly not have become a Board member in 1945 or, in all probability,
ever. As it is, with only brief periods when he has stood down, Sir Donald
has been a Board member for over 30 years, to the infinite benefit of Australian cricket.

The next year in the life of Don Bradman – leading up to the arrival in Australia of the first post-war side from England – was to be something in the nature of trial and error, as much in the matter of Bradman finding his feet afresh as a business man as with his health and his cricket prospects. His future as a cricketer was linked very much, of course, with his health: and as to this, there were rumours and counter-rumours, and Bradman himself could not be sure of his health from one week to the next. Writing from Australia in *The Cricketer* of 30 June 1945, Cecil C. Mullen said these interesting words:

> Little is known of Don Bradman's cricket intentions of the future but it is very doubtful if Tests will see him again. In his last appearance in first-class cricket in Australia just on the outbreak of the European war Bradman shaped poorly against O'Reilly which suggested that the turning point in his career had already begun.

When the new season of 1945–46 arrived, Bradman did not feel fit enough either to go to the nets or to play for his club, Kensington. One who spent an evening at his home with him at that time says he was *most* uncertain as to whether he would return to first-class cricket, but he planned to 'give it a go' before making up his mind. For all that, he did not think for one moment that he would play in the next series of Tests in Australia, as illness still troubled him – and, so far as a future tour of England was concerned, that, in 1945, was quite out of the question. He then expressed the view that he believed such a tour would be physically impossible. Nearly five years of fibrositis had left him thoroughly run down.

On 1 October 1945, Dr H. V. Evatt, the Australian Minister for External Affairs (and one of Australia's delegates at the I.C.C. in 1938) spoke at a luncheon at Claridge's Hotel in London and said how warmly Australia would welcome a Test tour by England in 1946–47. He was not speaking with the specific authority of the Australian Board, but Dr Evatt had many friends on the Board, not least his fellow Sydney lawyer, the powerful Aubrey Oxlade, and there is no doubt that that was what the Board earnestly wished. Dr Evatt had spent several months in England in 1938 and had established close contacts with English administrators. With what may be considered extraordinary haste from Lord's, M.C.C. reacted almost at once to Dr Evatt's speech and on 9 October announced that they would indeed be sending a side to Australia in '46–47. If anyone at this stage would have cared to nominate Australia's probable captain in that series, Lindsay Hassett would have got most votes. In August 1945 Denzil Batchelor called him 'an odds-on bet to be captain of the next Australian Test team'.[1]

---

[1] As to the sending of a side to Australia, Sir Pelham Warner had suggested in July 1945 that a tour by England should not be contemplated before 1947–48, so that England could use two full seasons to build up a side. Interestingly, earlier that same month Sydney Smith, talking at the annual meeting of the Randwick club in Sydney, had expressed the hope that a Test between England and Australia would be played in Sydney by Christmas 1946 – and of course his hope was to be fulfilled.

Ray Robinson, as the new Australian season got under way, said: 'Whether and when Bradman will re-enter cricket is still strangely hush-hush, as if it were a State secret.' In December 1945, Bradman was approached to play for South Australia against Hassett's Australian Services side at Adelaide at the end of the month. Though wholly out of practice, he agreed – this was his 'giving it a go' – as the three-day match was to be devoted to charity. He also decided not to play outside Adelaide that season. Shortly before, South Australia had lost to New South Wales by an innings, and were due to play Queensland at Adelaide starting on Christmas Eve. Bradman took the opportunity to play in this match, insisting that he was turning out only because South Australia lacked experience and needed his leadership. However, people believed he was trying himself out not only for the Services match immediately afterwards but before making up his mind about his future Test prospects. He scored 68 and 52* against Queensland (not a Sheffield Shield match – there were none that season), and though the two innings were described by Bradman himself as 'of a somewhat painstaking character', his fifty in his first serious innings for nearly five years came in 54 minutes, and his eyesight certainly was not troubling him. Then against the Services at Adelaide, he hit a chanceless 112 at a run a minute, reaching his century in 95 minutes before giving his wicket away. His footwork was quite splendid. After nearly six years he had hit a first-class hundred again and it was said to contain 'all his old scintillating brilliance'. Again, Bradman himself was not especially happy with it. The bowling had not really provided a true test, but he was at least satisfied with his physical reaction to the innings. And the occasion marked another Bradman hundred – and even though he was now 37, that was not something that could be passed over lightly by bowlers either in Australia or England. The interviewers flocked around him in Adelaide, remembering that M.C.C. were due out in 1946–47. 'Will you play against England next season?' he was asked, and with typical logical caution he replied: 'An answer cannot be given until next season. It depends on whether I am fit enough and whether I can spare the time from business to play.' Was he satisfied with his come-back? 'Yes. I stood up to it better than I expected', he said. 'I feel tired, and have torn a muscle, but it is only natural that something like that would happen after so long out of the game.' Those who still saw him as a legend with a magic bat forgot the barren years of war and looked at the scoresheet and the 112. Many optimistic minds were quickly made up. Bradman himself, however, refused to alter his previously announced intention not to make a decision on his cricket future until the following Australian summer.

If Bradman himself was not sure about his future, others were. R. S. Whitington, who had played in recent months with the Australian Services team in England and India, was on the field during Bradman's latest century and sent the following from Adelaide to the Sydney *Sun*: 'Bradman, making 112 for South Australia against the Services, batted better than anyone I have seen since I last saw Bradman. That word anyone includes Hammond,

Hutton, Compton and Amarnath. Bradman is still in a class of his own. It would take a Harley Street specialist's certificate to convince me he is not fit enough to score hundreds in Tests.' E. M. Wellings did not see Bradman's innings, but he opined in London: 'I fancy that we shall hear much, very much more of him.'

There were no more first-class matches in Adelaide that season, and Bradman accordingly played no more first-class cricket. He, Jack Ryder and E. A. Dwyer chose the Australian side to visit New Zealand early in 1946, but Bradman declared himself unavailable – and promptly suffered a most severe recurrence of his fibrositis. Perhaps the Australian winter brought it on, but it was severe enough for him to seek relief 400 miles away in Melbourne, from a masseur there named Ern Saunders. His treatment was unorthodox but effective. He was highly experienced and he manipulated Bradman's muscles back almost to normality. He was fit enough to be playing squash by September 1946. But that same month he entered hospital for a minor operation – while Walter Hammond's men were crossing the world to play a new Test series.

That new Test series – the first meeting between England and Australia for eight years – was going to be at the very top as a sporting attraction, whether Bradman would be playing or not. While the uncertainty remained, an inducement was put before Bradman which might have settled the matter for most men. In May 1946 he was made one of the biggest offers ever held out to any player if he would write on the forthcoming Tests. He turned the offer down. The story was revealed by the sports columnist of the Adelaide *Advertiser* in August 1946. He said:

> Bradman declined the offer solely on the grounds that he considered that his acceptance would have made him ineligible to play.
>
> I don't know whether Bradman will play next summer. It will depend, no doubt, upon his health, and nobody can blame him if he were to stand aside for that reason.
>
> But I am optimistic enough to think that while we may lose O'Reilly we may still see Bradman.
>
> After his experience in 1932 when his services were preserved for Australia, principally by journalism, and yet the Board of Control refused him permission to play and write, Bradman would be justified in resting on his laurels and accepting the rewards of cricket which could be his without even asking.
>
> That he had declined to allow a very substantial monetary reward to take precedence over other considerations shows an intense loyalty to the game.

The knowledge that Bradman had set his face against this temptation raised fresh hopes for Australians that he would play in the Tests – hopes not diminished by his known intentions to resume club cricket with Kensington. Before the season began some of his former Test colleagues frankly ridiculed the idea that Bradman would want to play Test cricket again after such a tiny amount of cricket during the war. But among the inner circle of Adelaide's cricket community there was a quiet belief that Bradman still had a firm eye on the Test match scene. And he was keeping as fit as possible. His name in any eleven was still a magnet to the public – and administrators knew that well enough as they awaited Bradman's decision. His appearance in even one or two of the Tests against England would be highly acceptable to them.

11 Rivalry Renewed

I thank whatever gods may be
For my unconquerable soul.
W. E. Henley

To the great pleasure of the Australian Board, anxious to resume Test match ties with England as soon as possible after the long hiatus of war, an M.C.C. side found itself sailing on the *Stirling Castle* from Southampton on 31 August 1946 en route for Fremantle. Who would be Walter Hammond's opposing captain in the Test series ahead? Would it be Bradman? Would it be Brown? Would it be Hassett? Or who? Neither Englishmen nor Australians knew the answer. No one knew – not even Bradman himself – who would be captaining even South Australia, let alone the Test side. But one thing was certain, it seemed: and that was that, if the Don, his fitness and form proven, was in the side, he would be captain.

Not for the first time in his career, Bradman's name was surrounded by speculation as an M.C.C. side landed in Australia. It was not the speculation of '32–33. Now the Don's health was in doubt. His ability to play in a six-day match was in doubt. His ability to marshal his physical resources was in doubt. In answer to a direct question about his Test prospects, he firmly replied: 'In no circumstances will I captain the side if my health and form are not up to scratch.' There were criticisms that Bradman was adopting a secretive attitude about his cricket future. Was he a rheumatic cripple? Or was he a squash-playing rheumatic cripple?

Those Englishmen who saw Bradman on their arrival in Adelaide in October 1946 remember him as a frail man, far from fit, and showing signs of strain. Vivian Jenkins wrote in 1950: 'I can vouch that in 1946–47 in Australia when we first saw him he looked too ill ever to play again.' He had last been seen by most Englishmen being carried from the field with a broken ankle in 1938. Now he was eight years older, his hair thinner, and hiding from no one the fact that he had been ill. His appearance certainly confirmed it. Denis Compton later recorded that so many and varied had been the stories the M.C.C. team had heard about Bradman that 'some of us wondered whether or not he was due for a nursing-home rather than a cricket pitch'.

The Don had indeed been in hospital. The previous months had been bad ones for him. Fibrositis had continued to plague him and his general health had been poor. More than one doctor had seen him and had advised against a return to big cricket. His health of course had prevented him going to New Zealand with the Australian side. Never exactly robust, he had lost weight. Gastric troubles worried his mind and his body. All this at a crucial juncture in Australian cricket, with Shield cricket about to start again and of course the first Test cricket on Australian soil for ten years.

The appointment of Hammond to lead England in Australia was seen as a formidable challenge. His utter eclipse as a batsman – not aided by domestic problems at home becoming public knowledge – could not possibly have been foreseen after his brilliant 1946 season in England. He was arguably the best batsman in the world when his name was announced as touring captain on 9 July. The response in Australia was immediately to look to Bradman to supply the necessary batting balance – and at once, frail and ill that he was, he began to be badgered to lead Australia in the forthcoming series. In inviting the 43-year-old Hammond to take the side, M.C.C. passed over all the younger candidates, like Brian Sellers – an early critic of Hammond's in Australia – Billy Griffith and Bryan Valentine. Hammond's vast talent, and his three previous tours to Australia, gave him the vote – whether or not Don Bradman would be opposing England.

To say the least, the Don was an uncertain starter so far as the Test series was concerned. He had been re-appointed a selector but would only allow his name to go forward if his own high standards were satisfied. At 38, a venerable age for an Australian cricketer, he might well have chosen to claim that business in Adelaide was consuming his time. He might easily have opted to play Shield cricket only in his own city, just as C. G. Macartney at the end of his career chose only to play in Sydney. Lack of practice, insistent press speculation and the continuing doubts over health placed Bradman in a dilemma. But in the first week of October he did accept the captaincy of Kensington and, though recovering from gastric influenza, said he would play as soon as possible. He had his first practice of the season at Adelaide on 17 October. Cricketers who watched him were quick to note he was seeing the ball as well as ever. Two days later he batted for the first time that season in a match, scoring 42* for Kensington, after fielding for most of the afternoon. The South Australian selectors were satisfied as to his fitness, for he was named the following day in the list of players to oppose the M.C.C. later in the week. (He took that innings of 42* to 117 when the match was resumed two Saturdays later. He scored his further 75 runs in 85 minutes, and he was said to be 'more like the old Bradman'.)

There can be no doubt there was still personal ambition left in the Don. Without that, the easiest course would have been to step down – and to walk out of Test cricket with an average of 97·94. To ambition was allied duty: and his potential contribution to Australia's cause as captain could not be lightly dismissed. No one knew better than Bradman, the selector, that Australia's Test sides would contain many new faces – a wholly different complement from the 1938 sides. His presence and influence were bound to make a difference. So stockbroking was put into second place, the prospect of sitting in the press-box logically put aside, and the jealous mistress called cricket given due obeisance.

He might have heard the whisper of those fearful for his reputation: 'But your average will be pulled down, inevitably.' Well, it was to be pulled down, it is true – from 95·82 (at the beginning of October 1946) to 95·14 (at the end of his career). The decline – 'inevitably' – was the sort that could have been achieved only by Don Bradman.

Bradman's reputation, by his own conscious act, was placed firmly at risk in October 1946. Australian spectators – and not least Australian treasurers – trembled at the thought of his absence. Practice was essential, and he took it both at the nets and in the middle with Kensington. Meanwhile Walter Hammond had scored a double-century at Perth. This put him one ahead of Bradman's 35 double-centuries in first-class cricket. Did this spur the Don to further effort? Did it awaken the old rivalries? At all events, all the resolve – and the artistry – were in evidence when he practised at the Adelaide Oval with two days to go before the State match with M.C.C. Harold Dale, who was in Australia for the *Daily Express*, was satisfied from this net that Bradman was still the complete master. 'He may have lost something of his forceful power because his physical strength is less great and his customary marathon innings may be too exhausting, but the cheerful, superbly competent player I met has not finished with cricket.' He was facing the South Australian Shield bowlers, and such was his rhythm and confidence that E. W. Swanton was moved to report that 'from a distance of 30 yards Bradman might have been having a brief knock before continuing one of his great innings at Leeds or the Oval'.

So Bradman played for South Australia in the four-day match against M.C.C. – his first confrontation with English cricketers since August 1938. The cricket at Adelaide on 25, 26, 28 and 29 October was naturally the focus of great attention, and for the whole of the first two days Bradman was obliged to field out to a big M.C.C. score. Sunday then intervened, and on the Monday Bradman actually made top score for his side. Short of practice or no, he scored 76 in 2½ hours, a faster rate of scoring than by any Englishman in the match except Compton. Bedser and Wright had been deliberately kept away from Bradman for the match: but his performance was still considerable, and he received a great ovation on his return. The innings was one of the most significant in Bradman's – and Australia's – immediate post-war cricket history. It was a revelation in view of his health troubles. The percipient E. M. Wellings that afternoon recognised that there was still a formidable power in the land named Bradman:

> He spent half an hour in reaching double figures. Then he began making the never-to-be-forgotten Bradman strokes, including powerful punches off the back foot on both sides of the wicket, and reached his 50 an hour later.
>
> Yet he was not quite the old scoring machine. He did not see where a ball was pitching as quickly as when he last toured England, but there is not the least doubt that he is still a great menace to our Test hopes.
>
> He nursed himself wisely, as he is still short of full health, but he seems likely to be his old dominating batting self by the end of November when the first Test is due.
>
> Write him down as a certainty to captain Australia again.

His critics nevertheless were ready to scoff. His fielding, his captaincy and his dismissal for 3 in the second innings (off his eighth ball) were all seized upon unfavourably. But the doubts were removed a fortnight later at Melbourne with a century for an Australian XI against the M.C.C., followed immediately with 43 and 119 in a Shield match against Victoria. On 19 November the name of D. G. Bradman was in Australia's 12 announced for the first Test.

Even that announcement – the result of the deliberations between the three Test selectors, Messrs Bradman, Ryder and Dwyer – aroused a wave of gossip around the name of Bradman, for no captain was named among the 12. One story sweeping Australia was that Bradman had taken exception to criticism of his captaincy in the recent Melbourne match against M.C.C., when he was accused of poor placing of the field and of taking McCool off prematurely. It may be, went the speculation, that he preferred to concentrate on his own game and let someone else assume the worries of leadership. Hassett's name was already being offered as captain. Such speculators did not know their Bradman; nor did they know the administrative rule whereby the Australian Board, and not the selectors, actually chose the captain. Within 24 hours the matter was publicly settled. Bradman was named as captain on 20 November.

It is trite to say that what Bradman did in the Test series of 1946–47 determined the pattern of Anglo-Australian cricket relations for some time to come. It did not only that (and, in its train, opened the door for Bradman's triumphant visit to England in '48) but set up Australia as the dominant power in post-1946 world cricket as no country's ascendancy had been established before, unless it be Australia's own superiority, engineered by Warwick Armstrong, immediately after the First World War. If this can be said to have fulfilled D. G. Bradman's sense of duty to Australian cricket, then it was fulfilled in abundance. A new generation of spectators, of players, and of readers – within Australia and outside it – were at once firmly conditioned to the fact that Australia was the greatest cricketing nation on earth. It may not have been the most palatable fact to some people, but the following brief table (limited to first-class matches) sets the matter in perspective. It shows the records of the first two touring sides in Australia after the war (from England and India) and the first two major tours abroad by the Australians:

	Matches Played by Australian Teams v non-Australian opponents	Matches Lost by Australian Teams v non-Australian opponents	Test Matches Lost by Australia
1946–47 in Australia	17	1	0
1947–48 in Australia	14	2	0
1948 in England	31	0	0
1949–50 in South Africa	21	0	0
	83	3	0

Australia's Test match record over the above four seasons was 15 wins out of 20 Tests, with five drawn. The West Indies, who are not included in the above table, had also by 1950 announced themselves as a world force: yet when they went to Australia in 1951–52 they lost six of their first seven first-class matches and ended with four wins out of 13 – two of them against Tasmania.

Much of the cricket played by Australians in this period, whether in Tests or on tour or against visiting opponents, was characterised by an efficiency approaching ruthlessness (Tasmanian sides always excepted). Opponents knew that Australians played 'hard', whether in their own country or away. Much of this ruthlessness stemmed directly from the influence of Bradman. He liked to win, and he liked even more not to lose. If success comes before all else in cricket, then the exalted position of Bradman the paladin cannot be questioned. His influence in this respect has never left Australian cricket. Australians were formidable opponents before Bradman, but never quite so consistently ruthless as they were after he emerged.

The foundations of victory meant more to Bradman than goodwill or popularity or almost anything else. Neville Cardus, in his brief flirtation with the *Sunday Times*, said of Bradman in 1948: 'He is the brain and the vertebra of Australian cricket, Government and executive. . . . Bradman bestrides them all; he bestrides the entire history of the game. . . . It is an error to think he is perpetually a grim Ironsides. He can relax and become quite playful after the foundations of victory have been more or less laid down.' It was of course partly Bradman's batting and in a great measure his captaincy that saw that those foundations were safely laid. It was not often that he was comprehensively defeated. But he most certainly was so at the Oval in 1938 (when neither he nor Fingleton could bat). And the next time he captained Australia on a Test match field was against England at Brisbane in November 1946.

Despite the holocaust of 1939–45, Bradman at Brisbane was the very last person to have the memory of the Oval, 1938, erased from his mind. His rival captain, moreover, was the selfsame Walter Hammond. If revenge indeed be a luscious fruit which you must leave to ripen, then eight years of enforced idleness can be said to have brought it to handsome maturity. The defeat at the Oval in 1938 was the most crushing ever inflicted on Australia in her Test history: the very next encounter between the sides was to see the complete reversal – the heaviest defeat ever suffered by England and the biggest victory ever recorded by Australia over any country. Bradman and the Brisbane weather joined forces in an irresistible combination.

One further matter must be considered. The Oval rout of 1938 was hardly the point at which Bradman could voluntarily have chosen to bring to an end a brilliant Test career. The bitter taste of that disaster was still lingering on Australian tongues in 1946, and there had been resentment of Bradman for what had happened, though of course he had been entirely without blame for the accident that removed him from the match. Moreover, other names were making their mark on Australian minds. Lindsay Hassett's star was high in the ascendant. Sidney Barnes had played some quite brilliant innings in 1945–46, distributing his hundreds around Brisbane, Adelaide, Melbourne and Sydney, and such was his panache and consistency that people were actually asking 'Is Barnes better than Bradman?' W. A. Brown, it was generally thought, had been groomed on the New Zealand tour for the captaincy against England in '46–47. Against this background it came about that Bradman defied his doctors and returned to Test cricket at the Woolloongabba ground on 29 November 1946.

The smiles that morning on the faces of the rival captains – put on for the photographers of Brisbane – was the last time the two men were ever to smile in each other's company. Hammond had said some nice things about Bradman earlier in the tour at an Adelaide reception, and Hammond hoped that this Test series in a new era would be graced with goodwill. In his brown felt hat he returned to the dressing-room, loser of the toss for the first time against Bradman, to lead out England to begin the series. Within less than 90 minutes of its start that Friday, all good intentions had been reduced to naught.

All that has been said and written over the years about the Bradman–Ikin incident just before lunch emphasises, but does not exaggerate, its importance. Bradman's form that morning was poor in the extreme. 'He began like a schoolboy', was Hammond's recollection. Facing Bedser for the first time in his life, he was in constant difficulty – so much so that Barnes, the Test novice, was actually shielding his great captain. 'Bradman's survival through his opening minutes', recorded J. M. Kilburn, 'was close upon miraculous.' Then Barnes got out, and a few minutes later Bradman, with his score at 28, attempted to chop a ball from Voce wide of the slips. The ball flew at chest height to Ikin at second slip who thought he had made a perfectly good catch. Hammond, at first slip, thought so too, as did the rest of the England side. Some of the fielders, of course, were not in the best position to see: but none of them has ever pronounced against the apparent legality of Ikin's catch. The bowler's umpire, however, *did* do so, and he was asked for a decision only after moments of silence while Bradman stood his ground. Hammond recorded: 'Bradman was idly looking away over the square-leg boundary, as if there was nothing to decide.' Borwick did not hesitate when the belated appeal did come. It was a bump ball in his judgment; and however divided was the large press contingent (watching from wide long-on, by the way) and the broadcasters, neither Borwick nor Bradman himself had any doubt. Bradman took the trouble afterwards to tell the press that if he had thought he was out he certainly would not have remained there. Scott, with commendable support for his fellow-umpire, wrote at the end of the series that the disputed ball was a bump ball: that information might have come to him via Borwick.

Hammond was described as 'blazingly angry' with Bradman for not walking – the words are those of one of Hammond's XI on the field – and at the end of the over he made the famous remark to his rival captain: 'A fine —— way to start a series.' Bradman went on and on. From positive uncertainty, his confidence flowed back gradually and surely. He batted a further four hours after the disputed incident, and on the second morning in particular he was in brilliant form until he was bowled for 187. Had the decision gone against him at 28, scored unimpressively, it is almost certain that Bradman would have had to play his second innings on the terrible sticky pitch that the violent thunderstorm produced at Brisbane. As it was, his innings guided Australia to the huge total that ensured England following on – and Bradman was spared the stress of that vile pitch.

In the view of some people Bradman might have ended his Test career had he suffered a double failure at Brisbane. That is impossible to know. What is certain is that after his escape he was a different batsman.

By the end of his first day in Test cricket for eight years, Bradman was 162 not out and batting at his best. The ominous significance of the pre-lunch Ikin affair was all too apparent. It seemed that Bradman, embarrassed by it all, decided to reply in his best, emphatic way – by punishing the bowlers without mercy. At the close of play E. M. Wellings wrote: 'Bradman's innings of 162 not out was of two shades, changing like the leaves of the bougainvillea from green to rosy magnificence. While scoring 28 before lunch he was really shaky and might have been out several times. He played more false shots than used to be a month's ration for him. Afterwards he was Bradman, the true Bradman, sure of himself and master of the glorious attack strokes.' Whatever ailments plagued Don Bradman, it seemed evident that the best of all medicines for them was runs from his bat – and plenty of them.

The truth of the Ikin incident can never be settled. Both Borwick and Bradman might have been wrong. Hammond certainly did not consider Borwick (or Scott) to be up to the standard of ten years before. Only evidence can be adduced, and never proof. In this regard one of the most vital participants in the drama seems consistently to have been ignored in the telling of the event – the next man in. That next man was Keith Miller, and he was moreover padded up to play his very first Test innings.[1] It was not just another cricket match for him:

> Clutching the ball to his chest, Ikin faced the field. His team mates close to the wickets applauded him. The great Bradman was out! That was the message conveyed to the 17,000 spectators who sat in shirt sleeves that hot, humid day.
>
> Oddly enough, I was padded up next man in to bat. As Ikin held the ball, I instinctively got out of my seat, picked up my gloves and grabbed my bat, my heart pumping like a runaway motor out of control. 'I'm in. My first Test innings.' I had played Victory Tests with the Australian Services team during the war, but this was the real thing.

---

[1] He had actually played v New Zealand at Wellington earlier in the year, but that match was not afforded Test status until a later I.C.C. ruling. Thus Miller was quite correct, at the time of the Brisbane Test, in treating that innings as his first in Test cricket.

But Bradman had not budged from the crease. Then came an appeal, a mere formality it seemed, but the umpire ruled Bradman not out. He believed the ball had rebounded off the ground into Ikin's hands.

The crowd were stunned. The English players looked at each other making signs that it was a fair catch. I sat down again. The Australian players started discussing the incident. Some agreed with the umpire that the ball had come off the ground. Others said it was a straight out simple catch. The game went on. So did the chatter.

One of those broadcasting at the moment of the incident was Clif Cary, of Sydney, a sports reporter and broadcaster. Cary was a trained observer. He was an experienced broadcaster, not only of cricket but most especially of horse-racing, where the accurate identification of detail is so important. His writings during the tour, however, especially a piece that appeared in a London Sunday newspaper (and swiftly quoted back to Australia) on the alleged laxness and habits of the M.C.C. side, were not always temperate. His book on the 1946–47 series, *Cricket Controversy*, is admittedly over-critical of both Bradman and Messrs Scott and Borwick, and it may be fair to say he is not always regarded as a reliable source, but the following paragraph is quoted without comment:

I was broadcasting at the time from a position directly behind the umpire at the bowler's end. I was looking at the play through powerful 10 × 50 Zeiss glasses. The whole scene was brought to within a few yards of me, and my exact words were: 'The next ball from Voce rises as it goes away and Bradman is out . . . Bradman out, caught Ikin at second slip, bowled Voce, for 28.' To me there was no doubt about the legality of the catch and when Bradman just stood there looking down at the ground, I was astounded, and at first thought it must have been a no-ball, and I had missed the signal. I quickly realised this could not have been the case and was at a complete loss for words. Seconds went by. Then came the belated appeal and the umpire's 'no'. Why Bradman stood there as if he had never hit the ball, as though there was nothing to worry about, is a question impossible to answer. He may have been undecided; may have been waiting for an appeal and hoping the delay would arouse some indecision in the umpire's mind, but I do know the Englishmen did not immediately request a decision because, as experienced cricketers, they felt the dismissal was so obvious that an appeal was totally un-necessary. To them Bradman was as plainly dismissed as if he had been clean bowled or caught high in the outfield. As one said to me, 'cricket is coming to a pretty pass if a side has to appeal for everything; when that happens it will mean the end of all those things for which cricket is supposed to stand.'

W. J. O'Reilly was another who watched the incident, and he too was in no doubt that Bradman was out. O'Reilly did not write a book on that tour, but he did write one on the 1948 tour of England (*Cricket Conquest*), where – despite the incident being somewhat out of context – he took the opportunity to perpetuate his version of Brisbane, 1946:

As far as the Bradman catch was concerned there was no doubt whatever in my mind. It was a legitimate catch absolutely. But Bradman had the right to wait for the decision because there was the doubt in his mind. I am quite sure, however, that the Australian captain must have had grave doubts as to the excellence of the decision when he thought over the facts of the case later on. To get a bump ball to go shoulder high at a speed sufficient to spin Ikin side-on as he effected the catch needs some uncanny propulsion seldom seen in cricket. . . . George Borwick, the Australian umpire who gave Bradman not out, must have been caught napping. He has had a long and honourable career in first-class umpiring in Australia and there has never been any suggestion that he is incompetent or one-eyed.

One of the men best situated on the field of play was Norman Yardley, fielding in the gully, and his version, too, is now given, even at the risk of prolonging this incident unreasonably, for it can fairly be said that it was one of the most vital incidents in the history of post-war England–Australia cricket. Yardley wrote thus in *Cricket Campaigns* (1950):

Bill Voce was bowling, Bradman had got 28, and suddenly attempting one of his favourite strokes, a drive just wide of cover-point, the ball flew from the *top edge* of his bat and straight towards second slip, where Jack Ikin caught it beautifully.

Now I want to be precise about this . . . I was in the best position on the field, even better than the umpire himself, to see exactly what happened. I watched the ball bounce from the turf on to the top edge of the bat and go from there straight to Ikin's hands. According to the Laws of Cricket, it was 'Out!' Ikin held the ball, waiting for Bradman to leave the crease. He stared at the ground and did not move. Astounded, Ikin called, ' 'Owzatt?' The umpire looked straight at him and said 'Not out!'

Everyone on our side looked in blank amazement, and Hammond in particular seemed to be wondering what to do next. Bradman still looked down. The point was this. The umpire, according to subsequent statements, supposed that the ball had been chopped down from the bat on to the ground, and had bounced. But you do not have to play cricket for years to know that a ball chopped down at that speed bounces *steeply up*. It does not travel parallel with the ground at chest height.

Don, in response to enquiries later from Australian Pressmen, apparently said: 'I did not know I had given any catch. I heard an appeal, the umpire indicated not out, so I batted on. Naturally, if I had thought I was out, I should not have stayed there.'

Without meaning to imply any unsportsmanship, I think most cricketers in a big match, in such a position, would not necessarily hasten to leave before the umpire's voice had been heard! I am not intending any slight to Don, nor suggesting anything except that Umpire Borwick made a mistake. All human beings make mistakes sometimes. All the same, it was an unfortunate moment at which to make one. Don Bradman was out, three wickets were down cheaply on a batsman's wicket in the first Test after the long war-time break. It might have made a world of difference if only . . .

D. V. P. Wright was at third man and saw the ball leave Bradman's bat. 'I thought it was a catch', he says. Likewise Alec Bedser, with firmness and certainty: 'I thought it was out.' Ikin himself is to this day as adamantly certain as he was at Brisbane in 1946 that he took the catch fairly and properly. Unambiguously imprinted on his mind, as if the incident had happened only yesterday, are what he considers the true facts – that Bradman attempted to put the ball past cover's hand, but that the ball flew sharply from the top of the bat straight to him, Ikin, at second slip; and flew from the bat crisply and straight, with all the characteristics of a 'legitimate' catch and with none of the characteristics of a ball impeded first by the earth. Bradman himself may well have been unsure: but it is Ikin's view that his hesitancy, combined with the fact that he actually stayed at the crease, provided sufficient time to allow the mind of the umpire to be influenced in Bradman's favour, consciously or unconsciously. Ikin is immovable in his conviction that the Don was out. (It was one of those issues that divided the cricket populace into two camps. C. B. Fry gave Bradman out, caught Ikin, from Hamble, Hants!)

Bradman's 187 was a new record score for an England–Australia Test at the Woolloongabba ground, beating the 126 of Maurice Leyland ten years before. If its achievement must be considered a triumph (as well as a land-mark) for Bradman, as was not untypical of the man there was more to come. Bradman had to nurse himself carefully that summer, with gastric trouble liable to bother him at any time. Apart from one Shield match in November, while he was testing his form prior to the Test series, his entire first-class cricket was limited to matches against Hammond's touring side. Bradman's health in 1946–47 was more of a national concern than the health of the Prime Minister. After all, if the Prime Minister were sick in bed, the Test chances of Australia were affected not a jot.

If Bradman was intending the Test match series to be warfare, his side's victory at Brisbane must have been as satisfying as Napoleon's victory at Jena. There was something of the same grim outlook between the two little men, not merely in generalship: the same capacity for planning, the same eye for detail, the same ambition and inflexibility of will. But just as Napoleon was ambitious not exclusively for himself but for France and for millions of Frenchmen, so Bradman was also ambitious for Australian cricket. The overwhelming win at Brisbane, much as it owed to the weather, put Bradman on terms with himself again. There was still a future for him at Test level, which he could only *hope* would be the case a week before.

The double-century that Bradman must have had his eye on at Brisbane – and indeed since 14 October, when Hammond scored his 208 at Perth – duly came in his very next innings. Oddly enough, Bradman had never scored a century against England at Sydney, though he had missed two possible Tests there through respectively a whim of selectorship and illness. In his only two previous Tests against England in his native New South Wales, he had both times been on the losing side. Sydney, her hotels now bursting at the seams, had not seen Australia win a Test match since as long ago as December 1931.

Bradman confounded everybody at Sydney – his doctors, his critics and his public. For one whose health had been described variously as between invalidism and merely shaky, he put up an astonishing performance by scoring 234 without a chance and taking part in a stand with Barnes of 405, which was – and remains – a Test and world record for the fifth wicket. It was the highest partnership Bradman ever shared in Australia. On exactly twelve occasions in his career did Bradman bat for six hours in an innings. Eleven of those times were as a young man, in his twenties – this was the one exception, at the age of 38, and he became the oldest cricketer, just as he was already the youngest, to score a double-century in England–Australia Tests. His stamina after the war may not have been the iron thing that bowlers had learned to dread in the '30s, and his speed of scoring appeared likewise to be not what it was: but the runs still came emphatically enough, and at Sydney at least the old stamina was still in evidence. Considering what Sir Donald himself has written about the innings, it assumes the proportions of a miracle:

> I was fortunate to bat at all. On the Friday I tore a leg muscle which prevented me fielding on Saturday. This was followed by an attack of gastritis which kept me in bed most of the weekend, and I felt far below par on the Monday. Even then my leg was heavily strapped and the whole innings was played off the back foot. I scarcely made one forward shot the whole day.

In the words of the old quip, if Bradman could score 234 on one leg, what could he have scored on two? He had spent 15 minutes inspecting the pitch two days before the start of the game, and then pronounced his verdict: 'It's a beauty.' He must have been hoping to win the toss again, but matches starting on Friday the 13th (as that Sydney Test was scheduled) had a strange habit of not being lucky for Australian captains. Up to then, seven Test matches in history had started on such a day, six of them involving Australia – and never once had Australia won the toss. Bradman duly lost the toss again on Friday the 13th of December 1946.

This match was Sydney's first sight of Bradman since the Patriotic Match of March 1940, and he had not scored a century there – or even a fifty – since before the war. (He was, incidentally, to average 81 in his five post-war matches on the Sydney Cricket Ground.) Now he was in the field, and at once showed his captaincy prowess by allowing his three fast bowlers, Miller, Freer and Toshack, to bowl only 23 overs between them in England's 255: the spinners took nine of the wickets. (Lindwall was absent recovering from chicken-pox, which he had developed at Brisbane, Bradman quickly summoning a doctor and getting him off to hospital. The second Test side might have been very strange had the infection spread, but after practice at Sydney the day before the match all the Australian players were medically examined and passed free of infection.)

Bradman's injured leg caused him to hold himself back to number six at Sydney. This was the celebrated match when Sidney Barnes, on the second evening, made repeated appeals against the light – five in all – in a very short space of time, before play was halted.[1] The Playing Conditions allowed an appeal after every ball – quite unlike what the England players had ex-

---

[1] Actually, the appeals were shared by Barnes and the stop-gap number three, Ian Johnson. But as the senior batsman at the wicket, Barnes was held primarily responsible.

perienced in the series with India a few months before, when *no* player could appeal. Had Bradman come out in his usual position of number three on the fall of Morris's wicket, he would not only have had to play on a pitch that was wet after heavy afternoon rain but would have been obliged to assume, in the role of captain, the part of appealer-in-chief against the light. Bradman thus, fortuitously or otherwise, spared himself the enormous opprobrium that was heaped on Barnes, who was loudly hooted off the ground when the umpires gave way. Barnes later admitted that it was the drying pitch and not the light that was the real cause for concern, and put the blame for the affair squarely on the shoulders of his captain. In the dressing-room, according to Barnes, 'Bradman told me to get my chin down, stay there at all costs, and appeal against the light at the first opportunity. The pitch was wet but not difficult. The ball was skidding through but every additional over we stayed in the middle meant that the pitch was drying with the prospect of becoming "sticky". Bradman told me he wanted us to bat as little as possible that day. He was willing to take the risk of it being fine on the third day. He told me to appeal against the light at every opportunity. . . . I was given my orders and I carried them out.'

In a radio broadcast from Perth at the end of the series, however, Barnes (then on his way to a league engagement in England), in dealing with the incident, made no mention at all of Bradman – the blame apportioned to his captain some years later. Perhaps he did not wish to jeopardise his chances for selection in 1948. But on the air in 1947 Barnes admitted making the appeals knowing there was nothing wrong with the light:

> We could have played on but it was a Test match and we just had to win. I realised something drastic had to be done or three wickets might be lost. So I appealed after every second ball. I complained of the people moving about, the light, and, in fact, anything, in an effort to get the appeal upheld. Hammond and Yardley were inspecting the wet pitch. I knew there was a chance of losing valuable wickets so I just kept on appealing until the umpires answered me.

Play actually ended on that second day at 4.54 p.m., so, if the light was really not at fault (as the Sydney crowd, including the members, felt) then England were deprived of bowling on a helpful pitch – and Bradman might have been obliged to make an appearance on it that evening. Bruce Harris remarked: 'I wondered why the fifth appeal was successful, for the light did not seem to have grown worse than at the first.' From the accounts of those there, first-class cricket in England had often been played without demur in worse light than at Sydney.

On Monday the pitch had rolled out perfectly, all in favour of the batsmen. Bradman's long innings – both his longest in time and his highest in runs in his post-war career – must be seen in the context of Barnes's innings at the other end. Throughout the entire 6½ hours that Bradman batted, Barnes was his sole partner. At Brisbane, where Barnes had gone for his shots, Bradman had taken him aside and criticised his approach to the job of opening the innings. 'You were looking for runs all the time', Bradman told him. 'I think what you want to watch as an opener is not getting out. . . . What is needed from my openers, and is most important, is patience and plenty of it.' That patience Barnes showed for ten hours 42 minutes at Sydney, to reach what was then the slowest double-century in Test cricket – an innings out of character but in accordance with his captain's wishes. Barnes had a start of four hours five minutes and 71 runs when his captain joined him just before tea on the third day: yet before they were separated Bradman actually overhauled Barnes. Bradman had limped in, impressed upon Barnes that he was not well, sometimes lay on the ground as if to emphasise it, but was still in possession at the close with 52 not out. As soon as he reached his hotel after the close he was ordered to bed.

The fourth day was a revelation. Before play began, there was endless talk about Bradman, who had allowed Hassett to captain the side for the whole of the second day and who had been limping during his 115 minutes at the crease on the third. He was said to be lame and to have stomach trouble. His wife revealed he had chronic gastritis, which had been troubling him for several months. He might not continue his innings, it was said; he might even retire from Test cricket. In the event, he came out again with Barnes, was very soon sprinting a third run and, whenever quickness of movement was required, he was not found wanting. He batted, without a runner, from start of play until 5.43 p.m. (17 minutes from the close) before Yardley had him lbw. His 234 – his eighth century in eight successive Tests in which he had batted – included 24 fours, and his last 16 runs came in a single over off Compton. He then ran off the ground to a great ovation and bounded up the pavilion steps. Spirit had triumphed over flesh. And in the dressing-room the adhesive bandages on his left thigh were ripped off with the same excruciating pain that is suffered by all mortals.

Barnes himself was out four minutes later for the same score of 234 – he always maintained he threw his wicket away deliberately not to exceed the Don's score. With 564 on the board, it was not especially rash. The Don was pleased with his innings this time, much more so than at Brisbane. (The Test average of Barnes, incidentally, is second among Australian batsmen to that of Bradman : but the margin is a vast one – 99·94 by Bradman and 63·05 by Barnes.)

While Bradman was at the wicket that day the spectators watched with increasing attention and wonderment. There were still some in Sydney who had resented his having left the State, but there was no denying the sheer spectator appeal of this cricketer. The moment he was out, the crowd got up as in a body and left the ground. The double-centurion Barnes was still then at the crease, but the magician had left the stage. Such was the mass exodus that the next man in, Colin McCool, who had sat with his pads on for two days, had to fight his way through the members to get on to the field. 'If I'd walked out to the crease wearing a false nose and smoking a cigar nobody would have noticed', mused McCool in later years.

The Don was well and truly back on top – 421 runs in his first two innings of the series and all but 12 hours in the middle without an actual chance. But to the Ikin incident at Brisbane had been added a similar one at Sydney, and once again it was a catch to Ikin that was in dispute, this time however on the leg side. Bradman, when 20, played a short ball from Bedser that travelled very quickly to Ikin at short-leg. Ikin gathered it, tossed it in the air, and he and Bedser both appealed. This time it was Scott who said not out, but once again not everyone was satisfied. This Sydney incident, either at the time or since, never seems to have approached the same degree of fervour as the Brisbane affair. The umpire's verdict in each case was bump ball, and at Sydney many more were in agreement with it than at Brisbane. Nevertheless it was unfortunate that one such incident should have occurred, let alone two. On the day after the second Test ended, E. M. Wellings cabled the following words to London: 'A Sydney paper yesterday remarked: "Test cricket is played hard these days." How true! It is particularly hard when you have to get the same star player out twice in each two of successive Test innings.' On the balance of evidence, the Don must be accounted lucky at Brisbane: had the umpire's finger gone up then, there would have been disappointment but no endless post mortems. At Sydney, again on the evidence, the umpire was almost certainly correct.

There were no more sensations in Bradman's cricket for the remainder of that Australian season. He played in only four more first-class matches – the last three Tests and the return game for South Australia against the tourists. He had a three-week break between the fourth and fifth Tests, standing down from his State's Shield matches at Sydney and Brisbane, P. L. Ridings (his eventual successor as captain of South Australia) leading the side.

In the fortnight between the second Test at Sydney and the third Test at Melbourne, Bradman's future – he was then of course 38 – was being pondered over by none other than the politicians. At that time persistent efforts were being made to induce him to turn to politics. With his name he would be a supreme asset to any party. Offers came to him from both Labour and the opposition, with assurances from both that a 'safe' seat could be found for him. It was noted that, not long before, Bradman had had a long talk with Dr Evatt, who was not only a cricket lover but Minister for External Relations. Up to then there was no evidence that Bradman had shown any liking for party politics or indeed for public life outside cricket. He had, of course, his livelihood as a stockbroker. The politicians were disappointed; then, as was to happen also a few years later, Bradman rejected their overtures.

In the New Year Test at Melbourne, where Bradman had thus far *always* scored a century in each of the seven Tests in which he had batted there, he lost his wicket twice to Norman Yardley (for 79 and 49), thus seeing Yardley capture his wicket three times in succession in the series. On the first morning Barnes had a start of some 50 minutes when Bradman came in, yet within *a quarter of an hour* Bradman had overtaken him. It was a feature of Bradman's batting that season that though he often seemed to start uncertainly – as he did at Brisbane, Sydney and Melbourne – the runs nevertheless accrued surely enough. In his 79 at Melbourne, before a crowd of more than 66,000, he hit only two fours in over 2¾ hours – one of them off a no-ball.

At the end of the third Test, with Australian wins at Brisbane and Sydney and a draw at Melbourne, Australia had retained the Ashes. It all made gloomy reading and listening for those who had high hopes of a closely fought series and who remembered Hammond's words on Waterloo Station that his side would not let England down. It was a bitterly cold winter in England, with power cuts and huge snowdrifts, canals freezing over – and even the bacon ration was cut from three ounces to two. Were the M.C.C., reluctant to send a side so soon after the war, right in yielding to the Australian Board and the mellifluous tones of Dr H. V. Evatt? Don Bradman, at the end of the series, had no doubt at all that they were correct, and said so in public. In retrospect it seems there can have been little change in the result of the series had it been delayed for twelve months. The tourists, with two more players – a fast bowler and a high-class middle-order batsman – could have been a powerful side. Bradman more than once warned his team that season: 'Don't feel you are so far on top of these boys that you can afford to give them a chance. Give them two more good players and they'd be a difficult lot to topple.'

Bradman himself was toppled neck and crop in the first innings of the Adelaide Test, when he was bowled by Alec Bedser for 0. He came in a quarter of an hour from the close on the Saturday, spurning the thought of a nightwatchman. The ball was swinging a little and Bedser was bowling to a short-leg field. After facing most of two overs from Bedser, Bradman was bowled by a magnificent ball which Bradman afterwards told Bedser – and confirmed it in his autobiography – was the finest ball ever to take his wicket. 'It was delivered', said Bradman to the bowler, 'on the off stump, swung very late to hit the pitch on the leg stump, and then came back to hit the middle and off.' Bradman's defence was breached and a roar of dismay came from the crowd. As Denis Compton later recorded: 'Depression was written on every face. You might have thought they'd lost their life-savings in a crash; apparently Bradman losing his wicket without scoring was almost as big a debacle.' It had happened before of course – it was actually his fifth Test duck – but was the first time that his home city of Adelaide had witnessed it. The next day on the beach at Glenelg, Alec Bedser was addressed by a small boy full of hurt and indignation: 'You've spoilt my week-end. I could hit you. Why did you bowl out Don Bradman for a duck?'

Robertson-Glasgow, strangely, as this Adelaide Test approached, remembered how Bradman had been run out by England there in 1928–29, and wondered whether perhaps, for Bradman, in the Book of Chance, this new match was marked as the Recurrence of Indiscretion. 'Perhaps', he concluded laconically. The fact that Bradman now got 58 fewer runs than his 58 run out of February 1929 was for many Australians the cruellest indiscretion of the decade.

W. A. Brown, Ben Barnett and Bradman were the only Australians ever to play against both Maurice Tate and Bedser in first-class cricket. Bradman, however, was the only one to face them both in Test cricket (and on Australian wickets) and at the end of his career he pronounced Bedser the more difficult to play. Bradman always had the highest admiration for Bedser's bowling, and rightly so. But of course he did not face Tate in 1924–25 and faced Bedser when his reactions were inevitably no longer those of a young athlete. The matter is impossible to prove, but it is the view of Ponsford (who never faced Bedser, but watched him in Australia after the war) that Bradman would not have ranked him above Tate had he played against Tate at his best.

The youthful athleticism of Bradman in the field was also inevitably missing after the war. He was sensible enough – as always – to realise that his great days as an outfielder or cover point in the tradition of Jack Hobbs were behind him. He was slower – but shrewder. So in 1946–47 he quickly concluded that Australia's interests would be better served by his presence nearer the wicket. Keith Miller was posted to cover point (with much success) and the Don captained Australia from mid-on or mid-off: in those positions he was still able to maintain a reputation as an above average fielder. The younger men in the side now naturally did more of the running, and Bradman was in correspondingly closer contact with his bowlers. He has admitted that the thrills of outfielding were, for him, never equalled when in a close-in position, but there is no doubt he was very good indeed there. In assessing the career of Don Bradman, one must never forget the immense number of runs his fielding saved, whether on the boundary, in the covers or close to the wicket. He dropped his occasional catches like any other man – but very few indeed, as it happens, while he was captaining a side – and characteristically observed that each dropped catch was something *more* than giving the other side an extra batsman because the batsman had by then usually become accustomed to the light and the pitch and the bowlers became progressively more tired.

But Bradman's contribution to the 1946–47 series did not lay in his fielding. It was his batsmanship and his captaincy that shone forth time and again. He was now a man of vast experience, steeped in the ways of Test cricket and wedded immovably to the concept of Test cricket as a matter of life and death. He certainly took up the cudgels precisely where he had laid them down, in some humiliation, eight years before. He was still the little giant, no less anxious than he had been in 1930 to make bowlers feel, as P. F. Warner then put it, that bowling at Bradman was like throwing stones at the Rock of Gibraltar. His knowledge of Australian wickets was intimate. His knowledge of opposing batsmen was a crucial aid to his bowlers. And of course he had a very talented side under him. The clash of personalities between Bradman and Hammond, which brought bad feeling to the first post-war series in

Australia, was the saddest thing of that series. Hammond was a changed man in Australia, without doubt, and both he and Bradman showed faults to create animosities. But if Walter Hammond, with or without instructions from Lord's on the matter, had chosen to anticipate a goodwill tour of Australia in '46–47, Don Bradman, the stern realist, did not go out of his way to accommodate him.

As for his batting, he was as difficult as ever to dismiss, despite his early uncertainties at the crease. He still believed that he, and not the bowler, must dominate the scene. The speedy co-ordination of mind and body was not there as it had been before the war, but his repertoire of strokes was none the less impressive – especially for one who had been 'written off'. The runs still flowed, and he scored considerably more than any other man in the series – 680, compiled at 33·33 per hour: not up to the golden years of the early '30s but, remarkably enough, faster than his runs in the series of 1936–37 and 1938. And his Test average was of course 97·14. Although he rationed his first-class cricket carefully, he still passed 1,000 runs for the season and topped the seasonal averages, ahead of any Australian or Englishman. He had achieved also the uncommon distinction of scoring 50 or over in at least one innings of all five Tests, ending the rubber with 12 and 63 at Sydney. The fifth Test over, Australia having won the series 3–0, Bradman announced he would be available to play against the Indians the following summer.

So Bradman's reputation, which he had put squarely at risk, was still intact. If anything, his stature was increased: and he had introduced himself, as a living legend, to a new generation of enthusiasts. A delightful and little-known story of that season must be recorded for its obvious significance. Between the second and third Tests Bradman took a holiday from his Adelaide stockbroking business, but it was a busman's holiday that took him to Melbourne. He went there from the Sydney Test, and when the Victoria–New South Wales Shield match was played, he was duly watching. The Davis Cup was the rage of Melbourne at that moment, and Bradman's interest in tennis was not minimal. One morning he was asked whether he would be watching the cricket or the tennis that day, and he replied: 'Cricket – where I shall learn something. I have never yet watched a day's cricket without learning something.'

12 Prelude to Triumph

*I love to play against him, and that goes for all my players, because he is such a
great sportsman and a thorough gentleman.*

> Lala Amarnath, India's captain, on D. G. Bradman,
> at Melbourne after the third Test, January 1948

In the Australian winter of 1947, Don Bradman, captain of Australia, had
ample time to take stock of things. He could look back, with something
approaching disbelief, at a wonderful summer against England in which he
had helped to rewrite the record books. His decision to play had been
triumphantly justified. Australian grounds still thrilled – and filled – to the
magic of his name. The spectacle of Test cricket was occupying its old place
on the cricket scene, and in England there was vast enthusiasm for Alan
Melville's South Africans and especially for the runs that Edrich and
Compton were taking off them. In a few months' time, the first touring side
ever to visit Australia from India would be arriving.

The programme of future tours also included an Australian visit to England
in 1948 – as to which the Don remained silent in announcing his availability
to play against the Indians. At this stage of his career the wisest course – and
in such matters Don Bradman would instinctively take the wisest course –
was to take the seasons singly and ensure that ambition would not o'erleap
itself. The dramatic eclipse of Walter Hammond had shown what one season
could do to a cricketer and his fame. Meanwhile, that Australian winter of
1947 witnessed an improvement in Bradman's health.

The prospect of playing against Bradman was something the Indians
looked forward to keenly, to a man. Pankaj Gupta, the manager, and
Amarnath, the captain, publicly declared their hope that Bradman would
play – they wanted to learn from him.[1] The dazzling form that Bradman was
to produce could have been anticipated neither by himself nor by the
tourists. It is a pity that Fazal Mahmood, an original selection for the tour,
could not go, being translated in Lahore from an Indian to a Pakistani
between the selection and departure of the side. Highly praised by Duleepsinhji, his duels with Bradman, like Bedser's the season before, would have
been interesting. V. M. Merchant, the originally appointed captain, also

---

[1] These remarks were construed by some Indian critics as deliberate flattery and a ruse to
gain popularity, calculated to lower the team's morale. Outstanding as Bradman was as a
cricketer, there were objections that the Indians – not least in their own eyes – should be going
to do battle with Bradman as 'students'.

could not tour; nor could Mushtaq Ali or Modi, and the side was accordingly weakened. Moreover India were to play a five-Test series for the first time ever.

Bradman was hardly tested at all seriously by the Indian bowling. Only Mankad came through the tour with any honour, and in the Tests even he was a failure. But against a weak or a strong side, Bradman's battle plan was unaltered – to win and to be the best. His ambition was still exceptional and insatiable. If records were there to be wrecked, the remorseless bat was as willing as ever.

Just as he had announced himself with a century against the first English side he ever met (Chapman's team in '28–29) and also against the first South African side he encountered (Cameron's in '31–32), so Bradman like-wise greeted Amarnath's Indians. In his first outing of the season Bradman reached his century in 98 minutes for South Australia against the tourists and took his score next morning to 156 at more than a run a minute – the aperitif, as it were, to the amassing of more than 1,000 runs that season off the Indian bowlers alone. In his heyday of 1931–32, when he was 23 years old, Bradman averaged three figures in both the Test series and in all first-class matches in the season. Now, at 39, he did it again, with the additional cares of captaincy, selectorship and business. Such was his astonishing form in 1947–48, when he scored eight centuries in the 12 innings he played, that it seemed a fresh Bradman heyday had arrived, tempered only by the know-ledge of the comparative weakness of the bowlers he faced.

But in his only Shield innings of that summer, against Victoria at Adelaide, he faced five bowlers who either were or by the end of that season had become Test match bowlers – and scored a chanceless 100. It was his 99th three-figure innings in the first-class game. That Shield match ended on Tuesday, 11 November, and on the Friday the Don was due in Sydney to captain an Australian XI against the Indians. Sydney was his favourite ground, where he had already scored 21 of his 99 centuries – more than on any other ground on which he had played. The prospect of reaching his hundredth there was as appealing to him as to the Sydney spectators, and with all the fuss made in the newspapers and on the radio no one was in any doubt about the significance of the occasion. Sydney forgot its dearer bread, the bitter struggle over the Banking Bill and that the New South Wales wheat crop was in jeopardy: all went to see Bradman. It so happens that Bradman lost the toss, but thereby, as though carefully stage-managed, he made his entry to the crease before a Saturday crowd. It was a huge crowd, containing many who had witnessed some marvellous feats by the Don on this ground, not least his triple-century as a 20-year-old and his world record score a year later. For 20 years his name had been on the lips of Sydney cricket-lovers.

Bradman was not to disappoint them on this auspicious day. He batted cautiously, but reached his half-century in 78 minutes, despite having hit only two fours. Miller was his partner. A risky second run in the nineties nearly spoilt all. Then he was 99, and hardly a spectator moved. It was the last over before tea. Amarnath summoned Kishenchand from the boundary – a man who had not bowled a ball so far on the tour, an unknown quantity. The Don matched shrewdness with shrewdness, but it would not have been in his nature to play out a maiden and go in to tea with 99. The second ball was pushed wide of mid-on for a single and the deed was done. Bradman had scored 100 out of 177 since he came in, in 132 minutes. The second fifty of this important innings had taken him only 54 minutes. He raised his cap to the applauding crowd and Miller shook him by the hand. It was a moment of great emotion and one to be treasured. Sir Donald himself has said of it: 'I think of all my experiences in cricket that was my most exhilarating moment on the field. The huge crowd gave me a reception which was moving in its spontaneous warmth.'

The innings was continued to 172 after tea, the last 72 coming in 45 minutes of most brilliant cricket. Bradman sped from 100 to 150 in only 29 minutes, he and Miller at one stage adding 50 in 16 minutes. Bradman was quite irresistible, and toyed with the bowling like a magician. The crowd were delirious with delight – more than 32,000 were watching – and after it was all over, there were some people who chose never to go to the Sydney Cricket Ground again but who rested content with the imperishable memory of a brilliant innings by a brilliant man. When Bradman was out, the crowd went home: and when stumps were drawn for the day, only a few thousand remained. A hit for six by Bradman that evening struck a young girl, not seriously, and she no doubt still boasts of the happening. Those who say that Don Bradman was not the same batsman after the war as before it are, in general terms, correct. But on that Saturday at Sydney, all the skills and all the stroke-play of the youthful conqueror cascaded forth again. The clock, for three-quarters of an hour at least, had been put back.

When he was asked after that intoxicating innings whether he was good for another 20 or 30 centuries in the first-class game, he wisely declined to comment. When asked if he was stiff, he smilingly replied: 'No. Why should I be?' He spent the Sunday at the home of friends and looked fitter than at any time during the previous season. W. J. O'Reilly had watched the 172 from the Sydney press-box and he knew well enough what the innings meant. On Monday morning his newspaper carried these words by him:

In his innings on Saturday Don Bradman showed not the slightest trace of the wear and tear of time so noticeable in his batting last year.

His running between the wickets, his extraordinary self-confidence, and his ability seemingly to read the bowlers' minds combined to make the innings a Bradman masterpiece.

There is no doubt that he has regained his health and strength and that he can, if he wishes, undertake the strain of another English tour.

The speed with which the runs came from Bradman's bat left the Indian bowlers and fieldsmen spell-bound.

They have found out, in the only way possible, that there is no effective answer, either with the ball or the placing of the field, when the real Bradman is going at full blast.

A film was made of the highlights of that hundredth hundred, and when it was shown in England R. C. Robertson-Glasgow joyously pointed out that at the historic and statistical moment, when Bradman was about to go from 99 to 100, there was the Indian bowler 'trying to deliver the ball with one hand and applaud with the other, a feat that is beyond the most enthusiastic practitioner'. It was quite an occasion!

Oddly enough Bradman was on the losing side in that match – the only time in his post-war career he experienced this against non-Australian opponents. Altogether after the war he played in 46 first-class games and was on the losing side in only three: the other two were Shield matches in '46–47 and '48–49 (his very last game).

The hundredth century, of course, was not unexpected. When he made up his mind to return to serious cricket in October 1946, he already had 93 first-class hundreds. Once his fitness and form survived that season (when four more hundreds were added) it was only a matter of time – and not too long a time at that, in Bradman's case – for the magical landmark to be reached. He reached it in the quite astonishing number of only 295 innings. His old adversary, Walter Hammond, on hearing the news, could hardly have relished the reminder that *his* hundred hundreds had taken him 680 innings. Nevertheless, Hammond had then been the record-holder. Frank Woolley had needed more than 1,000.[1]

Characteristically, Bradman went to his hundredth hundred at the earliest possible opportunity – in his very next innings after his 99th. Only Colin Cowdrey (at Maidstone in 1973) and Geoffrey Boycott (at Headingley in 1977) share this distinction. Most players have dawdled nervously as their hundredth hundred has come on the horizon, but Bradman, who began the season with 97, in his first four visits to the crease made 156, 12, 100, and 172, all in the space of 23 days. At the time that Bradman achieved his feat (and also at the time of his retirement), only one other Australian had reached even 50 first-class centuries – Warren Bardsley (53).

This may be a convenient moment to emphasise what all the world knows – that Bradman, on average, scored a century every third visit to the

---

[1] Bradman's unparalleled consistency, not only in relation to his own contemporaries, is illustrated by the following table embracing the 18 cricketers in history who have scored 100 first-class centuries:

	Innings required to reach 100th century		Innings required to reach 100th century
D. G. Bradman	295	C. P. Mead	892
D. C. S. Compton	552	L. E. G. Ames	916
L. Hutton	619	E. Tyldesley	919
G. Boycott	645	T. W. Graveney	940
W. R. Hammond	680	J. H. Edrich	945
H. Sutcliffe	700	F. E. Woolley	1,029
E. H. Hendren	740	M. C. Cowdrey	1,035
J. B. Hobbs	819	T. W. Hayward	1,076
A. Sandham	871	W. G. Grace	1,114

wicket in his career. At the start of the 1947–48 season his hundreds were 97 in 291 innings – one in three dead. He was actually to improve on that by the time he retired, so that his final percentage was 34·61. His dominance in this particular field is illustrated by the following table of those who have made centuries most frequently:

						Century Frequency
D. G. Bradman	–	117	centuries in	338	inns.	34·61%
G. A. Headley	–	33	,,	,,	164	,,	20·12%
W. M. Woodfull	–	49	,,	,,	245	,,	20·00%
W. H. Ponsford	–	47	,,	,,	235	,,	20·00%
V. M. Merchant	–	43	,,	,,	221	,,	19·45%
A. R. Morris	–	46	,,	,,	242	,,	19·00%
A. L. Hassett	–	59	,,	,,	322	,,	18·32%
A. F. Kippax	–	43	,,	,,	254	,,	16·92%
C. L. Walcott	–	40	,,	,,	238	,,	16·80%
W. R. Hammond	–	167	,,	,,	1005	,,	16·61%
C. L. Badcock	–	26	,,	,,	159	,,	16·35%

Bradman actually scored his 117 centuries in 234 matches – an average of precisely one century every other match. This, too, has been quite unapproached by any other player in the first-class game. (In four of the matches in which he appeared, he did not bat for one reason or another.) Given the same number of career innings as W. G. Grace, on this reckoning his hundreds would have been 517!

Centuries were very much on the agenda for Bradman against the Indians of 1947–48. After his memorable 172 at Sydney, he opened the Test series with 185 at Brisbane. This was an astonishing innings, in which he put all other batsmen in the match quite in the shade, not least the mercurial Keith Miller, one of those rivalling Bradman in public popularity. When Miller came to the crease during the final session of the first day, Bradman was 91 not out. Of the first 50 they put on together for the fourth wicket, Miller made 3. The stand was unbroken at close of play, having added 75 – of which Bradman made 69 and Miller 6. After passing his century, Bradman scored his next fifty in 33 minutes while Miller was almost impotent. Bad light ended play with the Don 160 not out, having scored 74 of Australia's final 90 runs of the day.

Within less than 24 hours Bradman was being hooted in best Australian fashion by the Brisbane crowd when the state of the pitch held up play until five o'clock. In fact it was he who wanted to play and Amarnath who did not, and in the end, in unpleasant conditions, there was another hour's cricket. On the third morning Bradman was out for 185, hitting his wicket down from behind – the one and only occasion in his entire career that he was out 'hit wicket' in a first-class match. The explanation for this apparent aberration, and for the extraordinary fact of the wicket being struck down *from behind*, is contained in the story that towards the end of his innings, with

324 Prelude to Triumph

the wicket rapidly becoming sticky, Bradman invited the wicketkeeper or a close fielder to nominate spots where he should hit the ball. After two successful sorties, Bradman then gave himself plenty of room and attempted an exotic cut over the head of point, with fatal results – or so the story goes. Once again the rains of Brisbane made conditions hopeless, and Bradman's individual 185 was comfortably in excess of the combined two-innings totals of India (58 and 98). This particular achievement was yet another Bradman record, for it was the third time off his own bat that he had engulfed his opponents in this way – the earlier occasions being his 452 not out and his 369. Percy Holmes, of Yorkshire, shares this unusual record.

Bradman's only failure of the season – bowled for 13 by an off-cutter from Hazare that sent one of the bails nearly 60 yards – came in the rain-ruined second Test at Sydney. On a rain-soaked wicket, Australia were all out for 107. Apart from the wholly abandoned Melbourne Test of 1970–71, there were fewer hours of actual play in this Test than in any other Test in Australia. This was a sadness, for it was the Don's farewell to Test cricket at Sydney.

On the first day of this Sydney Test, Bradman – for so many still the pride of New South Wales, for all his residence in Adelaide – received two presentations to commemorate his hundredth century in first-class cricket. During the luncheon interval, the New South Wales Cricket Association presented him with a handsome 39-piece set of cut glass; and at a dinner to Bradman at the Sydney Cricket Ground rooms after the day's play, attended by both the Australian and Indian players, he was presented with a canteen of cutlery from the S.C.G. trustees. During the luncheon presentation, in his reply of thanks, Bradman remarked: 'It can't be very long before I shall have to put my bat away for good.' But when he was taxed about the matter that night he said he had not decided to retire at the end of either that season or the next – his retirement, he said, would probably depend on his health and on his business. Informed circles were quietly confident, however, that he was planning his swansong in international cricket to be the English tour of 1948.

The one honour that had thus far eluded Don Bradman in his phenomenal Test career – at that moment his Test average was 97·88 – was the scoring of a century in each innings of a match, though he had already achieved this three times outside Tests. This omission was duly rectified in the New Year Test at Melbourne when, passing 6,000 runs in Test cricket, he emerged with scores of 132 and 127 not out, both of them chanceless. At 39 years of age he was, and remains, the oldest player to score two hundreds in a Test. He was also the first Australian captain to achieve this feat: up to then, only one Test captain in history had done it – Alan Melville, just a matter of seven months before. The one ball in the match that defeated Bradman (he was lbw to Phadkar in the first innings) was played immediately after an attack of cramp, when he swung wildly at the very next ball. Bradman played his 300th first-class innings in this match, and in it completed 25,000 runs – needless to say, far and away the fewest number of innings needed to reach this landmark.

It was little wonder that on the day after the Melbourne Test ended, with Bradman's average for the series now soaring into the 150s, Lala Amarnath should have said that without doubt Bradman was the greatest batsman he had seen. He considered his form on that tour – and the slaughter at Adelaide was yet to come! – to be as good as when he had seen him make a century at Lord's in 1938. Ominous words indeed to those English ears they might have reached!

With each successive innings this season the virtual certainty of Bradman making the trip to England became stronger. In all probability he had made up his mind before the season began, but with both common sense and a careful eye on his health, deemed it politic to let the season run its course before a public announcement. His tactical conversations with his players during that series with India led them to conclude that England was very much in the forefront of his mind: but of course Bradman could have been talking as much qua selector as prospective captain.

Bradman excelled himself at Adelaide in the fourth Test with a shattering double-century – 201 in 272 minutes before he threw his wicket away. For the sixth time (another world record) he had scored 200 or more runs in a single day's play in a Test. It all seemed too easy. The score occasioned no surprise, either in Australia or in England, where it was viewed – together with his other big scores that season – with an ominous foreboding.[1] It was the Don's 37th double-century of his career and the one he especially wanted, for it put him safely ahead of Hammond's 36. In the endless rivalry between Bradman and Hammond, the little man always seemed to edge in front.

The Adelaide innings marked also the sixth time he had scored 100 or more runs in a single session of play in a Test, yet another Test record, by an easy margin.[2] The first time he had done so – with great panache at Lord's in 1930 – he was only 21: now he was nearly 40, and scoring with such brilliance that he took his score from 100 to 200 in only 79 minutes – the fastest 100 runs he made in any of the 29 centuries of his Test career. Only a few of those centuries could be termed 'slow', and his individual rate of scoring over the whole of those 29 innings was 39·17 runs an hour. Now, at Adelaide, the oldest man on the field was scoring at 44 an hour off his own bat throughout the day and – after no more than the rest and refreshment of the tea interval – one golden spell of 75 an hour! It was the last time Adelaide was to see him as a Test cricketer, and it was the only ground in the world on

---

[1] The English public, ever since Bradman's performances against Hammond's side, were virtually satisfied that he would come to England in '48 – and come in good form. On the very first day of the series v India, a London paper announced Bradman's 24th Test century in its headline, and added the words: 'Our turn comes next.'

[2] The six occasions on which he performed this rare feat were as follows:

54*–155*	between tea and close on 2nd day in 254 v England	Lord's	1930
0 –105*	between start and lunch on 1st day in 334 v England	Headingley	1930
105*–220*	between lunch and tea on 1st day in 334 v England	Headingley	1930
169*–271*	between tea and close on 2nd day in 304 v England	Headingley	1934
43*–150*	between lunch and tea on 1st day in 244 v England	Oval	1934
94*–201	between tea and close on 1st day in 201 v India	Adelaide	1947-48

which he bade his farewell to the Test match scene with a double-century. The innings (which remains the highest ever played in Australia–India Tests) was his sixth century against Amarnath's side in six matches – precisely the ratio he recorded against the South African tourists when in his very prime in 1931–32. While Bradman was at the crease, he was scoring, as has been said, at 44 an hour, while his younger and by no means untalented partners, Barnes and Hassett, even with extras thrown in, could manage between them no more than 30 an hour. Bradman's 201 was the twelfth and last time he reached a double-century in a Test, his nearest rival in this respect being Walter Hammond, with seven instances – and among Australians R. B. Simpson with three. Bradman and Hammond played in an era when Test matches were nothing like so frequent as they became after their retirement: nevertheless, from 1950 to date, only a single player (Simpson) has made even three double-hundreds for his country.

C. R. Rangachari, of India, was making his Test debut in that Adelaide match, and meeting Bradman for the first time on the field. He was a useful fast bowler and claims that off his very first ball to Bradman, when his score was 2, a catch was edged to the slips. Amarnath's lumbago was supposed to be why it was not held. When Bradman was out for 201 and the Australian innings over for 674, Bradman sought out Rangachari in the dressing-room to congratulate him on having bowled 'like a Trojan' – a memory (and an inscribed photograph to go with it) that Rangachari has treasured ever since. Bradman, always generous in congratulating his opponents on the field for any special act of distinction, was the first to shake the hand at Adelaide of V. S. Hazare when he emulated the Don's own performance at Melbourne by scoring a century in each innings. Hazare's feat was actually unique in Test cricket, and is so still: for it is the only time that a batsman has scored two hundreds in a Test when his side has followed on.

That Adelaide Test against India was important for Don Bradman for another reason. He was on the verge of announcing his availability for England and, though there could hardly have been a scintilla of doubt at that stage, his double-century must have clinched the issue decisively. Though the Board, and not the selectors, would appoint the captain, it was a cricketing certainty that he would be captain if he went. The cornerstone of Australia's attack in England was to be the fast bowling of Lindwall, whose alleged tendency to 'drag' had flared into an issue in 1947–48. Lindwall's action was specially filmed during the Adelaide Test, and apart from Lindwall himself, the man most vitally interested in the film was Don Bradman, his captain. Indeed, the film was of paramount importance to Bradman if he was to give the proper advice to his key bowler to enable him to pass not only Australian umpires but, more importantly, English ones. Bradman attended a private showing of the film, together with members of the Australian Board. He then publicly declared he was satisfied with the fairness of Lindwall's delivery. This was certainly an honest expression of opinion, though officials of Lindwall's own State of New South Wales were not so satisfied on the evidence of an earlier film. At all events, the Don was armed with the facts and his diagnosis was ready, if needed. In due course he thrashed the matter out logically and lengthily with Lindwall – the boat ride to England was the ideal time for the talks – and under Bradman's captaincy Lindwall progressed through the '48 tour with virtually no mishaps, despite an unprecedented number of cameras at Worcester filming his feet in the hope of some early sensation.

At the Melbourne Cricket Ground on 6 February 1948 Don Bradman played his last Test innings on Australian soil. Everyone knew that this was his final Test in Australia, for on the evening before the Test began he informed the press of this fact – and also of the momentous decision they were all awaiting. The historic statement, read personally by Don Bradman to the gathering of pressmen in his hotel room in Melbourne that evening, was characteristically concise and to the point: 'I have today advised my co-selectors that I am available for the Australian tour of England. At the same time I wish to say that the game against India will be my last first-class match in Australia, as I shall retire from cricket at the conclusion of the English tour.'

The Bradman era was not yet over, but nearly so. The Don's decision – his two decisions – had not been made hastily. Each of course had an immense significance: the tour to England, with Don Bradman's name to the fore, almost guaranteed a summer of high interest; and then, thereafter, a certain emptiness. The news was at once joyous and sad. Bradman was quite unemotional over the announcement. He stated merely facts. But there was hardly a cricket-lover in the world, when the news became known, who was not moved by the impending departure from the scene of the greatest match-winner in history. But first there was a tour of England – and before that a Test match against India.

The best-laid plans of mice and men gang aft agley: and if Bradman had intended at Melbourne to win the toss, score a century and see Australia home by an innings in his final Test in his native land, he could hardly have been blamed. He very nearly pulled off all three, failing only in the final personal glory of a farewell hundred. He played in fine form to reach 57 in less than an hour and a half, then a torn muscle in his left side below the ribs caused him to retire hurt. The Melbourne crowd rose to him on his return – mindful that on this great ground he had scored more Test runs than on any other in the world; that here alone he had scored nine Test hundreds – more than Trumper or Hill or Macartney or Woodfull or Ponsford had managed in their *entire* Test careers; and that on this ground the little man's Test average, had they bothered to work it out, stood at 128·53. Bradman never returned to complete his innings (the necessity was not there anyway, with Australia comfortably passing 500) but he was able to take the field on the last two days to see the series to an end. Australia won it 4–0, with one match drawn, and, for Australian spectators at least, Bradman passed from the Test scene on the afternoon of Tuesday, 10 February 1948. Although he was committed to a tour of England, it is interesting that had Bradman actually retired from Test cricket at the end of the series against India, his Test average would have been 102·98. As it was, it dropped below the 100 mark – just!

The Indians had taken a very heavy beating at Bradman's hands, in his capacity as both batsman and captain. If he had looked forward to some easy pickings against a side of moderate bowlers, he certainly gathered in a cornucopia – 1,081 runs altogether off the Indians at 135·12 and 715 runs in the Tests alone at the marvellous average of 178·75. Despite all the glorious seasons of the past, he now set up one further record: his eight hundreds created a new record for an Australian season, and one that still stands. People noticed, too, a 'new look' about Bradman that season on the field that had not been the case the previous summer against England, when nothing at all was yielded. (Walter Hammond later said that he found Bradman 'tougher than ever' in '46–47.) Before the series against India started, one famous Australian critic wrote: 'If Bradman can't bring a better spirit to the game than that this season, then it would be better if he retired and concentrated on business.' But – perhaps because India were not Australia's traditional enemies and there was no equivalent of the Oval '38 to erase from the scene – Bradman *did* bring a better spirit to the game in 1947–48, when he was altogether more gracious and harmonious. This spirit, happily, was to continue in England in '48. The inevitable voices of criticism, for all that, were still audible. The former Australian captain, V. Y. Richardson, and Bradman's predecessor as captain of South Australia, reported on the 1947–48 series with India for the *Illustrated News* of Calcutta, and in writing of the fifth Test at Melbourne he said: 'Bradman has played this series of Tests in a very austere fashion and the Indian team has been given no quarter or privilege of any kind and has battled against a team eager to win by as big a margin as possible on every occasion.' The Indians let themselves down to some extent, but it must be also proper to say that Bradman's intention to build up a strong and confident side for the forthcoming tour of England was a motive as laudable as it was reasonable.

The criticisms of Bradman off the field also continued. Before his plans for 1948 were made known (but when he had already declared himself available against India) he was obliged in October 1947 to write a letter to the Adelaide *Advertiser* saying: 'It seems, as the season opens here again, that I am to be an Aunt Sally for certain people who endeavour to draw attention to themselves by criticising me.' He explained that he had refused an offer to write certain newspaper articles because he was asked to follow a contentious and provocative line. No sum, he said, would ever tempt him to write in that way. Bradman's primary consideration, both in 1947 and at all other times, was for the well-being of Australian cricket. And his actions, and those of his critics, must be judged by posterity in that light.

Bradman's mastery over Amarnath's side in 1947–48 was such that the Indian Board of Control, in the midst of that season, earnestly asked for a

29 Bradman the soldier. Lt D. G.
Bradman at the Army School of Physical
Training, Frankston, Victoria, in 1940.
He was invalided out of the Army in the
middle of 1941.

30 A trinity of batsmen who scored over
400 first-class centuries between them:
J. B. Hobbs, D. G. Bradman and C. B.
Fry at the Institute of Journalists' luncheon
at the Grosvenor House Hotel, London,
in 1948.

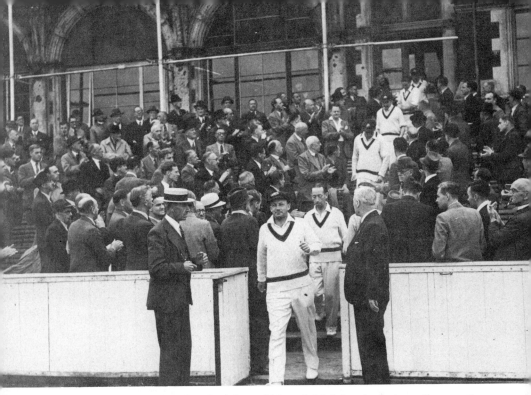

31 Don Bradman, a few days short of his 40th birthday, leads Australia onto the field at the Oval in the final Test match of his illustrious career. Australia won this match – the fifth Test of 1948 – by an an innings and 149 runs.

32 Don Bradman's arrival at the crease in his final Test innings at the Oval in 1948. England's captain, Norman Yardley, calls for three cheers. Was Bradman affected by the reception? Two balls later he was out for 0.

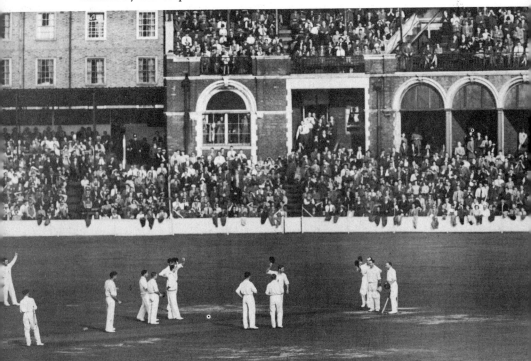

33 The final exit. Don Bradman's last moment as a batsman on a Test match field – bowled by Hollies for 0, second ball, at the Oval, 1948.

34 A Balmoral scene, September 1948. Don Bradman with the Queen, the King and Princess Margaret. On the right is Keith Johnson, the Australian manager.

35 Bradman the umpire. A rare picture of Sir Donald Bradman in the role of umpire, taken at the Adelaide Oval in January 1949 when he and Mr Tom Playford, Premier of South Australia, umpired a match between local industrial and commercial teams.

36 The Bradman family in Adelaide after returning from a holiday soon after the announcement of Sir Donald's knighthood in 1949. At the car window are John, then aged 9, and Shirley, aged 7.

37 Concentration of a different kind. Sir Donald Bradman practises with a
putter on the lounge floor of his home at Kensington Park, Adelaide. As a golfer,
Sir Donald has proved no mean opponent.

38 Sir Donald Bradman talks to England's captain, Len Hutton, on the first morning of the 1953 series at Trent Bridge. Sir Donald was in England to write on a Test series for the first time.

39 A piquant juxtaposition – Sir Donald Bradman and D. R. Jardine find themselves seated side by side in the press box at Headingley during the England–Australia Test of 1953.

40 A Bradman family scene in 1956 – Sir Donald and Lady Bradman and their two children, John and Shirley.

41 Two of the most trenchant cricket brains of modern times converse at Lord's during the Imperial Cricket Conference meeting of 1960: G. O. Allen, left, and Sir Donald Bradman.

42 A triumvirate of selectors – Dudley Seddon, Sir Donald Bradman and Jack Ryder meet in Melbourne early in 1956 prior to the announcement of that year's touring side for England.

43 Sir Donald Bradman, selector, in dark glasses, with R. B. Simpson, Australia's captain, at a practice session during the second Test against England at Melbourne, January 1966.

visit by Bradman to their country, either on an official or unofficial tour, so that Indian spectators might see him in action before he retired. Bradman was no longer in his pristine youth, and his energies had to be concentrated on a tour of England. But even so, one wonders what sort of carnage he may have wreaked had he batted on those marvellous batting pitches of India in the 1940s. (India had been deprived by the war of what was hoped to have been a four-month visit by Australia in 1940–41, on terms proposed by Frank Tarrant to the Indian Board of Control. Like the side Tarrant gathered five years before to visit India, the team would doubtless have been something of a mixed bag, but even if there had been no war, and if Bradman had not contracted fibrositis, he would still have been unavailable for Tarrant's side, for England were due to visit Australia in 1940–41 and Bradman would presumably have played in that series. Bradman, incidentally, more than once had offers from India to go there on his own terms, but he never yielded to them.)

13 Apotheosis '48

There's nothing new to say about Bradman, any more than there is about Moiseiwitsch, or the Tower of London.

R. C. Robertson-Glasgow in April 1948

The day after the series against India was over – on 11 February 1948 – the Australian team to visit England was announced. Bradman's name, naturally, was among them, and two days later the Board secretary, W. H. Jeanes, in Adelaide announced Bradman's appointment as captain. Bradman was, of course, one of the selectors who chose the party, once again with 'Chappie' Dwyer and Jack Ryder. He was also, of course, ten years older than on his last visit to England, when the strains of captaincy had proved considerable. Before the touring names were announced, Bradman said: 'I recognise that another tour at my age will be a heavy responsibility – one which I feel reluctant to accept – but if required to do so, I feel this would be my final opportunity to serve the game which has played such a big part in my life.' Once again Bradman had set his face against the implorations of Fleet Street. He could have commanded – and indeed was offered – the sort of fees paid by newspapers to the most distinguished of statesmen, if he had chosen to write on the 1948 tour. The advice of at least one close friend was to accept it. But as in 1946–47, Bradman said Australian cricket must come first. At one time rumour had been so strong that in August 1947 Bradman had had to issue a denial that he had actually signed a contract to write on the '48 Tests. The lure of the game won – as did the prospect (not an easy one) of adding further lustre to his great deeds on English soil by way of a golden farewell.

Bradman had many more reservations about his prospective run-getting in 1948 than the public had. English cricket lovers were delighted at the anticipation of his reappearance and gave no more thought to his being subject to mortal error than they had ten years before. A double-century at Worcester was freely predicted by professional critic and layman alike. As usual, it was Neville Cardus who expressed most exactly – and most felicitously – the prevailing mood of anticipation when he sent his first piece to begin his association with the *Sunday Times* in February 1948. He was still then in Australia and was to travel back to England with Bradman's team, and this is part of what he wrote:

Cricketers in England will rejoice that the last rays of Bradman's splendour will fall on the greenest fields in the world. He remains the absolute master, harder to get out than ever before, because he plays closer to the ball today than ever before. Also he has eliminated from his technique anything which in the past we could describe – with reckless use of language – as faintly approaching the empirical.

Bradman nowadays keeps within his limitations in a way that Goethe himself might conceivably regard as excessive . . .

No author of fiction for schoolboys would dare allow his hero to achieve chapter by chapter the consistent majesty and magnitude of Bradman; he would make him fail more often, if for no reason except from a conscientious artist's wish to respect Aristotelean notions of probability. A duck by Bradman is against nature; a duck by Bradman will next season be as momentous news as ever, and as taxing to the credulity.

The fact that Bradman was about to undertake a tour of England in his 40th year meant far less in 1948 than it might mean today. The age of 40 was decidedly not considered the veteran stage in English cricket 30 years ago, even though for most Australians it may have been 'old'. (In 1948 nearly 50 players appeared in first-class cricket in England at the age of 40 or over.) Bradman's past record – and especially his immediate past record against England and India since the war – was enough for most people still to hail him as 'the little wonder', in Fleetwood-Smith's phrase. If a later generation was to think of Ray Illingworth as Biggles and Batman rolled into one, Bradman in 1948 was certainly a combination of Hercules and Napoleon – even before the tour began. Just as Australian crowds sighed in gratitude at the very fact that he was able to turn out again in '46–47, so English crowds were prepared to welcome him just because his name was Bradman

The Australian touring team once again visited Tasmania – this time they flew there for the first time – before sailing for England. The muscle that Bradman had torn in his left side in the fifth Test against India was still worrying him, and Keith Johnson, the manager, admitted that the injury was not mending satisfactorily. Unnecessary risk was inadvisable, and at Hobart, in a two-day match, Bradman had no intention of repeating his 1938 century (he gave up his wicket to a catch in the outfield when 45, made in only 34 minutes) and withdrew from the match at Launceston. The sea trip to England would, it was hoped, effect a cure. 'This will be my last tour abroad', commented Bradman at the V.C.A. dinner to the Australian team at Melbourne on their return to the mainland, 'and I shall do my best to see Australia is well served.' One final match was played at Perth, when Bradman, though declaring himself not thoroughly fit when he practised there, did play and batted for a little over two hours for a chanceless 115, which seemed to dispel doubts about his condition. He thus set off for England with an average for the season of 129·60 and a record number of eight centuries in an Australian season. As in 1938, the second best average in Australia belonged to Lindsay Hassett, this time with 68·69.

The *Strathaird* left Fremantle on 19 March 1948 with Don Bradman coming to England for the second time as captain – a circumstance made possible only by the hiatus of the Second World War. That same hiatus, which had starved Englishmen of the sight of him for ten years, guaranteed him a reception on English grounds that was not to be entirely dependent on his

27—DON BRADMAN
All eyes will be on Don Bradman, greatest Australian cricketer, this summer. Will he smash more cricket records during the forthcoming Tests?

A 1948 pen and ink drawing of Australia's captain by Jack Dunkley of the London *Daily Mirror*.

success with the bat. If runs were to come, Bradman would certainly be received rapturously; if not, he would be received sympathetically and warmly. By the end of the tour Robertson-Glasgow was able to affirm that 'next to Mr Winston Churchill, he was the most celebrated man in England during the summer of 1948'.

Two receptions awaited Bradman before he arrived in England. At Colombo, the usual one-day game was played against Ceylon. The Colombo Oval was packed to see Bradman play his first match in the island since 1930. Under a fierce sun, he came in to a huge welcome, wearing a topee, when Brown was quickly out for 3. He scored a sedate 20 before being caught at cover off Russel Heyn. It was not until later in the day that it was discovered that the match was being played on a pitch of 20 yards!

At the Grand Oriental Hotel that evening a sumptuous dinner was given to Bradman and his team, before the *Strathaird* moved off to Bombay. Don Bradman's name in India was, if anything, even more of a legend than in other parts of the cricketing world, not least so soon after his tremendous feats against their own cricketers in Australia in 1947–48. Don Bradman had never been to India in his life – though the Indians had urged him more than once to honour them with a visit – and to travel via Bombay was not the usual route for an Australian touring side to England. It is no secret that the Indians were extremely disappointed when Bradman did not disembark when the *Strathaird* docked alongside Ballard Pier in Bombay. They had their magnificent Brabourne Stadium to show off, and Bradman was the very man they wished to show it off to. There were mitigating reasons which prevented Bradman (and many others of the team) from leaving the ship, but Vijay Merchant, A. S. de Mello (President of the Indian Board) and Pankaj Gupta were obliged to go aboard to meet Bradman for a brief presentation ceremony – while prolonged shouts of 'We want Bradman' rose up from several hundreds of voices gathered on the quayside. Eventually the great man had to yield to the demands, and he appeared at the rail of the liner and waved his hand in greeting, to the great joy – and even greater applause – of the crowd below. That Bradman-mad crowd had managed to get past the customs officials and make their way to the very edge of the boat. There were some thousands more who were not so lucky and were out of sight, but waiting anxiously and lengthily – and, alas, in vain – for Bradman to emerge.

Then on through Aden, the Red Sea, Port Said and to England. Bradman did not make many appearances on the deck of the *Strathaird* – so few indeed that many passengers wondered if he was truly on board. His time was engaged in mapping out the details of the months before him, preparing for his rigorous schedule of speeches, preparing for the interviews that would come his way, answering correspondence (he seemed to be doing this throughout his career) and choosing to leave as little to chance as he could. He was very much aware of his own role as captain, especially as captain of the first Australian side in England since the war. There was something of the Jardine resolution in him in his application to detail. He was now a modern captain in a modern world; and, so far as he could achieve it, he aimed to be the complete captain. The *Strathaird* docked at Tilbury on the morning of 16 April, the first time Bradman had arrived in England via the Thames estuary and Tilbury – and now to greet him and his team was all the post-war panoply of newsreel cameras, press photographers, journalists and radio interviewers, as well as many cricketing friends like Maurice Tate, Bill Bowes, Alec Bedser, and C. B. Fry on the verge of his 76th birthday.

The part of a touring captain's role that Bradman disliked most – the succession of public speeches, so often in competition with practised professional orators – marked the start for him of the 1948 tour. To those in his audiences it seemed that he took it all in his stride. A vast audience in their homes heard an absolutely brilliant speech by him at the dinner given by the Cricket Writers' Club, when the B.B.C. took the rare step of allowing the broadcast to overrun its scheduled time and encroach upon the sacrosanct area of the nine o'clock news. The plaudits they received were many. The day before, at the Institute of Journalists lunch at Grosvenor House, Bradman said: 'I appeal to the press to make this tour one of friendship and goodwill, free from unfortunate incidents and sensations.' In the main this appeal was to be heeded, but there was to be a definite element of anti-Bradman and anti-Australian writing as the tour progressed. Campbell Dixon, in the

Daily Telegraph, after hearing the speech at Grosvenor House, remarked that Bradman 'has become a very good speaker' – which caused C. B. Fry at once to sit down in the Savile Club and disagree. He did not like the suggestion that it was a *fresh* gift. 'He has always been one of the best after-lunch or after-dinner speakers – doing what comes naturally. He is witty.'

What came naturally, too, to Donald Bradman was scoring runs, a greater priority for him in 1948 than speech-making. When Denis Compton saw him at the nets at Lord's, Bradman joked that if he wouldn't be batting better than he was in the nets, he wouldn't be good enough for the Test side. Compton asked him about his health. 'I never felt better', replied Bradman, and Compton certainly thought he looked much fitter than when they had last seen each other more than a year before. 'We are going to do our best to make this one of the greatest tours ever made by an Australian cricket team', said Bradman.

It is strange how people manage to congregate on station platforms to catch a sight of a public figure even when there has been no inkling that he was to be on that train. A considerable crowd gathered at Paddington on 27 April to see the Australians leave London for Worcester – though they really wanted a glimpse of Bradman. Andy Flanagan, the Australian sports critic, who accompanied the side, later put it this way: 'To travel throughout England with Bradman is a unique experience. Cities, towns and hotels are beflagged, carpets set down, and dignitaries wait to extend an official welcome. He is the Prince of Cricketers.'

Before a record three-day attendance at Worcester of 32,500, Bradman led the Australians to an innings victory to get the tour off to a good start. His own contribution – before a full house of 15,000 on the second day – was a chanceless 107, though by common consent a fourth double-century in four tours was there had he wished it. As it was, he played on to Peter Jackson after 2½ hours, deliberately giving his wicket away, to end his career on the New Road ground with the wonderful average of 201·75. His form was now not in question; nor was his appeal – to judge by the battery of photographers who jostled to get his picture as he came out to bat. 'We had read by suggestion', said the Cricket Correspondent of *The Times*, 'that something had been lost, or slightly diminished, of his past glory. That is not true, for yesterday we were privileged once again to see the batsman who is the complete proof that a bowler can bowl only so well as the striker allows him to do. A field cannot be set to such genius with the ability, in the twinkling of an eye, to find the exact stroke to any chosen part he may select . . . If any man can believe that Bradman is past his best he is welcome to spend an hour or so in bowling to him.'

The innings of 107 against Worcestershire completed a sequence of five centuries in six innings, a feat performed by Bradman a record number of three times in his career (1931–32, 1937–38 and 1938, 1947–48 and 1948) – quite apart from his six hundreds in six innings in 1938–39. No other player in history has ever got five centuries in six innings more than once, and it has always been a very rare achievement.

The $2\frac{1}{2}$ hours that Bradman batted at Worcester was to be just about his average time at the crease on his farewell tour of 1948. He was going to attempt no heroics and no mammoth scores, and with so much powerful batting in the side under him, there was no need for either. At Grace Road, Leicester, he was out for 81, to give a new opening bowler from Middlesex, M. W. Etherington, his first wicket in first-class cricket. The bowler doubtless never forgot the occasion, for he took only two further wickets in the remainder of his career, and Bradman remained his solitary victim at Grace Road.

On his first appearance in London – on the ground of sad memories of 1938 – the Don was in splendid form. He hit 146 at 50 an hour against Surrey at the Oval. He batted quite beautifully as he went to his hundred, and on reaching it, Stan Squires offered him a 'Well played, Don.' 'Thanks, Stan', replied Bradman. 'It's nice to make a few now and again.' This from a man who had scored 107 centuries in 306 innings! Bradman sportingly gave Alec Bedser a congratulatory handshake on his return journey when he was out.

Bradman rested himself for the fixture at Fenner's (where he had always played on his previous tours) but brought himself back for the Whit week-end match against Essex, against whom, for one reason or another, he had never played in 1930, 1934 or 1938. Now, in this solitary appearance against the county, he was to leave his mark on them with a vengeance. There is a story that it was Bradman's avowed intention to make a hundred against every English county. That is probably not true, but no doubt he felt it his *duty* to play against every county: and so Essex came into his itinerary.

The run orgy at Southend on 15 May 1948, when the Australians amassed their 721 in a single day, was led by their captain's own innings of 187 in only four minutes over two hours – the fastest innings (at 90 an hour) of even Bradman's incredible career. 'Never have I seen Bradman annihilate an attack in such convincing manner in such a short space of time', recorded O'Reilly. He came in 22 minutes before lunch, and was 42* at the interval. He helped Brown add 219 for the second wicket in 94 minutes, and he himself scored 145 in the afternoon session, being out well before tea. His hundred had come in only 74 minutes. When he had scored but a single, he made his ground by a yard to escape being run out – three feet that proved expensive for Essex but a joy to the spectators. Bradman that day hit 32 fours and a five, and the Australians scored at 148 an hour while he was at the crease. 'Another grand stanza in his swan song', was how Thomas Moult described it, and he noticed something new about Bradman:

There were spells in which he seemed to be trying new variations of stroke-play, interesting and even fascinating to students of batsmanship. But hardly interesting or intelligible to the holiday spectators, of whom there must have been 16,000.

Then, however, he would suddenly get cracking again, and there were memorable moments when he hit Vigar and Price in turn for five 4s in each of two overs.

That evening people were again talking in terms of the Don making 1,000 runs before the end of May. He was unlikely to have another innings in the Essex match (!), but it was 15 May and his form was such that his four innings of the tour had yielded 107, 81, 146 and 187 – 521 runs at an average of 130·25. In such a phenomenally strong batting side, the chances of his batting twice in any match were not very high, and at this stage anyway he was deliberately missing some matches. In the event, the prospect of 1,000 by the end of May was never very real – he actually ended the month with 759 runs, average 94·87 – but, in his 40th year or no, he was still the first man in England to reach the 1,000-mark, which he achieved on the Saturday morning of the Trent Bridge Test (12 June), in only his tenth innings of the summer. On that same morning, at Lord's, 13 minutes later, Jack Robertson also reached his 1,000 – in his 23rd innings – the first Englishman to do so in the season. By reaching 1,000 when he did, Bradman had outscored Hutton, Washbrook, Compton, Edrich – and everyone else in the country.

Was the extravagance against Essex deliberate? Was it a show of strength that Bradman wanted to put on record early on in the tour? Some critics thought so, and Crawford White's Monday morning commentary in the *News Chronicle* was quite explicit:

> Bradman has not changed one whit. He is still the greatest batsman in the world and, good-will tour or not, he remains the coolest and most ruthless strategist in cricket.
>
> That mammoth 721 total against Essex on Saturday – the highest number of runs ever scored in one day – was far more than a holiday feast for the crowd. It was all part of his deliberate, merciless, efficient plan, brilliant in its execution, to build up the biggest possible psychological advantage for the Australians over English bowlers as a whole.
>
> Not that I blame Bradman for wanting that advantage. Confident and capable as the tourists are on hard wickets, he knows they will need it if the soft ones come along.

While the massacre of Southchurch Park was taking place, a new book by Learie Constantine happened just to come on the market in which the continuing ruthlessness of Bradman was precisely confirmed. In *Cricketers' Carnival*, Constantine said of Bradman:

> He pities none. If he can make any bowler look foolish, he will do it. If he can smash a man's averages so much that the man is dropped from big games for the season, he will spend his last ounce of energy and strain his wonderful sighting to do just that. No room for mercy, no standing back while a disarmed rival picks up his fallen weapon; the best of modern cricket is like that; and if you ask me, that is how the best cricket has always been.

Bradman 'pities none' . . . it was as true in 1948 as it was in 1928 or 1938, and already the bowlers of four English counties had had reason enough to know it was true. Only at Worcester had he shown a touch of mercy, by not caring to gather in his traditional 200 – and that was as much to preserve his energies and give his new players a taste of English conditions as anything else. That disregard for double-centuries – Walter Hammond, having retired, was no longer a neck and neck rival in this regard – was the only concession he was making to age. Even his scoring rate after his first four innings was as high as 55 an hour, though he was to reduce that to much less hectic proportions before long. Essex spectators, and especially the post-war Essex bowlers, have always smiled knowingly when it is suggested that Bradman in '48 scored a little more slowly than he had done in England in the '30s.

Bradman always tried to make a point of being on form – it was not too difficult for him – on his first appearance of the tour at Lord's, which was always the match against the M.C.C. In the corresponding fixture of 1938 he had made 278. As on that occasion, the gates were again closed in 1948. Bradman scored 98 before Edrich at first slip caught him off Captain Deighton, the Army fast bowler. No one in a first-class match had ever seen Bradman out for 98 before – whenever he had got that far, he had *always* gone on to reach a century. Bradman himself could hardly believe it until Frank Chester formally gave him out. He was no doubt disappointed at his fate, but this innings of 98 was his tenth successive innings of 50 or more in first-class cricket, equalling the world record of Ernest Tyldesley of Lancashire in 1926. No other player since 1948 has joined this pair. Bradman's actual successive innings, spread over the seasons 1947–48 (the first five) and 1948 (the last five) were 132 and 127*, 201, 57 ret. ht., 115, 107, 81, 146, 187, 98.[1]

It was in the M.C.C. match that Bradman first had to contend with public criticisms alleging that Sidney Barnes was improperly fielding at short-leg with one foot sometimes on the pitch itself. Some believed it to be contrary to the spirit of cricket. Bradman maintained a diplomatic silence, contenting himself to leave the matter to the umpires as sole judges of fair and unfair play and in the knowledge that there had been no protest by a batsman. Six months later, in a newspaper article (*Sunday Chronicle*, 28 November 1948), Bradman explained his silence: 'The article contained certain allegations which I badly wanted to refute and which I thought deserved a very harsh reply. But they went unanswered because I suspected that one aim was controversy – to try to draw me into a discussion which would attract attention and notoriety.' Barnes, of course, in 1948 was to regret his suicidal proximity.

---

[1] Tyldesley's 10 innings in 1926 were 144, 69 and 144*, 226, 51 and 131, 131, 106, 126, 81. This was perhaps a more meritorious performance, all the innings being scored in the same season (between 26 June and 27 July), Tyldesley thus scoring 1,209 runs within 32 days. Bradman, however, played four of his innings in Test matches, as opposed to only one by Tyldesley (the final one of 81). Tyldesley followed his world record spell with 44 v Essex, 139 v Yorkshire and 85 v Middlesex – only to find himself named as 12th man for the next Test match that season!

The unfortunate Tennyson 'snub' incident then broke immediately after the M.C.C. match. At first it was confined to the Australian papers, but, on being cabled back to England, the *Sunday Pictorial*, through Peter Wilson's column, brought it out with a great fanfare in its earliest possible issue, accompanied by a jovial top-hatted picture of Lord Tennyson and another of Don Bradman holding a telephone receiver, captioned 'He hasn't yet phoned to apologise.' The alleged apology was due for Bradman's refusal – on the grounds that he was 'too busy' – to see Lord Tennyson when he went to the Australian dressing-room at Lord's after Bradman's innings of 98 on the Saturday. In the Sydney *Daily Telegraph*, the columnist Dave McNicoll wrote:

> Tennyson told me he was so furious with this treatment that he immediately wrote to Bradman telling him that he did not consider his behaviour very commendable.
> Tennyson said: 'I told him I thought that as a former captain of England and a son of a former Governor-General of Australia he might have seen fit to spare me a moment. I also told him that I had merely wanted to congratulate him and to ask him and Hassett, Brown and Miller to dine with me at White's Club. I was so furious that I added that good manners cost nothing.'

McNicoll, who had got his version solely from Lord Tennyson, accused Bradman of 'needless brusqueness and lack of tact'. The *Sunday Pictorial* in London took it all up with great glee. They seemed glad that the incident had occurred. When the Australians had arrived in England the previous month, they had come out with a piece – also by Peter Wilson – with bold black headlines of: 'Relax, Mr. Bradman – Test Cricket is Only a Game'. Now the headlines were bold and black again. Bradman himself refused to comment, and still refused two years later when Tennyson called him 'this mannerless little man'.[1] He has always refused to comment. The facts behind the incident were known only to a small circle, and after years of injustice to Bradman, were revealed publicly in 1972 by E. W. Swanton in *Sort of a Cricket Person*. Lord Tennyson had lunched far too well and had gone first to the M.C.C. dressing-room and had spent some time there. 'Don knew this, was apprised of his state of health, and decided he did not want his team to meet the great man in these particular circumstances. With one eye on the field and one ear cocked towards another visitor who was present, he sent his message.' The whole matter in 1948 ought never to have been made public, and was anyway newsworthy only to a distinctly limited audience. But that audience seized upon it without any real desire to have the account properly balanced by the facts. The *Sporting Record* deplored the attack on Bradman: 'In our opinion it was an uncalled-for reflection on a captain who has done

---

[1] These words appeared when Lord Tennyson reopened the issue in his second volume of autobiography, *Sticky Wickets*, that came out with a certain flourish of trumpets in April 1950. Beyond regretting that Lord Tennyson had made the criticisms, Sir Donald refused to be drawn or to issue any statement. 'The whole thing', he said, 'is only a repetition of a statement made by Lord Tennyson back in 1948. I refused to make any comment at the time and I refuse to do so now.'

everything possible to make the tour a happy one. And you can take it that all his players almost worship the turf he treads on.'

Ever since Bradman had become a public figure, there were those anxious – some of them more than anxious – to cast slurs upon him as a person when they found they could not do so as a batsman. Only the law of libel prevented some writers going further than they did. Some of them indeed overstepped the mark and could well have been successfully sued had Bradman chosen to take what must always be a lengthy and distasteful step. Talk was less inhibited than the written word. 'Before we were married a year', recalled Bradman once, 'my wife overheard a conversation at a Test match about our alleged pending divorce.' There was also an occasion when he was accused of being drunk throughout a match 'when in fact the strongest drink I had ever tasted was lemonade'. No man's life is as pure as the driven snow, but it so happens that almost certainly Sir Donald's has been purer than most of his detractors'.

The temporary fuss over the Tennyson affair at Lord's – in reality a very minor matter indeed – fortunately had no adverse effect on the popularity either of Bradman himself or of the Australian team. Thus far there had been a complete absence of acrimony and untoward incidents, due not least to Bradman's own influence over the tour. On the very afternoon of the Tennyson incident, the London *Star*'s leader-writer had said:

> Bradman is not only the world's greatest batsman. As the years have added to his skill, he has become the perfect cricket ambassador.

Much of Don Bradman's life off the field never reached the columns of the newspapers precisely because of its ordinariness. But even the ordinary acts of Bradman were always much greater news than the extraordinary acts of many others, and he was often obliged to go out of his way to protect his privacy. When the Australians went up to Manchester for their match against Lancashire, Bradman performed a little service for a school in Manchester that is worthy of record, considering the demands on his time as captain of an outstandingly successful touring side. It showed Bradman in his role as ambassador. The Governor-General of Australia, William McKell, who in due course was to confer the accolade of knighthood on Don Bradman, had asked him before leaving Australia to deliver a panoramic photograph of the Sydney Cricket Ground to a Manchester school, in accordance with a long-standing promise. This Don Bradman arranged to do one morning before start of play at Old Trafford, when the children were told to be in their places strictly by 9 a.m. – leaving them to speculate on the reason why. Bradman arrived by taxi and met the delighted children in a basement gymnasium. He presented the photograph and, in addition, gave them a most entertaining address. He then left for Old Trafford, leaving behind an unforgettable impression of goodwill on many youthful minds.

This Old Trafford match was the celebrated occasion when Malcolm Hilton, aged 19, twice dismissed Bradman, for scores of 11 and 43. The fresh-faced Hilton, who bowled left-arm slow, was a virtual newcomer to the first-class scene, who had left his father's building and decorating business at Werneth the year before to become a professional cricketer. Hilton had gone out with orders from his fiancée to get Bradman's wicket. 'I don't care if you only get one', she told him, 'as long as it is Don's.' Bradman actually played on in the first innings via the inside edge of the bat, and gave Hilton a 'Well bowled'. Something approaching hysteria broke out the next day when Hilton got Bradman again, this time stumped. Detailed diagrams were published to explain the double downfall and Hilton was the most famous teen-ager in England. Years later Geoffrey Edrich, who was on the field, told Ralph Barker that his brother Eric did not take the bails off straight away. 'He waited for the great man to turn, see his wicket still intact, and try to scramble back. It must have been torture for Bradman, but if he'd taken them off straight away he'd have missed half the fun.' 'Anybody could have stumped him', protested Eric. 'I was lucky enough to be behind the wicket.' And when pressed, he confessed: 'I was just a bit slow getting them off.' In the 46 first-class matches that Bradman played between the end of the war and his retirement, this was the solitary occasion that he was twice dismissed for less than fifty. He was never again, incidentally, to be stumped.

Bradman changed his mind at breakfast-time about taking a rest against Nottinghamshire at Trent Bridge, and thus played in seven of the first ten matches. When F. G. Woodhead bowled him for 86, and also later bowled Hassett and Miller, the bowler overheard the Australians saying they could not understand how they could be bowled by someone with that name! It is interesting that during the previous Australian season, the only bowler who had managed to hit Don Bradman's stumps all season was V. S. Hazare. Now Frank Woodhead was the fifth to do so since the start of the '48 tour, and Jim Cornford became the sixth when Bradman played at Hove. Sussex had seen Bradman only once before, in 1934, for he had not played (though he was present) in 1930 and could not play after his Oval injury in '38. He now scored 109 in the final match before the first Test. The Australians were undefeated, and Bradman himself had captained the side in eight matches, which included six innings victories. Bradman's average when the first Test began was 96·44.

Ever since Bradman appeared on the Test match scene in 1928, the story of Test match cricket changed. England, of course, beat Australia several times since Bradman's emergence, and even contrived to win a rubber. But somehow the two countries never seemed to be playing on level terms when Bradman was in Australia's side. Thus it was once again in 1948, the little man bestriding the entire stage yet again, the fulcrum of all talk and speculation, no less than he had been in 1930 and in 1934 and in 1938. The magician's hair was a little thinner, but he could still perform wizardry beyond all others. He now dominated this post-war tour in spite of the galaxy of stars around him. It is strange how the British public almost *willed* him to do well at the expense of their own cricketers, having accepted his genius since the early days of 1930 and never daring to suppose that that genius could dim. No other touring cricketer had been so accepted – not Trumper, not Macartney, not George Headley, no one. The inevitability of Bradman was too powerful to fight against. He rewarded his public regularly and prolifically. When people decided to go to a match to see Bradman bat, he so frequently produced a performance that gained fresh converts to cricket. If a county crowd had the choice of a hundred by Bradman or one of their own players, the vote would almost always go for Bradman – always excepting of course a Hutton hundred at Bradford or Bramall Lane. When the Test series of 1948 opened at Trent Bridge, the score against the name of D. G. Bradman was 138.

N. W. D. Yardley was Bradman's opposing captain in '48, and no one knew better how hard would be the task to confront so palpably powerful an Australian side. Julius Caesar, before a battle, used to exhort his troops to remember their former prowess: but not a single one of Norman Yardley's troops had ever played in a winning series against Australia. As to Bradman himself, Yardley had no delusions. He knew he could expect relentless captaincy and relentless batsmanship. For the former he could do nothing, except hope to match it. But for Bradman's batsmanship a certain strategy was evolved after the team dinner on the night before the first Test which became known as the 'Bedser–Hutton Plan' and which had a certain amount of success. Yardley himself described it thus:

Alec was to bowl a certain sort of ball that Don was less positive against than he was against others; his weakness to make an opening single by tickling the ball round behind to the leg was to be exploited. With this in view we employed three short legs, of whom Len was one, who were to wait just on the spot for the catch we hoped would come from the late inswinging ball. I have said elsewhere that this theory was first attempted, under Wally Hammond's direction and advice, in the fourth Test in Australia in the previous rubber, and we got Don for a duck with it there, but it was not then formulated in such detail. Now we had seen it tried, and were able to modify it a bit, it worked extremely well; and, in fact, we got Don out twice with it at Nottingham, and then got him out at the Lord's Test . . . in just the same way. The great man's apprehensive feeling until he was fairly well off the mark was about the single weak joint in his shining armour!

Was it really, however, a Bradman chink? He was certainly very fond of getting off the mark with a single on the leg side, normally wide of mid-on, but how much more than mere hope could be placed on his pushing forward and edging the ball where he did not intend it? He was certainly caught 'round the corner' in both innings off Bedser at Trent Bridge, but in the first innings he did make 138! That hardly amounts to a successful exploitation of a chink in the Bradman armour. He himself called this dismissal an accident, coming off a ball he need not have played at. The picture of Hutton's hands awaiting the ball became one of the best known pictures of the series. In the second innings he was out in identical fashion, caught at backward short-leg by Hutton off Bedser – for 0, his first Test duck in England. But this duck came when it did not matter, for Australia needed only 98 to win.

The deliberate and persistent attack on the leg stump had slowed Bradman down considerably in his 138 – to the point even when he was barracked – and he frankly did not think much of this kind of attack. It certainly did not show off cricket as a spectacle. After nearly 4¾ hours on the second day he was 130*. Yardley's urgent desire to prevent Bradman getting off to a big-scoring start in the series had been frustrated. That night in the Black Boy Hotel, Alec Bedser (without a wicket so far) met Bill O'Reilly, and the famous Australian suggested how the leg-side field might be profitably changed when attacking Bradman. Bedser listened with due appreciation, and immediately next morning moved Hutton to 'O'Reilly's spot '– with the almost instant dismissal. No wonder Bedser raised his arm in the direction of the press-box, where O'Reilly was sitting.

The Hutton hands 'round the corner' dogged Bradman again in his next match, which chanced to be against Yorkshire at Sheffield. Bradman made 54 and 86, batting over four hours in all, the second innings ending in a Hutton catch off Aspinall. Then, in the second Test at Lord's, the scorecard once again had the entry 'c Hutton b Bedser' against Bradman's name, for the modest total of 38, he having almost been caught by Hutton for 13. The Yorkshireman of course was at backward short-leg. 'In all Bradman's career', commented O'Reilly, 'and I had seen a great deal of it, I had never known him to be guilty of falling into the same trap twice.' It was about this time that Walter Hammond described Bradman as passing from the ranks of the immortals to the ranks of the mortals. So there was something after all in Yardley's plan, and Bradman recognised it now by taking a special net at which he asked his bowlers to concentrate on inswingers at the middle and leg stumps, reproducing as closely as possible the style of Bedser. Never again could Bedser repeat his trick thereafter.

Bradman batted finely for 89 in the second innings at Lord's before Edrich, rolling himself into a ball, brilliantly caught him in the slips. Bedser's inswingers had been treated with caution, and none of them was prodded to leg. But actually it was Bedser who dismissed him in the end, completing a sequence of six successive dismissals by Bedser in innings in which the two men had met. Bradman's scores in these six innings were 63, 146, 138, 0, 38 and 89. So although Bedser's feat was quite remarkable (and unparalleled by any other bowler against Bradman), it cannot be held that Bradman was a failure. He did average 72 in the Test series of 1948 and a fraction under 90 in the whole summer!

It was now a virtual certainty that Australia would win the series, being two up after two Tests. Bradman had devoutly wished for this position – the more so in his final season as captain of Australia – and his superlative side had achieved it without undue strain. But even the best-regulated touring sides could never count their chickens, and Bradman no doubt remembered (without, perhaps, being unduly perturbed by the memory) how England had once been two up and lost.

At the Lord's Test, by the way, Lord Tennyson was again present – he was actually one of seven former England captains against Australia who watched the match. But there was no attempt this time to go to the Australian dressing-room and no meeting, of course, with Bradman. Douglas Jardine was another old England captain attending the game. He, too, did not meet Bradman.

By the end of June, quite irrespective of the state of the Test series, it was clear that Bradman's personal star was very much in the ascendant. Any fears he may have harboured in the early months of 1948 as to his ability to adapt to the rigours of another English tour had now been effectively reduced to naught. He was marching in triumph through the land, giving never a suspicion that he was lingering on the stage too long. And his triumph was being achieved without the double-centuries and the triple-centuries of old. The British public had never had the smallest doubt about what sort of tour he was going to have, and it was the happiest circumstance possible that Bradman was seeing out his career on the high plateau of achievement that had characterised his cricket for 20 years. To his batting prowess, of course, was added his stature as a captain, which served only to enhance his repute before the public. The huge match attendances and gate receipts wherever he played were evidence of his insatiable appeal. That this public interest extended as much (if not more) to Bradman personally as to the Australian team generally can be seen, for example, in the response of Yorkshire at Bradford when Bradman was absent. While fresh records were being established all round, the Australians emerged from the Bradford match with their share of receipts at only £534.16.6 (compared with £1,759 in 1938). When Bradman played against Yorkshire later in the tour at Sheffield, the Australian share was £2,757.5.10. Without Bradman at Bradford, the paying attendance was 12,128; with Bradman in the side at Sheffield, it rose dramatically to 51,824. The Australians were undeniably a highly attractive side. But it was Bradman who was still the magnet.

Instead of choosing to rest after the five days of Test cricket at Lord's, Bradman surprisingly played on the very next day in the return match with Surrey at the Oval – and moreover opted to field when he won the toss. Surrey were minus their three principal wicket-takers, Bedser, Laker and McMahon, and when he batted Bradman had little trouble in running up yet another century (128) at not far short of a run a minute. These were to prove the final runs of his career on the famous Oval ground, and Londoners who had watched him thus far on the tour, both here and at Lord's, had seen him average 99.80 on those two grounds alone. Quite what carnage he might have wreaked had he chosen to go to Bristol – where the Australians declared at 774 for seven against Gloucestershire at 79 runs per 100 balls –

can only be imagined. Instead he chose to be in Buckinghamshire with his old friend Walter Robins, now an England selector, before the third Test at Old Trafford which might settle the fate of the Ashes. Robins himself had been a contender for the England captaincy against Australia in 1948, having been persuaded to change his mind after saying he did not wish to be considered for the job. He led The Rest against England in the Test Trial at Birmingham, during which match he passed his 42nd birthday – and it had been precisely because he thought he was getting too old that he had resigned the Middlesex captaincy the year before, after winning the championship. If Yardley's lumbago had kept him out of the captaincy, Robins would very likely have pitted his nimble brains against Bradman's on the field. It was an interesting coincidence how closely Bradman and Robins resembled each other in physical appearance. Someone once suggested that they might well go to a fancy-dress ball together as the two Dromios in *The Comedy of Errors*!

Before travelling to Old Trafford (where, incidentally, Australia had not beaten England since 1902), Bradman had dinner at the Hind's Head Hotel, Bray, with Walter Robins. The staff at the hotel awaited Bradman's innings in the Test match with more than an ordinary interest. The reason was that Bradman had ordered a duck.

There was no duck on the field for England's bowlers to claim at Old Trafford, but on the ground where Bradman had conspicuously done little throughout his career he now lasted only seven balls in his 50th Test match before Pollard got an inswinger past his bat and practically the entire mass of the 30,000 spectators gave Bradman out lbw simultaneously with umpire Dai Davies. Pollard was a local hero, and the roar might have greeted the winning of the Ashes by England. (In the absence of that unlikely miracle, the dismissal of Bradman for 7 by a Westhoughton-born bowler was an acceptable substitute.) Rain and a subsequent draw ensured that the Ashes remained with Australia, and on the final day, when Bradman batted two hours for his undefeated 30, he was pinned down at nought for the longest period of his career – 28 minutes. That, unbelievably, was his highest Test innings ever at Manchester, where he aggregated altogether only 81 runs for Australia between 1930 and 1948 at an average of 27. It was the only one of the ten Test grounds he played on that he failed to score a Test hundred – and, of course, he never got even a fifty. The contrast with Headingley, which was the next major occasion on the agenda, was quite startling.

The combination of Bradman and Headingley had for 18 years been a magic mixture that was a guarantee of memorable cricket. Even before Bradman's availability for the tour of 1948 was known – but surely in anticipation of it – thousands had made up their minds to watch the Headingley Test: and had taken active steps to do so. The entire reserved accommodation was sold out *by the first post* on 1 January 1948 – the first day for the consideration of applications. So far as Bradman himself was concerned, he knew that fate was on his side at Leeds. In three Tests there he had scored

334, 304, 103 and 16. 'With ordinary human players', wrote Neville Cardus in 1948, 'we might say: "Well, he can't do it again – the law of averages is against him at Leeds this year"; but Bradman has usually created his own laws of average. Given a good wicket at Leeds, I shall expect from him, and he will go out to bat as though to an appointment with, a century – at least.'

What is still the record attendance for any cricket match in England – over 158,000 for five days, with many more thousands turned away – crowded into Headingley to watch Don Bradman and his team. They saw a wonderful game, which England should have won, but, with the aid of Bradman and his arithmetic, Australia eventually won 12 minutes from time. When Bradman walked to the wicket on the second evening, just under an hour from the close, one of the compelling reasons for the massed public concentration at the ground became apparent – Bradman, the idol of Leeds, was playing in his last Test in Yorkshire. In those days the dressing-rooms were still at the St Michael's Lane end of the ground, and not at square-leg, so Bradman found himself walking out through the long narrow opening, elongated for yards on to the field itself by an acclaiming crowd to his right and to his left, ushered through his admirers by three Yorkshire policemen, the sight of his small figure emerging at long last near the wicket giving the signal for yet louder applause from the rest of the ground. Bradman, noted E. W. Swanton, was 'greeted like an emperor by the crowd'. How Yorkshire-men loved him, and how positively did they endorse the Lancastrian Cardus's forecast of a century from the Bradman bat – at least.

There is no doubt that Bradman did intend to score a century on this splendid batting pitch; and coming in at 13 for one against an England total of 496, the situation called for one. By the close of play that Friday evening he was 31, and in superlative form. His partner was Hassett. The packed Saturday crowd could never have anticipated that within eight minutes of the resumption both these great Australians would be back in the pavilion. The pitch was a little lively after some early morning rain. Bradman took a two off Bedser's first over. Then Pollard, from the pavilion end, had Hassett caught at slip off his second ball. Miller took a three off his first ball, which gave Bradman the bowling. He was at once clean bowled, his off stump knocked right back. What a sensation, and what a roar! The only explanation is that Bradman did not see the ball out of the blackness of the football stand – there were no sightscreens at Headingley in those days. It was a perfectly straight ball – and Keith Miller said it was the first time he had ever seen Bradman bowled by a straight ball which did nothing either in the air or off the pitch. The day was most certainly considerably spoiled for a great many spectators, despite a memorable hundred in his first Test in England by Harvey.

The last day of this Test set the seal on Bradman's glory in 1948. On the penultimate evening Bradman made a note in his diary: 'We are set 400 to win and I fear we may be defeated.' On the final morning of the match, Bradman confided to his faithful scorer, Ferguson: 'Bill, I think we are going to lose this game. It is too many runs for any team to make in such a short time.' The fear was translated into practical effect that morning when Bradman instructed Fergie – the tale was told by Fergie to E. W. Swanton – to make sure the team's coach-driver was back at the ground to collect them by mid-afternoon. Bradman could not possibly have expected Australia to have won by then. He must only have believed – as did many Englishmen – that they might have lost.[1] Instead, on a worn wicket taking spin, Australia achieved their 404 for three between 11.46 a.m. and 6.18 p.m. Bradman's own role was crucial. He came in at one o'clock and was there at the end. On this particular pitch neither he nor his adulators could really have expected a hundred. But he was given, in his farewell Test innings at Headingley, another quite tumultuous reception. Again he had to be escorted – this time by a police sergeant – through the crowd of people who lined his way to the wicket, and the entire crowd stood and clapped him the whole way. Hats and cushions were thrown in the air, and the tunnel of spectators stretched almost three-quarters of the way to the pitch. (In September, at Scarborough, when Bradman was given honorary life membership of the Yorkshire County Cricket Club, Bradman said: 'I have learned to appreciate both the players and the public of Yorkshire and I know I shall never cherish any memory more than the reception at Leeds at the Test here. Not only was it the greatest I have ever received in this country, but the greatest I have ever received from any public anywhere in the world.' Bearing in mind that Bradman was not a Yorkshireman, the fervour of the reception accorded him at Leeds was something that far transcends either local pride or national patriotism. More recent memories of Headingley include the occasion of Geoffrey Boycott reaching his hundredth hundred in a Test match there in 1977. Within 24 hours of that memorable event, several spectators who had witnessed both receptions – and Yorkshire spectators at that – unhesitatingly opted for the Bradman reception as the greater of the two, despite the obvious emotion engendered by Boycott's feat. The occasions were quite different and not strictly comparable: but the results of a small opinion poll in Leeds did, as a simple fact, come down unanimously for Bradman.)

Bradman was lucky on that final day at Leeds to encounter England making more mistakes in the field than they can ever have made in a single day in Test cricket in modern times. He himself was missed in the slips off Compton when 22 and 30; during the afternoon he might have been caught at deep point off Cranston when 59, and just before tea, when 107, Evans should have stumped him off Laker. By the tea interval Australia were 288 for one, and a huge partnership had developed with Morris. By lunchtime, despite the wearing wicket, Bradman had realised the game could as easily

---

[1] In fact the Australians travelled to their next venue, Derby, by train from Leeds City Station. It is probable that the vehicle due at the ground was to collect the players' baggage rather than the players themselves.

be won as drawn: and he actually reached his hundred in the wonderful time of 145 minutes. He and Morris put on 301 for the second wicket at 83 an hour – Bradman's fifth triple-century stand in Test cricket – and Bradman himself ended with 173, including 29 fours, in 4¼ hours. It was his 29th and final century in Test cricket and, as it happened, his final runs on a Test match field. They were made, moreover, for much of the time in some discomfort, as he had suffered a recurrence of fibrositis in his side in early afternoon. Characteristically he engineered matters so that Harvey should hit the winning run. Bradman himself might have done that the previous over, off Pollard, but after hitting one four he methodically blocked the rest. At the winning of the game, Bradman was quickly alongside Harvey patting him vigorously on the back. It had been quite a day – even for Don Bradman. It was his considered view later on that if England had had a leg-spinner like Hollies or Wright in the side, Australia would not have made 250.

So, far from the touring side meeting their first reverse of the tour, the star of Bradman was still high in the ascendant. And for that position Bradman himself was entitled to very much of the credit. He seemed now to be not only captain and batsman but manipulator of fate.

The day after Bradman's great triumph at Leeds – where he seemed able to do no wrong – a proposal was being considered there that the city should recognise in tangible form his 963 Test runs there, and one suggestion was that the freedom of the city should be conferred on him. That did not happen, but he was, as has been stated, given honorary life membership of Yorkshire. A week after Yorkshire conferred the honour, Lancashire also elected Bradman a life member in appreciation of his services to English, Australian and international cricket. In 1948 Hampshire likewise honoured Bradman – and on the list of life members of all three counties, he was the only Australian.

Despite the physical and mental strain of the final day at Headingley, and despite some pain in his side which had called for emergency treatment, Bradman captained the Australians again next morning against Derbyshire. No Australian side had played at Derby since 1919, and a record crowd of 17,000 turned up. The Derbyshire captain E. J. Gothard's bowling figures for the season when he entered the match were five wickets at 38·80: yet he dismissed a trio of Test batsmen in Bradman, Brown and Hamence – Bradman for 62 in two hours. So, in four innings against Derbyshire in his career, Bradman never made a hundred. Derbyshire were strangely fortunate in this respect, for several other great century-makers in cricket history – and with far more opportunities than Don Bradman – never managed a hundred against them, including W. G. Grace, K. S. Ranjitsinhji, P. F. Warner, P. B. H. May and M. C. Cowdrey. It was also the only time on the 1948 tour that Don Bradman's opposite number as captain (E. J. Gothard) had the pleasure of obtaining his wicket.

Bradman then had four days off in London while his team spent the Bank Holiday week-end in Wales. That did not please Wales any more than it did any other venue from which Bradman absented himself in 1948, but not unreasonably Bradman felt he was entitled to an occasional rest. He then returned to the side at Edgbaston for his first encounter since 1938 with Eric Hollies. This was a fateful match indeed, for although Warwickshire lost by nine wickets, Hollies took nine of the 11 Australian wickets that fell in the match, all but one of them without assistance from the field. His first-innings feat of eight for 107 included the wicket of Bradman, bowled by a top-spinner for 31. Tradition has it that Bradman went out in the second innings (when the Australians needed only 22 more to win) in order to have another sight of Hollies, in case he should be chosen for the final Test, which of course he was. Hollies thereupon deliberately refrained from producing his googly and allowed Bradman a quarter of an hour of gentle batting practice. When Hollies indeed was chosen for the Test, he discussed with Tom Dollery Bradman's reading of his googly and they agreed Bradman had not spotted it during the first Edgbaston innings. 'I know I can bowl him with it', said Hollies, 'and I'll give it to him second ball at the Oval.' That, of course, is what happened; and Hollies's captain, R. H. Maudsley, quoted this as the only occasion on which a bowler has nominated how he would get Bradman out, and which ball.

Before the Oval Test came round, Bradman played in Cyril Washbrook's benefit match at Old Trafford, his notoriously unhappy ground. True to form, he played perhaps his worst innings of the tour, a very mundane 28 with two stumping chances; but atoned in the second innings with 108 out of the 184 added before lunch on the final day, when he declared with his score at 133*. He was kind to Lancashire in this match – he could have made them follow on, but as it was Washbrook's benefit (and Bradman was fond of Washbrook) he did not. 'Cranny, we'll strike again', he informed the Lancashire captain: and a good third day gate, with Bradman at the wicket, was ensured. So, good and bad innings mixed, Bradman entered the final Test with a tour average of 87·13.

On that Saturday at the Oval, when the fifth Test began – on 14 August – Bradman required only a further four runs to complete a career aggregate of 7,000 runs in Test cricket. His Test average when he went out to toss was 101·39, and against England alone 91·41. Those four runs – or anything beyond – would give him a final career average in Tests of three figures. He lost the toss – the 14th time in his 24 Tests as captain that he lost it – but by mid-afternoon England were all out for their sad total of 52.[1] This was comfortably passed by Australia's openers, and when Barnes was out at 117 Bradman emerged from the pavilion with the bowling in a ripe state for his plunder. His previous Test innings on the ground had been 232, 244 and 77. In 1948 he had already batted there twice (against Surrey) and had made

---

[1] The last time England batted against Australia at the Oval they had, of course, exceeded 900. The only thing common to the two innings was that Hutton was top scorer on each occasion.

146 and 128. He wanted very much to say farewell in a fitting manner. As
he walked out to the middle, his collar turned up as usual, the reception he
had been given at Leeds was repeated. There were some 20,000 present. It
was a memorable entry. In the middle Norman Yardley said to his team:
'We'll give him three cheers when he gets on the square.' Then he turned to
Hollies and said: 'But that's all we'll give him – then bowl him out.' Bradman
stood modestly, with his cap in hand, as the three cheers were duly given:
and Yardley shook him by the hand. Then the game went on. Hollies
(bowling, strangely, round the wicket) bowled him a leg-break which Bradman played defensively. The second was a googly, which drew Bradman
forward – but not far enough to smother the spin. The ball broke in and
removed the off bail. He was out! For o! The man who had come nearer to
mastering the art of batsmanship than anyone was out second ball. The
moment stunned the crowd as much as it did Bradman. As Jack Fingleton
put it: 'The game that had given him so much had denied him at the very
last Test appearance.' Then the crowd realised what had happened. Bradman returned amid fresh applause – at which Eric Hollies, perpetrator of
the deed, turned to Jack Young and lamented: 'Best ———— ball I've bowled
all season, and they're clapping *him*!' Sidney Barnes, whose cine camera was
put to consistent use on the '48 tour, filmed these historic moments from the
Australian balcony, and within a shorter space of time than he or anyone
else at the Oval could have surmised, he informed his captain that he had
captured the whole of his innings! That evening, when Hollies got home, he
telephoned Tom Dollery and told him triumphantly: 'He never saw it, Tom.'
The Melbourne *Herald* cartoonist depicted Hollies as 'the prickly fellow who
put the o in Don!'

Undoubtedly the Hollies duck – dramatic and decisive – is one of history's
most vivid noughts, only a little way behind Bradman's nought at Melbourne
in December '32. But Hollies *nearly* was not on the field at the Oval at all.
Leslie Duckworth, in his history of Warwickshire, has intriguingly related
the following:

> When the invitation to Hollies to play arrived he told Leslie Deakins he would
> rather play for Warwickshire. The rubber had already been decided and it would
> have meant that he would have missed two county games when he could ill be
> spared. It was the Warwickshire Committee who persuaded their 'home boy' to
> play; if they had not succeeded cricket history would almost certainly have been
> different.

Was the Oval occasion too much for Bradman? That is very doubtful in a
man of his experience. But Alec Bedser, who was only a matter of yards from
him when the three cheers were proffered, saw that he was deeply affected.
Bradman himself conceded the reception had stirred his emotions very deeply.
But did the enthusiasm affect his batting? That we will never know. Some
say there were tears in his eyes, but there is no evidence for that. 'Great
exaggeration', declared Bradman when asked about the matter years after-

wards. Let it remain one of the imponderables, to be debated in Elysium.

Despite the Oval duck, such was the enthusiasm by this time of the season for Bradman's performances that Fred Root, who resigned in mid-season from the umpires' list to write on cricket for the *Sunday Pictorial*, informed his readers next morning that they might profitably ignore the apparently firm prospect of Bradman's retirement at the end of the tour. The retirement, he said, 'must not be taken too literally'. Keith Johnson, the Australian manager, had told him: 'Don says his health has improved almost to the point of rejuvenation as a result of this trip to England.' On that evidence, and on some enigmatic and undisclosed plans that some sponsors allegedly had in Australia for Bradman's future, Fred Root declared: 'I can see the maestro scoring many more centuries before he finally hangs his boots on the pegs of a Sydney museum.' Good reading, perhaps; but hardly displaying an understanding of Bradman's character.

Australia won the fifth Test overwhelmingly, of course, the last rites on the final morning taking only 20 minutes. Bradman had triumphed in his final Test series as captain by four matches to none, with one drawn. It was the first time in history – and remains the only time – that England had lost four Test matches in a home series. The tributes to Bradman, and to his team, were profuse, and they began on that Wednesday morning on the players' balcony at the Oval when the Surrey President, H. D. G. Leveson Gower, spoke of Bradman's greatness as a player and called for three cheers for him and his team. 'This is rather a sad occasion for me', Bradman told the crowd of about 5,000 which gathered in front of the pavilion, 'because, whatever you may have read to the contrary, this is definitely the last Test match in which I shall ever play. I'm sorry my personal contribution was so small, but that was thanks to the generosity of the reception from the public and the English players and the very fine ball which Hollies bowled me.' He went on to express his thanks for the hospitality his team had received and their pleasure at playing in England, and paid a compliment to England's captain: 'In Norman Yardley', he said, 'I've found a very lovable opposition skipper. He has been very kind to us in every sense, and it has been a great pleasure to find him captaining the England team against us. Norman has been in an unfortunate position because the captain of a losing side has a very difficult job, a task I know only too well. I think he has been up against one of the strongest Australian sides ever to visit this country.'

In his reply Yardley said we were saying good-bye to the greatest cricketer of all time – 'a great cricketer and also a very great sportsman'. 'Future Australian sides will seem strange without Don Bradman', said Yardley. 'The only people who can be happy about his Test retirement are those who face the task of getting him out. For me, it is an honour and a pleasure to have played against him.' The crowd sang *For He's a Jolly Good Fellow* – and Don Bradman disappeared for ever as a player from the Test match scene. That afternoon one of his old rivals, Walter Hammond, went into print in the London *Star* with his own tribute:

I should like to offer my sincere and hearty congratulations to Don Bradman on his team's success and also his own particular achievements.

All cricket lovers in this country will be sorry to know that his Oval game marked his final appearance in a Test. It was fitting that the crowd should have given him such a hearty farewell.

The Cricket Correspondent of *The Times*, Beau Vincent, watched all the speeches and the cheers at the Oval: 'Whether, as was said, he is the greatest cricketer of all time will not be accepted by those who must retain that honour for "W.G." Let us say that he is the greatest of the present age, and can rank with Trumper, Ranji, Macartney, and Hobbs. Surely that is in all conscience sufficient praise.'

Not only had Bradman's side won the series handsomely but they achieved it by spirited and forceful cricket that gave the record crowds the fullest value for money. At Trent Bridge the gates were not again to be closed for a Test against Australia for a further 29 years. New record attendances were established in three successive 1948 Tests – at Lord's, Old Trafford and Headingley. A new generation was seeing Don Bradman for the first time – and, most sadly for them, for the last time too. Bradman's impact on them, as indeed on the more senior observers, was powerful and lasting. Most of the leader-writers sought to express the public feeling towards having Bradman in their midst, and all uniformly lauded him as an exceptional influence. Typical of the comment of the time were these words from a leader in the *News Chronicle* on the day after the series ended in 1948, the writer wondering what remedies were open to English cricket:

But perhaps the decisive answer is to be found in leadership. Norman Yardley, England's captain, has done almost all that could have been expected of him in adverse circumstances. But he was the first to admit that he was pitted against the greatest cricketer of all time.

Don Bradman is more even than that. He has shown himself to be a captain of unsurpassed skill. He has imbued the Australian team with his own single-minded determination to win. This amazing power of concentration was the determining factor.

Don Bradman has played his last game against England, but his influence on cricket, both here and 'down under', will be permanent. We salute his passing and thank him for the pleasure he has given us.

The opportunity for the ordinary man in the street to thank Bradman for the pleasure he had given them came when *The People* announced in their issue of 25 July (the Sunday of the Headingley Test) the launching of a Bradman Shilling Fund. It was the newspaper's belief 'that cricket-lovers of Britain would like to do more than send Bradman home for the last time with its thanks and good wishes'. No individual donation of more than a shilling was to be accepted – and the shillings poured in to Long Acre in London, many accompanied by simple letters of appreciation of Bradman's contribution to the game. The money was used to buy for Bradman, on behalf of the people of Britain, a magnificent solid silver trophy, one of the finest examples of the silversmith's craft. It was an exact replica of the famous Warwick Vase which came from the Emperor Hadrian's villa in Rome and was housed at Warwick Castle. The replica was mounted on a solid silver plinth and weighed 378 ounces. In due course, on 20 September, *The People* presented this trophy to Bradman at a sumptuous luncheon at the Savoy Hotel attended by the entire Australian team and about 200 guests. There were eight England captains in N. W. D. Yardley, G. O. Allen, A. P. F. Chapman, A. E. R. Gilligan, H. D. G. Leveson Gower, F. T. Mann, R. W. V. Robins and Sir Pelham Warner, as well as names like Frank Woolley, Wilfred Rhodes, Harold Larwood, Patsy Hendren, George Duckworth, Eddie Paynter, Ernest Tyldesley, George Geary, Maurice Tate and 'Tich' Freeman. It was the first time Larwood had seen Bradman since 1933. The gilt-tasselled menu card included a fine mounted colour portrait of Bradman in his blazer worn when he first became captain of Australia, and proclaimed that the luncheon and presentation was given 'as a tribute to a great sportsman'. It had been decided to use any balance subscribed for the benefit of cricket in England and to consult Bradman himself on how the money should be used. He opted for the laying down of concrete pitches for the encouragement of youth, something he had urged in his speech at the M.C.C. dinner to the Australians at Lord's earlier in the season.

Meanwhile the final stages of the 1948 tour of England were concluded on the field of play – in a blaze of triumph for Bradman himself. He scored 65 against Kent at Canterbury and then ended the first-class section of the tour with three successive centuries – for the tenth time in his career, very easily a world record. He bade Lord's farewell at the end of August with a chanceless 150, so dominantly acquired as to remind many of his greatest days. It was an occasion of tremendous nostalgia. 'The individual', wrote Beau Vincent in *The Times*, 'however illustrious he may be, must never be allowed to obscure the side, but in truth, as in the days when W.G. dominated the game of cricket, so one felt yesterday that this was Bradman's day at Lord's. And nobly he grasped the occasion. It is easy to say that the Gentlemen of England were slender in their bowling, and there is argument even among his greatest admirers whether Bradman is now the great batsman that he was. Sufficient is the answer that he scored 150 runs yesterday, runs made at long periods exactly as he chose to take them and apparently quite impossible to check.' He was in a most happy and relaxed mood, smiling and joking with the opposition, and calling loudly for runs. Colin Cowdrey was then 15 years old, and recalls the occasion thus: 'I also watched Bradman's last innings at Lord's, which was the only time I saw him bat. As he walked back to the pavilion for the last time, having made 150, he turned to the crowd, hung his gloves round his bat handle, raised them aloft and bowed farewell. I don't think that I have ever seen a more moving moment than this on the cricket field . . .' This innings, played two days before Bradman's 40th birthday and scored at a personal rate of 42 an hour, was played before an admiring crowd of nearly 18,000. It was Bradman's public farewell not only to Lord's but to London, where of course he had appeared more often than anywhere else in England. In his 25 first-class matches in London he had scored 12 centuries – impartially distributed, six to Lord's and six to the Oval – and 2,902 runs at the glorious round average of exactly 100. Had he been out for 147 that afternoon, his London average would not have reached three figures. Bradman presumably did not know that, but the fact is that as soon as he had passed it he at once threw his wicket away. Such was his mastery that he all but toyed with the bowling. This innings of Bradman's was especially remembered by the television and radio broadcaster, Barry Norman, when he was interviewed in 1976 about his cricket reminiscences: 'He scored 150 and then lofted up a catch and, long before anyone caught it, he was on his way back to the pavilion. He had just decided that that was what he was going to score and that was a moving moment because everybody stood up for him, applauding him (to and from the wicket) because it was his last match at Lord's.' When he had begun his innings in the morning, he had been applauded all the way from pavilion to crease by spectators and players alike, and that morning passed 2,000 runs for the season, to become the oldest tourist in England to reach that landmark. When he arrived back in Adelaide in October, Bradman said his biggest thrill was going out to bat at Lord's in his final match there.

On the second day at Lord's, after lunch, Bradman was presented with a special birthday cake, bearing kangaroos and other adornments, made by that old M.C.C. catering maestro, George Portman, who had then been at Lord's 46 years. It was a gift 'from all at Lord's' and weighed 60 lbs., being in the form of a book about 18 inches square. A ribbon of M.C.C. yellow and red divided iced pages overlaid with a birthday greeting to Bradman – mimosa for Australia and roses for England. Even a photograph of the hero managed to be incorporated. It was humorously remarked at the time that the book shape symbolised the story of Bradman's career – 'a piece of cake'. The Don also received a copy of Sir Pelham Warner's noble book on Lord's, and was toasted with champagne. The book bore the inscription: 'Presented to Don Bradman on the occasion of his fortieth birthday by the President, Committee and Members of the Marylebone Cricket Club in memory of the great pleasure he has given at Lord's since 1930 to countless lovers of cricket.' The presentations were actually one day premature – Bradman's birthday was on the scheduled third day of the match – but Lord Gowrie explained that no one could guarantee play lasting until mid-day on the Friday! In his gracious reply, Bradman said: 'To bid farewell to cricket on this great ground is for me a very sad occasion. I hope, however, to come to England again, though not as a player, and watch many Tests.' On Bradman's birthday itself, after the match ended in an innings win, the crowd gathered on the field in front of the pavilion and sang *Happy Birthday to You* and *Auld Lang Syne*. Bradman appeared on the Australian balcony and waved his farewell on his last day as a player at Lord's Cricket Ground. He admitted to feelings of pride and sadness as he passed through the Grace Gates that evening.

Bradman opened the innings only once on his four tours of England – when he was chasing his 1,000 before the end of May at Southampton in 1930 – but at Hastings in 1948, against the South of England, he was all but an opening batsman, for he came in when Barnes was out to the first ball of the match. Now he played another chanceless innings, this time of 143 in just over three hours – the only innings of his career on the Hastings ground. It was no secret that Bradman had set out on the 1948 tour with the ambition to see it through without defeat. That is why he probably played at Hastings, lest any 'festival' spirit might cause a sudden upset. He doubtless remembered that the only defeats suffered by the great side under Armstrong in '21 occurred after the Test series was over. One of those defeats had been at Scarborough, where indeed the 1938 side had also lost. H. D. G. Leveson Gower included ten Test cricketers in his XI in '38 (and the other man became a Test cricketer three months afterwards). Bradman, alive to the danger to his ambition, insisted that a maximum of six current Test men should oppose the Australians at Scarborough – while he himself, incidentally, fielded an Australian Test team! He need not have worried, but was nevertheless on his toes throughout until there was no possible chance of defeat. Such was Bradman's reputation that queues started forming outside the ground at 5 a.m. on the opening day. This was Bradman's last match in England, and when he left the pavilion on the final day (not out 30 overnight) he was escorted to the wicket, in the style Yorkshire had now perfected for Bradman, by two policemen who forged a way for him through a long line of well-wishers which stretched almost to the stumps. He appropriately made the highest score of the three days – 153 (chanceless, yet again) in front of nearly 17,000 people before he hit a ball from Bedser high to coverpoint. He had had enough, and Bedser deserved the wicket. He turned at once to run for the pavilion. Jack Fingleton was watching: 'By the time that Hutton's two safe hands had closed on the ball, Bradman was half-way to the pavilion. He did not turn to see whether the catch had been taken. He continued running, gloves, cap and bat fluttering from his hands, and almost before this huge Yorkshire crowd at the Scarborough Festival had had time to warm its hands in appreciation to him, Bradman was lost to view for ever as a first-class batsman on an English ground.'

Thus ended an era, the like of which cricket had never seen. It had spanned 20 years, and apart from the war the name of Bradman was the mightiest single influence of the time. It was Billy Murdoch who once said of W.G. that he had never seen his like and never would. Thousands said the same of Bradman between 1928 and 1948. Now, in a matter of moments, this miracle of batsmanship deserted the field at Scarborough, his magic bat now a memory. Later that afternoon, he bowled the final over of the match – an over of leg-breaks – the only time he bowled on the '48 tour. He was given a great ovation as he left the field.

That night at the Royal Hotel in Scarborough, where the Australian tourists stayed, a spontaneous and emotional scene took place. Crowds outside the hotel shouted for Bradman on this his final day as a first-class cricketer in England. As Bradman appeared at the top of the staircase on his way down to dinner, the entire assemblage in the lounge below – cricketers, cricket enthusiasts and ordinary guests – rose to applaud him as he descended the stairs. Don Bradman was certainly embarrassed – but at the same time deeply moved. It was a rare tribute, normally reserved for Hollywood film scenarios, and a form of tribute that may well be unique for a first-class cricketer.

Next morning, yet again, there were hundreds outside the hotel. And when Bradman appeared, with his team, to leave for Scotland, he was given a tumultuous farewell. For 20 years he had called his own tune in cricket, and his Scarborough swansong, when he left the field as in a flash after his 153, was not to be quickly forgotten.

There remained two minor matches in Scotland. It was announced that Bradman would not play in them, but it turned out that he played in both, perhaps again to ensure there was no minor mishap, even though they were not first-class games. At Raeburn Place, Edinburgh, he scored only 27. But at Mannofield, Aberdeen, his 123* is still remembered with the highest enthusiasm to this day, his stay of only 89 minutes (with two sixes and 17 fours) delighting a record crowd of 10,000 in splendid weather. This was Bradman's only visit to Aberdeen, and the elaborate and highly successful arrangements fully justified the Scottish Cricket Union's decision to stage the match there. The wicket was perfect and earned the praise of Bradman himself. He received a royal reception when he went in, reaching his fifty in 30 minutes and his century in 80 minutes. He then hit W. Nichol, of Kelburne, for two sixes in succession into the sightscreen, getting his last 23 in nine minutes. 'As a spectacle', Bradman said later, 'it must have been my best effort of the trip.' It was, of course, his last innings on British soil, on 18 September 1948 – and it is interesting that Bradman later officially reported that the hospitality extended to the team in Aberdeen was unequalled anywhere on the tour.

Thus Bradman saw his team through the tour without losing a match. Some said he was obsessional in his ambition, but success and ambition always attract criticism. The cachet of going through a full tour of England without defeat thereafter invested that Australian side with a glamour that perhaps no other touring side to England has ever been able to boast. Moreover the side won the record number of matches by an innings – 15 (as well as the two in Scotland). The 1930 side had won only six of its first-class matches by an innings. The average per wicket of the 1948 side was the astonishingly high one of 50·23. Against the side it was 19·66. It was interesting at the end of the tour to look back at the words Bradman used on the night of 10 March 1948, when he spoke at the Victorian Cricket Association dinner to the Australian team at the Melbourne Cricket Ground a week before they sailed for England. He said then that he thought no team had ever been selected with more mature consideration and greater deliberation than the one that was then going to England. 'It will take a good side to beat them', was his forecast.

In all matches on the 1948 tour Bradman scored 2,578 runs at 92·07. In first-class games alone he made 2,428 at 89·92. In the midst of a very brilliant batting side, he still finished very easily at the top – and indeed, by a big margin, ahead of any English batsman too. No other batsman in the country equalled his 11 first-class hundreds. Altogether he topped the fifty mark 19 times in his 31 innings. He uniquely passed 2,000 runs for the fourth consecutive tour of England.

It is worth recording that on the 1948 tour Bradman did not hit his first six *until September* (when he was well past his 2,000 runs). That was at the Hastings Festival, when he achieved his six by gliding Bailey, a fast bowler, over fine leg's head. Then at Scarborough he hit two more, off successive balls from Laker; and his final two at Aberdeen. Thus, outside festival-style cricket, his control was such that the lofted hit formed no part of his repertoire.

Argument continues to prevail as to his skill in 1948. The above figures to some extent speak for themselves, and it is a remarkable tribute to his own incredible standards that they should not in themselves settle the issue. Bill Edrich, who played in all five Tests, scored precisely the same number of runs that summer – *but in 24 more innings*. Robertson and Brown, of Middlesex, no mean performers with the bat, had 105 innings between them but could not jointly reach Bradman's tally of hundreds. Nor indeed could the joint efforts of Morris and Barnes.

It is true that Bradman was no longer the merciless killer who took each and every attack by the scruff of the neck. But he could still, as could few others, find the gaps between fielders. He had vast experience. And, despite his years (or because of them?), he seemed to use less effort than others. Bill O'Reilly was satisfied – as Bradman himself was well enough aware – that the 1948 Bradman was by no means the pre-war Bradman, high aggregates and averages or not.

He was still technical enough to outsmart most bowlers who opposed him [wrote O'Reilly in *Cricket Conquest*]. Knowing his own shortcomings as compared with his almost inhuman skill of former tours, Bradman never throughout the series tried to take liberties with any bowlers. He concentrated more than I had ever seen him concentrate before. If the bowling was accurate in length and pitched at the stumps he was content to bide his time and wait for the scoring chance to come without going looking for runs as he used to do in his pre-war days. Many times during the 1948 season I saw fieldsmen stationed in the short positions to Bradman's batting – places wherein it would have been impossible to have found any fieldsman foolhardy enough to go in other days. There were those kindhearted enthusiasts who greeted all Bradman's high scores of 1948 with the stereotyped rejoinder that 'He's just as good as ever.' That opinion was inspired perhaps by the speaker's sense of loyalty to a schoolboy idol. But no one in his proper senses could compare the Bradman of 1948 with the one of 1930 to 1938. He was slow to follow the moving ball. Spin bowlers, whenever he met one, found him allergic to the ball which moved away from his bat. Young Hilton, at Manchester, could hardly have believed his eyes when he saw the 'Great White Chief' make such a hash of trying to hit his inoffensive lefthanded leg-spinners round the countryside. Hollies, a straight-out righthanded leg-spinner, who had had experience of Bradman's prewar skill, found Bradman's wicket was not very difficult to obtain in 1948.

And O'Reilly again at the end of the tour: 'Not once since cricket has been resumed has "the little fellow" taken up the whole stage as he did before. He was still a fine batsman undoubtedly, but the "killer instinct" had gone completely. He, at most times, appeared quite human – if there is truth in the old adage "to err is human".' George Mann played against Bradman both before and after the war, and in his view 'the only difference seemed to be that he was comparatively human for the opening ten minutes or so of an innings. I think I heard him say that he felt he had to play from memory during that period. This consequence of advancing years, combined with the then new technique of bowling for catches at leg slip produced a slight Achilles heel (A. V. Bedser helping). One always felt that had he been presented with this problem a few years earlier, he would have solved it completely.'

For all that, there must still have been many bowlers in 1948 who must have felt that if Bradman *was* playing at any periods from memory, then he must have had a very good memory! His skill impressed itself on countless people, players as well as watchers. He made astonishingly few mistakes while batting in 1948, and it must certainly be true (as it is for many truly great batsmen) that he found it easier to bat faultlessly than to make errors. When he made his three centuries in successive innings at the end of the tour, all three were faultless – and in two of those scores he deliberately gave his wicket away. In a single day at Headingley, during his match-winning 173* v England, he literally gave more chances (four) than in all his other ten centuries on the tour combined (which contained only three chances). Trevor Bailey has said of him in 1948: 'I bowled against him then on three occasions, for Essex, for Gentlemen of England, and in the Hastings Festival. He was past his prime, but he scored 187, 150 and 143 and supplied me with three very good reasons for placing him as the finest batsman I have ever bowled against.' Jim Laker, too, at the end of a notable career of confronting many superlative batsmen, still has no hesitation in placing Bradman at the head of them all. 'Don Bradman', he has written, 'was the only batsman I have known to give me an inferiority complex. I was always a keen student of cricket in my youth, and I suppose that when I entered the first-class game I was more liable to be impressed by a "name" than, say, Brian Statham, who never saw a big match before he became a first-class cricketer. The fact that I was inexperienced and Bradman was still the mighty Don in 1948 might have had something to do with the feeling of awe I felt when bowling to him. Yet I never felt like that when I was bowling to Hutton, Compton,

Morris, Weekes and other fine batsmen, even in my comparatively "green" years. As I ran up to bowl, Bradman seemed to know what I was going to bowl, to know where the ball was going to pitch, and to know how many runs he was going to score. That was exactly the uncanny impression he gave.' Laker never had the opportunity to bowl to Bradman on a bad wicket. 'Even so', he says, 'Bradman was the greatest player I have ever seen or played against.'

After 30 successive seasons as Cricket Correspondent of the *Daily Mail*, Alex Bannister, in November 1976, said that of all the great post-war players he had seen on tour, Don Bradman was 'head and shoulders above them all' – a remarkable tribute over so great a span of professional watching. 'And let us admit it', said Norman Yardley once, speaking surely for many thousands – 'there is no shadow of doubt that he is the greatest cricketer of his generation!'

The balanced judgment of H. S. Altham, delivered after the close of the '48 tour, was that 'if Bradman no longer murdered the bowlers, their extinction, if less evident, proved almost as inevitable'. That really summed it up – the inevitability, the ruthless taking of the initiative from bowlers, the hopelessness of confronting him. W.G. in his prime was much the same. But what did Brian Sellers, for so long captain of Yorkshire and son of a first-class cricketer, say in 1948? 'In my opinion, the Don is the greatest player the game has ever seen or is likely to see for many years to come. My father, who played with W. G. Grace, thought the same.' To say that Don Bradman, even in 1948, was a phenomenon is merely to acknowledge the paucity of one's vocabulary.

The time of course will come when fewer and fewer people will remember the Bradman of the early '30s, or of the late '30s. His stature in those years will have to be accepted as we accept today the stature of W.G. There are many thousands still who remember the post-war Bradman, even though his aura then inevitably owed much to his pre-war charisma. But he never after the war gave the smallest sign of slipping from his lofty pedestal. And in England certainly, in 1948, he was the grand master – whether on the cricket field or in the banquet hall or indeed wherever he appeared. Was it luck that saw his skill stay with him to the end? Was it his own judgment of his personal capabilities? If the second war had lasted a year longer and Australia had come to England in 1949, what then? The future was uncertain for Bradman when he allowed his fellow-selectors to consider his name for the 1948 tour of England, and he had a great deal to weigh in the balance. That he did the weighing carefully – even meticulously – is certain. That the 1948 tour ran so smoothly was as much a tribute to Bradman as to his manager, Keith Johnson, and his splendid team. The social demands on Bradman in 1948 could well have swamped him had he allowed them to. The invitations, from the mightiest to the lowliest, called for a great deal of tact on his part. His mail was colossal, and so was his capacity for answering it – though in the early stages of the tour, when in one period of two days he received more than 600 letters, even Bradman found it impossible to reply to all personally, and the task had to be delegated. Apart from luncheons and dinners, Bradman made very few public utterances in '48 and very few reporters could corner him. As on previous tours, he could never be seen in the lounges or bars of hotels. He would take breakfast and dinner with his team, occupying whatever vacant seat there was. There were rumours of dissent between Bradman and Miller, and their temperaments certainly did not match – but neither could be said to have had a bad tour as a result. With the England players Bradman did not mix very much, but this was just his way, and he was always friendly. He encouraged good relations between the teams, as did his opposite number, Yardley. The teams exchanged ties and bats and the series was fought in a good spirit. Any of the old charges of unpopularity were rarely voiced against Bradman in '48. He took each ground that he played on by storm, and he was loved for it. His players recognised his burning wish to go through the tour undefeated, and they responded, especially after the final Test was over, with all the loyalty they could muster.

A little girl sent Bradman a birthday card in 1948 and was duly laughed at by her school-friends for doing so. She received back from Don Bradman a letter of thanks – and on the reverse were the signatures of the entire Australian team. Children were very rarely let down by Don Bradman – it was his habit nearly always to set aside their letters for his personal attention – though the enormous seeking after his autograph on that final tour inevitably caused some disappointments. A London schoolboy, after waiting several hours in the rain for the signatures of the Australians at Hastings in September, told his mother: 'I didn't get Bradman's autograph but he trod on my toe, though.'

Metaphorically, Bradman trod on few toes in 1948. The Tennyson incident, of which the public were unaware of the facts, was quickly submerged in the euphoria of the tour. The 'open letter' to Bradman that the *Daily Express* carried on 26 May and which said he was contravening the spirit of cricket by allowing Barnes to field with one foot on the edge of the pitch likewise came to nothing. At the end of the tour he upset some people by being photographed with his hands in his pockets while walking with the King at Balmoral – the picture can be seen in the 1949 *Wisden* at page 65. But King George VI, it should be remembered, like his father before him, always encouraged the most informal and friendly atmosphere in receiving Empire visitors. Rules and conventions which were strictly applied to residents in England were relaxed for them. This was the celebrated occasion on which Fergie, who scored in every one of the 52 Tests in which Bradman played, was asked by the King: 'Tell me, Mr Ferguson, do you use an adding machine when the Don comes in to bat?'

Few tourists have been personally better organised than was Don Bradman in 1948: and considering that he was captain, the sporting focus of a nation, and endlessly in demand, that was again no mean achievement, but one entirely in character. While still being able to reserve most of his energies for cricket, he was never caught unprepared in any situation. His speeches, as in 1938, he worked on most carefully – and well in advance. The speech he delivered when the team were the guests for dinner of the Lord Mayor at the Mansion House he prepared in Tasmania. He even had time to make a sight-seeing trip to Paris with some of his colleagues on the week-end between Hastings and Scarborough. On the final day of the tour, as the team were preparing to leave their London headquarters, the Piccadilly Hotel, virtually every room was in a state of confusion bordering on chaos – all except Room 326, the room of the captain. Don Bradman was perfectly in control. While others could not find shoes or shaving brushes, he was the first to be ready in a neat lounge suit. He was the first to be packed, the last item to go in being his latest trophy, a silver cup from Mr Stanislaus A. Santos, of British Guiana, who signed himself 'a true Australian fan'. That was on 23 September 1948, when Bradman and his team left St Pancras by train for Tilbury to board the S.S. *Orontes* for home.

'It had been without doubt in every sense', recorded Bradman, 'the grandest tour of all.' The British public were happy to echo H. D. G. Leveson Gower's last words on the Oval balcony at the end of the fifth Test: 'Well done, Don.'

The Times thought it incumbent to bid Don Bradman farewell with a leading article, part of which is here reproduced with permission:

If statistics were the last word in cricket, then it would be easy to prove that Donald George Bradman is the greatest cricketer who has ever lived. Happily they are not and memory, warm with summer days stretching back for nearly a generation, rather than pedantry brooding over decimals, prompts the good-bye and come back if only as a visitor that speeds the Australian captain on his homeward voyage. He sailed yesterday with an unbeaten team after making a century in his last match in England as he did long ago in his first. His own summing up of all that happened between was to express a mild hope that he had made 'some contribution to international cricket'. A fairer way of putting it is to say that no player, since history was made in the Hambledon era on Windmill Down, has contributed more to the game . . .

To have seen Bradman at the wicket is to have enjoyed the precision of the art of battting. Larwood's fierce attack and the cunning of Verity's spin – and, in the last chapters, Bedser's patient industry – tested his almost inhuman quickness and certainty of reaction, but only to remind spectators that he was a miracle of flesh and blood and not a little robot under a long-peaked green cap. Arthur Shrewsbury used to say, when he went out to bat after lunch, 'Bring me a cup of tea at half-past four.' Bradman, but for the dusk that causes stumps to be drawn at the end of even the longest afternoon, could with equal confidence have ordered his dinner in advance to be sent out on to the field. At the top of his form there was no getting him out. Some baby now toddling after a soft ball in New South Wales may grow up to be the scourge of English Test teams in the sixties. Old stagers who then watch him piling up a century will be able, however finely he plays, to murmur: 'Ah, but you should have seen Bradman.'

A Bradman happens once, and it had been heady champagne while it lasted.

14 Retirement:
The Elder Statesman

A politician thinks of the next election; a statesman, of the next generation.
James Freeman Clarke

Don Bradman returned to Australia in October 1948 immovably ensconced
as a national sporting legend, with never a hint that he could ever be toppled.
What a man, sighed his admirers. Some at once saw him as a future Lord
Mayor of Adelaide. Others saw him even as Prime Minister of Australia.
While he was still on the ocean, it was reported from Adelaide that Bradman
would be asked to stand as a Liberal Country League candidate at the 1949
Federal elections. (He had shown some sympathy in the past towards their
cause.) But when he reached Perth, he said he had not been consulted and
early in December he categorically stated: 'I am not at all interested in
entering politics.' He was a sportsman, not a politician, and he quietly
returned to his stockbroking business, with whose ways he was familiar, and
allowed parliament to get on without him. He had lost nearly a stone in
weight during the England tour and knew that the fresh exertions of a fresh
career were not for him.

Although it was his intention to play no cricket at all in 1948–49 – not
even for his club, Kensington – he did actually play in three testimonial
matches which marked his final appearances in the first-class game.[1] The
first of them was his own testimonial match, staged at Melbourne in December 1948 between his own XI and Lindsay Hassett's XI. At a reception
before the start he told the crowd that the happiest moment of his life was
watching Neil Harvey, aged 19, make the winning hit against England in
the Headingley Test. In surveying his career he puckishly picked out as the
highlight the occasion of his first century, as a 12-year-old for his school –
which got him into trouble for leaving the school bat behind on the ground.
The testimonial match itself was a huge success and ended in a tie (which
was certainly not contrived). Bradman himself scored 123 and 10, his century
being his fourth in a row in first-class cricket. A crowd of nearly 53,000
watched him score it, and he entered the huge arena to a standing ovation.
It was the last season any of them would ever be able to indulge in 'Brad-
mania'. When he was 97 he skied a 'dolly' off Johnston to Colin McCool at

---

[1] The idea was also mooted of staging an Australia v The Empire match at Melbourne in the
last week of October 1948 in Bradman's honour. Possible participants named included
Hutton, Compton, Evans, Wright, Nourse, Mitchell, Worrell, Headley, Hazare, Mankad and
Bert Sutcliffe. The proposal was discussed in Australia in July 1948 but proved impracticable.

wide mid-on – straight down McCool's throat, according to an eye-witness. McCool juggled with the ball and allowed it to fall to the ground, showing what most believed to have been mock chagrin. The Don ran three to complete his hundred, the incident provoking a great shout of mirth from the crowd, in which Bradman joined. Soon after he gave his wicket away. The match produced £A9,342 for Bradman. The previous record benefit in Australia had been £3,000, shared by Macartney and Ryder.

Between the playing of this match and his final two matches that season came the announcement on 1 January 1949 of Bradman's knighthood. It had not been entirely unexpected, even though it was breaking with all precedent to knight a cricketer primarily for his performances as a player. The Melbourne *Herald*, for one, had in the previous July certainly anticipated his knighthood. Sir Francis Lacey, Sir Frederick Toone and Sir Pelham Warner had preceded him, but even in Sir Pelham's case the honour did not come until 17 years after his last match for Middlesex. As long ago as ten years before, the *Daily Mirror* in London had speculated that Bradman was likely to be awarded the C.B.E. in the Birthday Honours List of June 1938. They were wrong, but certainly during the 1948 tour of England, the possibility of a knighthood for Bradman was freely talked about in cricket circles, and Andy Flanagan, of Sydney, who was writing on the tour, recorded these impressions at the time: 'Discussion is rife in England as to whether Bradman will receive a knighthood. One has only to observe how obsequious many in high places here, even lords and dukes, are in Bradman's presence, to know the answer. He could, it seems, receive a dukedom or a baronetcy for the mere asking, and here they are discussing whether he will be made a humble knight.' However, it must not be forgotten that knighthoods for sportsmen were not yet the habit in 1948. The official citation in the New Year Honours List was that Bradman was to be created a Knight Bachelor 'in recognition of his services over many years as a cricketer and captain of the Australian Test team, and for public services in several directions'. At the age of 40 he was easily the youngest of the seven new Australian Knights Bachelor announced that day, the next youngest being Sir Claude Plowman, the Tasmanian engineer, who was 53. By far the greatest majority of men who are knighted – whether Australians or Englishmen – are over the age of 50, and Sir Donald Bradman may well hold yet another record in being the youngest Australian to be so honoured. Since his time there have been a few younger sportsmen (outside Australia) who have been knighted, including Sir Garfield Sobers (aged 38), Sir Leonard Hutton (39) and Sir Frank Worrell (39), while Sir Edmund Hillary was only 33 when he reached the summit of Mount Everest in 1953 and was knighted.[1]

---

[1] Prior to 1949, knighthoods in modern times at a younger age than Bradman were very rare. In 1938 Sir Kenneth Clark was knighted at the age of 34, as Director of the National Gallery; and Sir Laurence Olivier appeared in the 1947 Birthday Honours List not many days after his 40th birthday – a few months younger than Bradman.

The Bradman knighthood was enthusiastically received throughout the cricket world as a fitting seal to a memorable career. Bradman himself received an avalanche of congratulations. He spent that first day of January as guest of the Victorian Cricket Association at the Melbourne Cricket Ground during the Shield match with South Australia. At lunch suitable speeches were made, and among those fortuitously present were the English women's touring side, thrilled to meet Don Bradman on this notable day, and both the captain and manager, Molly Hide and Netta Rheinberg, found themselves obliged to speak and add their congratulations publicly to Bradman – which both of them did, of course, most graciously. Bradman himself (who sat next to Molly Hide during lunch) appeared to take it all in his stride and he himself spoke of his knighthood and of the services he hoped to render to Australian cricket. He regarded the honour as a royal tribute to 'the wonderful game of cricket and its importance in Empire relationships'. His New Year resolution was to do everything possible, off the field now he was retiring, to promote the advance of cricket.

It had been hoped by Australians that anyone honoured with a knighthood in the New Year Honours of 1949 would have the accolade bestowed personally by King George VI during a proposed visit to Australia and New Zealand in the spring of 1949; and although the planning of the Royal tour had reached an advanced stage of preparation, on the advice of the King's doctors the tour did not take place. Bradman instead received the accolade of knighthood from the Governor-General of Australia, the Rt. Hon. W. J. McKell, at an investiture in Queen's Hall, Parliament House, Melbourne, on Tuesday 15 March 1949. Bradman knelt on a red plush cushion while the Governor-General touched him on the shoulder with a sword. After the conventional words, 'Arise, Sir Donald', the two men shook hands warmly and smiled. Lady Bradman was among the 500 guests who watched her husband receive his knighthood. He remains the only Australian to be knighted for cricket.

Meanwhile he had played in two further – and his two final – first-class matches. At Sydney, at the end of February, he played in the Kippax–Oldfield testimonial match – the first time since 1934 that he did not captain his side, Arthur Morris being captain. It was his farewell to Sydney, and he happened to come to the crease on the Saturday afternoon, before a crowd of 41,575. One of them, Arthur Reed, recalls the occasion: 'Never have I experienced anything more dramatic than the silence after the fall of the previous wicket, the Roman roar when that tiny figure appeared in the pavilion door, the silence again as he took guard, and the engulfing uproar as the first ball went with meticulous precision to fine leg for two.' Bradman scored 53 in just over an hour, which included the special relish of a Bradman v Miller encounter. This was a rare event, and in fact Bradman faced Keith Miller in only three matches in his career in first-class cricket. In this one Miller sent down bumpers, which Bradman – his 40 years notwithstanding – thrillingly hooked, with nimble footwork, 'as though it were nothing more than a fly-swat'. Eventually he mistimed a slower ball from Miller, who thus took Bradman's wicket for the only time in his life. But a few doubters had by then been satisfied.

March 4–8, 1949, marked Bradman's final game in the first-class arena. It was in his home city of Adelaide, where spectators had not yet had a chance to see him since his return from the triumphant tour of England. His own testimonial match might well have been staged there, but the South Australian Cricket Association felt the larger accommodation at Melbourne would be advantageous. This last appearance was also his last Shield match – South Australia v Victoria – and was played for Arthur Richardson's testimonial. Though without practice, Bradman's 30 was top score for his side. But sadly he did not last out the full extent of the match. On the second day, 5 March, he trod on the ball while fielding in Victoria's second innings, sprained his right ankle, and had to be helped off the field, limping. It was something of an inglorious exit, and first-class cricket never saw him again. It was the cruellest irony that at the very last a sprained ankle, of all things, should befall the very man whose footwork had thrilled so many thousands.

There it was, then, the playing career of Don Bradman behind him. As Ray Robinson was so dramatically to put it: 'Suddenly cricket was like a room with the light switched off.' Never since W.G. had any one cricketer so completely captured the public imagination. Bradman achieved what many believed to be impossible – and was disliked by some and envied because of it. Len Hutton was once asked, on a wet day at Cambridge, for his version of the Bradman legend: 'He's a good chap. He's so good a chap there's some people's jealous of him!' No other cricketer of his time was subjected to more barbs from his detractors. Yet, also, and more importantly, as R. C. Robertson-Glasgow once said: 'No artist has more shrewdly understood and satisfied his public. With a mind as keen and enduring as Toledo steel, a body that might have won a welter-weight boxing championship, and feet as nimble as Fred Astaire's, he answered the craving of the multitude to an almost inhuman degree.' Bradman's eminence – his almost superhuman eminence – made him an idol of countless thousands, but sadly rarely left him free from the envy of the few.

> *He who surpasses or subdues mankind*
> *Must look down on the hate of those below.*

There is always something about a man's success, as Oscar Wilde was not slow to point out, that displeases even his best friends.

At the time that he retired, Bradman's aggregate of 28,067 runs was easily the highest of any overseas cricketer in first-class cricket. It had been achieved without the benefit of regular play for an English county, and apart from his four tours with Australian sides to England, the aggregate had been amassed entirely by way of the limited opportunities offered by Australian seasons. Since 1949, R. E. Marshall, Hampshire's Barbadian, has retired with 35,725 runs, though he was hardly an overseas cricketer in the true understanding of the term, having played for 18 successive years in the County Championship. Almost unnoticed by all, while Zaheer Abbas was stealing the headlines with a double-century against England in a Test match at the Oval, Garfield Sobers, on a quiet afternoon at Newark on 23 August 1974, scored 58 handsome runs against Worcestershire before being caught at first slip, to take his aggregate to 28,068 – just one run ahead of the Don. This was at the very tail end of Sobers' career – he played in only two further first-class matches – and these runs had taken him 605 innings. (But he had over 1,000 wickets to his name at that time as well!) Mushtaq Mohammed, among overseas players, also passed Sir Donald's aggregate in his 755th innings while scoring 39 for the Pakistanis v Trinidad at Queen's Park Oval at the end of February 1977; and R. B. Kanhai did so during a century against Northamptonshire at Edgbaston on 30 May 1977. At the moment of writing B. A. Richards is within striking distance. But it seems safe to say that without the assistance of regular cricket in England, no overseas player will exceed the Don's 28,067 runs. The nearest approach by an Australian is the 21,699 total by R. N. Harvey. The Don's total of 18,230 runs in Australia alone seems destined to stand for all time.

When K. F. Barrington, not long ago, described Bradman as 'a genius, in a class of his own', he was not specifically thinking of his career average of 95·14, but he might well have been. The Bradman career provides the classic instance where figures *do* mean something. His average is, of course, easily the highest in history, and it is not without profit to note that only five men have reached even an average of 60 over a whole career in the first-class game:

	Runs	Average
D. G. Bradman	28,067	95·14
V. M. Merchant	12,876	72·74
G. A. Headley	9,921	69·86
W. H. Ponsford	13,819	65·18
W. M. Woodfull	13,392	65·00

Even if one were – purely as an arithmetical curiosity – to deprive Bradman's average of the benefit of all the not-outs of his career, his final first-class average would nevertheless be 83·03 – still a vast distance ahead of all other batsmen duly retaining the benefit of their not-out innings. This illustrates something of the colossal margin that separated Bradman from all others, a margin not just on paper but – as bowlers found for twenty years – real and undeniable enough on the field of play. 'If Grace put cricket on the map', said Vivian Jenkins once, 'Bradman held it there, and made it glow with incandescent heat. What a man, and what a record!'

Bradman's career average was more than three times that of such undoubtedly good batsmen as George Emmett, Joe Vine, C. P. McGahey, W. W. Read, Arthur Carr and A. O. Jones, all of whom played for England and made over 20,000 runs. And there are others. For even such a batsman as T. W. Graveney to swamp other batsmen's averages threefold, one would need to take in batsmanship of the type of J. G. Binks and Arthur Jepson.

After his 1948 tour of England Bradman obviously cried out to be one of the Five Cricketers of the Year in *Wisden* – but it could not be so, as he had already appeared once (after his 1930 triumphs), and once is the ultimate ration for any player. But Hubert Preston went as close as he dare to give him a second entry by including his portrait – a splendid picture taken by Walkers of Scarborough – and preceding the Five Cricketers of the Year with a special feature on Sir Donald's career by Raymond Robertson-Glasgow. Only twice before had a similar thing happened: in the 1921 edition, to mark Pelham Warner's retirement; and the 1926 edition, to mark Jack Hobbs' great summer the year before.

Meanwhile the Bradman mind – no less enquiring and no less restless for all his retirement as a player – had immersed itself in two major forms of activity. There were his regular labours in his stockbroking business in Adelaide. And there were his literary labours – for Bradman had again become an author. In the English winter of 1948–49 he wrote an exclusive series of six cricket articles for the *Sunday Chronicle* in England,[1] starting in their issue of 28 November 1948, and ending on 9 January 1949. (In Australia these articles appeared also in the Melbourne *Herald*.) These features looked at his career, at the 1948 tour, and at current problems – fine material and most trenchantly expressed. But they were really only a prelude to the more major literary effort before him.

It was inevitable that a cricketer of such status should be approached to write his life story at the conclusion of such a career as his. The first moves actually came in England in 1948. Bradman himself was not the instigator of them. He had no plans – especially in the middle of a strenuous tour in his 40th year – to do any writing. He had, moreover, done no serious writing (outside short articles) for some ten years, since his 1938 *My Cricketing Life*, which was effectively a collaboration. But there was no doubt about both the nimbleness of his brain and the enormous appeal with the public of his name on a book. Bradman had no agent in 1948, and did not have the need for one. He was then a cricketer and stockbroker. Whilst he harboured no serious ambitions in the literary field, he was sensible enough to know that he had both a power over words and much of interest to say. He once stated publicly that if he had not been a cricketer he would very much have liked to be a journalist.

By the time he left England in 1948 Bradman had got himself a literary agent. The initial idea was David Higham's. He was one of London's most distinguished authors' agents – he always preferred the term to 'literary agent' – who had started in that role as long ago as 1925 (and, sadly, who died on 30 March 1978). Higham arranged an appointment to see Bradman in

---

[1] He had also written some exclusive articles for them in the spring of 1947.

the Piccadilly Hotel. This was in mid-tour. Higham put the proposition that Bradman should write his memoirs, with Higham to act as his agent. 'I'll think about this', said Bradman, who temporarily left it at that. Bradman discussed the proposition with Denzil Batchelor, then steeply immersed in cricket journalism, and Batchelor soon afterwards wrote to Bradman to persuade him why he needed an agent. Batchelor could write a very persuasive letter – he was a practised professional with a mellifluous pen – and from all accounts he wrote a very impressive letter indeed! When Bradman returned to London he again met Higham in the Piccadilly Hotel, and this time Bradman knew exactly what he wanted to do. He would write the book; and terms were agreed. Higham was very impressed by the two interviews. He remembered Bradman as 'a remarkable man'. Such was Bradman's incisiveness of thought at the second meeting that Higham at once concluded: 'This man is a captain.' More than that, he believed that 'he could have been a general'.

The result of these deliberations was that Bradman in due course delivered his typescript, all very methodically prepared, and *Farewell to Cricket* was published on 22 June 1950, by Hodder and Stoughton – 320 pages at 12/6d. By a special arrangement Theodore Brun Ltd, of Great Russell Street, brought out simultaneously a limited de luxe edition of 500 copies, beautifully bound in full morocco, of which 150 copies, numbered 1 to 150, were signed by the author and were available only to members of The Collector's Book Club. The price was a modest 28 shillings (or, with gilt top, 30 shillings). (In addition, five copies of the de luxe edition, numbered I to V, were struck off as presentation copies.) The exclusive British serial rights of the book were sold to *The People*, where extracts appeared on several Sundays during July and August 1950. The book, needless to say, was written entirely by Sir Donald himself, and he appeared on the title-page as plain 'Don Bradman'. Many of the English reviewers were none too friendly; and while Bradman's opinions were respected, they were not necessarily agreed with. Charles Bray, in particular, was somewhat tart, and listed a catalogue of points that he proceeded to disagree with seriatim. Vivian Jenkins was upset that Bradman chose not to forget hardly a single pinprick he had suffered: 'If there is one thing Bradman dislikes more than another it is to be proved wrong about anything. Prima donna-ish, he bristles like a flouted Carmen at any assault on his ego.' D. R. Jardine, given a platform in *The National and English Review*, said of the book: 'A good deal of its interest lies in what the writer might have said and did not say, but it gives a picture of rather a lonely traveller.' The book nevertheless remains an important document in the Bradman story and one that no student of his period can afford to ignore. One of the most perceptive of all the reviews was one of the least publicised – hardly, one surmises, read at all outside the midlands. It was by the Cricket Correspondent of *The Birmingham Post*, W. E. Hall, who did not think too highly of the book – his own standards forced him to dub it 'poorly written' and 'journalese', perhaps over-harsh assessments – but he ended with a quite superb evaluation of Bradman's place in the development of twentieth-century cricket:

> In due course we shall come to see Bradman as an inevitable part of the evolution of the game. From Grace's integration of forward and back-play the art of batting advanced until, in Hobbs, a technique was perfected to master the 'new' bowling, as it has been called. It was the last of the qualitative changes in cricket, a fact realised by one writer who said that the game needed a new kind of ball to do what the 'googly' once did. But there has been no new kind of ball, and the only development left to batsmen between the wars was the quantitative one which followed, as surely as mass production followed the start of the Industrial Revolution. By the time Bradman arrived cricket had its hierarchy of the high priests of style, each of whom was held to be unassailable in his own line. There was one place left – for a batsman who should score more runs than anyone had ever done before. Bradman took that place, and if he had not, someone else would surely have done so. He made runs quickly, too, and he reminds us that the charge of slow scoring made against Australia in Tests is ill-founded. The reason why his batting did not always please those who saw it is that he did it too well. He was so much the master that he destroyed that sense of contest between bat and ball which is vital to cricket. All of us will concede that a tractor is the most efficient means of ploughing a field; but all of us would prefer to watch a team of horses. Bradman was a phenomenon. But we shall remember him as Bradman the cricketer: not Bradman the author.

Inevitably Sir Donald Bradman dropped out of the public eye after his retirement, though his name always continued to make news in a variety of ways. He now took more seriously to golf, and won the Mount Osmond Club championship in July 1949, just as he had done in July 1935 (as his first attempt). When he played in England in 1948 his handicap was eight, but his style was such to leave no doubt he would be hard to beat. He was asked then if he found it easier to hit a stationary ball: 'It would be if it was cricket-ball size.' Within three years of his retirement from cricket his handicap went down to scratch. To achieve that he had pursued a relentless course of practice and dedication, but it was precisely the sort of challenge that he most relished. Many years later, Colin Cowdrey was to write of Sir Donald: 'We also played golf together on his home course at Kooyonga, Adelaide, where he embarked on every round as though he were driving off for the World Match-Play Title.'

Cricket administration now began to occupy more and more of Sir Donald's time. It was especially fortunate – not only for Australian cricket but for world cricket – that he should have taken to administration so readily, especially in view of his early clashes with authority as a player. But very few Australians understood the game so deeply or were able to apply so piercing a mind to its problems. The administration of cricket over the last 30 years has been a succession of hurdles and puzzles, some technical, some moral, some political, and some personal. To some extent, too, they have interwoven and have had implications outside Australia and beyond the game of cricket itself. To be at the hub of the cricket scene, whether in

Australia or elsewhere, has been as much a responsibility as a privilege. Sir Donald undertook that responsibility – voluntarily and with no sense of self-advancement – alive at all times that the highest traditions of Australian sportsmanship were partially entrusted in his hands.

The pre- and post-retirement Bradman really reveals two separate careers. The first, of course, as a player, with a certain amount of selectorship and administration thrown in. Then as a selector and administrator alone. In the one he was before an adoring public week after week. In the other he was behind closed doors, taking decisions of various degrees of momentousness in concert with others. There were now no scoresheets by which to judge his prowess. As he himself wrote in 1977:

> One's efforts as a player are easily discernible but it is much less obvious in the other spheres. The confidences of selection committees mask success or failure. So too in administration, where decisions are by majority vote and rarely is the view of an individual recorded so that one's influence for good or bad is not known to history.

The entire career of Sir Donald Bradman the administrator has of course been an honorary one (as well as, it need hardly be added, an honourable one). Quite how many hours he has spent, and how many miles he has travelled, in the cause of Australian cricket, can never be computed. When he retired from being an Australian selector in February 1971, Sir Donald himself estimated that he had spent 'about eight years' away from home on duty as a Test selector. And that takes no account of the enormous number of years he has devoted to committees of both South Australia and the Australian Board stretching from before the war to the present time.

As a selector alone, he served Australia at Test level from the start of the 1936–37 series against England to the end of the 1970–71 series against England, with only a short gap in between, when he stood down on 18 August 1952 (as both an Australian and State selector) because of the illness of his son, John. He did no selecting at all during the 1952–53 South African tour of Australia and further played no part in selecting the 1953 side for England. Bradman was always one of three selectors for Tests and touring sides, and after the war he acted as chairman, though the actual position of chairman was not officially created by the Australian Cricket Board until five years after Bradman's retirement as a selector (when P. L. Ridings was so appointed in September 1976 to chair the selection committee in choosing the 1977 team for England).

At the time of his retirement as an Australian selector, Sir Donald had been involved in the selection of very nearly half of all the Test sides that had ever taken the field for Australia in the whole of history. Australia lost only 21% of the matches in which he was one of the selectors, the full playing record in such matches being as follows:

	Tests Played	Won by Australia	Lost by Australia	Drawn	Tied
In Australia	71	35	14	21	1
Away from Australia	80	33	18	29	0
	151	68	32	50	1

The measure of success against each of Australia's Test opponents is thus:

	Tests Played	Won by Australia	Lost by Australia	Drawn	Tied
v England	70	27	15	28	0
v South Africa	24	9	8	7	0
v West Indies	25	13	5	6	1
v New Zealand	1	1	0	0	0
v India	25	16	3	6	0
v Pakistan	6	2	1	3	0
	151	68	32	50	1

The above figures relate to matches from 1936–37, when Bradman first acted as an official selector. Though he played no part in selecting the 1934 touring side for England, he did form one of the selection trio (together with Woodfull and Kippax) when the team were actually in England, and thus had his first experience in helping to select Test elevens at the early age of 25.

In addition, Sir Donald was one of the selectors for the five Australian sides that visited New Zealand, without playing Tests, under W. A. Brown in 1949–50, I. D. Craig in 1956–57 and 1959–60, L. E. Favell in 1966–67, and S. C. Trimble in 1969–70. As a Test selector, Bradman's name was for a dozen years – from 1954–55 – linked with Jack Ryder, of Victoria, and Dudley Seddon, of New South Wales. They proved themselves a powerful and successful triumvirate, transacting much of their selectorial business – so legend has it – by swiftly conducted three-way telephone calls linking the three men in Adelaide, Melbourne and Sydney. Bradman was, of course, the South Australian on the committee, but no charge of parochialism can be proffered against him, for South Australian players chosen for their country during Bradman's selectorship were very firmly in third place behind Victorians and New South Welshmen. The earlier selectors with whom Bradman worked were E. A. Dwyer (New South Wales) and W. J. Johnson (Victoria) – the latter was Ian Johnson's father – and towards the end he helped pick Test sides with R. N. Harvey (New South Wales) and S. J. E. Loxton (Victoria). Richie Benaud, at the time of Bradman's retirement as a selector, remarked: 'Sir Donald was easily the best selector I came across in the game anywhere in the world, not just in Australia.'

As a Sheffield Shield selector – again as one of a trio – Bradman served South Australia for 28 seasons, starting in 1935–36 and ending in 1969–70, missing only 1952–53 (when South Australia in fact won the Shield).

Altogether, in the 28 seasons involved – five before the war and 23 after – South Australia won the Shield four times and finished second five times. They were never a particularly potent force, except perhaps when Bradman and Grimmett were in their ranks, and, later on, when Sobers arrived.

When the 1971–72 season began, Sir Donald Bradman was not selecting any sides at all, either for Australia or South Australia. He was still only 63 (a long way short of Jack Ryder, who had been an octogenarian selector) – and Sir Donald's retirement ushered in an era of more youthful selectors in Australia, as had already become the pattern in England. Indeed, although there were various reasons – family, business and health – which caused Sir Donald to give up State and national selectorship, he was prompted also by the desire to make way for a younger man. He was succeeded as South Australia's representative on the Australian selection committee by Phil Ridings, ten years his junior. At the same time the Australian Board of Control placed on record its appreciation for 'the long and valued service' rendered by Sir Donald as an Australian selector.

Like any selector in any part of the world, Bradman did not escape criticism during his long tenure of office. Especially when his playing career was over, and when the centuries were no longer inexorably paraded before a doting public, he attracted an element of opposition that was prepared – often anxious – to place on his shoulders the blame for any alleged selectorial shortcomings as if he himself comprised the entire selection committee. The criticism permeated from the press to the man in the street. Selectors do not divulge their confidences, but there can be no doubt that Bradman qua selector was as conscientious in that role as in all else of responsibility that he undertook. He has himself said that he more than once fought for the inclusion of a man who was eventually omitted – and yet suffered the public censure for his omission. It no doubt gave a good many people a malicious pleasure out of the ordinary to know that Bradman could no longer hit back at his detractors with the magic of his bat.

It is impossible to say in which role, off the field, Sir Donald has served cricket best. It would be undesirable – as well as unprofitable – to make the attempt. Apart from his career as selector, he has given unstinted service to both the Australian Board of Control and the South Australian Cricket Association. Both these bodies have derived decades of benefit from the presence in their midst of Sir Donald, who has never chosen to give either of them less than the maximum fruits of his endeavours.

His services as an administrator have been so varied that to put them on record in any composite form must smack of the nature of a catalogue. On the Australian Board of Control itself – which changed its name to the Australian Cricket Board in September 1973 – he has served continuously, apart from two brief breaks, as one of South Australia's delegates from his first meeting in September 1945 to the present time. In May 1953 he resigned due to his impending overseas absence that year to write on the Test matches in England, resuming his place on the Board in December that year on the

death of another South Australian, H. H. M. Bridgman. He resigned again –
for the same reason – in April 1956, taking his place again in September
1957, since when he has had an unbroken spell as a delegate exceeding 20
years.

Sir Donald was elected unopposed as Chairman of the Australian Board –
the first Test cricketer to hold this post – on 13 September 1960, at the annual
meeting of the Board in Sydney, in succession to W. J. Dowling, of Victoria.
This was the start of his first three-year term as Chairman, the Board's
constitution precluding a man holding the office for more than three consecutive years. He therefore on 11 September 1963 vacated the Chairmanship, but was elected for a second three-year term from September 1969 to
September 1972. Thus he was Chairman during the prolonged South
African crisis which led to the cancellation – announced by Sir Donald
himself in a judicial statement issued on 8 September 1971 – of the proposed
tour by South Africa of Australia due to begin a few weeks thereafter. Sir
Donald had been one of the three members of the Board's Emergency
Committee which had grappled with this emotive issue, and until the last
moment that committee had done everything practicable for the tour to
proceed. Sir Donald was a member (and Chairman) for many years of the
Board's Emergency Committee.

For South Australia, quite apart from representing them on the Board for
over 30 years, his functions have been enormous. His membership of the
Cricket Committee of the S.A.C.A. dates back to 1938–39, when he was
already of course a State selector, and continued until 1965. In 1943 he was
elected a member of the South Australian Ground and Finance Committee,
on which he is still serving. By the time Shield cricket was resumed in 1946–47,
he was also on the Emergency sub-committee and the Oval sub-committee.
He was one of South Australia's representatives at the Interstate Conference
of Sheffield Shield States from 1945 until that body was merged into the
Australian Board in September 1973.

He was made an honorary life member of the South Australian Cricket
Association in September 1947, and two years later was elected honorary
treasurer. He was a Vice-President from 1950 to 1965, and was elected
President on 28 July 1965 in succession to R. F. Middleton. He was elected
unopposed and held the Presidency until 1973, when he announced his
voluntary retirement to make way for a younger man. He was appointed a
trustee in September 1957, and is still so serving. At the same time he caused
some surprise – and some speculation – when he took on the post of honorary
State coach for one season, but this was only because G. Noblet was not
available to act as coach. He did actually perform the duties of a coach –
but was quick to dispel any rumours of a suggested come-back! He has
served on numerous South Australian committees of varying degrees of
significance, and was Chairman of the important Select Committee on
Throwing set up by the State in 1959 to report on that problem, which of
course was of moment not simply within South Australia.

It was the chairmanship of this committee (which included, among others, Mel McInnes, Colin Egar and Phil Ridings) which fitted him so ably to be one of Australia's delegates at the Imperial Cricket Conference meeting at Lord's in 1960 and which also was of inestimable value when he assumed the reins of the Board of Control, as Chairman, soon after. Sir Donald's attendance at the I.C.C. meeting of 1960 was an important departure from practice, for Australia had normally been represented by 'local' proxies (at that time Walter Robins and Ben Barnett, then living in England). With the throwing problem high on the agenda – as well as dragging and the use of bumpers – the Australian Board, after some indecision, sent over their Chairman, Bill Dowling, and Sir Donald, both ably briefed. When they arrived at London Airport from Sydney, Dowling, though Chairman, was all but ignored as reporters rushed to question Sir Donald on the pressing subject of throwing in particular. 'My opinion is not important in this matter', he protested. 'What is important is the umpire's opinion. The umpire must be the sole judge. Otherwise it is like trying a fellow for murder and then disagreeing with the verdict.' But, of course, Sir Donald's opinion *was* important – and that is why he was in London. He knew, too, that Australian interpretation of the law was not the same as England's. He and Mr Dowling did not merely attend the Conference. They stayed behind and spent a good deal of time at Lord's discussing the throwing problem with senior English administrators and examining films of suspect actions. Sir Donald also had an opportunity of seeing Geoffrey Griffin in the nets at Lord's. He watched the Saturday of the Middlesex–South Africans match from the Committee Room, sitting beside Sir Pelham Warner, and on the last day of the match watched from the South Africans' balcony. He also watched the Trent Bridge Test – and one morning took out a bat to give some catching practice to the players.

On his return to Australia in August, Sir Donald admitted that the following year's (1961) Australian tour of England could lead to 'the greatest catastrophe in cricket history' if the throwing controversy was allowed to get out of hand. 'It is the most complex problem I have known in cricket', he said, 'because it is not a matter of fact but of opinion and interpretation. It is so involved that two men of equal goodwill and sincerity could take opposite views. It is quite impossible to go on playing with different definitions of throwing. This was the great hurdle of the Conference and it unanimously and amicably agreed on a uniform definition. It was the major achievement, but it still has to run the gauntlet of time. We must find some answer which places due regard on the integrity, good faith and judgment of all countries, their umpires, players and administrators. I have good reason to think certain proposals under examination might lead us into calmer waters. I plead that a calm, patient attitude be exercised while we pursue and resolve the problem.' Sir Donald henceforth played his part to the full in finding that answer and, with patience, the throwing menace was wiped out of Australian cricket, as it was by administrators elsewhere in the world.

When he came to Lord's in July 1960, Sir Donald stepped into the venerable pavilion for the first time in his life as an honorary life member of the Marylebone Cricket Club. The news became known on 5 August 1958, and was described in Adelaide that day by Alan Lyon, secretary of the South Australian Cricket Association, as a great honour for Australian cricket and a fitting reward for a lifetime of wonderful service to the game. Up to then, honorary life membership of the M.C.C. had been conferred only upon members of the Royal Family and famous statesmen, like Mr Menzies, the Australian Prime Minister. Sir Donald's election was under a new rule of the club, that had only recently been brought into use, whereby the committee were empowered to elect as an honorary life member any person whose membership was considered to be particularly desirable in the interest of the club. In a letter to the M.C.C., Sir Donald expressed 'my deep gratitude for the great honour which has been conferred upon me'. In his own country he is a life member of the two district clubs – St George in Sydney, and Kensington in Adelaide – for which he played with such brilliance when not engaged in first-class games. His election to life membership of St George was somewhat belated – more than 31 years after he played his last game for them. But it was passed with great acclaim at the club's annual meeting at Hurstville on 14 July 1964.

What sort of administrator has Sir Donald been? According to Tim Caldwell, of Sydney, who has served for many years with Sir Donald on the Board and succeeded him in 1972 as Chairman, he is a man who is 'incisive in thought, who does his homework thoroughly – more so than others – and is an outstanding administrator because of his aggressive attitude in those matters in which he believes'. He is as positive in his cricket thinking in committee as he was with his bat on the field. Jack Fingleton, in 1960, acknowledging his greatness as a batsman, said: 'I sometimes wonder whether Bradman, now a legislator, is still not prone to dominate the field as he did when a player.' It is true that Sir Donald does stick to a point when he believes it to be right. He *does* often dominate the thinking, because of the homework he has done. He is willing to learn if evidence is produced: but, as one of those who has known him well has said: 'The little — is so often right.' Administrators *do* argue with him, but his views are highly respected and count for much, stemming from his great knowledge and favoured background as a player. He can take decisions, is unafraid to shirk difficult issues – 'drag', the front-foot rule, throwing, and the South African crisis were all tackled boldly by him – and whilst he has not always been infallible, he has at least attempted to be scrupulously fair.

The laws of cricket in particular – ever since that day in 1933 when he passed the New South Wales umpiring examination – have been his great interest. 'What does Bradman think of that?' has been the frequent question when a problem on the laws has come up for debate. He has always maintained a great channel of correspondence all over the world on matters pertaining to the laws, and will gather responsible views from many quarters before weighing an issue in the balance. He is judicial as well as incisive in his approach to cricket's problems.

How has he seen his own role as a selector and administrator? 'In those areas', he has said, 'I endeavoured to encourage all that was best for the development of the game.' Few will choose to question that. If he saw the presence of Garfield Sobers and Barry Richards as a benefit to South Australia, he encouraged their coming. If he saw the relationship between players and administrators becoming too delicate, he sought to strengthen it. If he saw a weakness in the lbw law, he sought by legislation to amend it. Ever since 1933, when he first wrote a letter to the M.C.C. advocating a change in the lbw law to include a ball pitching on the off side (then excluded from the law), he has consistently proposed an extension in favour of the bowler so that a batsman might be out to a ball pitched outside the line of the off-stump even though he might not be in a straight line 'between wicket and wicket' (i.e., where the pads too are outside the off-stump, provided of course that the ball would have hit the wicket). This, of course, has been aimed at preventing excessive pad play. One day this may become law, and for some years now an experiment has applied whereby a batsman can be so out provided the umpire believes he has made no genuine attempt to play the ball with his bat. As a lucid exponent of lbw reform, Sir Donald has always been to the fore, recognising its supreme importance 'because it establishes the whole groundwork for batting and bowling'. In 1947, in reply to an enquiry on this point from E. W. Swanton, Bradman said: 'Batsmen, who are generally in the majority, oppose alterations to the lbw rule which would assist the bowler, but the laws should be framed to make the game as attractive as possible, not to please the batsmen.' His advocacy to widen the scope of lbw did not, be it noted, stem from his closing days as an active player. It started in 1933. At times, too, Sir Donald has advocated embracing the *leg* side in the lbw law, but this has not gained wide favour and has always been rejected by the M.C.C. In 1957 Keith Miller, never exactly an off-the-field devotee of Bradman, asserted that the Bradman attempt to alter lbw was aimed at preserving his own records – a view which met with a hostile reception in Australia. It is true that the Australian Board some months before had discussed the leg-side extension – after a communication from New South Wales. And, again, it was sent to the M.C.C. at the request not of South Australia, but of Victoria.

Bradman never assumed the role of manager of an Australian side on tour and seemed consistently opposed to this at all times. 'Under no circumstances', was his reply at the end of Walter Hammond's tour of Australia when he was asked if he might consider managing the 1948 side to England if he did not go as a player. In July 1952 there was a strong body of opinion which held that he would be manager of the 1953 side to England, and he began being pressed to accept the post on the grounds that his managership would do much to pull cricket out of its financial doldrums. Then in August 1955 he was freely being spoken of in Australia as manager of the 1956 side.

The job could have been his for the asking, but he never considered applying for it. He was also publicly spoken of as manager of the Australian sides to the West Indies in 1954–55 and to South Africa in 1957–58. Indeed, for the latter tour, when the appointed manager, Mr Jack Jantke, of Adelaide, became indisposed, hopes rose swiftly – especially in South Africa, where Bradman had never been received in any capacity – that Sir Donald would replace him and provide a wonderful 'personality boost'. But Mr Jack Norton, of Sydney, went instead. Rumours surrounded him afresh in the early months of 1956 when he was publicly tipped as a possible future Australian High Commissioner in London. 'I know nothing about it', said Sir Donald in Adelaide. Talk in Canberra was that his old friend, Robert Menzies, would appoint him; and the tales became so persistent that Sir Thomas White, the current High Commissioner, who was due to retire in May 1956, was sought out in London for his comment. 'Yes', he said, 'I've heard it said that Bradman will take over from me. But this is a job for a senior Cabinet man. A tough job, too. There's about as much chance of Bradman coming here as High Commissioner as Len Hutton getting a similar job in Melbourne.' The rumours then fizzled out.

But Bradman did come to London in both 1953 and 1956 to write exclusively for the London *Daily Mail* on the England–Australia Tests. [1] The news was announced – with great pride – by the *Daily Mail* on 7 May 1953, and was welcomed both by the Australian team already in England and by Englishmen. The touring side's manager, George Davies, said: 'Sir Donald is looked upon with possibly more affection than anybody else by the Australian team and officials. On behalf of the team I can say we shall be very happy to have him among us again.' And Len Hutton, the England captain, said: 'He probably knows more about cricket than anyone else. I shall be very happy to renew our acquaintance.' He decided to come to England only because of the remarkable recovery made by his son John, who in 1952, aged 13, had contracted poliomyelitis, and in order to carry out the engagement Sir Donald resigned as a delegate on the Board of Control. It was on the initiative of the *Daily Mail*'s own cricket correspondent, Alex Bannister, that Sir Donald was procured in 1953, and the relationship between the two men was completely harmonious throughout the tour, as it was to be also in 1956. They have remained close friends ever since.

If Indians considered themselves unlucky in not seeing Don Bradman during his playing career, and if they were disappointed at his not setting foot on Indian soil when the *Strathaird* docked at Bombay in 1948, they took the fullest advantage when he and Lady Bradman passed through Calcutta on their way to London at the beginning of June 1953. Indian Cricket Board officials and local cricketers met him at the airport, where 1,000

---

[1] The *Daily Mail* had exclusive rights in England, though Sir Donald's material was syndicated to many parts of the cricketing world. A report from Sydney in the first week of March 1953 said that Sir Donald had been offered a fee of over £5,000 to write on the Tests but had then decided against the tour because of his son's illness.

cricket enthusiasts broke through a police cordon. Sir Donald and his wife had to be driven off in an army car! They arrived in London on 5 June after being delayed by engine trouble at Karachi, accompanied by Tim Wall's wife, Mrs Evelyn Wall, from Adelaide, who acted as Sir Donald's secretary during the tour and attended the Tests with him. He wrote quite masterly commentaries on the Tests so that even a *Times* leader at the end of the tour paid a generous tribute to him by remarking that 'his analytical comments in the *Daily Mail* were for those interested in the strategy and tactics of the game, a distinguished feature of the season'. He wrote in longhand in a small book, with several sheets of carbons. His contract stipulated that once his writing left him, it could not be altered, and he never failed to go through the printed version each morning to check it word for word. He wrote about 1,200 words on each day's play, as well as a preview and summary of each Test. He did not write on any of the matches outside the Tests.

When it was announced in April 1956 that he would again come to England to write for the same newspaper, Alex Bannister set down some words about the 1953 tour that were so intriguing as to merit reproduction here:

Many times during the memorable season of 1953 I was asked if Sir Donald Bradman, alone and unaided, wrote the brilliant commentaries on the Tests which appeared in the *Daily Mail*.

The answer is an unqualified 'Yes.'

Clearly, the batsman who upset all values with his record scoring; the captain with the strategic reputation second to none – in short, the world's greatest cricketer – needed no help in assessing individual form and the state of the game. Indeed, it was fascinating to sit next to him and see how long it took the captains to arrive at Sir Donald's thoughts.

He would observe: 'Fine leg is not fine enough.' Or: 'The slips are too deep.' Sure enough fine leg or the slips would ultimately be moved. He would anticipate bowling changes long before they happened.

During the second Test at Lord's Len Hutton, England's captain, asked if Sir Donald could spare a moment. It was to thank Sir Donald for the daily advice, sympathy, and penetrating tactical wisdom in the *Mail*.

As for Sir Donald needing a literary ghost . . . well, few professional writers could express themselves so clearly and lucidly.

I remember the last occasion when it was announced Sir Donald Bradman was to write for the *Daily Mail*. Lindsay Hassett's Australians were playing Yorkshire at Bradford and an experienced Australian newspaper man drily observed: 'Well, that means none of us counts now.'

How true. Sir Donald was pre-eminent as a player and he carries his genius to the Press Box.

He arrived in England again by air on 30 May 1956, for his second series as commentator for the *Daily Mail*, which was no less successful than the first. He set an unusual precedent (which had not been the case in 1953) in that he wrote critical observations on a touring team he had helped to select. There has been no subsequent instance of such a practice – at least not by an Australian – and it is worth remembering that on the very grounds that he had been one of the selectors, Jack Ryder declined several offers from English papers to go to England to write on the 1930 matches. In neither 1953 nor 1956 did Bradman play any cricket in England, but had he arrived in England in time he would have been invited to play for the Duke of Norfolk's XI against the Australians in the opening tour match at Arundel in 1956. It is not certain if he would have accepted, for he had many approaches to play in England – as indeed he did later on, in 1960, when he came for the I.C.C. meeting – and declined them all. But he did accept a few other less exacting invitations. He and Colin Cowdrey read the lessons at a special service for cricketers in 1956 at Islington Town Hall, where the preacher was David Sheppard, then a curate. And in 1953, two days after landing in England, he appeared as guest celebrity in television's 'What's My Line?' – and was duly 'recognised' by Gilbert Harding on the blind-folded panel!

On 28 June 1954 the surprise announcement was made that Sir Donald Bradman, on doctor's orders, was retiring immediately from his stock-broker's business in Adelaide. He was still only 45. He would continue to hold his cricket offices. He said he had received 'a serious warning' – the words were his own – from his doctor the previous week. It prompted him to hand in his resignation from the Adelaide Stock Exchange and he was closing his firm of Don Bradman and Co. the following Friday. 'For nearly 30 years', he told a reporter, 'I have been subjected to stresses and strains of a somewhat abnormal character which only those closest to me thoroughly understand. Therefore my doctor's advice to ease up is not altogether a surprise, even though unpalatable. I shall be sorry to relinquish my Stock Exchange work, which I loved very much, but as soon as circumstances permit I will take a complete rest.' And so the firm at 23 Grenfell Street changed its name, but continued as stockbrokers, with Sir Donald retaining a business link. Actually his right-hand man, Leonard Bullock, took over the goodwill of the business. By this time, too, Sir Donald was a director of many companies – today he is a director of at least 30 – and in due course he went back as principal of the new firm (Len Bullock and Co.), attending to busi-ness matters on most days when he was not at Tests or cricket meetings.

What sort of a business man has Sir Donald been? From his earliest days – certainly from his first tour of England – he was keenly aware that business could, indeed should, run hand in hand with cricket. He had shrewd commercial instincts. Those envelopes with Folkestone postmarks in 1930 did their job, as did many a subsequent envelope thereafter. One of the remarks attributed to him in 1930 was that his main ambition was to become Australia's Selfridge. It was estimated that he probably made £3,000 on each of his first two tours of England – which, for the 1930s, and for a young man in his twenties, was remarkably good. Up to the time that he left Sydney for Adelaide, his sports store work, his journalism and his radio talks brought him in about £1,500 a year. In May 1937 a London report said he had built up a fortune of £50,000 as a result of six years of first-class cricket, but this can only have been fantasy. Bradman himself reacted to it by remarking that it was regrettable that the paper publishing the report had become confused in quoting the total runs scored by W. G. Grace. But by then he had assets of probably £10,000, mostly in house property in New South Wales and Adelaide. He was rather more than less thrifty than others, and saved more than most cricketers. Yet his expenses were heavy, particularly in respect of provision he made in the 1930s for his parents.

As a stockbroker, he was a shrewd investor both for his clients and for himself. It was a common expression by those who knew him in his post-war stockbroking days that 'everything he touches turns to gold'. That view wasn't very wrong. He has always had a wonderful head for figures that he has turned to advantage time and again. But inevitably there were some members of the Stock Exchange who were jealous of the publicity his business received from his cricket.

He once turned down an offer by the *Sunday Express* in London of £1,000 for four 1,500-word articles – and that was during his playing career, when that sort of money was not often bandied about. He also once received an incredible offer of £1,000 a week, and fares for himself and family, to visit South Africa. That too was declined. But there were other occasions when he did earn large sums from newspaper articles and his books, not least from *The Art of Cricket* – perhaps the finest exposition of cricket technique ever written – published by Hodder and Stoughton in 1958. His ten-roomed house in Kensington Park is a handsome luxury home, with squash court and swimming-pool and a huge billiard-room, with walls covered with cricketing photographs and mementos, where his friends have been entertained for years. If he has done well for himself, it can be no more than a man with his gifts has deserved.

After his formal retirement from the game, Sir Donald played only very occasional games of cricket, and those of a social nature. On 6 February 1957 he scored 85 in as many minutes (with 13 fours, showing much of his old precision) and also took two wickets when he captained a team of share-brokers against their clerks at Adelaide; and he played in a similar match, organised by the Adelaide Stock Exchange, to celebrate his 50th birthday, when he again captained the stockbrokers and this time scored 89 before he was caught by a spectator, who finished with a pint of beer in one hand and the ball in the other – while Bradman ran off as though he were genuinely out.

His last match of all was on 6 February 1963 when, at the invitation of Mr Robert Menzies, he captained the Prime Minister's XI against E. R. Dexter's M.C.C. side in a one-day match played on a fine pitch, in beautiful sunshine, before a record 10,000 crowd at Manuka Oval, the premier ground of Canberra. The occasion brought forth the most rapturous prose from the critics. John Clarke began his report for the *Evening Standard* in London with: 'This was the day of Sir Donald, the day Bradman came back to cricket. And in cricket it rated as would a re-appearance of Michelangelo in the art world, or Keats among the poets.' Sir Donald fielded first at extra cover and later at first slip through M.C.C.'s innings of 253 for seven declared, and eventually came in to bat shortly after tea, at number five in the order, at 108 for three, a few minutes after four o'clock. He was wearing his Australian cap. He was given a prolonged ovation by the crowd and the M.C.C. team and seemed to be enjoying the occasion immensely. This is how John Woodcock, watching the match for *The Times*, recorded the next few minutes:

> Graveney, who was bowling, offered him a wide long hop to begin with, followed by a straight full toss which Bradman clipped back to the sightscreen. At the other end Dexter gave Statham another over.
>
> The first ball Bradman had from Statham he met with the middle of the bat, although it kept a shade low. Playing back to the second, he was slightly late with his stroke. The ball spun from his bat on to the top of a pad and thence into his stumps, with just enough impetus to remove the off bail. This was decidedly unlucky – 'It mightn't have happened one in a thousand times', he said – but there was nothing anyone could do about it except regret it.

The bowler's umpire, Alan Davidson, might just have saved the situation had he called 'No ball' very promptly. But he did not! Brian Statham, who had never before seen Don Bradman bat, later called the dismissal the most disappointing cricket experience of his life. 'Magnificent proof', declared Bradman himself a decade afterwards, 'that you can't rig a game of cricket.'

So, at the age of 54, Sir Donald Bradman walked back from the crease for the last time, out for 4. He had received five balls in all. His last partner at the wicket was a cricketing politician, Don Chipp, the Liberal Federal Government member for Higinbotham, Victoria. On that day, at least, Don Chipp outlasted the greatest run-gatherer of the twentieth century. Sir Donald, on his way to Canberra, had looked in for a few hours on the last day of the Victoria v M.C.C. game at Melbourne and conferred with one of his fellow-selectors, Jack Ryder: but any hints he might have wished to gather from the M.C.C. bowling did not result in any personal advantage! On the eve of the match at Canberra, Mr Menzies entertained most members of his team to dinner, and the captain of his own side, Sir Donald, and the reigning Australian captain, Richie Benaud, were his guests that night and the following night at The Lodge, the Prime Minister's residence in Canberra. Arthur Mailey was among the guests at dinner. On the morning of the match itself, Mr Menzies officially opened the new pavilion at Manuka Oval – the Bradman Pavilion. That night the Prime Minister entertained both teams at dinner at the Hotel Canberra. The following day Sir Donald declared: 'I have just played my last game of cricket. The cricket bat has seen the last of me.' And he kept his word.

Sir Donald then occupied himself with the companies of which he was a director, with his golf, and with his family. His son John had recovered completely from the attack of poliomyelitis he had suffered as a 13-year-old in 1952. It happily left little effect on him. He attended St Peter's College, Adelaide, and became a useful schoolboy cricketer who played for his school and for Kensington in the South Australian Cricket Association's Schoolboys' Competition and scored at least two hundreds in schools cricket in Adelaide. But he disliked his cricket through the constant publicity he attracted and concentrated on athletics. He became a fine hurdler, at one time holding the South Australian records for both the 120 yards and 220 yards hurdles, and, as a sprinter, ran the 100 yards in ten seconds and the 220 in just over 22 seconds. In March 1972, when he was 32 years old and a lecturer in law at Adelaide University, he changed his surname by deed-poll to Bradsen to escape the endless pressures of being identified as 'the son of' a famous man. 'I was popped into a metaphorical glass cage to be peered at or discussed', he complained. 'And I am no longer prepared to accept being seriously introduced as simply someone's son. I'm an individual, not a social souvenir.' It was a sad episode, but one that his father – who had himself been so ruthlessly exposed to the glare of publicity and endless comment for so many years – could well understand. 'Only those who have had to live with the incessant strain of publicity can have any idea of its impact', commented Sir Donald. As late as 1964, when John Bradman came to England during the Test series, he was on holiday in North Wales and signed in at a small guest house in Llanberis as 'John Bradman' – and at once came the enquiry 'Are you the son of Sir Donald?' He was never left alone by the other guests for the rest of the evening. Sir Donald would have understood that, too. He once said that when he went away with his family it was no holiday for them; he would rather stay at home.

The other child of Sir Donald and Lady Bradman is their daughter, Shirley. She, alas, has been a sufferer since early childhood from cerebral palsy. But she has led a reasonably full life; has come to England for holidays, drives a car, and, like her brother John, is married.

Sir Donald has sought to live a quiet life in recent years. He has always been ready to talk to players and help them with their problems. He is starting to go grey and wears glasses. But his interest in cricket is as great as it ever was. He is still sought out for a publishable opinion, for editors are aware enough that his name still has a glamour that cannot wear off. He is no confirmed *laudator temporis acti*. He dislikes public appearances and avoids being interviewed. His mail is still a large one – not only from people he knows but from those he has never heard of. The fanatical followers of cricket in India are particularly prone to write to him. The letters flow whenever his name appears in print. They flowed, for example, when he and Lady Bradman attended the Sydney Cricket Ground on 5 January 1974 for the opening of the new and splendid Bradman Stand – 'The Don has come home', was the verdict of those present. He received a rich reception when he walked on the ground, and quite delighted the crowd gathered for the

Test match against New Zealand when, in his neat suit, he played a stroke or two in the middle with a solitary stump.

A few months later Sir Donald and Lady Bradman made a special journey to London, where Sir Donald was guest of honour of the Anglo-American Sporting Club at a boxing-dinner evening at the Hilton Hotel in aid of the Lord's Taverners' Fund on 13 May 1974. Sir Donald, an honorary member of the Lord's Taverners since 1954, was invited 'in recognition of his unique and unforgettable contribution to world cricket', and the occasion was a personal triumph for him (as well as yielding proceeds of about £10,000 for the Taverners). A few days before, Sir Donald had attended an M.C.C. dinner at Lord's where, to the disapproval of some present, he was inevitably pestered to sign a good many menu cards. Before the Hilton dinner Sir Donald anticipated events and spent the preceding week-end personally signing all the 900 menu cards to be set before the capacity attendance. It was a characteristic piece of Bradmanism, and those menu cards, bearing the signature against a Roy Ullyett depiction of the Don, have found their way into many homes as personal treasures. Sir Donald left soon after with his wife for a brief holiday in Norway, and paid a private visit to South Africa on his way back home.

If the 22-year-old Bradman had been unable, at the end of his great tour of England in 1930, to get himself on to a postage stamp, the 67-year-old Bradman most unexpectedly did so in March 1976. Moreover, it was not even an Australian stamp, but one issued by South Africa to mark the centenary of the Champion Bat Tournament (the forerunner of the Currie Cup), first held at Port Elizabeth in 1876. Sir Donald was not named as the cricketer depicted, but an old photograph of him was actually used.

In September 1976 Bradman went back to Bowral, where everything had started. He returned to the Bradman Oval, to re-open the ground, rebuilt at a cost of $25,000, and to open the new Bradman Stand there. Cricketing fever gripped Bowral, especially as O'Reilly was due to be there too. Sir Donald and Lady Bradman shook hands with 230 guests at a dinner at Bowral Golf Club the night before – including many who had been to school with Bradman more than half a century earlier. On the day itself, before television cameras and a posse of photographers, O'Reilly bowled a single ball to Sir Donald which sped low down outside the leg stump – and which Sir Donald, attempting to hook, missed! The last time the pair had been in contention on that ground, Bradman had scored 234 runs in a day.

Sir Donald was back in the news again. He was invited by the Board of Control for Cricket in Pakistan to visit that country to attend a series of one-day matches there against an International XI in November–December 1976, to celebrate the centenary of the birth of Mr Jinnah, but he was unable to accept. At about the same time, in Adelaide, it was decided that the South Australian Cricket Umpires' Association Player of the Year award (for the cricketer with most umpires' votes in the district competition) should be given a new title – the Bradman Medal: and Sir Donald himself in due course presented it to the first recipient, Kevin Griffiths, captain of Adelaide University.

Sir Donald, naturally attended the Centenary Test celebrations at Melbourne in March 1977 and took his place among the former Australian captains who walked on to the field. He was in splendid spirit throughout those memorable days. At the Australian Cricket Board's sumptuous dinner at the Melbourne Hilton Hotel on the Monday of the match, he gave a fascinating and typically thorough historical survey of one hundred years of Test cricket between England and Australia, 40 minutes of oratory that brought a standing ovation from a full house of about 300, of whom some 200 were former England–Australia Test cricketers. The occasion served as a reminder of the camaraderie of cricket and that Donald George Bradman, for all his uniqueness, was but one of a great galaxy of players who have adorned the game throughout the ages.

Rumour, right up to 1977, still had a habit of surrounding him. When Sir Douglas Nicholls, Governor of South Australia, was contemplating stepping down from his post through ill-health, Sir Donald Bradman's name was one of several put out in the press as possible candidates – in the hope, perhaps, that there would be a denial (which there was not). Sir Douglas did indeed stand down, and was succeeded by the Rev. Keith Seaman, a Methodist minister – to put rumour once again in its place.

15 The Style and the Secret

About his batting there was to be no style for style's sake . . . His aim was the making of runs, and he made them in staggering and ceaseless profusion.
R. C. Robertson-Glasgow on Sir Donald Bradman, 1949

The story was often told before the war of how Archie MacLaren, after watching Don Bradman score a hurricane hundred at Lord's and being asked what he thought of it, replied, after slow consideration: 'I wouldn't give sixpence to bat like that.' The methods of MacLaren and Bradman were certainly vastly different, and each man – certainly each former England captain – is entitled to his view.

Bradman himself never made the smallest pretence towards style, and even as a 21-year-old, writing for the London *Star* in 1930, he said: 'Style, as style, I have never studied; my batting is dictated by the needs of the moment.' This was a tenet that Bradman held for the whole of his career. Years later he remarked: 'Style? I know nothing about style. All I am after is runs.'

Statistics can be made to mean anything, but the figures of Don Bradman's career must take a great deal of explaining away. That he set a new standard in batsmanship is undeniable: but it was a *standard* he set rather than a style. He was, of course, the greatest challenge to bowlers of his generation, and had he chosen to model himself on any batsman – which he decidedly did not do – his pre-eminence might not have been so marked. The pre-war Bradman, at least, was merciless in his appetite for runs. His limitless stroke range and power produced runs on a scale that the great stylists could not match. His resource made up for what he lacked in grace. Anything bordering on looseness was dealt with in a ruthless manner. He was so quick of eye, foot and bat that he could play strokes from positions that would have been impossible (and more often than not humiliating) for lesser player. He found his satisfaction as a batsman in achievement rather than in method.

Much as he might have chosen to deny it, Bradman certainly possessed the 'killer instinct' as a batsman up to the war. Bowlers knew it, fielders knew it, and spectators knew it. No man could have scored over 7,000 runs in all cricket in less than 12 months without it. 'I was never happier', said Bradman once, 'than when at the wicket facing a bowler. It was a challenge that never once lost its appeal.' *Never once.* That insatiable appetite for runs made run-getting for Bradman his method of self-expression. This certainly was the view of O'Reilly, who observed that Bradman expressed himself 'long and loud':

There was no escaping the Bradman bat when it was charged with the responsibility of smashing down all opposition. Off-theory bowling to a packed field was chicken feed to him, whereas the packed on-side field set for the leg-theory bowler was as nought. I have seen him step wide of his stumps and hit the leg-theory merchant past point where there was no fieldsman at all, and the off-theory bowler must often have wished that he had twenty fieldsmen instead of ten. That was the pre-war Bradman.

Bradman simply exuded confidence. Of that there can be no doubt. Having discovered that he was good, he made sure that others knew it and never forgot it. The legend of invincibility that grew up around the name of Bradman was helped firmly along its path as much by his own confident smile as he walked to the crease as by his subsequent feats in the middle. Like many young Australians he had a grin – certainly in the early '30s – that Jack Fingleton later described as 'the cheekiest, the most challenging, and the most confident thing I have ever seen in sport. It was such as to rip the innards out of any bowler . . .' That smile certainly went part of the way towards winning many a battle: and one battle having been won, the next was correspondingly less difficult. On this matter of the Bradman temperament, Ray Robinson has said that in his early years he 'almost burst at the seams with self-confidence'.

Dr Dickinson Priest, now of Jersey, was travelling through Australia around 1936 and chanced to sit one day beside Bradman at lunch. It was at the Adelaide Oval. The young and unknown Englishman, to the curiosity of all, was taken into Bradman's confidence, and one remark has stayed over 40 years: 'When I am set, and seeing the ball absolutely, I don't know how I could ever get out – I don't – until I get tired.' This was not mere arrogance, but a straightforward statement of fact.

It was Woodfull who always maintained that the secret of Bradman the batsman was his consistent ability to send the *good-length* ball to the boundary. It was this that set him apart from all other batsmen. It was this that made it so difficult to bowl to him a maiden over. It was this that made it so difficult to restrict his scoring rate. And it was the very feature most calculated to induce that feeling of despair in bowlers on which Bradman thrived so healthily and for so long.

That was not the only secret, of course. Many people tried to discover what it was that made Bradman pre-eminent. 'I'm just lucky', he once protested. But that was only shrugging off a questioner. A doctor in Sydney said he was born with a highly developed muscle sense. Another said it was the afferent and efferent nerves, which control the body actions. 'The afferent nerve telegraphs from eye to brain, the efferent nerve from brain to limbs. In my opinion, Don Bradman's efferent and afferent work quicker than most people's.' Perhaps. The South Africans under Cameron asserted his uniqueness was because he did not sweat.

Was it his wrists? Possibly they had something to do with it. But in the

Queen's Hotel, Leeds, on the Monday morning after his shattering 334 in 1930, an *Evening Standard* sports writer, Clyde Foster, and the Australian Press Association man, Geoffrey Tebbutt, had a 'wrist contest' with Bradman. Foster came first, Tebbutt second, and Bradman third! 'Compare my wrists with the wrists of Hobbs or Tate', said Bradman, 'and I suppose you would find theirs twice as big.' The two newspapermen pressed him for his secret. 'I am trying all the time to find out', replied Bradman, 'what is in the bowler's mind as he delivers the ball. It is a constant battle, one man against another – I to hit him and he to beat me.' That also had something to do with it, but not everything. Many men, by the way, with wrists like steel do not make good batsmen. Bradman also possessed exceptional muscles between the thumb and first finger of each hand. By a very early stage of his career, use had hardened them and made them of abnormal size. He gripped the bat as in a vice.

Don Bradman's secret was not one single attribute but a combination of several. They were quite divorced from the matter of style, in which he was inferior to many, but taken together within the personality that was Bradman, these attributes became a peerless mixture.

The ingredients of his genius may be listed as follows:

1 Unwavering concentration.

This was developed with a stump and a golf ball at the back of his home in Bowral and has never left him throughout his life, whether on the cricket field or off it. It was far more natural for him to concentrate at the crease than not to. Accordingly, the amount of 'loose' play (i.e. dangerous play) was eliminated to almost negligible proportions. 'The two most important pieces of advice I pass on to young batsmen', Sir Donald has said, 'are (*a*) concentrate and (*b*) watch the ball.'

2 A magnificent sportsman's eye.

In his playing days he had the eye of a hawk. His visual acuity enabled him to read an ophthalmic surgeon's chart right down to the bottom line. He had perfect eye muscle balance to discern a ball's direction and flight half a second before ordinary players. Some bowlers were sure that he could even see the way the ball was spinning as it came through the air.

3 Quickness of foot.

His superb footwork was variously likened to Anton Dolin and Fred Astaire. By moving so quickly he achieved the extraordinary power that characterised his strokes, for he was always in perfect position to make the precise shot he intended. He could not be confined. He virtually never needed to improvise (with the attendant risks) and for the same reason so rarely put the ball in the air. Allied to his magnificent eye, his speed of movement allowed him to move into the ball with perfect timing and certainty. C. B. Fry pointed out that all his strokes, however short, were swung, not pressed.

4 Temperament.

He possessed the perfect temperament for all occasions: relentless and imperturbable. Cricket was his life, not just his hobby. The pinnacle of success had no effect on his single-mindedness and rigid self-discipline. Self-adulation was unknown to him. His temperament marked him as a man apart. In a confrontation with a bowler, there was never any doubt in Bradman's mind who was master. Temperament was not the least of his attributes of genius.

To these basic ingredients there went also, in abundant supply, self-confidence; patience beyond the average; ambition; increasing experience; nimbleness of brain; spirit of aggression (the 'killer instinct'); fitness and stamina; strength of forearm and wrist; and a thorough understanding of the tactics of cricket. It was indeed the co-ordination of all these ingredients that made Bradman what he was. Some players have had some of these attributes; and a few players have had many of them. But none has been able to co-ordinate them to the degree Bradman did. Of only this one batsman in the whole world has it been possible to say, as Jack Fingleton once said of him, that 'every bowler, every fieldsman, every spectator in Bradman's heyday sensed that he was using not a bat so much as an axe dripping with the bowler's blood and agony'.

In Bradman's case there must be added, too, the encouragement and opportunity he received, the rapid promotion he – like so many Australians – was given, and the complete absence of any part played by his financial or other standing in life. To give youth an early chance has been age-long Australian policy.

One other valuable asset of Bradman's should be mentioned. He had an instinctive knowledge where every fieldsman was positioned. More than any other batsman he seemed to be able to place the ball to beat the field. No captain was ever heard to say he had discovered a field to frustrate the Don. In December 1938 both Jack Fingleton (captaining New South Wales) and Bill Brown (Queensland) thought they had discovered such a field, but Bradman scored 143 and 225 against them respectively. Bradman once gave a momentary glance round the field before receiving his first ball and said to the wicketkeeper: 'There's one missing. Oh, no. There he is. I lost him in the sun.' The number of occasions were absolutely legion when an opposing captain moved a fielder to block a scoring-stroke and Bradman promptly placed the next ball through the gap that had been created. He was, in addition to all his other attributes, equally at home on the off-side and the leg-side – as masterly a cutter as he was a hooker, as brilliant a hitter through cover as a driver through mid-on.

When P. F. Warner, who was never in Australia at any time in 1928–29, saw Don Bradman for the first time with a cricket bat in his hands – at the nets at Lord's on 24 April 1930 – he said: 'Bradman is not exactly a stylist, but he watches the ball closely and hits hard.' By the end of the tour, that initial judgment had been confirmed, and this is what Warner wrote in his book on the tour in 1930:

One would not call Bradman exactly an attractive bat, but he was undoubtedly a most interesting one. It will be seen from diagrams of his great scores that he very seldom drove straight, but he had at his command every other stroke. His cutting was extraordinarily fine, and safe. He was a master of the hook; he seldom, if ever, missed a ball on his pads, and he off-drove brilliantly. No batsman that I have ever seen has watched the ball more carefully. He seemed to follow it right on to his bat, with his nose well over the ball on every occasion. I was reminded of what Tom Emmett used to say: 'Smell her, sir, smell her!'

Bradman used his bat as an uncompromising weapon of offence and was irrevocably dedicated – at least up to the middle '30s – to the ruthless acquisition of runs. It was as much, if not more, a matter of mental state, where failure was quite out of the question, as a matter of stroke-play, stylish or otherwise. His batting was more of the staccato than the effortless. But let it never be thought that he was all function and no style. He was no 'flannelled mechanism', any more or less than any other cricketer has ever been. Jack Fingleton has always believed that Bradman not only could play pretty strokes but *did* play them when he wished: but he far more frequently wished to punish the ball with the full face of the bat to produce a resounding four rather than a graceful two or a single. 'His style may be open to criticism', wrote Neville Cardus on Bradman's 131 in the Trent Bridge Test of 1930, 'but it is his own and he knows his own limitations – at least until he has been keeping the bowlers at work for an hour or two.' In that same year Geoffrey Tebbutt defended Bradman against the charge of gracelessness: 'Do not assume . . . that young Bradman is a batsman without delicacy of touch. I have seen him score a good many hundreds in his many thousands of runs by strokes of a delicacy which a billiardist might envy. He is pre-eminently a batsman of the positive, hard-hitting type, but he has *finesse* too.'

The individual timbre of Bradman's style was never easy to define or to categorize. C. B. Fry once saw him as an amalgamation of Jessop and Abel. Others instinctively linked him with Trumper and Macartney – and others, just as instinctively, rejected that. On the morning that Bradman scored his triple-century in a day at Leeds in 1930, Ranji had gone into print with the words: 'This young Bradman, of the Australians, looks to me as if he should become a very fine bat in time, but I like the look of their other youngster, McCabe. I would call Bradman a miniature Macartney, but a long way behind Macartney yet.' Lord Tennyson, with no incident yet at Lord's to prompt his thoughts, said at the annual dinner of the Ferrets Cricket Club in London in 1931 that he thought Bradman had a great deal to learn. He was not in the same class, he said, as Trumper or Hill, and he thought he had not half the strokes of men like Hobbs, Woolley and Sutcliffe. But were his lordship's criteria based on style? Even he, bold sportsman that he was, must have trembled at Bradman's future prowess when the Australian had duly learnt the 'great deal' more that was in front of him! By then Robertson-Glasgow had already put the matter in settled perspective by asserting (at the end of 1930) that Bradman 'is not a Grace, a Trumper, a Hobbs, a Macartney, or a Ranji – he is simply Don Bradman'.

Bradman's style and Bradman's secret were each complementary to the other. The richest dividends accrued precisely because he was not like Hobbs or like Woolley or like Sutcliffe. This was through no conscious choice. Nature ordained that he should be unique. His personality and his skill fused into his own brand of batsmanship – a brand that seared bowlers' hearts for year after relentless year. Whatever bowlers bowled to him was usually wrong. To find a length to disconcert him was impossible. To set a field to tame him was never achieved. He would not have cared to be described as D'Artagnan and Mercutio in one (the Cardus appellation of Macartney) if only on the simple pragmatical grounds that neither of those gentlemen knew the first thing about batsmanship. But let it be from Neville Cardus that the final words should come by way of reply to the Bradman detractors who could find no grace in his style:

If, as often happens, people say 'Oh, but he hasn't the charm of McCabe, or the mercury of Macartney, or the dignity of Hammond', the objection is a little unintelligent, as though a lion were criticized for lacking the delicacy of the gazelle, the worrying tenacity of the terrier, and the disdainful elegance of a swan or a camel. Or we might as well sigh, at Bayreuth, not for the sweep and dynamic energy of Wagner, but for the poignant delicacy of Mozart as heard in the Residenztheater of Munich. We must pick and choose – and all sorts are needed to make the world's fairground.

16 The Don on Wet Wickets

*To be truthful, I would prefer to see all matches played on dry wickets. It would
be a fairer test of skill for both sides.*

Sir Donald Bradman in 1950

A single failure by Bradman against Verity at Lord's on the last day of the
Test match in 1934 seems conclusively to satisfy most people of his inability
to bat on a difficult pitch. This is as unfair and irrational as condemning a
motorist whose car may go into a sudden slide on a treacherous stretch of
icy road. The irrationality stems from the passing of a judgment from a
single event. The raindrops on Verity's hotel window which awakened him
with Australia's week-end score at 192 for two may certainly have been
music to his ears and it was certain that his Monday would be a good one.
He took 14 wickets and brought the match to a summary conclusion. The
critics cannot agree whether Bradman batted perfectly soundly or perfectly
execrably for half an hour, the length of his innings, that afternoon. Then
he attempted to hit Verity off his length. He paid the price at once and no
writer has ever allowed him to forget it. It was at once the cry that he was
'hopelessly at sea' against Verity on a difficult pitch. Verity for his part, let
it be said, always maintained that Bradman was great on any pitch. Verity
bowled more balls against Bradman in first-class matches than any bowler
in history. He was in the Yorkshire side at Sheffield in 1938 – a side that had
a superlative bad-wicket bowling attack – when Bradman batted for an
aggregate of $3\frac{3}{4}$ hours on a really difficult rain-affected wicket, a genuine
'sticky dog', to score 59 and 42 (the second and third highest innings of the
match), playing, on Verity's own admission, his sharpest spinners in the
middle of the bat. Bradman in unfamiliar conditions had to apply himself
with great resolve, and even *his* great resolve faltered momentarily on the
second day when his predicament was such that he offered his bat to Brian
Sellers, the Yorkshire captain, fielding nearby, with the words: 'How *do* you
play this stuff?' That was the match, watched by about 60,000 persons (and
noisy ones at that) in which the Australian batsmen, except Hassett, shuffled
in and out, in the words of Jack Fingleton, like electors at the ballot-box.

Nobody has ever relished playing on vicious turf, and it is true that on
such turf Bradman's bat was not always as flawlessly straight as the bats of,
say, Trumper and Macartney. Trumper in Australia used to try to get
practice in the nets on a deliberately watered batting surface, from which
his fellow-batsmen chose rather to stay away. Trumper on wet wickets in
England was superlatively good. Bradman, though he had the same quick-
footedness, was less commanding – perhaps because he had had less practice.

He played virtually all his Sheffield Shield cricket on covered wickets – compulsorily covered from the mid-'30s and optionally covered before that. Sydney, while he was a New South Wales player, was one of the grounds that chose not to cover in the optional days: but for all that the Shield matches he played in on rain-affected wickets can literally be counted on the fingers of one hand.

It is often claimed that Bradman was lucky in touring England in four good summers (during which, incidentally, he scored 9,837 runs at an average of 96·44 and headed the English batting averages all four times). His phenomenal success in 1930, when he took England by storm, blinds people to the fact that that was *not* a good summer. Apart from June, it was a wretched summer. The championship was ruined by rain and a great portion of the Australian fixture-list was dogged by rain. Of the Australians' first ten matches, only two (those at Worcester and Oxford) escaped interruption to some degree by the weather. By the end of the Warwickshire match in early August, unfavourable weather had caused the Australians the loss of more than 100 hours of cricket on the tour. 'Remember, it was a wet summer', said Oldfield when he spoke about the tour on arrival back in Sydney. In as many as 13 of the 26 matches in which he batted – precisely half – Bradman played one or other of his innings either wholly or in part on a wet wicket. When he scored 98 before lunch on the fourth morning of the Oval Test, he did so on a wet wicket. The ball was kicking and lifting off a decidedly nasty pitch, but one commentator said of the England bowling that morning that 'Bradman often made it look like club stuff'. When a man has upset all previous standards of batsmanship, with six double-hundreds, a record 974 runs in the Test series, and a hitherto unprecedented average of 98·66 at the end of the first-class season, how could he possibly have played in a wet summer? In fact almost exactly one third of Bradman's 2,960 first-class runs in 1930 were scored on wet or drying wickets and his average of 98·66 was highways ahead of the next best in England – 64·22 by Herbert Sutcliffe and 58·04 by Kippax. Philip Mead in 1930 averaged 29·65 (from 49 innings) and Charles Hallows, of the champion county – and maker of 1,000 runs in the May of 1928 – averaged 25·03 from 30 innings. It must be remembered that not every wet wicket was necessarily difficult to play on and some measure of explanation may be found in the fact that the Don, strangely, found a slightly damp wicket in England – so far as his personal methods were concerned – easier to play on than a perfectly dry one. This is not to suggest he welcomed anything more than *slightly* damp! Writing home to a friend in Goulburn on 11 June 1930, Bradman said that no two wickets were the same in England. Compared with Australian wickets, they were treacherous, but offered 'fine experience to a young player'. Bradman always believed that Australians generally had less difficulty in adjusting to English wickets than vice versa. He once interestingly observed: 'I certainly admit that for perfect batting conditions give me a warm but reasonably dull day in England.'

Bradman certainly had his failures on bad wickets, just as he had them on good wickets. But he had his successes too. A Bradman success was nothing more than expected, but a failure brought instant charges of faulty technique, unorthodox grip of the bat (which stood him in good enough stead in all conscience!) and all manner of allegations that were suffered by no other cricketer when he failed. Bradman was a subject to be exploited by the critics, and they did so without mercy when they had the chance. A Bradman dismissal in England at least, at any time, was a matter of national importance – *a fortiori* for a low score. It rarely took long, however, before another century or double-century from Bradman's bat silenced the detractors, and the chances were that the shrewd Bradman filed away what he had learnt from his failure and filed away what he had learnt about his critics.

Like all Australians, Bradman learnt his cricket on good wickets – in his case on the hard, matting wickets of Bowral. The vagaries of the uncertain pitch were still before him. Despite a career average hovering almost mechanically in the nineties, when he encountered them he more than once went so far as to condemn the sticky wicket as unfair. 'You might as well expect Inman to play on a torn table', was his analogy – which was itself an 'unfair' analogy, but one could see the point of the perfectionist batsman. The sticky wicket is now in practice a thing of the past – much to the regret of some. Legislation has outlawed it in the interests of gate receipts. Outside the Shield, in Test matches in Australia alone Bradman had his taste of them: notably at Brisbane in 1928–29 (he scored 1), at Sydney in 1930–31 (43 and 0), at Brisbane in 1936–37 (a duck), and at Sydney in 1936–37 (a duck again). To what further heights might the batsmanship of Bradman have soared had he known no such thing in his own career?

Only a regular number of consecutive seasons as a county cricketer in England would have settled the issue once and for all as to the Don's ability on uncertain turf. As it is, he retired with not all of his critics satisfied. At the approach of the 1948 season, with the Don about to play in England for the last time, Neville Cardus opined as follows of Bradman: 'I find it hard to believe that he could not, if he set himself to the task, play great cricket on a "glue-pot"; his eye, his footwork, the main and general style of his stroke-play, are the signs of a born great batsman, in any and all weathers, here or overseas.' To those qualities Sir Neville might have added single-mindedness, for the key may surely lie in the phrase *if he set himself to the task*. Was it rather that in conditions which the Don's mind, rightly or wrongly, could not accept as 'fair', he did not choose to play seriously? The evidence seems to suggest that undoubtedly there was something psychological in Bradman's approach to a bad pitch – the approach, for example, that J. B. Hobbs never adopted. If a great batsman is to be judged in his periods of ordeal, rather than in his periods of ease at the wicket, then Bradman does not come out on top. His limitations on most bad pitches were apparent. Robertson-Glasgow's knack of finding the right simile summed it up as follows: 'You could see, watching him go in to bat on a "sticky" pitch, that he wasn't jobbing easily. He was like a schoolboy with castor-oil. He just took it.'

Jack Fingleton's view was that for each of the few times Bradman succeeded on a bad pitch one could name half a dozen when he failed. 'His whole demeanour changed on a sticky pitch.' The Don seems instinctively to have resented them, or at least to have resented being judged by his performance on them. But they were part of the cricket scene; as, incidentally, a torn table was not part of the billiards scene. If the boot had been on the other foot at Lord's in 1934, would Sutcliffe or Hammond or Leyland have lost his head and his wicket at a crucial moment to Grimmett or O'Reilly?

Just as it is unfair to judge the Don just on his failure at Lord's in '34, so it is unfair to judge him simply on his success at Bramall Lane in '38. In that pulsating match against Yorkshire, at least, the Don's demeanour did not change to the uncaring. Verity again was in the opposition, and it may well have escaped the great mass of persons throughout the world – but almost certainly not Bradman himself – that this was the first occasion since that 1934 débâcle that Messrs Bradman and Verity were in contention on a bad wicket in England. Four years and a week was but a bagatelle to wait to put the balance right. Though it has never been suggested before, that was exactly, it is here submitted, Bradman's intention at Sheffield. An English pitch was necessary to do the balancing, and the Don merely bided his time. 'Don't ever tell me', Verity used to say after that match, 'that Don is just ordinary on the sticky ones.'

A certain amount of nonsense is spoken by those who become passionate about Bradman's difficulties on sticky wickets. The matter is certainly capable of unreasonable exaggeration – and these very words add to that state of affairs – but it is considerable tribute that men should subject the Don to such analysis at all. It is the view of Ben Barnett that if Bradman had gone to England and played cricket six days a week, he would have quickly become as great a batsman on sticky wickets as has ever been.

Let the last word be that of Jack Hobbs: 'My candid opinion of Bradman? Well, it is this: He is the best batsman in the world on dry wickets, and probably on all wickets if given the opportunity to get used to wet ones.' In Australia, virtually all Don Bradman's cricket was played on covered wickets, so his opportunities were, to say the least, not many.

17 The Don and the Price of Fame

A celebrity is one who is known to many persons he is glad he doesn't know.
H. L. Mencken

A man who becomes a legend in his lifetime – and in particular the sporting hero of a nation – has burdens to bear and penalties to pay above the ordinary. He is not a 'simple' citizen; not 'one of the crowd'. If you are Sir Donald Bradman, you are the potential subject of talk or gossip whenever you step out in public. 'That's Bradman' has been said not thousands of times but tens of thousands of times: and more often than not, some comment, adulatory or derogatory, will accompany it. 'Great man', some people will say. 'Not a good mixer', some others will say. 'I saw him play his last innings, you know', and so on. The American humorist, 'Kin' Hubbard – who did *not* know Bradman! – once summed it up with typical acumen: 'After a fellow gets famous it doesn't take long for someone to bob up that used to sit by him at school.'

Ever since the assumption by Bradman of the captaincy of Australia, and more so than ever since the conferment of his knighthood, he has had to suffer endless interruptions and approaches by persons who seek the most trivial of pretexts to talk to him. 'I met you at Scarborough in 1930', they will say, as though the Don should show instant recognition and embrace them as long-lost colleagues. It has happened – and still happens – so frequently as to be almost expected: but hardly welcomed.

Even the Bradman residence in Holden Street, Kensington Park, is one of the sights of Adelaide, to be pointed out with respectful awe (or disrespectful curiosity?) to newcomers to the city, along with Parliament House, the two handsome cathedrals and the State Observatory. In the same way taxi-drivers in Bridgetown will point with pride to the home of Everton Weekes, just as Yorkshiremen will to the homes of Brian Close and Raymond Illingworth, regardless of their defections southwards to play their cricket.

Bradman has never ceased to be news and has never ceased to be publicly recognised in all the 30 years that have elapsed since his playing days. This is an astonishing tribute to the Bradman legend. Of only W.G., among other cricketers, can this be said – his enormous physique and big black beard made him the best-known figure in Victorian England after the Queen herself. W.G. was news from a teen-aged boy till his death at 67, but he enjoyed only seven years of retirement after his final first-class game. He was still taking part in good and regular club cricket right up to 1914, the year before he died. He played in no fewer than 20 matches that season. Don Bradman virtually severed his connection with all forms of active cricket from the moment he walked from a first-class field for the last time in March 1949. Yet the lustre has never dimmed. And were he to be brave, or fool-hardy, enough to go to the crease – or even the nets – as a septuagenarian, the size of the crowd could be assured well in advance. Not just the crowd, but the cameras and the gossip-columnists and the publicity men and the interviewers: everybody from the connoisseur to the merely curious. The Don was – and is – big news.

When the Don was at the summit of his early fame and the term 'bodyline' had not yet been coined (though it was ominously around the corner), he journeyed from Sydney to Perth in October 1932 to make his first acquain-tance with Jardine's Englishmen. He was due to play for a Combined Australian XI in the first important match of the tour, though due to a Sheffield Shield fixture no Victorians were included in the side. Bradman's State colleagues on the long train journey were Fingleton and McCabe. At that stage his career average was 93.83 and he was within touching distance of 10,000 first-class runs, which he was duly to reach before the year was out, only five years after his debut. Perth had seen him only once, just before the Australian side of 1930 had sailed for England: on that occasion he scored 27 out of 31 in under half an hour. Since then he had torn England's Test attack to ribbons, as also he had done those of the West Indies and South Africa. The story of the journey from Sydney and the entry into Perth is just the sort of thing that might have been concocted by Hollywood for one of its more lavish productions. Actually Bradman had been in Hollywood only a few weeks before, but it is doubtful whether the experience prepared him for his own bout of celebrity-worship.

When the train was on its long run across the Nullarbor Plain [wrote J. H. Fingleton in *Cricket Crisis*] lonely men and women of the outback travelled many miles to catch a glimpse of this cricket magician. Piping little voices travelled the length of the train calling 'Bradman, Bradman, Bradman', when infrequent stops were made at night along that desolate, dreary line. At Quorn, a sleepy little hamlet drowsing in the hot sun, the Mayor came down to the train to accord us a civic reception in the shade of peppercorn trees.

Kalgoorlie, with its famous, bearded 6 ft. 6 in. Mayor Leslie, wearing a som-brero hat (he was always remembered by the Prince of Wales), gave us another reception. Further down the line at Coolgardie hundreds of enthusiastic miners flocked to the station calling for Bradman. His patience had worn thin by this time. He locked himself in his cabin, but the miners were determined to catch a glimpse of him. They began to ransack the train, several windows were broken and the conductor thought it time he moved out of Coolgardie. The train drew out from a tumultuous scene . . .

No prince could have had a more regal entry into Perth. As the long and dusty eastern train jolted to a stop thousands crammed the station, the adjoining roofs and buildings, the exits and the streets outside. Police had to force a passage for Bradman, and the Palace Hotel, where we stayed, was in a constant simmer by day and night.

It is easy for someone who has never experienced this sort of situation to imagine its discomforts can be exaggerated. Bradman had intelligence and wit and sensitivity. He also had nerves which, like anybody else's, could be frayed. On the field he had had, and was to continue to have, his full share of adulation – the worthy and proper response to high skill. Off the field, he detested it, and his detestation left a trail of ill-feeling in its wake by those who accused him of rudeness or aloofness or both. His private life was considered the property of all. When Bradman visited Adelaide in 1934 to discuss his prospective move to that city from Sydney, he made the journey under the pseudonym of 'Lindsay'. How many other cricketers have ever been reduced to this expediency?

The Don's entry into Perth in October 1932 coincided with all the alarm and pother about whether he would be playing in the forthcoming Test series or sitting in the press-box. At last he admitted that he *would* be playing in the first Test, if selected. 'I'm glad all the fuss about it is over', he said. 'The publicity has nearly turned me crazy.' If Australians were then in love with their Bradman, they did not do him the best of services – either in 1932 or at any other time – by turning him 'nearly crazy'. How many who saw him were indifferent to him? There must have been some, but they are anonymous. A most touching instance occurred on the train journey back from Perth after the Combined XI game. At a tiny desert halt, Bradman was at the window playing bridge. Outside the train, stretching up her hands appealingly to him, was an old aboriginal woman, dirty and dressed in rags. 'She wants your autograph, Don', someone remarked. She did not. She did not know it was Don Bradman. 'Takka my photograph', she said. 'Seexpence. No seexpence, no photograph.'

The old lady in the desert could not strictly be called indifferent to Bradman if his fame was unknown to her. But what a welcome relief the reversal of the roles must have been. Here was somebody straightforwardly putting the Don in second place in a confrontation between individual and individual! It could not last, of course. When the Don got to Sydney things were back to normal. And when the Don played in a picnic match that season at Rushcutters Bay for a press side (his contract with the Sydney *Sun* qualified him) against the Australian Navy, 3,000 turned up to watch him.

The endless intruders on his privacy and the endless interlopers on his conversations have always taken it for granted that cricket is the sole subject he can talk about or wants to talk about. This displays a woeful ignorance of Sir Donald Bradman. The country boy from Bowral may have had a wholly unprivileged youth: so, for example, did Ramsay MacDonald and James Callaghan, who each became Prime Minister of Great Britain. But the keenness of his intelligence was never in doubt, and he had the will to learn not only on the field. The young Don Bradman once sought out Neville Cardus to procure from him a list of books to develop his mind and enlarge his outlook – not exactly the sort of action that every young sportsman at the top of the tree might take. Cardus's list, while it may not have taxed Bertrand Russell or Einstein, was no easy course. But Bradman eventually read every book on it. Colin Cowdrey, who in six tours of Australia got to know and admire the Don closely, recently wrote of him: 'If he begins to expound on rose-growing, Australian wine, building a swimming pool or the local rateable value it is worthwhile listening because he does not venture opinions unless he is master of the subject.' Sir Robert Menzies once ventured the view that Don Bradman knew more about certain aspects of Australian finance than any other man in the country.

There was a time when Bradman could not post a letter or buy a morning paper without being molested by 'well-wishers'. That was when he was an active player. Mercifully, things did not stay that way. In London in 1974 he actually walked through West End streets, in his neat suit and hat, totally unmolested – recognised perhaps, but not molested. Once upon a time, in 1930, he had had to almost fight his way through the throng to get from the Oval to the underground. He was obliged later to remedy that and have a motor waiting for him: but even so, he was able to jump into it only with difficulty on the last day of the Test series, when he was pounced on by a group of young women. Geoffrey Tebbutt wrote in 1930 that 'if he has a rest from a match, the spectators feel a personal sense of injustice and partiality'. When Bradman left London for home towards the end of September that year, 20 cameras were present at St Pancras Station: a few days later, when the rest of the party (including Oldfield, Jackson, a'Beckett, Hurwood and the manager) left Victoria Station, not a single camera was there.

After the turmoil of 1932–33, P. F. Warner observed: 'The Press in Australia never leave him alone. Either he is a hero or the reverse. It must be very trying, and I am certain he would be happier if less limelight were thrown on him.' That was rarely to be his good fortune, and many cricketers felt genuinely sorry for Bradman and his endless limelight. 'He has had no private life in the last twenty years except that which he can commandeer by his own and his wife's obstinacy in keeping away from the prying eyes of supposed well-wishers', wrote Bill O'Reilly at the end of the 1948 tour. 'I venture a guess that after His Majesty the King and Winston Churchill, Bradman is the best known man in the British Empire.'

Some of his feats in 1936–37, when he captained Australia for the first time, turned Bradman into a semi-god. Even a farmer's parrot in Cronulla that season used to ask for Bradman's scores! 'Bradman is news', an Australian editor said to William Pollock on that tour. 'If he cuts himself shaving it would be a front-page story.' Everyone was grateful to Bradman in their own large or small way. The man from whom Pollock bought his newspaper remarked: 'He's my best spinner. Doesn't matter if he gets a duck or 200, he's money.' The news-vendors in Brisbane did a roaring trade by shouting

'Don's duck'. To the players in the dressing-room Bradman may have been 'Braddles': to the public he was 'the King of Australia'.

Sir Donald Bradman is the only cricketer in the world whose fame has prompted the idea of a film on his life. The Australian actor, Ron Randell, a useful schoolboy cricketer himself in Sydney, came to London in 1952 from Hollywood to seek someone with £170,000 to invest in such an enterprise. He did not succeed, having also tried unsuccessfully for years to get the film made in America. Randell himself wished to play the role of Bradman.[1] Sir Donald is also the only cricketer whose boots are preserved on display at Lord's. In 1930 P. F. Warner had said that he thought Bradman should present his boots to the Australian nation, 'to be placed in the pavilion at Sydney, there to be kept in a glass-case for future generations to gaze on, and to inspire them to something like his own nimbleness of foot!' Instead, just before he returned to Australia from England in 1953, Sir Donald – having just had a letter from 'Plum' Warner about the speed of his footwork – responded by presenting the Memorial Gallery at Lord's with the pair of cricket boots (size six) that he wore during the 1948 tour of England. Sir Donald sent them personally, and they were duly placed in the Memorial Gallery on 3 September 1953. Since then, a noble portrait of Sir Donald Bradman, as an elder statesman, has been placed in the Long Room at Lord's. The Commercial Bank of Australia (who had commissioned R. Hannaford to paint it) handed the portrait over to the President of M.C.C., Aidan Crawley, on 3 July 1973, in the presence of Lady Bradman. The South Australian artist, Ivor Hele, had painted Sir Donald's portrait in 1949, a reproduction of which was distributed to cricket clubs all over Australia. There have been occasional portraits painted since.

Don Bradman also had a lengthy spell on exhibition at Madame Tussaud's in London. The archives there show him to have been exhibited from 8 June 1934 (the first day of that year's Test series) until 1967, a spell of 33 years – perhaps a record for a cricketer. (However, there is some evidence that Bradman had already made it before 1934.) The original model of Bradman was made by Bernard Tussaud, the great-great-grandson of Madame Tussaud, and until his death in 1967 the chief modeller and in charge of the studio.

Fame, deriving of course from his great skill, has made Sir Donald Bradman one of the imperishable sporting figures of the twentieth century. When many others have fallen by the wayside, his name will still blazon forth. The man who was born on the same day as Sir Donald Bradman, Lyndon Baines Johnson, was for ever in search of hints as to his fate at the hands of posterity, always worried about how historians would treat him after he was dead. Sir

---

[1] Bradman had himself made an instructional film, *How I Play Cricket*, which was sold to Metro-Goldwyn-Mayer in November 1932 for distribution in the U.K., South Africa, Canada and the Far East. Various other short films, including one filmed at his Bowral home, were also made.

Donald need entertain no such worries – that is, if the historians know their sources and can distinguish the mendacious from the frank. Every man of genius is considerably helped by being dead, said Robert Lynd: and if that be true, then the living legend that is now Sir Donald Bradman – and may the legend remain a living one for many, many years – is destined to soar to an unassailable height in the gallery of great cricketers and great Australians.

With other cricketers, when journalists look back and seek to say something really impressive about them, the tendency is to exaggerate, tell a small white lie, or at least embellish a fact or two in the cause of reader interest. Keith Miller, for example, to quote a fine writer who shall be nameless, used always to 'arrive at cricket grounds just before the toss, hang his dinner jacket on somebody else's peg and still score a century before lunch'. With Sir Donald Bradman no such embellishments have ever been necessary. The dazzling impressiveness of the true facts have been sufficient for most journalists and their readers. Who else could score 100 runs in three overs? Who else could pass a triple-century on the first day of an England-Australia Test? Who else could score a century every third time he went to the wicket in his first-class career? Who else could score 7,000 runs in less than a year? Who else, on no fewer than 27 occasions in first-class cricket alone, could score 200 runs in a single day off his own bat? Who else could average 99·94 in a Test career spanning 20 years?

When all is said and done, it must be Sir Donald's brain and Sir Donald's temperament that contributed so very much to every stage of his triumphant career. One who knew him well, the former State cricketer and selector, Dr Eric Barbour, said in 1934: 'Bradman is the greatest batsman of his day, not because he can make better strokes than others, but because he has a wonderful cricket mentality, and a wonderful control of his own emotions and his own powers.'

'I have known him for many, many years', said Walter Robins to the present writer a year before he died, 'and no one I can think of has equalled him as a player, as a thinker or as a citizen. He's an astonishing man.'

Let us accept that verdict – an astonishing man. Sir Donald Bradman, at least as a player, was a genius – which is a convenient word to express admiration for someone whom we cannot explain or understand. He had one of the greatest careers in cricket history; and yet it is doubtful whether his greatness can be discovered by the closest research into his public deeds. The man behind the glittering public pageant seems somehow greater and more alluring than his fellow-players and fellow-citizens may ever have understood.

18 A Few Figures

Figures can lie, but in cricket, taken in the large, they tell the truth, and in his case defy all argument.

H. S. Altham on D. G. Bradman, 1941

This book is not intended to be a statistical work, and any effort that sought to improve on the tables in B. J. Wakley's *Bradman the Great* would be an impertinence.

However, some statistical record, however brief, is called for, at least for Sir Donald Bradman's first-class and Test career.

'There seem no limits to this extraordinary young man's possibilities', concluded Aubrey Faulkner on watching Bradman's first Test century in England, at Trent Bridge, in 1930. How far Bradman indeed stretched those limits can be gathered in some measure by the figures of his career.

Much of what follows, though initially compiled independently, owes confirmation to B. J. Wakley's work, which is here warmly acknowledged.

First-Class Career

	Matches	Inns.	N.O.	Runs	H.S.	Av.	100s	50s	Ct.
1927–28	5	10	1	416	134*	46·22	2	1	1
1928–29	13	24	6	1,690	340*	93·88	7	5	3
1929–30	11	16	2	1,586	452*	113·28	5	4	4
1930	27	36	6	2,960	334	98·66	10	5	12
1930–31	12	18	0	1,422	258	79·00	5	4	7
1931–32	10	13	1	1,403	299*	116·91	7	0	5
1932–33	11	21	2	1,171	238	61·63	3	7	6
1933–34	7	11	2	1,192	253	132·44	5	4	4
1934	22	27	3	2,020	304	84·16	7	6	9
1935–36	8	9	0	1,173	369	130·33	4	1	7
1936–37	12	19	1	1,552	270	86·22	6	2	10
1937–38	12	18	2	1,437	246	89·81	7	5	13†
1938	20	26	5	2,429	278	115·66	13	5	8
1938–39	7	7	1	919	225	153·16	6	0	3
1939–40	9	15	3	1,475	267	122·91	5	4	11
1940–41	2	4	0	18	12	4·50	0	0	0
1945–46	2	3	1	232	112	116·00	1	2	1
1946–47	9	14	1	1,032	234	79·38	4	4	4
1947–48	9	12	2	1,296	201	129·60	8	1	9
1948	23	31	4	2,428	187	89·92	11	8	11
1948–49	3	4	0	216	123	54·00	1	1	3
	234	338	43	28,067	452*	95·14	117	69	131†

† Also one stumping in 1937–38.

Of his 131 catches, four were made as wicketkeeper. He made one further catch in first-class cricket while fielding as substitute in the second Test at Sydney in 1928–29.

Summary

	Matches	Inns.	N.O.	Runs	H.S.	Av.	100s	50s	Ct.
In Australia	142	218	25	18,230	452*	94·45	76	45	91
In England	92	120	18	9,837	334	96·44	41	24	40
	234	338	43	28,067	452*	95·14	117	69	131

Double-Centuries

340*	New South Wales v Victoria, Sydney	1928–29
225	W. M. Woodfull's XI v J. Ryder's XI, Sydney	1929–30
452*	New South Wales v Queensland, Sydney	1929–30
236	Australians v Worcestershire, Worcester	1930
252*	Australians v Surrey, Oval	1930
254	Australia v England, Lord's	1930
334	Australia v England, Headingley	1930
232	Australia v England, Oval	1930
205*	Australians v Kent, Canterbury	1930
258	New South Wales v South Australia, Adelaide	1930–31
223	Australia v West Indies, Brisbane	1930–31
220	New South Wales v Victoria, Sydney	1930–31
226	Australia v South Africa, Brisbane	1931–32
219	New South Wales v South Africans, Sydney	1931–32
299*	Australia v South Africa, Adelaide	1931–32
238	New South Wales v Victoria, Sydney	1932–33
200	New South Wales v Queensland, Brisbane	1933–34
253	New South Wales v Queensland, Sydney	1933–34
206	Australians v Worcestershire, Worcester	1934
304	Australia v England, Headingley	1934
244	Australia v England, Oval	1934
233	South Australia v Queensland, Adelaide	1935–36
357	South Australia v Victoria, Melbourne	1935–36
369	South Australia v Tasmania, Adelaide	1935–36
212	Rest of Australia v Australia, Sydney	1936–37
270	Australia v England, Melbourne	1936–37
212	Australia v England, Adelaide	1936–37
246	South Australia v Queensland, Adelaide	1937–38
258	Australians v Worcestershire, Worcester	1938
278	Australians v M.C.C., Lord's	1938
202	Australians v Somerset, Taunton	1938
225	South Australia v Queensland, Adelaide	1938–39
251*	South Australia v New South Wales, Adelaide	1939–40
267	South Australia v Victoria, Melbourne	1939–40
209*	South Australia v Western Australia, Perth	1939–40
234	Australia v England, Sydney	1946–47
201	Australia v India, Adelaide	1947–48

In Australia	25 double-centuries
In England	12 double-centuries
	37 double-centuries

Highest Partnerships

451 for 2nd wkt. with W. H. Ponsford	Australia v England, Oval	1934
405 for 5th wkt. with S. G. Barnes	Australia v England, Sydney	1946–47
388 for 4th wkt. with W. H. Ponsford	Australia v England, Headingley	1934
363 for 3rd wkt. with A. F. Kippax	New South Wales v Queensland, Sydney	1933–34
356 for 3rd wkt. with R. A. Hamence	South Australia v Tasmania, Adelaide	1935–36
346 for 6th wkt. with J. H. W. Fingleton	Australia v England, Melbourne	1936–37
334 for 2nd wkt. with A. A. Jackson	New South Wales v South Australia, Adelaide	1930–31
301 for 2nd wkt. with A. R. Morris	Australia v England, Headingley	1948
296 for 2nd wkt. with W. H. Ponsford	Australians v Tasmania, Hobart	1929–30
294 for 2nd wkt. with W. A. Brown	New South Wales v Queensland, Brisbane	1933–34
277 for 4th wkt. with C. L. Badcock	Australians v Worcestershire, Worcester	1938
276 for 3rd wkt. with A. L. Hassett	Australia v England, Brisbane	1946–47
274 for 2nd wkt. with W. M. Woodfull	Australia v South Africa, Melbourne	1931–32
272 for 3rd wkt. with A. F. Kippax	New South Wales v Queensland, Sydney	1929–30

He took part in 41 double-century partnerships in first-class cricket, and 164 century stands in all.

Dismissals in First-Class Cricket

Caught	in 58·983%	of his dismissals	(174 times in career)
Bowled	in 26·441%	„ „	„	(78 „ „ „)
Lbw	in 9·152%	„ „	„	(27 „ „ „)
Stumped	in 3·729%	„ „	„	(11 „ „ „)
Run out	in 1·356%	„ „	„	(4 „ „ „)
Hit wicket	in 0·339%	„ „	„	(1 , „ „)

Test Career

	Tests	Inns.	N.O.	Runs	H.S.	Av.	100s	50s	Ct.
1928–29 v England	4	8	1	468	123	66·85	2	2	2
1930 v England	5	7	0	974	334	139·14	4	0	2
1930–31 v West Indies	5	6	0	447	223	74·50	2	0	4
1931–32 v South Africa	5	5	1	806	299*	201·50	4	0	2
1932–33 v England	4	8	1	396	103*	56·57	1	3	3
1934 v England	5	8	0	758	304	94·75	2	1	1
1936–37 v England	5	9	0	810	270	90·00	3	1	7
1938 v England	4	6	2	434	144*	108·50	3	1	0
1946–47 v England	5	8	1	680	234	97·14	2	3	3
1947–48 v India	5	6	2	715	201	178·75	4	1	6
1948 v England	5	9	2	508	173*	72·57	2	1	2
	52	80	10	6,996	334	99·94	29	13	32

Summary

	Tests	Inns.	N.O.	Runs	H.S.	Av.	100s	50s	Ct.
In Australia	33	50	6	4,322	299*	98·22	18	10	27
In England	19	30	4	2,674	334	102·84	11	3	5
	52	80	10	6,996	334	99·94	29	13	32

Test Record v Each Country

	Tests	Inns.	N.O.	Runs	H.S.	Av.	100s	50s	Ct.
v England	37	63	7	5,028	334	89·78	19	12	20
v South Africa	5	5	1	806	299*	201·50	4	0	2
v West Indies	5	6	0	447	223	74·50	2	0	4
v India	5	6	2	715	201	178·75	4	1	6
	52	80	10	6,996	334	99·94	29	13	32

Centuries in Test Cricket

112	v	England	Melbourne	1928–29
123	v	England	Melbourne	1928–29
131	v	England	Trent Bridge	1930
254	v	England	Lord's	1930
334	v	England	Headingley	1930
232	v	England	Oval	1930
223	v	West Indies	Brisbane	1930–31
152	v	West Indies	Melbourne	1930–31
226	v	South Africa	Brisbane	1931–32
112	v	South Africa	Sydney	1931–32
167	v	South Africa	Melbourne	1931–32
299*	v	South Africa	Adelaide	1931–32
103*	v	England	Melbourne	1932–33
304	v	England	Headingley	1934
244	v	England	Oval	1934
270	v	England	Melbourne	1936–37
212	v	England	Adelaide	1936–37
169	v	England	Melbourne	1936–37
144*	v	England	Trent Bridge	1938
102*	v	England	Lord's	1938
103	v	England	Headingley	1938
187	v	England	Brisbane	1946–47
234	v	England	Sydney	1946–47
185	v	India	Brisbane	1947–48
132 } 127* }	v	India	Melbourne	1947–48
201	v	India	Adelaide	1947–48
138	v	England	Trent Bridge	1948
173*	v	England	Headingley	1948

Highest Partnerships in Test Cricket

451 for 2nd wkt. with W. H. Ponsford	v England	Oval	1934
405 for 5th wkt. with S. G. Barnes	v England	Sydney	1946–47
388 for 4th wkt. with W. H. Ponsford	v England	Headingley	1934
346 for 6th wkt. with J. H. W. Fingleton	v England	Melbourne	1936–37
301 for 2nd wkt. with A. R. Morris	v England	Headingley	1948
276 for 3rd wkt. with A. L. Hassett	v England	Brisbane	1946–47
274 for 2nd wkt. with W. M. Woodfull	v South Africa	Melbourne	1931–32
249 for 3rd wkt. with S. J. McCabe	v England	Melbourne	1936–37
243 for 4th wkt. with A. A. Jackson	v England	Oval	1930
236 for 2nd wkt. with S. G. Barnes	v India	Adelaide	1947–48
231 for 2nd wkt. with W. M. Woodfull	v England	Lord's	1930

He took part in 14 double-century partnerships in Test cricket, and 35 century stands in all.

Test Record on Each Ground

In Australia

	Tests	Inns.	N.O.	Runs	H.S.	Av.	100s	50s	Ct.
Adelaide	7	11	2	970	299*	107·77	3	3	6
Brisbane (Exhibition Ground)	2	3	0	242	223	80·66	1	0	2
Brisbane (Woolloongabba Ground)	5	7	0	736	226	105·14	3	1	4
Melbourne	11	17	4	1,671	270	128·53	9	3	9
Sydney	8	12	0	703	234	58·58	2	3	6
	33	50	6	4,322	299*	98·22	18	10	27

In England

	Tests	Inns.	N.O.	Runs	H.S.	Av.	100s	50s	Ct.
Headingley	4	6	1	963	334	192·60	4	0	1
Lord's	4	8	1	551	254	78·71	2	1	1
Old Trafford	3	4	1	81	30*	27·00	0	0	2
Oval	4	4	0	553	244	138·25	2	1	1
Trent Bridge	4	8	1	526	144*	75·14	3	1	0
	19	30	4	2,674	334	102·84	11	3	5

Sheffield Shield Career

For New South Wales

	Matches	Inns.	N.O.	Runs	H.S.	Av.	100s	50s	Ct.
1927–28	5	10	1	416	134*	46·22	2	1	1
1928–29	5	9	3	893	340*	148·83	4	1	0
1929–30	6	10	2	894	452*	111·75	1	4	2
1930–31	4	6	0	695	258	115·83	3	1	0
1931–32	3	5	0	213	167	42·60	1	0	3
1932–33	3	5	1	600	238	150·00	2	3	1
1933–34	5	7	2	922	253	184·40	4	2	3
	31	52	9	4,633	452*	107·74	17	12	10

For South Australia

	Matches	Inns.	N.O.	Runs	H.S.	Av.	100s	50s	Ct.
1935–36	6	6	0	739	357	123·16	3	0	6
1936–37	4	6	1	416	192	83·20	2	0	0
1937–38	6	12	2	983	246	98·30	4	4	6†
1938–39	6	6	1	801	225	160·20	5	0	3
1939–40	6	10	2	1,062	267	132·75	3	4	9
1946–47	1	2	0	162	119	81·00	1	0	0
1947–48	1	1	0	100	100	100·00	1	0	2
1948–49	1	1	0	30	30	30·00	0	0	2
	31	44	6	4,293	357	112·97	19	8	28†

† Also one stumping in 1937–38.

Summary

	Matches	Inns.	N.O.	Runs	H.S.	Av.	100s	50s	Ct.
For New South Wales	31	52	9	4,633	452*	107·74	17	12	10
For South Australia	31	44	6	4,293	357	112·97	19	8	28†
Total in Sheffield Shield	62	96	15	8,926	452*	110·19	36	20	38†

† Also one stumping.

Career in Minor Cricket

D. G. Bradman's batting record in *all* cricket, first-class and minor, was given in a publication of the Australian Broadcasting Commission as follows:

	Inns.	N.O.	Runs	H.S.	Av.	100s
	669	107	50,731	452*	90·26	211

This may accordingly be divided as follows:

	Inns.	N.O.	Runs	H.S.	Av.	100s
First-class cricket	338	43	28,067	452*	95·14	117
Minor cricket	331	64	22,664	320*	84·88	94
	669	107	50,731	452*	90·26	211

'Sir', observed Dr Johnson, talking about Alexander Pope, 'a thousand years may elapse before there shall appear another man with a power of versification equal to that of Pope.'

So might one make a claim, too, about the batsmanship of Donald Bradman.

Index